BIRTH, MARRIAGE, AND DEATH

BIRTH, MARRIAGE, AND DEATH

Ritual, Religion, and the Life-Cycle in
Tudor and Stuart England

David Cressy

OXFORD UNIVERSITY PRESS

1997

Oxford University Press, Great Clarendon Street, Oxford OX2 6DP

Oxford New York

Athens Auckland Bangkok Bogota Bombay Buenos Aires
Calcutta Cape Town Dar es Salaam Delhi Florence Hong Kong
Istanbul Karachi Kuala Lumpur Madras Madrid Melbourne
Mexico City Nairobi Paris Singapore Taipei Tokyo Toronto
and associated companies in
Berlin Ibadan

Oxford is a trade mark of Oxford University Press

Published in the United States
by Oxford University Press Inc., New York

British Library Cataloguing in Publication Data
Data available

Library of Congress Cataloging in Publication Data
Data applied for

ISBN 0–19–820168–0

1 3 5 7 9 10 8 6 4 2

Typeset by Graphicraft Typesetters Ltd., Hong Kong
Printed in Great Britain
on acid-free paper by
Biddles Ltd., Guildford and King's Lynn

To Keith Thomas

Acknowledgements

This study has taken many more years to complete than I originally envisioned. From an original ambition to tackle all kinds of ritual its focus has narrowed to the landmarks of the life cycle. At the same time its scope has expanded to encompass a wealth of social, cultural, and religious concerns. I hope it is better as a result. Along the way I have incurred many debts to individuals and institutions, only a few of which can be mentioned here. I wish to thank the president and fellows of Magdalen College, Oxford, and the master and fellows of St Catherine's College, Oxford, for appointing me to visiting fellowships in 1990 and 1991. A fellowship grant from the National Endowment for the Humanities allowed me to take that year as a sabbatical away from teaching. Another NEH Fellowship in 1996 helped bring the project to completion. I am grateful too to the American Philosophical Society, the British Academy, and the Huntington Library for supporting my travel to English archives, and to the Scholarly and Creative Activities Committee at California State University, Long Beach, for released time and summer stipends. Most of this book was written in the interstices between teaching, and I thank my students for their patience and their curiosity.

Among the many scholars who have responded to parts of this work while it was taking shape, I particularly wish to thank Patricia Cleary, Elyse Blankley, Lori Anne Ferrell, David Harley, Roger Schofield, Kevin Sharpe, and William Weber. John Morrill generously agreed to read the typescript and to warn of inconsistencies and mistakes. Lisa Ford helped check the footnotes. The design and execution, however, is mine, and I am responsible for all remaining errors.

To every thing there is a season, and a time to every purpose under the heaven: a time to be born, and a time to die. (Ecclesiastes 3: 1)

We see it verified by experience that all earthly and transitory things have their end, to the which they tend. Our very years are limited, God hath measured out our months, the days of our lives are dated, how long we have to live. So that our first lesson (even at the beginning) that we have to learn is this, to think of our ending. We see that the longest day passeth, and the night succeedeth; how summer followeth winter, and winter summer. The sun it hath both his rising and his setting, his shining and his shading. The spring time hath his course in covering and clothing the ground with fruits. Summer it ripens them, harvest gathers them, and winter spends them. Thus one thing followeth another, and both one and another pass swiftly to their end. The generation of one thing is the destruction of another, and the death of one thing is the life of another; first is our generation, then our conception, after comes our birth in wonderful weakness, our cradle is our castle, when we have once crept out of that, we come to a little strength; yet long is the time ere we come to ripeness. And here (behold) we never continue in one state; for as our strength increased at the first, so by little and little it diminisheth at the last. As youth succeedeth childhood, and age youth, so childhood, youth and age have all their end.
(John More, *A Lively Anatomie of Death* (1596; STC 18073), sigs. B–Bᵛ)

Birth, and copulation, and death.
That's all the facts when you come to brass tacks.
(T. S. Eliot, 'Sweeney Agonistes', in *Collected Poems 1909–1962* (1963), 131)

He not busy being born is busy dying.
(Bob Dylan, *Writings and Drawings* (New York, 1973), 171)

Contents

DEATH

List of Illustrations

DEATH

INTRODUCTION

Themes

The period from the middle of the sixteenth century to the end of the seven-teenth century—encompassing Renaissance, Reformation, Revolution, and Restoration—saw intense debate and sharp conflict in England over the mean-ing and conduct of routine rites of passage. Politicized disagreement about religious behaviour and social practice contributed to the national divisions of the Civil War and Interregnum as well as to countless parochial disputes, and were barely resolved in the reigns of the later Stuarts. Godly protestants of the post-Reformation era objected to 'popish' elements that they thought still stained the life-cycle services in the Book of Common Prayer, while epis-copal disciplinarians prevented puritan nonconformists from simplifying or subverting established ceremonies. Traditionalists clung to patterns of beha-viour that the official church was reluctant to countenance. Furthermore, the rowdiness and irreverence associated with some of these rituals—such as chris-tening festivities after baptisms, gossips' feasts following churchings, wedding parties after marriages, and funeral dinners accompanying burials—brought rites of passage within the purview of the campaign for the reformation of manners. The dispute was fought out in public and private, in sermons and pamphlets, diaries and letters, as well as in court cases and in poetic and dra-matic literature. This book sets out to interrogate the widest possible range of sources in order to examine the social, cultural, and religious history of the ceremonies associated with birth, marriage, and death.

Every stage of the life cycle in early modern England was accompanied by ritual activity. The major episodes of birth, marriage, and death, in particu-lar, were intensely scripted, marked by customary social performance as well as the regulated routines of religious liturgy. The Book of Common Prayer, in its various editions and revisions from 1549 to 1662, contained the services for the ministration of baptism to infants, the churching of women after childbirth, the ceremony for the solemnization of matrimony, and the order for burial of the dead. These were powerful protocols, with their prayers and incantations, exchanges and interrogatories, and the rubric of ritualized action—sprinkling with water, signing with the cross, kneeling at the altar, giving the bride, placing the ring, meeting the corpse, and casting earth upon the body. Even under protestantism, within the reformed Church of England, the spiritual and social drama of birth, marriage, and death was graced with elaborate ceremony. Negotiation, challenge, and defence of this body of ritual, both in religious discourse and local community practice, provided much of the documentary foundation for this study.

Life-cycle rituals exposed society's raw nerves. Each of the major rituals of baptism, churching, marriage, and burial was potentially an arena for argument, ambiguity, and dissent. Ideally, as classic rites of passage,[1] these ceremonies worked to bring people together or to assign everyone their place. But they also set up traps into which people could stumble, and tests which not everybody could pass. Ritual performance, in practice, revealed frictions and fractures that everyday local discourse attempted to hide or to heal. The making and remaking of ritual formed part of a continuing conversation, sometimes strained and occasionally acrimonious, that ranged over important areas of sixteenth- and seventeenth-century life.

Every time a child was baptized, a couple married, or a body buried in Elizabethan and Stuart England—the figures are in the millions—the religion of protestants was both taught and tested. Routine religious observances— the weekly and seasonal round of services and the life-cycle offices of baptisms, weddings, and funerals—served as primary points of contact between family and community, centre and periphery, and between men or women and God. Their rhythms and messages were made familiar through frequent reiteration. This framework of uniformity provided recurrent opportunities to challenge as well as to sanction the established order.

In addition to the formal requirements of the church there were multiple matters of custom involving childbirth and lying in, midwifery and gossiping, christening cakes and veils at churchings, espousal rituals and exchange of courtship tokens, wedding parties and bridal possets, funeral doles and mourning dress, noise-making, costuming, and neighbourly bestowing of food. These rites of passage gave cultural meaning to natural processes, and constructed a social and religious framework for biological events. These activities too drew contemporary criticism and comment. But only when something went wrong, or when the overarching social and religious framework was under challenge (as it was in the sixteenth and seventeenth centuries), would rites of passage become sites of contention.

Baptism, for example, was a frequently performed service that repeatedly posed problems. Tudor and Stuart theologians grappled with the mystery of baptism and explored its twin elements of transformation and initiation, while ordinary parents and godparents attempted to do their duty. In parish life, where official formulations of religion met the vagaries of local practice, crosses in baptism and fights over fonts reveal the unresolved legacy of the Reformation. Even when there was general agreement about what baptism meant, there was recurrent controversy about its conduct. Should the clergy alone be permitted to baptize, or was there room for lay baptism or baptism by women, especially midwives? Should the ceremony take place in private or in public, at home or in church? And if held in church, in what part of the building, before what assembly? Should the minister use a font or a basin, and how should he apply the water? Should any other substance besides water be permitted in the service, such as the chrism, oil, salt, spittle, or cream associated with traditional catholicism? Should the minister always make the sign of the cross over the infant, as the prayer book insisted, and if so where, how often, and in what manner? How much time should elapse between the birth of a child and its coming to be christened? What befell the soul of a child who died unbaptized, and how should the community dispose of its body? How much mingling of the secular and the sacred was permitted in any accompanying in a christening festivity? And what should be done about offenders?

These may seem like minor matters, but they were capable of polarizing a parish or dividing a church. It was the genius of early modern disputants to turn adiaphora (matters theologically indifferent) into key tests of conformity and discipline. As the authors of the Book of Common Prayer insisted, 'the keeping or omitting of a ceremony, in itself considered, is a small thing; yet the wilful and contemptuous transgression and breaking of a common order and discipline is no small offence before God'.[2]

The thanksgiving of women after childbirth, commonly called the churching of women, caused countless minor problems. As the successor to the catholic ritual of purification, it was fraught with ambiguity and subject to contention. Was it 'indubitably a ritual of purification closely linked with its Jewish predecessor', as Keith Thomas once wrote, or was churching rather, as Natalie Davis has suggested, a ritual of feminine empowerment, a moment of 'women on top'?[3] How should the woman present herself, in what garments, with what degree of gravity or mirth? Should she be kneeling or sitting? Should the priest church her at the altar, or his desk, or her seat? Should an unchurched woman be excluded from the sacraments, or from her husband's bed, and be shunned by her neighbours as in some way unclean? What should be done when a woman was churched irregularly by her husband, or in the case of the Bedfordshire woman in 1617 who churched herself? How did the implications of the ceremony vary according to the religious viewpoint, authority, role, and gender of the parties involved, and how did it change over time? Churching, I will argue, had more to do with the politics of ecclesiastical conformity than with any lingering notions of female pollution, but the politics of the ceremony and the intensity of concern altered considerably over the sixteenth and seventeenth centuries. The requirement that women wear veils at their churching, not specified in the prayer book but insisted on by some of Charles I's bishops, created circles of resentment and disagreement that were still being worked out at the outbreak of the Civil War.

Courtship was not governed by the church but none the less followed unwritten rules of conduct. How courtship might begin and develop, what difficulties had to be surmounted, and how courtship led to marriage, were open to scrutiny and comment. The questions at issue included freedom and initiative, privacy and obligation, and the gendered and inter-generational aspects of discipline, ambition, consent, sexuality, and love. Courtships that culminated in betrothal, or the problematic rituals of espousal, left a trail of documentation if the intended union of two people went wrong.

Like other life-cycle ceremonies, the solemnization of matrimony signalled important changes for those most closely involved. The ritual marked the passage from one state to another, assigning new social and sexual roles, rearranging patriarchal obligations, and conferring new duties of status, authority, and dependency. Marriage for a man meant mastery, responsibility, and the prospect of fathering a lineage. Marriage for a woman was, perhaps, the major defining moment of her life, determining her social, domestic, and reproductive future. In the words of the wedding service, marriage joined husband and wife together 'for better for worse, for richer for poorer, in sickness and in health' until death they did part. As the Jacobean puritan William Gouge observed of the ceremony of marriage, 'by it men and women are made husbands and wives. It is the only lawful means to make them fathers and mothers. It is the ordinary means to make them masters and mistresses.'[4]

Marriage, however, was as contentious a matter as baptism. While catholics considered marriage a sacrament, radical puritans thought it more a matter for the magistrate than for the minister. The Church of England struggled to impose its discipline on marriage, and in the process generated an extensive documentary record. Disputes turned on the timing, setting, and conduct of the ceremony, and the impediments of age, consanguinity, affinity, pre-contract, and consent. Should marriages only be performed in public, after publication of banns, or were private or clandestine marriages equally valid? How could an irregular marriage be legitimized or undone? Countless real-life dramas, as well as works of dramatic literature, turned on these considerations. Nor was the ceremony itself beyond contention. Countless arguments revolved around the ritual exchange of the ring, which the prayer book required but puritans argued was 'popish' and superstitious. The secular accompaniments to the marriage ceremony have barely been studied, yet a vast amount survives in diaries and reminiscences to expose the domestic, communal, and sexual dimensions of nuptial feasts and wedding suppers. We need to discover what these rituals meant to various social groups and how their observance changed over time.

The rituals of death and burial pose similar problems of meaning and conduct. What was the fate of the soul and what was the proper disposition of the body? How should a corpse be handled, and where and how should it be buried? How much 'pomp' was appropriate in the course of a funeral, and how should the mourners and survivors behave? Could the departed soul benefit from sermons or ceremony, and was it piety or superstition to offer prayers for the dead? How did the secular and the sacred elements intertwine, and what parts did clergy and laity play, in theory and in practice? What do these rites of passage show about customary behaviour, religious discipline, nonconformity, and the shifting social and cultural stresses of Tudor and Stuart England?

Glossed by theologians, governed by episcopal disciplinarians, administered by clergy, and experienced by men and women of all sorts, the life-cycle rituals associated with birth, marriage, and death constitute an interlocking array of actions and meanings at the centre of the interdisciplinary humanities agenda. Our understanding of these complex issues can best be advanced through a wide-ranging, eclectic, and ecumenical approach. It should be particularly interesting to see what can be learnt from the juxtaposition of high theology and popular ballads, church court records and private correspondence, sermon literature and the texts of dramatic comedy. By linking the high-culture concerns of church and state to the experiences of ordinary families and individuals, by relating theology and politics to demography and ethnography, we may be able to write a more integrated history of England that sheds the constraint of being labelled 'social', 'cultural', 'religious', or 'political'.

Passages

In a tradition reaching back to the ancient world, Tudor and Stuart authors imagined the life cycle in terms of a succession of ages. Infancy gave way to childhood, childhood to youth, youth to maturity, and maturity to old age. Different schemes offered particular additions and refinements, such as adolescence, adulthood, and dotage. Some writers assigned years to the pattern, seeing youth, for example, as lasting from the age of seven to the age of thirty. Historians have recently argued that the most momentous event in anyone's life, apart from parturition and dying, was entry into marriage.

Anthropologists have encouraged us to see not ages but stages, separated by ritual markers of transition from one stage to the next. An important body of theoretical literature has grown up in the past one hundred years that classifies and illuminates the principal rites of passage.[5] I have striven to be informed by this literature but not to be in thrall to it. I wear my social theory lightly, so lightly, perhaps, that it barely shows.

Social-science theory can readily be brought to bear on to English historical material to identify rites of aggregation and separation, and states of liminality and 'communitas'. The model works well for the ceremonies of childbirth and churching, as well as the rituals of baptism, betrothal, marriage, and death. It helps us to see that the sites and spaces, costumes and accessories, phases and processes of post-Reformation rituals conform to a wider framework. Once applied, however, it is neither useful nor interesting to keep playing the 'liminal transformation' game. The effort suffers from diminishing returns and risks becoming unfocused or dislocated, anachronistic, or boring.

Historians interested in the cultural problems of early modern England will find it much more fruitful to examine the differences between ritual performances, and the particular participants' explanations of their variant courses of action. Like modern anthropologists, who seem now to be more attuned to diversity, particularity, and change than to universal cross-cultural characteristics, they may come to delight, as I do, in the complexities of circumstance and context.

There were, of course, more life-cycle rituals in Tudor and Stuart England than those associated with birth, marriage, and death. Women in pregnancy and childbearing enjoyed ritual gatherings and ceremonies that are barely glimpsed in the male-dominated records. Parents may have given ritual recognition to a baby's progress from swaddling to weaning, and to a child's development from walking to putting on gender-specific dress. The beginning and ending of 'sucking' and the male child's achievement of 'breeching' were matters of concern or satisfaction in several diaries and letters. Children in devout households experienced the ritual instruction of catechism, and many underwent the religious ceremony of confirmation at the hands of a bishop or his surrogate. There may have been rituals associated with leaving home, of entering service, and starting employments, just as there were academic rituals of matriculation and commencement. Young couples revitalized the rituals of courtship, and some of them proceeded to the solemnities of espousal or betrothal before marriage. Husbands and wives may have ritualized their start of a household, their birthdays and anniversaries, their blessing of heirs, and their readiness to retire. There are signs of a rich and inventive ritualization of the life cycle, at all social levels, alongside the landmarks of baptisms, weddings, and funerals. These petty rituals, however, lacked structure, scripting, and coherence. Less was at stake in them, compared to the validating, testing, and incorporating rituals of the prayer book. I have left them alone, for the most part, to concentrate on the main rites of passage.

Sources

This work draws on a wide range of manuscript and printed sources, including prayer books and proposals for liturgical revision; canons, laws, injunctions, and articles of religion; episcopal visitation books and the records of local ecclesiastical administration; parish registers and churchwardens' accounts; presentments, citations, and the answers of parties brought before the church courts. It also incorporates sermons, pamphlets and other contemporary publications, letters, diaries, autobiographies, and occasional works of literature.

These are not necessarily reliable sources, and none is free of problems. Most are heavily weighted to the clerical, to the male, and to the literate élite. The immediate circumstances that produced them have often faded from view, and even the most generous sources leave much of the background opaque. Behind the cramped writing and brief entries in the ecclesiastical records lie stories of village confrontations whose passions can be more readily imagined than revealed. We know only those cases which came to court and for which documentary evidence has survived. It is often hard to tell how serious an offence had been committed, who, exactly, was offended, and how a particular episode became a matter of record and discipline. In the rare cases when personal testimony survives to amplify the allegation we are faced with problems of truth and diction, what had to be said to get the case into court, what had to be said to conform the story to the law, and the demands of judicial process. We may choose to call this surviving material 'evidence', in accord with established historical principles, so long as we recognize the mixture of reportage, prescription, book-keeping, special pleading, selectivity, and fiction that so often renders evidence intractable.

Similarly diaries, tracts, and sermons employed codes and conventions that render their modern reading problematic. It is by no means a simple matter to catch and to calibrate the nuances of language, rhetoric, argument, and assumptions that shaped religious writing in an age of Renaissance, Reformation, and Revolution. Taken together, however, these sources reveal the range of issues and the spectrum of voices that ran through the religious culture of Elizabethan and Stuart England. Through careful handling they can show the alteration of concerns over time and may also be made to illuminate the behaviour and opinions of the laity, the lesser folk, and of women.

From time to time I cite poetry and ballads, and fragments of speeches from plays. Works of the imagination have long been thought 'off-limits' to historians, and historians have kept their distance by declaring creative literature to be unreliable and unrepresentative. We were warned, on the one side, that we lacked the necessary literary, textual, or theoretical acumen, on the other that we risked looking 'the wrong way through the telescope'. Guardians of the craft will see that I make no claims to literary criticism, but I do insist that sixteenth- and seventeenth-century verse can be read historically by an historian. My reading of Herrick, for example, locates him in a particular cultural conversation in the reign of Charles I, concerned with the social and religious conduct of contested rites of passage. I am less concerned with Herrick as a poet, than as a distinctive or corroborative historical voice.[6]

Spelling and punctuation have been modernized, except in the titles of printed sources. All printed works were published in London unless otherwise noted. For works printed up to 1640 I have also provided the STC number from the revised *Short Title Catalogue*.[7] Dates are given 'old style', but the year is taken to begin on 1 January.

Territories

This book introduces a large number of individuals, many below the level of the gentry and the clergy, who would not otherwise find their way into works of historical scholarship. It is populated by men and women who have been temporarily dislodged from obscurity. Here they are not subsumed in demographic tabulations, nor eclipsed by fixation on the élite. Through judicious handling of sources we may occasionally be privileged to hear their voices, or at least a mediated version of what they are purported to have said. Their engagement with the authorities and with each other, as recorded in church court records, letters, and diaries, may stimulate us to reflect on complexity and diversity within the routines of birth, marriage, and death. Too often their stories are incomplete. Their voices are tantalizingly laconic, their tales interrupted by other business. None the less, by allowing them to strut and fret, by giving them their moment on stage, we may find our way towards a richer and more variegated picture of the past. Elizabethan and Stuart England, like Piers Plowman's England before it, appears here as 'a fair field full of folk', many of them with tales of joy and trouble.

This is not, however, 'history from below'. It does not set out to delineate 'popular culture' or to reconstruct the lives of ordinary people, both of which may prove to be historically irretrievable. It traces, rather, a history of transactions and engagements, including collisions and misunderstandings, between various sectors of post-reformation society. It investigates the variety of social interaction—top down, bottom up, and in all directions across the middle—amongst clergy and laity, men and women, governors and governed, at critical points in the life cycle. It is concerned with the interplay of secular and religious activity, the spiritual meanings of birth, marriage, and death, and the performance and critique of mandated and customary ceremonies. What follows is a blend of voices, including familiar voices, unheard voices, and the voices of the unheard of. My voice, inevitably, is part of the current. Like it or not, the historian's gaze is ever-present, with varying degrees of effacement and self-consciousness.

The work ranges widely over society, space, and time. Driven by my sources as well as my questions, I concentrate sometimes on the gentry and aristocracy, sometimes on the marginal and poor. Though wealth and status kept people apart, and some of the gaps were widening, their biological circumstances were not dissimilar and religion gave them a common liturgical ground. Only in the later seventeenth century, when the élite grew wealthier and more genteel and their rituals became more private and select, did the privileged classes withdraw from the customs of the wider community. Parish clergymen, the link between hierarchy and populus, feature prominently in this book as targets or instigators of investigation or as authors of tracts and sermons. They, after all, were central participants in the principal rites of passage, professionally involved in the rituals of hatching, matching, and dispatching.

I take all of England as my territory, and even venture occasionally to Ireland, Scotland, and Wales. I have drawn on the records of more than a dozen dioceses, covering more than thirty English counties. Diaries and other sources fill some of the gaps. If many of my examples come from London or Essex, Leicestershire or Oxfordshire, Yorkshire or Durham, that reflects the quality of the surviving records as well as the convenience of access to them. Though sensitive to regional variation, and as interested as any in bringing local cultures under scrutiny, I feel justified in treating England as one cultural area.[8] Church and state, and above all the Book of Common Prayer, provided a common framework for religiously scripted rituals, while secular behaviour and customary festivity, though locally nuanced, were recognizable and comparable from place to place.

I trace this history over almost 250 years. Ranging from the reign of Henry VIII (1509–47) to the reign of Queen Anne (1702–14), I concentrate on controversies from the Act of Uniformity of 1559 to the Toleration Act of 1689.

A social and cultural history of rites of passage cannot be written without the traditionally dominant framework of politics and religion. The establishment of protestantism under Elizabeth I and the subsequent challenges of puritans and traditionalists, James I's Hampton Court Conference and the balancing of consensus and discipline, Charles I's embrace of high ceremonialism and the collapse of his regime into revolution and war, the splintering of the English church in the 1640s and the confusions of the 1650s, the discords of the Restoration and the challenges of political and religious dissent: these provide a background for this book, just as they did for the millions of subjects and inhabitants who were trying, in difficult times, to get on with their lives.

Positions

This book is not constructed as an historiographical polemic. I am less interested in challenging the positions of other historians, and much more interested in evoking and commenting on a wide range of fascinating historical material. However, as readers will also discover, I find myself at odds with several well-entrenched academic views. The early modern period did not see, so far as I can tell, a growth of individualism. Individualism and communitarianism were entwined in tension throughout this time, as they had been for as far back as the evidence allows us to go. Nor do I discern significant changes in the structure of the family that have any bearing on the conduct of birth, marriage, and death, or anything to do with 'modernization'. The families I have encountered were nuclear in structure though fruitfully connected to their wider kin. Patriarchal ideology prevailed, though parents did not always control their children or husbands their wives. Gender created recurrent strains, though rarely so acute as to suggest a sex-gender system in crisis. Far from there being a paucity of emotional warmth in these families, I find their emotional lives to have been complex and intense, especially affected by grieving and loving. The control and performance of emotions became particularly fraught in courtship and marriage, death and mourning, and were further complicated by divisions between religious reformers and traditionalists, clergy and laity, educated and uneducated, and men and women. There is grist here for many mills, and readers will find useful chains of reference in my notes.

Puritans crop up repeatedly, especially in the period before 1640, but never as a party or movement. Some were critics of the Elizabethan church, who sought a stricter purge of ceremonies; some advocated a presbyterian ecclesiastical polity; a few embraced radical sectarianism. Most, however, were godly ministers or pious layfolk who could thrive within the established church, so long as they were permitted their own adjustments. This might mean that a minister dispensed with the surplice, though not necessarily on all occasions. In baptism, it might mean withholding the sign of the cross, or preferring a baptismal basin to the font, and perhaps some hesitancy about the role of godparents. In churching it could mean conducting the ceremony in the most comfortable part of the church, the woman attired as she pleased, along with a willingness to allow some churchings to be done at home. More puritans were moderate than zealous, and most took part in the solemnization of holy matrimony, even if they frowned on the use of the ring and thought 'giving the bride' an odd idea. They had few objections to the burial service, so long as there was no hint of prayer for the soul or undue stress on the certainty of glorious resurrection. From the accession of Queen Elizabeth to the collapse of the Caroline regime, a modest diversity of practice was accommodated within the uniform structures of the Church of England, only sometimes detected or disciplined by an unwinking archdeacon or bishop.

The polarities that some historians see between conformists and nonconformists appear less acute and less confrontational in much of the material analysed here. Mediation, brokering, and adjustment was more common than out-and-out intransigence. Of course, there were uncompromising bigots as well as determined disciplinarians, who generated lots of noise and paper; but for most of the time more moderate voices prevailed. Only when the hierarchy tilted toward Arminian theology and high ceremonial churchmanship in the 1620s and 1630s were mainstream puritans tarred as sectarians. The Laudian emphasis on the altar—which was to be re-edified and railed, carpeted and reverenced, and attended by communicants on their knees—may have convinced some critics that the protestant Reformation was coming undone. So too did the Caroline reimposition of the Declaration Concerning Lawful Sports, with its embrace of traditional merriments at the expense of strict Sabbatarianism. The Laudian approach to life-cycle ceremonies, especially baptism and churching, only exacerbated the problem by making them tests of conformity. These, by themselves, were no stirs to rebellion, but they built a legacy of bitterness and frustration that poisoned the community of Christians and did damage to the community of the realm.

As the Church of England fell apart and was then disbanded in the 1640s, a variety of experimental liturgical practices arose in its place. People continued to be born, to marry, and to die, and most still sought ceremonial sanctification for their baptisms, weddings, and funerals. In the confusions of the revolution, some families clung to the accustomed Anglican services, many adopted a less formal ceremony, while radicals gave up infant baptism and rejected religious ministration of marriages and funerals. The cultural matrix of the mid-seventeenth century was aflame with enormities and enmities that still await detailed investigation.

By the time the Church of England was revived in 1660 and re-established in 1662, an unknown proportion of the population had lost the habit of church attendance, had abandoned respect for episcopal discipline, or fallen prey to apathy or cynicism. The prayer-book ceremonies of the post-Restoration era were similar to those of the early seventeenth century but they no longer commanded near-universal acceptance. Pious and conscientious dissenters could now establish their own congregations and conduct their rites of passage how they wished, and by the reign of James II they could worship with impunity. The established church held on to its buildings and property, and probably held on to the bulk of its congregations. Most people still resorted to church for baptisms, marriages, and burials, though increasingly these services were private, unceremonial, or clandestine. Few of the issues that divided English protestants in the 1570s or the 1630s were resolved, but most people thought they no longer mattered.

In every period, from the mid-sixteenth century to the beginning of the eighteenth century, a minority could be found evading customary social conventions or dissenting from established ceremonial rules. Individuals abnegated their domestic duties when they engaged in sexual activity out of wedlock, or chose partners without parental consent. Couples defied community standards when they married secretly without licence or banns. Families fell short of neighbourly expectations if their hospitality was deficient at christenings, weddings, or funerals. Parishioners clashed with their ministers if they refused to follow the rubric in the Book of Common Prayer. Ministers gained the attention of the authorities if they themselves objected to the ceremony or circumvented some aspect of baptism, churching, matrimony, or burial. The records are filled with exceptional cases. Each violation tested the tolerance of authority and custom. Each challenge and defiance offered room for negotiation. Each act of deviance underscored the norm.

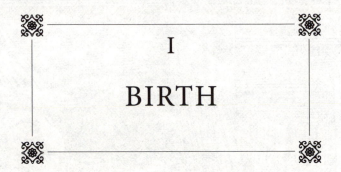

I

BIRTH

FIG. 1 'Birth room scene' from Eucharius Roesslin, *Der Schwanngeren Frawen und Hebammen Rosegartten* (Augsburg, 1529)

1

CHILDBED MYSTERIES

Childbirth was a private event with public significance, a domestic occurrence of which the commonwealth took note. In the household, as in the kingdom, the birth of a child established new relationships and new prospects as men and women and children negotiated their roles as parents, offspring, successors, and heirs. Without childbirth there could be no patriarchy, without human procreation no social reproduction. The woman's work of childbearing made mouths to feed and hands to work, new subjects, citizens, and Christians.

The primary work of childbearing, however, was not the production of a child but the deliverance of a woman. Attention focused on the female body and its punishing trials and tribulations. As all around her knew, the childbearing woman underwent a series of transformations affecting her physical, hormonal, emotional, social, domestic, and cultural condition. From conception to quickening, through all the anxieties of carrying and gestation, to the climax of labour, parturition, and recovery and the rewards of suckling and motherhood, each woman participated in a series of commonly shared experiences, performances, and ceremonies. Nature governed the biological parameters of her progress but culture gave childbirth its social meaning. Each stage of the transformation was nuanced by social scripting and social construction. Every phase of the process was invested with emotional, cultural, and religious significance. Though not formally ritualized or liturgically performed like the life-cycle services in the Book of Common Prayer, the ceremonies of childbirth were deeply embedded in the popular culture of Tudor and Stuart England. Women of every social background understood the protocols of pregnancy, midwifery, and female fellowship around the childbed. Indeed, many of the social and economic differences between élite and humble women were dissolved in the primal activity of birth.

Childbirth was women's work, in which men played distant supporting roles. Very few men gained intimate entry to the birthroom or knew what happened behind the screen. The transformations belonged to a powerfully gendered domain in which women relied on each other. Women were the central figures in childbearing, sharing the pain and the peril. Women were the guardians of its mysteries, the custodians of its lore. This poses particular problems for historians, regardless of their gender, since the bulk of the documentation of early modern society was generated by men. Women, for the most part, were illiterate, and they rarely set forth their experiences in writing. With a few remarkable exceptions, our sources are confined to the viewpoints of husbands, fathers, ministers, doctors, and scribes. Gynaecological handbooks and medical manuals, domestic conduct books and herbals, religious exhortations and diaries, and court records and correspondence, are all heavily weighted to the male point of view. Exploiting this evidence and seeing beyond its limits requires an unusual effort of empathy and imagination. Most of what we know about the childbed mysteries comes from the other side of the veil.

The ceremony of childbirth began with the recognition of pregnancy, gained pace with the sensation of quickening, progressed to preparations for labour, developed urgency with the ministrations of the midwife and her attendant women, and climaxed with the deliverance of the woman and the birth of the child. Its ritual aftermath included lying in, gossips' feasts, the child's christening, upsitting, the woman's 'month', and the ecclesiastical ceremony of churching or thanksgiving. Each stage involved a host of procedures and traditions, that varied in detail between social groups and regions and were subject to subtle modulations over time. Every aspect of the ceremony was subject to complications and controversies.[1]

God's Babies—the Spiritual Construction of Childbirth

The Christian culture of early modern England provided the master narrative for understanding the mystery of childbirth. Other systems of explanation—especially the learned traditions of ancient science, medieval medicine, and renaissance anatomy—addressed the physiology of childbearing, but fell short in describing its deeper spiritual significance. Indeed, thought Elizabethan churchmen, to construe childbirth as merely 'a natural and ordinary work of nature' was to deny God his honour and to deprive Christian parents of limitless spiritual comfort.[2] For the sixteenth and seventeenth centuries the miracle of reproduction was swathed in religious meaning. The Christian church, predominately a male institution, provided the language and told the stories that governed thinking about human reproduction. But the extent to which the public Christian discourse on childbirth was echoed within the private womanly domain of the birthroom is something we may never know.

From the point of view of the church, a woman in childbirth experienced both the curse of Eve and the grace of Christ. Motherhood, from the pulpit perspective, recapitulated the entire spiritual history of humankind. The woman bore children and suffered because she was stained by original sin. Yet miraculously, through Christ's redemption, she could be saved. Childbirth involved sorrow, shame, and chastisement; yet under Christ the woman's labour was part of a covenant of sanctification, mercy, and eternal comfort. Sermons, prayers, and pious meditations reiterated this theme in countless disquisitions on childbearing in Elizabethan and Stuart England.

The Old Testament set forth the story of God's punishment of Eve's transgression and the consequent curse that descended to all womankind through the ages. 'Unto the woman he said, I will greatly multiply thy sorrow and thy conception; in sorrow thou shalt bring forth children; and thy desire shall be to thy husband, and he shall rule over thee.' The pain and the peril of childbearing, the exercise of patriarchal authority, and the politics of reproduction all descended from this awful judgement. Characteristically, the New Testament offered fresh hope, though no diminution of female subordination. 'The woman being deceived was in the transgression. Notwithstanding she shall be saved in childbearing, if they continue in faith and charity and holiness with sobriety,' explained St Paul to Timothy. This epistle, according to one seventeenth-century clergyman, offered 'heart-reviving words to every drooping woman'.[3]

Religious writers usually insisted that sexual activity, conception, and childbearing were joyful and lawful activities, so long as they took place within marriage. They were part of God's plan (at least the revised post-lapsarian plan) for his creation. 'We are plainly taught of God that the seed of faithful parentage is holy from the very birth,' opined Richard Hooker. 'The fruit of marriage is birth, and the companion of birth, travail.' The newborn child was the 'pledge of love' between husband and wife, 'a joyful benediction' to be welcomed as a future Christian, repeated many a seventeenth-century sermon. It became a commonplace of English protestant instruction that 'children are a blessing, an inheritance, a crown, a reward unto us of the Lord'. William Hinde in his eulogy of the puritan squire John Bruen repeated that 'children are the inheritance of the Lord, and the fruit of the womb his exceeding rich reward'.[4]

Nor was this exclusively a male or clerical perspective. Guided by faith, the devout Elizabeth Joceline wrote in 1622 that she 'earnestly desired of God that I might be a mother to one of his children'. Elizabeth Clinton, the Countess of Lincoln, wrote after eighteen pregnancies that 'children are God's blessings', though she also saw childbearing as the consequence of Eve's transgression. 'It pleased God to give me the blessing of conception,' wrote Alice Thornton of her first pregnancy in 1652, and God was her constant companion whenever she was big with child or came to term. 'God gave her conception,' wrote John Angier of his wife in 1642, though he himself surely had something to do with it. 'Blessed be to God for his mercy to her,' exclaimed John Evelyn when his wife was 'bearing' again in 1664.[5] Pious lay men and women shared with the clergy this popular theology of reproduction.

Using biblical imagery more resonant of the Mediterranean than the temperate environment of northern Europe, early modern preachers likened a man's productive wife to 'the fruitful vine, and the number of his children like olive branches round about his table'. Adopting this imagery, the childless Sarah Savage in the 1680s longed to be 'a fruitful vine'.[6] It was a common conceit in religious writing, as well as in literature and folklore, that the woman was like a tree or a vegetable, her offspring the fruit of her womb. God was a gardener and with his husbandmen on earth (husbands indeed), set out to shape the branches and tend the vine. 'A man's yard [i.e. penis] is, as it were, the plough wherewith the ground is tilled, and made fit for production of fruit,' observed the seventeenth-century midwife Jane Sharp, adding, 'man . . . is the agent and tiller and sower of the ground, woman is the patient or ground to be tilled'. Under God's guidance, in popular medical writing, the seed became flesh, in a ferment of water, blood, and milk. It was through the woman's body, through its ingoings, outcomings, and cultivation, that mankind could go forth and multiply.[7]

Childbearing, everyone agreed, was an obligation for married women. Matrimony existed, so the wedding service reminded everyone, 'for . . . the procreation of children'.[8] Giving birth was a Christian duty that was fully consonant with God's law. Avoiding pregnancy was a sin. But a tension existed between interpreters who emphasized the spiritual rewards of procreation and those who stressed the inherent sinfulness of the carnal act. Religious ambivalence about the godliness or sinfulness of childbirth reflected similar strains between the New Testament and the Old, between joy and despair. The familiar words of the baptism service, repeated in countless sermons, reminded listeners that 'all men be born and conceived in sin'. The ninth of the Thirty-Nine Articles, on the subject 'Of Original or Birth Sin', explained 'that the flesh lusteth always contrary to the spirit, and therefore in every person born into this world it deserveth God's wrath and damnation'.[9]

Few preachers went so far as to suggest that lawful sexual intercourse was unclean or that childbirth inherently involved pollution. But some of the sterner sort drew attention to the fundamental corruption in which all human beings were conceived and born. This sinful state, of course, was a consequence of humankind's post-lapsarian condition and had nothing directly to do with the processes of reproduction. But some godly writers were

so overwhelmed by the discourse of sin and salvation that they could not mention childbirth without reference to defilement and the 'spot of child-bed
taint'. The Jacobean preacher Daniel Featley reminded a christening congregation in 1619 of 'that filth and corruption which we draw from the loins of our
parents'. Similarly Sampson Price, in a sermon of 1624, associated birth with
nakedness, sin, and shame. 'Man . . . enters into the world bathed in blood, an
image of his sin . . . our nativity is miserable because vile and unclean.' The
remedy was to be born again. In the same vein, though with a different religious
sensibility, the puritan artisan Nehemiah Wallington grieved that he was 'born
in sin and came forth polluted into this wicked world'.[10]

John Donne's preaching on the subject of childbearing emphasized the
sinfulness, uncleanness, and filthiness of human origins. 'Our mothers conceived us in sin; and being wrapped up in uncleanness there, can any man
bring a clean thing out of filthiness?' Donne asked at the churching of Lady
Doncaster in 1618. 'We come into this world as the Egyptians went out of it,
swallowed and smothered in a red sea, *pueri sanguinum, et infirmi,* weak and
bloody infants at our birth.' The newborn babe was contaminated by spiritual and material stains, its physical loathsomeness, *a maternis visceribus,* a
symbol of the vileness of the human condition. One can imagine the charmed
discomfort of his auditors as Donne piled on extravagant references to dung,
excrement, blood, and rottenness, as well as falsehood, treachery, and deceit.
This may seem strange for a sermon of thanksgiving after childbirth, especially one preached before members of the Jacobean aristocracy; but the point
of Donne's rant was to emphasize the horror of sin which was common to
all, and to indicate its partial remedy in baptism.[11]

Some of the ministers who associated childbirth with defilement, Donne
included, did so in the course of polemical, historical, and liturgical discussions about purification, thanksgiving, and the churching of women. This
was a controversial subject, reaching to the heart of religious ceremony and
ecclesiastical discipline, as we will see later. References to childbirth in this
context might then be understood to have more to do with theology, liturgy,
and church politics than with close observation of natural processes. The
language of religious polemic shaped this part of the spiritual construction
of childbirth. Unfortunately, we seldom hear this debate from a lay point of
view, and rarely from that of a woman.

In unreformed popular culture as well as in fastidious high-church circles,
the opinion still circulated that childbirth involved some kind of pollution,
and that an unchurched mother was in some sense 'green' or unclean. Reacting
against the view that there was something loathsome or corrupt in natural
reproductive processes, puritans often argued that it was absurd to treat a

recently delivered woman, in the month before her churching, as if she had committed 'some grievous offence'. But the mainstream Church of England never regarded the thanksgiving ceremony of churching as purification. No 'purification' was necessary if nothing impure had taken place, though each newly delivered mother was obliged to give thanks. Full discussion of the complexities of purification, thanksgiving, and the churching of women is reserved for a later chapter.[12]

Like their early Stuart predecessors, high Anglican clergy of the later seventeenth century sometimes made reference to 'the stains of childbirth', especially when preaching their Candlemas sermons. But Candlemas (2 February), commemorating the Purification of the Blessed Virgin, invoked unreasonable comparisons between the purity of Mary under ancient Judaism and the condition of ordinary childbearing women in early modern England. Once again, the rhetoric of preaching supplied language about childbirth that was not necessarily applicable to the birthroom. When the church discussed childbirth it talked about godliness, not gynaecology.[13]

Sermons were not the best place to discuss the physical details of procreation, and at least one preacher admitted that treating the topic at all required exceptional delicacy. Public discussion of childbirth by men would be considered an indelicate intrusion into the female domain. The Jacobean preacher John Day, in a Christmas sermon commemorating that most remarkable of all childbirths, cut short his classical, historical, and biblical disquisition by saying, 'but I spare your ears in this place, and so much the rather for that sin hath made our bringing forth so full of shame, that we can hardly speak thereof, though never so warily, but we may be thought by women kind to pass our bounds'. Day's discomfort may also have been shared by some of the parishioners of Much Totham, Essex, whose vicar, Ambrose Westrop, was said to 'profane the ordinance of preaching, by venting in the pulpit matters concerning the secrets of women'. Westrop was acutely misogynistic, well beyond the Caroline ministerial mainstream, and he was said to have regarded both marital sexual intercourse and normal menstruation as sources of pollution. Not surprisingly, radical puritans took the opportunity to remove him from his parish in the sequestrations of 1643.[14]

Eve's sin explained women's pain, but not everyone received the story of the fall with due awe and reverence. The Stuart minister John Ward tells the story of

a woman in Warwickshire, being in travail and sorely afflicted with pain, they could not rule her, but sent for my Lady Puckering to try what she could do; when she came she exhorted her to patience, and told her that this misery was brought upon her sex by her grandmother Eve, by eating an apple. 'Was it?' says she, 'I wish the apple had choked her,' whereupon my lady was constrained to turn herself about, and go out of the room and laugh.

In May 1662 Samuel Pepys 'heard a good sermon of Mr. Woodcock's at our church. Only, in his later prayer for a woman in childbed, he prayed that God would deliver her from the hereditary curse of childbearing, which seemed a pretty strange expression.'[15] Popular Pelagians, amongst whom Pepys might be numbered, were disinclined to worry about original sin and more prepared to treat childbirth in sexual than in spiritual terms. This may have been the most widespread view among the laity, but it is slenderly represented in the surviving records.

Comforts for Childbearing Women

Whether the pain of childbirth was natural or spiritual in origin, a consequence of female physiology or the ancestral curse of Eve, women took measures to lessen its intensity and reduce its accompanying peril. Midwives, wise women, and many of the sorority of matrons who gathered in the birthroom, knew special phrases as well as concoctions, and applications of sympathetic magic, that would help a woman through pregnancy and labour. The female subculture of childbirth included intimate practices and beliefs that were barely suspected by husbands or priests, were long resistant to reform, and which remain virtually inaccessible to historians. Late medieval midwives are said to have used the following Latin charm: 'O infans, sive vivus, sive mortuus, exi foras, quia Christus te vocat ad lucem,' which sounds more learned than popular. A Leicestershire midwife was reportedly heard intoning, 'In the name of the Father and of the Son and of the Holy Ghost, come safe and go safe, what have we here,' during the course of a difficult delivery in 1569. Others may have used less recognizably Christian prayers.[16]

Herbal medicine, primarily in the female domain, offered a variety of remedies for hastening or easing delivery. 'Kitchen physic' yielded salves and caudles that could be administered with or without accompanying prayers. A diligent midwife's physic garden would include lilies and roses, cyclamen or sowbread, columbine or aquilegia, all of which were believed to ease the pains of birth or to hasten delivery. Traditional herbals included remedies 'to help conception', 'to nourish the child in the womb', 'to stay the longing of woman with child', 'to procure an easy and speedy delivery to women in travail', 'to bring down the afterbirth', and 'to increase milk in women's breasts'. Printed herbals, which were frequently refined and republished in the sixteenth and seventeenth centuries, served as botanical histories and pharmacological reference works for apothecaries and physicians, but they also gave scholarly botanical precision to the folkloric general knowledge of wise women and midwives.[17] In addition to traditional herbal concoctions for women in labour, laudanum became available in late Elizabethan London, to be joined in the seventeenth century by such questionable remedies as the exotic maldiva nut.[18]

Traditional Roman Catholicism offered an armoury of comforts to the childbearing woman, many of which were discredited with the Reformation. Under the old dispensation, a woman in labour could call on St Margaret or the Virgin or one of a host of local supernatural helpers, and could supplement this saintly intercession by clutching religious relics, girdles, amulets, and fragments of the consecrated host. Only through enquiries at the dissolution of the monasteries in 1536 do we learn that the convent of Bruton, Somerset, treasured 'our lady's girdle of Bruton, red silk, which is a solemn relic sent to women travailing which shall not miscarry *in partu*'. Other monastic houses loaned out holy girdles or belts, necklaces, and relics as aids to women who were pregnant or lying in. Bishop Nicholas Shaxton of Salisbury thought it necessary in 1538 to prohibit the use of 'any girdles, purses, measures of our Lady, or such other superstitious things, to be occupied about the woman while she laboureth, to make her believe to have the better speed by it'. In some places, it was believed, a woman's own girdle would serve to ease labour if it had been wrapped around sanctified bells. Village wisdom and folk religion provided additional assistance in the form of special stones, charms, and potions that promised a safe deliverance or relief from childbed pains.[19]

In traditional popular catholicism, the holy sacrament was the most powerful medicine of all. The Sarum Missal, one of the most popular formularies of pre-reformation worship, included masses 'on behalf of women labouring with child' and supplications to St Mary, 'the benign assister of women in travail'. The catholic Bishop Bonner admonished childbearing women in mid-Tudor England 'to come to confession and to receive the sacrament especially when their time draweth nigh'. Some people believed that attendance at mass in this condition helped the unborn child as well as the expectant mother, and that its spiritual benefits extended to a child who might die before baptism. If the woman could not come to mass then the mass, or some part of it, might be taken to the woman.[20] Alice Thornton, a staunchly protestant Yorkshirewoman, took the sacrament in 1665 in readiness for lying in. 'After this great mercy in the renewing of our vows and covenants with God,' she declared, 'I was fully satisfied in that condition, whether for life or death.' In later seventeenth-century variants on this tradition, Margaret Godolphin 'received the heavenly Viaticum' (her name for the eucharist) at the onset of labour in 1678, and John Evelyn's daughter took the sacrament a week after giving birth in September 1694. Like the mass a century or more earlier, the eucharist served to settle the soul in preparation for an unpredictable outcome.[21]

The Elizabethan Jesuit John Gerard told the story of Lady Grisell Wodehouse, who seemed to be dying after childbirth. 'An old priest, one of those ordained before the beginning of Elizabeth's reign [came] to give the lady all the last rites of the church. After making her confession she was annointed and received Viaticum and (this is the wonderful thing) within half an hour she was recovered and was out of danger.' Gerard marvelled that her husband, Sir Philip Wodehouse, a protestant, 'wondered how it had happened. We explained to him that one of the effects of the holy sacrament of Extreme Unction was to restore bodily health when God judged it to be for the soul's good. This completed the husband's conversion.' Protestants would have been shocked by this recommendation of unction, and by other signs of resurgent catholicism.[22]

Reforming churchmen sought to suppress traditional practices they deemed superstitious, including women's semi-secret rituals surrounding childbirth. The protestant attack was most ardent during Elizabeth's reign, when 'superstitious' customs were still deeply entrenched. But unauthorized practices continued in the perilous intimacy of the birthroom long after the establishment of the reformation, and not only in the much maligned 'dark corners of the land'. Protestant hostility to potions and charms formed part of the larger campaign for the reformation of manners and the expunging of superstition. It was not explicitly misogynist, although it stripped away some female comforts. The Church of England no longer countenanced a woman's promise to go on pilgrimages if God gave her an easy labour, or her employment of 'purses, measures of our Lady, or such other superstitious things . . . to make her believe to have the better speed by it'. Bishop Barnes of Durham instructed his clergy in 1577 to discipline 'all such women as shall . . . at the child's birth use superstitious ceremonies, orisons, charms or devilish rites or sorceries'. Midwives were put on oath not to 'use any kind of sorcery or incantation' and to inform against any who so offended.[23]

Many traditional practices survived the reformation, and not all were corrected by protestant instruction. Richard Greenham, ministering to his parishioners in Elizabethan Cambridgeshire,

observed many things to be corrupted by superstition which were good in their first original, as, when women drawing near the time of their deliverance do require the prayers of the church, as in a farewell commit themselves to the intercessions of the saints, partly for that they are about to enter into a dangerous travail, partly for that they shall be long without the public means of the assembly, and therefore stand in need of the grace of God watching over them.[24]

Though it was perfectly understandable that women should clutch at whatever helped sustain them through the travails of childbirth, it was offensive to
advanced protestant sensibilities if those props were tinged with catholicism
and superstition.

Catholic families were especially instrumental in keeping traditional practices alive, including recourse to holy girdles and invocations of the saints.
But one did not have to be a follower of the old religion to turn to eagle
stones or other childbirth talismans. One such wonder was offered to Margaret Cavendish, the Countess of Newcastle, to ease her labour in 1633. Anne,
Viscountess Conway, secured another which she wore while pregnant in 1658
for its 'great virtue in hard labour'. So-called 'eagle stones' (aetites, a stone
within a stone) reputedly came from Cyprus or Africa but they were readily
'to be had in London' and were strongly recommended. The seventeenth-
century midwife Jane Sharp advised expectant mothers to wear one, 'for I
have proved it to be true, that this stone hanged about a woman's neck and
so as to touch her skin, when she is with child, will preserve her safe from abortion, and will cause her to be safe delivered when the time comes'.[25] Other
medical manuals repeated this advice. The nested stones apparently worked
through the principles of sympathies and signatures, the stone within the stone
signifying the security of the child within the womb. Alternatives to the eagle
stone included therapeutic lodestones and 'the skin of a wild ox' tied to the
woman's thighs.[26] Rather than deriding such practices as superstitious, the
more thoughtful commentators commended the goodwill shown by friends
who provided these items and the solicitude of husbands who sought to protect
their wives and future offspring by every means their culture afforded.

English protestantism continued to provide a powerful range of spiritual
comfort and assistance to women in need. Although the Church of England
no longer countenanced special masses for childbearing women or prayers to
the saints on their behalf during labour, it strenuously encouraged the use of
prayer. In the crisis of childbirth, when life and death walked hand in hand, a
pious family had but one place to turn. Domestic prayers and religious exercises were designed to attract God's attention; they petitioned, they assuaged,
they explained; and they provided a pathway to reconciliation if anything
went seriously wrong. Thomas Bentley's massive *Monument of Matrons*, published in 1582, includes model prayers for 'women with child, and in childbed, and after their delivery', as well as prayers for midwives and prayers of
thanksgiving.[27]

Devotional exercises for use during pregnancy and labour formed part of
the revived religiosity of early Stuart England. They were written by mainstream Calvinists as well as by advanced Arminians. Though framed by

reference to Eve's transgression, their prayers did not dwell on pain and punishment, but stressed instead the blessings of fruitfulness, the honour to women, divine deliverance, and the prospect of salvation. Popular devotional manuals such as Robert Hill's *Pathway to Prayer and Pietie*, which went through eight editions between 1606 and 1628, included model prayers and meditations for women in travail. So too did Samuel Hieron's *A Helpe Unto Devotion*, which reached its twentieth edition in 1636. Daniel Featley's *Ancilla Pietatis: or, The Hand-Maid to Private Devotion,* which went through six editions between 1626 and 1639, similarly offered prayers and admonitions to the childbearing woman. Addressed to the middling and better sort, the message of these handbooks was invariably one of stern comfort. For the woman commencing labour, Hill observed, 'her sin is great, her danger is not small, her pains will be grievous, and the hour of life is now at hand'. 'Religious women', Featley advised, 'ought patiently and comfortably to endure the pains of childbirth', not least because 'child-bearing hath a promise annexed unto it of a blessing temporal/spiritual if the mother be faithful and so continue'.[28] Neither Featley nor Hill would wish these trials and rewards for themselves, but their mainstream Christian perspective gave high value to the reproductive fulfilment of women and re-emphasized the spiritual construction of childbirth.

Competing directly with Featley, John Cosin's *Collection of Private Devotions,* which went through five editions between 1627 and 1638, also featured prayers 'to be used by women that travail with child' and for 'thanksgiving after childbirth'. The expectant mother would pray for protection 'against all the dangers and pains of my labour and travail' and ask God that 'I may be safely delivered of this happy fruit which thou hast created in my womb'. The newborn child, 'a joyful benediction, even the fruit of mine own womb', would 'forthwith' be readied to be 'born again by baptism'. In a similar vein Samuel Rowlands printed 'a prayer for a woman in time of her travail', and George Wither composed hymns for 'when a woman hath conceived' and 'when a woman is safe delivered'.[29] A later work, John Oliver's *A Present for Teeming Women*, included 'a prayer before childbirth' and 'scripture directions for a woman with child' written for Mrs Bridget Seymour of Hanford House, Dorset. This was printed by a woman, Sarah Griffin, and published by another, Mary Rothwell, as a further commendation to the ladies.[30]

Surviving diaries and letters sometimes show lay men and women adapting these prayers, or making their own, in stressful domestic circumstances. 'Childbirth is God's work,' Lady Massingberd counselled her daughter, 'pray spare yourself as much time as you can for meditation and prayer to acquaint yourself with God.' The pious Elizabeth Egerton, Countess of Bridgewater, typically turned to prayers and meditations to ease her through childbearing.

'Oh God, to thee I give all praise and glory, that thou hast been pleased to bless me, that I have conceived again with child . . . I beg of thee to have compassion on me in the great pain I am to feel in the bringing forth of this my child.' Even when praising God her mind did not stray far from reflection on 'the great torture of childbirth'. She died in childbed in 1663 aged 37 after bringing forth several children.[31]

Other godly families engaged in prayer, together with more mundane preparations, at the critical moments of a pregnancy. Devotional handbooks were unnecessary if the prayers came freely from the heart. In 1638 the Northamptonshire puritan diarist Robert Woodford raised his own heartfelt prayers for 'my dear wife who is now in travail'. During each of Hannah Woodford's pregnancies her husband self-consciously looked to the Lord; her own spiritual preparations are unknown. In July 1640, amidst the burgeoning crisis of the kingdom, Woodford prayed for those closest to him: 'Lord look upon my dear wife in her present condition now great with child, Lord give her a gracious delivery, give her strength to bring forth, preserve her life, give the child right shape and form, continue her life of it and of the rest, make them instruments of thy glory and vessels of mercy.' And the following year, awaiting the outcome of his wife's fifth pregnancy, Woodford prayed, 'Lord order every conveniency, give her a gracious delivery in thy due time, the sentence on her is to bring forth in pain and on me to get my bread by the sweat of my brows, Lord stand by her thy servant and support her graciously. Lord, many have lately died in childbed . . . Lord build up and continue our family still.'[32]

The Essex clergyman Ralph Josselin likewise 'sought to God' on the eve of his wife's labour in 1645, and prayed that 'God would order all providences so as we might rejoice in his salvation.' In 1654, after another satisfactory outcome, the diarist recorded, 'I am persuaded my particular earnest prayers were moving for her in the very moment of her delivery.' In 1657, at the time of Jane Josselin's quickening, 'the women met with her in prayer', but since Josselin himself was not with them, there is no indication of what they said.[33] Typically the male diarist was concerned to prevent loss, while his wife prayed to endure pain. It was his burden to beget and multiply, hers to suffer the curse of Eve.

Seventeenth-century dissenters, like their conforming brethren, argued that the pain and the peril of childbearing could be alleviated by religious exercises and attention to prayer. Richard Adams, a nonconformist under Charles II, advised that a godly life laid 'a sure ground of a comfortable exemption from the curse in childbearing, and of the removal of that original guilt which otherwise greatens the sorrows of women in such a case'. It was Adams who glossed the words of Paul to Timothy as 'heart-reviving words to every droop-ing woman'.[34]

Later Stuart nonconformists conducted days of prayer and fasting on be-half of women in childbed. In December 1661, the Manchester minister Henry Newcome recalls, 'I was sent for out to the poor woman that was in labour and prayed with her, but she died this evening.' In November 1672 Newcome went 'to Benjamin Booker's to a private day, on the account of his wife who is with child'. Oliver Heywood 'sought God' while his wife lay in and 'praised God' when she brought forth a son. And in his public ministry Heywood 'kept a private fast at Mr Dawson's house for his wife to beg mercy for her in childbearing' in May 1673. In May 1678 Heywood and his wife visited Isaac Balmes at Boulin, Lancashire, and 'kept a fast there for his wife near her time', adding, 'God helped.' In September he 'kept a private fast for young John Kershaw's wife in Wyke, great with child', and the following August again 'kept a fast with many women for Esther Kershaw's safe deliverance in childbearing'.[35] These nonconformist gatherings provided spiritual fellow-ship and material support at critical moments, and needed neither handbook nor prayer book to guide their religious rituals.

Just as devout households prayed for the safety of the mother and the happy deliverance of her womb, so the kingdom—the family writ large—was similarly called to prayers during the pregnancy of a queen. In 1605, for example, the government of James I printed prayers 'for the queen's maj-esty's safe deliverance in her childbirth', and appointed them 'to be used in the church at morning and evening prayer by every minister'. Those who com-plied found seven variant prayers asking God to preserve Queen Anne from 'the great pains and peril of childbirth'. They prayed God that 'through thy heavenly protection she may be safely delivered of the blessed fruit of her body, and become a joyful mother of a happy issue'. So might any husband pray for his wife, or any minister for his parishioner. God had appointed 'to all the sons of Eve one and the same entrance into life through the sorrows and pangs of childbirth', and the royal family was not exempt. A short while later came another little prayer book containing prayers of thanksgiving 'for the queen's majesty's safe deliverance' on 9 April, which proved to be just one of the deliverances of 1605. The nation was likewise asked to join in prayer during the reign of Charles I to seek God's protection of Queen Henrietta Maria as she produced her 'long desired' and 'happy issue'.[36]

The vocabulary of deliverance linked public and private blessings. Chris-topher Hooke's lecture on the occasion of Elizabeth Savile's deliverance in childbirth in 1590 made explicit reference to the nation's 'miraculous deliver-ance from the Spanish invasion' two years previously. England's deliverance from the Gunpowder Plot could be likened to the deliverance of the Stuart queens. The official prayers of thanksgiving printed after 5 November 1605 exactly matched the design of those for the safe deliverance of the queen six months before.[37]

Suffering and Death

Conventional Christian counsel considered the two most likely outcomes for the woman in childbed, 'a comfortable sanctified deliverance here, or a blessed translation to heaven', the former 'to reap in joy what was sown in tears', the latter joy everlasting.[38] Two lives were at stake, that of the mother and her newborn baby, and death was a prospect for them both. But childbirth meant more than a calculus of souls.

Every stage of the childbirth experience exposed the woman's vulnerability and summoned intimations of mortality. Even uncomplicated childbearing involved laborious travail, sharp discomfort, and the prospect of lingering distress. Women otherwise blessed with robust good health often feared that childbirth might kill them. The pain and the peril—Eve's legacy and nature's course—was a rite of violence through which all mothers passed and which a minority would not survive. This was no time for subtle discussion of predestination or the possible torments of hell (although strict Calvinists spoke of both), but rather for soothing words about deliverance and salvation.

Hearing the screams from the birthroom, some men were astonished that their women came through alive. Others accepted the continuance of life as a matter of routine. Pain was to be expected, death to be feared. The Elizabethan separatist Henry Barrow thought 'the safe deliverance of these women . . . though a singular benefit of God, yet a thing natural, ordinary, and common'. The Jacobean puritan William Gouge was more impressed by the mystery of survival and more inclined to give praise, considering the safe deliverance of women from childbed 'near a miracle . . . wherein the Almighty doth so evidently manifest his great power and providence'.[39] Most of the popular devotional manuals included prayers of thanksgiving after childbirth as well as prayers for its successful outcome.[40]

Male diarists report their wives' fears and their own anxieties at these critical junctures. Richard Rogers, the puritan minister of Whethersfield, Essex, learnt of a neighbour's death in childbed in 1588 and worried that his own wife Barbara might die likewise. 'I, seeing by much pain in wife and near childbirth many likelihoods of our separation, considered how many uncomfortablenesses the Lord had kept from me hitherto by those which I then saw must needs come if he should part us.' Among his concerns was the complication of having to marry again. Fortunately Rogers could follow this diary entry with another a few weeks later, '*Natus est Ezechiel meus* and my wife hardly escaped.'[41]

Ralph Josselin recorded that his wife Jane was 'oppressed with fears' at the onset of labour in 1645. She 'was wonderfully afraid and amazed' and experienced 'great fears' and 'sad pains and sadder fears' during subsequent deliveries. Yet Mrs Josselin brought forth ten children from at least fifteen recorded pregnancies, and outlived her husband. In June 1654, as Jane Josselin struggled to deliver her seventh child, her husband struggled with the Lord. 'My heart was sensible in some measure how great a loss it would be if God took her from me, and yet my spirit was borne up in expectation of the mercy.'[42] Fear was a recurrent companion, though obviously different for women and men.

The Cambridgeshire minister Isaac Archer likewise noted in his diary in 1670, 'my wife growing nearer her time was troubled with fears she should die, and I feared it too. She was much taken up, I saw, with such thoughts, and I was glad, because it was an occasion of seeking God.' After giving birth again in 1672 Mrs Archer experienced 'the very agonies of death, as she thought, and was seized all over with intolerable pain, and possessed with a persuasion she should die that night. Her father and mother were with her, and we all had grief enough.' Once again she recovered. Archer's diary, to be examined in detail below, shows Mrs Archer surviving nine completed pregnancies and several miscarriages, yet her fear, and the fear of those around her, was real enough.[43]

Several diarists saw some of their worst fears fulfilled. Nicholas Assheton recorded in February 1618, 'my wife in labour of childbirth. Her delivery was with such violence, as the child died within half an hour and, but for God's wonderful mercy, more than human reason could expect, she had died; but he spared her a while longer to me, and took the child to his mercy.' John Angier's wife Ellen had premonitions of dying in childbed and indeed died soon after giving birth in 1642. According to the diarist, 'after her conception her weakness and weariness increased, and was not mitigated, as usually, after she quickened, so that she feared she should not come to her time, and often said it would be her death'. She was delivered on 21 November 1642, 'in the evening after hard labour'. The child survived, but Mrs Angier never recovered and died three weeks later.[44]

John Evelyn's friend, Margaret Godolphin, was similarly unfortunate. She appeared 'exceeding well laid' in 1678, but 'so careful and provident she was to prepare for all possible accidents that, as if she foresaw her end, she received the heavenly Viaticum but the Sunday before, after a most solemn recollection; and putting all her domestic concerns in the exactest order, left a letter

directed to her husband, to be opened in case she died in childbed.' Mrs
Godolphin gave birth on Tuesday, 3 September, and died six days later, most
likely of puerperal fever.[45]

The classic story of Christian fortitude, forbearance, and spiritual preparation concerned Elizabeth Joceline, a godly Jacobean gentlewoman, who looked
on her first pregnancy in 1622 as a likely sentence of doom. 'When she first
felt herself quick with child, as then travelling with death itself, she secretly
took order for the buying a new winding sheet,' and called for this winding
sheet to her childbed. She survived parturition, giving birth to a daughter,
but died nine days later of 'a violent fever' at the age of 26. Mrs Joceline's
pious meditations, published posthumously as *The Mothers Legacie to her
Unborn Child*, were frequently reprinted with a eulogy of her life, and the
account of her morbid preparation was often retold. The tale provided a
model of faith and fortitude for all expectant mothers.[46]

Fearful expectations abound in the records, and examples of women dying
in childbed are not hard to find. But it would be misleading to deduce from
this evidence that childbed mortality was common. In fact the opposite is true.
Most women survived childbirth without complications and most mothers
quickly recovered. Childbirth was a natural occurrence, notwithstanding the
pain and the peril, and emphatically had more to do with life than with
death. A leading Jacobean medical manual, repeating ancient wisdom, asserted
optimistically 'that of a thousand births, there is scarce one found that is
amiss'.[47] Modern demographic calculations also suggest that early modern
childbirth was not so dangerous as was feared, though the chance of death
was more like one in a hundred.

In an important essay titled 'Did the Mothers Really Die? Three Centuries
of Maternal Mortality in "The World We Have Lost" ', Roger Schofield cal-
culates that 9.3 per 1,000 or just under one per cent of mothers died in
childbed in Elizabethan England. The rate deteriorated in the seventeenth
century, as demographic conditions generally worsened, to a peak of 15.7 per
1,000 in the reign of Charles II. Conditions were always worse in London—
sometimes twice the national rate—with maternal mortality as high as 23.5
per 1,000 in Aldgate parish in the 1590s. But London is a special case, in this
as in so many other things. Contrary to popular myth, women were not in 'a
state of virtually perpetual pregnancy' in the early modern period. On average
they could expect six or seven pregnancies (not all successful), and therefore,
according to Schofield, 'a woman . . . would have run a six to seven per cent
risk of dying in childbed at some time in her procreative career'. But mothers,
like other people, also died of other things. Schofield has calculated the risk
to women of dying during their non-childbearing intervals, and concludes,

'the risk she ran of dying in childbed was no greater than the risk she ran every year of dying from infectious disease and a whole variety of other causes'.[48] If we accept this evidence, we have a broad demographic framework in which to set particular experiences. Most pregnancies turned out successfully for both mother and child. But one does not need actuarial precision to be frightened.

The Archers: A Family History

Isaac Archer's account of his wife's childbearing experience is worth reporting in detail. Not yet widely known, though as lively and informative in some areas as the celebrated diary of Ralph Josselin, Archer's diary provides a candid and conscientious account of successive childbirths as well as spiritual and professional difficulties.[49] Inevitably, Mrs Archer's childbearing is reported entirely from her husband's point of view. Isaac Archer was the vicar of Chippenham, Cambridgeshire, and Freckenham, Suffolk, during the reign of Charles II. Born in 1641 and educated at Trinity College, Cambridge, during the Protectorate, he became a godly Anglican minister with pronounced sympathy for nonconformists. Married in November 1667, Archer expressed delight in his change of estate. 'I found my wife perfectly devoted to please me, and I bless God for giving me one with a meek and quiet spirit, and well disposed,' he wrote the following February.[50] Like many other seventeenth-century diarists Archer never writes his partner's name, referring to her throughout as 'my wife'.

Anne Archer became pregnant in 1668 and on 3 April 1669 'she was delivered of a lusty girl . . . after six hours pains'. After greeting his firstborn daughter Archer confided to his diary, 'I prayed for a boy.' A frightening incident occurred three days after the birth, when the house caught fire as Mrs Archer lay in helpless in her enclosed chamber. After the blaze was quenched her husband declared it a deliverance, comparable to Mrs Archer's deliverance from the pains and perils of childbearing. This child died one year later.[51]

Anne's second pregnancy in 1670 prompted her husband's morbid reflections. 'My wife growing nearer her time was troubled with fears she should die, and I feared it too. She was much taken up, I saw, with such thoughts, and I was glad, because it was an occasion of seeking God, as I know she did.' These fears were almost realized, for shortly after giving birth to another daughter on 27 November 1670, Mrs Archer came close to death. 'About one o'clock my wife began to faint, through an overflow of blood, and was without sensible pulse or colour; we gave her over and she took leave of me (which much concerned me); the women told me she would lose all her blood.' Fortunately

the haemorrhage ceased and she recovered, though not without general distress.[52] Her own thoughts and fears on this occasion are unrecorded.

A third pregnancy quickened in 1672. On 1 June 1672 Archer wrote,

my wife was newly with child when we came from Chippenham, and had many pains
for a week; and we had the midwife with us because we live in a solitary place. This
night, at 10 of the clock, she was delivered of a boy, lusty and large, but lean; this was
the eve of Trinity Sunday, and as we had counted, the time was just come about.

Once again Mrs Archer came close to death. Two weeks after giving birth, on
13 June, 'my wife fell grievously sick and faint by reason of some noxious and
venomous impurities that nature should have cleaned her of; she had the
very agony of death, as she thought, and was seized all over with intolerable
pain, and possessed with a persuasion she should die that night. Her father
and mother were with her, and we all had grief enough.'[53] Fortunately, once
again, Mrs Archer recovered. The long-wished-for son lived less than three
years.

Mrs Archer gave birth to another daughter in December 1673 after four
hours of labour. The diarist had little else to say on the matter except that the
child was 'fat and lustier than usual'. Next came another short-lived son who
was born prematurely in August 1675. Archer wrote on 25 August 1675, 'I had
taken a nurse into the house to suckle it because my wife was not able, as
having suckled the last too long. The woman knew of its illness, and yet told
us not of it, so it died while she slept, and unbaptised.' The minister agonized
over the spiritual consequences of this neglect but managed to convince
himself that the child would still be taken to God's bosom.[54]

By the spring of 1676 Anne Archer was pregnant for the sixth time. On 25
April the diarist noted, 'my wife was with child, it seems, and had gone about
three months'. Sadly, she miscarried on August 22, 'through a sudden fright,
upon an unhappy occasion'.[55] Within a few months, however, she was bloom-
ing again, and by 10 June 1677 the signs of impending delivery appeared secure.
'My wife is now with child, and we hope past the danger of miscarrying, having
been let blood twice,' wrote Isaac Archer, adding, 'I have in an earnest manner
begged a son.' Then on 6 October, 'about four of the clock in the afternoon
my wife was delivered, two months before her reckoning, and of a girl, which
came wrong, and stuck so long with the head in the birth, that it was dead
when fully born, though alive in the time of travail, and so next day 'twas
buried in Freckenham chancel on the north side of the little boy, under a
stone'.[56]

Chastened by this loss, Archer prayed for his wife. 'I thank God she is
hearty, and I hope may be healthful in time, after so much cleansing.' And

he reflected on himself, the father of so many dead babies, 'perhaps I am not worthy of a son . . . the loss is the less because 'twas a girl, though we could have wished the life of it. God's will be done.' Archer continued to brood on his losses, lamenting children as 'chastenings sent by God for the good of parents'. 'Since God took away my two boys I ceased not privately to pray for another to make up my loss. My wife miscarried twice, and then had a girl dead, and now after all God's time is come.'[57]

The longed-for second son was born on 14 February 1678 after another painful delivery. Archer relates, 'my joy however was somewhat damped when the women thought the child would not live because it changed colour and frothed at the mouth', but the boy lived to be baptized Isaac like his father, a son of prayer. This baby Isaac died on 29 July 1678 at the age of five months, and his 6-year-old sister Frances died two weeks later.[58]

Mrs Archer miscarried once more in October 1680, 'when she reckoned she had gone about eighteen weeks'. Predictably, within a few months she was pregnant again. Isaac Archer spent an anxious summer, fearful of a further miscarriage, 'for she was quick', and no doubt hoping for a boy. Then on 21 August, after three hours labour, his wife was 'delivered of a girl'. Again the birth was premature, 'eight weeks before her reckoning', and again it went badly. 'She came wrong and was wasted; it lived half an hour, and died.' In his prayers Isaac Archer begged good health for his wife and reproached himself, 'I have too eagerly desired children'.[59]

Finally, in September 1682, Mrs Archer came to term once again, and was 'delivered of a lusty girl, fatter and larger than any yet'. Archer wrote in his diary, 'I bless God that we have a living child; I never so much as asked of God a son, though we thought it would have been one by all signs.' But this daughter, named Frances in memory of her lost sister, was also dead within three months.[60]

After fifteen years of marriage and at least ten pregnancies, the Archers had one surviving daughter. Mrs Archer had been racked with pain and had known dire peril. Several times she came close to death. Twisted with hopes and disappointments, the family accommodated itself to grief. The Reverend Isaac Archer had buried most of his offspring, some of them before they could be baptized. Mrs Archer would have two more miscarriages, in January and July 1684, but no more live children. Her procreative career was at an end, despite Archer's egotistical patriarchal prayers. 'I begged a child if God saw good . . . the loss to me is very unkind; but God's will be done.'[61] Clearly the husband cared for his wife, the carrier of his children; but his happiness was incomplete until God spared him a son, a male child to serve the Lord and carry the Archer name. She lived until 1698.

Isaac Archer's diary captures the urgency and anxiety in this minister's attempts at family formation. It provides valuable glimpses of the management of pregnancy in the seventeenth century, together with insights into the emotional religiosity, humility, and vanity of the man as husband and father. This particular family's history should not be regarded as typical, but several features of its childbearing regime were common: the shared recognition of pregnancy and the husband's gendered preference for a son; fear of miscarriage and preparations for labour; supervision by the midwife in company with other women; the wife's experience of pain and fear of dying; the hours of labour and danger of complications; the loss of blood and risk of infection; lying in; occasional wet-nurses; and the premature death of young children. Archer himself would not normally have entered the room where his wife was giving birth, but relied on 'the women' to give him reports. While the diarist wrestles with his self-consciousness, the mystery of childbirth remains veiled.

2

THE MANAGEMENT OF CHILDBIRTH

Childbearing was a curse as well as a blessing. It was an experience that young couples wished for to start their families, but one that older couples feared might bring their family life to an end. For both husband and wife the childbearing period involved a special phase of altered relationships. Households of the middling sort looked forward to a topsy-turvy time when the wife lay in at leisure (provided she was not seriously ill), while the husband temporarily took responsibility for some of the woman's domestic duties. Wealthier families hired a nurse or 'keeper' at this time, or brought in kinswomen to assist as managers. Humbler households experienced much less change. In principle, the woman was withdrawn from the outside world, absent from church, relieved of most household tasks, and excused sexual relations in the weeks immediately preceding and following childbirth. She suffered great pains and lived through serious dangers in the course of her confinement, but she would not endure them alone. Female neighbours and relations provided almost constant companionship, bringing with them a wide range of wisdom, experience, and advice concerning precautions, procedures, and protocols.

Books for the Birth of Mankind

Every childbirth was unique, though childbearing was one of the most common events in the world. Deliverance could be 'easy and uneasy, difficult or dolorous', as doctors and midwives knew well. The outcome was in God's hands, and, under him, in the hands of women. For a man to witness a birth was virtually unheard of, but most men would have heard 'the screeches and outcries' that accompanied their women's 'pains and pangs'.[1] In order to know more they would have to negotiate the frontiers of women's gossip, or turn, if they could, to texts. Sixteenth- and seventeenth-century writers collected and published a broad range of recommendations for the successful management of childbirth.

Like the herbals, popular medical textbooks drew heavily on Galenic and Aristotelian systems of explanation and were slow to abandon the ancient theories of humours and signatures. Obstetrical treatises were especially conservative. Childbirth manuals plagiarized unmercifully and repeated each other's venerable observations. Well into the seventeenth century they continued to repeat the theories and lore of the ancient and medieval world. Translations and adaptations connected European and Arabic wisdom to the English gynaecological heritage. Reiterations of ancient cases, abstracts of Aristotle, Galen, and Avicenna, treatises by distinguished French and German physicians, and compilations of gynaecological nostrums, all served to guide readers who obtained their information from books. Most books of this kind were written by physicians in order to advertise and advance their careers. Most were surprisingly tolerant of the traditional practices of midwives. Only later in the seventeenth century, as doctors became more professional and persuaded themselves that they knew better, did the tone of their writing become more censorious. Only then did authors turn to ridicule village wise women and midwives, and berate them for delays in summoning expert (male) physicians.[2]

Country midwives themselves had little use for such books, since their knowledge was based on experience rather than on reading. Like other village women, they had minimal command of letters. Urban midwives were more likely to have been literate, especially later in the seventeenth century, and may even have read some of these publications, but their skill too came from practice and tradition rather than printed texts.[3] Midwives learnt from each other, by attending births, by using their ears, their eyes, and their hands.

The proliferation of books on obstetrics and gynaecology points to a growing public interest, but it does not necessarily reflect the actual practices of women in childbed. A late seventeenth-century volume declared all previous publications on this subject 'strangely deficient, so crowded with unnecessary notions and dangerous mistakes'.[4] When we turn to these works, alongside other sources, for guidance on the management of childbirth in early modern England, it is vital to bear in mind their prescriptive, medicalized, and somewhat archaic flavourings.

Frequently reprinted handbooks, such as Eucharius Roesslin's *The Birth of Man-Kinde, Otherwise Named the Womans Booke* and James Guillemeau's *Child-Birth Or, The Happy Deliverie of Women* appealed to a diverse range of readers. Both were products of the early sixteenth century, appeared in several European languages, and were still going strong a century and a half later. Roesslin's book was first published in Frankfurt in 1513, was available in English by 1540, enlarged by Thomas Raynold in 1545, and frequently reprinted from 1552 to 1676. Guillemeau's was first published in France in the reign of Francis I and published in England in 1612 and 1635. These two

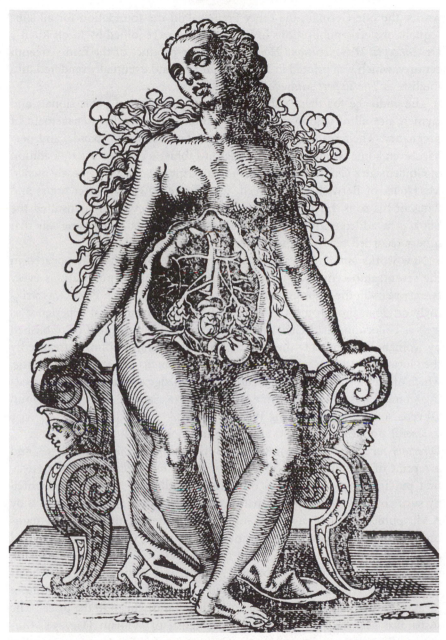

FIG. 2 'The female urogenital system' from Jacob Rueff, *De Conceptu et Generatione Hominis* (Frankfurt, 1580)

works, the one German, the other French, laid the foundation for all subsequent obstetric publications in English. They were joined by Jacob Rueff's
De Conceptu et Generatione Hominis, another product of the mid-sixteenth
century, which was printed in Frankfurt in 1587 and eventually rendered into
English as *The Expert Midwife* in 1637.[5]

The audience for these publications included medical professionals and
laymen, not all of whom were directly concerned with the management of
pregnancy. Their readers included anxious fathers and husbands, and perhaps even some women. The Huntington Library's copy of the 1612 edition
of Guillemeau's *Child-Birth* includes manuscript notations by an early owner,
Mr Holles of Berwick upon Tweed, who wrote down the exact hours and
dates of his sons' births in 1621 and 1622. He had evidently consulted the
book as he added to his family, and entered the results in the same way that
others recorded births in their diaries or the family Bibles.[6]

New works aimed at demystifying the miracle of childbirth appeared in
the seventeenth century, with clusters of gynaecological publications every
twenty years in the 1630s, the 1650s, the 1670s, and the 1690s. None was strik-
ingly original, though most claimed to be based on practical experience as
well as collections of ancient authorities. Several were printed or published
by women, most notably the firm of Anne and Sarah Griffin. A treatise by
the Norwich physician John Sadler, *The Sicke Womans Private Looking-Glasse*,
which offered a summary of conventional knowledge about the care of 'breeding women' was printed by Anne Griffin in 1636. Sarah Griffin printed John
Oliver's *A Present for Teeming Women* in 1663.[7]

Useful publications of the interrregnum included Nicholas Culpeper, *A
Directory for Midwives* (1651), Richard Bunworth, *The Doctoresse* (1656), and
a reprint of the Elizabethan Philip Barrough, *The Method of Physick* (1652,
first published 1583). Technical obstetrical handbooks were complemented
by such compendia of lay information as *A Rich Closet of Physical Secrets* by
A.M., published in 1652. The identity and gender of the author remains
unknown but this work was also printed by a woman, Gertrude Dawson, and
contained a variety of remedies and recipes that women would find useful,
including 'the child-bearers cabinet'.[8] Another publication of 1652, Nicholas
Fonteyn, *The Womans Doctour*, promised a volume 'safe in the composition,
pleasant in the use, effectual in the operation, [and] cheap in the price'. The
1650s also saw the first publication in English of William Harvey's *Anatomical Exercitations, Concerning the Generation of Living Creatures* (1653), a
revolutionary work that would have signalled the end of Aristotelian and
Galenic biology if the rest of the medical community had chosen to pay
attention.[9]

The Restoration saw several important publications on midwifery, including the first indisputably written by a woman. Jane Sharp, *The Midwives Book* (1671), was an invaluable blend of traditional learning and practical experience, especially useful for its herbal recipes. William Sermon, *The Ladies Companion, or the English Midwife* also appeared in 1671, advancing the professional interests of the physicians. To this could be added the man-midwife Hugh Chamberlen's translation of Francis Mauriceau, *The Diseases of Women with Child* (1672 and 1683) and the same author's *The Accomplisht Midwife* (1673), as well as such compendia of recipes and remedies as *The Queens Closet Opened* by W.M. (1674) and Hannah Woolley, *The Gentlewoman's Companion* (1675).[10] Percival Willughby's 'Observations in Midwifery' were written about this time but were not published until the nineteenth century. Later Stuart responses to the public appetite for books on female subjects included *The English Midwife Enlarged* (1682); John Pechey, *A General Treatise of the Diseases of Maids, Big-Bellied Women, Child-bed Women, and Widows* (1696) and *The Compleat Midwife's Practice Enlarged* (5th edn. by 1698); and the surgeon Robert Barret, *A Companion for Midwives, Child-Bearing Women, and Nurses*, published in 1699.[11] The late seventeenth century accumulated a vastly expanded literature on human reproduction and the business of childbirth, yet many of the day-to-day secrets of the birthroom remained behind the veil.

Medical literature that dealt with human reproduction offered technical scientific information but it also risked pandering to prurient interest in the slippery passage between gynaecology and pornography. Authors and readers, most of them male, had to negotiate the discursive boundaries of indecency and decorum.[12] In 'a prologue to the women readers', *The Birth of Man-Kinde* announced its intention to explain 'how everything commeth to pass within your bodies, in the time of conception, of bearing, and of birth'. Roesslin's conjectured audience was illiterate midwives and women 'of the better and more sober sort' who were recommended 'to hear the book read by some other, or else, such as could, to read it themselves'. But the author also recognized that 'the secrets and privities of women', especially when accompanied by anatomical illustrations, could be a source of male titillation, and he felt it necessary to warn against 'light' or 'lewd' reading. The widely disseminated *Problemes of Aristotle* (not Aristotle's work at all but a pastiche of ancient and medieval writers) contained 'divers questions, with their answers, touching the estate of man's body'; but many of its most-thumbed passages had to do with the bodies of women. John Banister's Elizabethan anatomy text dealt frankly with 'the generative parts' of man but declined to deal similarly with women because, he said, 'I am from the beginning persuaded that, by lifting

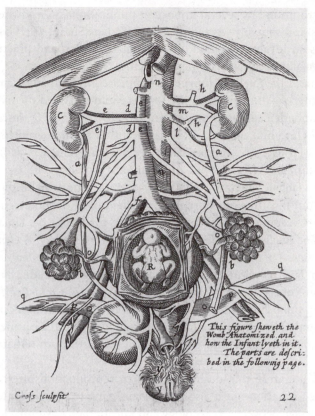

Fig. 3   'The womb anatomised' from Wolveridge, *Speculum Matricis Hybernicum or The Irish Midwives Handmaid* (London, 1670)

up the veil of nature's secrets, in women's shapes, I shall commit more in-decency against the office of decorum, than yield needful instruction to the profit of the common good.'[13]

Seventeenth-century writings faced similar problems of readership and response. Helkiah Crooke's *Microcosmographia*, a comprehensive anatomy text which included a long discussion of childbirth, announced the author's unease in discussing 'the natural parts belonging to generation, as well in men as in women'. In the interest of modesty, and to guard against some men's 'lewd and inordinate affections', he decided to proceed 'by honest words and circumlocutions to mollify the harshness of the argument'. The explicit detail of Nicholas Culpeper's *Directory for Midwives*, especially his depiction of 'the organs of generation', prompted one seventeenth-century critic to call it obscene, 'Cul paper, paper fit to wipes one's breech withal.' When discussing the 'generative parts' of men and women in *The Midwives Book* of 1671 the experienced midwife Jane Sharp cautioned 'the courteous reader to use as much modesty in the perusal of it as I have endeavoured to do in the writing of it'. Another author of 1671, James Wolveridge, promised 'no scurrilities . . . to please lascivious, wanton eyes', and hoped, with veiled lasciviousness, that his *Speculum Matricis Hybernicum; or, The Irish Midwives Handmaid* would 'be dandled in the ladies lap'.[14]

The growing female readership of the later seventeenth century found a clamour of voices offering gynaecological advice, although women did not necessarily become more adept at having babies or midwives more skilful in delivering them by reading books. Educated women had access to a widening choice of handbooks, but it still seems likely that the primary readership of most of these works was male. *The Ladies Dictionary, Being a General Enter-tainment for the Fair Sex* (1694) was clearly pitched to a curious male reader-ship despite its explicit appeal to women. This work delighted in subjects that might 'be in the least imputed immodest by the wise and discreet', includ-ing mildly salacious entries on 'big-bellied' women, conception, childbearing, and female sexual anatomy. Its compiler, N.H., remains anonymous, but the work fits the style of its printer, John Dunton, an energetic popular author and bookseller.[15] Through textual inscription the secret world of womanhood was partially opened to the erotic gaze of men, in a manner akin to popular 'medical' works that featured genital anatomy and the mysteries of concep-tion and parturition.

Signs of Conception

Husbands and wives, neighbours and kin, medical advisers and midwives, all were interested in the signs of conception and the progress of pregnancy. Med-ical manuals and popular handbooks addressed this interest in the develop-ing foetus, 'the signs to know it, and whether male or female, and of false conception'. Observers watched for 'signs to know whether a woman be with child or no', while women anxiously monitored their own bodies.[16] Then as now, the signs could be ambiguous. As one doctor commented, 'there is nothing more ridiculous than to assure a woman that she is with child, and afterward that her natural sickness or store of water should come from her, and instead of child some windy matter should break from her, and so her belly fall and grow flat again'. Even more embarrassing was for a woman not known to be pregnant unexpectedly to give birth. Such was the fate of Lady Anne Effingham in 1602, who fell ill while playing shuttlecock and 'was brought

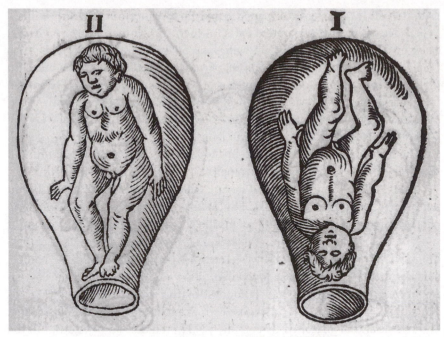

F IG. 4 'Foetal presentations' from Eucharius Roesslin, *The Byrth of Mankynde* (London, 1560)

to bed of a child without a midwife, she never suspecting that she had been with child'.[17]

Subtle alterations of moisture and motion, known only to the woman herself, announced the beginning of pregnancy. Other signs became apparent to the people around her, making pregnancy a social as well as a personal experience. The eyes (wan), the nipples (hard), the veins (swollen), and the urine (clouded), all provided clues to her altered condition. If she felt 'a kind of yawning and stretching, and feels within her a shaking or quivering', it might signify that 'the matrice' was embracing 'the matter of generation', as did the tightening of the neck of the womb revealed by the midwife's digital probe. If the woman 'falls a vomiting and spitting, distastes her meat, groweth dull, careless and qualmish, (and) longeth after strange things', the household could expect an addition. If 'her belly swells' and 'her courses appear not', the pregnancy would be confirmed. Cessation of menstruation, however, was not firm evidence, and it was well known that 'some have them when they be with child'. The stirring of the baby, from the third or fourth month, gave the most positive indications, which the midwife might confirm by means of a physical inspection.[18]

The evidence of diaries suggests that women often knew within a month or two that they were pregnant, though their calculations of when they were due to deliver were not always accurate. Jane Sharp's years of practical midwifery taught her that 'young women especially of their first child are so ignorant commonly, that they cannot tell whether they have conceived or not, and not one in twenty almost keeps a just account, else they would be better provided against their lying in, and not so suddenly be surprised as many of them are'. Mrs Josselin and Mrs Archer both experienced 'misreckoning'. Dorothy Rawdon, another experienced mother, wrote to her husband in 1664, 'I am very uncertain in reckoning this time'. Miscalculation and 'a false conceit of their being with child' accounted for some women's claims, and some doctors' beliefs, that a pregnancy could last for ten months or longer.[19]

As the pregnancy progressed families learned to watch for 'tokens and signs whereby ye may perceive whether the time of labour be near'. The woman, her husband, her midwife, neighbours, and friends all had parts to play in securing a satisfactory outcome. Those interested in guessing the sex of the child, particularly those wishing for a boy, could follow the humoral system of diagnosis in which things hot, dry, hard, thick, dexter, ruddy, and ascending indicated masculinity, and matters cool, moist, soft, slender, sinister, pale, and descending represented the female. The brightness of the woman's right eye, the swelling of her right breast, and the blush of her right cheek were all hopeful indications of a male. Uroscopic analysis also played a part, a reddish tinge indicating a boy, a whitish colour suggesting a girl.[20] Seventeenth-century medical authorities repeated this popular wisdom, but increasingly played safe by admitting their scepticism, and acknowledging that it was impossible to know whether the child would be a boy or a girl.[21]

Judicial astrology provided an alternative system for diagnosing the beginnings of pregnancy and predicting the sex of the child in the womb. In astrological theory, all aspects of development depended on the configuration of the heavens, so that astral arrangements at the time of conception, as well as at the moment of birth, and even at the time of consultation, had an influence on future outcomes. Horary questions of this sort, relating to childbirth, dominate the case books of early Stuart astrologers.[22] Nicholas Culpeper, writing in the mid-seventeenth century, further popularized theories of stellar and lunar influence on the development of the unborn baby. Following this system, the scientist Robert Hooke noted in 1672, 'Dr. Bradford assured Dr. Wren that his next child would be a boy, this being born in the increase of the moon.'[23]

That astrology and midwifery were not good bedfellows is suggested by

John Ward's story of 'one Mr Early in Warwickshire, who had some skill in astrology, and his wife being ready to be delivered of a child, he consulted his books when she was in travail what was the aspect of the stars, and finding it bad, he bid them hold their hands but the woman could not, she must be delivered, and so she was'.[24] Nativity was destiny. But most medical practitioners knew that childbirth could not be stayed until the astrologically propitious moment.

Care of the Expectant Mother

It was a common conceit that a woman with child was like 'a good pilot who being embarked on a rough sea and full of rocks, shuns the danger if he steers with prudence'. The late Stuart surgeon Robert Barret compared the womb 'to a rough sea, in which the child floats for the space of nine months. The labour of delivery is the only port, but full of dangerous rocks'.[25] Husbands, close relations, and friends concerned themselves with the welfare of the expectant mother throughout her dangerous journey, but became especially watchful as she approached her final haven. At stake was the woman's health and safety and her ability to continue as helpmeet and partner, as well as the economic, legal and emotional consequences of her bearing a child. At such a time a man might think of heirs and expenses, as well as the comfort of his marital companion, while a woman might dread the ordeal and wonder if she was going to die.

Men as well as women had important roles in the management of pregnancy. 'Husbands also in this case must be very tender over their wives and helpful to them in all things needful', advised the Jacobean minister William Gouge. It was the husband's responsibility, according to Gouge, to provide 'such things as are needful for (the woman's) travail and lying in childbed', even if he was only following her instructions. At this time the man might be expected to assume a greater share of domestic duties, including matters of household management that were normally the woman's preserve, 'because it is a time of weakness, wherein the woman cannot well provide for herself'.[26] In practice, however, the wife often made her own arrangements or relied on the support and experience of female relations or neighbours, or even made no preparations at all.

Domestic conduct manuals as well as medical handbooks offered plentiful advice on the care of pregnant women, and diarists and correspondents maintained an anxious commentary on this matter. According to William Gouge, 'the first part of a child's infancy is while it remaineth in the mother's womb. Here, therefore, the duty lieth principally upon the mother; who so soon as she perceiveth a child to be conceived in her womb, ought to have an especial care thereof, that, so much as in her lieth, the child may be safely brought forth'. Though most of John Oliver's *Present for Teeming Women* was concerned with spiritual solace, he too recognized that women advanced in pregnancy 'must be taken off from such manual employments in which they were busied before, and must allow for some rest and retirement'.[27] Gentlemen of this era commonly described their wives in stock-rearing terms as 'bearing', 'breeding', or 'teeming', but recognized that they needed special consideration while in that delicate condition. The Yorkshire gentleman Ralph Thoresby recalled in 1688, 'I was most concerned for my dear wife, who was in the family way.'[28]

Renaissance physicians were more confident than some of their modern counterparts in asserting when human life began. According to Jacob Rueff, following Hippocrates, 'the seed conceived even unto the forty and fifth day is changed into the due and perfect form and shape of the infant; and then by the judgement of some learned men it receiveth life, and therefore afterward ought not to be called a feature but an infant, although as yet by reason of his tender and feeble condition and state he wanteth motion'. The forty-fifth day, by common opinion, saw the birth of the soul, though others thought ensoulment came with conception. By James Wolveridge's calculation 'the infant . . . will stir in ninety days', a third of the way through the pregnancy.[29] This was the moment of quickening, when the mother could feel her baby moving in her womb. It was also a time, some moralists urged, when the woman should 'quicken' to repentance, as religious and physiological concerns became fused. When body and soul were united in the womb, John Donne remarked, 'we become in that instant, guilty of Adam's sin'.[30]

Quickening was a time for joy, but it also marked a new stage of anxiety. Diarists like Angier and Archer report quickening as the critical time of their wives' pregnancies, when the risk of miscarriage was most acute. A royal quickening gave promise of an heir or rearranged the claims of lineal succession. Londoners prayed and celebrated in November 1554 when Queen Mary's false quickening appeared to indicate that she was with child. They gave thanks again in 1629 when Henrietta Maria quickened with the future Charles II, and again in 1688, with emotions mixing dynastic joy and religious dread, when Mary of Modena quickened with another prince James.[31]

Medical literature and popular wisdom agreed that pregnant women should avoid violent passion or motion, maintain moderation in diet, and guard against distempers of the body and the weather.[32] 'Let them take heed of cold and sharp winds, great heat, anger, perturbations of the mind, fears and terrors, immoderate Venus, and all intemperance of eating and drinking', advised *The Expert Midwife* of 1637. The same treatise urged caution that no peril and danger may happen to them which are with child by any manner of means, either by sudden fear, affrightments, by fire, lightning, thunder, with monstrous and hideous aspects and sights of men and beasts, by immoderate joy, sorrow and lamentation; or by untemperate exercise and motion of running, leaping, riding, or by surfeit or repletion by meat and drink; or that they being taken with any disease do not use sharp and violent medicines using the counsel of unskilful physicians.

John Pechey added 'the noise of guns or great bells' to the list of frights that pregnant women should avoid.[33] James Wolveridge advised childbearing women to avoid 'mourning and careful anxiety', to 'abstain from all hard labours', to forebear 'overmuch venery', and to dispense with the questionable medical benefits of blood-letting, cupping, and scarification, especially in the first four months. These shocks to the mind and body might dislodge a child from the womb, or else imprint it with some baleful influence. It is not hard to imagine the inversion of this regime of care by any who wished to induce an abortion, as we shall see below. The seventeenth-century minister John Ward noted in his commonplace book that 'midwives say that it is good for a woman after seven months to walk much, pretending that it facilitates birth'.[34]

Orthodox medical opinion advised couples to limit their sexual activity during pregnancy. Since conception was the primary aim of love-making, Christian commentators similarly urged moderation once that goal was achieved. Popular manuals on childbirth recommended abstinence from 'Venus' or 'venery' in the first four months of pregnancy 'for fear of shaking the child and bringing down her courses'. The sixth and eight months were similarly regarded as vulnerable to miscarriage, 'but in the seventh and ninth month she may boldly use it, especially toward the end of the ninth month, which some are of opinion will help and hasten the delivery'. Such a regime, of course, depended on fairly accurate calculation of the months between conception and deliverance, as well as a degree of self-control. Part of the father's duty at this time was to 'fashion' his child, to set his influence on it, and it was thought that this could best be done through judicious sexual intercourse. There was little that anyone could do, however, to guard against 'virulent tinctures contracted by the infant in the nutriment of the womb'.[35]

In traditional lore the womb-child was also threatened by evil spirits and myriad dangers that required specific action or avoidance. A pregnant woman might not attend funerals in order to avoid harmful influences; she might refuse to engage in winding or grinding activities for fear, sympathetically, of strangling the child; she should be shielded from the sight of monsters lest her foetus became deformed. The best-documented evidence for these fears and taboos comes from later periods and from rural France, but they are assumed to have been deep rooted and widely observed in early modern England. It was not necessary to have a fully developed theology of evil spirits in order to take customary precautions.[36]

Antenatal care included positive applications or ingestions of herbal remedies, as well as avoidance of shocks to the womb. Sage in particular was known as 'the holy herb, because women with child if they be like to come before their time, and are troubled with abortments, do eat thereof to their great good; for it closeth the matrix, and maketh them fruitful, it retaineth the child, and giveth it life'.[37] During pregnancy, wrote Jane Sharp, a woman should apply concoctions of tansy and muscatel to her navel, take glisters made with boiled mallows, hollyhocks, honey, and sugar, and drink sage ale to strengthen her womb. Other authorities recommended drinking syrups with tansy and sage.[38] These herbal preservatives no doubt made a woman feel better and caused no harm. The same, perhaps, could be said for the 'eagle stones' and holy girdles which we have already discussed.

Prayers and precautions did not always work, for one in every two conceptions ended in miscarriage. Even with God as its guardian, a fertilized ovum had no better than a 50 per cent chance of going to term.[39] Miscarriage was a frequent occurrence and was often described with anguish. Robert Woodford noted in March 1638, after walking with his wife to Abingdon, 'my wife found some alteration this morning and I fear lest she went too violently yesterday, which if she be with child may cause her to miscarry, and I am somewhat melancholy'. John Angier's wife Ellen feared miscarriage and 'a full month before her deliverance God confined her to her chamber, when both days and nights were wearisome, she being unable well to sit, to go or to lie in her bed'. Ralph Josselin's wife Jane had at least five miscarriages as well as ten live births. Alice Thornton's sister, Lady Danby, who brought ten pregnancies to term, also suffered six miscarriages 'upon frights by fire in her chamber, falls, and such like accidents happening'. A Buckinghamshire man, Jonas Reading of Amersham, explained the loss of his baby in 1635, telling the archdeaconry court that his wife, 'by reason of a fall or slip from off a pair of stairs, was delivered of a child a month or thereabouts before her time, and that the child was still born'.[40]

Abortion

Abortion, often called 'abortment' in early modern texts, could be naturally or artificially induced. From a medical viewpoint, an abortion was 'either the issuing of an imperfect infant or his extinction and death in the womb'. The Jacobean physician Helkiah Crooke added that 'some there are who will not have it called an abortment before the infant hath moved, so that a woman shall not be said to abort but from the third to the seventh month, and that before the motion it shall be called an effluxion or miscarriage'. If there had been no quickening there could be no abortion, and therefore no crime in ejecting an unwanted foetus.[41] This, apparently, was the thinking of Henry Eaton of Holme Hale, Norfolk, who tried to persuade the servant he had made pregnant to obtain an abortion, saying 'that it was no sin to do so except the child was already quickened within her, and that it was such a common thing in London for such women to use such practices in such cases'.[42]

Knowledge of abortion was widely distributed in the female subcultures of early modern England. It was available from 'wise women' or 'cunning women' and, presumably, also from co-operative midwives.[43] Contraception and abortion were closely related in the spectrum of fertility control. The playwright Ben Jonson imagined the collegiate ladies in his comedy *Epicoene* exchanging recipes to prevent their 'bearing of children' and modern research shows Tudor and Stuart gentlewomen sharing similar knowledge. Lady Grace Mildmay described a medicine based on the tropical plant guaiacum, to be applied to the 'matrix, being tied upon a stick . . . even until it bleeds', but added the cautious comment, 'I take this medicine to be very dangerous and evil to be applied unto women in this manner.'[44] The physician Jacob Rueff warned women who wished themselves free of pregnancy 'that they use not the wicked arts and policies of old witches and harlots' who knew how to murder an infant in the womb. Towards the end of the seventeenth century *The Ladies Dictionary* acknowledged 'those bad women who . . . use ill arts, either to prevent conception or procure abortion, which must needs be very displeasing to God'.[45]

Practitioners of such arts were not hard to find. When Elizabeth Francis of Chelmsford, Essex, became unwillingly pregnant in the early 1560s she turned to her 'grandmother Eve' of Hatfield Peverel who (through Satan, according to the report) 'bade her take a certain herb and drink it, which she did, and destroyed the child forthwith'. Elizabeth Bowyer of Cuckfield, Sussex, in 1578 prescribed her pregnant servant 'a cruel hot drink' based on 'dragon water' (from dragonwort or *dracunculus*), which led to her prompt evacuation of a stillborn child. As late as the nineteenth century in fenland Cambridgeshire women who wished to terminate their pregnancy could turn to 'Granny' Gray of Littleport, who distributed pills of hemlock, pennyroyal, and rue. Many of these pot-herbs and roots had significant anti-oestrogenic properties, which made them effective antifertility agents and abortifacients.[46]

Apothecaries and physicians could also help to end unwanted pregnancies. Reluctant fathers—adulterers and fornicators who did not want to be forced into marriage or to have bastards laid to their charge—sometimes contrived to destroy the fruits of their illicit sexual activity by procuring abortions. Evidence of this sort is hard to find, but it leaves occasional traces in the records of local courts. Alice Butcher, a Cheshire woman, reported in 1612 that potions for this purpose could be obtained from the apothecary in Warrington. A Berkshire yeoman, Robert Brooks, took a sample of urine to Stephen Bridges, a physician at Corpus Christi College, Oxford, in 1635 to determine whether his adulterous lover was pregnant, and if so, 'desired to have some pessary to destroy the child that she was forward withal'. James Bowrey of Holt Chapel, Cheshire, similarly pressed Margaret Royden in 1667 to drink a concoction of bearsfoot and water germander or hellebore, which, reputedly, 'would cause a mare to drop its foal and a woman her child'.[47] Such remedies did not necessarily work, of course, and many a desperate woman must have suffered acute discomfort in unsuccessful attempts to dislodge a foetus. Lydia Downes confessed to the borough court at Colchester, Essex, in 1638 that she had tried savin and physick to end her unlawful pregnancy 'but it prevailed not', and even after taking poisonous ratsbane 'yet the child was not killed within her'.[48]

Attempting to be rid of her womb-child a pregnant woman might reverse all the advice designed for its care, and subject her body to violent shocks and purges. 'Instructed with evil arts, they make the first experiments by lacing in themselves straight and hard, that they may extinguish and destroy the feature conceived in the womb.' If this failed, as usually it did, they would approach 'some old witch very skilful in curing these diseases and famous by long experience, asking and questioning with them about the cure and remedy of the stopping of the terms, desiring a medicine and counsel to procure them to issue'. A sinful woman carrying an unwanted child might 'contrive ways of preventing its birth by wicked adventuring on such expulsive recipes', observed the Restoration minister John Oliver.[49] If she was successful, who would ever know?

Medical practitioners, both male and female, knew ways 'to procure the months' and 'to draw down the flowers', and might also advise, in secret, how to terminate a pregnancy. Blood-letting, vomits, and electuaries were recommended, along with medicines based on laurel, madder, pepper, sage, and savin.[50] After describing ways in which abortions might happen, the Tudor physician Andrew Boorde advised 'every good woman to beware of all manner of things above rehearsed' and 'to beware what medicines they do take'. He then described how to expel a dead child from the womb and how to provoke the terms. After listing herbal remedies to stimulate or induce menstruation, Nicholas Culpeper cautioned, 'give not any of these to any that is with child, lest you turn murderers'. Jane Sharp's chapter on 'women's miscarriages or abortments, with the signs thereof', warned that 'violent purging before the fourth month or after the seventh causes abortment', and that 'great labour, as dancing, leaping, falls or bruises' had like effect. Her recipes 'to provoke the terms' included madder, orris, savin, and senna, all with known abortifacient qualities. Women who successfully induced an abortion by one of these methods might themselves be sought out as experts, thought Jacob Rueff, so that 'they impart and communicate likewise those murdering arts and cruel practices to others'.[51]

Hints and warnings about various natural abortifacients appeared in most of the printed herbals. More than a hundred plants were known for their oils or juices that when drunk, inserted, or applied induced miscarriage or brought down women's courses. Spurgewort, darnell seed, horehound, motherwort, horse-tongue, parsley, mugwort, madder, dittany, and trefoil were among those commonly mentioned, along with germander, hellebore, pennyroyal, savin, and rue. These were often the same plants used to ease the labour of childbirth or to accelerate delivery. Stinking gladdon, a kind of iris, was known to be a general purgative, with a powerful propensity for purging the womb. 'If it be drunk with wine it provoketh the terms, and being put in baths for women to sit over, it provoketh the like effects most exquisitely . . . It profiteth being used in a pessary, to provoke the terms, and will cause abortion.' Similarly dragonwort 'scoureth and cleanseth mightily' and was known to induce miscarriages. Cyclamen or sowbread, which served to relieve the extreme pains of childbirth, could also have dangerous effects in the earlier stages of pregnancy. The leading herbal warned of cyclamen, 'it is not good for women with child to touch or take this herb, or to come near unto it, or stride over the same where it groweth, for the natural attractive virtue therein contained is such that without controversy they that attempt it in manner aforesaid shall be delivered before their time.' A seventeenth-century editor glossed this, 'I judge our author somewhat womanish in this, that is, led more by vain opinion than by any reason or experience.' But anyone seeking to terminate a pregnancy might wilfully ignore the disclaimer, and expose themselves to the herb's more baneful effects.[52]

Preparations for the Birthroom

Most expectant mothers approaching the end of their term turned their attention to the setting in which they would give birth. With other women to assist them, they attempted to secure clean clothes, fresh bedding, and appropriate supplies and furnishings in readiness for the time of their travail. The luxury and scale of these preparations varied, of course, with wealth and social position, but nearly every woman made some shift to get ready. The preacher Richard Adams noted that women at this time were 'usually busy about in preparing (their) child-bed linen'. Indeed, he observed, some expectant mothers were 'apt to be over curious in the washing of their linens for their lying in' but neglected to take similar preparations for their spiritual condition. Another religious writer, John Oliver, remarked that 'women will make no other preparation for lying in than what is common, if they only get linen and other necessaries for the child, a nurse, a midwife, entertainment for the women that are called to their labour, a warm convenient chamber, etc.' He too wanted more focus on spiritual preparation, especially since some women would 'need no other linen shortly but a winding sheet, and have no other chamber but a grave'.[53]

The traditional equipage included a white linen sheet to cover the woman's bed during her lying in, an item that the separatist John Canne associated with superstitious rites and customs. The Elizabethan minister Richard Greenham, however, thought it 'civil and seemly in all sickness that the bed should be comely adorned with whites, but especially that this was comely in the sickness and after the travail of women, so superstition be avoided'.[54] By the later seventeenth century the popish associations of white bed linen were mostly forgotten. 'Women that are come to their labour' should have their 'childbed linen at hand', advised the midwife Jane Sharp. Another seventeenth-century manual urged the expectant mother to have 'the linen about her body clean, and what linen is necessary for other occasions got ready, and in its proper place'. The aristocratic Margaret Cavendish took note of the 'care, pains, and cost, in getting, making, and buying fine and costly childbed linen, swaddling clothes, mantles, and the like' among her childbearing friends at the time of the Restoration.[55]

There may have been regional patterns and local preferences in birthing practices, as in so much else, but these are most difficult to document. Popular medical books noted that 'all women are not delivered after one fashion; for some are delivered in their bed; others sitting in a chair, some standing being supported and held up by the standers by; or else leaning upon the side of a bed, table, or chair; others kneeling being held up by the arms'. Some practitioners recommended a board for the woman to brace her feet on, or piles of pillows on the bed. One advantage of giving birth on a stool or kneeling, rather than lying in bed, was that the bed would not be immediately soiled by 'the blood, waters, and other filth which is voided in labour'. But delivery in a bed avoided 'the inconvenience and trouble of being carried thither afterwards'. Midwive's stools—plain or furnished—were depicted in books on childbirth and were popularly known as 'groaning stools'. Physicians

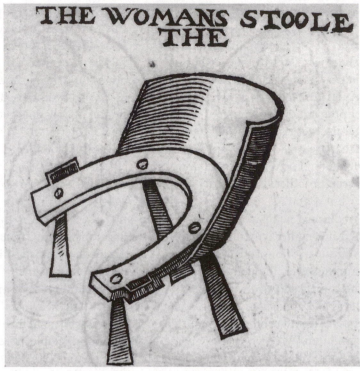

THE WOMANS STOOLE
THE

FIG. 5 'The woman's stool'—birthing stool from Eucharius Roesslin, *The Byrth of Mankynde* (London, 1560)

had been promoting the use of the birthing stool since the sixteenth century but, as one writer of the 1680s conceded, 'few midwives have them or use them'. In a rare diary entry from colonial America, the Massachusetts merchant Samuel Sewall recalled accompanying the midwife home through the streets of Boston in 1677, 'carrying her stool, whose parts were included in a bag'.[56]

Standard handbooks on childbirth advised that a bed be set up 'like a pallet . . . of a reasonable bigness, strong and firm' and of a height convenient for the work of the midwife and her helpers. This bed should be 'so set and placed that they may conveniently come and go round about her'. Ideally, it should be close to the fire for warmth, and far enough from the door to avoid draughts. This advice was repeated almost word for word in successive manuals on midwifery by different authors for over a hundred years. How it was followed in practice is almost impossible to tell. Tradition called for the women to remove all rings, laces, knots, fastenings, and buckles, as a way of sympathetically easing labour and removing constrictions on the birth, or merely to avoid them getting in the way.[57]

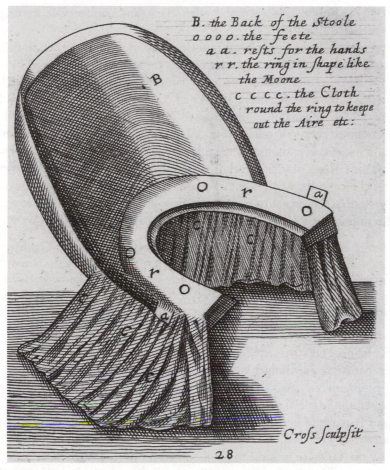

FIG. 6 Birthing stool, Wolveridge, *Speculum Matricis Hybernicum or The Irish Midwives Handmaid* (London, 1670)

It is striking that birth in early modern England took place in a closed and muffled environment, whereas death was followed by a throwing open of windows and doors. The birthroom was supposed to be kept warm, dark, and snug for the duration of labour and lying in. According to standard medical opinion, the childbed woman 'must be kept from the cold air because it is an enemy of the spermatical parts . . . and therefore the doors and windows of her chamber in any wise are to be kept close shut'. Royal and aristocratic birthrooms were accordingly hung with arras, the doors guarded, and the windows covered.[58] A seventeenth-century manual advised, 'you must lay the woman in a dark place, lest her mind should be distracted with too much light'. The room became a womb, warm, dark, and comfortable, restricting entry to evil spirits.[59]

Most women gave birth at home in their own parlour or chamber. But some, especially those expecting their first child, arranged to be delivered in their parents' home rather than in their matrimonial establishment. There they might find supportive female relations and comfortable surroundings, as well as domestic arrangements uninterrupted by the temporary disability of the principal housekeeper. Women advanced in pregnancy must have been among the most important and most vulnerable travellers on England's difficult roads, though the stresses of such travel increased the risk of miscarriage.[60] Vagrants had no choice in the matter, but a surprising number of respectable married women embarked on journeys as their pregnancies drew to a close.

The shipwright Phineas Pett recorded that early in 1601,

presently after Christtide my wife, being great with child, fell sick at Chatham and grew so weak that I was forced, about the 10th of March following, to remove her, not without hazard, to London, and from there to her father's house at Highwood Hill in Middlesex, where the 23rd day of March after, thanks be to God, she was delivered of her first born son, John Pett, from whence she returned to Chatham in safety some two months after.[61]

Most of Ann Pett's subsequent babies were born under her own roof, and in her mature years younger kinswomen journeyed to her house to complete their confinement.

Higher on the social scale, Isabella Twysden travelled home to Kent to give birth in 1645 while her husband Sir Roger was a prisoner in the Civil War. On 8 February she writes, 'I came to Peckham great with child, and ride all the way on horse back, and I thank God had no hurt.' Four weeks later, 'between one and two in the morning I was brought to bed of a boy'. The child was christened Charles (to honour the king) and nurse Jane 'had 12d. for a month' for his nursing. On another occasion Isabella wrote that 'my cousin Henage Finch's wife was brought a bed of a son . . . at her father's at Lambeth'. Travel in this condition sometimes took its toll, for one of John Evelyn's nieces 'miscarried of a son in the coach as she came up to lie-in at London'. More often the pregnant woman stayed at home and friends and relations gathered about her. Late in the seventeenth century the Derbyshire yeoman Leonard Wheatcroft recorded, 'my daughter Anna sent for her sister Betty to be with her when she lay in. She went to her April 4, 1693. And Anna was brought to bed of a daughter May 12, 1693, whose name was called Elizabeth.'[62]

3

CHILDBED ATTENDANTS

Before it was taken over by medicine (mostly an eighteenth- and nineteenth-century development), childbirth took place in a closed and mysterious world from which men were conventionally excluded. The marital bedchamber, the heart of patriarchal prerogative, became a gossips' parlour, busy with bustling women.[1] It is hard to discover exactly who was present in the birthroom but fragments of evidence sometimes help to reconstruct the roster. This chapter is concerned with the witnesses and assistants who attended the crisis and climax of labour and birth, and in particular with those misunderstood specialists in the childbed ritual, midwives.

'Who ought to be at the birth?' asked the Elizabethan doctor John Jones. His answer, shaped by concern for good order and domestic propriety, was 'a few rather of godly, expert and learned women . . . than a rude multitude given either to folly, banqueting or bravery, as in the towns of the west country is too much used'. In the 'north parts of late years', according to Dr Jones, the problem of unruly women in the birthroom was especially acute. A century later the surgeon Robert Barret echoed Jones's recommendation. The midwife should come with 'some sober wise women among her neighbours, such as have gone through the like hazard before; but above all, take care there be no frightful, whimsical, resolute, headstrong drunken, whispering, talkative, sluttish women amongst them . . . One of such women may do more harm than three modest wise women can do good.' Coached in prayer by ministers like Samuel Hieron, 'those which are employed in the assistance and help of a woman in travail' were reminded to 'put far from [them] all superstitious conceits and idle fancies' and to remember that God too was present in the room.[2]

From the viewpoint of ministers and physicians, and perhaps too for many husbands, the gathering of women at childbirth was exclusive, mysterious, and potentially unruly. In the interests of health and decorum, and perhaps also to control costs and to reassert masculine authority, some men mocked at the meetings of midwives and gossips and sought to curtail their excesses. (Gossips, of course, were female companions, the word being derived from 'god-sib' or sister in the lord. Evolving from the fifteenth to the seventeenth

FIG. 7 'Midwives attending a woman in childbirth' from Jacob Rueff, *Ein Schone Lustig Trostbuchle* (Zurich, 1554)

century, the word incorporated reference to baptismal co-sponsorship, participation in childbirth and christening ceremonies, and only in the later period took on the pejorative connotations of idle chatter.[3])

The misogynist *Batchelars Banquet* of 1603, an English rendition of *Les Quinze Joyes de Mariage*, includes a satiric depiction of 'the humour of a woman lying in childbed'. This particular passage is not in the French original, but is entirely the work of the late Elizabethan author. *The Batchelars Banquet* is a bitter entertainment, more sardonic than good-natured, but it reflects the cultural practices, if not the moral values, of the metropolitan middle class. By these lights, when the wife withdraws from her domestic role into the mystery of motherhood, the man 'is fain to play both husband and housewife'. With his pregnant wife the centre of attention, the husband loses mastery in his own home yet runs up abnormal expenses because of the ravenous congregation of women. It is the wife who specifies which friends she wants around her, and the husband who sets out to fetch them. 'When the time draws near of her lying down, then must he trudge to bid gossips, such as she will appoint, or else all the fat is in the fire.' The husband must find money for the midwife, and also for 'her nurse to attend her and keep her, who must make for her warm broths and costly caudles enough for herself and her mistress, being of the mind to fare no worse than she; if her mistress be fed with partridge, plover, woodcocks, quails, or any such like, the nurse must be partaker with her in all these dainties'. Soon the poor husband must dip deeper into his purse, for the women will return for the christening feast and the festivities of upsitting and churching. Post-Restoration reworkings of this motif offered sardonic comfort to the new father whose household was overrun by 'sisters, wives, aunts, cousins' and other women who assembled to assist the midwife and 'the woman in the straw'.[4]

'Mother Wright the midwife of the parish and . . . nine other honest women' were present at the birth and emergency baptism of George Brown at Bobbingworth, Essex, in 1569. When the unmarried servant Agnes Bowker was in labour at Harborough, Leicestershire, the same year, there were six other women beside the midwife in the birthroom. Several of these women were themselves newly delivered, and attended the birth with their babies in their arms. At the opposite end of the spectrum, a cluster of gentle and noble ladies converged on the Countess of Essex when she 'expect(ed) her time' in January 1591. Tudor household ordinances for a queen's deliverance required 'all the ladies and gentlewomen to go in with her, and after that no man to come into the chamber'. The royal 'gossips' were lodged nearby, with women of noble rank in close attendance.[5]

When a suspected recusant gave birth in Lincolnshire in 1607, 'there were many women of the parish' present but, suspiciously, 'none at the christening'. Mother Watts of Sandwich 'called in her neighbours, being women all of a willing forwardness in such a business', as well as the midwife, 'goodwife Hatch the younger', to assist at a delivery in Kent in 1609. A roomful of female villagers joined the midwife Francis Fletcher for the delivery and lying in of Eleanor Rymel at Great Tew, Oxfordshire, in 1633.[6] 'My Lady Cholmely and my dear aunt Norton, my Lady York and Mrs. Watson, with my sisters Denton and Francis Thornton, were with me', as well as the midwife and maid, Alice Thornton recalled, at her delivery in 1662. During her lying in in 1675, Elizabeth Freke reports, 'my sister Norton and a great many of my friends were met together at my dear father's to be merry, which mirth soon turned to mourning' when the company received news of the death of Elizabeth's sister. Male diarists repeatedly recorded the arrival of 'the women' and their mysterious attendance on the segregated 'woman in the straw'.[7]

Attending other women's childbirths and taking part in their gossipings was an important part of some married women's routines. Lady Margaret Hoby took medical knowledge and Christian comfort with her to the birthrooms of her Yorkshire kinsfolk and neighbours. On 15 August 1599, she writes, 'I went to a wife in travail of child, about whom I was busy . . . 'til one o'clock, about which time, she being delivered and I having praised God, returned home and betook myself to private prayer.' On 4 February 1602 'I was sent for to Trutsdale to the travail of my cousin Ison's wife, who that morning was brought to bed of a daughter.' As soon as Robert Woodford's wife was recovered from her own lyings in, she joined in the confinements of neighbours. In December 1637 she attended goodwife Crutch, 'who had sent for her to her labour'. In April 1638 she 'was called to Mrs Danby's labour this morning between three and four'. Robert Woodford, the diarist, did the best a man could do on such occasions by offering a prayer, 'Lord stand by the poor woman, give her a gracious delivery and comfort her for the lord's sake.'[8]

Skilled and experienced matrons liked Lady Margaret Hoby supplemented the work of midwives. Margaret Roos, a gentleman's wife, advised on childbirth in Elizabethan Leicestershire, as did Mrs Mary Mildmay in mid-seventeenth-century Essex and Lady Puckering in later Stuart Warwickshire. When Jane Josselin was prepared to give birth to her first child in 1642, Ralph Josselin writes, 'my wife called her women and God was merciful to me in my house giving her a safe deliverance'. Among those present was Mrs Josselin's mother. In February 1648, the diarist continues, 'my wife was delivered of her second son, the midwife not with her, only four women and Mrs. Mary [Mildmay]'. When a third son was born in May 1649, Josselin writes, 'my wife was alone a great while with our good friends Mrs. Mary and her mother, some few women were with her, but the midwife not'.[9]

Like most married women, the reverend Henry Newcome's wife looked forward to her neighbours' childbirths and lyings in. Her husband wrote in his diary on 1 March 1662, 'it was a pretty vanity of my spirit to be concerned as I felt myself to be this day, in that Mrs. Holbrooke was in labour and my

wife is not called . . . What should be the reason?'[10] Whether this was slight
or oversight we may never know, but Richard Holbrooke was a neighbouring
presbyterian minister and Newcome was about to lose his pulpit for nonconformity. By the 1660s the politics of religion had set up extra cleavages within
the local community that cut across the customary solidarity among women.
Sharpening social divisions may have had a similar effect as social fissures
reached into the circles of gossip. The communal dimensions of childbirth,
as well as other primary rites of passage, appear to have diminished as English
society became more compartmented in the course of the seventeenth century. In contrast to their Elizabethan forebears, later Stuart women may have
attended childbirths and gone a-gossiping by select invitation rather than by
social obligation or customary right. Baptisms too were increasingly private,
as we shall see, and weddings and funerals also became closed to all-comers.

Reputable Midwives

Historical writing about midwives has sometimes been sensationally mis-
guided. Fortunately this is beginning to change. We are beginning to see a
new appreciation of the midwife's skill, and a positive reappraisal of her role
in the local community.[11] But misrepresentations still abound, based on uncrit-
ical acceptance of hostile caricatures, wilful misreading of legal and medical literature, and a remarkable eagerness to believe the worst about gender relations
and childbirth conditions in the past. Discussion of midwives is further ham-
pered by confusion of historical periods, by reading the medical prejudices
of the eighteenth and nineteenth centuries back into the sixteenth and seventeenth, and by a failure to examine the records of actual midwives going about
their normal business.

Popular historical literature has both vilified and sentimentalized midwives, associating them in one tradition with filthiness, bawdry, and witchcraft, in another with ancient goddess wisdom and resistance to patriarchal
oppression. Both these assessments are wrong. According to Thomas Forbes,
early modern midwives were characterized by 'ignorance, incompetence, and
poverty', were mired in superstition, and easily tempted to 'the delights of
witchcraft'. Lawrence Stone repeats the charge that 'midwives were ignorant
and ill-trained, and often horribly botched the job'. These views echo the
most hostile assertions of the midwives' worst enemies, past and present, and
are light on historical analysis.[12] On the other hand, efforts to elevate midwives and to see them as victims of misogynist domination has driven some
feminist scholars to the realm of fantasy. Midwife-witches, according to one
influential survey, formed 'part of an organized underground of peasant

women' locked in struggle with the male power establishment. They belonged, says another, to 'the sacred sisterhoods of the *med-wyf*', whose skill was 'passed down in the matrilineal clans from pre-Christian times'. This is not history but wishful thinking, akin to belief in the survival of pagan religions.[13]

There is no evidence to support the notion that midwives, more than any other women, were involved in witchcraft, or that witches were commonly midwives. Indeed, to the contrary, the authorities employed midwives to examine the bodies of suspected witches for witch marks, with no suspicion that the midwives themselves were engaged in *maleficium*.[14] Nor is there anything to suggest that midwives had links to an occult pre-Christian religion, despite their employment of charms and potions. Again, quite the opposite is true.[15] Midwives acted as agents of respectability and upholders of sexual propriety. In support of both secular and ecclesiastical courts, they gave evidence in cases of rape, bastardy, and infanticide. They were foremost in the jury of matrons to determine whether female offenders were virginal, pregnant, or recently delivered of child. For example, the Canterbury ecclesiastical court took action in 1573 because 'Agnes Hollway, single woman, is with child as the midwife saith', and members of the privy council took note of the Sussex midwife Denis Clarke's denunciation of a bastard-bearer in 1578.[16]

Most midwives were respectable married women or widows, almost all churchgoers, with years of practical experience. They were supposed to be licensed by the church. Had they been subversive or malicious they would soon have fallen foul of the civil and ecclesiastical authorities. Had they been grossly incompetent their clients would surely have refused to use them. The preponderance of evidence from Tudor and Stuart England reveals midwives to have been dutiful, respectable, and well-appreciated members of their local community, leaders in the sisterhood of women, needing nothing illicit or supernatural to sustain their position.[17]

The little we can learn of the social status of midwives sets them in the heart of the social order, towards the middle of the economic scale. Mrs Gataker, the midwife at Kirkham, Lancashire, in 1645, was the widow of the parish minister. Jane Webster, the midwife of Downham Market, Norfolk, in 1677 was the wife of a barber surgeon. Northern midwives in the reign of Charles II included the wife of a master clothworker, an innkeeper's widow, and several widows of yeomen. Of three midwives at Eccleshall, Staffordshire, in the late seventeenth century, one was married to a shoemaker who was also an overseer of the church, and the other two were her mother and her sister. London midwives of this period were wives or widows of tradesmen and craftsmen, city officials, and even gentlemen, and enjoyed a social status no lower than that of most of their clients.[18] Only in the eighteenth century, when popular and genteel cultures drew awkwardly apart, did the social status of midwifery undergo a precipitous decline.[19]

Early modern midwives were neither marginal nor sinister, but were vital participants in the reproductive cultural system. The rising numbers of births kept them busy. Midwives advised on the management of pregnancy and preparations for delivery, took charge of labour and its aftermath, and fulfilled a host of associated gynaecological tasks. They were, in the words of a Civil-War petition, 'highly respected in our parishes for [their] great skill and midnight industry'. Some parishes even reserved a special seat in church for the midwife, for her use at baptisms and churchings. Midwives were formidable women possessed of exceptional authority, and this may have made some men uneasy. Humorous literature (entirely men's work) sometimes ridiculed the midwife as 'mother midnight' or 'old mother grope', but this was an uncomfortable male representation of skilful women whose specialties were gender-specific and mysterious.[20]

Some scholars have depicted early modern midwives as besieged and disparaged by a misogynist medical profession. This applies especially to the eighteenth and nineteenth centuries, when the social standing of midwives underwent a precipitous decline, but earlier ages allowed the midwife much higher esteem. Most Renaissance physicians deferred to midwives for routine deliveries and primary care, and only the most assertive doctors, in alliance with the new man-midwives of the later seventeenth century, challenged their good faith and utility. Their most severe criticism was that traditional midwives were dirty, incompetent, and old-fashioned, and were too slow to call for expert help in emergencies. But since very few physicians could ever have seen midwives in action it is hard to credit the objectiveness of these complaints.

Midwives were summoned as servants but performed as officiants. They crossed social boundaries and entered homes of all sorts. In the crisis of labour they supplanted husbands as the principal support for their wives, and took temporary command of the intimate core of his household. The midwife's office allowed her to pass thresholds and open doors, to reach day and night to the heart of *materia materna*. She alone could touch the labouring woman's genitals. Ministers sometimes looked upon midwives with suspicion because alone among women they occasionally performed a priest-like function, administering the sacrament of baptism *in extremis* to a child who seemed likely to die.[21]

It was the midwife who swaddled the child and presented it to the waiting father. If she followed tradition, she would address the lucky man with the formula, 'Father, see there is your child, God give you much joy with it, or take it speedily to his bliss.'[22] At normal church baptisms the midwife carried the infant to the font, proudly displaying the success of her endeavours. And in the subsequent ceremony of churching, when the mother came to give thanks for her deliverance, the midwife again enjoyed a prominent place as principal supporter and attendant to the woman who had recently given birth. None could match her ritual significance in bridging the domestic world of childbirth and the public realm of organized religion.

The midwife took charge of the birthroom. The other women present deferred to her knowledge and experience. She controlled the heat and light, arranged furnishings, and issued confident instructions. An important part of her task was to give counsel and encouragement while nature did its work. Her ministry, according to an Elizabethan prayer for midwives, was 'to comfort [women] in their sorrows, cherish them in their child-beds, ease them in their pains, and to further them in their deliverance'. To this end an experienced midwife would come equipped 'with a convenient stool or chair, with a knife, sponge, binders, and with oil of lilies warmed, with which she may profitably annoint both the womb of the labouring woman and her own hands'.[23] As a courtesy and precaution she would keep her nails trim and remove all rings and bracelets before bending to her task. Removal of constricting ornaments also served, sympathetically, to ease constrictions on the womb. Neither she nor the physicians knew the benefit of washing one's hands, though some seventeenth-century doctors believed that midwives caused damage if they did not trim their finger nails.[24]

As the birth progressed the midwife would probe and pull, advise and comment, intervening as she considered necessary. The midwife employed clisters, purges, liniments, poultices, ointments, and herbal infusions to relieve the woman in labour. She would bathe her, lubricate her, talk to her, comfort her, and administer fortifying beverages. For Jane Sharp, following Jacob Rueff, 'the midwife must annoint her hands with oil of lilies, and the woman's secrets, or with oil of almonds, and so with her hands handle and unloose the parts, and observe how the child lieth and stirreth, and so help as time and occasion direct'.[25]

Early modern doctors agreed with ancient authors that the easiest childbirths were those requiring the least intervention. Modern obstetricians feel the same. James Guillemeau's often-reprinted *Child-Birth or, The Happy Deliverie of Women* advised 'neither the midwife nor any of the woman's kinsfolk or assistants ought to do anything rashly, but suffer nature to work'. As Galen said, 'nature surpasseth all'. The most popular books on the subject recommended trust in nature's course and the midwife's customary skills.

They promoted no aggressive medicalization of childbirth, no male professional encroachment on the women's domain; rather they recognized that
the midwife had primary supervisory responsibility and that in normal circumstances her knowledge would be sufficient. Only in case of severe complications would there be a role for a male physician, and in most English
parishes no such person could be found.[26]

Helkiah Crooke, an early Stuart court physician, allowed that nature was
aided by 'the skilful hand of the heads-woman or midwife as we call them,
for she setteth the woman in a due posture or position of parts, receiveth
the infant gently which falleth betwixt her knees, directeth it if it offer itself
amiss, and finally draweth away as easily as possible the afterbirth which
stayeth behind'. A generation later his fellow physician William Sermon
thought midwives needed better instruction, but not that they ought to be
replaced.[27] For her part, the Restoration midwife Jane Sharp granted physicians and surgeons their 'honour due . . . when occasion is', but gave prime
obstetric responsibility to her own gender and profession. It was, she argued,
'the natural propriety of women to be much seeing into that art'. In rural
England, 'where there are none but women to assist . . . the women are as
fruitful, and as safe and well delivered, if not much more fruitful and better
commonly in childbed, than the greatest ladies of the land'. Testimonials
written on behalf of midwives by later seventeenth-century physicians and
surgeons support the notion that, in provincial England at least, male and
female practitioners of childbirth medicine were more likely to be allies than
opponents.[28]

Midwives and Ministers

Midwives, like schoolmasters, came within 'ecclesiastical cognizance' and were
supposed to obtain episcopal licences to practice. The origins of the licensing
procedure are obscure, but it seems to have developed between the reigns of
Henry VIII and his daughters. A statute of 1512 made bishops responsible for
licensing male medical practitioners. Andrew Boorde, in the mid-Tudor
Breviary of Health, urged bishops to extend this oversight to midwives. And
a late Stuart writer not implausibly attributed the first licensing of midwives
to the Marian Bishop Bonner.[29]

In order to obtain a midwife's licence a woman had to satisfy diocesan
officials of her religious orthodoxy and good reputation, and pay a small
fee (in the diocese of Norwich in the seventeenth century 1s., though fees as
high as 18s. 8d. were charged in the Diocese of Chester).[30] This licence was by
no means a check on her gynaecological or obstetric skill, but rather a way

to weed out those most wedded to unreformed superstitious practices. If a midwife was to baptize an ailing newborn child in the name of the Father, the Son, and the Holy Ghost it was important that she did so with Christian understanding, especially in the period of the Reformation. If the mother was unmarried the midwife acted as agent for the parish to learn the name of the father, so that punishment and financial responsibility could be assigned. The church acknowledged that midwives performed a vital role and set out to ensure that the women were fit for the social and spiritual dimensions of their task.

Rather than seeking to suppress the practice of emergency baptism by midwives, reforming bishops of Henry VIII's reign sought to regulate it, to conform it to Christian principles, and to ensure it was done with decency and without superstition. According to Nicholas Shaxton's Injunctions for the Diocese of Salisbury in 1538, the priest was supposed to

instruct his parishioners, and especially the midwives, the essential manner and form how to christen a child in time of need; commanding the women when the time of birth draweth near to have a vessel of clean water ready for the same purpose; charging also the midwives to beware that they cause not the woman, being in travail, to make any foolish vow to go to pilgrimage to this image or that image after her deliverance, but only to call on God for help. Nor to use any purses, measures of our Lady, or such other superstitious things to be occupied about the woman while she laboureth, to make her believe to have the better speed by it.[31]

Elizabethan reformers divided on the question whether midwives should be allowed to baptize. Some wanted to reserve all priestly functions to the ordained male ministry, and mocked the old tradition that the women at a birth should have 'water in readiness to christen the child, if necessity so require it'.[32] Others were unwilling to risk the souls of unbaptized children, and, though uneasy about entrusting sacramental work to women, allowed the custom of baptism by midwives to continue. Attitudes hinged on whether churchmen thought baptism a necessary prerequisite to salvation, or primarily a mark of membership in the Christian community. As we will see in a later chapter, baptism by midwives became much less common in the seventeenth century, as ministers themselves became more willing to perform baptism in private.

When the Elizabethan midwife Eleanor Pead took her oath in 1567 she promised,

that in the ministration of the sacrament of baptism in the time of necessity, I will use apt and the accustomed words of the same sacrament, that is to say, these words following or the like in effect, 'I christen thee in the name of the Father, the Son, and the Holy Ghost', and none other profane words. And that in such time of necessity, in baptizing any infant born, and pouring water upon the head of the same infant, I will use pure and clean water, and not any rose or damask water, or water made of any confection or mixture; and that I will certify the curate of the parish church of every such baptizing.[33]

In its seventeenth-century form, however, the midwife's oath makes no mention of her performing baptisms, but instead subordinates her to the parish priest. 'The oath that is to be administered to a midwife by the bishop or his chancellor of the diocese, when she is licensed to exercise that office of a midwife' is worth recording in full for the little light it throws on the practice of midwifery, and for the potent range of fears it reveals concerning its darker side: social inequity, contested paternity, fraud, conspiracy, infanticide, witchcraft, abortion, extortion, and the revival of Roman Catholicism.

You shall swear, first, that you shall be diligent and faithful, and ready to help every woman labouring of child, as well the poor as the rich; and that in time of necessity you shall not forsake or leave the poor woman to go to the rich.

2. Item, Ye shall neither cause nor suffer any woman to name or put any other father to the child, but only him which is the very father thereof indeed.

3. Item, You shall not suffer any woman to pretend, feign or surmise herself to be delivered of a child who is not indeed, neither to claim any other woman's child for her own.

4. Item, You shall not suffer any woman's child to be murdered, maimed, or otherwise hurt, as much as you may; and so often as you perceive any peril or jeopardy, either in the woman or the child in any such wise as you shall be in doubt what shall chance thereof, you shall thenceforth in due time send for other midwives and expert women in that faculty, and use their advice and counsel in that behalf.

5. Item, That you shall not in any wise use or exercise any manner of witchcraft, charm or sorcery, invocation or other prayers than may stand with God's laws and the king's.

6. Item, You shall not give any counsel, or minister any herb, medicine or potion, or any other thing to any woman being with child whereby she should destroy or cast out that she goeth withal before her time.

7. Item, You shall not enforce any woman being with child by any pain or by any ungodly ways and means to give you any more for your pains or labour in bringing her to bed than they would otherwise do.

8. Item, You shall not consent, agree, give or keep counsel, that any woman be delivered secretly of that which she goeth with, but in the presence of two or three lights ready.

9. Item, You shall be secret, and not open any matter appertaining to your office in the presence of any man, unless necessity or great urgent cause do constrain you so to do.

10. Item, If any child be dead born, you yourself shall see it buried in such secret place as neither hog nor dog nor any other beast may come unto it, and in such sort done, as it be not found nor perceived, as much as you may; and that you shall not suffer any child to be cast into the jakes or any other inconvenient place.

11. Item, If you shall know any midwife using or doing any thing contrary to any of these premises, or in any other wise than shall be seemly or convenient, you shall forthwith detect, open to show the same to me or my chancellor for the time being.

12. You shall use yourself in honest behaviour unto the woman being lawfully admitted to the room and office of a midwife in all things accordingly.

13. That you shall truly present to myself or my chancellor all such women as you know from time to time to occupy and exercise the room of a midwife within my foresaid diocese and jurisdiction of—without my license and admission.

14. Item, You shall not make or assign any deputy or deputies to exercise or occupy under you in your absence the office or room of a midwife, but such as you shall perfectly know to be of right honest and discreet behaviour, as also apt, able, and having sufficient knowledge and experience to exercise the said room and office.

15. Item, You shall not be privy, or consent, that any priest or other party shall in your absence, or in your company, or of your knowledge or sufferance, baptise any child by any mass, Latin service or prayers than such as are appointed by the laws of the Church of England; neither shall you consent that any child born by any woman who shall be delivered by you shall be carried away without being baptised in the parish by the ordinary minister where the said child is born, unless it be in case of necessity baptised privately according to the Book of Common Prayer; but you shall forthwith upon understanding thereof either give knowledge to me the said bishop or my chancellor for the time being. All which articles and charge you shall faithfully observe and keep. So help you God and by the contents of this book.[34]

Like other attempts at ecclesiastical regulation, the supervision of midwives was piecemeal and erratic. Many women practiced midwifery without licence, and only took the oath when forced before the diocesan authorities. Elizabeth Wyatt told the London archdeaconry court in 1635 that 'she hath practiced as a midwife for the space of these five years and that she is not yet licensed, for she is a deputy to one Mrs. Brown with whom she conditioned to serve seven years, and at the expiration of the said years she intendeth to obtain licence'. Licensed or 'professed' midwives were obliged by their oath to help all women in travail, whereas those who simply 'used the office of a midwife' and helped from time to time could bestow or withhold their services as they chose. An unlicensed midwife at Thame, Oxfordshire, who had formerly 'helped some of her neighbours at their travail', justified her refusal to help a woman in labour in 1637 because she was 'no professed midwife, and she intends not to meddle any further therein'.[35]

Bishops commonly asked at their visitations whether each parish had a midwife who was duly authorized, but rarely followed up presentments on this topic. Archbishop Whitgift's visitation articles for the Diocese of Winchester in 1590 covered the principal points of ecclesiastical concern. Each parish would be asked

whether midwives be of sober life and uncorrupt religion, not suspected of papistry; whether any of them use in time of woman's travail any witchcraft, charms, Latin prayers or invocations, or take upon them to baptise; whether when they be present at the delivery of any child known or suspected to be begotten in unlawful matrimony, (they) do not straightly charge the mother to declare who is the father and where it was begotten, and immediately certify the ordinary or the least the curate and churchwardens of the parish thereof.

More succinctly, William Laud asked of the Diocese of London in 1628, 'how many midwives have you in your parish, which do exercise that office, how long have they so done, and by what authority? Of what skill are they accounted to be of in their office and vocation?'[36]

The scope of episcopal visitation returns can be judged by the following sample from the diocese of Chichester in 1579 during the regime of Bishop Richard Curteys. Eighteen out of thirty-four parishes in the West Sussex deanery of Boxgrove reported the presence of active midwives. Nearly all these women were represented as honest, sound, and necessary, though very few of them could show an epsicopal licence. None was alleged to use illicit practices or charms, none was implicated in witchcraft. Simply citing their names helps to restore them to history.[37]

Boxgrove: 'There is two named Agnes Fawkner and Isabel Jape that execute the office of midwife but not so allowed.'

Compton: 'We have a woman that deals as a midwife which is of good and sound religion, whether she be authorized we know not.'

Eartham: 'We have a very godly matron in our parish, Joan Peachy, which doth use the office of a midwife in the time of necessity, whether she be licensed we know not.'

North Mundham: 'There is one honest poor widow who in extremity and necessity is ready being called with the best help she can and is thought to be a very necessary woman and such a one as might ill be spared.'

Birdham: 'Joan Hiberden, widow, doth execute the office of a midwife, whether licensed or no we know not.'

Chidham: 'There is an honest woman ... one Alice Wheeler in our parish which doth serve the office of a midwife but not thereunto licensed.'

Singleton: 'We have one Alice Peachy (mother Peachy) which for her good and honest behaviour hath been allowed a long time.'

East Dean: 'We have a midwife but not sworn.'

East Marden: 'We have an honest woman (Joan Sylvester) to supply the office of a midwife when need is . . . being not licensed.'

Funtington: 'We have an honest old woman that hath been midwife there a long time.'

West Wittering: 'One Hoskins widow doth take upon her to execute the office of a midwife and is thought a woman very meet but not licensed.'

West Itchenor: 'Alice Aylmer being midwife and not licensed.'

East Wittering: 'Midwives be not sworn nor will not be sworn.'

Selsey: 'Joan Gearing doth execute the room or place of a midwife being not licensed.'

Aldingbourne: 'the midwife saith she was admitted by bishop Barlow [1559–68] and so hath since remained; she baptised infants.'

Hunston: 'Gillian Caplan of a good and honest report doth exercise the office being licensed thereto by word of Dr Worley.'

Hampnett: 'Goodwife Legatt admitted a midwife by Dr Worley once did baptize a child which died.'

Stoughton: 'we have a midwife and whether licensed we know not.'

The same visitation revealed midwives in nine of the thirty parishes in the deanery of Midhurst, in six out of twenty-nine parishes in the deanery of Arundel, in nine of twenty-seven parishes in Storrington deanery, and four in the city of Chichester. Noteworthy among them were 'an honest woman' of Petworth who 'hath good report of all her neighbours and hath executed the office here above twenty years'; a licensed midwife of Bury who 'medleth not with baptism'; the midwife of Pulborough who 'baptiseth infants in time of great peril and danger at home'; and widow Alice Mallat of Wiggenholt who 'executeth that function for charity sake when she is requested'. Barely a third of these parishes admitted the presence of midwives, and few of them were licensed.[38] Like their sisters elsewhere, these Sussex midwives may have served several neighbouring communities, caring more for their clients than for the formal licensing requirements of the church. Elizabethan Sussex was notoriously troubled with catholic recusancy, and that, along with an aversion to ministerial oversight and fees, may partially account for the low ecclesiastical compliance.

Ecclesiastical licensing of midwives continued until the Civil War and was revived, with sporadic bursts of energy, after the Restoration. The spate of publications on the medical aspects of childbirth may have persuaded some bishops that midwives needed particular attention. And amidst the religious divisions of the early 1660s it was important to ensure that newly licensed

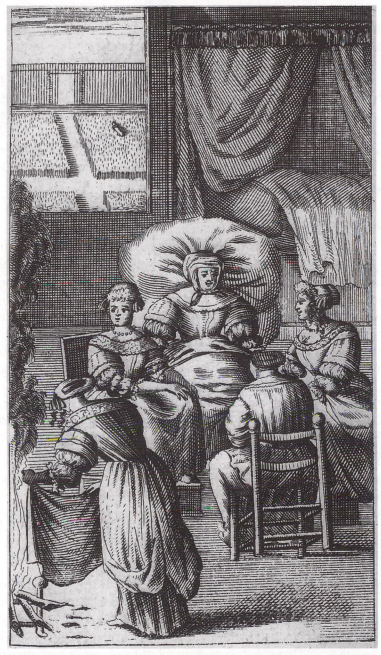

FIG. 8 'Woman in labour with midwife and assistants' from *The Ten Pleasures of Marriage* (London, 1682)

midwives, like parish officials, were 'of an orderly and sober conversation and well affected to the doctrine and discipline of the Church of England'. Diocesan records of the reign of Charles II frequently preserve testimonials to show that such or such midwife was indeed 'of honest life and conversation' and 'a dutiful and obedient daughter of the Church of England'. Anne Knutsford of Nantwich, Cheshire, was exceptional for earning a negative testimonial in 1663. Though evidently an accomplished midwife, she offended her neighbours 'by her scandalous speeches, that (contrary to her profession of midwife) she hath revealed the secrets of women [and] that she is ordinarily addicted to lying, swearing and cursing'. The minister, two churchwardens, and fifteen women subscribed this remarkable certificate.[39]

Midwives in Action

In aristocratic households, where childbirth was closely implicated with lineage and power, the selection of a midwife was almost as important as the choice of a tutor or a steward. Both male and female networks operated to secure the most renowned or most advantageous services. Account books record that 'the midwife came' to take up temporary residence in the Earl of Derby's household a month before Lady Strange gave birth in December 1588. Lesser gentle families shared information about the availability and reputation of suitable midwives. Joan Thynne, for example, wrote to her husband from Longleat in March 1590, 'if my sister be in London I pray you entreat her to provide me of a good midwife for me against Easter or a ten or twelve days after, for I think my time will be much thereabout. Here is none worth the having now goody Barber is dead.' Francis Tilghman thanked Richard Oxinden of Kent in January 1621,

for your mindfulness of my wife for a midwife; the time draws nigh at hand, and therefore have thought fit to send unto you, entreating you to write by my man that she may come away with him, if you think fit, or otherwise to direct him by some token to the same end, for I am altogether stranger unto her. I think she shall serve my sister Saunders' turn also, who hath mind thereto if God give opportunity to both.[40]

Diaries sometimes yield vivid accounts of the midwife's summons to the birthroom. These entries, written by anxious husbands, provide dramatic counterpoint to the somewhat impersonal prescriptions of the childbirth manuals. Men may not have known much of the intimate mysteries of childbirth but they understood their responsibility to secure proper attendance for their wives. 'Help, neighbours, help!' was a familiar cry announcing the onset of labour.[41]

The Northampton puritan Robert Woodford recorded how about seven in the morning on 29 August 1638 his wife Hannah 'began to fall in travail, so the midwife was sent for, and came', and speedily brought forth a baby girl. A year later Hannah Woodford was again close to confinement, and her husband worried lest the midwife 'be fetched away [to other clients] before we shall use her'. On 13 August 1639, Woodford wrote, 'between two and three o'clock in the morning my wife was very ill, and I rose and sent for the midwife Mrs Parsons to Mr West and called some friends, and my wife hath since been somewhat better and doth yet continue ill'. Two days later, 'Mrs Parsons is here but my wife is pretty well and doubtful she shall stay till the midwife be gone.' Not until 16 August were Woodford's prayers answered, for 'this day my dear wife brought to bed of another girl between eight and nine at night, the lord graciously ordered all conveniences'. The midwife, who had stayed throughout this crisis, departed the following day to another client, while God remained to smile his blessings on the Woodfords. August, apparently, was Hannah Woodford's month for childbearing, for on 17 August 1640 her husband recorded, 'my wife is fallen very ill and the women are with her and we suppose it is her travail and the midwife goodwife Edwards is now come, blessed be God'. And on the next day, 'my dear wife is brought to bed between two and three of the clock this morning of a son'. The following August she was expecting yet another child, this time with the preferred midwife Mrs Parsons in attendance.[42]

Another diarist of the 1640s recorded the midwife's midnight business in revolutionary London. The haberdasher John Greene's wife gave birth to a son on the evening of 8 March 1644. 'She had been in labour all that day and all the night before, the midwife being sent for at twelve of the clock on Thursday night.'[43]

Ralph Josselin's famous diary includes remarks on the midwives and other women who attended his wife, and dramatic accounts of their summoning. On 24 November 1645, he wrote,

about midnight on Monday, I rose, called up some neighbours, the night was very light, goodman Potter willing to go for the midwife, and up when I went, the horse out of the pasture but presently found, the midwife up at Buers, expecting it had been nearer day, the weather indifferent dry; midwife came, all things even gotten ready towards day; I called in the women by daylight, almost all came; and about eleven or twelve of the clock my wife was with very sharp pains delivered . . . we had made a good pasty for this hour, and that also was kept well,

so nobody went home hungry.[44]

In 1658 Ralph Josselin records another urgent night-time search for the midwife. On the night of 12 January the midwife was already with the Josselins, my wife thinking she might use her; but being sent for, my wife let her go, that another that was in present need might be holpen . . . But within half an hour, as soon as I had done family prayer, my wife had so sure a sign of her labour and speedy that put us all to a plunge. I sent two messengers after her and it was at least four hours before she came. Mr. Richard Harlakenden's man fetched her, but she came time enough for us, God be praised. My wife was wonderfully afraid and amazed but help was speedily with her and in particular young Mrs. Harlakenden, who put forth herself to the utmost to help her, and her presence was much to my wife.

After a brief intermission, Jane Josselin lay quaking and trembling in bed at two in the morning on 14 January, so her husband 'called up the midwife and nurse, got fires and all ready, and then her labour came on so strongly and speedily that the child was born, only two or three women more got in to her, but God supplied all, young Mrs. Harlakenden got up to us very speedily, and some others'. On this occasion Jane Josselin 'judged her midwife did not do her part, but God did all', and she was delivered of a daughter after labour that was 'exceeding sharp'.[45]

Elizabeth Freke's account of the birth of her son in June 1675 is one of the few descriptions of seventeenth-century childbirth written by a woman. She was attended by no less than four midwives as well as by one of the newly fashionable and controversial man-midwives. Mrs Freke writes,

Wednesday, June the second, my dear son Mr. Ralph Freke was born about three in the afternoon, at my father's at Hannington, and by him with my Aunt Freke and Sir George Norton, he was christened Ralph Freke of my dear father's name. I were four or five days in labour of him, and had four midwives about me when he was born, the man midwife affirming he had been long dead to my husband, aunt and sister Norton with my Lady Thynne, all who were with me several days in this my extremity. My great and good God that never failed me or denied my reasonable request, raised me up a good woman midwife of my Lady Thynne's acquaintance, one Mrs. Mills, who came in at this juncture of time, and, by God's mercy and providence to me, I was safely delivered. And though [apparently] of a dead child, my God raised him up to me so far as the same night to baptise him of my dear father's name, Ralph Freke, for which mercy to him and me I beg I may never forget to be thankful. I put my son into the hands of a good surgeon for at least six weeks, who came every day from Highworth, a mile from my dear father's, I being almost all the time confined to my bed; and at last, by my God's great goodness and mercy to me, he recovered him, for which great God make me ever thankful, for sparing my child and raising up his poor servant, Elizabeth Freke.[46]

Mrs Mills outperformed the man-midwife, the consulting obstetrician, and more than earned her money.

Payments to midwives were more like a reward than a fee, and varied with the resources of the establishment rather than the extent of the midwife's efforts. The reward could be a few pennies or a few pounds, and sometimes included payment in kind, such as a gift of a piglet or chickens. Jane Magham of Hull, Yorkshire, bequeathed four sheep to her midwife in her will of 1584. Goodwife Hatch, the Kentish midwife, earned 7s. for her 'diligent pains' in delivering a monstrous birth in 1609. Mrs Turner, the midwife who attended the Hayne family of Exeter, received 20s. from John Hayne and 10s. more from his wife after helping to deliver a daughter in 1637. She received 25s. after the birth of a second daughter in 1639, and 30s. when a son was born in 1640.[47]

Joyce Jeffries, a Hereford gentlewoman, paid 20s. to the midwife when her 'god-daughter Walsh was brought to bed' in April 1638. After her cousin Jane 'was delivered of a daughter' in December 1647 Joyce Jeffries 'gave the mid-wife Hughs of Upper Tedstan the christening day ten shillings', and the like amount to nurse Nott. With less money to dispose, and less pressing claims of kinship, the Sussex clergyman Giles Moore paid 5s. to 'goodwife Moore, midwife', 2s. to 'goodwife Ellis, wetnurse', and 1s. to 'the widow Vinall, dry nurse' after a neighbour gave birth in 1672. Later that year he gave 2s. to the midwife, 2s. to the nurse, and a shilling to the 'tender' on the occasion of another neighbour's childbearing.[48] Such payments were often made at chris-tenings, when godparents and others gave tips that augmented the midwife's income.

The surviving account book of an anonymous London midwife who prac-tised between 1694 and 1716 lists dozens of women 'laid' and children deliv-ered, with details of dates and fees. The writer was evidently a busy professional midwife, whose fees ranging from a few shillings to several pounds reflected a socially varied practice. The following entry is typical: 'laid Mrs. Chaste of a daughter on the 20 day May being on a Monday at one o'clock 1695, living in Glass House Yard in Aldgate Street. Given me 7s. 6d.'[49] The fees these women earned simultaneously recognized and enhanced their standing in the local community.

Bastard Births

About one out of every forty babies was born out of wedlock. Bastardy rates varied from time to time, place to place, and across the social scale, but the best available statistics point to an overall rate around 2 or 3 per cent, rising to a peak of 4 per cent around 1600, then falling in the early Stuart period and remaining below 2 per cent for the rest of the seventeenth century. These statistics are derived from parish register entries, but they stand up well

alongside evidence from the ecclesiastical courts and other sources. Late Elizabethan and early Jacobean England experienced the highest rate of bastardy,
along with other social and economic problems, while the incidence of illegitimacy rose and fell in phase with general fertility patterns. Court records
point to 'a more rigorous attitude to bastard-bearing and bastard-begetting'
in the 1620s and 1630s, at a time when the actual incidence of illegitimacy was
in decline. Bastard births appear to have been somewhat more common in
the highland areas of the north and west where parochial discipline was
weaker.[50]

The most common profile of a bastard-bearer was a single woman in her
twenties, employed away from home as a domestic maid or servant in hus-
bandry, who succumbed to the pressures or promises of her master or fellow
servants. Few single women who became pregnant were sexually promiscuous
and most hoped or expected soon to be married. Rather than being 'wanton
wenches' who enjoyed uninhibited sexuality, the great majority of unmarried
mothers were casualties of exploitative relationships or of prenuptial contracts
that came apart. Their average age—in their middle twenties—was almost
exactly the same as that of women entering lawful matrimony. The estimate
that up to a quarter of all brides were already pregnant at the time of their weddings suggests that many began sexual congress when they became contracted
or betrothed.[51] Since contract or betrothal was often informal, unwitnessed,
or improperly performed, and since there was little to ensure that the parties
to a promise were unimpedimented or sincere, it is little wonder that some
expected marriages never came to pass. Mortality as well as amnesia claimed
some prospective husbands.

The patriarchal Christian norms of early modern England required that
every child should know its father. Paternity was the key to lineage, position,
substance, and name for females as well as males. Bastards suffered legal limitations in regard to property and title. Some jurists argued that only children
born in wedlock could inherit, but in practice the law allowed bastards to
receive legacies through wills. Whether illegitimates suffered shame in consequence of their birth and begetting, and whether bastard men suffered differently than bastard women, is still a matter for research.[52]

Both the secular and ecclesiastical authorities investigated and punished
the parents of bastard children. Not surprisingly, a double standard applied.
The father, if identified, was supposed to assume financial responsibilty for
the maintenance of his child. If he was a servant or a person of subordinate
social position he might also be whipped. The mother, who faced the usual
pangs and perils of childbirth without the normal system of domestic and
social support, was subject to whipping, public humiliation, and even

imprisonment in the house of correction. Her punishment was liable to be more severe if she refused to name the father, and if the child became a burden to the parish. Justices of the peace had discretion to investigate cases of bastardy and to punish those responsible 'as they think convenient'. Bastardy orders, recorded at Quarter Sessions, usually specified who should make payments for the maintenance of the child, with imprisonment for those in default.[53]

Single or married, supported or alone, a pregnant woman went through the same stages of breeding and quickening, carrying and bearing, as the most respected matron. Fragments of evidence from the ecclesiastical court records point to a pattern of discovery, despair, coming to term, and lying in. Few single women were completely alone when they came to give birth, and most secured some attendance by neighbouring women and assistance by midwives, like their more respectable sisters. The main difference was that in cases of bastard birth the midwife sought to ascertain the name of the father as well as to deliver the child, and there was no grateful husband at hand to acknowledge the child or to give the women their reward.

Agnes Bowker, a servant of Harborough, Leicestershire, quit her employment when she became pregnant in 1568 and took to wandering the lanes. The father of her child was either Randall Dowley, a fellow servant, or Hugh Brady, the local schoolmaster. Agnes tried at least twice to kill herself, according to her testimony, but when she tried hanging, her girdle broke, and when she tried drowning, the water was too shallow and some strangers pulled her clear. She scrounged for support, failed to secure an abortion, and eventually placed herself in the hands of a local midwife and gave birth in a room full of women. Agnes Bowker's story would be commonplace were it not for the extraordinary outcome of her pregnancy and the amazing stories she told to explain it. Allegedly she gave birth to a cat, fathered on her by a diabolic shape-shifting beast, though it would not be unreasonable to suspect this story was a cover for infanticide.[54]

Mercy Gould, another single woman of Cuckfield, Sussex, was dismissed from service in 1578 when she was no longer able to hide her pregnancy. She went home to her parents, but after they both died of plague she took refuge in the house of one Boniface. Mercy became seriously ill after swallowing a 'metredation of dragon water' (which doubled as a plague remedy and an abortifacient), and gave birth to a stillborn child. During labour she was attended by 'the goodwife of the house and her servants', but not by the Cuckfield midwife, Denis Clarke, who only turned up after news of Mercy's deliverance went abroad. In this case the midwife was denied the chance to exercise her skills, but did not stint to discover the name of the father, 'John

Orgle, Mr. Bowyer's man', or to besmirch the reputations of Mercy Gould and her employer.[55]

One more brief story will illuminate the plight of unmarried pregnancy and the legal and moral complications attendant on bastard birth. Rose Arnold, a servant of Scraptoft, Leicestershire, became pregnant in 1608 after her master's son, Francis Lane, promised to make her his wife. Francis intended no such course and his first thought on learning that he was to be a father was how to get rid of the baby. He pushed poor Rose into a well, intending either miscarriage or murder but achieved neither. Eventually, in Rose's words, 'my fault beginning to be apparently seen', she left the house with a small sum of money, and then 'wandered up and down in Northamptonshire until I was delivered of childbirth'. This child died, in circumstances that are not revealed, and the newly delivered single mother returned to Leicestershire. Although she had no baby she could not conceal the fact that she had recently borne one. The rest of the case turned on Rose naming Francis Lane as the father and Lane trying to lay the child to somebody else. Despite her mistreatment Rose insisted Francis fulfil his promise of marriage, calculating, no doubt, that it was better to be miserable as a wife than single, abandoned, and ruined.[56]

That none of these three cases involved a child who survived to baptism may heighten suspicion that the parish register evidence underrepresents the scale of illegitimate fertility. Unmarried women who struggled with pregnancy appear to have been disproportionately vulnerable to natural or deliberate miscarriages and failure to produce a live birth. Jacobean legislators looked on these women with such deep suspicion that they passed 'An act to prevent the destroying and murthering of bastard children', which construed concealment of the body of an illegitimate child as murder unless a witness could testify that the child had been born dead.[57]

Pregnant single women commonly attempted to conceal their plight for as long as possible by judicious arrangement of aprons and skirts. Suspicions aroused by the normal signs of pregnancy might be confirmed by inspection by the midwife. 'Agnes Hollway, single woman, is with child as the midwife saith', reported the churchwardens of Alkham, Kent, in 1573.[58] Ejected from her place of employment, the pregnant woman might then move away to give birth in a parish where she was not known. Women heavy with child must have been common sights on the fringes of towns and villages, though most found shelter, at least a roof and a bed, by the time they went into labour. Only the most desperate, or most unfortunate, gave birth alone in a field or a hedge, or dragged themselves to a church porch, and even they would, most likely, soon find assistance from other women. Even vagrant women are alleged to have banded together when one of them was 'in the straw'.[59]

References to these matters are scarce. They appear from time to time in the church court records in connection with allegations of 'harbouring' disreputable bastard-bearers. In 1592 'a strange woman . . . being a vagrant person going from door to door' reached the house of John Potter in Sussex, 'where pitifully she cried because she was presently to be delivered. And when his wife, who was with him, heard her cry, she opened the door and perceiving her case, for charity's sake, let her in, where forthwith she was delivered.' This act of charity, initiated by the woman of the house, led to John Potter's appearance before the Chichester diocesan court, as well as much ignominy, expense, and inconvenience. The woman moved on as soon as she was fit to travel, after threatening to leave her bastard in the parish.[60]

In a similar case from the outskirts of London, 'one Elizabeth' (surname unknown) 'being unmarried and in travail in the field' was rescued and brought to the house of Juliana Pinckham of Stepney, Middlesex, in 1620, 'where after she the said Elizabeth had continued about half an hour she . . . was delivered of a child', and as soon as she was able she stole away with the child without it being christened. Margaret Hanford, a sturdy beggar, 'run away' after 'being delivered of a man child in the street' of St Botolph, Bishopsgate, in 1638. William Whiteway, up from Dorset, was astonished to see 'a woman delivered of a child' in Morefields in 1634, a rare example of a man witnessing a birth in a public place.[61]

In the suburbs of London, and throughout rural England, there were alehouses, victualling houses, and guest houses well known as places where women in trouble could be 'harboured' while they gave birth. Thomas Heywood's eponymous character, *The Wise Woman of Hogsdon,* boasts about her profit from this traffic:

Those be kitchen maids, and chamber maids, and sometimes good men's daughters, who, having catched a clap, and growing near their time, get leave to see their friends in the country, for a week or so: then hither they come, and for a matter of money here they are delivered. I have a midwife or two belonging to the house, and one Sir Boniface, a deacon, that makes a shift to christen the infants; we have poor, honest, and secret neighbours, that stand for common gossips.[62]

Several of the midwives in the teeming east Middlesex riverside parishes of Stepney and Whitechapel operated what amounted to private nursing homes with few questions asked. Alice Mathews in 1612 and midwives Halloway and Baker in 1640 were reported for activities of this sort. Among their male accomplices, John Sachell of Stepney was reported to the bishop of London's commissary in 1632 as 'a common entertainer of women to lay their great bellies'. The citation of Abraham Barkins of Stepney in 1638—'for having a woman delivered in his house of a child not known to be married; he had thirty pounds for conniving at the business; she came in a coach by night'— suggests that not all bastard-bearers were distressed serving women.[63] One wonders what aristocratic drama lay behind this entry, and who among the London élite made anonymous use of the services of the East End.

The church courts repeatedly cited those involved in harbouring bastard-bearers on suspicion of bawdry, but in the absence of foundling hospitals or other welfare provisions for unwed mothers the authorities could do little to stem the practice. Typically, those charged with harbouring claimed ignorance of the unmarried mother's background or subsequent history. They were surprised, they said, to discover that some of their guests were pregnant, and more surprised to learn that they were unmarried. Such a one, said a plaintiff at Stepney in 1589, 'came to her house for succour and presently did fall in labour'. In 1602 came another, 'saying herself to be weary and glad to rest herself there a space, and presently after her staying there it appeared . . . that she . . . was with child and that her time of delivery was so short that she could not well be removed to any other place without great danger'.[64] For some it was an act of charity, as well as a source of income, to shelter bastard-bearing women. Most plaintiffs were able to satisfy the court that the baby was baptized and the mother churched and reprimanded before she went on her way.

Bastard births, like normal childbirth, took place in a closed environment where the historian has difficulty squinting behind the veil. Testimony in ecclesiastical court cases throws some light on the circumstances, though it must be treated with circumspection. The little we know comes from interrogations designed to learn something else, such as the identity of a bastard's father. Isobel Warner, a midwife of Thame, Oxfordshire, testified in 1589 that 'at the delivery of Joan Felloe she demanded of the said Joan in the time of her labour who was the father of her child, and the said Joan answered her that she would tell her at another time', and later named a journeyman clothmaker 'who was gone for a soldier'. Sybil Bowden of Towersey, Oxfordshire, in 1605 'was brought to bed of a woman child' suspected to belong to her father's servant, 'as the women which were at her travail did affirm'. In support of his denial that he fathered a child on his servant Ann Edwards, Robert Gardener of Wapping, Middlesex, reported in 1606 'that the said Ann at the time of her delivery being in great peril of death did confess unto the midwife and divers other women being then present with her that one Paddon, a sailor, was the father of her child and none else but he'.[65]

Elizabeth Glover, the midwife of Banbury, Oxfordshire, testified in 1630 that during the labour of Elizabeth Barnes, late servant of Lawrence Styward, she (the midwife) did very strictly examine her concerning the father of that her child, putting her to extreme pains, at which time the said Elizabeth did oftentimes affirm, being in great danger of death, with very deep protestations as she hoped for salvation, that John King . . . of Banbury was the father of her child, and that none other had the knowledge or carnal use of her body.

Four other women who were 'present at the labour' supported the midwife's testimony, and Margaret Haynes, a mercer's wife, recalled the midwife 'purposely putting her to the more pains thereby to find out the right father of the child'. Anne Hawbie, another midwife, and three women who assisted her testified to the bishop of Lichfield's chancellor in 1636 that Elizabeth Lomasse of Minster, Derbyshire, 'in the extremity of her childbirth' did absolutely father her child upon one John Backe.[66]

At the very least these citations show that bastard-bearers, like married women, normally enjoyed the service of a midwife and the company of other women. They show too that in cases of illegitimate birth the midwife's service to the mother was complicated by her obligations to the community, the law, and the church. By eliciting the name of the father at this time of crisis the midwife laid the foundation for the baby's social identity and helped to assign financial responsibility for its support.

MOTHER AND CHILD

Delivery of the child meant deliverance for its mother. From the moment the baby emerged the management of childbirth divided into two paths, one to look after the infant, the other to care for the newly delivered woman. Each had different needs, producing a division of labour in the birthroom, though the midwife remained in charge. Both mother and child would receive applications of oils, powders, warm water, and dressings, and both would most likely be the subject of blessings and prayers. Each began a process that would lead to baptism for the one, churching or thanksgiving for the other. 'While the midwife is doing her office about the child, the nurse or some other woman' provides refreshment and ointment to the mother, advised a standard treatise.[1] This chapter examines the experience of mother and child immediately following a birth, paying particular attention to the circle of womanly gossip that enlivened a lying in and the question of whether a newly delivered mother should nurse.

As soon as a baby was born, anxious onlookers, as well as the mother, would examine the infant for wholeness and take immediate note of its sex. A boy generally earned higher regard, though parents would be satisfied with any child that was well made. The midwife would 'take notice of all the parts of it, and see all be right'. She would clear all passages and make sure that the baby was breathing freely. Then it was the midwife's duty to cut the umbilical cord and to tie the navel string, and to extract and bury the placenta or afterbirth.[2]

Cutting the navel string was a delicate matter. As Jane Sharp proudly said, 'a midwife's skill is seen much if she can perform this rightly'. It is not surprising that the midwife's knife, reserved for this purpose, became the standard emblem of her office. The physical separation of mother and child became a ritual process involving a complex range of beliefs and anxieties. Some people held that the future size of an adult male's penis or the tightness of female 'privities' depended on the closeness of the midwife's knitting of the navel string.[3]

The navel held the key to future fertility. By tradition, the women at the birth would inspect the child's navel, especially that of a firstborn, to predict the mother's future childbearing: 'if it have any wrinkles in it, then so many children shall the woman have in time to come'. Medical authors smiled on such superstitious divination, believed to date from the medieval Arabic world of Avicenna if not from ancient Greece, observing, 'these sayings be neither in the gospel of the day nor of the night'. 'Our modern writers jeer at' such beliefs, wrote Nicholas Culpeper in 1651, but that did not eliminate them from the privileged enclosure of the birthroom. An associated belief was that carrying a piece of navel string would protect the wearer from the falling sickness or even defend against witchcraft and devils. Jane Sharp, who repeated this wisdom without subscribing to it, added dryly, 'one may try this if they please'.[4]

For the practical midwife it was more important to dress and protect the child's navel than to consider its prophetic value. An astringent powder of aloes and frankincense might be useful here. A skilled midwife would open the infant's nostrils 'and purge them of filthiness', bathe the child in warm water, then swaddle it in bands of cloth and lay it in the cradle. The child had to be cleansed of the birthing fluids, blood, and water *a materna visceribus*.[5] The Elizabethan doctor John Jones recommended bathing a newborn child in a lukewarm mixture of ten parts water and one part milk to which mallow and salad oil or sweet butter had been added. Juice of rue, herb-race, myrrh, linseed, fenugreek, and barley meal made a useful ointment, advised *The Expert Midwife*. Other handbooks recommended the midwife to 'annoint the child's body with the oil of acorns; for that is singularly good to confirm, steadfast, and to defend the body from noisesome things which may chance from without, as smoke, cold and such other things'.[6] The midwife might delegate some of these tasks to a nurse or assistant while she devoted her primary attention to the mother.

The classic *Expert Midwife* allowed a brief period of bonding between mother and child before proceeding with other tasks.

Many say that the child being washed and wrapped in his swaddling clothes, before he suck the breasts or take any meat, must be laid by his mother, lying in her bed, on the left side near the heart first of all; for they think, as they are persuaded, that the mother doth attract and draw to her all the diseases from the child, and that she doth expel and void again by the flux and issue of her womb what evil soever she hath attracted, without any hurt to herself.[7]

Many modern parents follow this suggestion, even if they no longer accept the humoral principles on which it was based.

Traditional catholicism encouraged the practice of crossing the child after swaddling, sprinkling it with protective salt, and placing a coin in the baby's cradle or hand. The Reformation discredited these practices, but they may have continued unmentioned in attenuated folkloric forms. As late as the nineteenth century in Cambridgeshire some households placed a sixpence on a newborn baby's buttocks to drive the devil away.[8] We should not be surprised that people sought the most comprehensive protection for their newborn children, regardless of the strictures of reformed religion or scientific medicine.

Early modern England continued to swaddle its babies, wrapping them tightly in linen bands before laying them in a cradle. University-trained medical men like the Elizabethan John Jones disapproved of excess swaddling, but the practice persisted beyond the seventeenth century. Handbooks like *The Birth of Mankind* insisted that special care be taken to ensure that the binding was done right, to foster the child's proper physical development. It was the midwife's task at this time to massage the child's body, especially the head, to ensure its proper growth.[9] Protestant religious advisers sometimes borrowed this image for didactic purposes, 'as the midwife frameth the body when it is young and tender, so the parents must frame the mind while it is green and flexible'. The puritan William Gouge did his best to advise what to do for a newborn baby 'while it is in swaddling bands and remaineth a sucking child'. But his experience of such matters was limited, as he readily conceded: 'what the particulars be, women better know than I can express'.[10]

Swaddling received less attention in later childbirth manuals and seems gradually to have gone out of practice. But for Jane Sharp in 1671, as for generations of midwives before her, it must have been one of the most satisfying parts of their practice to handle the child 'very tenderly and wash the body with warm wine, then when it is dry roll it up with soft cloths and lay it into the cradle'. Jane Sharp also advised providing a sheltered sleeping place for the newborn child. 'Let not the beams of the sun or moon dart upon it as it lieth in the cradle especially, but let the cradle stand in a darkish and shadowy place.' This continued the darkness of the womb and the subdued light of the birthroom, but it also invoked the words of Psalm 121, traditionally used at the churching of women after childbirth, 'the sun shall not smite thee by day, nor the moon by night'.[11]

The Woman in the Straw

Like the child in the cradle, the woman recovering from childbirth was supposed to remain in the same dark, snug environment in which she had given birth. Jane Sharp's regime for the newly delivered woman involved a period of quiet rest and recovery. 'Let her for three days keep the room dark, for her eyes are weak and light offends them; let all great noises be forborne, and all unquietness, remembering to be praising God for her safe delivery.' Learned doctors agreed 'that there is nothing worse to childbearing women than the cold air' which risked entering and injuring the womb. Preachers acknowledged, with regard to newly delivered mothers, 'it is a long time after that they recover their former strength'.[12] But the time taken for this recovery varied from a couple of days to several months. Modern childbirth practitioners know that the puerperium, the period between the delivery of the placenta and the recovery of the woman's reproductive organs to their pre-pregnant condition, may last from six to eight weeks.[13] Some women, victims of haemorrhage or puerperal fever, never recovered at all.

In the hours immediately following childbirth the midwife would offer restorative drinks, broths, and caudles to speed the mother's recovery and plasters, dressings, ointments, and salves to quell her bleeding and reduce inflammation. Once again she would draw on local herbal knowledge for concoctions that were specific to the womanly world of the birthroom. The Stuart physician James Primrose remarked on the practice of dosing newly delivered mothers with 'burnt wine . . . brewed with hot spices, cinnamon water and the like, to wit, to strengthen them, for ever the by-standers are solicitous of those strengthening meats and drinks'. Dr Primrose was unusual in thinking this practice 'pernicious' because, in his view, 'those strong and hot drinks are very hurtful, for they inflame the inward parts and amend not the morbous humours at all, but increase and corrupt them'. Here was a medical argument to augment the reformist and misogynist critique of the tippling childbed gossips.[14]

Commonly called 'the woman in the straw' by reference to her bloody straw mattress, the childbed woman experienced uterine contractions or 'afterpains' and coped with lochia, the bloody post-partum vaginal discharge.[15] These afterpurgings could flow for six weeks (though for a shorter time among nursing mothers) and complex cultural conventions addressed the woman's condition at this time. Traditional wisdom, derived from Hippocrates and Leviticus, prescribed a thirty to thirty-three day period of purgation and cleansing after the birth of a boy, and a period of forty-two to sixty-six days after the birth of a girl. But this was not followed in early modern England. As Jane Sharp commented, 'Hippocrates's rules may be calculated chiefly for his own country of Greece, and the Levitical law most concerns the seed of Abraham.' As far as the English were concerned, 'you shall know if a woman be well cleansed by her health, for if she be not she cannot be well and lusty'. James Wolveridge repeated the traditional number of days, but added 'that a woman is passed all danger after twenty days purgation'. Clinging to the gendered humoral system, others anticipated twenty days of cleansing after the birth of a male child, considered to be hot and dry, and twenty-five days after the birth of a female, whose humours were cool and moist.[16]

By general consensus a full month was necessary for a woman to complete recovery from childbearing. But this too varied with medical and domestic circumstances. How the woman should conduct herself during this period, how many friends should visit her, what gossipings might occur, and whether she might resume sexual relations with her husband, were all subject to custom and debate. Similarly, whether she was housebound or could go outdoors, whether she could resume full domestic and economic activities, whether she could attend church and take part in services, and whether or not she was in some way contaminated or unclean, were all points of religious and cultural contest. As will be seen in our discussion of 'churching', Tudor England regarded a newly delivered mother as a 'green' woman, perhaps by reference to her chlorotic pallor. Traditional superstitions constraining her social activity at this time became bound up with post-Reformation debates about purification, thanksgiving, and the churching of women.[17]

Childbed Gossips

From the time of lying in to her eventual return to full domestic duties, the childbed woman was a centre of social attention. The women who attended the birth would stay for 'good cheer' and would return periodically with others for gossiping and good fellowship. Standard advice held that in the first few hours after delivery a woman 'must be kept from sleeping, though she be very desirous thereof, and let her be entertained with some discourse'. During the period of her recovery, common opinion continued, the woman should 'banish all grief and heaviness, having regard only of her health, and to be merry, praising God for her delivery'. Here was a prescription to justify the gossips' chatter.[18] The festivity of gossips was just what the doctor ordered. Husbands and moralists might pray that it was not too loud, too long, or too lacking in decorum. Husbands and other male friends and relations were not necessarily excluded any more, but female gossips, midwives, and nurses dominated the period of lying in. Post-natal gossiping transformed a biological event into a communal affair, bonding women among women and incorporating family and neighbours, baby and kin.

Removed from male supervision and distracted from godly prayer, gossipings could be construed as potential sources of disorder. Moved by this threat, some town governments of the sixteenth century undertook to control the gadding of gossips and to regulate childbed celebrations. The Tudor city of Chester took order against such gossipings, 'for as much as great excess and superfluous costs and charges hath and doth daily grow by reason of costly dishes, meats and drinks brought unto women lying in childbed'. At Leicester in 1568 the councillors voted to regulate 'the superfluous charge and excess' of feasts 'for gossips and midwives'. Kirkby Kendal, Westmorland, limited to twelve the number of women permitted at such gatherings, but allowed 'that wives may present one another with presents during only the time of being in child bed, but not after purifying'.[19] Reforming ministers also sought to constrain these childbed gatherings. On behalf of the newly delivered woman, the Jacobean preacher Robert Hill prayed God to teach 'all that are about her to avoid at this time effeminate speeches, wanton behaviour, and unseasonable mirth, which often doth accompany such meetings as this'.[20]

According to *The Batchelars Banquet,* the wives of the neighbourhood invaded the house of a newly delivered woman with eager appetites and wagging tongues. As soon as the woman was safely brought to bed, 'the gossips, kinswomen, and neighbours come in troops to visit and rejoice for her safe delivery'. One can almost hear the poor husband's groans.

Then every day after her lying down will sundry dames visit her, which are her neighbours, her kinswomen, or other her special acquaintance, whom the goodman must welcome with all cheerfulness, and be sure there be some dainties in store to set before them; where they about some three or four hours (or possibly half a day) will sit chatting with the child-wife, and by that time the cups of wine have merrily trolled about, and half a dozen times moistened their lips with the sweet juice of the purpled grape.[21]

The husband had to get used to this, for the women would gather throughout the period of his wife's lying in, expecting additional refreshments to celebrate the baby's christening and the mother's upsitting and churching.

The Batchelars Banquet, though satire, is not lacking in verisimilitude. Other sources play on a similar theme. Margaret Cavendish observed at the Restoration that a newly married woman would often be visiting 'other married wives, and her time will be spent at labours, christenings, churchings, and other matrimonial gossipings and meetings', consuming sweetmeats, junkets, and other refreshments laid out for the gossips and guests. A later seventeenth-century writer quipped that 'for gossips to meet . . . at a lying in, and not to talk, you may as well dam up the arches of London Bridge as stop their mouths at such a time. 'Tis a time when women, like parliament men, have a privilege to talk petty treason against their husbands.'[22] The tattling boozers in Henry Parrot's satire *The Gossips Greeting* were visiting a woman in childbed, as were the gossips in Michael Drayton's savage poem 'The Moone-Calfe'.[23]

Two or three weeks after the birth, if all went well, the woman would be bathed and changed, and removed from her soiled bedding 'in the straw'. Professional medical advice again matched common practice.

And when three weeks of her time are expired, she having been neither troubled with ague, pains or gripings, nor any other accident extraordinary, and being likewise cleansed from all her afterpurgings, before she go abroad it will be very good for her to bathe, cleanse, and wash herself, being first purged with some easy medicine according to the physician's direction.[24]

This marked her 'upsitting', when her family might arrange a further feast to mark the progress of her recovery, and when neighbours might come bearing gifts. Other writers referred to 'footing time . . . when the childbed woman gets up'. In the late Elizabethan citizen's world of *The Batchelars Banquet* the husband provides a second 'gossips supper . . . because it is your upsitting, and a fortnight at the least since you were brought to bed'. His wife acknowledges 'the month indeed is half expired, and I fear the rest will come before we be ready for it'. Contemporaries understood that 'the month' was the notional accepted time for the woman's post-natal privileges.[25]

Ecclesiastical court records permit glimpses of childbirth festivities at different points in the social scale, usually when somebody committed an offence. Testimony in a defamation case in the Elizabethan diocese of Canterbury told how 'the goodwife Egglestone and goodwife Cotterell went to one Browning's wife of Burmarsh (she there lying in childbed) a-gossiping, and to make merry . . . and one Hawke's wife followed and came thither a-gossiping also'.[26] When George Wilcocks of Stepney was charged in 1620 with disorderly drinking during service time on the sabbath, he explained that 'his wife lying in childbed, some of his friends and acquaintances came to visit her', and a party ensued. Thomas Salmon, a servant of Great Tew, Oxfordshire, was so keen to sample the 'good cheer at the house of Eleanor Rymel who was then lately brought a-bed' in 1633 that he disguised himself in women's clothing to join in the gossiping and drinking. Salmon's case is a rare and fascinating example of early modern cross-dressing, but it also illuminates the closed world of ceremony and celebration in the birthroom.[27]

Diaries and correspondence reveal further traces of the rituals of lying in, presenting, gossiping, and upsitting. Nicholas Assheton, the squire of Downham, Lancashire, went 'a presenting my cousin Assheton's wife that lay in' in July 1617. The following spring it was Mrs Assheton's turn to enjoy this customary post-natal visiting and gift-giving. On Sunday, 8 March 1618, three weeks after she had lost her baby in childbed, the diarist recorded, 'Downham wives and Worston wives presented my wife'. 'Presenting' of this sort raised £7 in cash for the Reverend Henry Newcome's family in 1656 when, he reports, 'my wife then lay-in on Peter, and several of the women would needs send tokens to her'.[28]

Making slow recovery from childbearing, Lady Mary Verney had to delay her upsitting, in 1647. Baby Ralph was born on 3 June, but three weeks later on 24 June Mary Verney wrote, 'since I was brought to bed I have never been able to sit up an hour at a time'. The outstanding memory of 5 November 1709 for the Somerset physician Claver Morris was, 'my wife went out of the parlour chamber and walked a little while in the hall chamber, being the 17th day after her delivery'. A royal upsitting, like a royal quickening, was cause for celebration. John Evelyn observed the fireworks in July 1688 'which were prepared for the queen's upsitting' after Mary of Modena had given birth to the Prince of Wales.[29]

The Blessings of the Breast

Maternal breast-feeding reconnected mother and child, but the common practice of wet-nursing kept mother and baby apart. Elizabethan and Stuart England saw a continuing debate about the virtues of mothers' milk and the advantages and disadvantages of wet-nursing. Much of this debate was designed to persuade fashionable women of the middling and upper classes to overcome cultural inhibitions and to behave as God and nature intended. Puritan ministers were especially insistent that nursing was a godly responsibility.[30]

Humoral theory on the circulation and conservation of fluids associated milk with blood, and lactation with menstruation. The one substance supposedly turned into the other. The Norwich physician John Sadler was one of many who followed Aristotle, he thought, when he wrote in 1636 that woman's milk 'is nothing but the menstruous blood made white in the breasts'. Experience showed that 'so long as the woman giveth suck to the child, and hath store of milk in her breasts, her terms be of little or no quantity . . . forasmuch as the ebbing of the one is the flowing of the other'.[31] The preacher Robert Cleaver similarly taught that 'God converteth the mother's blood into the milk wherewith the child is nursed in her womb. He bringeth it into the breasts furnished with nipples'.[32] Medical and gynaecological manuals were generous with advice about how to stimulate the flow of milk or how to dry it up, and most of the herbals offered similar information.[33]

Standard gynaecological handbooks urged that 'it shall be best that the mother give her child suck herself, for the mother's milk is more convenient and agreeable to the infant than any other woman's'. Maternal feeding allegedly passed the mother's own good qualities to her child. However, *The Birth of Man-Kinde* continued, 'it shall be best that the child suck not of the mother's breast by and by as soon as it is born, but rather of some other woman's for a day or two, for because that the cream, as they call it, straight after the birth, the first day in all women doth thicken and congeal'. Colostrum, in other words, was indigestible and possibly harmful.[34] Some doctors would lengthen this period of precautionary wet-nursing to a week or a month, 'by reason (the mother) hath been troubled and tired in her lying in, and because she is not as yet well cleansed and purified of her after-purgings'. General opinion was that 'a year is long enough to give suck to a child, it being ordained by nature no longer than the child is weak, and cannot digest anything else', though evidence from autobiographies suggests that breast-feeding lasted longer.[35]

Moral and medical advice concurred that 'mothers should nurse their children' themselves. Poorer women had no alternative, but the privileged and prosperous sort commonly resorted to wet-nurses. Elizabeth Clinton recited the most common objections to breast-feeding among the gentry: 'that it is troublesome, that it is noisesome to one's clothes, that it makes one look old, etc. All such reasons are uncomely and unchristian to be objected, and therefore unworthy to be answered.'[36] Other justifications for preferring a wet-nurse were that the mother was following fashion, obeying her husband, attending to her comfort, securing her health, or taking best care for the well-being of her children. The irony was that the women who nursed suppressed their fertility, while those who used wet-nurses were susceptible to more frequent pregnancies. People observed, but did not understand, the contraceptive aspects of lactation.[37]

In the opinion of Elizabeth Clinton, the remarkable Countess of Lincoln who published a tract on the subject in 1622, breast-feeding was a Christian duty 'which all mothers are bound to perform'. It was, she argued, 'the express ordinance of God that mothers should nurse their own children'. Biblical examples and Christian precepts supported her position. 'God provideth milk in our breasts', she wrote, so that it was unnatural and ungrateful for women to go against his providence. The spiritual construction of childbirth extended to infant feeding, so that 'keeping God's ordinance, they are sure of God's blessing'. Unfortunately, Lady Clinton observed, 'now women, especially of any place and grace, do not hold this duty acceptable to God, because it is unacceptable to themselves . . . This is one hurt which the better rank do by their ill example egg and embolden the lower ones to follow them to their loss.' She herself felt remorse for failing to follow these precepts, and wished her daughter to do better by suckling her babies herself.[38]

Puritan authors made it a Christian duty for mothers to nurse their own children. Why else had God provided women with breasts? Nursing earned the good woman commendation, thought Robert Cleaver, while not to nurse was 'nice and unnatural'. Refusal to nurse made women 'but half mothers' who 'break the holy bond of nature in locking up their breasts from their children, and delivering them forth like the cuckoo to be hatched in the sparrow's nest'. William Gouge added an argument of practical charity, derived from his observations in Jacobean London, that 'mothers ought to nurse their own children', if only to lessen the great number of 'nurse-children' that die while being put out to wet-nurses. The godly mother, wrote Daniel Rogers, 'seeks not breasts in her husband's purse, but in her own bosom'. She owed it to God, to nature, and to her child to nurse the infant herself.[39] Despite this stream of advice, women of fashion were most reluctant to nurse their babies themselves. Alice Thornton, a Yorkshire gentlewoman, may have been unusual for women of her class in attempting to suckle her children, writing in 1654 that she was 'overjoyed to give my sweet Betty suck'. The midwife Jane Sharp observed, 'the usual way for rich people is to put forth their children to nurse, but that is a remedy that needs a remedy . . . because it changeth the natural disposition of the child, and oftentimes exposeth the infant to many hazards'.[40]

Writing towards the end of the seventeenth century the minister Henry Newcome railed against 'the luxury of our age' and 'the triumphs of brutish custom over reason and religion' displayed in the common practice of wet-nursing.

Children of our nobility and gentry . . . in their infancy generally are more unhappy than the sons of country peasants. The poor tenant's child is for the most part nursed in its own mother's bosom, and cherished by her breasts, whilst the landlord's heir is turned out, exiled from his mother's embraces as soon as from her womb, and assigned to the care of some stranger.

Newcome's pamphlet, *The Compleat Mother*, listed the 'mischiefs' and 'inconveniences' of wet-nursing, ranging from the loss of affection between mother and child, and the risk of disease and death, to the prospect of child-theft or substitution. His ultimate appeal was to husbands, who purportedly ruled their wives, and his strongest case was that wet-nursing threatened the continuity of lineage and inheritance.[41]

Notwithstanding their preference for maternal feeding, the writers of medical works and books of domestic conduct recognized that many mothers

would engage a long-term wet-nurse for their children. A newly delivered
mother might be seriously ill, or her milk might be insufficient. She might be
averse to breast-feeding, or culturally conditioned not to perform it. Choosing a substitute was no light matter, for all sorts of moral qualities as well as
physical nourishment were believed to pass from breast to lip. *The Birth of
Man-Kinde* advised that a wet-nurse

be of good colour and complexion, and that her bulk and breast be of good large-
ness . . . that it be not too long after her labour, so that it be two months after her
labour at the least, and that, if it may be, such one which hath a man child . . . that she
be good and honest of conversation, neither over hasty or ireful, nor too sad and tim-
orous: for these affections and qualities be pernicious and hurtful to the milk, corrupt-
ing it, and pass through the milk into the child, making the child of like condition.[42]

Jane Sharp agreed that the finest milk came from a nurse 'of a sanguine complexion . . . not a woman that is crooked, or squint-eyed, nor with a misshapen nose or body, or with black ill-favoured teeth or with stinking breath,
or with any notable depravation', for such deformities risked affecting the
child. And if possible, 'a female child must suck the breasts of a nurse that had
a girl the last child she had, and a boy must suck her that lately had a boy'.
This last belief was false, according to Dr James Primrose, but it thrived 'not
only of the people, but some physicians also'.[43]

Whoever was feeding the child—wet-nurse or natural mother—was advised
'to abstain from venery or man's company; for if she use that, it shall spend
and consume the milk, and make it unsavoury and unwholesome'. A popular
seventeenth-century publication explained that 'copulation of the nurse exceed-
ingly offendeth and hurteth the child, as that which chiefly retracteth and
diminisheth the milk . . . for which cause, in times past, husbands were driven
away from their wives and restrained from the company'.[44] In times of distraction, it implied, such courtesies had gone by the board. Once again, diaries
and personal histories bring precepts to life and give gynaecological nostrums
a social context. Given the social bias of these sources it is not surprising that
they have more to say about wet-nursing than maternal feeding.

The Cheshire landowner Sir Edward Fytton was delighted to learn that his
daughter Anne Newdigate had given birth in May 1598, but was less pleased
with the news that she intended to suckle the infant herself. 'God bless your
little one,' he wrote, 'and grant thee as much comfort I beseech him as ever
mother had of a child, but I am sorry that yourself will needs nurse her.'
Lady Fytton was less alarmed, and sent 'a nurse's reward' to her daughter.
But the courtier Sir William Knollys, standing as godfather by proxy, tried to
counsel the young mother from her folly 'that you play the nurse. I confess

it argueth great love, but it breedeth much trouble to yourself and it would more grieve you if sucking your own milk it should miscarry, children being subject to many casualties.'[45] Disregarding this conventional advice, Anne Newdigate embarked on a career of celebrated motherhood, described by a kinsman as 'green and flourishing'. Court physicians at this time were choosing a wet-nurse for James's Queen Anne 'by tasting of their milk, etc.' and after the birth of her fourth child in 1604 Anne Newdigate was considered a candidate for the position of royal nurse.[46]

After Sir John Oglander's son was born in 1609, he recalled, 'we put him to nurse to George Oglander's wife, my tenant then living at Upton, and gave a great rate for the nursing of him. When he was fit to be weaned we took him home and bred him carefully under our own wings.' As a landed gentleman as well as a loving father it was a matter of honour to do the best for one's heir. The Evelyn family similarly put young John Evelyn out to nurse after his birth in 1620. Reflecting back on this Evelyn noted that he was put to a wet-nurse for a year and a quarter, 'in regard of my mother's weakness, or rather custom of persons of quality'.[47]

The puritan Woodfords of Northampton wanted their children to suckle from their natural mother but were forced to fall back on wet-nurses. Indeed, one of the themes of Robert Woodford's diary from 1637 to 1640 is the drama of milk and prayer. Woodford's wife had trouble with her breasts after the birth of her son on 8 August 1637 and was unable to nurse him properly. The child suffered and was undernourished. Woodford's prayers were answered on 31 August when the child 'awakened and hath sucked Mrs. Rushport this morning, blessed be God'. Mrs Woodford persevered but with little success. The diarist wrote on 11 September, 'my wife's breasts are not well, and the child is hardly brought to suck. Good lord, I pray thee give us the blessing of the breast as thou hast of the womb.' This was also the day, a month after the birth, when 'nurse Woodnot went away'. Mrs Woodford struggled on, her right breast especially pained, until 25 October when Woodford wrote, 'little John not well, nor my wife, and so we are advised to have one to suckle the child, so after much debate we are resolved on it, and the lord in his providence hath sent us one goodwife Emerson that pleased us very well, and the child hath sucked daintily, blessed be the name of the lord'. The wet-nurse Emerson evidently took care of young John until the following March when, Woodford recorded, 'nurse Emerson who suckled John hath an ague, so we are forced to wean him; Oh lord preserve him and bless him and my whole family for the lord's sake'.[48]

Mrs Woodford tried again to nurse her daughter Sarah, born 29 August 1638, but by 18 October the diarist observed, 'my wife's milk gone, which

grief lord help us'. Sarah became 'very ill' but recovered after 22 October
when 'we have got a nurse today . . . for our child'. Half a year later on 13
May 1639 Woodford noted, 'I paid the nurse 40s. and gave her 2s. 6d. Sarah
went away today, oh lord let thy blessing rest upon her.' The wet-nursing
went well, despite the separation. On 4 July Woodford wrote, 'I went to see
my sweet child Sarah at nurse near Edmonton in Enfield Chase and left her
very well, I bless the lord.' The Woodfords followed a similar course with
their third child, a daughter, born on 16 August 1639. Two weeks later on 30
August, the diarist wrote, 'this day my poor child is gone to nurse to goodwife
Iblethy; oh lord, you who denied the blessing of the breast to us, blessed be
thy name, thou providest the breasts of others for us'.[49]

Jane Josselin was more fortunate, her husband writing in 1642 after the
arrival of their firstborn, 'God blessed my wife to be a nurse.' Isaac Archer's
wife suckled her first few children, but had difficulties with the baby boy born
in 1675 and so engaged a nurse. Unfortunately, the nurse was neglectful and
the child 'died while she slept, and unbaptised'. Alice Thornton employed
wet-nurses for most of her children, but after one such nurse fell asleep with
the child at her breast and almost crushed it, she attempted to suckle them
herself. She was delighted in 1660 when 'my pretty babe was in good health,
sucking his poor mother to whom my good God had given the blessing of
the breast as well as the womb'. Sadly, the child died two weeks later.[50]

Lady Anne Clifford, unusual for an aristocrat, recorded her approval of
family breast-feeding after the birth of her great-grandson in 1654.

My daughter of Thanet was there at the birth and christening of this first grandchild
of hers. So as he sucked the milk of her breast many times, she having with her her
now youngest child, the Lady Anne Tufton, being about nine weeks old. But my
grandchild, the Lady Margaret Coventry, after my daughter of Thanet's departure
from Croome, gave this child of hers suck herself, as her mother had done most of
her children.[51]

The Wet-Nurse and the Martyr

Since so much of our evidence about child-rearing practices is anecdotal I
make no apology for concluding this section with another story. In *The Life
and Death of Mr. E. Geninges,* a hagiographical biography of a catholic martyr
published in 1614, we read prophetic wonders concerning the circumstances
of his first feeding as a baby.

For scarce had nature cleansed his silly corpse from such uncleanness as it brought
a maternis visceribus, from his mother's bowels, but presently within an hour or two

Nuntia Christicolis venturæ cladis, inermes
Æthere ab armatis nocte perire videt. *M. 6. 3.*

FIG. 9 'The wetnurse and the martyr' from John Geninges, *The Life and Death of Mr. E. Genings* (St Omers, 1614)

appeared a sign . . . The midwife and other women having accomplished everything belonging to their office in the birth of the infant, the nurse sat her down by the fire to give the child his first food; and directing her dug into his mouth, he presently bit the same. At which unexpected pain, the simple woman sent forth loud shrieks and cries, which she no sooner had done but the child bit her again. Which unwonted accident so bereft the nurse of all patience, that she was ready to have done the child some mischief had not the women then accompanying his mother run to succour him; who inquiring the cause, they perceived the lamb to have played the lion, and searching his mouth they found him to have a very fair white tooth in the forepart thereof. Which strange spectacle worthily put them all in admiration.[52]

This story hardly seems to have the supernatural muscle to presage a saint, but it does take us briefly into that most secret of chambers, the birthroom. The compiler of *The Life and Martyrdom* thought the incident remarkable enough to deserve illustration, and the accompanying picture (Fig. 9) includes details that are often mentioned but rarely depicted. We see a darkened room with a bed draped with hangings, on the bedside table a cup for the caudle, the midwife's knife for cutting the navel string, and what appears to be a saintly girdle for the woman in labour to pray by. The child's mother, or possibly his nurse, sits with the swaddled baby, preternaturally alert, next to a canopied cradle on rockers. Warming the room is a blazing and smoking fire, and by the fireside sits a cat.

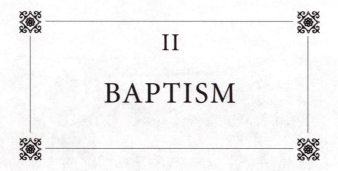

II

BAPTISM

FIG. 10 The baptismal party around the font. Detail from a copper engraving 'taken out of St Mary Oueris Church in the Lectureship of the late deceased Doctor Sutton 1624' entitled, '*The Christians jewell [fit] to adorn the hearte and decke the house of every Protestant.*'

BAPTISM AS SACRAMENT AND DRAMA

Being born into the world was but a prelude to the social and spiritual ritual of baptism. The struggle of mother and child in the relative privacy of the birthroom soon gave way to the more public ceremony of incorporation into the community and the church. This section examines agreements and disagreements about the sacrament of baptism in England in the century following the Reformation. Like other parts of this study of the rituals in the life cycle, it attempts to relate the theological, ecclesiastical, liturgical, and political arguments of high culture to the varied experiences, disturbances, and contentions of families and individuals in the parishes. It deals with the interactions of élite and popular culture, compares prescription and performance, and explores some of the social and cultural aspects of religion. Discussion extends from theology and worship to ritual and discipline, encompassing the material substances of the sacrament, the physical setting of the ceremony, and the changing nexus of familial and ecclesiastical expectations. I hope to show how baptism operated as a domestic and community ritual as well as a sacrament of the church, and how religious emphases and social ritual altered among successive generations.

It would not be a difficult exercise to borrow the concepts of social anthropology and to categorize English protestant baptism as a classic rite of passage.[1] Following the pioneering theorist van Gennep, we may see that the central participant (the child) was brought from one space (home) to another (church), and through the performance of ritual actions and the application of sanctified substances was transformed from one state (original sinner) to another (recipient of grace.) The ceremony involved rites of separation (forsaking the devil) and rites of aggregation (membership in Christ), and ended a period of liminality (the ambiguous state of the unbaptized baby). The ritual took place at a reserved location using dedicated equipment (the font), involved special helpers (the minister and godparents), and often concluded with celebratory refreshments (the christening supper). Ritually transformed and released from liminality, the child became a participant in the religious life of the community, with a new Christian identity and a name.

There is little more to be gained, however, from an anthropological analysis that delineates standard characteristics rather than particular historical features. An exercise of this sort risks ending discussion by classifying human behaviour and then closing the box. Much more can be learnt by trying to be receptive to difference, by listening to individual stories, and by examining particular circumstances as they developed over time. Baptism is worth studying not only for its exhibition of ritual activity but also for what it shows about social and cultural tensions, frictions, and proceedings. It will be treated here as part of a continuing conversation, sometimes strained and occasionally acrimonious, that ranged over important areas of sixteenth- and seventeenth-century life. It was a conversation that embraced the associated topics of childbirth and churching, marriage and death, the ligaments of the life cycle and the intersection of the natural and supernatural worlds. Baptism concerned adults and children, men and women, pastors and parishioners, and laymen and theologians. Notwithstanding the conformity and continuity implied by the Thirty-Nine Articles and the Book of Common Prayer, the social rituals of Christian initiation in England varied with wealth and status as well as religious inclination, and altered over the course of time. Changes in public policy and alterations in taste and style imposed strains on accustomed practice, while arguments about religious discipline exacerbated underlying social and cultural stresses.

Questions of Contention

Baptism laid the foundation for Christian life. It was held to be a sacrament of fundamental importance, securing immeasurable spiritual benefits to all concerned. Both the individual recipient and the community at large were supposed to profit through participation in its mystery. It operated, like most rites of passage, in both public and private dimensions. The ceremony signified the covenant between Christ and his people, and entered the newborn child into the congregation of the Christian faithful. As a solemn ceremony of the church, baptism opened the doors to the kingdom of heaven and bestowed the badge of membership in the universal body of Christ. The retention of baptism as one of just two post-Reformation sacraments in the protestant Church of England (the other being holy communion) is testimony to its central position.

Yet the church harboured many streams of opinion, and spoke with varied voices. A common sacrament could carry multiple messages. Without diverging too far from approved theological positions, English churchmen expressed a broad range of thought, with different shades of emphasis, on what baptism meant, what it signified, how to perform it, and what the ceremony achieved.

Within the framework of official uniformity there were myriad local challenges and negotiations over liturgy, conduct, and discipline. In parish life, where official formulations of religion met the vagaries of local practice, the sacrament of baptism was a frequently performed and contentious service. Crosses in baptism and fights over fonts reveal the unresolved legacy of the Reformation and illuminate the processes of negotiation and accommodation required to prevent strains from developing into fractures. The English church was usually adept at the containment of controversy, but repeatedly, at critical moments, disagreements erupted into view. The Restoration churchman Thomas Comber characterized baptism as 'that universal, plain and easy rite . . . exceeding proper, and very innocent',[2] but this was an attempt to defuse a century of controversy.

Like their medieval catholic predecessors, Tudor and Stuart theologians grappled with the mystery of baptism and explored its twin elements of transformation and initiation. Clergy and laity expressed varied views on what the sacrament meant and how the ritual should be conducted. Puritans in particular kept up a stream of criticism, more often directed to the liturgical practice of baptism than to its theological underpinnings. The matter was not confined to Convocation or the universities but concerned all parishioners, men and women. Baptism was a fundamental ritual in the life cycle that touched every family and was expected of every child. Almost everybody in Tudor and Stuart England had been baptized.

Even when there was agreement about what baptism meant, there was recurrent controversy about its conduct. Arguments flared about when and where the ceremony should be conducted, and about how it should be performed. Was the prayer-book form of baptism sufficiently reformed or fatally contaminated? Was the service of the Church of England congruent with the practice of primitive Christians, as apologists insisted, or was it still polluted with the dregs and residue of Rome? Should the sacrament be confined to infants, or did scripture provide an ordinance for adult baptism, as the anabaptists believed? How much time should elapse between the birth of a child and its coming to be christened? Was every infant eligible for baptism, or only the children of the faithful? What befell the soul of a child who died before being baptized, and how should the community then dispose of its body? How should cases of medical necessity be treated, compared to matters of routine? Should the clergy alone be permitted to baptize, or was there room for lay baptism or baptism by women, particularly midwives? Should the ceremony take place in private or in public, at home or in church? And if held in church, in what part of the building, before what assembly?

Questions of theology and liturgy led to questions about procedure and practice. Should the minister use a font or a basin, and how should he apply the water? Should he sprinkle or dip the infant, and if dipping, how many times and how deep? Should any other substance besides water be permitted in the service, such as the chrism, oil, salt, spittle, or cream associated with traditional catholicism? Should the minister always make the sign of the cross over the infant, as the prayer book insisted, and if so where, how often, and in what manner? What words should be spoken, what gestures performed? Who was to be present at the service, the entire congregation or just those connected to the child? What was the father's role in the ceremony, and should the mother be present if she had not yet performed her churching or thanksgiving? Who would hold the baby, and who would give it a name? What kind of name was suitable? Should there be sponsors, witnesses, or godparents, and why did it matter what such helpers were called? How many godparents were permitted, of what sex, and with what roles or duties? Was it reasonable for godparents to make promises on behalf of an uncomprehending infant, or to undertake for his or her renunciation of the devil? Should the minister or his assistant expect a fee for their service? How much merry-making was permitted after the service, how much mingling of the secular and the sacred? And what should be done about offenders?

Every one of these questions provoked a babble of answers and argument. Like other life-cycle rites of passage, the ceremony of baptism was fraught with ambiguity and subject to contention. By comparison, the rituals of child-birth seem relatively straightforward. In the mid-Elizabethan period it was the sign of the cross, in the mid-seventeenth-century infant baptism, and in the later Stuart period baptism at home that stimulated the greatest controversy. Throughout the period one heard a low-grade murmur, sometimes rising to an impassioned frenzy, about the efficacy and authority of the sacrament, the elements and substances to be employed, and the gestures and equipment required for the proper performance of baptism. Most baptisms passed smoothly, without comment, but every time the sacrament was conducted it risked stirring this cauldron of issues and questions.

Timing, Refusal, and Neglect

By the time of the Reformation the early Christian practice of grouping baptisms at Easter and Whitsun had long since yielded to baptisms throughout the year. There was no religious calendar constraining baptism, as there was for marriage, although there was none the less a distinct seasonality, tied to the seasonality of births, with peaks in early spring and early autumn.[3] There was no set day for baptism, no particular age when it had to be performed, although it was supposed to be done at a time when the congregation was gathered for worship. Like so much else in the Church of England, the timing of baptism was a matter of custom and convenience, a matter of local discretion. Richard Hooker acknowledged, 'We have for baptism no day set as the Jews had for circumcision; neither have we by the law of God but only by the church's discretion a place thereunto appointed.'[4]

The Elizabethan prayer book instructed pastors and curates to 'admonish the people that they defer not the baptism of infants any longer than the Sunday or other holy day next after the child be born, unless upon a great and reasonable cause declared to the curate and by him approved'.[5] This was a reasonable provision in the light of high infant mortality rates and concern for the baby's spiritual and physical health. In normal circumstances the child would be just a few days old on that first Sunday at the font, but thousands of baptisms took place on other days of the week, and many after the first week of life. Higher status families often delayed their infants' baptisms in order to complete necessary social arrangements, and delays between birth and baptism generally stretched longer towards the end of the seventeenth century. Elizabethan babies were usually baptized two or three days after their birth, but in later Stuart times the median interval was eight days, growing even longer in the following century.[6]

The cultural pressure to baptize newborn babies was overwhelming. Very few families refused baptism for their children on the basis of explicit religious principles, and any who objected before the 1640s were likely to face stiff penalties. Mainstream protestants, from high ceremonialists to strict presbyterians, were adamant that there should be no avoidance of infant baptism, no rebaptizing of adults, no anabaptism. This was a fundamental tenet of the Church of England.[7] Actual anabaptists were thin on the ground in early modern England, although diocesan officials were continuously watching for them. The word 'anabaptist' was sometimes used as a slur on all kinds of radicals or puritans without discriminating the niceties of religious division.

None the less, the Elizabethan church saw several dramatic tussles over the enforced ministration of baptism. These rare episodes reflect the failure of compromise and the exercise of discipline when determined conscience met unyielding demands for uniformity. Involving puritan radicals and episcopal officials, they pitted laity against clergy, family against community, and parents against ministers, and invoked the coercive authority of the state. Objections to particular features of the ceremony could grow into refusal to have any part of it at all.

After Elizabeth and William Whiting of Cirencester, Gloucestershire, refused to have their child baptized in 1574, an ecclesiastical commission ordered the minister, churchwardens, constables, and five leading citizens to go to their house 'and there to take the said child' to public baptism. Elizabeth reported that 'she was not present' at this enforced baptism, which was done 'contrary to her husband's will', and therefore she could not say how it was conducted. William Whiting protested that he would follow the Queen's majesty's laws and her highness's proceeding, 'so far forth as the same did agree to God's word and not otherwise'. His radical objection to the Church of England's baptism led to ever more dangerous statements. Offered the chance of reconciliation, if only he would take communion, Whiting dug in deeper 'and said there was more tyranny now in these days used than ever was; and unreverently crying out with a loud voice, said that God would take vengeance upon the magistrates, rulers, and governors of this realm, and would root out both prince and people for the maintenance of idolatry, superstition, and all other abomination and wickedness'. Beginning with a dispute about fonts and godparents, Whiting's anger had risen to challenge royal and ecclesiastical authority. His foolhardy ranting over baptism drove him headlong into sedition, and, not surprisingly, he was committed to the common gaol at Gloucester. He was still there a year later while the authorities decided what to do with him. Elizabeth Whiting, after two weeks custody in the castle, returned home to look after her forcibly baptized child.[8]

Another case from the 1570s indicates the passion that could arise over issues of religious conformity. William Drewett and his wife of Gloucester were cited in February 1576 for refusing to have their newborn baby baptized. The ecclesiastical commission threatened to take the child by force and have it baptized against the parents' wishes, as they had done so recently with the baby Whiting. William Drewett answered that 'if their child were taken from them by violence and christened, that they would never receive it again nor take it for their child any more'. If the church insisted on baptizing the child against their will, the hard-line Drewetts would disown it.[9]

A dramatic scene unfolded at Gloucester on 24 March 1576 when William Drewett appeared before the commissioners, 'holding his child in his arms, and his wife with him'. He still refused to allow the child to be baptized, and refused the court's instruction to hand it over to the midwife.

Whereupon they commanded the midwife to take the child off him, and she laid her hands on it to have received it; but Drewett would not suffer her to have it out of his arms, saying that he will not deliver it to be polluted. Whereupon the commissioners forewarned him that they intend to commit him to one prison, and his wife to another, wishing and commanding him to deliver his child to his wife to remain with her, that she may give it suck in prison. And he said he would carry it with him to prison and would not deliver it to his wife.

Three times more the court commanded him to yield the child to the midwife, to the minister, or to his wife, and each time Drewett refused. Who knew best where lay the interest of the child? The patriarchal authority of the husband clashed with the patriarchal authority of the state, while the wife and the midwife struggled with contradictory instructions. For his obstinacy Drewett was sent briefly to prison, then released to await questioning before the Privy Council. Further details of his case are missing, but its outcome is indicated by a list of recusant prisoners in Newgate in 1581, one of whom was William Druet 'of the precise sort', almost certainly the same man.[10]

The Whitings and Drewetts were radical lay puritans within the diocese of Gloucester who thrived under the lax regime of bishop Richard Cheyney. It took the might of a royal commission to bring them to light. Stories like theirs were rarely heard from the 1580s to the 1620s, when extremists were less vocal and the authorities more accommodating. Puritans were more likely to object to particular elements of the ceremony rather than to reject the sacrament altogether. A radical sectarian at Sturston, Suffolk, was heard to say in 1627 'that it is not fit for children to be baptised until they be able to come to answer for themselves', but the minister of Swavesey, Cambridgeshire, reported in 1638, 'our anabaptists are dead long since and gone' and all was well.[11]

Simple neglect was far more common than outright objection. Fathers occasionally faced charges for delaying the baptism of their child beyond 'eight days' or longer than 'the sabbath next' after its birth. Citations of this sort are scattered through the ecclesiastical court records.[12] The father, not the mother, normally faced censure in such cases because patriarchal duty assigned him the responsibility of arranging his child's baptism. John Petchie of Frierning, Essex, delayed the baptism of his child for three weeks in 1587. John Minors of Barking, Essex, kept his child unbaptized 'a whole month' in 1597. William Osborne of Launsing, Sussex, was cited in 1623 'for delaying the christening of his child two several Sundays'. John Rawling's child was 'born about seven weeks since and not yet christened', reported the churchwardens of Eyton, Hereford, in 1637. Thomas Alexander of Elwall, Staffordshire, had a child aged six months and still not baptized in 1639, and was reported to the bishop of Lichfield.[13] These delays were more often the result of accident and circumstance than scrupulous religious objections. That, at least, is how offenders commonly answered their citation. It is hard to tell when plausible excuses were covers for principled opposition.

Baptism required material as well as spiritual preparation and often entailed some cost in the form of fees, gifts, and refreshments. Not every family was ready on time. A Norfolk couple resettled in London explained in 1596 that their seven-week-old child remained unbaptized because 'their friends that should be witnesses at the christening were not come to town'. When cited in 1597 for keeping his child unbaptized a month, Edmund Bates of Ingham, Norfolk, explained, 'that he had requested one Richard Bailey, his brother-in-law dwelling in Norwich, to be godfather to his child, who happening to fall sick, he kept his child for him, and not otherwise'. Charged with similar offences in the same visitation, Thomas Bishop of Wreningham, Norfolk, said 'that it was for gossips, and not for any reasons of religion'. Robert Clerke of Huntingfield, Suffolk, similarly blamed 'the deferring of the baptism' of his son on unavoidable delays by the godfathers.[14] A similar circumstance befell the family of William Draper at the high end of the social spectrum and at the very end of our period. Mrs Draper (John Evelyn's daughter) was 'well layed' of a son on 13 September 1694, but the baptism was deferred until 11 October because of the 'indisposition' of one of the godfathers, Sir Thomas Draper, 'which hindered him from coming abroad', and also because the mother 'had not been recovered of her so late dangerous sickness'. No ecclesiastical court at this time was likely to reprimand the parents for deferring the baptism, but the diarist John Evelyn recorded that the delay was 'much against my desire'.[15]

Bastard children and babies born to vagrants were particularly at risk of escaping baptism. Most bastard babies were baptized, and their christenings recorded in the parish register.[16] Indeed, episcopal authorities threatened punishment to any minister who let such unfortunates fall through the net. But too often the woman withdrew to her lodgings or took to the road again, without tarrying for the sacrament; and sometimes the sacrament was withheld until she had shown proper penitence, or until the parish was indemnified for the child's upkeep.

The Reverend Anthony Anderson of Stepney, Middlesex, for example, would not christen a harlot's child in 1589 'because none would be bound for to save the parish harmless for the child'. Margaret Shield of Danby, Yorkshire, was presented in 1575 'for bearing two children [out of wedlock] and both of them died unbaptised, although the one lived four days and the other ten'. That she had risked her babies' entry into heaven was a far more serious offence than not providing them with a father. Isabel Romsey of Tanfield, Durham, was presented in 1579 for having 'a child in fornication, being four or five years old and not yet christened'.[17] At Leintwardine, Hereford, in 1617 the churchwardens cited Anne Davies who was 'unlawfully begotten with child . . . and the child is not yet baptised being two or three months old'. The churchwardens of Milverton, Somerset, reported in 1624 'a child born in the house of Elizabeth Alderman, widow, which was never brought to be baptised; who were the parents and what is become of the child it is un-known'. The churchwardens of Barnston, Essex, acknowledged in 1664 that 'we have one infant, the child of Joan Little, a base born child that remains unbaptised for want of godfathers; she will not confess the father of it'.[18] It is not clear whether the mother was at fault here, or whether the minister was withholding baptism until she confessed.

Occasionally a minister was presented for refusing to administer the sacra-ment, or even worse, for allowing a child in his parish to die without bap-tism. Behind these presentments lay conflicting views about the necessity of baptism for salvation, anxiety about the souls of unbaptized children, and anger that the clergy were not doing their job. The clergy themselves were divided and the laity often confused over the urgency, efficacy, and absolute importance of the sacrament. What for some was a matter of custom and convenience was for others a vital prerequisite to salvation. Ministerial rigid-ity upset neighbourly and charitable expectations. Parental desires to secure prompt baptism could be frustrated by ministers who valued pastoral flexibility less than sacerdotal precision. The fragmentary record of cases shows a dif-ferent sense of urgency among the laity and clergy.

At Turkdean, Gloucestershire, in 1563, for example, the churchwardens reported, 'our curate did stubbornly refuse to christen a child which was born and in danger of life, nor would not by no means nor entreaty that the wives and neighbours could make until it was the Sunday following, the child being born on the Monday before'. Parishioners at Woolastone, Gloucester, reported in 1563, 'for lack of a priest we have children died unchristened which lived considerable time to have been christened'. Thomas Clarke, the minister of Barnard Castle, Durham, in 1587, 'refused to christen one John Cook's . . . child upon a workday, when he had christened others that was wealthy men's children'. In a strict interpretation of the prayer-book rubric, Clarke would only deviate from christening the children of humble parish-ioners on Sundays or holy days if the father swore the child was likely to die.[19]

Other cases add to the pattern of friction and frustration. John Dawson, cootman of Billingham, Durham, brought his child to be christened on a Sun-day in 1587, but was kept waiting from eight in the morning until two in the afternoon, 'saying the curate tarried so long he was forced to seek one new godfather', although the other was prepared to wait. Alexander Read, rector of Fyfield, Essex, refused to baptize a child on a Sunday morning, despite hav-ing advance notice, and despite earnest warnings by the father, the midwife, 'and diverse other neighbours' that the child was 'very weak and sick'. Read told them 'he would not baptise it until the afternoon, and so it was carried away again unbaptised'. The puritan rector of Beetley, Norfolk, was presented in 1597 'for denying the christening of a child of John Farewell, except the said John and the godfathers would confess at the time of the christening their faith. And he never signs the children at the christening with the cross.'[20] Withholding baptism on these terms was completely contrary to the policy and discipline of the Church of England.

Similar clerical neglect could be found in the seventeenth century, and perhaps in every other era. A Durham minister, Thomas Harriman, was allegedly 'so drunk that he could not stand' when a child was brought for christening in the 1620s, and the child (a bastard) died unbaptized. Anthony Wright, the rector of Linwood, Lincolnshire, did his best at a christening in 1631 but was so 'in drink' that he 'flung down the water and then he did christen the child as well as he could utter out his words'. Emmanuel Macie, curate of Bruton, Somerset, refused to christen the child of Susan and Edward Young in 1633, perhaps because he was busy bowling (as he was a month later when Susan came to be churched). The vicar of Witham, Essex, restored in 1660 after sequestration, was also too drunk on some occasions to perform baptisms. Parishioners claimed in 1664 that his scandalous life drove them to seek baptism for their children elsewhere, though his personal inadequacy was not supposed to affect the validity of the sacrament.[21] Clerical offences like these were perhaps inevitable amongst a priesthood more than 8,000 strong, but their very rarity makes them stand out in the records.

Liturgy

Baptism had various layers of meaning, some internal and spiritual, others external and social. At one level the sacrament signified the mystical Christian covenant and the promise of redemption from sin; at another it marked the initiation of new members into the community of the church. Its performance involved a demonstration of faith, a test of conformity, and fulfilment of social and familial obligations. Like most religious ceremonies, the ritual of baptism involved inward grace and outward form, matters essential and things accessory. Richard Hooker alluded to some of the complexity of the sacrament when he explained, in the 1590s, that 'baptism is an action in part moral, in part ecclesiastical, and in part mystical: moral, in being a duty which men perform towards God; ecclesiastical, in that it belongeth unto God's church as a public duty; finally mystical, if we respect what God doth thereby intend to work'.[22]

The multiple and miraculous properties of the sacrament were most readily suggested to the laity by the service for 'the ministration of baptism' in the Book of Common Prayer.[23] The words and the ritual would have been familiar to every churchgoer in Elizabethan and Stuart England. Even in the smallest parishes they could expect to hear it several times a year, and in large communities several times a week. The theme of the service was regeneration and new birth. Short prayers gave condensed expression to the Christian interpretation of the Old and New Testaments, a summary and encapsulation of standard religious beliefs. They explained that mankind was fallen and sinful, but the incarnation and resurrection of Christ held out the prospect of everlasting life. Baptism was the means to this transformation, though it did not, of course, automatically guarantee salvation.

The English protestant service for the ministration of baptism was adapted from earlier catholic liturgies. The Elizabethan prayer book of 1559 (in use until 1645 and in many places much longer) was modelled closely on the second Edwardian prayer book of 1552; its predecessor of 1549 was essentially an anglicization of the older Latin missals. The Restoration prayer book of 1662 (still familiar to some twentieth-century churchgoers) was a modified form of the Elizabethan Book of Common Prayer.[24] Like most other services, the order for baptism included a set of instructions (sometimes printed in red ink, hence 'rubric'), and set forth the standard form of words to be spoken by the priest and other participants. The Act of Uniformity of 1559 allowed no other form of worship than the Book of Common Prayer, though room still remained for local unofficial variation in matters of custom, convenience, and discretion. The Jacobean canons of 1604 reiterated Elizabethan ideals of uniformity and discipline, and included a lengthy disquisition on the sacrament of baptism and the use of the sign of the cross.[25]

The minister began the service of public baptism by reminding those present that 'all men be conceived and born in sin, and that our saviour Christ saith, none can enter into the kingdom of God except he be regenerate and born anew of water and the Holy Ghost'. Through the sacrament of baptism, it was hoped, the sinner would be 'delivered from [God's] wrath', and 'received into the ark of Christ's church; and being steadfast in faith, joyful through hope, and rooted in charity, may so pass the waves of this troublesome world' and finally 'come to the land of everlasting life'. Baptism was the beginning of a journey, a rite of passage indeed, awash with aquatic and fluvial images, through symbolic waters, floods, and waves. The minister called on God, that those to be baptized 'may receive remission of their sins by spiritual regeneration', and that Christ 'will embrace them with the arms of his mercy'. The priest prayed, 'that they may be born again and be made heirs of everlasting salvation', and 'that the old Adam in these children may be buried, that the new man may be raised up in them'.[26] This was powerful language, appropriate to a mystical transformation.

The climax of the service involved actions as well as words. The liturgy spoke to the eyes as well as to the ears, but the critical movements could only have been seen by the people closest to the font. According to the rubric in the prayer book, 'the priest shall take the child in his hands, and ask the name; and naming the child, shall dip it in the water, so be it discreetly and warily done, saying: N, I baptize thee in the name of the Father, and of the Son, and of the Holy Ghost.' If the child was weak, it was enough to pour water upon it instead of dipping. 'Then shall the priest make a cross upon the child's forehead, saying: We receive this child into the congregation of Christ's flock, and do sign him with the sign of the cross, in token that hereafter he shall not be ashamed to confess the faith of Christ crucified.' Utterance of the phrase 'I baptize thee . . .' was the crucial part of the ceremony; at this point, and through these words, the child was actually baptized.[27] The other ingredients—the dipping in water and signing with the cross—were ritual accompaniments that gave rise to endless difficulties, disagreements, and problems.

The liturgy made clear that the service was one of incorporation as well as transformation. Those baptized were 'received into Christ's holy church and . . . made lively members of the same'. They were 'grafted', 'adopted', and 'incorporate(d)' as new Christians into 'the body of Christ's congregation'. Henceforth they would be members, not only of the local and national congregation of worshippers, but also engaged with the wider spiritual community of Christians in all times and places, both the quick and the dead. The popular word 'christening', though not used in the Book of Common Prayer, exactly captures this process.

The 1552 service for public baptism continued in use until the twentieth century, with minor modifications. Yet almost from its inception there were demands that it be changed. To Elizabethan puritans it was clear that the Church of England was but half-cleansed, and that much of the work of Reformation remained undone. Ecclesiastical vestments, the font, the sign of the cross, private baptism, and permissive attitudes to emergency baptism by women, were all 'abominations' left over from popery, according to *The Admonition to the Parliament* of 1572. The *Admonition* claimed that among early Christians, 'it was enough with them if they had water, and the party to be baptised faith, and the minister to preach the word and administer the sacraments'. But now, in accordance with the prayer book, 'we must have surplices devised by Pope Adrian, interrogatories ministered to the infant, godfathers and godmothers brought in by Higinus, holy fonts invented by Pope Pius, crossing and such like pieces of popery, which the church of God in the Apostles' times never knew'.[28] Selective historical scholarship supplied powerful partisan ammunition for current ecclesiastical controversies.

Even more than the presbyterian proponents of the *Admonition*, Elizabethan separatists like Henry Barrow despaired of 'this heap and dunghill of
Romish trumperies' that continued to contaminate the Church of England.
John Canne, writing from Amsterdam in the early 1630s, held similar separatist ideas. In his view the surviving church ceremonies in England were
'inspired by Satan, invented by man, commanded first to be practiced by the
beast and his bishops; therefore they are idols of Rome, Babylonish rites, part
of the scarlet woman, her inventions, popish fooleries, accursed remnants,
and leaves of the blasphemous priesthood, known liveries of Antichrist'.[29]
Baptism was included in this attack.

From an orthodox point of view, of course, the ceremonies of the Church of
England were congruent with primitive Christianity, shorn of popish superstition, and were eminently pleasing to God. Banished from baptism were such
popish elaborations as the figure of a 'dove let down of old upon the baptized
. . . for a sign of regeneration by the spirit' (which Robert Parker claimed to
have seen in Cambridgeshire in Elizabeth's time), and lamps or candles put
in the hands of the baptized 'to act the parable of the virgins' lamps'.[30] But
drama and ceremony remained, even if the flamboyant theatricality of the
old catholic service had been subdued. The Book of Common Prayer provided
a standard script for performances that could vary with the actors, the circumstances, and the setting.

Theology

A compressed summary of the theology of baptism appeared in the twenty-
seventh of the Thirty-Nine Articles of religion adopted by Convocation in
1563. This set forth the standard position of the Church of England:

Baptism is not only a sign of profession and mark of difference whereby Christian
men are discerned from others that be not christened, but it is also a sign of regeneration or new birth, whereby, as by an instrument, they that receive baptism rightly
are grafted into the church; the promises of forgiveness of sin, and of our adoption
to be the sons of God by the Holy Ghost, are visibly signed and sealed; faith is confirmed, and grace increased by virtue of prayer unto God. The baptism of young
children is to be retained in the church, as most agreeable with the institution of
Christ.[31]

The Elizabethan bishops adopted the articles of religion in the hope of 'avoiding diversities of opinion, and for the establishing of consent touching true
religion', a hope espoused with no greater success by their Stuart successors.
Every minister in every parish was held answerable to the Thirty-Nine Articles, and, according to the canons of 1604, both clergy and laity alike were

liable to excommunication if they impugned or disputed them.[32] Enforcement, however, was often slack and haphazard.

Alexander Nowell's *Catechism*, the standard text of Christian instruction first published in 1570, attempted to explicate the mystery of baptism. Through baptism, it explained, 'we are born again'. Helpless sinners, 'the children of wrath', were received into God's household and were 'joined and grafted into the body of Christ, and become his members and do grow into one body with him'. Baptism was, almost literally, incorporation. It was not, however, a certain grant of salvation. The baptismal water *signified* forgiveness and regeneration but did not automatically ensure it. As a good Calvinist, Nowell knew that only God's grace, sustained by faith, opened the doors of heaven. 'The unbelieving in refusing them the promises offered them by God, shut up the entry against themselves and go away empty. Yet do they not thereby make the sacraments lose their force and nature.'[33] The first part of the explanation was generally acceptable, the second part fraught with problems.

Churchmen of all sorts could agree with the Jacobean bishop Thomas Morton that baptism was 'a token and sign of a covenant and stipulation between man and God'. The high-church minister and poet John Donne taught that baptism was 'a seal' of our 'union with God, which is also our salvation'. The ceremony established 'a covenant, a contract' between the soul of the baptized and God.[34] The presbyterian *émigré* Robert Parker similarly recognized baptism as 'the seal of the heavenly king', though he would not go so far as to connect it with salvation. The puritan casuist William Ames allowed that baptism consecrated the child to God, and that it signified 'the covenant between Christ and the child'. The Calvinist theologian William Perkins explained that through this sacrament, through 'the outward sign of washing . . . is sealed and propounded the marvellous solemn covenant and contract' which made possible the prospect of everlasting life.[35] Baptism, for the Restoration-era presbyterian Oliver Heywood, was a doctrinal seal, an initiating sign, a discriminating badge, and a binding obligation, and with this at least his Anglican colleagues would have agreed. The seal of baptism was so important for Heywood that instead of marking his birthday, like more worldly mortals, he observed the anniversary of his baptism, his Christian beginning, as a day of prayer and meditation. So too did other nonconformists, like Henry Newcome, who wrote on 27 November 1661, 'This is my baptising day. I am now thirty-four years of age complete.'[36]

The language of 'sign' and 'seal' became a commonplace of protestant teaching, as ministers glossed the words of the prayer book and reiterated the articles of religion. In a culture imbued with the law it was no accident that the imagery of attestation, contract, and covenant should be applied to the sacrament of baptism.[37] But there was much less agreement about the additional properties of the sacrament, especially whether baptism operated as an instrument of salvation. English protestantism harboured competing theological tendencies—from rigid Calvinism to popular Pelagianism, from exclusive to inclusive views of salvation—with room for varying shades of opinion. The debate was by no means settled whether baptism was something more than a 'sign', what were the limits of its transformational efficacy, and what befell the soul of anyone unfortunate enough to die unbaptized. Contingent on the answers to these questions were political and procedural matters of enduring controversy, such as whether lay folk or women could perform the ceremony of baptism, exactly where it should be conducted, how long after a child's birth, and with what degree of awe and urgency.

Consensus within the Church of England on the spiritual significance of baptism eroded on the question of its efficacy, and threatened to disintegrate over matters of liturgical conduct. Positions shaped by opposition to Roman Catholicism in the sixteenth century became strained or modified in the face of changing conditions in the seventeenth century. English Calvinism lost ground. High ceremonialists tended to stress the importance of baptism as a sacrament of regeneration, and gave reverent attention to the full performance of the ritual. Those with more puritan views emphasized the role of baptism in the public initiation of Christians, and sought ways to simplify the ceremony. Sectarian extremists proposed to jettison it altogether.

The mainstream position of the Church of England was that baptism had limited efficacy, and did not wash away all sin. Anyone who suggested that the ceremony itself, or any of its particular elements, automatically secured forgiveness of sins would surely be condemned as superstitious. Puritans in particular stressed that 'the mystical washing away of sin' was not achieved by the water, still less by the sign of the cross, but only by 'the work of God in the blood of Christ'.[38] Yet despite many years of protestant instruction, there were still lay folk who believed in the magical effectiveness of baptism, and ministers whose views on the subject verged on papism. One reformer warned the bishop of Lichfield in 1570, 'if you were in the country . . . your ears would tingle to hear the gross and superstitious speeches of the people'. Later in the reign of Charles II, John Aubrey encountered countrymen who still thought of baptism as an exorcism, a driving out of devils, as well as an act of consecration. Was it any wonder that such views survived when the ministry itself set forth conflicting doctrine? Echoes of these debates could still be heard in the nineteenth century amidst arguments about justification, sanctification, and baptismal regeneration.[39]

Unreformed beliefs were encouraged by traditionalist priests like the rector of Fobbing, Essex, who was called before the authorities in 1576 for saying 'that a child before he be baptised is not the child of God, but the child of the devil', and like Thomas Staple, vicar of Mundon, Essex, three-quarters of a century later, who taught 'that children dying without baptism are all damned'. Jeremiah Ravens, the Caroline rector of Great Blakenham, Suffolk, offended strict Calvinists by claiming that 'all shall be saved that are baptised, and that all being baptised are the children of God'.[40] John Cosin, the controversial Caroline Arminian, required his clergy in the East Riding of Yorkshire in the 1620s to instruct the people 'in the nature, necessity, benefit, and efficacy of this holy sacrament'. Through baptism, he maintained, a child 'undoubtedly received both remission of original sin, and all things necessary to salvation'. At the time of the Restoration, Cosin proposed amending the prayer book to say, 'that children being baptised have all things necessary for their salvation, and be undoubtedly saved, if they die before they commit actual sin', implying that sacramental action was somehow responsible for this state of grace.[41]

These were extreme views, however, and more moderate clerics would not accept them. Both Oxford and Cambridge Universities were divided in 1629 over the issue whether 'all baptized infants are undoubtedly justified', the rising Arminians tending to affirm it while Calvinists opposed the proposition.[42] Another leading Arminian, Richard Montague of Norwich, sought citations against any in his diocese in 1638 who held 'that the sacrament of baptism is not of absolute and indispensable necessity unto salvation in God's ordinary course and dispensation with man, but that either eternal election sufficeth or original sin, which infants only have, condemneth none'. This was well outside the mainstream of the early Stuart church. Robert Herrick's poetic aphorism was, perhaps, more acceptable. 'The strength of baptism, thats within; | It saves the soul, by drowning sin.'[43]

What was the sacrament supposed to achieve? Was baptism an effective instrument as well as a symbolic sign, a mechanism as well as a token? According to the Jacobean preacher John Day, through baptism 'the flesh is washed, that the soul may be cleansed'. John Donne, a few years later, taught that human beings were born in filthiness and sin, but the remedy lay in 'the water of baptism'. It was at the font, said Donne, that 'we discharge ourselves of all the first uncleannesses, of all the guiltiness of original sin'.[44] Donne came close to arguing that the ceremony itself was a means to salvation, and some of his less careful colleagues evidently went overboard in this direction. Edward Cherry, rector of Much Holland, Essex, and John Wilson, vicar of Arlington, Sussex, were among the 'scandalous, malignant priests' of Charles I's reign who were cited for teaching 'that baptism utterly taketh away original sin'.

Arminians, with a high regard for the sacraments and an optimistic view of salvation, were inclined to treat baptism as an entry ticket to paradise. The Restoration bishop Anthony Sparrow, who had been a Cambridge fellow in the 1630s, saw baptism as 'the only ordinary means of our regeneration or second birth, which gives us a right and title to heaven'.[45] Such a view could have led to his sequestration had he held a parish in the early 1640s.

Puritans were naturally uneasy about linking baptism and regeneration. The connection seemed too automatic, and risked making the ceremony a *means* to regeneration rather than a mere sign of it. Instead, they tended to emphasize a different aspect of the sacrament, its role in joining Christians together as members of the universal church. This was made most explicit in a puritan petition of 1585 which used images of corporate, collegiate, and civic membership to argue that 'baptism is an incorporating of us into the body of Christ, a matriculating of us into the body of the church, and an enrolling of us into the number of the citizens of the holy city'.[46] William Perkins described baptism as 'the first sacrament . . . whereby Christians are initiated and admitted into the church of God'. It was, said the godly Jacobean William Gouge, 'a pledge of our incorporation into the body of Christ and communion of his saints'. Few seventeenth-century Christians would disagree with this, although some would lay their emphasis elsewhere. Nor would many agree with the extreme puritan position, reportedly preached in the 1630s, that the outward sign of baptism 'did no more to the making of Christians than the washing of a dog's leg', a view to make the ceremonialists shiver.[47]

A poignant personal perspective is found in the diary of Robert Woodford, a puritan layman of Northampton, who began his diary in August 1637 with reflections on the solemnity of baptism. The Christian initiation of his firstborn was surely an auspicious occasion on which to commence a record of his own actions and thoughts. 'I prayed alone, and I and my dear wife prayed in private this morning to beseech the Lord for his blessing upon the sacrament of baptism to our poor child this day, that inward grace might go along with the outward sign.' And in preparation for the baptism of his next child a year later, Woodford prayed, 'Lord, sanctify my child for the ordinance of baptism, and sanctify the ordinance to the child.'[48] For Woodford, as for other moderate puritans, the ceremonial trappings were less important than the sacramental covenant. A theory of sacramental grace was not incompatible with a Calvinist belief in predestination. Woodford's diary indicates that his children's baptisms took place privately at home in the presence of the mother, with witnesses rather than godparents, and most likely without the sign of the cross.

Lost Souls

Variant views on the efficacy of baptism came sharply into focus with the immediate, personal, and practical crisis of an infant dying without benefit of the sacrament. Were such children lost souls, consigned to hell for mankind's original sin, or would Christ in his mercy embrace them to his bosom? Were their souls imperilled for want of the Christian sacrament, or would they find grace regardless of prayers and sprinkling? Were they lost to some ill-defined limbo? This was not just a matter which exercised theologians, for it directly concerned parish priests in their pastoral role and was an anguish for parents who lost a newborn baby. The official position of the church was awkward and ambiguous, while local reactions were coloured by guilt, recrimination, and confusion. Clergy and laity might blame each other for the possible forfeit of eternity, or might comfort each other with dubious doctrine about salvation. The Church of England had no consistent or satisfactory answer to the problem of 'infants which die unbaptised'. And ministers were sometimes uncertain whether to use the Christian form of burial in such cases, and whether to inter the infant in consecrated ground.

Conscientious Elizabethan reformers, like Bishop Richard Barnes of Durham, tried to transmit complex theological positions to the local level as they exercised their pastoral and disciplinary roles. Barnes instructed his clergy to teach their parishioners,

that if any infant die without public baptism first to it ministered, that the same is not to be condemned or adjudged as a damned soul, but to be well hoped of, and the body to be interred in the churchyard, yet without ringing or any divine service or solemnity, because the same was not solemnly professed and received into the church and congregation.[49]

Parents of such children were no longer to despair, but they were still denied the satisfaction of a Christian burial. Could they look forward to reunion at the resurrection, as bereaved family members were encouraged in less problematic circumstances?

The judicious Richard Hooker acknowledged that in such cases, 'the judgement of many hath gone hard against them'. But 'seeing grace is not absolutely tied unto sacraments', and bearing in mind both 'the lenity of God' and the Christian purpose of the parents, he was inclined to argue that children who died unbaptized were not irredeemably jeopardized.[50] This was certainly the most charitable view, and one which fostered optimism, but it was by no means a consistent position within the Church of England.

The issue resurfaced at the Hampton Court Conference in 1604 in the context of ambiguities and disagreements over occasional baptism by women. Richard Bancroft, bishop of London, defended such baptism in case of necessity, the state of the infant, dying unbaptised, being uncertain, and to God only known; but if he die baptised, there is an evident assurance that it is saved; who is he that having any religion in him, would not speedily, by any means, procure his child to be baptized, and rather ground his action upon Christ's promise, than his omission thereof upon God's secret judgement?[51]

An unbaptized child was not necessarily condemned to perdition, but given the odds and the opportunity there was every incentive to make sure that baptism was accomplished. Alongside this view was argued the importance of priestly mediation, an issue on which radical presbyterians and episcopal ceremonialists could agree. It was better to be baptized than not baptized, and better by far that the ceremony be performed by a priest than by a woman.

Bishops sometimes asked at their visitations whether any child had died without baptism, and required those involved in such a scandal to explain themselves. Edmund Binder, curate of Blackmore, Essex, was cited in 1584 because 'two children . . . died unchristened by his negligence, for that he would not christen them before the Sunday following, and died in the mean time'. A Sussex father, Edward Leeds of Westfield, was presented in 1600 because his child died before being brought to baptism. Anthony Armitage, the vicar of Ellington, Huntingdonshire, refused to baptize a child on a weekday despite being told by the father and 'ancient women of the parish that the child was very weak and in peril of death, in so much the child died without baptism, to the great grief of the parents'. At Racton, Sussex, in 1623 'a child of Mr. Richard Peckham's died suddenly and unbaptised because the minister was upon earnest occasions then at London'. And 'divers children died unbaptised for want of a minister' at Selsey, Sussex, so the churchwardens reported in 1625.[52] These were serious derelictions of paternal and clerical responsibility which had to be examined. Doing everything possible to secure baptism was considered so important that if any infant died unbaptized as a result of the minister's refusal or negligence, 'the said minister shall be suspended for three months', according to the new church canons of 1604.[53]

The convolutions of casuistry and conscience in such cases can sometimes be traced in the local records. A dispute arose at Kingston, Surrey, in 1586 when the minister, Mr Udall, asserted, 'that it does not matter if a child die before baptism'. Udall upset traditionalists by preaching 'against those who think a child is damned if it die unbaptised, and have the ceremony performed hastily in a corner, and not before the congregation'. He argued that 'haste in baptism, and baptism by midwives, show a belief in popish doctrine of the efficacy of baptism', but such radical views brought him trouble with the episcopal authorities.[54] Similarly, when a parishioner asked the nonconformist vicar of Timberland, Lincolnshire, to hasten to baptize his child in 1623, 'it being then so very weak and likely to die', the minister responded,

'What if it die in the mean time? Is that such a matter? Was it not born of a Christian woman? Did not a Christian man get it?' The vicar, Tristram Hinchcliffe, was no doubt arguing the primacy of faith over ceremony, and advancing the genealogical theory of the covenant, but he seems not to have succeeded in comforting the anxious parents.[55]

Laudian ministers of the reign of Charles I were sometimes alleged to have taken more extreme positions on the opposite side. We have already met Thomas Staple, vicar of Mundon, Essex, with his view 'that children dying without baptism are all damned'. In the same vein James Buck, vicar of Stradbrooke, Suffolk, 'hath often preached that if a child die baptized it is undoubtably saved, but if it die before baptism it is undoubtably damned'. Acting on this principle, Thomas Bailey, rector of Brasted, Kent, 'refused to read the burial service of some children because they died before baptism'.[56] These ministers of the 1630s were not cited to their bishops, who may even have shared some of their views, but they were singled out for censure and sequestration by puritan opponents a few years later when their unreformed views on baptism were used against them.

A crisis with spiritual, professional, and domestic dimensions beset the Reverend Isaac Archer in 1675 when his newborn son died without baptism. We are permitted to enter into this crisis through the remarkable record of Isaac Archer's diary. As minister of Freckenham, Suffolk, he of all people should have taken steps to safeguard his child's spiritual welfare. As a father, Archer was responsible for arranging a prompt baptism for his child; as minister, he was liable to be cited for permitting a parishioner to die unbaptized. The baby was born prematurely on 7 August, and soon fell sick with a fever. The mother, too, was seriously ill. The household faced multiple distractions. On 20 August Archer wrote in his diary, 'my wife had been very sick, which made us put off the baptism of the little one'. When the child died on 25 August, two and a half weeks old and still not baptized, Archer turned to his diary with explanations.[57]

I had taken a nurse into the house to suckle it because my wife was not able, as having suckled the last too long. The woman knew of its illness, and yet told us not of it, so it died whilst she slept and unbaptised, which I could not in the least help as knowing nothing of its illness. I know God is a god of the faithfull and their seed, and baptism is a sign of it; and I no more question the child's happiness (whatever St. Austin thought) than that of the Jewish children who died before the eighth day. I take God to witness, I do not, did not, despise the sacrament; but now 'tis fallen out so, not through the fault of the infant, or our wilfull neglect, but through an unavoidable necessity. . . . I laid it in Freckenham chancel near my seat; and I expect to meet it at the resurrection of the just, Amen.[58]

The unnamed child was buried in holy ground, in a part of the church controlled by the incumbent, alongside the bodies of his brothers and sisters who had been baptized.

In practice, in most cases, children who died before baptism were given decent burial in the churchyard. Some ministers, like Archer, allowed them to be interred alongside family members in prime positions, others consigned them to marginal ground. When a severely deformed child died unbaptized at Sandwich, Kent, in 1609, the minister 'very charitably gave it burial'.[59] Babies whose mothers also died in childbirth were sometimes buried in their mothers' arms with the one funeral service doing double duty. Thomas Comber, a leading churchman of Charles II's time, acknowledged the ultimate uncertainty regarding those who died unbaptized, but advised 'the parent may take comfort in his having done what he could, and ought to hope in divine mercy'. Further relief could be found in Richard Baxter's argument that through baptism 'the children of true believers consent to the covenant by their parents, and are as certainly saved if they die before baptism as after'.[60] In other words, they were made Christians by inheritance as well as by receipt of the sacrament, as Tristram Hinchcliffe had argued earlier. A late seventeenth-century *Companion for Midwives* suggested that parents should not 'despair of God's mercy to poor children that die without baptism'. But as late as the nineteenth century (and perhaps more recently) hard-line churchmen continued to refuse Christian burial to babies who died unbaptized.[61]

As ever, there was room for compromise and negotiation. The potential scale of the problem is indicated by figures for neonatal mortality. Demographic estimates show that approximately 2 per cent of babies born in the Elizabethan period died before the end of their first day of life. Death claimed a cumulative total of 5 per cent within a week, 8 or 9 per cent within a month, and 12 or 13 per cent within a year, with slightly higher rates of infant mortality in the later seventeenth century.[62] Very few of these children escaped baptism.

Baptism by Women

Baptism was part of priestcraft. The ceremony belonged to the ecclesiastical domain. It was the privilege and duty of the clergyman, presiding in his surplice, standing at the font, and reading from the Book of Common Prayer, to administer the sacrament to the laity. But in emergencies, when no priest was available and an unbaptized child appeared likely to die, any Christian, male or female, was permitted to conduct a baptism. The Book of Common Prayer even included an abbreviated version of the service for private use 'when great need shall compel them'. It was enough, in cases of necessity, to say the words, 'N, I baptise thee in the name of the Father, and of the Son, and of the Holy Ghost'.[63] Since childbirth was largely a female affair, attended by gatherings of women, it might fall to one of them, most likely the midwife, to perform some kind of baptism *in extremis*. This was one of the principal reasons that midwives were examined for their religious conformity. Baptism by women was not unusual in Tudor England but became increasingly rare in the seventeenth century after the Jacobean church took measures to prevent it.

Traditional catholic practice required parishioners to know 'in what manner children should be baptised in time of necessity', how to apply the water, and to say the appropriate words in English. This tradition continued, though somewhat abated, after the Reformation.[64] Reforming bishops of the 1530s fully expected women to baptize children 'in time of need'. Far from suppressing the practice of christening by the midwife, they sought instead to regulate it, to make sure that it was done properly and without superstition. Bishop Rowland Lee enjoined his clergy in the Diocese of Coventry and Lichfield in 1537, 'ye shall teach and instruct your parishioners, at the least twelve times in the year, the spiritual manner and form of christenings in English; and that the midwife may use it in time of necessity; commanding the woman when the time of birth draweth near, to have at all seasons a vessel of clean water for the same purpose'. The Henrician bishops of Salisbury, Gloucester, and York set forth similar Injunctions, 'that every curate instruct his parishioners, and especially the midwives, the essential manner and form how to christen a child in time of need'.[65] Such instructions disappeared from the later visitation articles of the Church of England, but the popular knowledge they referred to survived.

The established church harboured mixed opinions about baptism by women, as it did about so many other things. Churchmen who believed in the efficacy of baptism and the necessity of the sacrament for salvation were inclined to permit emergency baptism by women in order to safeguard souls. Those who regarded the ceremony as a mere token, at best a ritual initiation, could find little to support the traditional baptismal practice of midwives. Sacerdotalists were torn on this issue, for many hard-line clergymen, traditionalists as well as reformers, bridled at the notion of women performing any kind of religious office.[66]

The authors of the puritan *Admonition* of 1572 saw 'baptism by women' as one among many popish abominations that had to be eradicated. Yet, they added, 'it is used almost in all places . . . as common practice without controlment'. Lay practitioners, primarily midwives, should be warned 'not to meddle in ministers' affairs'. Anglican apologists insisted that it really did not matter. Archbishop Whitgift endeavoured to disarm puritan criticism by arguing that 'the sacrament remaineth in full force and strength, of whomsoever it be ministered, or howsoever by ceremonies or other additions it is corrupted'.[67] But far from settling the matter, such lukewarmness among the bishops convinced puritan radicals that their fundamental objections were correct.

The separatist Henry Barrow, writing in 1590, described the practice of 'hasty baptism done by the midwife; who if she see the child in peril and like to die before it can be brought to the church, then is she to bestir her, and give the child the Christendom, least it never come in heaven'. Did this imply, asked the Oxford puritan Thomas Sparke, 'that the children not baptised should be in danger of damnation, and that the outward baptism with water, even for the work wrought, saveth the child that is baptised?'[68] If so, it undercut the theological and liturgical basis of the English service of baptism. Again there was ambiguity, dispute, and contradiction, with traditionalists allowing the practice to continue and radicals urging that it stop.

Richard Hooker defended the practice of the Church of England, where 'women's baptism in private by occasion of urgent necessity' was allowable. He also acknowledged part of the puritan complaint, without addressing its wider implications: 'it may be the liberty of baptism by women at such times doth sometimes embolden the rasher sort to do it where no such necessity is'.[69] If there were abuses they could surely be solved by the pastoral oversight of the bishops. But the fundamental problem, to which this issue constantly referred, remained whether a child's soul was imperilled if it died unbaptized.

The records of Elizabethan episcopal administration show the same ambivalence towards baptism by women that is found in the controversial tracts and pamphlets. Given a choice, Elizabethan bishops would have preferred all baptisms to be performed in the church, on Sundays or holy days, by ordained ministers, in exact accordance with the Book of Common Prayer. But they also recognized, if only reluctantly, the demands of necessity and the ingrained strength of custom. Most parishioners wanted their babies baptized, by minister or midwife, because they believed that without such action the infant would not be able to enter into heaven. The general line of the Elizabethan church was that baptism by women was undesirable, but not absolutely intolerable.

Typically, the Elizabethan hierarchy fudged the issue. Matthew Parker, Queen Elizabeth's first archbishop of Canterbury, recommended in 1559, 'that private baptism in necessity, as in peril of death, be ministered either by the curate, deacon, or reader, or some other grave and sober man, if the time will suffer'. Only in the last resort might the sacrament be performed by a woman, but not before exhausting the preferable hierarchy of minister, deacon, reader, 'or some other grave and sober man'.[70]

Richard Barnes of Durham took a harder line, ordering in 1577 'that no midwives, nor any other women, be suffered to minister baptism; but if the infants be weak and the parents likewise, that they cannot expect the sabbath day, that the minister, or some other godly and discreet person (in that extreme necessity only) do baptise such infants at home'. If any woman should 'enterprise to baptise' she should be reported to the diocesan officials, especially if she used 'superstitious ceremonies, orisons, charms, or devilish rites or sorcery' at the birth.[71] The bishop suspected the worst of midwives and wanted to prevent them performing Christian ritual, but baptism by women did not invalidate the sacrament. Bishop Thomas Cooper of Winchester argued that 'the Church of England . . . doth not maintain either the baptism of midwives as a thing tolerable in the church, or else the condemnation of those children that depart this world unbaptised, but doth account them both erroneous, and not according to the word of God'. But the Church of England spoke with many voices, in Convocation and in the parishes. The practice of baptism by midwives might be 'erroneous' in the bishop's view, but none the less 'also of rashness by some is done'.[72]

Private emergency baptisms by midwives were supposed to be recorded in the parish register, with equal weight to those performed at the font. A few Elizabethan registers give additional details, such as the entry at Staplehurst, Kent, in 1564 that the twin sons of William Simon, 'being weak were named and baptised by the midwife', and at Bobbingworth, Essex, in 1569 that 'George Bourne the son of William Bourne was christened at home by mother Wright the midwife of the parish and in the presence of nine other honest women of the parish then being present according to the law, through great peril and danger'.[73] The unusual amount of detail here, in records that were notoriously laconic, suggests a need to apologize for actions that the authorities might find mildly irregular.

Midwives operated at the boundaries of life and death, with skills few men could fathom. They were, as we have seen, vital practitioners in the field of human birth. Bishops commonly enquired at their visitations whether midwives 'take upon them to baptise', but it was extremely unusual for any to be punished for so doing. In a survey of the Diocese of Chichester in 1579, recording the names of forty-two midwives serving 120 parishes, only three were acknowledged as performing baptisms: the midwife of Aldingbourne who 'baptised infants', Goodwife Legatt of Hamptonet who 'once did baptize a child which died', and the midwife of Pulborough who 'baptiseth infants in time of great peril and danger at home'. At Bury the churchwardens noted, 'we have a midwife which is licensed but she medleth not with baptism'.[74]

Were people who had been baptized by women truly baptized, or did the irregular circumstances of their christening debar them from admission to holy communion? Should the few children christened by women be baptized again by a minister, or should they at least be brought to church as soon as possible for Christian recognition? Questions of this sort hovered round some clerical discussions well into the seventeenth century. Strictly, of course, baptism was baptism no matter who performed it, but, as the Elizabethan John Greenwood insisted, where there is no ministry there is no sacrament. Greenwood was a sectarian conventicler, executed for sedition in 1593, but in this at least the Laudian ceremonialists of the 1630s would have agreed with him.[75] Any formal public baptism that followed emergency baptism by a parent or midwife risked the horrors of anabaptism, if the original baptism was valid, so an optional conditional form of service was devised. 'It is expedient', said the Book of Common Prayer, that survivors of emergency baptism 'be brought into the church, to the intent the priest may examine whether the child be lawfully baptised or no'. Then followed an adaption of the service for public baptism, with the extraordinary formulation, 'If thou be not baptised already, I baptize thee'. Critics thought this absurd, but in some circles, as late as the nineteenth century, the survivors of emergency baptism by midwives were considered to be only half-baptized.[76]

Episcopal policy mirrored the confusions within the church. According to Archbishop Whitgift, speaking at Hampton Court in 1604, 'the administration of baptism by women and lay persons was not allowed in the practice of the church, but enquired of by bishops in their visitations and censured'. Bishop Babington of Worcester argued further that lay baptism was neither legal nor necessary. But Bancroft of London and Bilson of Winchester, by contrast, insisted on the antiquity and lawfulness of baptism by 'private persons in cases of necessity'.[77] Left unresolved was the gender of those 'private persons' and the practical definition of 'necessity'. Prominent in these discussions was a sacerdotal notion of priestly authority, in which none but the lawful minister could perform God's sacraments except in the most extraordinary circumstances.

A minor revision to the Book of Common Prayer following the Hampton Court Conference signalled major changes in the sacramental capacity of women. In its Elizabethan version the rubric for 'the ministration of private baptism' allowed any 'one of them . . . that be present', condition unspecified, to perform the office; here was the midwives' charter. But after 1604 it fell only to 'the lawful minister' to dip the child in water and to say the instrumental words. The clerical victory seems to have been complete, for there is little evidence of baptism by women in the remainder of the seventeenth century. Parish registers no longer drew attention to baptisms by midwives. The oath administered to midwives referred baptisms to 'the ordinary minister' and the Book of Common Prayer. Midwives' manuals, which proliferated in the seventeenth century, make no mention of this traditional sacramental practice. The revised prayer book of 1662 insisted that performance of the sacrament belonged to 'the minister of the parish', further removing the possibility of baptism by women.[78]

Adjusted rubrics notwithstanding, Jacobean visitation articles imply that traditional practices continued, sometimes with semi-official blessing. John Overall of Norwich enquired in 1619 whether any children had been 'baptized in private houses by any lay person, or midwife, or popish priest, or by any other minister, but upon urgent occasion when the child was in danger of death?' If the intent was to restrict baptism to the lawful minister, it was undermined by the let-out clause invoking 'urgent occasion'. Bishop Miles Smith of Gloucester similarly asked about baptism 'at home' by any midwife, in his visitation of 1622, but allowed no concession to urgency or necessity. Matthew Wren's interrogation of the Diocese of Ely in 1638—'Have any children been baptised in private houses (except upon great necessity, and if so, what was the same?) or by any lay person, or midwife, or popish priest, or by any other than your own minister?'—reflected concern about irregular rituals and popish recusancy, and was as much an attempt to impose ecclesiastical discipline as to prevent the practice of baptism by women.[79] Yet when a poor woman in London was delivered in 1635 of a premature child that was 'so weak it was not like to live an hour', the midwife 'sent her maid to get a minister to christen it' rather than risking censure by performing the baptism herself. Fortunately the maid encountered 'Mr Barnes, an ancient minister', in Newgate market, who named the short-lived infant Edward. A generation earlier the midwife would most likely have said the sacramental words herself.[80]

That women could baptize at all was so inconceivable to the ceremonial sacerdotalist John Cosin that he left out all consideration of it in the dozen questions dealing with baptism in his archdeaconry visitation articles of 1627. Baptism was a sacrament of the church and therefore could only be performed by a priest. 'In case of necessity . . . as when the child is in peril of death and cannot safely be brought to the church', it was up to the minister to 'hasten' to baptize it. Too bad if he did not get there in time. And afterwards, to compensate for the lack of 'ceremony or solemnity' in such cases, 'if the child grow well and live' it was to be brought to church to be publicly

certified as a Christian, and for 'due supply . . . of all things before omitted'.
Thomas Bedford, writing in 1638, rejected earlier arguments for emergency
baptism by women and reminded readers that the Hampton Court Conference had appropriated the act of baptizing 'to the lawful minister', and him
alone.[81]

Questions regarding baptism by midwives were dropped from later Stuart
visitation articles. The sacrament, wherever it was performed, was now exclusively the business of the lawful minister of the parish. The change reflects
the assertive sacerdotalism of the post-Restoration church as well as a restrict-
ive redefinition of lay and female roles. But, as we shall see, the price for this
was some erosion of baptism as a public ecclesiastical ceremony, and the rise
of the baptizing minister who made house calls. The post-Restoration laity
seem to have been more relaxed about baptism, more willing to postpone the
sacrament, and less anxious about the souls of the unbaptized. As the pressure
was removed, as 'necessity' and 'extremity' became less urgent, the rationale
for emergency baptism by midwives disappeared, although the practice no
doubt continued in 'backward' areas.

CROSSES IN BAPTISM

The Sign of the Cross

One of the longest-running disputes among early modern churchmen concerned the sign of the cross in the sacrament of baptism. The Book of Common Prayer specified that 'the priest shall make a cross upon the child's forehead' while saying out loud, 'we receive this child into the congregation of Christ's flock, and do sign him with the sign of the cross, in token that hereafter he shall not be ashamed to confess the faith of Christ crucified'.[1] This might seem like an unexceptional piece of symbolism, congruent with belief and tradition. Indeed, most people appeared content with it. But some ministers and parents vehemently objected to the cross in baptism as a superstitious and contaminated remnant of Roman Catholicism, and did all they could to prevent its use. The ceremony of baptism was supposed to be performed with goodwill and dignity, but occasionally, because of disagreements over crossing, it degenerated into contentious disorder. This chapter examines controversies about the *conduct* of baptism and pays particular attention to the gestures, substances, and equipment associated with the sacrament.

The old catholic service was rich with sanctified gestures. In baptism the priest crossed the infant with oil on the shoulders and breast, made the sign of the cross in the infant's right hand, and again crossed the child with chrism on the forehead. Each application of the sign of the cross betokened a particular signification of faith, and was accompanied by adjurations to the devil to depart. The drama of priestly recitation, questioning, and stylized application of holy substances—water, oil, chrism, spittle—echoed the larger drama of Christ in combat with the devil.[2]

The reformed protestant rubric removed most of this rigmarole, but did not go far enough for puritan fundamentalists. Some of the more radical Tudor churchmen would gladly have abandoned the residual gesture of the cross in baptism, but maintained it in the interest of conformity and discipline. Some hoped for further reform of the Book of Common Prayer, while others quietly modified the ceremony when they performed it in their parishes. One view, apparently common among scrupulous mainstream ministers, was that the sign of the cross could be retained, as the service book insisted, so long as it was stripped of traditional catholic significations. Differences within the upper reaches of the early Elizabethan church were accentuated in 1563 when a proposal at the Canterbury Convocation, that the sign of the cross in baptism should be omitted 'as tending to superstition', was rejected by a majority of one.[3]

In 1565 James Calfhill, the Calvinist archdeacon of Colchester, published a lengthy treatise ridiculing Roman reverence for the sign of the cross. His adversary, the Louvain priest John Martial, advanced the traditional claim that 'the cross is given us as a sign upon our foreheads, like as circumcision was to the Israelites; by this we Christian men differ and are discerned from infidels. This is our shield, our weapon, our banner and victory against the devil. This is our mark that the destroyer touch us not.' Calfhill replied, as reformers often did, that there was no scriptural foundation for this conceit, no biblical commandment to that end. Several generations were known to have passed from the time of Christ before Christians adopted the cross as his symbol, and then under papacy the sign was abused and corrupted. Calfhill insisted that the true sign of the Christian, and his only true armour, was faith. If the sign of the cross was retained in the Church of England's baptism it should be understood as a man-made addition to the sacrament, a mere external device, 'for otherwise, the crossing without believing is mere enchanting'. The forehead, many said, was the appropriate place for this symbol because it was the physical seat of shame.[4]

Richard Hooker agreed that 'it is not . . . the cross in our foreheads, but in our hearts the faith of Christ that armeth us with patience, constancy, and courage'. This, of course, was the standard sixteenth-century protestant position. But Hooker would not agree with the radicals that the sign of the cross, or other ceremonies of that nature, were displeasing to God. Though made by man and unfounded in scripture, these ritual actions were none the less acceptable as 'helps' and 'memorials of duty' with 'good and profitable use'. Any 'offence and scandal' that attached to such actions under popery, he argued, was happily 'now reformed', so that 'touching the sign and ceremony of the cross, we no way find ourselves bound to relinquish it'. The task of the Church of England was to maintain respect for the sign of the cross without encouraging the belief, reportedly common among ignorant country folk, that it formed 'the essential part of baptism'.[5]

As ever, a gulf yawned between learned theology and popular opinions and practice. The moderate puritan Richard Greenham worried that ignorant parishioners would get the wrong idea, like the old woman in Cambridgeshire 'who seeing the minister baptise children with a cross, thought that she might cross herself when she came to pray'. If the gesture was allowed in baptism, where else might it ignorantly continue? 'Admit once the aerial cross in baptism,' warned the Jacobean presbyterian David Calderwood, 'ye cannot refuse to set up the material cross and the rood in the kirk, nor the wooden or stone crosses in the highways.'[6] In the eyes of godly critics, these ceremonial gestures invited the return of resurgent Roman Catholicism.

The standard baptismal rubric remained unchanged under Elizabeth and the early Stuarts but the ceremony did not go unchallenged. Disciplinarians, apologists, critics, and casuists would argue the matter over several generations. Thomas Cooper, the Elizabethan bishop of Lincoln, offered in defence of the ceremonies of the reformed Church of England his opinion that the sign of the cross was 'made only in the air' and that no superstition attached to it. Whitgift quoted the Reformation hero Martin Bucer to the effect that the sign of the cross was 'neither uncomely nor unprofitable . . . so that it be purely understood and religiously received'.[7] Not so, responded puritan objectors. Rather, the cross was an offensive gesture, a superstitious remnant, and a symbol of all that connected the worship of God in England to the discredited practices and doctrines of Rome. 'Marking the child in the forehead with a cross, in token that hereafter he shall not be ashamed to confess the faith of Christ', was wicked and superstitious, according to the authors of the *Admonition* to the Parliament in 1572. It was another of those 'hundred points of popery yet remaining, which deformeth the English reformation' according to Anthony Gilby in 1581. Nicholas Standon prepared a list of 'particular reasons against the crossing of children in baptism'. And a chorus of puritan criticism reiterated the charge throughout Elizabeth's reign.[8] Especially outspoken was Owen Rydley, vicar of Battersea, Surrey, who was indicted before the Assize court in 1588 for saying

that crossing in baptism was of the same nature that other superstitious and devilish ceremonies used by the papists in the celebration of that sacrament, to wit, salt, cream, spittle, oil and candles, and that it was brought in by man's tradition contrary to the first institution and was the pride of man's brain; and that of those superstitious abuses all were abolished saving that of crossing, that we should have good cause to praise God if it would please him also to take it away out of his church.[9]

Addressing King James in 1603, the moderate puritan authors of the Millenary Petition asked politely 'that the cross in baptism . . . as superfluous, may be taken away'. The Suffolk puritan John Knewstub led the fight against the sign of the cross at the Hampton Court Conference in 1604, asking what power the church had 'to institute an external significant sign'. The King and the bishops claimed antiquity and respectability on behalf of the cross in baptism, and asserted that now under protestantism it was free from contamination by popery and superstition.[10] The Elizabethan use survived, with support from the new church canons, but conformity would be hard to maintain.

The *Constitutions and Canons Ecclesiastical* of 1604 are, for the most part, pithy restatements of Elizabethan church practice. But the thirtieth canon, the lengthiest of them all, stands apart as topical and argumentative. The canon tackles the cross in baptism and insists on its unquestioned use.

We are sorry that his majesty's most princely care and pains taken in the conference at Hampton Court, amongst many points, touching this one of the cross in baptism, hath taken no better effect with many, but that still the use of it in baptism is so greatly stuck at and impugned. For the further declaration therefore of the true use of this ceremony, and for the removing of all such scruple . . . we do commend to all the true members of the Church of England these our directions and observations.

Here was an uncompromising call for 'true use' by 'true members', which made liturgical precision a touchstone of conformity. The canon then reviewed the origins and history of the sign of the cross and the 'cautions and exceptions against all popish superstition and error' in its employment. As soon as the minister applied water and said the words, 'I baptize thee', the text explained, the infant was 'fully and perfectly baptized. So as the sign of the cross being afterwards used, does neither add any thing to the virtue and perfection of baptism, nor being omitted doth detract any thing from the effect and substance of it.' Furthermore, the infant was 'received into the congregation of Christ's flock, as a perfect member thereof' by virtue of baptism, 'and not by any power ascribed unto the sign of the cross'.[11]

That being so, one is inclined to ask what all the fuss was about, and why making the sign of the cross could not be left to ministerial discretion. (This is what Knewstub and his puritan colleagues requested at Hampton Court.) The answer was that, though a thing 'indifferent', it was none the less 'prescribed by public authority'. The same was true of kneeling, bowing, and other liturgical gestures, of veils to be worn at churchings and rings to be exchanged in marriages. 'Things of themselves indifferent do in some sort alter their natures when they are commanded or forbidden by a lawful magistrate; and may not be omitted at every man's pleasure, contrary to the law, when they be commanded, nor used when they are prohibited.'[12] What counted in the end was not theology but power. A liturgical gesture of dubious value was maintained as a test of conformity, a hallmark of ecclesiastical discipline. The argument may have been conducted in terms of biblical and historical scholarship, but at heart it was a question of power.

Nonconformists remained unimpressed. Some continued to omit the sign of the cross, or used it intermittently; others kept up the argument in print. For William Bradshaw, writing from Amsterdam, there was nothing harmless or indifferent about the cross in baptism, and its use should 'be crossed out or cursed out of our liturgy'. Presbyterians, presumably, would have preferred the Scottish rite for 'the order of baptism', which required the minister to lay water upon the child's forehead, without making any sign of the cross.[13] Neither the Hampton Court Conference nor the new ecclesiastical canons closed the subject, but they did enable bishops to press harder for uniformity of practice. Approximately 150 ministers refused to subscribe that the prayer book contained 'nothing contrary to the word of God', and some eighty or ninety lost their benefices as a consequence. The *Abridgement* of the Lincolnshire ministers' petition of 1605, reprinted in 1617 and 1638, became a classic formulation of moderate puritan grievances against the Book of Common Prayer.[14]

A new book entitled *A Scholasticall Discourse Against Symbolizing with Anti-Christ in Ceremonies: Especially in the Signe of the Crosse* appeared in 1607. This handsome folio carried no imprint, no name of printer, author, or place of publication, but it is known to be the work of the radical puritan Robert Parker and was apparently printed in Amsterdam. The high quality of its production suggests that the *Scholasticall Discourse* was directed to a courtly, episcopal, or collegiate audience, while its studied anonymity indicates the sensitivity of its subject-matter. Parker argued at great length that the sign of the cross was 'a part of the devil's worship, a character to effect things supernatural and devilish miracles, an instrument of witchcraft, an enchanting rod, a magical sign', and an utterly intolerable 'idolatry against God'. It was worse than other images, of the kind already removed from most English churches, because it was more subtle and deleterious in its effects. 'The aerial cross is worse than another image . . . because the intelligible and contemplative credit, which the sign of the cross hath gotten, striketh deeper than the sensible corpulency of a common image, and more decayeth more sorts of men.'[15]

The separatist John Canne went further, blasting the sign of the cross as 'the mark of the beast, a juggler's gesture, a magical instrument, a rite and badge of the devil, a harlot which stirreth up to popish lust'. As an action that had been 'idolatrously used in popery', the cross in baptism should be 'scandalous and offensive to good Christians'.[16] Such charges were completely untrue in so far as they applied to the official beliefs and practices of the Church of England. But they may have hit home with regard to popular beliefs in the quasi-magical efficacy of the external elements of baptism. The heated language and lurid imagery reflects the polemical intensity of this debate. Though George Herbert's country parson 'willingly and cheerfully crosseth the child, and thinketh the ceremony not only innocent but reverend', a good number of his brethren thought otherwise.[17]

Apologists for the Church of England were keen to answer puritan objections to the retention of the sign of the cross. Hooker's work provided useful answers, and variations were readily forthcoming. Thomas Sparke, a conformist of broad sympathies, wrote *A Brotherly Perswasion to Vnitie* in 1607, in which he attempted to settle puritan anxieties about the cross. Its use in baptism, he argued, though none the less a man-made thing, was 'far ancienter than antichristian popery'. Its purpose, he reminded everyone, was as 'an admonitory sign' or token, 'an honourable badge of our Christian profession'. Sparke agreed that some writers 'attribute too much unto it', and he recognized the danger of superstitious usage, 'making it a sign of itself not only significative, but also operative and effective of wonderful things'. But the thirtieth canon, to Sparke's satisfaction, explained its proper usage as 'a lawful outward ceremony'. Though not essential to the sacrament (witness the validity of private baptisms performed without it) the sign of the cross retained a proper place in the public rituals of the Church of England. Thomas Morton, in a treatise dedicated to the Marquis of Buckingham, likewise asserted in 1618 that the sign of the cross was 'only a token of protestation between particular men, the members of the church of Christ . . . The cross in the forehead is only a sign of man's constant profession of Christianity.' Its use, he insisted, was devout, not superstitious.[18]

John Burges, whose *Answer Reioyned* of 1631 so pleased the government that it was 'published by his majesty's special command', took pains to distinguish the lawful practice of the Church of England from the 'superstitious conceits' of Rome. 'With us,' Burges explained, 'the minister . . . may not cross himself, or the people, or font, water, communion table or cups, or the bread and wine, or any other of God's ordinances, all of which in popery the priest is bound to do for their consecration.' The English church allowed none of the promiscuous crossing or notorious abuse of oils and other substances that contaminated Roman Catholic services. 'With us,' Burges continued, 'the minister may not cross [the child] before baptism on the forehead, breast, or any part, which in popery the priest must do to drive away the devil . . . After baptism, the minister of Christ's baptism with us may not cross the child with oil or chrism, or without on the crown, as in popery is required.' In sum, the baptismal cross was neither 'operative upon the child, or necessary at all to the efficacy of the Lord's sacrament'. It was, rather, 'an outward badge and ceremonial cognizance of the constant profession of Christ crucified, which belongs to all Christians'.[19]

Every issue raised by the learned controversialists had its counterpart in the stirs and frictions of parish life. Fundamental concerns about the meaning and efficacy of baptism became points of contention among clergy and laity. Matters of conformity set neighbour against neighbour, churchwardens against ministers. It would be wrong to imagine that every community was energized by religious controversy, or that there were frequent collisions; but problems of theological interpretation and ecclesiastical discipline were never confined to the Convocation and the universities, and could arise at any time. While scholars argued over the history and theology of baptism, parish clergy had the routine responsibility of performing and interpreting the sacraments, and parents had the duty to bring forth their children to the font. From time to time a few of them fell into neglect or error, or encountered gradations of resistance from neighbours. The records of such incidents, disputes, and deviations indicate what was supposed to happen as well as what sometimes went wrong.

Episcopal visitors checked on the use of the cross in baptism as a standard test of clerical conformity. Bishop Cotton of Exeter, for example, asked in 1599 whether each minister 'doth reverently say service and minister the sacraments according to the Book of Common Prayers, without any alteration thereof, and namely, use the ring in marriage and the cross in baptism'. Jacobean bishops commonly enquired about conformity to 'the rites and ceremonies appointed by the laws now in force, and particularly the cross in baptism'. John Cosin was characteristically rigorous in his Yorkshire archdeaconry in 1627, demanding of each minister, 'doth he not only sometimes, or commonly, use the sign of the cross, but doth he always use it, and never omit the use of it, making the sign of the cross upon every child's forehead, as is commanded?'[20]

Though never more than a minority, hundreds of Elizabethan and early Stuart churchmen were presented at visitations for omitting the sign of the cross in baptism. Often these same men compounded their offence by failing to wear the surplice while performing the sacrament, or by other marks of nonconformity. Among them were Thomas Larkin of Waltham Parva, Essex, in 1583; Hugh Tuke of Silk Willoughby, Lincolnshire, in 1585; Thomas Clarke of Barnard Castle, Durham, in 1587; William Addister of Gosberton, Lincolnshire, in 1594; John Hill of Great Yarmouth and Robert Jeckles of Ketteringham, Norfolk, in 1597; John Tillney of Holton St Peter, Suffolk, in 1597; Anthony Armitage of Ellington, Huntingdonshire, in 1602; Thomas Harpe of Marbury, Buckinghamshire, in 1603; John Waterhouse of Cuckfield, Sussex, in 1605; Meredith Mady of Blagdon, Somerset, in 1612; Mr Leedes of Holt, Norfolk, in 1627; William Wilson of Heddon, Durham, in 1628; William Brearcliffe of North Cave, Yorkshire, in 1634; Lemuel Tuke of Greasley, Nottinghamshire, in 1638, and many more.[21]

Some of these clerics were outspoken and confrontational puritans, supported by networks of co-religionists in league with notorious offenders; but others were only occasional and contingent offenders, neighbourly and peaceable men who expressed their willingness to conform in the future. The irregularity of some of these 'puritans' was occasional and tentative, rather than wholehearted and deep-rooted; it reminds us that despite the historian's bold definitions, puritanism and clerical nonconformity could be tentative, slippery, and loose-edged. Far from being clear cut, the boundaries between orthodoxy and nonconformity were often permeable and indistinct.

Despite the pressure for conformity it seems clear that compliance was sometimes occasional and discretionary, and that some ministers reshaped the service to their own or their parishioners' consciences. Godly ministers were inclined to 'overskip the cross in baptism, ring in marriage, or any such needless ceremony' if they could get away with it, if they enjoyed sufficient community support, and if their episcopal superiors left them alone.[22] The evidence increasingly suggests that baptismal arrangements involved negotiation between clergy and parishioners, each making allowance for the other's scruples and preferences. Liturgical discipline could be contingent, variable, and adjustable in practice, at least so long as nobody brought it to the attention of more zealous authorities. Scrupulous lay puritans with strong opinions about sacramental practice sought ministers to accommodate them, if not in their own parish then elsewhere. Such people clearly intended to remain within the Church of England, if only the church could be Christianlike and flexible in its discipline. Only when agreement broke down, foundering on unshifting principle, or when a parish priest complained about intrusions upon his monopoly, would matters come to the attention of the courts.

Something of this sort seems to have happened in Norfolk in 1573, when John Allen's child was to be baptized, 'one of the godfathers, in beginning of service time, came to Thomas Gladon requesting him to change the words of the book . . . and to leave out the sign of the cross'. Similarly in Wiltshire in 1588, Thomas Baslyn, a godly layman, 'offered his child to be baptised' by the parish minister, but only if he did it without godparents or the sign of the cross. When the parson refused to administer the sacrament on these irregular conditions, Baslyn arranged for another minister to perform a private baptism 'at his dwelling house . . . in the presence of divers other faithful people'.[23]

Complaints drawing attention to these irregularities brought the offending parties into trouble. John Hawksbury, Ralph Josselin's predecessor as vicar of Earls Colne, Essex, willingly baptized the Harlakenden children without the sign of the cross, at his patron's request, but begged forgiveness and promised conformity when cited at Archbishop Laud's visitation in 1636. Richard

Clayton, the puritan rector of Shawell, Leicestershire, 'omitted the sign of the cross when baptising one of his own children', but, the record suggests, he employed it on other occasions according to his parishioners' requests. Ezekiel Rogers of Rowley, Yorkshire, acknowledged with regard to the cross in baptism, 'that sometimes it hath been used, and sometime omitted'. In 1635 his disregard for ecclesiastical ceremony brought him before the High Commission, and soon after he moved to New England.[24]

It took sharp eyes to determine whether or not the gesture was properly performed. There was an art to confusion and dissembling, and some liturgical actors knew well how to protect themselves from charges of irregularity. A Buckinghamshire minister in 1622, 'having the child in his arms when he should be signed with the cross did a little withdraw himself, but whether of purport or not (the witness) cannot tell, neither did (the official) find any fault with it at that time'. It was in response to actions of this sort that John Selden observed, 'in England of late years I ever thought the parson baptized his own fingers rather than the child'.[25]

The articles against William Brearcliffe in 1634 reveal another level of veiled nonconformity, another way of coping with the disputed cross. The High Commission charged Brearcliffe, vicar of North Cave, Yorkshire, with having

baptized divers children and infants without the sign of the cross; and if at any time you did offer or make the sign of the cross, you never with your fingers touched the child's forehead, but as it were in contempt and dislike thereof you made a show with your fingers to make some such demonstration in the air, never lying your hands upon the forehead of the said children; and . . . thereby have deceived the spectators and persons then present, to the manifest violation of the canons and constitutions and the laws ecclesiastical in that case provided, and the evil example of others.

Brearcliffe's behaviour, almost indistinguishable from full conformity, was apparently acceptable to his parishioners until the authorities decided to throw the book at him for speaking favourably on behalf of William Prynne. His laxity, or his sleight of hand, might have been tolerated a generation earlier, but under Charles I it cost him suspension from his parish.[26]

Without sophistication and goodwill, negotiations between clergy and laity could degenerate into ugly confrontation. Stirred by an unfortunate mixture of obduracy and passion, baptism services were even known to break up in disorder as parishioners attempted to interfere with the ceremony. We have already referred to the disruptions in Gloucestershire in the 1570s when sectarian parents tried to halt the baptism of their children. A lesser drama of this sort occurred at Thetford, Norfolk, around 1595 when Elizabeth, the wife of William Jenkenson, interrupted the minister Robert Browne in his christening of a child of Sir Edwin Ritch. Elizabeth, the churchwardens alleged, would not suffer [the minister] to sign the child with the sign of the cross, but pulled the cloth over the face thereof; and the same being again by the said Mr. Browne taken off the face of the child, and offering to sign the same again with the sign of the cross, she again covered the face of the child, and would not suffer him to do it, thereby giving great offence to many those inhabitants of Thetford then and there present.

Elizabeth Jenkenson seems actually to have been holding the baby during this altercation, but it is not clear whether she was godmother, midwife, or nurse.[27]

A few years later in 1597 Elizabeth Cantrell of Norwich was excommunicated, 'for that she, having a child at baptism, turned away with the child, whereby the minister could not sign it with the sign of the cross'. Likewise Mrs Aris of Chesham, Buckinghamshire, 'did offend in withdrawing her child from the cross in baptism' in 1605. Nor was this the worst that could happen. In 1626 or thereabouts (in the words of a Victorian editor) 'the Lady Lawrence, for a gross act of indecency at the font, was recommended to the High Commission; when a child should have been signed in its forehead, she presented its hinder parts', perhaps not in their cleanest state.[28] Scenes like these fuelled the authoritarian ceremonialist nightmare, in which lay irreverence, female disobedience, and nonconformity compounded each other to compromise the sacrament and promote disorder in God's holy house. Repeatedly, in these cases, it was a woman who seized the initiative, disparaging the sacrament and posing a challenge to male and ecclesiastical power.

Oliver Heywood, who grew up to become a leading nonconformist, recalled a similar though more modest altercation at his own baptism at Bolton, Lancashire, in 1630. Again, it was thanks to a woman that 'I had not the vain ceremony of the aerial cross upon my forehead'. Just as the minister was about to say the words 'I baptise thee', etc., 'Mrs. Andrew of Little Leaver being the person that held me stepped back off from the steps, and so prevented my being signed with the cross, she did it purposely to prevent it.' In later years on the anniversary of his baptism, Heywood took to reflecting on this 'providential presage of my proving a nonconformist minister'. He claimed it as a source of satisfaction, 'though I have not the aerial cross of men's devising, yet I had water sprinkled on of divine institution', and this was the model for his own baptismal practice as a dissenting minister in the 1670s.[29]

Disrespect for the sacrament of baptism was not necessarily a matter of principled religious opposition, but could also be attributed to impatience or rough manners. The ceremony was supposed to take place in public, for the mutual advantage of the child and the whole congregation, but not everyone had the patience to sit through it. Parishioners sometimes got up to leave, as they left other parts of worship that did not interest them. Problems between the minister and churchwarden of Preston Parva, Northamptonshire, were exacerbated in 1584 when Peter Hastings 'caused a tumult in the church by prattling and talking during the baptism of Henry Ryght's child'. Similarly David Ap David was presented at Alderbury, Hereford, in 1617 'for disturbing the sacrament of baptism and for jangling and talking in time thereof'. An Essex woman complained in 1623 'that Mr. Sabridge did put her child's neck out of joint when he did christen it, and that he did preach of women's matters things which were not fitting'. A baptism at Kayningham, Yorkshire, became a ruckus in 1633 when four women disturbed the minister, claiming that the child was a bastard and one of the godmothers a whore.[30]

At another Yorkshire baptism in 1663 a women tried to snatch the child from the minister, and her 'violence, incivility and wilful rapture' so upset the ceremony that the child fell into the font. It is not clear from the record whether the woman involved was the midwife or the mother, and whether her action was intended to prevent the baptism or to thwart the signing with the cross. Nor is it clear that the child's baptismal immersion was accidental as the minister made out. The Reverend John Noble told the court that

he would only have easily dipped the face of the said child in the water . . . but in case it did fall into the said water, it was through the violence and wilful rapture of the mother [midwife, crossed out] of the said child then and there present, who snatched at the said child, to have gotten it from the said Mr. Noble, and thereupon betwixt them both the said child casually and accidentally was more than ordinarily dipped into the said water.[31]

In 1664 the churchwardens of All Hallows on the Wall, London, reported that 'a maid servant . . . did make a disturbance at the administration of the sacrament of baptism, by unseemly or reproachful language touching the same'. Since the court made no record of this language we can only speculate about the nature of her objection.[32]

Elements and Substances

It is important to remember that baptism, while primarily concerned with initiation and redemption, with the making of Christians and the lifting of sin, was also a matter of solids and liquids, equipment and substances, requiring the ritual handling of water and the upkeep and re-edification of fonts. Theology led to liturgy, and liturgy needed equipment. In the following section I wish to direct attention to the material circumstances of baptism, the substantial accoutrements of the sacrament, and the physical setting of the ceremony. All were contested, and all contributed to the continuing cultural discourse between community and church.

Traditional catholic baptism involved the ritual application of a variety of sanctified substances. Each was reverently applied and devoutly explained in the various missals and rationales. When the priest put hallowed salt into the mouth of the infant at baptism it was 'to signify the spiritual salt, which is the word of God, wherewith he should be seasoned and powdered that thereby the filthy savour of stinking sin should be taken away'. The child was like rancid meat being prepared for God's table. When the minister 'wetteth with spittle the nose thurles [nostrils] and ears of him that shall be baptised' it was 'to put us in remembrance of the miracle of the deaf and dumb wrought by Christ who looking up into heaven put his spittle with his fingers into the ears and touching his tongue said *Ephphatha,* that is to say, be opened'. The holy oil or unction applied to the child's breast and shoulders 'signifieth that our heart and affections should be wholly dedicated to Christ and . . . that we should be steadfast, stout and strong to bear the yoke of our lord'. The holy chrism (a mixture of oil and balm) applied after baptism signified anointment 'with the spiritual unction of the Holy Ghost', and so on.[33]

Protestants rejected these substances and accoutrements, as well as most of their accompanying words and actions. A remarkable reminiscence from the sixteenth century indicates how conscientious some godly parents could be in this regard. Rose Hickman, wife of an Edwardian protestant merchant, faced a serious dilemma after her child was born in Oxfordshire during Mary's reign. Should she suffer her child 'to be baptised after the papist manner', or could she lawfully save it from contamination by superstitious substances and practices? Writing her autobiography half a lifetime later from the safe vantage point of established Elizabethan protestantism, Mrs Hickman (by this time remarried as Mrs Throckmorton) explained that she posed this question to the protestant Bishops Cranmer, Latimer, and Ridley, then in prison at Oxford,

who answered me that the sacrament of baptism, as it was used by the papists, was the least corrupted, and therefore I might. But therewithall they said that I might have been gone out of England before that time if I had done well. And so my child was there baptised by a popish priest; but because I would avoid the popish stuff as much as I could, I did not put salt into the handkerchief that was to be delivered to the priest at the baptism, but put sugar in it instead of salt.

This is an extraordinary account of a quasi-magical or anti-magical subterfuge undertaken in the interest of protestant purity. Through the mother's scrupulous ingenuity, the popish priest's superstitious salt was countered by the innocuous sugar, the popish ritual mitigated by a secret substitution of substances. This was a story to relate with pride in later years, and perhaps to embroider; it was the stuff of family legend.[34] The story compares well to that of the Marian martyr, Thomas Hawkes, who rejected the 'oil, cream, salt, spittle, candle, and conjuring of water', and 'would not suffer [his son] to be baptised after the papistical manner' despite being warned by the archdeacon of London that both he and his son would be damned if the child died unchristened.[35]

The horror that some Elizabethan protestants expressed at the miscellaneous substances contaminating the Roman practice of baptism was akin to their aversion to popish images and superstitious gestures. This distaste was modified, or perhaps sharpened, by the realization that most of them, including their rulers, had themselves been subjected to the popish ceremony. Queen Elizabeth and King James had both experienced the catholic form of baptism, though James's protective mother would not let her 'pocky' priest spit in his mouth.[36] The reformer James Calfhill, writing in the 1560s, likened the old priests who consecrated 'crosses and ashes, water and salt, oil and cream, boughs and bones, sticks and stones . . . to the vilest witches and sorcerers of the earth'. The catholics, he charged, 'not sticking to the ceremonies of the received fathers, have chosen rather, of their own fantastical and idle brain, to use crossing and conjuring, begreasing and bespewing of the poor infants' in baptism. They had corrupted the service with 'conjuration, consecration, or insufflation', and the introduction of honey, milk, wine, oil, salt, spittle, and tapers.[37]

Most Elizabethans were freed from worrying about such details. Apologists for the reformed church, Calfhill among them, prided themselves on achieving a purity of liturgical practice not known since the time of the early Christians. Through their reformation they claimed to have stripped away the many corruptions introduced into worship during the long ascendancy of Rome. The new common prayer book 'alloweth neither spattle nor salt, cream nor yet stinking oil, with other pilled peltries of the pope', asserted the acerbic John Bale. Each of these alien substances was removed by 1552. 'In baptism,' wrote Elizabeth's first bishop of Durham, James Pilkington, 'we follow Christ Jesus his apostles, Austin and Pauline, whom Pope Gregory sent into England, in the chief points; which all christened in unconjured water, without salt, spitting, oil, and chrism, etc.' Popish 'blowing, censing, salting, spitting, oil and cream' were emphatically banished, although the retention of fonts and the sign of the cross convinced some forward protestants that their church was still insufficiently reformed.[38]

Traditional catholic practices could not be eliminated overnight, as Arch-

bishop Grindal appreciated in his long battle against the 'relics and monuments of superstition and idolatry'. Grindal's Injunctions for the Province of
York in 1571, repeated in his Articles for Canterbury in 1576, insisted that no
clergyman 'shall use any oil, or chrism, tapers, spattle, or other popish ceremony in the ministration of the sacrament of baptism'. Too many people,
both laity and clerics, still cherished these traditional substances. 'The chrism,
as it is superstitiously called', was still used 'in sundry places' in the Welsh
Diocese of St David's in the 1580s. 'The triple submersion of the infant all
naked, and . . . the devout use of the popish chrism' were among the 'manifold enormities' delaying reform in Lancashire in 1590.[39] Full reformation
was slow to take root in these outlying districts. Even within the progressive
orbit of London, Oxford, and Cambridge, traditional views on the efficacy
of baptism never completely disappeared, and unreformed catholic practices
were never entirely suppressed. Jacobean nonconformists feared that rituals
like the sign of the cross in baptism would 'open a gap to images, oil, lights,
spittle, cream, and all other popish ceremonies', while opponents of the new
ceremonialism of the 1620s and 1630s feared that all manner of discredited
substances were creeping back into favour.[40]

Protestants of the 1620s were again reminded that popish baptism had
been 'depraved and defiled . . . by conjurations, exorcisms, mixtures of salt
and oil, wax candles, extreme unctions, breathings, babies or puppets with a
thousand cruzadoes in the forehead, in the eyes, on the back, on the stomach,
on the shoulders, and at the mouth, and all to drive away devils'. Their service
was contaminated by the use of salt, oil, wax, spittle, drivel, creams, milk,
and honey, all of which contrasted with the alleged purity of the reformed
Church of England. Reiteration of distinctions like these was important to
the forming of firm protestant identity.[41] The puritan William Gouge stressed
that water was 'the only element sanctified to this purpose' in the baptism
service of the Church of England, at which point an early owner of the 1634
edition of *Of Domesticall Duties* added emphatically in the margin, 'no salt'.[42]
It would not be extreme to suggest that anxiety about material substances,
along with friction over fonts and associated liturgical practices in the reign
of Charles I, contributed to the cultural and religious tensions that sparked
the Civil Wars.

Even after a century of protestant practice the concern for elements and
substances would not go away. The great presbyterian divine Richard Baxter
considered the question whether one may lawfully 'offer his child to be baptised with the sign of the cross, or the use of chrism, the white garment, milk
and honey, or exorcism?' This was a curious combination for consideration
in the 1670s, for most of these ancient practices had long been abandoned in

England, and only the sign of the cross was retained. Roman Catholic baptisms were necessarily private, and few people would have seen the ritual uses of chrism, cream, or exorcism; but memory, history, travel, and revived catholic fortunes kept the nightmare of popery alive. Samuel Pepys, a guest at a catholic baptism in 1666, found the unfamiliar Roman practices strange.[43]

Baxter's question catered to scrupulous Christians who found all popish remnants offensive, who yet wished to abide peacefully with their neighbours in the ritualistic Church of England. What should such a Christian do if no other form of baptism was available than that set forth by law in the Book of Common Prayer? Baxter's answer was typically reasonable and accommodating. These 'ceremonial accidents', he explained, were of ancient and uncertain origin; though certainly prone to abuse, their inclusion was not necessarily sinful. His counsel to the Restoration godly was not unlike that of the Marian martyrs to Mrs Hickman: better to have baptism with excess ceremony than no baptism at all. And in this as so many aspects of post-Restoration parish life, Baxter counselled, 'being peremptorily commanded, I cannot prove it unlawful to obey'.[44] As in the 1550s, so in the 1620s and again in the 1670s, liturgical issues which hinged on the mystical and sacred were resolved in terms of performance, equipment, and discipline. Accommodation was always possible, though the ghost of conflict hung in the air.

Dipping and Sprinkling

There was much less dispute about the use of water in baptism, for that at least seemed to rest on secure scriptural foundations. Special prayers in the baptism service recalled God's use of water with Noah's flood, the Red Sea, and the sanctified waters of Jordan. Water was especially suitable for this sacrament, thought the Jacobean preacher John Day, for this was 'the element wherein [God's] wrath was once declared, whenas he drowned the whole world'. Now, 'what will he work for our sakes, who can turn the sea itself into dry land?'[45] Most English protestants could agree with William Perkins that 'the external and visible matter of baptism is water, for the minister may not baptise with any other liquor, but only with natural water'. No other liquor washed so clean as water, observed the Caroline divine Thomas Bedford, 'and therefore none other so fit to signify the blood of Christ, which cleanseth the soul from all sin'. Water also symbolically cleansed the blood of childbirth, the sanguine impurities that troubled divines like Sampson Price and John Donne.[46]

Given room for disagreement, however, early modern Englishmen would be sure to find it. Elizabethan administrators sought to prevent the use of 'rose water or damask water, or water made of any confection or mixture' from contaminating private baptisms. The bishop of Norwich's enquiry in 1638, whether anyone used 'rose water or other liquor than pure, mere water from the well' for the sacrament of baptism, implied that deviant practices were still to be found.[47] At the other extreme some sectarians of the Civil-War period went so far as to argue 'that John's baptism which was by water did end at the coming of Christ, and that there is no baptism by water instituted by Christ'. The Lancashire catholic William Blundell was shocked to learn in 1665 that Quakers 'did not use baptism by water at all', although dry baptism was rarer than complete abnegation of the sacrament.[48]

How much water should the minister use, and how should he apply it? Even this simple question could open wounds and spark contention. In the old catholic liturgy the priest dipped the child three times, with its face to the north, to the south, and towards the water, and this practice was reintroduced during Mary's reign after the brief experiment of the second Edwardian Book of Common Prayer. Liturgical discipline turned on such matters as language, timing, action, and the application of material substances during the central rituals of Christian life. As a leader of the Marian counter-reformation, Bishop Bonner sought to restore the traditional manner of trine (triple) immersion that had so recently been subverted. Were there any in the diocese, he asked in 1554, 'that will not suffer the priest to dip the child three times in the font, being yet strong, and able to abide and suffer it . . . but will needs have the child in the clothes, and only to be sprinkled with a few drops of water?'[49] In the interest of purity and simplicity English protestants eschewed this 'thrice dipping' of popish baptism and sought to punish it if it occurred. The 1559 Book of Common Prayer, like that of 1552, required the priest to dip the child in water, 'so it be discreetly and warily done', but immediately offered an alternative, 'if the child be weak, it shall suffice to pour water upon it'.[50]

To William Perkins it mattered little how the infant received the water, whether by sprinkling or dipping, so long as it signified 'the outward sign of washing'. The difference was that in dipping the child was put to the water, whereas with sprinkling the water was applied to the child. Dipping or immersion required a font, whereas sprinkling could be achieved with a smaller and more portable basin. Most ministers followed their preference, or did what was pleasing to their parishioners, but in this aspect of the ceremony too there was room for controversy. Conformists stuck to their fonts and were generally more disciplined about dipping. Puritans favoured sprinkling and were more likely to use basins. Some ceremonialists of the 1630s reverted to thrice-dipping, asserting, with Thomas Bedford, that 'the number . . . is held indifferent'.[51] Immersion, affusion, and aspersion all had their partisans, though fortunately, for the most part, the church treated this as a matter of theological indifference.

The Jacobean puritan William Gouge thought that the most that was required of the water was a moderate sprinkling. The child came not for a bath but for baptism. 'The party to be baptised is not brought to the font to have his face or any part of his body made clean, but to have assurance of the inward cleansing of his soul.' Rather, 'the proper rite be used if applying the water to the body of the child, so at least the face of the child may be sprinkled therewith'.[52] An associated concern was that applying cold water in a draughty church might be unhealthful for newborn infants. Parents sometimes said as much when explaining their delay in bringing their children to baptism. The Restoration ceremonialist Mark Frank countered this excuse, claiming 'the child will get no cold by the way it goes to God. Our niceness makes the trouble, and betrays us to the fear. The child gets no hurt by being carried to the font; nor did it in devouter times when it was wholly dipped.' Another Restoration churchman, Anthony Sparrow, the explicator of Anglican common prayer, referred to 'dipping or sprinkling . . . either of which is sufficient', while his colleague Thomas Comber remarked that 'it is not a matter worth contending for', for 'divine grace is not measured by the quantity of water'.[53]

Water was pure and proper, especially without admixtures of chrism or other oil, but promiscuous sprinkling with holy water could be too much of a good thing. High ceremonialists like Lancelot Andrewes, one of James I's favorite bishops, allowed that sprinkling holy water on the congregation 'for remembrance of their baptism' was permissible as 'a moral ceremony'. If that was true, worried William Ames, the door lay open to the return of popish ceremonies of the sort already seen at Durham; it might then be a short step to the reintroduction of 'chrism, salt, candles, exorcisms, ephata, and the consecration of the water, so well as the cross' and the rest of the ritual apparatus of Rome.[54] The immediate problem, from the point of view of zealous protestants, was not so much that these abominations were actually used, but rather that the official episcopal position against them was insufficiently robust and emphatic. Even ground that was cleared had fertile soil for the tares and briars of superstition.[55]

Fonts and Basins

Clashes of style, belief, and devotional practice, which often turned on vestments, gestures, altar rails, or the liturgical calendar, also embraced the material equipment of baptism. Problems arose about the location, decoration, maintenance, and deployment of fonts, which were cherished and neglected, reedified and abused, removed and relocated at various times between the 1550s and the 1680s. Disagreements about such apparently trivial matters as fixtures and fittings point to serious struggles for control of the faith and control of the parish. Church furnishings, clearly, were neither neutral nor innocuous, but were significant items in an unfinished argument about religious culture and ritual.

Like the eucharistic sacrament at the communion table or altar (another highly contentious area), the baptismal sacrament had its special architectural setting.[56] In most churches the font sat toward the west end, nearer to the south door than the altar, though other locations were possible. Usually the font commanded a clear space with room for people to stand around, a step for the officiating minister, and stools or benches for the baptismal party. The seats or pews that the congregation used for their other services would be separate from the baptismal area, facing in the opposite direction, although some fonts were moved to accommodate changing liturgical preferences.

As far as John Whitgift was concerned, the font could be found as well 'in the midst of the church' as in 'the nethermost part', and its precise location mattered little so long as it was orderly and convenient.[57] But for some of his successors the location, condition, and use of the font became topics of sharp contention. Like parish plate, surplices, and other liturgical accoutrements, fonts were easy to enquire after, and could be used as a yardstick of ceremonial order. Radical puritans tried to dispense with fonts altogether, while high ceremonialists reverenced them to the point of superstition. As with the sign of the cross, so with baptismal equipment, it was the achievement of authoritarian ceremonialists to convert adiaphora into key tests of discipline.

Traditional catholic worship, laid out in the Sarum Missal, included a ritual hallowing of the font, though strictly it was not the masonry but the water that was consecrated. The priest divided the water three times in the form of a cross, cast water from the font in four directions, breathed three times into the font in the form of a cross, dripped a cross formation of wax into it from a candle, stirred the water with the candle in the form of a cross, and further sanctified the font before baptism by the infusion of oil and chrism. It was no wonder that protestants regarded this as spell-making or conjuring, and that radicals sought to do away with fonts altogether as objects that were hopelessly contaminated.[58]

Both traditionalists and mainstream reformers of the mid-Tudor period sought to maintain the salubrity of the font. The protestant Nicholas Ridley enquired at his visitation of the diocese of London in 1550 'whether the water in the font be changed every month once'. His catholic successor, Edmund Bonner, asked similarly whether the water was changed monthly, 'according

to the old custom of the church'.[59] There agreement ended. One man's sanctification was another man's pollution. It was one thing to maintain the
equipment, another to use it properly in liturgical practice. For protestants
there would be no more hallowing of the font, no special devotions at the
font on Easter eve; yet the font would continue as essential equipment in the
critical sacrament of baptism.

Archbishop Matthew Parker had the difficult task at the beginning of Elizabeth's reign of advancing English protestantism against traditional beliefs
and practices, while also restraining those activists who wished to take the
Reformation further. Against the one he opposed the popish hallowing of
fonts, against the other he ordered 'that the font be not removed'. Parker's
'Advertisements' of 1564 gave clear notice to ministers who baptized from
basins instead of fonts that such practices would no longer be tolerated,
while instructing all parishes to keep their fonts in good repair.[60]

The puritan objection to fonts was that they were man-made implements,
a popish invention, and an inducement to superstition. Their customary location at the western end of the church separated the service of baptism from
the rest of Christian worship. It was hard to edify the congregation and remind
those present of their own baptismal vows if the people were detached from
the action and facing the other way. This architectural problem could be
overcome by applying the water of baptism from a portable basin, and by
conducting the ceremony at the communion table rather than at the ancient
accustomed place. Presbyterians preferred to have baptisms performed 'in the
face of the congregation, where the people may most conveniently see and
hear, and not in the places where fonts in the time of popery were unfitly and
superstitiously placed'. But they were not able to advance this as national policy
until the adoption of the Directory of Public Worship in the aftermath of the
Civil War.[61]

According to the Elizabethan separatist Henry Barrow, the 'conjured font'
retained by the Church of England was 'an abomination . . . an idolatrous,
popish, enchanted hallowed relic'. A bucket or basin would do just at well,
anything that held water, for the font 'is not an instrument of any more necessity or use . . . than any other clean and decent vessel'.[62] Ecclesiastical authorities learned to look for basins as material clues to the disorderly practices of
puritans.

An argument broke out in the parish church of Wolsingham, Durham, in
1570 as to who should christen a child of John Bierlay. The new minister,
Richard Rawling, 'standing at the communion table there ready to christen
the child', no doubt equipped with a portable basin, faced the old priest,
John Peirt, who may have positioned himself at the font and who seems to

have been the parents' preference. We can picture the factions facing each other at opposite ends of the church in a dispute that began over impropriations, but was articulated through liturgical practice and equipment and carried over into performance of the sacrament.[63]

In another serious confrontation at Cirencester, Gloucestershire, in 1574, the sectarian Elizabeth Whiting 'saith she will not have her child christened in the font, for that it is a superstition and not agreeable to God's word, and for that it was devised by Pope Pius'. Her husband, William Whiting, was more forthright and 'called the font, the which he misliked of, a trow, and said . . . it was wicked and abominable'. A 'trow', in West of England dialect, was a watering trough for cattle; the word also referred to a worthless discarded trifle. Alarmed by such 'disobedience and breach of order', the authorities committed both husband and wife to the castle gaol.[64]

The condition and use of baptismal equipment became a standard item of enquiry in Elizabethan visitation articles. The font became another touchstone for evaluating orthodoxy. Richard Barnes's Injunctions for the diocese of Durham in 1577, for example, required every church to have a 'decent baptistery or font'. Archbishop Whitgift asked in the deanery of Shoreham in 1597, 'whether you have a large and decent font, being no basin or bowldish, wherein to baptise children; and whether the same be sweet and clean kept; and whether your minister doth baptise therein?' Bishop William Chaderton demanded of the Diocese of Lincoln in 1598, 'whether your font be sweetly kept and renewed from time to time with clean and fresh water, and whether any minister leaving the use of the font do christen or baptise in any basins or other profane vessels?'[65] Questions like these invited the local authorities to present suspected offenders.

Visitation returns reveal the variety of practices uncovered and the excuses that were offered to explain irregularities. At Boughton Munchelsea, Kent, in 1573 the visitors noted the relatively minor problem that 'their font lacketh a good covering', but at Hothfield they encountered a nonconformist minister who 'doth use to minister the sacrament of baptism in basins'. At Whitstable in 1591 they learnt that John Halfnoth, while serving as churchwarden, had 'plucked down . . . our font made of stone and lead, very comely and handsome, and instead thereof hath placed a worse made of a piece of wood or timber or joiner's work, and also a basin in it, which also our minister misliketh'. Halfnoth, in his defence, told the court that he dismantled the old font because it was

broke in the bottom, both in the lead and stone work, and stood very unfitly and unseemly in the church there, not being used for the administrations of the sacrament of baptism by the space of twenty years together; and instead thereof he set up a new one in the church, with the consent of the parishioners, much better and more convenient than the other, being of wainscot and covered decently, but he said that the water therein is held in a basin.[66]

Without more information it is hard to tell whether this report simply reflects unhappiness about the remodelling of parish equipment, whether it was connected to a continuing dispute between clergy and laity over management of the parish, or whether it was symptomatic of the struggle between puritans and conformists for control of the liturgical practice of the Church of England. The care with which Halfnoth's testimony was collected is indicative of the sensitivity of the topic.

In 1597, in the course of a similar visitation, the bishop of Norwich discovered that 'a basin is set into the font in the time of baptism, being a profane vessel and used in baptism', in the parish of St George Colgate. He also found that Robert Selby, the minister of Bedfield, Suffolk, 'did baptise a child in a basin, the basin standing in the font'. Selby replied that he did it, 'not knowing anything in the Book of Common Prayer to the contrary'. And indeed, strictly speaking, he was right; the baptismal service required participants to be 'ready at the font' for the dipping or sprinkling, but it did not expressly rule out basins. At Sudbourne, Suffolk, the bishop discovered, 'at the time of baptising of children a porringer or basin is set in the font, and the child is baptised therein'. The rector, Thomas Agas, answered 'that the font is broke and will not hold water'. But knowing that Agas was also cited for omitting the surplice, it seems likely that the dilapidation of church fabric (for which, in any case, he was partly responsible) was a cover for puritan scruples. John Sagar of Trimley St Mary, Suffolk, made a like reply to a similar charge in the 1597 visitation, but added subsequently that 'the said font is amended and the basin forborne'.[67]

The ecclesiastical canons of 1604 specified that 'there shall be a font of stone in every church and chapel where baptism is to be ministered; the same to be set in the ancient usual places: in which only font the minister shall baptise publicly'.[68] (Significantly, the canon specifies places, not place.) This was a restatement of pre-existing orthodoxy, but also a reproof to nonconformists who favoured baptismal basins. Seeking conformity to these new canons, seventeenth-century bishops frequently asked whether every parish had a 'font of stone for baptism, set in the ancient usual place', and 'does your minister baptise any children in any basin or other vessel than in the ordinary font, being placed in the church according to the 81st canon, or doth use to put any basin in it?' Officials who were sympathetic to the godly would not press the matter, but others went further and demanded that the font be 'decently covered and cleanly kept' so that baptisms could be conducted with maximum decorum.[69]

With the rise of religious ceremonialism in the 1620s, parishioners were urged once again to recognize the sanctity of fonts, to plug their leaks and clean their stonework, and to beautify them with appropriate ornamentation. Medieval font covers, last refurbished during Mary's reign, were repaired and regilded in the 1620s and 1630s, and some fonts were clad in elaborate painted panelling. It was fully in keeping with the new ceremonial style that 'a decent and comely cover' be ordered for the font at Castle Donnington in Leicestershire in 1633; that 'a fit covering for the font' as well as 'a fit carpet for the communion table' should be required for the peculiar of Tredington within the Diocese of Worcester in 1634; that the font should be railed as well as the altar at Edington, Wiltshire, in 1635; and that the font be 'set upright and a new cover provided' at Adstock in Buckinghamshire in 1637. The archdeacon of Nottingham similarly insisted in 1638 on font covers that were 'decent' and 'convenient'.[70] Font covers, like altar cloths and pulpit coverings, were nowhere required by rubric or canon, but they featured increasingly in the ceremonialist drive for the beauty of holiness. They also served the practical function of keeping debris from defiling the sacramental water while adding to the ornamentation and honour of God's house. The cost of this refurbishment was borne by parish funds (and usually recorded in churchwardens' account books) so the ceremonialist focus on liturgical equipment had economic as well as religious implications.[71]

Several churches in Norwich were equipped with new font covers after an archdeacon's visitation in 1622. A report on the church of St John Maddermarket in that year shows the interweaving of material conditions and liturgical practice. 'The font standeth undecently and very unfittingly, so that at the administration of the sacrament of baptism the parishioners have no sight thereof.' The churchwardens were ordered to 'remove it from the place where it stands, and to place it in the lower end of the middle aisle toward the west, in decent and comely manner according to the custom of the Church of England'. The font at Great St Mary's church, Cambridge, was one of many that was reconstructed, painted, and railed in 1633.[72]

Inspection of the Diocese of Chichester in 1636 found many of the fonts in Sussex churches still not up to standard. At Upmander 'there wanteth a new cover for the font and it wanteth to be whited'. At West Hampnett 'the font will not hold water and they christen in a bucket'. At Whiston 'the font is in decay and will not hold water, so that the minister is forced to baptise in a basin'. Out of 120 parishes examined, twenty-two needed repair or replacement of their font covers, and fourteen needed correction of leaks so that the minister would have no excuse to baptize with a basin. One would undergo relocation. At Eastbourne, the bishop ordered, 'the font is to be removed from the south side of the church where it stands inconveniently and set near to the north door of the church; it will gain room enough for thirty or forty persons to sit and hear divine service and sermons, there being as the font standeth not room enough to receive them all.'[73]

Seeing the substantial stonework and monumental masonry of the ancient fonts in many English churches, it is hard to imagine that they were not forever fixed to the spot or that their condition and use caused controversy. But for a century and more after the adoption of the Book of Common Prayer the font provided the symbolic focus for a range of associated liturgical and theological problems. Physical relocation or refurbishment and competing aesthetic economies could alleviate or exacerbate these concerns. For Caroline ceremonialists in particular the spiritual significance of the font was bound up with its physical location, material condition, and use. At Chesham in Buckinghamshire 'a font was built in the church there near unto the minister's seat, that he might stand in his seat and baptize' without traipsing down to the west end. John Williams, the bishop of Lincoln, had apparently approved this arrangement. But in 1633 the Laudians gained control of the parish and 'caused [the font] to be removed and set it upon the low end of the church', as tradition and discipline required.[74] Though intended to teach respect and devotion, the action exacerbated resentment and suspicion and hardened divisions within the church.

As prebendary of Durham in the late 1620s, John Cosin scandalized traditional godly protestants by moving the cathedral font 'from the ancient usual place in the choir . . . and placed it out of the choir, where divine service is never read'. Cosin's opponent Peter Smart complained that 'they removed the font from place to place, from the east end of the church to the west end, from the north to the south, where lately it stood'. Cosin explained in his defence that 'the font was removed many years before his time from the upper part of the choir, where it was conceived to stand inconveniently, to the lower part of the church, where all fonts used to stand, by the order of the late Dean and Chapter'. The cathedral community was divided, as was much of the country, between innovators whose reforms suggested an accommodation with papism, and traditional protestants who were stung into reaction. It may be significant that Cosin was a quarter-century younger than his principal accuser and was backed by the ascendant Arminian Bishops Howson, Montaigne, and Neile.[75]

The relocation of the font was not the only offence alleged against the Durham ceremonialists, for 'the sacrament of baptism also, they will not suffer it to be administered without an hideous noise of music, both of voices and instruments'. On 7 September 1628, Peter Smart reported, when they baptized a child 'at evening prayer, after the second lesson as the rubric directs', the organ played and the choir sang 'with such a noise that they could not hear one another at the font, to the great offence of many'. John Cosin's enemies furthermore accused him of 'setting up pictures about the new font amongst which was a dove carved, and the four evangelists, and John the Baptist baptising Christ in Jordan', imagery which more austere protestants construed as superstitious.[76]

Beautifully redecorated fonts were a feature of high ceremonial churchmanship, as shown by Cosin's projects in his parish church at Brancepeth, Durham, and at St Botolph's, Cambridge, opposite Peterhouse where he became master in 1635. Clad in ornamental woodwork and decorated with expensive gilding and paint, the Cambridge font was an emblem of ceremonial churchmanship and the 'beauty of holiness'. It also symbolized the ascendancy of a viewpoint on baptism that many mainstream Calvinists abhorred. John Warner, bishop of Rochester, similarly set up an elaborate new font at Canterbury cathedral in 1636, displaying carvings of Christ with children, saints, and angels, and both royal and ecclesiastical arms, and a font cover featuring the figure of a dove. Not surprisingly, this ensemble was among the first to be vandalized by iconoclasts in 1641.[77]

Archbishop Laud's visitation instructions of 1634 insisted that all fonts be restored 'to their ancient place wherever they are removed'. Matthew Wren gave 'particular orders, directions and remembrances' to churches throughout the Diocese of Norwich in 1636, 'that the font at baptism be filled with clean water, and no dishes, pails, nor basins be used in it or instead of it'. His successor Richard Montague demanded to know in 1638 whether the font was 'fixed unto the Lord's freehold, and not moveable . . . near unto a church door, to signify our entrance into God's church by baptism', whether it was decently covered, and whether, heaven forbid, 'some basin, bowl, or bucket filled with water [is] set therein'. John Cosin asked, characteristically, 'when any child is brought to the church to be christened, hath not your minister got the new device to baptise it in a basin, or some other vessel brought from private houses, leaving the ancient use of the font, which is consecrated for that purpose?'[78] Although some puritans regarded the font as an unfortunate relic of popery, to ceremonialists like Cosin and Montague it belonged, with the altar, as the fulcrum of reverence and devotion.

Even redundant fonts deserved reverent treatment as dedicated sacramental equipment. Laudians of the 1630s rescued the font, which had been used as a horse trough, from the decayed chapel of Montsorrell in Leicestershire, and put it into service again. At Royden, Wiltshire, they ordered re-edification of the decayed chapel and restoration of its font stone which had been used for a cheese press.[79] The lavish attention ceremonialists paid to these ancient stones may partially explain the vehemence of the attack on them during the iconoclastic outrage of the 1640s.

THE PEOPLE WITH THE CHILDREN

Parents and Godparents

Baptism was a social activity as well as a sacrament of the church. The ceremony built bonds of neighbourliness, community, and kindred, while also
conveying complex spiritual benefits to the child, the family, and the parish.
Godparents were involved in networks of honour and obligation with other
members of the laity, and their role was only partially regulated by the church.
This chapter considers these social and communal aspects of baptism, some
of which excited religious controversy, and examines the festive activity of
christening feasts that brought this stage of the life cycle to a close.

Mothers had no part to play in the baptism of their children, and fathers
were permitted no more than a shadowy role. The parents' formal obligation
ended when they contacted the minister. Law and custom made it the man's
responsibility to arrange for his child's baptism. He, after all, was the 'principal governor' of the household, according to the Jacobean puritan William
Gouge.

The mother at that time by reason of her travail and delivery is weak, and not in case
to have her head much troubled with many cares; much less able herself to take order
for such weighty matters. Only the husband is to make known to the wife (if she be
not extraordinary weak) what his purpose is concerning the place, time, manner, and
other like circumstances of baptising the child, and to advise with her about the
name, witnesses, and such like points.[1]

Mothers stayed at home, lying in after childbirth, and usually waited the customary month before coming to be churched. The rubric of the 1549 prayer
book instructed godparents to warn the mother that the chrisom cloth, in
which the child was wrapped at baptism, should be returned to the church at
the time of her purification. No such reminder would have been necessary if
the mother herself was presumed to be present. This instruction was removed
after 1552 because chrisom cloths were no longer required, not because mothers
could henceforth attend baptisms.[2]

Of course, there were exceptions and violations. Some mothers delayed
the christening of their children until the time of their churching, or found

some other way to be present at the font. Margaret Barber of Reddisham, Suffolk, 'came to church to give thanks the time her child was christened, and stood by the font when it was christened' in 1597. So too did Jane Minors of Barking, Essex, in the same year. The curate of Funtington, Sussex, cited John Cutfold in 1621 for keeping a child unbaptized 'until his wife goeth unto church; no such thing accustomed to be done in the parish before'. At Chichester, Sussex, in 1625 the authorities learnt: 'Thomas Lampard kept his child unchristened a month after his wife was brought abed, and the child christened and the mother churched both on a day at the month's end.'[3] Neither the baptism nor the churching was invalidated by these irregular arrangements, but they were affronts to ecclesiastical propriety and discipline. These problems of attendance and participation could be overcome by arranging a private baptism, in domestic rather than ecclesiastical space, even in the mother's chamber. As we shall see, such arrangements became increasingly common in the later seventeenth century.

Fathers might witness the sacrament, but they were not permitted to speak. The important spiritual work was done by proxies. The Book of Common Prayer was characteristically vague about the composition of baptismal parties, referring only to 'the godfathers, godmothers, and people with the children'. The twenty-ninth canon of 1604 insisted, 'no parent shall be urged to be present, nor be admitted to answer as godfather for his own child'.[4] Godly ministers encouraged the fathers to take on more responsibility, but offered them no ceremonial role. Richard Greenham, the Elizabethan rector of Dry Drayton, Cambridgeshire, insisted 'that the father should promise privately that he would labour in the child's godly education', even though technically this was the obligation of the godparents or witnesses.[5]

Custom called for two godfathers and a godmother for a boy, two godmothers and a godfather for a girl, but sometimes there might be other combinations. In Stuart England it was irregular, though not unusual, for a child to have two godparents of each sex.[6] A seventeenth-century etiquette book advised, 'at a christening, the midwife, the godfather, the godmother, and the child, and all that are essential to the ceremony, go before'. As the principal participants in the ritual, they were to take precedence, even though 'their conditions be inferior' to others who might be present. Significantly, the parents are not mentioned.[7]

The significance and duty of godparents occupied yet another area of contention, hot in the early Elizabethan period, simmering for a century after, and periodically prone to eruption. The Church of England maintained godparents in both public and private baptism, and most families seemed happy to engage them. Puritan critics repeatedly protested, however, that godmothers and godfathers were another groundless popish invention. In 1560 the minister at St Olave's, Southwark, 'did christen a child without a godfather, and the midwife asked him how he could do it, and he answered her and said it was but a ceremony'. Archdeacon James Calfhill reminded his readers in 1565 that godfathers were invented by Pope Hyginus and, though not necessarily offensive, were not an original component of early Christian practice. In the heroic first age of the church, from which the reformed Church of England drew much inspiration, 'ye shall not lightly read of any gossipping'. John Selden, a generation later, also acknowledged that godparentage was a relic from 'primitive times'.[8] Yet few were inclined to throw over so useful and so venerable an institution.

The authors of the puritan *Admonition* of 1572 predictably repeated that godfathers and godmothers were popish inventions, not part of 'the ancient purity and simplicity' on which England should model its church. It was 'childish and superstitious', these presbyterians argued, for godfathers and godmothers to promise on behalf of the infant that 'which is not in their powers to perform'. Instead of the procedure prescribed in the prayer book, the *Admonition* proposed that infants should be brought to baptism by their parents, by implication both mother and father. Only if the parents were absent 'upon necessary occasions and businesses' (such as recovery from childbearing) should 'some of the congregation' stand in their stead. In an appendix to the *Admonition* this procedure is modified and the mother drops out of sight. Ideally, in this version, 'the father should and might, if conveniently, offer and present his child to be baptized, making an open confession of that faith wherein he would have his child baptised'. This, it went on, was the practice 'in well reformed churches' elsewhere in Europe.[9] John Whitgift, in reply, asserted that scripture said nothing to prohibit godparents, and their usage was lawful, ancient, and appropriate. Local ministers and laity joined in this discussion, arguing among themselves about godparents and sometimes seeking advice from such renowned spiritual arbiters as the martyrolgist John Foxe. Anthony Gilby included the promise by godfathers and godmothers among his 'hundred points of popery yet remaining, which deform the English reformation'.[10]

Just as priests could be called ministers, parsons, pastors, or clergymen, so godparents could be referred to by different terms. The alternative language promoted reformed ideas of their function, and attempted to dissociate them from discredited popish practices. Elizabeth Whiting told a Bristol and Gloucester commission in 1574 that she 'utterly misliked' the words 'godfathers and godmothers' and 'would not have them so termed, but called witnesses or sureties to the baptism'. The learned Richard Greenham referred to baptismal attendants as 'promisers', 'sureties', 'delegates', 'witnesses', and 'assistants', studiously avoiding the word 'godparents'. Others referred to 'sponsors' or 'susceptors', an educated term more commonly used in the later seventeenth century. In popular parlance they were 'gossips'. Thomas Comber's *Brief Discourse Upon the Offices of Baptism and Confirmation*, published in 1675, referred to 'spiritual guardians', 'sureties', 'godfathers and godmothers', 'monitors', 'witnesses', and 'new and spiritual relations', all within one paragraph.[11]

The choice of terminology is indicative of changing religious sensibilities. William Whiteway, the Dorchester bailiff and diarist, referred simply to those who named or stood for his children born in 1621 and 1622; his daughter born in 1624 was attended by her 'godfather' and 'godmothers'; but the people performing those functions at the baptisms of Whiteway's children in 1625, 1628, 1630, and 1633, when he came under the influence of Dorchester's 'godly reformation', were distinctly designated as 'sureties'.[12] The London minister William Gouge made no mention of godparents, only witnesses, in his treatise *Of Domesticall Duties*, and he gave them a minimal role. Even the Book of Common Prayer mentioned 'sureties' at one point (in an address to the godparents), although the baptismal rubric repeatedly referred to 'godfathers and godmothers'.[13] Robert Woodford, the godly steward of Northampton, named 'the witnesses', not godparents, at the baptism of his children in 1637 and 1639, and served himself as a 'witness' at neighbours' baptisms in 1638 and 1640. In one last example, the devout Yorkshirewoman Alice Thornton referred to the 'witnesses' at her children's baptisms in the 1650s, mentioned 'sureties' at a christening in the unsettled spring of 1660, then wrote only of 'godfathers and godmothers' at the baptisms of three more children born after the Restoration in the 1660s.[14] Selective renaming was agreeable to religious inclinations, but it did not resolve the underlying problem of what these godparents, witnesses, or sponsors were for.

The primary business of godparents was to answer on behalf of the child when the minister asked about forsaking the devil and all his works, on the reasonable assumption that the child was too young to answer itself. 'This form of interrogating the godfathers in the name of the child is very ancient and reasonable,' thought Anglican apologists like Anthony Sparrow.[15] But radicals thought it ridiculous. The separatist Henry Barrow sneered at the 'special gossips called and chosen which are godfathers and godmothers' in the Church of England.

What need more witnesses of the matter than the whole congregation? But how wicked and impious is that law of their church which forbiddeth the parents to answer and undertake for the bringing up their own children in the true faith and fear of God, and driveth them to bring popish gossips and sureties, who must both undertake, vow, and answer for their child, that he doth forsake the devil and his works. etc.. What can be more vain, foolish, and ridiculous?[16]

More moderate puritans consulted their consciences but most continued to work within the law. As with the sign of the cross, they were often ready to negotiate a local compromise. Richard Greenham, rector of Dry Drayton, Cambridgeshire, told his followers in the 1580s that the interrogatories in baptism were 'corrupt' but that none the less they should 'say nothing'. William Gouge as rector of the London parish of St Ann, Blackfriars, performed scores of baptisms with the child 'accompanied only with the midwife and three witnesses'; but his preference was for a ceremony that embraced the entire family and congregation. 'It belongeth to parents to give the name to the child,' Gouge maintained.[17]

Seventeenth-century attempts to modify the prayer book in this direction came to nothing. The Millenary Petition of 1603 sought, among other reforms, the abolition of 'interrogatories ministered to infants' at baptism, but the petitioners were disappointed. Nothing came of attempts to broach this matter at the Hampton Court Conference. Only with the Directory of Public Worship, adopted by Parliament in 1645, were godparents abrogated, and even then many families continued to provide them.[18] Presbyterian negotiators at the Savoy Conference in 1661 asked again that parents be permitted to stand as sureties to their own children if they wished, and that the employment of godparents be optional; but Anglican orthodoxy was reasserted with the prayer book of 1662. Once more under William and Mary in 1689 a royal commission entertained serious proposals to permit 'the suretieship of the parents', but again the episcopal hierarchy closed ranks in favour of traditional uniformity.[19]

The established church would brook no change. On godparentage as on so many other matters, the leading bishops sought to guard against superstitious practices while holding the line against unlawful innovations. Archbishop Parker warned his clergy in 1564 against 'charging the parent to be present or absent at the christening of his child, although the parent may be present or absent, but not to answer as godfather to his child'. The canons of 1604 set forth the qualifications of godparents and prohibited them from making 'any other answer or speech, than by the Book of Common Prayer is prescribed in that behalf'.[20] Visitation articles frequently enquired whether any baptisms had taken place 'without godfathers and godmothers', or with irregular numbers or combinations. Lancelot Andrewes's articles for the Diocese of Winchester in 1619 were typical in asking, 'whether hath any parent been urged to be present, or admitted to answer as godfather for his own child, or hath any godfather or godmother made any other answer or speech than is prescribed by the book?'[21] Archdeacon Cosin gave detailed instructions to godparents on their qualifications and duties, and went so far as to require that their names, as well as the names of the parents and children, be entered into the parish register. In his own parish at Brancepeth, Durham, Cosin maintained a model register of this sort in the 1630s, but there was no legal requirement to record the names of godparents, and few other parishes followed suit.[22]

All sorts of things could go wrong. Godparents could be found to be the wrong age, the wrong number, or to say the wrong things; even more serious, they might be omitted altogether by nonconforming fathers who preferred to answer for their children themselves. This problem was particularly acute during the puritan agitation of the late sixteenth century, though minor irregularities of all sorts could be found in every period. Errors and shortcomings, like other problems associated with rituals in the life cycle, expose the desires of ordinary parishioners and illuminate the concerns of the ecclesiastical authorities.

Deficiencies resulted from accidents as well as ignorance or principle. At Frierning, Essex, in 1587 the minister allowed the baptism of a baby boy to proceed with only one godfather, despite his knowledge that it was 'contrary to law', because the father 'was disappointed of the other godfather'. When charged in 1597 with keeping his child unbaptized a month, Edmund Bates of Ingham, Norfolk, explained, 'that he had requested one Richard Bailey, his brother-in-law dwelling in Norwich, to be godfather to his child, who happening to fall sick, he kept his child for him, and not otherwise'. Charged with similar offences in the same visitation, Robert Clerke of Huntingfield, Suffolk, blamed 'the deferring of the baptism' of his son on unavoidable delays by one of the godfathers who was 'earnestly occupied about other urgent business and could not so come'.[23]

Godparents were supposed to be old enough to have taken holy communion, presumably aged at least 16. In exceptional circumstances the curate of Barking, Essex, apparently permitted an under-age child to stand as a godparent in 1579, 'contrary to the queen's majesty's injunctions'. David Smith of Worlingworth, Suffolk, was similarly cited for permitting young teenage godparents in 1597. At Churchstock, Hereford, in 1616 the curate 'admitted Richard Clerke being but thirteen years of age and never received the communion to be godfather of Edward Griffith's child'.[24] Most godfathers and godmothers, however, belonged to the parents' generation, and some were significantly older.

The requirement that godparents be communicants was designed more to ensure their conformity than their maturity. Diligent ministers, if they could not examine the child, could at least examine its sureties for conformity and understanding. But this too could pose problems, if ministers and laity held different notions of religious qualification. The rector of Chignal, Essex, was cited in 1567 'for not examining the godfathers and godmothers prior to baptism'. But a Laudian minister at Oxford in 1640 was alleged to have gone too far the other way when he 'refused one to be godfather to a child that would not bow at the name of Jesus'.[25]

John Tillney, the puritan rector of Holton St Peter, Suffolk, came to the attention of the bishop of Norwich in 1597 because 'he suffereth the father to answer for the child at baptism, and he useth not the sign of the cross'. Mr Byrd of Ipswich offended likewise. A layman, Philip Ward of Banbury, Oxfordshire, was cited in 1605, 'for naming his [own] child at the font'. Similarly, Aaron Ealsmeare of Burstead Magna, Essex, stood godfather to his own child in 1621, 'openly naming his child and answering for it, contrary to the twenty-ninth canon'. The court accepted his explanation 'that by error he did stand, for that Mr. Pease did not tell him to the contrary'.[26] Without better evidence we cannot tell whether this was artless simplicity or veiled puritan nonconformity. Acknowledgement of error was usually more politic than rigid confrontation.

Rather than accepting the Book of Common Prayer without question in this regard, or aligning themselves with puritan objectors, these lay men and women seem to have engaged in an open-minded exploration of appropriate Christian behaviour at times of baptism. This was an important topic for discussion for Lady Margaret Hoby and her pious circle of friends in Yorkshire at the end of the Elizabethan era. On one cold day in March 1600, Lady Margaret records, 'I kept my chamber and had some of my neighbours, with whom I took occasion to speak of divers needful duties to be known: as of parents choosing for their children, of the charge of godfathers, and of the first instituting of them.' A short while later, in May 1600, an opportunity arose to put these theoretical issues to the test.

Mr. Daunie . . . invited me to be a witness at his child's baptising, which I refused, in regard that my conscience was not persuaded of the charge I was to undertake, nor thoroughly taught touching the perverting the end of witnesses from a Christian institution . . . but I will enquire more of this matter, God willing, with the next faithful divine, being loath to deny, if I may, any friend such a courtesy.

And not long afterward she records in her diary a discussion with her husband and Mr Rhodes, the minister, 'touching baptism'. Their ministerial and patriarchal advice evidently overcame Lady Margaret's pious scruples, for

both she and Mr Hoby went on to serve as witnesses or godparents at several
of their kinsfolk's christenings.[27]

The negotiable quality of Anglican ritual is shown once again in the diary
of the Restoration minister Isaac Archer. One of his parishioners at Chippenham, Cambridgeshire, in 1663 'had a child to be baptised but would not
have godfathers, etc. For peace sake, and that the ordinance should not be
omitted, and at his request, I yielded to do it without any sureties but father
and mother . . . This gave much satisfaction to the nonconformists of the
town who were present.'[28] This was a violation of ecclesiastical discipline but
so long as it was not widely publicized it did not draw down the wrath of the
authorities. Archer's compromise would have found approval with many of
his Jacobean predecessors.

The closing words of the baptism service charged godparents to see that
their godchildren were brought up virtuously in Christian life; but this
was an exhortation without teeth. The church had no way to monitor such
commitments. Godparents were often chosen for their relationship to the
parents—as neighbours, patrons, or kin—and many would have died before
the children came of age.

In practice the spiritual aspects of godparentage were easily submerged
beneath social and secular considerations. Many families treated godparentage
as a matter of social respect and esteem, rather than as surety for renunciation of the devil. To stand at the font was as much an honour to the parents
as a favour to the child. Letters and diaries from the literate and privileged
classes reveal the manœuvres and negotiations involved in securing a godparent or in agreeing to be one. Testimony in court cases suggests that similar considerations prevailed among the common sort. Parents were sometimes
willing to delay the ceremony of baptism, risking censure before ecclesiastical
officials, in order to secure a particular sponsor for their child. Far from
showing contempt for the sacrament, they appear to have taken it very seriously, though not necessarily sharing the nuanced theological and liturgical
understandings of the clergy.

Godparentage established or re-established links of fictive kinship and social
and spiritual interest among parties of several generations. The child, the
child's parents, and the men and women entrusted with godparentage were
bound together by obligation, prayer, and ritual, at least for the duration of
the ceremony. In many cases there was nothing fictive about these ties, for
godparents were frequently selected from the pool of consanguinal and affinal
kin. Diaries and letters, especially those of the gentry, demonstrate how godparentage formed part of a matrix of kinship and clientage. Unfortunately
there was no requirement that the names of godparents be entered in parish

registers, and only a few incumbents took it upon themselves to record this information, so a systematic study of font-fellowship connections is almost impossible. It seems likely, however, that common people as well as aristo-crats favoured kinsfolk, if available, to perform this intimate honour. Personal writings also reveal traces of continuing relationships and reciprocal obligations operating between godparents and godchildren, though nothing as formal or binding as has been alleged for late medieval Europe.[29]

At the christening of his daughter Hester in 1615, Sir William Ashcombe noted, 'Sir Peter Temple (was) her godfather, my old lady and my sister Sir John's lady godmothers.' Kinsfolk similarly obliged when the Lancashire squire Nicholas Assheton's daughter Margaret was baptized in 1619; Eleanor Assheton, wife of cousin Assheton of Whalley, 'and my cousin Braddyll's wife Millicent, godmothers', noted the diarist. John Evelyn's grandfather and two other 'near relation(s)' served as godparents at his christening in 1620. More than sixty years later Evelyn recorded his visit to 'my yet living godmother and kins-woman Mrs. Keighly, sister to Sir Thomas Evelyn and niece to my father, being now 86 years of age, a spiritfull woman and in perfect health'. Evelyn himself served as godfather to nieces, nephews, and grandsons, as well as to the chil-dren of neighbours and friends, and his diary reports other baptisms where cousins, aunts, uncles, nephews, nieces, and grandparents filled the office.[30]

It is easy to multiply these examples. When William Whiteway's daughter Mary was baptized at Dorchester in 1621 the godparents were Whiteway's uncle John, his own mother, and his mother-in-law, all kin and all of a senior generation. At another daughter's baptism in 1624 Whiteway's uncle, sister, and cousin did the honours. Samuel Newton, alderman of Cambridge, stood as godfather to a cousin's younger son in 1667. The 'head of the family', Sir William Godolphin, was principal godfather to baby Francis Godolphin in 1678 and the child's aunt was godmother. When John Cannon was christened in Somerset in 1684 his grandfather and another male relation were god-fathers, and his aunt Sarah Walter and Lucia Knowles, also a relation, were godmothers. 'This Mrs. Knowles was forty years before godmother to (John Cannon's) mother, which perhaps was an inducement for her being one of the sureties now,' remarked Cannon in his memoirs.[31]

Serving as a godparent, or securing such services, involved the accumu-lation or expenditure of social credit. Diarists and correspondents acknow-ledged these minor investments of affection and respect. Simon Forman marked his rising position in the 1580s, 'I had great power in making friend-ship, and was bid godfather to a child, and I did prosecute mine enemies in law.' John Evelyn's high social position brought frequent invitations to stand as a godfather. In February 1664 he noted, 'I was godfather to Dr. Breton our vicar's son John, and was the same day sent to be godfather also to Mr. Christopher Wase's son, which I did by proxy.'[32] The extended family circle drew in new allies and friends by these invitations to participate in baptisms.

In January 1669 Sir John Reresby wrote to the Duke of Newcastle to remind him 'of the honour your grace promised me of being a godfather'. The elderly Newcastle had previously told Reresby 'that he hoped to see five generations of my family, that he knew Sir Thomas Reresby very well, and desired to be a godfather to my son, if he lived till one was born to the family'. Reresby's son would be named William, as a mark of respect to his lordship William Cavendish. In 1678 Charles Allestree, vicar of Daventry, Northamptonshire, wrote to a kinswoman, Mrs Rachel Goodwin at Derby, regarding her invitation 'to stand at the font in my representative and to be a godfather' to her son: 'By this act you have not only doubled my relation to your child, and made me both uncle and godfather too, but, by joining me with so worthy a partner [the other godfather Mr Smith, a gentleman of higher rank] have done me an honour which I durst never aspire to.'[33] Honour was furbished, circulated, and displayed in these socio-religious ceremonies.

Busy godparents could even perform their duties by proxy using deputies or stand-ins. Sir William Knollys accepted the post of 'gossip', or godfather, at the baptism of a child of John and Anne Newdigate, but could not spare time from his duties at court. His letter of 1598 assured the family 'how desirous I am in person to perform the office of a godfather mine own heart knoweth . . . but such is my bondage to this place as I have neither liberty to please myself nor satisfy my good friends' expectation'. The remedy lay with a proxy. 'I have entered my brother (Sir Christopher) Blunt to supply my place in making your little one a Christian soul, and give it what name it shall please you.' Thereafter in his letters Knollys addressed Mrs Newdigate as 'fair gossip', an intimate greeting, even though he had not attended her child's baptism. After standing as deputy godfather in place of Archbishop Sheldon, Sir Edward Bagot wrote to him in 1665, 'not only to give you an account . . . of my performance thereof, but also to render my many thanks for the favour you were pleased to do both the families therein'. Samuel Pepys's wife 'was urged to be godmother' at 'Mr. Pierce's wife's child's christening' in 1660, but, Pepys, noted, 'I advised her beforehand not to do it; so she did not, but as a proxy for my Lady Jemimah.'[34]

Families of this elevation were experienced in the niceties of protocol and social balance, and knew that godparents should not be of grossly disproportionate rank. Consciousness of these distinctions seems to have been especially acute after the Restoration. In 1664 Pepys 'was to have been godfather' at the christening of a child of William Griffith, the doorkeeper at the navy office, 'but Sir John Mennes refusing, he wanted an equal for me and my lady Batten and so sought for others'. On another occasion Pepys was invited 'to be godfather' in company with Lady Penn and Lady Batten, 'which I accepted out of complaisance to them'.[35] A demurral based on different principles came from Thomas Brockbank in 1698, responding to a neighbour's request for a 'kindness . . . that you would please to be a witness to our son, which we intend to christen on Thursday next. Your partners will be brother William Wilson and cousin Phillipson's daughter of Hayrigg.' Brockbank excused himself, citing the seriousness of the obligation. 'I have always looked upon the charge that lies upon the godfather to be so great that hitherto I have studiously avoided to take it upon me.' By this time he was an ordained minister, but had not yet settled to a place,

and upon that account not likely to see any children instructed and brought up to Christianity . . . Ere your son be grown up to such discretion as may fit him for the imbibing of the principles of religion and good manners, 'tis probable that I may be removed hence and not in a capacity to the least care over him . . . I do earnestly beg to be excused.[36]

Serving as godparent could be a costly business. Gifts were expected at the time of the christening, not only among the gentry, and a lifetime of obligations could follow. Amongst the élite it was customary for godparents to bestow silver spoons, if they could afford them, plus gilt bowls and silver plate according to their financial resources.[37] Expenses of this sort sometimes show up in diaries and financial accounts. Walter Bagot, for example, ordered silver plate worth between four marks and three pounds to take to the baptism of a new godchild in 1617. Sir Francis Foljambe presented 'a large silver salt' to his godson John Reresby in 1634. Joyce Jeffries, a gentlewoman of Hereford, gave ribbons and silks, silver tankards, bowls, and money to thirteen godchildren between 1638 and 1647 and recorded their values in her books.[38] Samuel Pepys bought silver spoons, plate, and porringers for the godchildren he answered for in the 1660s. Dr Thomas Cartwright, bishop of Chester, paid £3 'for charges at the christening of my cousin Ives's son Thomas Ives, to whom I was godfather', in 1687.[39] Lower down the social scale godparents might bring gifts of food or drink, or decorative accessories or favours.

As might be expected, the strongest ties lay between parents and godparents who had social, familial, and generational links in common; but the very act of standing as surety also established connections that the growing godchild might later exploit. There is no way of telling how strong such links were in ordinary circumstances, especially among the humble and illiterate majority, but letters, diaries, and wills reveal the operation of expectations and obligations among the propertied classes. Visits and correspondence greased the connections. Lady Elizabeth Grey sent 'my most dearest love to my sweetest god-daughter' in a letter of 1611. Walter Edge, a student at Trinity College, Oxford, wrote a Latin letter thanking his godfather for his continuing interest in 1612. Leonard Wheatcroft's 16-year-old son John went 'to Glapwell and Bolsover to see his godfathers and godmothers, where he was born', before moving to London to take up an apprenticeship in 1682. Doubtless the godparents gave him a token of their affection. Thomas Brockbank's godparents were also important family connections and one at least, a gentleman schoolmaster, was in a position to help young Thomas when he was a student at Oxford in 1688. His father wrote to inform him that 'your godfather Mr. Lodge is very richly married'.[40]

Godparents, if properly cultivated, could be called upon to act the part of a kinsman. The dynamics of this relationship are still in need of research, but the available evidence suggests that baptismal ties, though weak, were susceptible to being pulled. Regardless of genealogical connections, godparents belonged to that circle of latent or dormant resources that could be made effective in times of need.[41] Unfortunately, we have no way of telling how many godparents survived to be of service to their godchildren, or how many had the resources to help, even if they were willing.

One of the Bagot letters of 1589 shows a godfather assisting in arrangements for his godson's marriage. Another of 1597 invokes the bond of godparentage to facilitate the execution of a writ of seisin. Leonard Shalcross addressed Richard Bagot, 'Right worshipful, because of your conceived goodwill toward your godson my grandchild I have at this present presumed of your friendly countenance and good favour.'[42] From the petitioner's point of view it was not an unreasonable assumption. Godparents were expected to behave like avuncular benefactors. Minor cash gifts were common. The Devonshire yeoman William Honeywell gave 12d. to his goddaughter in the course of a dinner visit in 1602, and bequeathed £6 to his godson in his will. The Yorkshire yeoman Adam Eyre gave a shilling to his godson in 1648, assisted the boy with his school expenses, and left him £10 in his will. Joyce Jeffries adopted one special goddaughter as a companion, and provided her with a wedding dress, a riding horse, and a portion of £800 when she married. The Sussex lawyer Timothy Burrell paid 10s. for a coat 'for my godson Luxford' when the boy was put in coats in 1699 (a ritual of childhood maturation), and later contributed to his godson's school expenses. When Sir John Reresby's brother-in-law died in 1679 he left 'all the land he had in England' to his godson, Reresby's four-year-old son John.[43]

Humbler wills show similar patterns of behaviour. Godsons were rarely the principal beneficiary, but they were not completely forgotten. The Essex yeoman Richard Man left legacies of between 1s. and 10s. to four named godsons in his will of 1571. The Wiltshire miller William Glasse bequeathed in 1684 'my flagon which I give to William the son of John Glasse, who is both my grandson and godson'. Almost a fifth of Elizabethan yeomen's and clothiers' wills mentioned godchildren, but the numbers were much reduced a century later.[44]

Naming the Child

After offering to renounce the devil, the godparents' most important cere-monial task was to supply the child with a name. The opening questions of the Catechism which prepared most children for confirmation asked 'what is your name?' and 'who gave you this name?' The proper answer to the second was, 'my godfathers and godmothers in baptism, wherein I was made a member of Christ, the child of God, and an inheritor of the kingdom of heaven'. When, in the course of the baptism service, the minister asked the name of the child to be christened, the godparents were expected to provide it. The minister then recited that name along with the essential words of baptism.[45]

In most cases the chosen name was no surprise. Parents and godparents usually agreed in advance what the child should be called, selecting from a conventional repertoire of Richards and Johns and Sarahs and Elizabeths.[46] Names like Elizabeth, Anne, James, and Charles may also have marked re-spect for the monarchy, akin to the way that catholics chose names for their association with patron saints. Saints' names, associated with saints' days, did not completely disappear. In Elizabethan Yorkshire a high proportion of boys baptized on 26 December, St Stephen's day, took the name of the saint.[47]

Names often ran in families, so that a newly baptized infant would be the namesake of its grandparent, aunt, or uncle, or perhaps a predeceased sib-ling. It was common, though by no means necessary, for a senior godparent to give the child his or her own name. A goodly number of Samuels, for example, were named for Samuel Pepys. When Isaac Archer christened his firstborn son William, he noted, 'I named the child of my father's name in honour of his memory.' A few years later he baptized another son, 'my child of prayer, desire, and hopes . . . my name [Isaac] given it'.[48] Between a half and three-quarters of children baptized in three Yorkshire parishes in the reign of Elizabeth took the name of a godparent, though evidence from the seventeenth century suggests a decline in this pattern.[49]

Naming was a serious business, securing legal, social, religious, and semantic identity. According to conventional commentators, the name given at baptism was indeed one's Christian name, a sign of 'our regeneration' and 'a badge that we belong to God'. It also put one in fellowship with all others who had worn that name before, to be 'recorded not only in the church's register, but in the book of life, and stand there forever'. The Anglican John Evelyn approved of 'the religious custom of the primitives, to impose such names on their children as might mind them of either their duty or the imitation of holy persons after whose name they were called'.[50] The name could serve as an inspiration and a mnemonic device as well as an identifying label.

Zealous puritans, never a large number, sometimes went in for earnest, godly, and biblical names, leaving a sprinkling of Praisegods and Nehemiahs in English parish registers. John King, the Jacobean bishop of London, felt it necessary to ask in his visitation of 1612 whether any godparents 'give the children baptised any name absurd, or inconvenient for so holy an action'. Reacting against similar excesses, the poet-parson George Herbert urged the country priest to admit 'no vaine or idle names'.[51]

In the vast majority of cases, the naming of children was unexceptional. But here too, as in almost every other aspect of baptism, the frictions of parish life and the strains of religious culture caused problems. A zealous minister in Elizabethan Northamptonshire 'refused to baptise the child of one Hodgkinson, because it was to be called Richard, not a godly name'. Amongst other complaints against Anthony Armitage, vicar of Ellington, Huntingdonshire, in 1602, was that 'in the baptising of Mr. John Dyckering's child [he] did refuse to give or repeat the name the godfathers did give the child, but did name the child at his pleasure without consent of the godfathers'. The minister's action appears less unreasonable when we learn from a sympathetic witness that the godfathers would have named the boy Edward Maria, 'and Mr. Armitage would not name it any more than Edward, leaving out Maria'.[52] Robert Evans, vicar of West Wycombe, Buckinghamshire, in 1633 'did christen the daughter of John Child Sarah when the godfather and godmother named it' Barbara. Richard Locksmith, rector of Loddington, Leicestershire, faced suspension by the spiritual courts in 1634 for christening a boy by the name of Millstone. His neighbour, Mr Avery, the vicar of Fleckney, was cited the same year for christening 'divers children without giving any names to the said children, although the godfathers and godmothers have distinctly signified what the name should be'.[53]

These were minor problems, of little weight in themselves, but they easily contributed to a pattern of deteriorating relationships between ministers and parishioners. In another local crisis, John Bradford of Thurlaston, Lincolnshire, caused his child to be named Ichabod in 1611, to the great scandal of community and church. Bradford, so the rector, Thomas Wood, explained, was a supporter of the former minister, Mr Sharewood, who was deprived for nonconformity, and after his departure the local puritans lamented 'the glory is gone . . . Upon which, as it is commonly said and thought in those parts, he caused his said child to be called as aforesaid, Ichabod, viz. the glory is gone'.[54]

Ichabod was not a common name, but it caused uncommon problems. The seventeenth-century Warwickshire minister John Ward tells the story

of a certain woman who having had a hard labour, would have her son which she brought forth called Ichabod. The woman that carried the child, having drunk plentifully, fell asleep all sermon time, and after sermon time the minister came to baptise the child, the woman went off very briskly to the font, the parson, when she came, asked her the name of the child, she rubbed her forehead and could not tell; at last she cries out she could, he bid her name it, she calls it—'Incombob'. The parson wondered at it, but under that name he baptised it, and afterwards the woman remembered it, and went back with the parson, who baptised it Ichabod.[55]

Chrisom Cloths and Christening Sheets

Though not required by scripture or rubric, it was customary to wrap a child at baptism in a clean white cloth which could be taken for 'a token of innocency'. Here was yet another item susceptible to controversy. In the old catholic service the newly baptized child was clad in a white chrismal robe, 'holy and unstained', which also served the practical purpose of mopping up drips of chrism, oil and water. Though not required by the protestant prayer book, chrisom cloths were still standard equipment, at least in the Elizabethan period, and their use continued occasionally under the Stuarts. It was traditional for a child who died within a month of birth to be shrouded in the chrisom cloth when buried; and in happier circumstances it was customary for the mother to present the cloth (or its cash equivalent) to the minister at her churching. According to a helpful seventeenth-century dictionary, 'chrisom . . . signifies properly the white cloth which is set by the minister of baptism upon the head of a child newly appointed with chrism after his baptism; now it is vulgarly taken for the white cloth put about or upon a child newly christened, in token of his baptism.' Chrism oil was no longer applied, of course, in the reformed Church of England, but the use of the chrisom cloth endured.[56]

According to puritan critics, to lay 'a white garment . . . upon the body of the baptised, to act the wedding garment and the armour of light', was yet another carryover from catholicism.[57] But principled objections stood little chance against popular practice in an area the established church deemed adiaphora or indifferent. Even today a white christening robe is the garment of choice for a baby's baptism.

Records of baptismal garments sometimes appear in domestic accounts. Among the items sent out to be washed from the Yorkshire household of Henry Best in June 1640 was 'a christening sheet with buttons'. This was evidently a special item, reserved for ceremonial use within the family. On this occasion it would seem to have been lent to a kinsman or close neighbour, for the last of Best's own children had been christened seven years earlier in 1633.[58]

Christening Cheer

Ample evidence survives among diaries and account books, and in literary and documentary sources, of the secular and festive aspect of baptisms. Just as the cycle of the seasons and the anniversaries of protestant England provided occasions for public celebration,[59] so the renewal of life and the expansion of families sparked rounds of domestic merrymaking. In early modern England, as in cultures around the world, conviviality and commensality fostered social cohesion. Religious disagreements about the meaning or practice of baptism were offset by delight in the greeting of a newly baptized child.

Festive drinking might begin as soon as the baby was born, with the gossips in the birthroom and the menfolk in the parlour. But it often reached its peak on the evening of the baptism. The scale of celebration varied with the status and means of the family, but it was rare for a christening to pass without some display of good cheer. Lavish hospitality attended aristocratic baptisms, while humbler households celebrated in parlours, alehouses, or taverns.[60] As a greeting and celebration, an introduction of the child to the society of kindred and community, the christening supper was a fitting counterpart to the child's mystical introduction to the congregation of Christians. Learning about baptismal festivity is difficult, however, because the activities that followed the service were of little direct interest to the church.

Among the propertied classes in particular, a christening operated as an important secular celebration. Quite apart from its sacramental benefits, a baptism allowed a household to demonstrate power, to show off a firstborn, to greet an heir, or to present other extensions of lineage. Wetting the baby's head, a profane pastiche of the christening ceremony, pledged neighbours, friends, and guests to a strengthened association with the family. The gathering gave wider recognition to the status and accomplishments of the parents, to the potency of the father and the fecundity of the mother. Each parent would receive separate congratulations, and the child would be welcomed as the fruit of their loins. The secular setting of the christening feast, rather than the sacred enclosure of the church, was the place to acknowledge the newly initiated child as a nephew or niece, grandchild, cousin, or neighbour. The occasion called for the exchange of cordiality, hospitality, and deference, and for the bestowal of christening gifts and kisses.

Christening parties were notorious for their sexual banter. Discussion of parenting and begetting, access to alcoholic refreshment, and a generally merry mood, were prompts to mild lasciviousness. We should not make too much of this, for decorum was always the ideal, but the porter's remark in Shakespeare's *Henry VIII*—'Bless me, what a fry of fornication is at door . . . this one christening will beget a thousand'—may have been pertinent to more than royal occasions. Observations by Samuel Pepys, William Lawrence, and Ned Ward in the later seventeenth century point to a tradition of sexual playfulness at Stuart christening parties.[61]

Aristocratic baptisms were especially elaborate. The 'Orders and Regulations for an Earl's House', drawn up in 1525 but still used by the Earl of Huntingdon in 1589, specified decorations for the church, processional order for the guests, and protocols for obeisance and gift-giving at a noble child's christening. Liturgical procedures altered with the Reformation, but the aristocratic concern for cushions and carpets continued. The 1589 baptism took place at a parish church, with the party returning for further festivities at the earl's great house. In readiness for the ceremony the church was adorned with tapestry and cloth of arras, and the benches covered with similar fabric. Benches reserved for the godparents were covered with silk or cloth of gold, suitable to their degree and estate. The font was decorated with 'a fine frontal of cloth of gold or silk', and framed by heraldic emblems and banners. Conveniently nearby was 'a cushion for her that beareth the child to sit upon with the child'. Inside the church was a curtained-off area, 'for the child to be made ready in against it shall go to the font', and here the child was attended by the midwife and appropriate gentlewoman. Following convention the mother—the countess—stayed at home in her chamber. Under the midwife's supervision, the child was mantled in silk, lawn, and wool, and carried in state to the font with attendants on either side 'for jeopardy of falling'. By virtue of her office the midwife, a woman of humbler birth, took precedence over the gentlewomen who followed two by two, arm in arm, 'after their degrees'.[62] This was a public occasion, employing the prayer-book order for public baptism. The aristocratic accoutrements drew attention to rank and lineage, but they did not mask the essential parts of the ritual.

Following the completion of the service the party would retire in due order. Back at the house the principal guests would be shown to the new mother's chamber to thank her, 'after the custom and manner that is used, for the honour they have done her', and they would make their final obeisance to the child. The mother, excluded from the ecclesiastical ceremony and still in the early days of her lying in month, was reintegrated into the life of the household. Gifts bestowed by the godparents were placed on formal display while guests were eating and drinking, then taken up to the lady's bedside. The entire celebration was stage-managed and scripted, revealing the involvement of the heralds.[63] Though by no means the norm, such noble rites of passage set the scale for others of descending order.

Other records of the gentry and aristocracy show their elaboration of the baptism ceremony with items of luxury and display. At the baptism of Sir Thomas Chamberlayne's son in London in 1559, 'the church was hung with cloth of arras, and after the christening were brought wafers, comfits, and divers banquetting dishes, and hyopcras and muscadine wine to entertain the guests'. Household records show that 3 January 1588 'was the christening of my Lord Strange's daughter [the Lady Elizabeth] . . . and many gentle women came to the christening'.[64]

Sir John Oglander recalled a particularly lavish baptism party among the Jacobean gentry. Bowyer Worsley's wife presented him with a son John,

at whose christening was the greatest drinking and uncivil mirth that ever I knew. The Earl of Holderness [John Ramsay, d. 1626] was one of his godfathers. After dinner they were to drink healths, and he had provided one hundred musketeers, fifty in the garden and fifty in the court, and at every health these must come and discharge into the parlour doors, where they drank as much smoke as wine.

Oglander himself could not compete with this display when his own first son was baptized in 1609, though he had two knights for godfathers and a distinguished kinswoman as godmother. One priest performed the baptism ceremony and another preached a sermon. But, Oglander recalled with satisfaction, 'all the better sort in the country were at his christening'.[65]

More muted celebrations continued lower down the social scale. A London tradesmen provided two gallons of French claret and two quarts of Spanish canary wine for a christening party in 1640. The Essex clergyman Ralph Josselin spent £6. 13s. 4d. 'at least' to celebrate the baptism of his first child in 1642, almost 10 per cent of his annual clerical income. On the day of his son's christening in 1644 in Civil-War London the gentleman-lawyer John Greene noted, 'I had a great banquet: stood me in about £4. I had not much company.' When another child was baptized at home in 1648, Greene records, 'we had about twenty-five guests at the christenings'. Many families continued to celebrate this important rite of passage despite the religious confusions of the revolution. Dr William Denton attended a christening in Cheshire in 1656 that was 'not without a fiddler and the merry cup, and the toast of Sir Ralph [Verney]'s health'.[66]

Removed from the solemnity of the church, it was hard to tell whether christening parties were more famous for their food or their drink. At the end of the Elizabethan period, according to contemporary satirists, the prosperous citizen would be sure 'to have all things fine against the christening day, what with sugar, biscuits, comfits and caraways, marmalade and marchpain [marzipan], with all kind of sweet suckets and superfluous banquetting stuff, with a hundred other odd and needless trifles which at that time must fill the pockets of dainty dames'.[67] The aristocratic Margaret Cavendish referred approvingly to the 'banquets of sweet-meats and other junkets' that would be expected at 'a good gossiping'. The antiquarian John Aubrey reported in the later seventeenth century that 'we still use cakes at christenings. At Burchester (=Bicester) in Oxfordshire at a christening the women bring every one a cake, and present one first to the minister if present. At Wendlebury and other places they bring their cakes at a gossiping, and give a large cake to the father of the child, which they call a rocking cake.' Henri Misson, a French observer of patrician life in London in the time of William and Mary, remarked that at christenings, 'they drink a glass of wine, and eat a bit of a certain cake, which is seldom made but upon these occasions'.[68] Everyone would be expected to tuck in.

Sometimes it took an unfortunate accident, such as occurred at West Bilney, Norfolk, to illustrate the common activity among women of preparing cakes and pies for their neighbours' christenings. Elizabeth Freke records in her diary in 1687, 'Goody Mamon's house next to mine was, about ten o'clock at night, burnt down to the ground with over-heating her oven for Goody Saywell's christening, and the poor widow woman burnt to death in it by the treachery of Goody Cheny persuading her to fetch out a dish on Saturday night.'[69] The tragedy had absurd and ordinary origins, just like the Great Fire of London.

Tudor and Stuart christening parties were notorious for male carousing and female gossiping. Men and women were said to have consumed abnormal amounts of alcohol, in both mixed and separate company. John Paynton of Ludgershall, Wiltshire, recalled 'that upon occasion of baptism of a child of his, he invited [Dr. Andrew Reade, the Laudian minister] to dinner; and after dinner the said doctor went to an inn in town, and continued there till supper time', becoming so drunk that he was incapable of conducting evening prayer. Oliver Heywood noted with disgust in 1674 that Mr Richard Beaumont of Lassel Hall 'had laid up nineteen gallons of wine against his wife lying in', and several neighbouring gentlemen came round to drink their way through it. Seven men consumed the whole nineteen gallons, so that afterwards, not surprisingly, 'they lay like swine'.[70]

Popular misogyny was more likely to depict women as drunkards at christenings. A catch-phrase of the time was 'as drunk . . . as women at a gossiping'. The tone is best captured in a literary satire of 1647, cousin to *The Batchelars Banquet* of 1603, in which Mother Bumbey, grandmother to a newborn child, invites the 'witnesses and gossips' to return to the house after attending the baptism. 'Come my good neighbours, let us home. I have already prepared an hogshead of nappy ale, with a gammon of bacon and other good accoutrements, which today we'll make merry with.' The company takes pleasure in feasting, drinking, and telling stories in the sexual afterglow of the christening. 'Having sated themselves sufficiently with meat, and waxing something warm with ale, Mother Bumbey motioned that each gossip should sing a catch; but Gammer Grumble replied, they in doing so should lose much time which they might thriftily employ in tippling.' Attended by 'gossips' and 'old crones', and directed by the formidable Mother Bumbey, the party is depicted as heavily if not exclusively female and well on its way to a drunken stupor.[71]

A correlate to this is Thomas Shipman's 'Gossip', satirizing the greed and gluttony of those invited to private baptisms during the era of the Restoration.

> Especially since gossips now
> Eat more at christenings than bestow;
> Formerly they used to trowl
> Gilt bowls of sack, they gave the bowl;
> Two spoons at least; an ill use kept;
> 'Tis well now if our own be left.

The costs could be formidable, according to Shipman:

> And christening feasts are but a toll
> Exacted, or an earlier dole.
> A font brings far the heavier doom
> To a poor father, than a tomb.[72]

Christenings were no less useful for displaying important connections in the later seventeenth century. Godparentage, especially among the élite, was notoriously a matter of ambition and fashion, a paying of social respect rather than taking of spiritual responsibility. ' 'Tis well known', observed Philip Stubs in an address to the Lord Mayor of London, 'that persons of any fashion are . . . ambitious of playing that complimental piece of respect . . . to our shame be it spoken, 'tis too frequently look'd upon as no more.'[73] Diarists and autobiographers were proudly attentive of this interchange of compliments, noting who stood for whom in the ceremony. In May 1672, for example, Thomas Isham recorded that Sir Edward Nichols invited 'many people of rank' to the baptism of his son, and that Lord Montague was one of the godfathers, alongside other representatives of the Northamptonshire gentry. The diaries of John Evelyn and Samuel Pepys are particularly rich in their description of marks of favour and gatherings of pleasure at baptismal celebrations. So too are the humbler family records of the Derbyshire yeoman Leonard Wheatcroft and the Lancaster clergyman Thomas Brockbank. In 1681, Wheatcroft wrote, 'I stirred very little abroad, but only to feast and banquet at neighbours houses, at weddings and christenings.' Whenever news arrived of a kinswoman brought to bed, preparations would begin for the merriments of christening, gossiping, and welcoming. Wheatcroft took great pleasure in the 'sporting . . . mirth and melody' occasioned by family rites of passage. Brockbank ministered baptisms and afterwards 'dined . . . with the gossips'. After one such christening in 1701 he noted, 'the good wife in the straw is well for the time'.[74]

Samuel Pepy's diary, though extremely well known, is worth recalling again for its detailed pictures of social practices among the later seventeenth-century élite. Pepys has much to say about the activities of godparents and the festive occasions on which they performed their office. On 29 May 1661—already a day of festivity as Royal Oak Day, the King's birthday, and the anniversary of his formal accession—Pepys dressed himself finely for his role as a godfather at Mrs Browne's house in Walthamstow.

And there, before and after the christening, we were with the women above in her chamber; but whether we carried ourselves well or ill, I know not, but I was directed by young Mrs. Batten. One passage, of a lady that eat wafers with her dog, did a little displeasure me. I did give the midwife ten shillings and the nurse five shillings and the maid of the house two shillings; but for as much as I expected to give the name to the child, but did not, it being called John, I forbore then to give my plate, till another time, after a little more advice.

Pepys had earlier gone to the trouble of ordering a piece of plate to give to Mrs Browne's child, and had set off in high spirits with 'six spoons and a porringer of silver in my pockets to give away today'. He was evidently put out that neither he nor the other godfather (Sir William Penn) were permitted to give their name to the child.[75]

Another entry in November 1661 reveals some of the social, gender, and kinship dynamics of the christening party. Pepys and his wife took part in the baptism of their cousin Benjamin Scott's new son. Samuel Pepys and his namesake cousin from Ireland were godfathers, and gave the child their name. The diarist continues,

> there was a company of pretty women there in the chamber; but we stayed not, but went with the minister into another room and eat and drank. And at last, when most of the women were gone, Sam and I went into my cousin [Judith] Scott, who was got off her bed; and so we stayed and talked and were very merry, my she-cousin Stradwick being godmother; and then I left my wife to go home by coach,

Mrs Pepys evidently staying on by the bedside with the mother's most intimate female companions. Pepys's final comment was, 'it cost me twenty shillings between the midwife and two nurses today'.[76]

In March 1663 Pepys and his wife attended a Sunday afternoon christening at Westminster, and then returned to the house where the new mother, Anne Ferrers (daughter of a Scottish earl, married to Captain Ferrers), 'lies in in great state'. The mother received guests in her chamber, and the father provided 'very pretty and plentiful entertainment'. Much satisfied, Pepys and his wife 'could not get away till nine of night'. At other christenings in the 1660s Pepys remarked 'much company, good service of sweetmeats', that among many guests at table 'I got a piece of cake', and that he drank the wine 'and kissed the mother in bed'.[77]

What did people talk about on such occasions? There is nothing in the post-Restoration record to suggest that the spiritual transformation of the child or the ineffable efficacy of baptism formed the dominant line of discourse. Rather, from our urbane and well-bred sources, the topic seems to have been gossip (the tattle of god-sibs) with a mildly sexual flavour. Margaret Cavendish writes,

> I was invited to be a gossip, to name the lady B.R.'s child, of which she lies in; and at the christening, and being most married women as is usual at such gossiping meetings, their discourse was most of labours and child-beds, children and nurses, and household servants, and of preserving, and such like discourses as married women and mistresses of families usually have.

The women also talked about their husbands.[78]

William Lawrence's letters of the 1670s reveal the lightest view of spiritual matters. In May 1675, in a letter written to amuse his brother who was a merchant in the Levant, Lawrence recalled, 'I did once by your deputation stand as a godfather to Jenny [his sister], and this godman was appointed to carry on the work of the day; but you'd have laughed to have seen how silly was his matter and how wildly expressed; his prayer was so full of holy bawdy, that I dare swear there were many things stood in the room beside the godfather.'[79]

The popular writer Ned Ward offered a comprehensive account of a private baptism and christening party in London at the end of the Stuart period. Titled 'a comical description of a christening; with the humours of the gossips', it displays a mixture of stereotypical misogynism and cynical urbane irreverence. Part pastiche, part close observation, and heavily wrought by art, it reveals details that are missing from more conventional reports, and is therefore worth reviewing at length. The world it describes is that of the metropolitan commercial classes, far removed from the earnest religiosity of the godly controversialists.[80]

'A relation in town' brought news of his firstborn son, and solicited Ward 'to do the penance of a godfather'. Ward agreed, 'to stand as a Tom-Doodle for an hour or two, to be bantered by a tittle-tattle assembly of female gossips'. Clean-shaven and in clean bands, and with a fair degree of apprehension, he set off 'for the solemnization of this ancient piece of formality'. Entering the house, amidst 'a confusion of women's tongues', Ward enquired 'after the welfare of the woman in the straw'. He learnt that the new mother was surrounded by her female companions, leaving the outnumbered men a few moments of relief. 'The women, heaven be praised, were ushered upstairs, so that I was in no great danger of having my ears stretched upon the rack of verbosity, till the administration of the sacrament was over.' Ward chatted briefly with his fellow godfather, a man with more experience in these matters, who advised him how to flatter the women: 'lard your talk now and then with a little waggery wrapped up in clean linen'. Restrained flirtation was the order of the day.

'In came the parish sprinkler with Amen at his heels [the minister and parish clerk], who were ushered upstairs among the assembly of help-meets. Now, thought I, the curtain's to be drawn, and the show is ready to begin.' The baptism was performed upstairs in the mother's chamber, where everyone soon assembled. 'We came into the room and . . . bowed our backs to the old cluster of harridans, and they in turn . . . bent their knees to us.' Then, 'the parson plucking out a pocket tool belonging to his trade [presumably the prayer book], began in solemn-wise the preface to the business in hand, whilst old Mother Grope [the midwife] stood rocking of the bantling in her arms, wrapped up in so rich a mantle'. The formal part of the business passed quickly. 'At last the babe was put into my hands to deliver, though not as my act and deed, to the parson.' The child went from the mother to the midwife, the midwife to the godfather, the godfather to the minister, and then back to the arms of 'old Mother Grope'.

'The religious part was concluded; and now kissing, feasting, and jocular-
ity were to follow in their proper places.' With sacramental business discharged, the festivities could begin. Godfathers kissed godmothers, and all
raised their glasses. 'As soon as the parson had refreshed his spirits with a
bumper of canary, dedicated to the woman in the straw, and the clerk had
said Amen to his master's good wishes after the like manner, each of them
accepted of a paper of sweetmeats for his wife or his children, and away they
went, leaving the rest of the company behind.' There followed more kissing
and greeting, more drinking and tittle-tattle, as the company prepared for
the next stage of the proceedings.

The action upstairs with the minister was the formal climax of the occasion, but there was more social action to follow in the dining-room. Leaving
the mother to her rest, the guests moved 'into the next room where was a
very good hot supper ready upon the table, and two or three dozen of several
sorts of wine'. Somebody said a ribald grace, and the party turned to eating,
drinking, gossip, and bawdy chatter. 'In this sort of hopeful tittle-tattle they
tired their lungs and wasted their time, till they were most of them got as
boozy as so many bumpkins at a wake, or tipling loyalists upon the king's
birthday.' There were healths and jokes about 'the woman in the straw',
but neither mother or child had any further part in the action. The guests
departed with tokens of their visit, 'a service of sweetmeats which every gossip carried away in her handkerchief'. Finally, 'what remained for me to do,
was to go upstairs to bid my bed-ridden relation much joy of her new Christian, and to receive thanks for the trouble she had put me to' in the form of
kisses. That done, Ward made his escape, 'having now struggled through
every difficult part of these accustomary formalities'.

CHANGES AND CHALLENGES

Baptism in Times of Distraction, 1642–1660

It is apparent, from all the sources at our disposal, that the rituals of baptism were sensitive and complex. Elements of controversy hovered around the font. Yet notwithstanding the differences of religious style and taste which exercised controversialists between the accession of Queen Elizabeth and the demise of the later Stuarts, the service set forth in the Book of Common Prayer provided a framework for continuity and consensus. The order for the ministration of baptism served as a standard script, even if the partici-pants disagreed about some of the protocols of performance. All of this was disrupted during the disturbances of 1640s and the distractions of the 1650s when the Church of England was temporarily swept aside. Traditional objec-tions to Church of England ritual, and radical rethinking of ecclesiastical organization and conduct, combined together in the revolutionary era to transform, and in many places to obliterate, the customary form of baptism. This chapter investigates these disturbances and examines both conservative and radical responses.

Even before the outbreak of war in August 1642 there were increasing reports of desecrations, repudiation of Laudian practice, and of parishioners taking control of the liturgy. Several fonts fell under the hammer in 1641 and 1642, and more would follow. As the authority of the established church unravelled during the opening years of the Long Parliament, for example, radical parishioners at Radwinter, Essex, offered 'affronts and insolencies' to their conformist minister, Richard Drake. As the aggrieved minister tells it, the parish was severely divided and baptism services broke down in disorder over attempts to impose or to prevent the signing with the cross. On one occasion John Smith, a blacksmith, 'violently snatched [his] child out of the curate's arms, before he had signed it with the cross, to the great offence of the sober minded and to the encouragement of others in disorder'. John Traps, a tailor, 'coming up close and standing in a daring manner by him', thwarted the minister's attempt to christen another child in April 1642 and 'told him that he should not have her out of the godmother's arms, nor sign her with the cross, and to that end flung the cloth over the face of the child, keeping his hand upon it and saying, "it is the mark of the beast"'. When the minister attempted to make the sign of the cross on Giles Alton's child in June 1642, one woman 'covered the child with the linen and kept it down with her hand', while another woman 'laid hold of one of the curate's hands which was kept behind him by the father of the child'. The parish was in uproar, the minister dishonoured, and the dignity of the sacrament severely diminished. Liturgical disagreements that might earlier have been dealt with by selective accommodation or sleight of hand now risked plunging the community into anarchy.[1]

Nor was that the worst that could happen. In that same troubled summer of 1642, according to a contemporary printed account, Mary Wilmore, wife of a rough mason of Mears Ashby, Northamptonshire, became so convinced that the cross in baptism was 'pernicious, popish and idolatrous' that she wished her baby to be born without a head rather than have it baptized in that manner. Her husband sought advice from neighbouring ministers, and might have been persuaded to accept the ceremony, but Mary remained adamant; and sure enough, goes the report, she was rewarded by giving birth to a deformed monster, 'a child without a head, and credibly reported to have a firm cross on the breast'. The pamphlet reporting this 'strange and lamentable accident' pits wife against husband, laity against clergy, rebellion against concord, and places it in the Elizabethan tradition of prodigies and judgements. It was a warning of worse horrors to come, when the world turned upside down. Regardless of the truth of the matter, it was symptomatic of the news and opinions in circulation as the country descended into war.[2]

There was no clear pattern to this surge of disorder, though local contentions sometimes mirrored national divisions. Stories multiplied of incivility towards ministers, travesties of the sacrament, mock baptism of animals, rebaptism of adults, and urination in the font.[3] Reports of such outrages horrified some observers, entertained others, and added to the heightened instability following the collapse of episcopal discipline. Most diocesan administrations ground to a halt before 1642, and church courts ceased to function. A parliamentary bill of 1643 abolished the episcopal hierarchy, and three years later the office, title, and authority of bishops was formally extinguished.[4] The crisis of the early 1640s ushered in a decade and a half of freedom, experiment, and confused recrimination. Baptism was one of the issues that split families, communities, and congregations.

Parliamentary leaders sought to establish a reformed national church along presbyterian lines, but their efforts collapsed in the face of radical independency and sectarianism on the one side and Anglican conservatism on the other. Guided by the Westminster Assembly, Parliament passed an ordinance in January 1645 'for taking away the Book of Common Prayer and for establishing . . . the Directory for the Public Worship of God'. This included new instructions for baptism which attempted to preserve the dignity of the occasion while meeting mainstream puritan objections.[5]

As in Anglican worship, the presbyterian ceremony was held to signify both cleansing from sin by the blood and resurrection of Christ and the child's reception 'into the bosom of the visible church'. But the conduct of the sacrament was radically transformed. Baptism, the Directory insisted, was

not to be administered in any case by any private person, but by a minister of Christ . . . Nor is it to be administered in private places, or privately, but in the place of public worship, and in the face of the congregation, where the people may most conveniently see and hear; and not in the places where fonts in the time of popery were unfitly and superstitiously placed.

The service could now come forward to the front of the congregation, in close proximity to the Lord's table. The child was to be presented 'by the father, or in case of his necessary absence by some Christian friend'. There was no mention of godparents, and still no place for the mother. There would be, of course, no crossing, and no set form of prayer. 'In these or the like instructions, the minister is to use his own liberty and godly wisdom, as the ignorance or errors in the doctrine of baptism and the edification of the people shall require.' At the climax of the ceremony the minister should baptize the child 'by pouring or sprinkling of the water on the face of the child, without adding any other ceremony'. Presumably he would use a basin for this purpose, while naming the child and pronouncing the only immutable words, 'I baptize thee in the name of the Father, of the Son, and of the Holy Ghost.'[6]

The Directory of Public Worship never took firm root. It satisfied neither traditional ceremonialists nor radical sectarians. Only a minority of parishes acquired the new book, and its prescriptions were weakly enforced. Instead, most parishes seem to have adopted their own form of service, loosely derived from the Directory or the Book of Common Prayer and infinitely adaptable to varying community needs and shifting religious concerns. Some ministers wore surplices and baptized in fonts, others discarded the contested liturgical trappings, some eschewed ceremony altogether. Critics in Kent complained of 'the roundheaded kind of christening'.[7] Theological speculation ran rampant alongside religious experimentation, as people sought insight into God's inscrutable demands. Congregational Independency jostled with dour presbyterianism, modified Anglicanism, antinomian illumination, and the rising community of Quakers, in a welter of religious creativity and confusion.

Baptists and Anabaptists, virtually unheard of in England since the sixteenth century, emerged among the most numerous of the post-puritan sects to challenge the very notion of infant baptism. Baptism, Baptists argued, was the mark of the born-again Christian, and full immersion the declaratory ceremony of the mature believer.[8] Quakers rejected ceremony altogether. The demography of religious affiliation in this period has so far resisted scholarly investigation, so we can do little more than guess at the strength of various religious factions, but the printed output of their controversy is vast and readily available for study. Those with a taste for such things can turn to *A Treatise of the Vanity of Childish Baptism* by A.R. (1642), *The Dippers Plunged in a Sea of Absurdities* by Thomas Bakewell (1650), or *The Font-Guard Routed* by Thomas Collier (1652), and the dozens of similar treatises, confutations, vindications, replies, and responses on the meaning and conduct of baptism. The London bookseller George Thomason collected over 125 titles specifically addressing this topic between 1642 and 1660.[9]

The issues involved not only the question of how to baptize and when to baptize, but also whom to baptize and whether to baptize at all. Every aspect of the sacrament was subject to challenge. Some godly communities embroiled themselves in the kind of divisive sectarianism that also threatened to turn the American New Canaan into a land of Babylon. On the northern frontier of New England proponents and opponents of infant baptism confronted each other in the street with Bibles fixed on halberds. These American factions, led by the Independent Thomas Larkham and the Particular Baptist Hanserd Knollys (both of whom returned to England), had their followers and counterparts in dozens of English parishes.[10]

Thomas Jolly's puritan congregation at Altham, Lancashire, set forth restrictions on baptism in their 'particulars of church discipline' of 1652 which rejected the notion of an open universal church.

Concerning admission to baptism, we cannot understand that the children of such as are not members of the church, and will not submit to the ordinances and ways of Christ, have any right to this ordinance, unless their predecessors that are worthy will covenant for them, and engage they shall be educated in the nurture and admonition of the Lord.

They further agreed that,

at the admission of any child by baptism, it is to be required that the parent, or who undertakes for the child as their own, shall not only promise the good education of the child, but covenant in behalf of it to do the things required at the admission of members, and that the child when it comes to the years of discretion shall confirm this covenant or be refused.[11]

More typical, perhaps, was the situation in Devonshire where, wrote Susanna Parr in 1659, 'we were . . . in a bewildered condition, without either of the sacraments: some not having their children baptized in a long time, others did procure some congregational minister to do it'. Susanna Parr suffered excommunication from her Exeter Independent congregation as the community splintered among radical and conservative factions.[12]

Changes in religious belief and alterations of ecclesiastical organization required changes in liturgical practice. Fonts became officially redundant after 1645, to be replaced by portable basins, but they did not suffer so badly as has sometimes been suggested. It was not necessary to deface or remove the font to meet the new liturgical arrangements; simple neglect would suffice. Nor would it be difficult to refurbish the font if the religious climate should change. Medieval fonts were often massive pieces of masonry, hard to damage and expensive to move; though some took a battering, most remained in place. During the Civil Wars and Interregnum some fonts were neglected, others moved or despoiled. Most survived unscathed, however, and after 1660 could again be used as they were intended.

Cathedral fonts were particular vulnerable, caught up in the anger against episcopacy, though parochial fonts were also at risk. The elaborate new font at Canterbury cathedral was attacked in 1641. At Peterborough cathedral the font was 'pulled down, and the lead taken out of it by Cromwell's soldiers' in 1643. The cathedral font at St Asaph was used as a hog-trough. At Marden, Kent, the Baptist minister Mr Cornwell, is said to have found infant baptism 'a delusion and a snare contrary to scripture' and smashed his font with a hammer.[13] At Houghton-le-Spring, Durham, the churchwardens paid 4s. 'for taking away the font' in 1651, but the job could not have been completed for they paid another 6d. 'for removing the font' in 1657. The churchwardens of Wilmslow, Cheshire, sold the lead lining of their font for 3s. and bought instead 'a pewter basin to baptize in'. At Aldwincle St Peter's, Northamptonshire, they bought a basin for 6d. in 1655 and sold the font for 3s. 6d. in 1657.[14] Stories of this sort are rare. In the parish accounts of the period it is more common to find payments for taking down the royal arms (pursuant to official instruction) than for dismantling the font (a matter of local discretion). Scores of fonts had to be rebuilt after the Restoration and many more refurbished, but the evidence does not suggest that fonts became as widespread targets of iconoclasm as is sometimes suggested. The Parliamentary iconoclast William Dowsing only attacked fonts if they featured offensive religious images, although at Southwold, Suffolk, in 1644 he also took down the font cover.[15]

Godparents continued to serve at baptisms in the 1640s and 1650s, and in many churches they still stood next to fonts. It proved impossible to prevent the presence of godparents at private ceremonies despite the official suppression of their office. Among the conservative gentry, Sir John Oglander served as 'godfather' to his granddaughter in 1646, and Antony Blagrave was 'godfather' at a neighbour's 'christening' in 1653. Robert Beake, Mayor of Coventry, recorded in his diary for 1655, 'a man travelling from Ryton to Exhall to be godfather was distrained and paid ten shillings'. The offender, like many others in the 1650s, was ostensibly punished for journeying on the Lord's day, but the record makes clear that godfathers were still in demand.[16]

Entries in diaries suggest some of the difficulties posed by the changing conditions of the 1640s and 1650s. They indicate, too, that people of means and conscience made private arrangements to secure whatever elements of ceremony they regarded as satisfactory. Local negotiation became more important than ever. When a nephew of the London lawyer John Greene was baptized in 1643 the diarist thought it worth recording that 'Mr Higgins christened it without the sign of the cross'. When the time came for the baptism of his own son in 1644, 'the child was baptised . . . by my uncle, Dr. Jermyn, in the house. He used the common prayer book, but signed it not with the cross.' Following this occasion, Greene noted, 'I gave 5s. to our minister, 2s. 6d. to Allen [the parish clerk?] and 1s. 6d. to the sexton; and our minister neither baptised the child nor churched my wife.' (She was churched at the lecture a week later.) Making the customary payments, even though the parish minister had not performed the service, may have been a professional courtesy, a way to maintain harmony, and perhaps an inducement to overlook irregularities. Greene's second child, a daughter, 'was baptised upon Monday the 24 of February [1645] being St. Matthias Day, privately at home by Mr. Burdale the minister of our parish'. After another son was born in 1648, 'we had about twenty-five guests at the christenings and Mr. Henshaw our lecturer baptised it in the chamber'. Godparents—Greene tends to call them 'gossips' before 1645, 'witnesses' thereafter—performed their customary duties on each of these occasions; usually they were close relations.[17]

Another glimpse of changing practices in the 1640s comes from the diary of Lady Isabella Twysden of East Peckham, Kent. Her own son, born in March 1645, was christened with godparents in the usual manner. But the following month when her sister Twysden 'was brought a bed of a girl at Malling, it was christened . . . and named Ann without gossips'. Two years later, in September 1647, Isabella writes, 'my sister Twysden was brought a bed of a girl at a quarter past five o'clock in the morning, being Friday; it was christened that afternoon, and named Margaret . . . it was christened without gossips, the new way'. And sister Twysden's next two children were similarly christened in London 'without gossips' on the afternoons of their births in 1648 and 1649.[18] In noting this absence of godparents, Isabella Twysden reveals her attachment to the old order as well as her awkward conformity to the new.

Less willing to compromise, Sir Ralph and Lady Verney made advance plans for christening the child they expected in the summer of 1647. Lady Mary promised to 'get a minister in the house that will do it the old way, for 'tis not the fashion here to have godfathers and godmothers, but for the father to bring the child to church and answer for it'. Sir Ralph offered more cautious advice, appropriate for the temper of the times.

Now for the christening, I pray give no offence to the state; should it be done in the old way perhaps it may bring more trouble upon you than you can imagine, and all to no purpose; for so it be done with common ordinary water, and that these words, 'I baptise thee in the name of the father, and of the son, and of the holy ghost,' be used with the water, I know the child is well baptised. All the rest is but a matter of form and ceremony which differs almost in every country.[19]

Alice Thornton would most likely have agreed, although she took pains to secure proper baptism for her children born in the 1650s. Michael Siddall, the minister of Kirkington, Yorkshire, or Charles Anthony, the vicar of Catterick, usually performed the office, with close relations serving as 'witnesses'. Earlier in 1645, Alice Thornton recalled, her sister died in childbirth of 'a son named Francis, whom I baptised'. This seems to suggest that she assumed the traditional duty of the midwife and administered emergency baptism, though it could also mean that she simply served as a godmother. Since the sister's house was occupied by Scottish presbyterian soldiers at the time, Alice Thornton may have had no choice but to undertake the sacrament by herself.[20]

Four of John Evelyn's children were born in the 1650s, at a time when the Church of England was abolished and the prayer book overthrown. In these trying times Evelyn kept his Anglicanism alive through private patronage of suspended ministers and private use of the Book of Common Prayer. Having baptisms performed at home was, for gentlemen of Evelyn's class, a common practice, not an expedient forced on them by the revolution, but the special circumstances of the Interregnum taught them to behave like nonconformists. Evelyn even adopted some of the language of godly discrimination, referring to godparents as 'susceptors'.

On 2 September 1652, Evelyn writes, 'Mr. Owen, sequestered parson of

Eltham, christened my son by the name of Richard . . . susceptors my brother George and sister Evelyn, about four in the afternoon, in the little drawing room next the parlour in Sayes Court, many of my relations and neighbours present.' A year later in October 1653 Mr Owen performed a similar service, christening Evelyn's second son John; this time the baptism was administered in the library. A third son, another John, was christened in January 1655, 'Mr. Owen officiating at Sayes Court according to the rite of the Church of England.' And in June 1657 Evelyn's fourth son was baptized George, 'Dr. Jeremy Taylor officiating in the withdrawing room at Sayes Court'.[21] The house provided a refuge from presbyterianism or independency, an alternative liturgical venue to the parish church. Evelyn himself stood as godfather at baptisms in 1648, 1649, and 1658, at services conducted as close as possible to the suspended usage of the Church of England. On 29 November 1649, he writes, 'I christened Sir Hugh Rilie's child, with Sir George Ratcliffe, in our chapel, the parents being so poor that they had provided no gossips; so as several of us drawing lots it fell on me, the dean of Peterborough, Dr. Cosin, officiating. We named it Andrew, being on the eve of that apostle's day.'[22] With John Cosin in attendance one can be sure that the service was as lavish as circumstances permitted.

Since the social and cultural history of Interregnum England is still largely unwritten, it is hard to gauge how typical were the strategies of these diarists or how strongly attached people became to alternatives to the Book of Common Prayer. One recent study concludes that 'we can only guess how many' used Anglican baptism. Historical demographers have determined that registration of baptisms was disrupted during the period of Civil Wars and Interregnum, as might be expected, but underrecording was no worse than during Mary Tudor's reign. An act of 1653 required civil registration of births, marriages, and burials, rather than ecclesiastical registration of religious rites of passage, but only a minority of parishes complied. Most places continued to use their old parish register to record baptisms.[23]

Perhaps the most profound consequence of the mid-century disruptions, in this regard, was to license a wide variety of practices unhindered by episcopal discipline. Key elements of the baptismal ceremony were sustained by community custom and family preference. Though performed by a minister and recorded in the register, the ritual was increasingly conducted in private, removed from public scrutiny, and physically separated from the church. John Beadle, an Essex minister, may have spoken for many of his brethren when he complained in 1656 that, despite the eradication of 'offensive ceremony', many 'care not whether their infants be admitted into the church by that sacrament or no'.[24]

Baptism after the Restoration

The conventional mainstream history of the later Stuart church may be summarized in a paragraph. The Church of England was restored at the Restoration, complete with the royal supremacy, episcopal hierarchy, and Book of Common Prayer, though deprived of the High Commission. The majority of clerics and most of the laity accommodated themselves to this order, but a scrupulous minority dissented. Nonconformist clergy lost their pulpits and benefices after 1662, but some remained active as ministers to dissenting congregations. Baptists, and congregationalists quietly flourished, eventually securing toleration, while Roman Catholicism gained new adherents, especially in the 1680s. Quakers endured bouts of persecution before they too came to terms with their neighbours. Calvinism faded from the established church, and Arminianism too declined, as religion became tinged with latitudinarianism and moderation. Apathy and indifference became widespread. High-church and low-church positions emerged, while the Church of England clung to its privileges, served the state, and guarded itself against enthusiasm.[25]

Children still had to be baptized, couples married, and bodies buried. The church still claimed authority in these areas, but after a generation of religious turmoil could no longer count on dutiful adherence to its ritual practices. The culture of conformity, never securely cemented, was now severely fractured, and an untold number of families loosened their ties to the church. The following section explores some of the ways in which the church reasserted its authority. Its also considers how people explained and approached the sacrament and how baptism worked at the local level in the later decades of the seventeenth century.

During the 1640s and 1650s the revolutionary view had flourished 'that paedobaptism is unlawful and antichristian, and that 'tis as lawful to baptise a cat, or a dog, or a chicken, as to baptize the infant of believers'.[26] All established liturgical practices were challenged at this time, but that does not mean that they were extinguished. By the time of the Restoration in 1660 the uniform established church was shattered, and a host of sectarian practices and anticlerical sentiments jostled alongside each other. Though orthodox public baptism was again made mandatory with the Act for the Uniformity of Public Prayers in 1662,[27] strict enforcement proved impossible. There is no way of knowing how widespread were the views of Thomas Twentiman, a nonconformist at Kirkhampton, Cumberland, who was cited in 1665 'for spreading contemptuous words of the sacrament of baptism, saying the gracewife might have cast a dishfull of water upon the child at home; and for the Lord's Supper the people might rather stay at home and take bread and water'. They were, perhaps, shared by the Leicestershire rowdies, later charged with dissent, who in 1663 fouled the water in the font at Redmile 'and threw it up and down the seats and washed themselves and others with it'.[28]

Under Elizabeth and the early Stuarts the episcopal authorities had demanded adherence to every detail of the baptism service; their main disciplinary task was to secure liturgical uniformity, especially against nonconformist priests. But after the Restoration the bishops faced a different measure of difficulty: polarization between Anglicans and dissenters, dwindling regard for ecclesiastical authority, and large pockets of cynicism and indifference.

A Representation of the State of Christianity in England, published in 1674, expressed the fear that neglect and contempt of baptism was so severe that 'the cockle will soon overspread the wheat, and instead of Christians our towns and villages will become the herds of heathens and infidels', but similar alarmist rhetoric had been heard for decades. A parliamentary move in 1677 to enforce baptism and catechizing came to nothing. It is a mark of the change in religious culture that discussions in the later seventeenth century turned not on the efficacy and power of the sacrament, but whether baptism was a matter of routine or indifference. Referring in 1699 to the duty of parents to bring their children to baptism, Robert Barrett, a medical writer, called it 'a duty nowadays too much neglected and slighted'.[29]

In the fractured religious culture of Restoration England, Baptists, Quakers, and other sectarians who had gathered strength in the 1650s took principled stands against infant baptism. Presbyterians rejected godparents, the sign of the cross, and other popish remnants of the Church of England. Many others of indifferent religious persuasion had simply fallen from the habit. Many families neglected to offer children for baptism in church, and increasing numbers, including Anglican conformists, preferred to have the ceremony performed privately at home. Episcopal authorities of the later Stuart period faced the compound problem of bringing recalcitrant families back to the parish church, and then making sure that they followed the rubric in the Book of Common Prayer.

After the confusions of the revolution there were many people in England who could not tell if they had ever been properly christened. The restored Church of England attempted to remedy this through its visitation processes, to ensure that every adult was eligible to receive holy communion and Christian burial. Year after year in the 1660s the church courts heard that such a one had a child aged 10, 'and never was yet baptised by any lawful minister as we can hear of', or 'four children born in our parish, we do not find they are registered or baptised'. In such cases the parties involved would be charged to make enquiry, to scour records, and to interrogate local memories. William

Strange of Turweston, Buckinghamshire, 'knoweth not whether his child be christened or not, but his wife perhaps can tell', advised the churchwardens. 'Diligent enquiries amongst her friends and neighbours' were organized on behalf of a 14-year-old girl in Oxford 'to learn so far as they can whether she were baptised or not, and if yea, where and by whom'.[30]

Church court records of the 1660s list page after page of laymen 'refusing baptisement' for their children. Nonconformist and recusant families from Cornwall to Cumberland refused to have anything to do with the Church of England's public baptism. The only part a Durham Quaker, John Hall, played in the service was disruptive, 'disturbing our rector . . . going from his seat to the font to baptise children' in February 1665. The churchwardens of Great Parndon, Essex, regretted in 1664, 'many children as yet unbaptised which were born in that notorious rebel's time'. Officials at South Mimms, Hertfordshire, cited clusters of Anabaptists and Quakers 'whose children are not baptised'. At the nonconformist stronghold of Weathersfield, Essex, the churchwardens listed dozens of families who 'have had children many weeks, yea many months and many years and are not baptised'. At nearby Wakes Colne, John Turner, comber, 'refuseth to baptise his child or come to church, and speaketh scandalous words against his majesty's court and officers ecclesiastical, saying they are all a company of ridiculous fools'.[31]

There was little the later Stuart church could do about such recalcitrance, for its sanctions of penance and excommunication held minimal terror.[32] Community pressures may have been more effective, as neighbours grew more comfortable with conformist routines. Occasionally the clerks expressed triumph when a family returned to the fold. At Great Dunmow, Essex, they reported with satisfaction that Mr Daniel Thaines and his wife 'by much ado brought their children to be baptised, one of them eight years old'. But several other families in the parish held out. Christopher Buckmaster of Slapton, Buckinghamshire, with one child aged ten months and another almost 4 years old, was able to certify in October 1662 'that he hath brought his children into the public congregation to receive the outward badge of Christianity'. James White of Coggoe, Oxfordshire, reputedly an Anabaptist, had two of his children baptized by September 1662, and promised to attend to the others 'so soon as it shall please God to remove the infectious disease of the smallpox from his family'. The churchwardens of Waltham Magna, Essex, informed the bishop of London in 1664 that 'Thomas Parker, labourer, living in a part of our parish called Northend, who hath three or four children unbaptised, hath refused the advice and persuasions of our minister to baptise them.' A little later they reported that 'Thomas Parker does submit, and seriously promise to our minister that he will present his children to baptism within ten days.' Not since the first era of Christian conversion among the Anglo-Saxons would there have been such work for the baptizing minister, such a spectacle of children of all ages gathering at the font.[33]

The reign of Charles II saw renewed disagreement over the sign of the cross, though not with the intensity that had troubled previous generations. Officially dropped from the presbyterian Directory of Public Worship, this controversial gesture returned with the restored Church of England. Inevitably there were frictions and confusions. After attending an aristocratic christening in London in 1661, Samuel Pepys confided to his diary, 'to my and all our trouble, the parson of the parish . . . did not sign the child with the sign of the cross'.[34] Presbyterians at the Savoy Conference in 1661 pleaded to be permitted discretion in this area, but they had no more success than the puritans at Hampton Court in 1604. 'These ceremonies', argued the Savoy reformers, 'have for above an hundred years been the fountain of manifold evils in this church and nation, occasioning sad divisions between ministers and ministers, as also between ministers and people, exposing many orthodox, pious and peaceable ministers to the displeasure of their rulers.'[35] Sadly, they would soon be exposed to official displeasure again with the reimposition of uniformity in 1662.

Baptismal ceremony was one of the most visible 'matters in dispute' between Anglican apologists and their 'dissenting brethren' in the reign of Charles II. Whether the sign of the cross was more ancient than papism, and whether its usage implied affinity with Rome, still called up 'immeasurable bias of prejudice and fervency of opposition', at least in combative clerical circles. It was 'scrupled by some and reviled by others as abominable superstition', in much the same terms as a century before.[36] There was nothing new to add to the argument, but that did not prevent divines and controversialists from displaying their commitment and exercising their erudition. What was new in the later seventeenth century was the sense among some leading divines that English protestants were being distracted by disagreements about the practice of baptism, and that with papism unvanquished there were far more important matters at stake.

'It will be much more profitable for us all to join against real idolatry and superstition, than to contend about the shadows of it,' wrote the Yorkshire minister Thomas Comber in 1674. The great presbyterian divine Richard Baxter was inclined to agree, conceding that baptism with the sign of the cross was better than no baptism at all. 'I do not indeed think any of our church so fond of this ceremony particularly, but that, if the laying of it aside might turn to as great edification in the church, as the serious use of it might be improved to, our governors would easily enough condescend to such an overture,' ventured the academic churchman Nathaniel Resbury in 1684.[37]

One more chance to debate the issue arose in 1689, when the bishops in Convocation considered 'the usefulness of the cross in baptism, not as an essential part of that sacrament, but only a fit and decent ceremony'. Parliament also took up the question, offering to make the cross in baptism and ring in marriage 'indifferent things, so that people that would have them might, and those that would not might not'. But again and forever, as far as the Church of England was concerned, the customary ceremony was retained. Dissenters already had their toleration, and proposals to alter the prayer book produced only irritation among conservative country priests. The Cambridgeshire minister Thomas Hewardine contributed to a long tradition of Anglican self-satisfaction when he insisted during the reign of William III that the official service of baptism was perfectly cleansed of popery; 'not the least jot or tittle of it remains with us'.[38]

As in earlier generations, ingenious and well-meaning ministers of the later seventeenth century sometimes compromised between the strict requirements of the church and the varying wishes of their parishioners. Henry Newcome records that the Manchester minister Mr Johnson either made or omitted the sign of the cross in baptism as the parents requested, in a flexible interpretation of his office. In May 1662, before the new Act of Uniformity took effect, Johnson 'baptised . . . eight or nine children, crossed all but three which he spared with much ado. One child he baptised with the cross without the words of institution, I baptise thee in the name of the father, etc.'[39]

A similar account comes from Isaac Archer, who as vicar of Chippenham, Cambridgeshire, sought reconciliation and accommodation in the polarized religious climate of the 1660s. In 1663, he recalled in his diary,

I was very tender of nonconformists, and had the love of them all. I did not sign with the cross because it gave offence, and the bishop, Dr. Reynolds, did not require it in his articles; and I did as little as was possible without incurring danger, and so kept myself very moderate, and displeased, I think, none by so doing.

Ministers like Archer maintained local harmony by their flexible performance of the sacraments; but harmony of this sort could easily be broken by a parishioner's complaint or a bishop's visitation. Archer himself faced suspension later in 1663, but was able to keep his position. Later as minister of Freckenham, Suffolk, he was further protected from episcopal oversight, the parish being a peculiar of the bishop of Rochester within the Diocese of Norwich.[40]

Quasi-puritan or barely conformist religious practices continued from place to place despite passage of the Act of Uniformity, so long as nobody complained. William Barton, the barely conforming vicar of St Martin's, Leicester, neglected the sign of the cross throughout the 1660s despite being twice charged with violations. The minister at Peniston, Lancashire, kept peace with his semi-dissenting parishioners by omitting the sign of the cross in baptism, and by churching women from the pulpit (instead of by the altar), until Mr Brigs of Burton (a 'very troublesome' fellow, according to Oliver Heywood) 'ordered a citation to be read against' him in 1682. Others, like the dissenter Henry Newcome, turned to private baptisms in nearby houses, a practice increasingly shared with Anglicans.[41] Episcopal visitors continued to press for full conformity but increasingly, as the seventeenth century drew to a close, they were lucky to get begrudging compliance. Anyone choosing private baptism could evade all the ritual requirements of surplices, fonts, and the sign of the cross, thereby rendering the long-drawn liturgical controversy moot.

Another problem, with roots deep in parish discourse, related to the provision of fonts. Old arguments returned, as officials and parishioners debated their provision, position, and use. In a spirit of compromise in 1661 some presbyterians conceded that the font might be acceptable, so long as 'it may be so placed as all the congregation may best see and hear the whole administration' of baptism. The bishops at the Savoy Conference were prepared to make minor concessions in this regard. 'If the font be so placed as the congregation cannot hear, it may be referred to the ordinary [usually the bishop or his chancellor] to place it more conveniently.' Fonts might move again, but only with official permission. That such permission might not be readily forthcoming was signalled by their observation that 'the font usually stands, as it did in primitive times, at or near the church door, to signify that baptism was the entrance into the church mystical', and that this should set the standard.[42]

To Restoration bishops, fonts represented antiquity and continuity as well as decent liturgical practice, and warranted special attention after the abuses of the previous twenty years. Bishop Robert Sanderson's visitation of Lincoln in 1662, like several of this period, included the standard question, 'is there a font of stone, with a good cover thereunto, standing in a convenient place towards the lower part of your church, for the administration of baptism?'[43]

A visitation of the diocese of London in 1664 found dozens of fonts in disrepair, but many more undergoing refurbishment. At Stow Maries, Essex, the font was broken. At Weathersfield, Essex, 'the font was taken down by Mr. Coale's command to the churchwardens in the times of distraction, and some parts of the stones dispersed about in the parish, and the rest remain in the belfry, but the lead melted'. At Witham, Essex, 'we have a decent font newly built, being formerly spoiled'. Leaking fonts were common. At Foxton, Cambridgeshire, in 1663 the font was found to leak water into the church, and this was ordered to be amended. At least four out of twenty-six parishes reporting from the Diocese of Canterbury in 1663 had no fonts at all.[44]

Payments for this restoration of the liturgical fabric of the Church of England can often be found in churchwardens' accounts. The churchwardens at Houghton-le-Spring, Durham, paid 'for setting up the font' in 1660 only three years after they had paid to remove it. The churchwardens of Rous Lench, Worcestershire, reported in 1663, 'the font which was by some disorderly persons formerly demolished, now again set in order and repaired'. During the Interregnum John Ledgerd, the minister of Kirk Heaton, Yorkshire, did 'pull up, remove and deface the said font, and sold the stones thereof', and, befitting the shift from visual ceremony to auditory worship, installed seats in its place. Now in 1663 the font would be restored, at considerable expense to the parish. New fonts were also set up at Chalfont St Giles, Buckinghamshire, and Bunbury, Cheshire, to replace those previously damaged.[45]

But within a generation neglect set in again. Subsequent visitations of the Diocese of London found fonts in every parish, but some of them had been neglected and would not hold water and were clearly not being used. The font at Preston, Sussex, was said to be in poor repair in 1674, while the decayed church of St Thomas in Winchelsea, Sussex, had 'no font for baptism'. In enquiries from 1683 to 1686 the archdeacon of Essex noted dozens of fonts out of repair and several more in need of covers.[46] The implication is that either ministers had taken to using basins to hold the baptismal water, or that public baptism in church was now infrequent, with the rise of nonconformity and the growing practice of private baptism at home. Later seventeenth-century clergymen were increasingly inclined to baptize away from the font, without fear of rebuke, while many more baptisms were conducted in domestic chambers where no font of any sort was required.

An episcopal visitation of the archdeaconry of Ely in 1685 found fonts in forty out of sixty-eight parishes which were 'useless', 'nasty', 'foul', 'abominable', or in some other way defective. Many of them would not hold water, and apparently had been abandoned. At East Hatley the 'old font' was 'used to make steps to the stable'. Instead, in many of these Cambridgeshire parishes, the minister made do with a basin, or, as at Barton, 'a nasty black dish'. Against this clear demonstration of changing liturgical custom, the bishop and his chancellor demanded dignity and conformity. As in Essex, this pressure brought results, at least in the short run, and once again the majority of fonts were refurbished.[47]

A common compromise was to baptize from a basin set in the font. This fixed the service in its ancient position but allowed some flexibility in the actual administration of water. The minister of Hillingdon, Middlesex, made a special note in the parish register in 1672 recording the baptism of Elizabeth Pratt, 'the first that in eleven years was baptized with water in the font, the custom being in this place to baptize out of a basin, after the presbyterian manner, only set in the font, which I could never get reformed till I had gotten a new clerk, John Brown, who presently did what I appointed to be done'.[48] This confession of postponed conformity is an eloquent comment on the balance of authority between laity and clergy on the outer reaches of the diocese of London.

High-church and low-church positions were developing within the framework of Anglican conformity. Laudian ceremonialists would have relished, as puritans would have abhorred, the newly installed font at St James in the Fields in the 1680s. This fashionable new church, in the environs of the court, boasted

a rare piece of workmanship, where the hand of the artist has set forth to the life upon the font the history of original sin, and its cure in the water of baptism. Adam and Eve stand beneath, confessing the guilt of that sin, for which infants are brought thither to be cleansed. Round the basin is seen Christ under the hand of the Baptist in Jordan, authorizing the institution of that salutary laver. And over it is an angel, as it were descending to move the waters, and to signify that the efficacy of that sacrament is from above.[49]

Humbler parishes made do with their ancient stone fonts, or, if nobody objected, a simple dish or basin. With so much else to worry about it must have been a relief to hear from a leading Restoration churchman that the previously vexed issue of dipping or sprinkling was 'not a matter worth contending for'.[50]

The Rise of Private Baptism

Baptism was intended as a public performance, introducing a new Christian to the community at large. The child was supposed to be brought to the church, and the ceremony was designed to be conducted in the face of the entire congregation. One of its purposes was to remind everyone present of their own baptismal vows. However, as we have seen, these intentions were often thwarted. Baptisms had long been conducted on days other than Sundays and holy days, and at times when none but the baptismal party was present. The service could be low-keyed in tone and select in composition, even if performed at the font in general compliance with the prayer book.

The Book of Common Prayer recognized that some babies were too frail to withstand the journey to church, and that other occasions of necessity might prevent normal public baptism. It therefore provided an alternative service, intended for ministration by a priest but *in extremis* available to any layman (or laywoman), which allowed for a private baptism at home.[51] Throughout the Elizabethan period and under the early Stuarts, such private baptisms were relatively unusual. They were, at least, the exception to the rule. But beginning in the 1640s, and increasing to the point of notoriety following the Restoration, parents planned private domestic baptisms in cooperation with the officiating clergymen.

Late sixteenth-century nonconformists like Henry Barrow had agreed with the Elizabethan bishops that baptism was a public duty, 'to be delivered openly in the assembly when the whole church is met together'. The pledge should be performed, thought the Jacobean puritan Gouge, 'with the more solemnity, as a matter of great moment, before many witnesses', and preferably in the face of the whole congregation. Gouge criticized 'their practice who bring their child to church to be baptised accompanied only with the midwife and three witnesses. It were almost as good to be baptised in a private house; for it is not the walls of the church, but the assembly of saints, that addeth to the honour of the sacrament.'[52] Ceremonialists and episcopal disciplinarians might demur at Gouge's depiction of congregational saints, but they agreed on the importance of public baptism. Early Stuart bishops railed against parishioners who baptized their children 'privately according to their own fantasies' or 'according to their own fancies'. Services conducted away from the church, feared the Restoration churchman Anthony Sparrow, 'may be an occasion of mischief, that the form of baptism may be vitiated and corrupted'.[53] Who knew what slackness or irregularity might befall, what superstitions might creep back in, if baptism moved out of the public sight?

This, exactly, was the point. The problem lay not with those cases in which a child might die before a full ecclesiastical baptism could be scheduled, but rather in the deliberate avoidance of the many disputed aspects of baptism which we have been discussing. Parents and ministers could collaborate in a private baptism, and the service, though conducted without surplice, interrogatories, font, or sign of the cross, would be completely valid. Such a ceremony could be constructed as a domestic occasion, for the family and household rather than the common congregation, allowing the newly delivered mother to take part. Taking the sacrament indoors, from public to private space, was an easy way to achieve liturgical simplification while maintaining the sanctity of the ordinance. This seems to have been the strategy of post-Restoration dissenters, even more than of pre-Civil War puritans. Though building on earlier traditions and precedents, this domestication of the sacrament constituted a significant relocation of religious activity. Catholic recusancy could also flourish in these circumstances, along with puritan irregularity.

Private baptism also gave privileged families greater control of the ritual setting. It allowed for a more select gathering, removed from public view, with more comfortable seating and speedier access to the refreshments. When conducted in private chambers the religious baptism ceremony could blend smoothly into the secular christening supper. Members of the élite were among the first to value these benefits. John Evelyn, for example, was baptized in 1620 in the family home at Wotton, Surrey, the rites being 'performed in the dining room by parson Hingham'.[54] The aristocratic Evelyns had no quarrel with the ceremonies of the Church of England, but enjoyed the convenience of a minister who made house calls. There were, therefore, two distinct advantages of private baptism, one a way of dispelling liturgical scruples, the other a matter of social exclusiveness and convenience. It could also be argued that making the minister come to the child was safer and healthier for the infant than taking the child to the church. Furthermore, in a culture shrugging off priestcraft, it indicated who was working for whom.

During the 1640s and 1650s, when confusion was in the air and when ecclesiastical ceremonies were overthrown, an untold number of households maintained the traditional baptismal ritual by bringing it indoors. The evidence of diaries and letters suggests that this was mainly an upper-class practice, particularly strong among the defeated royalist élite; but humbler families may also have found ministers to conduct baptisms and churchings according to the Book of Common Prayer. Private baptism had long been practised by scrupulous nonconformists but, as William Sherlock explained in retrospect, 'when the Church of England was pulled down, and the use of the ceremonies forbid, those who still retained their reverence and obedience to the constitutions of the church, and would not partake in a prevailing schism, were forced to retire into private too'.[55] Defenders of Anglican ceremony now discovered the advantages of private services that had long been known to its critics. The domestic services of the Evelyn family, discussed above, may be the best-documented examples of a widespread liturgical conservatism.

Once established the practice was hard to break. In the 1660s, when the Church of England was triumphantly restored, the Evelyn family continued to arrange for their baptisms to be conducted at home. John Evelyn's son Richard was christened in January 1664, 'Mr Brereton officiating in the great chamber at Sayes Court.' On 8 October 1665, the diarist writes, 'before dinner was my daughter christened Mary in the chamber called the red chamber where born'. Evelyn's second daughter, Elizabeth, was christened in September 1667, 'by Dr. Breton, our vicar, in my house at Sayes Court'. And a third daughter, Susanna, was christened in May 1669, presumably in similar circumstances. Evelyn's grandchildren were also baptized privately at home.[56]

Most of the baptisms Evelyn attended as a guest or godparent were also private occasions, suited to the high social status of the parties involved. In November 1674 he attended the christening of 'Mrs. Watson's son . . . in its mother's lodging in King Street (London)'. In September 1678 he was an honoured guest when Mrs Godolphin's son 'was baptised in the chamber where it was born, in the mother's presence, at Whitehall, by the chaplain who used to officiate in her pretty family'. An exception to these private events was the public baptism 'in Greenwich church with much solemnity' when Sir John Chardin's son was baptized in 1687. The godparents included the Earl of Bath and the Countess of Carlisle, and celebrations concluded at the Queen's house in Greenwich.[57] Leading families never completely abandoned the parish church for ceremonies of this sort. Through choice of time and company the public rite of baptism could still be made to serve both their spiritual and their social needs.

Private christenings combined with christening suppers were common events among Samuel Pepys's circle of gentry, merchants, and officials in Restoration London. Some took place in the afternoon, others in the early evening after dinner, on various days of the week. Their characteristic features included polite discourse and mild flirtation, a light snack with moderate drinking, and bestowing of gifts by godparents. The sacramental high point, the actual religious baptizing, was sometimes submerged amidst these lively and noisy actions. Samuel Pepys memorialized such a christening at the house of Michael Mitchell, liquor-seller, in May 1667. It was an idyllic scene,

his little house full of his father and mothers and the kindred, hardly any else, and mighty merry in this innocent company; and Betty mighty pretty in bed, but her head aching, not very merry; but the company mighty merry, and I with them; and so the child was christened, my wife, his father, and her mother the witnesses, and the child's name Elizabeth. So we had gloves and wine and wafers, very pretty, and talked and tattled.

In its modest way, the scene was similar to that described more artfully by Ned Ward.[58]

Although the pattern cannot be quantified, it appears that private baptism became increasingly fashionable among leaders of society during the reign of Charles II. Provincial civic elders and families of the middling sort followed suit, especially in urban areas. In 1669 Alderman Samuel Newton of Cambridge and Mr Hughes the Esquire Bedall stood as godfathers to young Roger Thompson. The child was 'baptised at home in [the mother's] chamber by Mr. Christopher Bainbrigg of Christ's College'.[59] Such a ceremony would have taken several days to plan, and could not have been justified in terms of medical necessity. Nor is there a whiff of nonconformity. It was consonant with the wider round of private dining and socially select entertainment that these Restoration dignitaries often preferred. This is yet another indication of the separation of social classes in the second half of the seventeenth century, in which the high-born and powerful removed themselves from community scrutiny. It fits with the erection of locked pews to segregate congregations, travel by closed coach instead of by horseback or open carriage, domestic architecture which secluded betters from their inferiors, the rage for clandestine weddings and night-time funerals, and the conversion of open parish festivities into select indoor junkets. The rise of private baptism also accords with a privileging of select social activity over communal religious fellowship, and the dislodging of the church from its central place in the lives of the laity.[60]

Defenders of ecclesiastical discipline complained about 'the shameful disuse' of public baptism, and set out to cajole families back to the font. The bishop of London circularized his clergy in 1679 and urged them to exhort parishioners to bring their infants to church. In the last resort, suggested Bishop Compton, 'if they will not bring their children into the congregation, supposing they have health to bear it, we ought to refuse the registering of them'. Some country ministers also threatened to refuse to register baptisms they had not themselves conducted in church, but there is little evidence that such sanctions were often applied.[61] Whether performed in church or chamber, a baptism was still supposed to be recorded in the Anglican parish register. Dissenting ministers who performed private baptisms were also supposed to register them, and the majority seem to have obliged. Historical demographers who have examined large numbers of registers believe that defective registration of baptisms was no worse in the post-Restoration period (1660–95) than it had been under Elizabeth and the early Stuarts (1558–1640) when some 4 or 5 per cent of baptisms went unrecorded.[62]

William Sherlock, a leading London minister, wrote in 1682 that

public baptism is now very much grown out of fashion; most people look upon it as a very needless and troublesome ceremony, to carry their children to the public congregation, there to be solemnly admitted into the fellowship of Christ's church. They think it may be as well done in a private chamber, as soon as the child is born, with little company and with little noise.

Against what had become the 'prevailing' custom of private baptism, Sherlock urged a return to the traditions and constitutions of the church. So too did Edmund Arwaker in a 'dissuasive from baptising children in private'.[63] The bishop of London's campaign for public baptism was further promoted in visitations of the Dioceses of Bath and Wells, Chichester, Lincoln, and in sermons by the archbishop of Canterbury. Country clergy picked up the theme, such as Martin Strong, vicar of Yeovil, Somerset, who preached and published on *The Indecency and Unlawfulness of Baptizing Children in Private*.[64]

Countering the common justification for private baptism, that 'the child is at present indisposed' or that 'the gossips are now in the way who cannot so well attend another time', Philip Stubs retorted,

to be plain, 'tis not the child's real indisposition, but the unhappy bent of the parents' too perverse inclinations oftentimes that makes them take these measures; since 'tis notorious, that of those who dared not venture their infant two or three doors to church in the cold air of this city, many have speedily after sent it out some miles in a much colder, to be taken care of in the country. And then, as for the excuse of wanting those who will stand godfathers and godmothers, 'tis well known that persons of any fashion are not without numbers ambitious of paying that complemental piece of respect to them; for, to our shame be it spoken, 'tis too frequently looked upon as no more.

Poor people made similar excuses, Stubs alleged, preferring baptism at home as a way to keep down expenses; 'being unable to provide things handsome enough for their company and a public appearance, they don't care to be ridiculed and laughed at by their neighbours'.[65]

The ecclesiastical campaign for a return to public baptism made some surprising converts. John Evelyn's long experience with private baptism does little to prepare us for the position he took at the end of the seventeenth century opposing baptism in private chambers. By 1689 John Evelyn had become an advocate of public baptism, in support of the traditional usage of the Book of Common Prayer and against the prevailing customs of his age. In conference with the archbishop of Canterbury in April 1689, Evelyn urged, 'that when they went about to reform some particulars of the liturgy, church disciplines, canons, etc., the baptising in private houses without necessity might be reformed'. The common practice, he now claimed, proceeded 'merely from the pride of the women, bringing that into custom which was only indulged in case of necessity, during the rebellion and persecution of the clergy, in our late civil wars, etc.' Evelyn had clearly misremembered the experience of his own family. The other culprits, besides women, were the clergy themselves, who, Evelyn said (and he would know), 'were paid with considerable advantage and gifts, for baptising in chambers'.[66]

Sermons by Roger Wye in 1691 and by William Stringfellow in 1693 further convinced Evelyn that baptism should be timely and solemn. Stringfellow convinced him that children should be brought to baptism 'at farthest' by the eighth day following their birth, 'and that in regard of the infinite benefits and advantages of that sacrament, admitting the child into all the privileges of the Christian religion, it concerned parents not to defer the christening of their children'. Stimulated by another Stringfellow sermon in 1699, Evelyn returned to the topic of baptism. The sacrament, he understood, required 'inward holiness, with promise of spiritual and heavenly blessings and fruitions'. But too many of his contemporaries thought otherwise. Too many people, 'by their neglect and slightly regarding baptism but as a ceremony . . . think it enough and all done when the christening is over'. As for 'private baptism in their houses, as the mode of late is, though permitted in times of persecution, schism, sickness, that else it ought to be public and before the congregation'.[67]

At present we cannot tell how successful was this campaign for reform, nor how serious was the problem outside of London. Our primary evidence for the rise of private baptism comes from complaints by the diocesan clergy and entries in half a dozen diaries. Its significance lies in the withdrawal of élite groups from the common parish assembly, the accommodation of religious ritual to social convenience, and the remaking of a major life-cycle event as a domestic, rather than an ecclesiastical occasion.

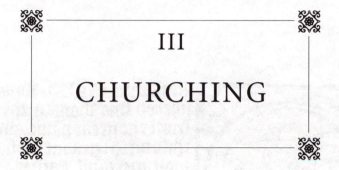

III

CHURCHING

Almightie G⚙D, which haſt
liuered this woman thy ſerua
from the great paine and peril
child birth : graunt we beſeech t
moſt mercifull Father , that t
through thy helpe, may both fa
fully liue , and walke in her bo
on, according to thy Will, in thi
preſent, and alſo may bee parta
of euerlaſting glory in the lif
come, through Ieſus Chriſt our Lord, Amen.

FIG. 11   Detail of the initial and prayer for the Churching of Women, *The Book of Common Prayer* (1603)

PURIFICATION, THANKSGIVING, AND THE CHURCHING OF WOMEN

The social and cultural activities of childbirth did not end with the safe delivery of a baby, or with the infant's christening, but extended for several more weeks while the newly delivered mother adjusted to her new lease on life. Another ritual performance, almost as complex and as contested as baptism, secured a ritual closure to the extended process of childbearing. It celebrated the woman's survival and marked her return to everyday circumstances. This chapter deals with the religious ritual required of women after childbirth, and with its social accompaniments.[1] Known by several names, the religious aspect of this ritual was variously referred to as 'Purification', 'Thanksgiving', and the 'Churching of Women'. The various names remind us that three separate issues were involved, three distinct activities with different meanings and different histories. For convenience I will commonly refer to the churching of women, or simply churching; but it is important to keep in mind the idea that the ecclesiastical ceremony, itself ambiguously named, had different resonances and implications according to the religious viewpoint, authority, role, and gender of the parties involved.

Churching was a ritual process that connected the semi-secret domestic world of women and childbirth with the public ecclesiastical and communal business of religion. Like the related ceremony of baptism, churching became embroiled in the liturgical and disciplinary contests of English protestantism and the struggles of religious politics; but it also had social, sexual, and festive associations that lay beyond the reach of the church. As a post-partum ceremony, churching occupied a special space in the womanly world of fecundity and matronhood.

Like other ritual performances and rites of passage, churching opens a window into some sensitive and opaque areas of early modern culture. The history of this ceremony—of people's understanding of it, participation in it, or rejection of it—illuminates several important clusters of issues. One such cluster includes the progress of the Reformation; the maintenance or suppression of allegedly Jewish, popish, or superstitious practices; the development, adaptation, and ossification of liturgy, and the tensions of liturgical practice; the shaping and defence of an Anglican ecclesiastical polity, with its distinctive theology and discipline; and the shifting weight and shifting concerns of nonconformity, puritanism, and religious dissent. Churching, from this perspective, is connected to the mainstream history of religion.[2] The liturgical politics of churching were driven by the same array of nuanced religious opinion that fuelled contention over other ecclesiastical ceremonies.

A related set of issues includes the interaction of clergy and laity; the local politics of ecclesiastical power; the role of the church (and behind the church, the state) in sustaining customary practices at key passages in the life cycle; the relationship of family and parish, household and community, and the intersection of the domestic and public domains; also the relations of rich and poor, respectable and reprobate, established and marginal; how disputes over churching related to the reformation of manners; and the degree to which England experienced a common religious culture. Churching, along with other cultural practices related to childbirth, marriage, and death, was bound up in a discourse about behaviour, propriety, and discipline.[3]

There are also complex gender relations to sort out: the relationship of male priests and female mothers; the interaction of husbands and wives; the roles of other women, midwives and gossips, in both the religious and secular aspects of the ceremony; and the problem of churching an unmarried mother. The shaping and regulation of the ceremony reflected the national religious politics of Tudor and Stuart England. Its conduct involved the politics of community relations, and the politics of gender. Churching, then, provides another topic in which liturgy, law, and custom come together as part of the recombination of social and traditional history.

Viewpoints

What little discussion of churching one finds in the secondary sources has largely been shaped by Keith Thomas. In *Religion and the Decline of Magic* Thomas emphasized the split between the official position of the church, which 'chose to treat the ceremony as one of thanksgiving', and the views of people at large, for whom 'churching was indubitably a ritual of purification closely linked with its Jewish predecessor'. Popular superstitions, so-called 'taboo' and 'magical elements' in the ceremony, and puritan objections to the ecclesiastical service, all confirm that we are witnessing a ritual of purification. And Thomas concluded that 'resistance to churching or to wearing the veil became one of the surest signs of puritan feeling among clergy or laity in the century before the Civil War'.[4] A summary might suggest that something very old and primitive was at work here, which took on political dimensions when it became part of the puritan agenda.

Most scholars have absorbed the work of Keith Thomas on this subject, and quote him (and some of his sources) to the effect that churching was a ritual of purification and an arena of conflict. Thomas's characterization of late medieval attitudes is taken to apply equally to early modern England. Some scholars have also adopted the anthropological language and interpretive schema of van Gennep, and see churching as a rite of reintegration after the ritual isolation of childbearing, the ritual closure to a period of liminal transition. The Polynesian word 'taboo' appears frequently in these discussions without much self-consciousness or criticism. Churching is presented as a classic *rite de passage* dealing with female pollution, as a cultural response to the fear of women, and as a man-made instrument for their control.[5] It has been treated as a ceremony of restoration and cleansing after the impurity and sequestration of childbearing. One recent essay on churching concludes that 'the rite, its trappings and focus were almost penitential', a reflection of the 'endemic mistrust of womankind'. Another considers churching as an unpopular practice to which 'the majority of women submitted'.[6]

The most common view seems to endorse those early modern puritans who criticized churching as an unreformed purification, while at the same time arguing, with certain feminists, that churching was a patriarchal or misogynist instrument for the subjugation of women. My reading of the evidence leads me to neither of these conclusions. Indeed, an alternative case can be made that women normally looked forward to churching as an occasion of female social activity, in which the notion of 'purification' was uncontentious, minimal, or missing.

I am much more persuaded by Susan Wright, in her thesis on Salisbury, who notes that 'for many women churching represented little more than an opportunity to meet and celebrate with their peers'.[7] This is an important observation which shifts attention from the priests who performed the ceremony, and the controversialists who argued about it, to the experience of the women themselves. By paying attention to the context and circumstances of churching, aside from its theology and theory, we may find the way to a fresh interpretation.

Adrian Wilson has gone furthest in this direction, dissenting from the view of churching as 'an imposition from without, as a male and clerical burden laid upon mothers'. He too resists the identification of churching with purification. Neither the newly delivered mother nor the women who accompanied her to church behaved 'as if *they* felt her to be impure', nor is it clear that her husband or neighbours thought in terms of pollution or defilement.

Churching was, rather, a social gathering, a collective female occasion, and the conclusion to the privileged month that women normally enjoyed after child-birth. For Wilson, however, churching was more than a thanksgiving; it marked a zone of sexual politics and gendered conflict. Churching, in his model, was struggle, where women took initiatives and achieved victories. 'Women's resist-ance to patriarchal power' through the ceremonies of childbirth and church-ing is said to exemplify the alternative feminist tradition of 'women on top'.[8] And of this too I have yet to be convinced.

Gail Paster, a literary scholar, has offered a sensitive rereading of the church-ing ceremony in light of the conservative medical discourse on women's bodies. Although, as she points out, the English religious ceremony makes no expli-cit reference to the subject of purification, a powerful rhetoric about unclean fluids hovered behind the text. Overt and latent meanings intermingled. The popularity of churching among women, Paster suggests, 'may argue just as forcefully for their internalization of shame and embarrassment as for their pride, relief, and self-congratulation'.[9] Unfortunately for the historian, inter-nalizations of this sort leave little trace in the records.

The documentary material that might permit a re-examination of purifica-tion, thanksgiving, and the churching of women comes from several sources. It includes biblical exegesis, religious debate, and sermons; liturgy and the arguments for liturgical revision; ecclesiastical visitation articles and the records of visitation processes; accounts of parochial administration covering fees and church fabric; and family papers, diaries, and letters. The majority of this evidence comes from male clerical authors, of course, and it reflects their concern with worship and discipline; only a few sources depict churching in practice, and rarely from the viewpoint of the woman in the pew. As usual, people's behaviour and thinking must be inferred from fragments. None the less, we can construct a history that traces several clusters of issues from the mid-Tudor Reformation to the later seventeenth century.

Too often, discussions of this sort draw evidence eclectically from different periods, as if all issues and problems were at all times equally present; the synchronic prevails over the diachronic. In the short review that follows I want to suggest that religious and disciplinary concerns altered over the course of the Elizabethan and Stuart periods, and that changing attempts to regulate churching produced varying responses at the local level. Veils, for example, which are often adduced as sure signs of taboo and purification, remained a marginal issue in most dioceses until high ceremonialist bishops of the 1620s and 1630s began once again to insist upon them. And churching, in the decades after the Restoration, had more to do with the politics of conformity than with any lingering notions of female pollution. Churching was about many things, but not necessarily always the same things. Like many other rituals, its outward form could mask a variety of meanings.

Gossipings

The formal religious ceremony of thanksgiving formed part of a larger social ritual with complex secular dimensions. One did not have to be a devotee of the Book of Common Prayer to celebrate the social reappearance of a women recovering from childbirth, or to join in offering thanks for her safe deliverance. Like the christening feasts that celebrated baptisms, the wedding suppers that accompanied marriages, and the funeral dinners following burials, the 'gossipings' associated with the churching of women provided opportunities for hospitality, conviviality, and display.

The scale of the celebration varied according to circumstances and social status, but usually included feasting and drinking. When Lady Strange was churched in January 1589 the guests included the bishop of Chester and his wife, Baron Walton and his wife, and a glittering company of aristocratic and gentle couples. At the opposite extreme of society, when Jane Minors of Barking, Essex, came to be churched in 1597, she 'feasted at a tavern four or five hours in the forenoon' and returned for more drinking later. When asked why she had not completed the formal business in church, 'she answered it was [but] a ceremony'. Agnes Turner, a Hampshire woman, similarly 'had wine and cakes in the morning before she went to be churched' at Basingstoke in 1635.[10] In London in 1561 the churching of Mrs White, wife of an alderman and grocer, concluded with 'a great dinner' with 'many worshipful ladies and alderman's wives and gentlewomen'. In March 1563, reports the diarist Henry Machyn, 'a great company of gentlewomen had a great dinner as could be had as for Lent, as for fish', to celebrate another London churching.[11]

In some towns the corporation attempted to control expenditure on 'dishes, meats and wines' at churchings as well as baptisms, as part of their campaign of reform. Thanksgiving gossipings and associated childbirth gatherings had allegedly got out of hand. At Leicester in 1568 it was ordained that, 'for the eschewing of the superfluous charge and excess of the inhabitants . . . there shall be no feasts made at any churching within the said town saving only one competent mess of meat provided for gossips and midwives'. In 1575 the aldermen of Kirkby Kendal restricted to twelve the number of wives accompanying a woman to her churching, and set limits on the drinking and feasting that followed.[12]

Churchings formed part of the townswoman's round of 'daily gadding with her gossips to banquets and bridals'. According to Margaret Cavendish, a newly married woman might spend much of her time 'at labours, christenings, churchings, and other matrimonial gossipings and meetings'. Foreign visitors remarked on the freedom of English wives to gad outside the house, 'making merry' at 'child-births, christenings, churchings, and funerals'.[13]

Most of our information about this aspect of the ritual comes from literary and anecdotal sources, and applies to the middling sort of people and their betters. In the misogynist satire *The Batchelars Banquet* of 1603, the wife found 'great cheer, and no small company of wives' when she attended a neighbour's churching. All the women wore their most fashionable outfits. Preparing for her own churching, she tells her husband, 'it be a thing which ought both by reason and custom to be done'. The husband, easily manipulated, promises her a new gown and assures her he will not 'break custom' by cancelling the gossips' feast.[14] The author shows us gossips 'prattling and tattling', indeed gossiping, as they work their way through the household supplies of wine and sugar. Actual expenditures of this sort may sometimes be found in domestic accounts. The festivity was considered to be the woman's occasion, even if paid for by her husband and attended by male relations and friends. Alcohol flowed so abundantly on these occasions that writers of Stuart comedy could joke about characters 'as drunk as women at a gossiping'.[15] This crude characterization embraced the entire sequence of womenly gatherings from lying in to thanksgiving after childbirth.

References to thanksgiving gossipings in diaries indicate that they were often mixed occasions, though generally dominated by women. After initial formalities the men and the women may have retired to separate rooms. Thomas Crosfield of Oxford went 'gossiping' in 1626 at the house of a child he had baptized three weeks earlier, and stayed drinking until one o'clock in the morning. Robert Woodford invited the minister and his wife and several close friends, both men and women, to share a dinner of venison pasty to celebrate his wife's churching in 1639. Samuel Pepys and his wife attended similar post-churching gossipings in the 1660s.[16] Other diaries mention social excursions and parties on the days of a churching, and even the nonconformists of the later seventeenth century enjoyed gatherings of joyful thanksgiving (usually with dinner) a month after one of them had given birth.[17]

For the woman and her friends, churching provided a social occasion, a sisterly outing with wives and midwife escorting the newly delivered mother. The same women who had gathered to attend the birth—'those who serve the child-bed mysteries' in Herrick's supple phrase[18]—would now share in the thanksgiving for the mother's deliverance. Midwives, as we have seen, served as keepers of custom, and may have helped organize the traditional parts of the ceremony; their prominence at churchings also advertised their skills in the birthroom. Dressing for the occasion, wearing fresh clothes, gadding with gossips, and consuming food and drink, were important accompaniments to this ritual, as to so many others, although it could be done simply and quietly. Ministers warned against 'effeminate speeches, wanton behaviour, and unseasonable mirth, which often doth accompany such meetings'.[19] Indeed, the solemnities of the service could be offset by chatter and giggles, making it a moot point whether childbirth warranted purification or thanksgiving. Evidence of this sort is scant, but Katherine Whitehead of Danbury, Essex, was cited in 1578 because at her churching she 'with a loud voice demanded of Mr. Doctor Withers if he were ready to do his duty, she was ready to do hers; whereby she troubled him in his sermon and caused the people to make a laughter'.[20]

Green Women

Churching marked the end of the woman's privileged 'month', and for the man the end of what contemporaries sometimes called their 'gander month'.[21] It concluded a period of physical recovery, and also a time of sequestration and abstention during which (at least in some cases) the husband took charge of domestic duties while being excluded from the matrimonial bed. 'The mother at that time by reason of her travail and delivery is weak, and not in case to have her head much troubled with many cares', advised William Gouge. It was a time, enjoined the preacher William Whately, 'when lust should be laid to sleep, and pure good-will be most wakeful and working'.[22] The merchant John Hayne of Exeter normally allocated monthly household funds to his wife, but on four occasions in the 1630s when his wife lay in he assigned the money 'into a bag for house expenses' on his own account. A 'monthly nurse' or 'keeper' attended Mrs Hayne after each confinement until she was able to return to her normal duties.[23] Even unmarried women who were 'harboured' illicitly during childbirth commonly lay in for a month before moving on.[24]

Throughout this time, in popular opinion, the woman in childbed was considered to be 'green'. The term was used partly with the sense of her being unwell or unready, but was primarily related to the condition of 'greensickness', amenorrhoea, the stoppage of the menses or terms.[25] Sixteenth-century folklore held that an unchurched 'green woman' should stay at home, refrain from sexual intercourse, and not participate in the sacraments of the church.[26] An Elizabethan countrywoman, Joan Thrussell of Danbury, Essex, excused herself from coming to church after childbirth in 1586, 'by reason of being a green woman'. In 1624 the churchwardens of Ferring, Sussex, reported, 'we have divers green woman that yet have not given thanks'.[27]

The ceremony of churching established a ritual closure to this state of affairs, allowing the resumption of sexual relations between husband and wife and the restoration of normal domestic order. The erotic ramifications of the thanksgiving are clearly suggested in Robert Herrick's verse, 'Julia's Churching, or Purification' written in the 1620s or 1630s.

> All Rites well ended, with fair Auspice come
> (As to the breaking of a Bride-cake) home:
> Where ceremonious Hymen shall for thee
> Provide a second Epithalamie.

The poem (from the man's point of view, of course) concludes with the restored wife offering her husband 'not one but many a maidenhead'.[28]

Medical opinion advised that a month was needed for a woman to recover from the pains of childbirth. Lochia, the bleeding discharge from the uterus, persists for up to six weeks (though for a shorter time among nursing mothers), and the discomforts of this 'afterpurging' may also have inhibited sexual intercourse. Conventional handbooks such as *The Birth of Man-Kinde* urged breast-feeding women too 'to abstain from venerie or man's company; for if she use that, it shall spend and consume the milk and make it unsavoury and unwholesome'.[29] Demographic evidence is inconclusive about the effect of these inhibitions on fertility,[30] and we have little hope of finding out how consistently they applied in practice. An intriguing fragment occurs in the diary of Ralph Josselin, the Essex clergyman, who wrote on 8 March 1648, three and a half weeks after Mrs Josselin had given birth, 'at night my wife in kindness came and lay in my bed'. The Lancashire gentleman Nicholas Blundell similarly noted in 1704, 'my wife's month being now out we lay together'.[31]

In a dialogue published in 1601 a spokesman for the Church of England is made to suggest that abstinence from sexual pleasure in the month after childbirth, in regard to the woman's 'weakness and uncleanness', is one of the differences 'betwixt reasonable creatures and beasts'. But his female puritan adversary knew better: 'How doth your churching of women restrain a carnal and licentious appetite from executing his villainous and beastly desire? Hath he not his full swindge and liberty to do what he list for all that?'[32]

In practice, the woman's 'month' may have been notional and prescriptive, more an ideal than an actual period of sequestration. For depending on their needs, health, and circumstances, newly delivered women did go out, could attend church, and perhaps even engaged in sexual intercourse before the month expired. Richard Hooker noted that the law said nothing to bar a green woman from going to worship, 'although her abstaining from public assemblies and her abode in separation for the time be most convenient'. None the less by custom, as Shakespeare's Hermione insisted in *The Winter's Tale,* 'the child-bed privilege' was one 'which 'longs to women of all fashion'. Leontes' cruelty to his wife was compounded by denying her the childbed privilege of seclusion, dragging her from her chamber and subjecting her to public examination and humiliation while she was still 'green'.[33]

Blessing and Cleansing

From the earliest times, the churching service was attended with ambiguity. In pre-Reformation practice the ceremony was as much a blessing as a cleansing, a comfort as well as a purification. In some versions of the Sarum Missal one finds the 'ordo ad purificandum mulierem', in others, and perhaps more commonly, 'benedictio mulieris post partum ante ostium ecclesie'. Some have the priest saying 'Thou shalt purge me, O Lord, with hyssop', after sprinkling her with holy water, and before leading her into the main part of the church; others omit those words. The priest recited psalms, spoke of deliverance from the peril of childbirth, and concluded with the prospect of eternal life.[34] In traditional catholic practice the woman to be purified wore a white veil, carried a lighted candle, and was accompanied by two married women, but this was not formally required by any rubric.[35]

Protestants maintained that this ceremony was a continuation of Jewishness, a superstitious adherence to Mosaical and Levitical law. From the progression from the church porch, through the sprinkling with holy water, to the reference to purging with hyssop (the herb used to cleanse sacramental vessels), the ceremony was filled with priestcraft and popish superstition.[36] Though the service was substantially rewritten for the Church of England, puritan agitators of the 1570s (and later) asserted that little had improved.

Edward VI's reign saw important changes in the liturgical conduct and in the larger religious significance of this service. What appeared in 1549 as an anglicization of the Latin 'ordo ad purificandum mulierem' (the order for the purification of women) became in 1552 and all subsequent editions of the prayer book, 'the thanksgiving of women after childbirth, commonly called the churching of women'.[37] The three words circulated around each other, each with their attendant connotations. Officially, after 1552, the service was no longer a purification; all notion of a penitential cleansing was disclaimed. As Nicholas Ridley assured the more austere protestants at Zurich, 'I ween the word purification is changed, and it is called thanksgiving . . . the matter there said all tendeth to give God thanks, and to none other end.'[38] The Church of England preferred to label the service a thanksgiving, but it acknowledged the popular understanding of the process of public ecclesiastical reception, that is, churching.

The service announced the woman's deliverance and preservation from 'the great danger of child-birth'. Its words, including the majestic Psalm 121— 'I have lifted up mine eyes unto the hills, from whence cometh my help'— have more to do with survival than cleansing. Several Edwardian protestants, including the future Bishop Robert Horne, wondered 'whether should the office for the churching of women be retained' at all, when it had been abandoned by other reformed churches.[39] Could the impulse for its retention in England have came from women's delight in the social and religious attention they received at their churching, rather than from male or clerical anxieties about unpurified women? We should at least keep open the question whether purification was something done *to* women, or *for* them.

In the old catholic service the priest met the woman before the church porch, and only moved inside the church after sprinkling her with holy water. In the rubric of 1549 'the woman shall come into the church, and there shall kneel down in some convenient place, nigh unto the choir door'. By 1552 that convenient place had moved from the threshold and margins of the church to its ritual centre: now the woman should kneel 'nigh unto the place where the table standeth'.[40] These may seem like minor adjustments, but they were enormously significant. They transformed the woman from a penitent to a celebrant (or 'gratulant'), from a petitioner at the margin to the focus of community attention. There was no more sprinkling with holy water, no mention at all of veils or candles, and, after 1552, no reference to the customary offering of chrisoms, the cloth wrapped round a newborn child at baptism. Custom might retain some of these trappings, and custom could be enforced with discipline, but the rubric is simple. The service is introduced with the instruction that the priest 'shall say these words, or such like as the case shall require'.[41] Nowhere else in the Book of Common Prayer is the minister given such latitude.

A well-known sermon by Hugh Latimer, preached in 1552 before the Duchess of Suffolk (Latimer's patron, the dowager Catherine Bertie, who remarried that year), points to some competing traditions. Latimer told of a woman in prison at Cambridge who had recently given birth and who was now waiting to be executed for the crime of infanticide. 'She made great moan to me, and most earnestly required me that I would find the means that she might be purified before her suffering; for she thought she should have been damned if she should suffer without purification.' Latimer took the opportunity to explain the new protestant position, and counselled her 'that that law was made unto the Jews, and not unto us; and that women lying in childbed be not unclean before God; neither is purification used to that end, that it should cleanse from sin; but rather a civil and politic law, made for natural honesty sake'.[42] What Latimer and his like meant by 'natural honesty sake' in this regard is a matter to which we should return.

According to Latimer,

a woman before the time of her purification, that is to say, as long as she is a green woman, is not meet to do such acts as other women, nor to have company with her husband, for it is against natural honesty and against the commonwealth. To that end purification is kept and used, not to make a superstition or holiness of it, as some do, which think that they may not fetch neither fire nor anything in the house where there is a green woman; which opinion is erroneous and wicked. For women, as I said afore, be as well in the favour of God before they be purified as after.[43]

This was a sermon at court before the high-born; but it was also an opportunity to display and dispose of some popular superstitions. The Cambridgeshire woman seems to have wanted a sacramental cleansing, *in extremis*, to prepare her soul for death as much as to cleanse it of the stain of childbearing. It is noteworthy that Latimer uses neither the term 'churching' or 'thanksgiving'.

Another source just a few years later points to some different problems. At his visitation of the diocese of London in 1554 Edmund Bonner asked whether newly delivered mothers were, 'after a convenient time . . . purified according to the old ancient and godly ceremonies and customs of the catholic church'. Or were there any women who 'by themselves or by sinister counsel have purified themselves after their own devices and fantasies, not coming to the church according to the laudable custom heretofore used in the same, where the parish priest would have been ready to do it, and some of the multitude to have been witnesses accordingly?' The issue was not whether anyone refused purification, or even what purification meant, but whether the ceremony was properly performed. Elizabethan protestant bishops would ask similar questions.[44]

With shifting emphasis and scope for additions, the issues raised by Latimer and Bonner would resound for more than a century: the efficacy of the service, on both spiritual and social levels; its role as a marker between clean and unclean states, as a sign of altered condition, and of renewed sexual contact between husbands and wives; whether the ceremony was a matter of law or custom, and the degree to which ecclesiastical authorities were concerned with its regulation; whether it could be performed in private or needed public display to the congregation; and how much of the responsibility for its conduct and interpretation came from the established church, 'sinister counsel', or from women themselves. Latimer's sermon recounts his pastoral work in the protestant ministry, Bonner's articles belonged to his exercise of catholic episcopal discipline; but both point to a disputed ground that would become further contested under Elizabeth and the Stuarts.

Complaints and Objections

The *Admonition* controversy of the 1570s raised alarms about the Jewish and popish remnants in the Book of Common Prayer. The widely read puritan *Admonition to the Parliament* claimed that 'churching of women after child-birth smelleth of Jewish purification'.[45] Another manifesto cited eight borrowings from 'Jewish religion' that lingered in the 'popish custom' of churching.[46] Thomas Cartwright insisted that the 'accustomed offering' that the woman made at her churching was 'most Jewish', and 'carrieth with it a strong scent and suspicion of a sacrifice'.[47] Christians were supposed to be free from the strictures of Jewish ceremonial law, and God was said to be offended by their retention. Echoes of these views could be heard from radical ministers such as William Sanderson of King's Lynn, Norfolk, who was presented by his parishioners in 1574 for calling the churching of women 'Jewish purifications'.[48] The separatist Henry Barrow later characterized the churching ceremony as 'absolutely Jewish' or 'a mixed action of Judaism and popery'. In either case, he continued, 'this trumpery is so gross, as it deserveth no refutation, but a dung fork to cast it out'.[49] An unauthorized pamphlet of 1601 continued the puritan attack. Churching, it insisted, contained 'no one word, matter or form of thanksgiving', but was rather a 'Jewish or popish purifying shadowed and varnished over' and continued 'under the pretence and colour of a service of God'.[50]

But this was never a popular argument; its most vocal adherents were radical churchmen. Few lay people knew or cared whether their religion had Jewish analogues or Jewish ancestry. Some might object to particular aspects, like the use of Psalm 121, the veil, or the offering, but few were prepared to dismiss churching altogether as the relic of an alien religion. Thomas Baslyn, a lay puritan from Wiltshire, protested in 1588 'that purification of women is a Jewish ceremony', but this seems to have been unusual.[51] The Jewish issue was soon set aside, though it could always be revived in the course of clerical and academic disputation. It came up at Hampton Court in 1604; and presbyterians at the Savoy Conference in 1661 again objected that the churching of women 'may seem too like a Jewish purification than a Christian thanksgiving'.[52]

Most of the brief ceremony of churching was taken up with recitation of Psalm 121. This was a psalm of praise and thanksgiving for divine protection, which included the strange promise 'that the sun shall not burn thee by day, neither the moon by night'. Puritans could not denounce these words of David, but claimed instead that they were 'childishly abused' in the context of women recovering from childbirth. Radical critics leapt on this phrase about the sun and the moon to ridicule the service as vain and superstitious. The puritan 'kinswoman' who debated with the Church of England 'chancellor' attacked the use of this psalm as 'a plain abusing and profaning of the word'. John Milton, whose own first wife was churched, derided this reference to 'sunburning and moonblasting, as if she had been travelling not in her bed, but in the deserts of Arabia'. Attacks of this sort were finally defused in 1662 by substituting Psalms 116 or 127 for for the problematic Psalm 121.[53]

For some Elizabethan reformers the multiple names for the ceremony revealed its contamination. A presbyterian treatise of the 1570s included 'certain considerations about the churching of women, otherwise called purification, and covered with the name of thanksgiving after childbirth, to prove the same no thanksgiving indeed but a disorderly custom'. The naming was a way of hiding the underlying corruption.[54] Thomas Cartwright inveighed against 'the churching of women, in which title yet kept there seemeth to be hid a great part of Jewish purification'. The very word 'churching' was thought to suggest a ritualistic end to 'banishment' and 'excommunication', implying thereby that the ceremony operated as a purification. Whitgift answered these 'cavils', as he called them, by insisting that the ceremony was, and was properly styled, a thanksgiving. 'Churching' was simply 'the common name customably used of the common people, who will not be taught to speak by you or any man, but keep their accustomed names and terms'.[55] The 1601 pamphlet concluded that the service of churching was a mingle-mangle, 'neither fish nor flesh nor good red herring'.[56]

Popular usage shared ground with the more orthodox term, and Elizabethan bishops more commonly referred to 'churching' than to 'thanksgiving'. Whitgift's own visitation articles for Worcester in 1577 ask about 'the form of thanksgiving or churching'. Bishop Richard Barnes of Durham referred to churching. Thomas Cooper as bishop of Lincoln referred to the woman's 'thanksgiving', but his successors William Wickham and William Chaderton called it 'churching'.[57] Only one Elizabethan bishop took serious exception to the term 'churching', and this was the eccentric and unfortunate Marmaduke Middleton of St David's. Middleton thought 'churching' a 'superstitious' term, 'as if for . . . conceiving and bringing a child into the world (and that in lawful wedlock) a woman should be unclean and profane'. 'The thanksgiving for the deliverance of women' would be the only terminology permitted in his administration.[58]

'Churching' and 'thanksgiving' were used as interchangeable terms in the seventeenth century, combined in everyday usage and in ecclesiastical government as they were in the title in the prayer book. If there was a distinction, it would be made by an Arminian ceremonialist like John Cosin. Correctly considered, 'the churching of women' was an ecclesiastical action, performed by the priest, in which the role of the woman being 'churched' was passive. 'Thanksgiving', by contrast, was the woman's active duty to participate in the service, to recognize God's mercy, and to make her offering at its end. In William Laud's usage, and Matthew Wren's, the minister 'use(s) the form of thanksgiving to women after their childbirth'; he churches her; she renders thanks.[59] None of their visitation articles refers to this action as purification; to do so would be to concede to the puritans that the ceremony was indeed an unreformed survival. Some churchmen continued to talk of 'purification', but this was loose and casual usage that left few traces in the record.[60]

Rates and Fees

To radical Elizabethan puritans the churching of women was 'heretical, blasphemous and popish foolerie . . . knavish presumption and presumptious knavery . . . idle babblement' and altogether unnecessary. An early Stuart separatist, John Canne, charged that churching was 'a horrible mocking of God', and listed it as number fifty-five among seventy principal errors of the Church of England.[61] But there was little popular support for this position. There is, on the other hand, strong evidence from visitation processes that many women wanted the ceremony in some form or other, and that in most cases they conformed to the Book of Common Prayer. Susan Wright's calculations from a remarkable 'chrisom book' show churching rates of 75 to 93 per cent in late Elizabethan Salisbury.[62] Similar evidence from Jacobean London indicates that 92 to 96 per cent of all 'women who gave birth and had their child baptised underwent the ceremony of churching'; even among women whose babies died before they could be baptized the churching rate exceeded 76 per cent. Jeremy Boulton finds that 'neglect of the ceremony, either from religious dissent or simple indifference, appears to have been insignificant'. And this high level of participation prevailed among rich and poor, 'across the social structure'.[63]

The Book of Common Prayer required that 'the woman that cometh to give her thanks, must offer accustomed offerings'. The rubric from 1552 onward left these offerings unspecified, but custom required either the chrisom cloth in which the child had been wrapped at baptism or its cash equivalent. At Wickenby, Lincolnshire, 'the chrisom and a gracepenny is always to be given at the woman's churching. The chrisom must be half a yard of fine linen long and a full yard in width.' Elsewhere the chrisom was customarily commuted for cash. Archbishop Parker's 'Interpretations' of the Injunctions of 1559 advised, 'to avoid contention, let the curate have the value of the chrisom, not under the value of fourpence, and above as they can agree, and as the state of the parents may require'.[64] At Salisbury between 1569 and 1592 the 'church wives' paid 1d. to 4d. for their churching, and made additional offerings of 4d. to 6d. 'for her chrisom'. The fees seem to have been calibrated according to ability to pay, with exemptions such as that recorded in 1574, for 'a church wife poor, *nihil*.' In 1585 one woman offered 'her chrisom in cloth', rather than cash, and the parish later sold it for 3d. In two cases where women were churched at home (in 1584 and 1585) they were excused the offering for the service but paid 6d. each for their chrisom. If the child had already died the mother still paid her fee for the churching service but offered no chrisom, for custom required the use of the chrisom cloth as a winding sheet for children who died within a month of being born.[65] Some parishes loaned a communally owned chrisom cloth to poor families at the time of a baby's christening, and the payment of 'accustomed offerings' at churching was a way to get it back.

Fees from churchings made useful additions to parish funds; at St Thomas's, Salisbury, the quarterly receipts from churchings in 1585 were 16s. 2d., 24s. 7d., 17s. 9d., and 16s. 9d.—a total of £3. 15s. 3d. Income from churchings bolstered the 'casualties' of London parishes in the 1630s.[66] The willingness of so many people to pay fees for this service may be taken as further evidence for its popularity; on the other hand, routine fee-paying may just as well reflect the pecuniary diligence of the clergy and the force of custom. The sectarian Katherine Chidley wrote scathingly of the practice of churching in 1641, but her special anger was reserved for the minister's collection of fees. Unpaid fees were regarded as outstanding debts; an account book kept by the rector of Stow Bardolph, Norfolk, in 1691 noted that John Bosse was in arrears for his church rate and still owed 6d. for 'his wife's churching'.[67]

Arrangements for churching left other traces in the parish records and in the material fabric of the church. Since the churching party normally included the midwife and the month-old child, as well as the recently delivered mother and her gossips, considerations of probity, decorum, and comfort combined to secure them a privileged but segregated space. Some parishes furnished special stools, benches, or even an enclosed 'churching pew' or 'childwife pew' for the woman and her attendants. The churchwardens of Pittington and Houghton-le-Spring, Durham, in 1597 and 1598 provided mats 'for the wives to kneel on when they come to be churched'. The parish inventory of St Oswald's, Durham, in 1605, included 'a covering cloth for covering the form before women at churchings', which was replaced in 1638 by 'two yards of kersey for a churching cloth' costing 7s. Great Yarmouth, Norfolk, purchased new mats 'for the stool wherein women sit to give thanks'. The parishioners of Cundall, Yorkshire, paid 26s. 8d. in 1636 for the construction of 'a childwife's pew'. At Wisbech, Cambridgeshire, the churchwardens complained in 1638 that 'the churching seat under the pulpit doth somewhat encroach upon the middle alley'. It became a source of merriment, as well as a sign of irreverence, when single women or young men mischieviously seated themselves in the childwife's pew.[68]

Cases and Collisions

In the Elizabethan period, objections to churching came more frequently from the clergy than the laity, when reforming ministers set their scruples against community expectations. Friction arose at Downham, Essex, in 1580 when the rector was charged with refusing to church four women; at Kingston, Surrey, in 1586 when John Udall and his 'faction' were cited for showing contempt for the order of churching by turning women away; and at Winscomb, Somerset, in 1615, 'when John Attwood's wife came to be churched [the minister] would not let her in the door'.[69] In each of these cases the routine demand for churching occasioned or exacerbated a conflict between ministers and parishioners, traditionalists and reformers, involving troublesome personalities as well as religious principles.

A Northamptonshire case from 1584 shows how disputes over churching could build on existing animosities and in turn precipitate more serious collisions. John Elliston, the reforming minister of Preston Capes, had already upset some parishioners by not wearing the surplice and by omitting the sign of the cross in baptism. His patrons, the puritan Knightleys, were locked in a struggle with conservative villagers, and the vicar soon became involved in a dispute over tithes. In December 1584, Elliston reported, 'a butcher did beat me in the street because I yielded not to a superstitious coming to church, which his wife used after her deliverance in child-birth'. The butcher's wife was determined to be churched according to custom and the Book of Common Prayer, and her husband was ready to use violence on her behalf against the recalcitrant clergyman. Elliston had the butcher bound over to good behaviour, and he retaliated by citing the minister to the bishop of Peterborough as a nonconformist. The case eventually moved to the ecclesiastical courts of

London and Canterbury, and even Star Chamber, threatening Elliston with fines, expenses, imprisonment, and deprivation.[70]

A review of church court records (from a dozen dioceses) suggests that the majority of women, like the butcher's wife, wanted to be churched, but problems sometimes arose over irregularities in their performance. They came at the wrong time, in the wrong clothes, with the wrong demeanour or companions, and positioned themselves in the wrong place in the church. Some neglected to come to church, or came weeks after they were supposed to; but neglect is not the same as objection. Cases involving churching are too few and too scattered to be treated statistically, yet the citations and answers provide a rich vein of suggestive evidence.

The Essex courts provide some easily accessible examples. One woman in 1587 'came . . . to give thanks for her delivery' but not 'as she ought to'. Jane Minors of Barking came be churched in 1597, 'very unwomanlike' after four or five hours feasting at a tavern, and departed unchurched because the minister was busy with a funeral. When the wife of Robert Aylet of Hornchurch came to give thanks in 1592 it was 'without any other women with her, to the offence of her neighbours'. The wife of one Collins of South Benfleet came to church in 1602 'to give God thanks for her delivery' but 'came very undecently and contrary to order . . . without kercher, midwife, or wives, and placed herself in her own stool, not in the stool appointed'. Her excuse was 'that in places from whence she came, the use is such, neither did she at any time otherwise'. She accomplished her churching, but not 'according to the book'.[71] And the book itself was remarkably vague and flexible, with its references to 'convenient' places and such words 'as the case shall require'.

Goody Collins's comment about different uses in different places raises interesting questions about cultural geography and social practices in early modern England. Much more needs to be learnt about variations from parish to parish and from region to region, as well as changes over time. At one level it would seem that the liturgy was remarkably standardized, under the eye of a national church; but activities not covered by the rubric may well have varied from place to place, and much was a matter for the minister's discretion. Conformity was locally negotiable except when busy bishops intervened, so that churchings took place in different parts of the church, with variable costumes and company, and could even take place informally at home. It was this very variety that upset hard-line bishops, and their drive for uniformity that convinced some reformers that parish godliness was under attack.

Private churchings involved matters of discretion and connivance, medical necessity, and sometimes aversion to strict liturgical form. They raise questions similar to those posed by private baptisms, clandestine marriages, and hugger-mugger funerals. Sometimes their irregularities came to the attention of episcopal authorities. William Frith of Upminster, Essex, was said to have been upset when the minister refused to church his wife at home when she was too ill to give thanks in public. On Frith's urgent appeal, the vicar of nearby Hornchurch performed the ceremony at his wife's bedside. Richard Matthew of Lambourne, similarly obtained permission from the archdeacon of Essex for his wife to be churched at home in 1606, 'in regard of her weakness'. When the curate refused to do it, the husband 'procured . . . a strange minister taken up by the way to solemnize that duty, in his own house and after his own manner . . . in the presence of many neighbours'. The authorities disapproved of such practices, but might 'wink at many things' so long as they were not disruptive.[72]

The wife of Robert Woodford, a Northamptonshire puritan, was churched at home on at least two occasions in the reign of Charles I; she may have been too ill to attend the parish church, but by arranging the ceremony at home she could secure her choice of minister, and would be constrained neither to kneel at the altar nor to wear a veil.[73] A woman at Hampden, Buckinghamshire, stayed at home in 1635 instead of going out 'to be churched publicly'; her husband, Thomas Timberlake, 'said a long grace at dinner, and so [she] was not churched at all'. The local minister, Mr Lea, was so outraged by this neglect of ecclesiastical thanksgiving that he cited the couple before the archdeacon's court. But a neighbour, Ellen Birch, protested, asking 'what should they make such a matter of it, for she had had children and was churched of eight of them?'[74]

Rather than evincing hostility to churching, the records show some families so eager for some version of the ceremony that they risked offending against ecclesiastical discipline. William White of Charlbury, Oxfordshire, explained to the court in 1596, 'that his wife being delivered of a child, could not be churched for that she was excommunicated, and he, being desireous that she shall serve God, did say and read certain prayers unto her'. For a husband to church his wife was most disorderly, but it is not clear from the record whether this took place in church or at home. Other records point to churchings by irregular ministers, or by clergy from outside the parish, and occasionally by laymen such as the parish clerk.[75]

In a remarkable case from Bedfordshire, the wife of Richard Chaw of Elstow was presented to the archidiaconal court in 1617 'for churching herself'. The court heard 'that she coming to the church to thanksgiving, and the minister having warning overnight and not coming to church accordingly, she did take the Book of Common Prayer and read the thanksgiving herself openly in the church'. Here was a woman who was determined to have her moment, and whose literacy is attested as well.[76]

We know nothing about Richard Chaw's role in his wife's self-churching, but some of the records do illuminate relationships between husbands and wives. When one Essex woman 'went to church to give thanks disorderly in her petticoat' and sat 'not in the right seat' her husband 'maintained her therein'. His support for his wife was comparable to, though not so violent as, the Northamptonshire butcher's. Elizabeth Shipden, whom we shall meet later, enjoyed the full support of her husband. Other cases reveal less solidarity. At Hatfield Peverel in 1586 Edmund Fanning was 'a hinderance to his wife being churched'. A Buckinghamshire court heard in 1607 that Nicholas Nell of Iver 'doth keep his wife from churching'. A Sussex court cited William Osborne of Launsing in 1622 'for not churching his wife'.[77]

Thomas Yardley of Grantham, Lincolnshire, was presented in 1588 'for denying the laudable customs of the church'. The court ordered him to confess his faults in public 'and to lead his wife to the accustomed place where women are used to sit while they give thanks after child-birth, and there give thanks'. His neighbour Richard Morley said in the same year that 'the churching of women is a beggarly ceremony . . . and if he could have persuaded his wife she should never have given thanks'. In a gender-charged insult in Essex in 1589 it was said that a woman going to churching was 'like . . . a sow with pigs following of her or like a bitch that went to salt'. But the author of this opinion was a woman![78] Fragments like these point to low-intensity struggles between clergy and laity, divisions within the community, and a continual testing of patriarchal authority against female independence. Even against the objections of their husbands, most of these women were determined to make their public thanksgiving. Even unmarried women were routinely churched after giving birth, provided they had not left the parish.

Elizabethan bishops commonly threatened to deny bastard-bearers their thanksgiving, as a form of punishment, until they had named the father and performed proper penance. Visitation articles and injunctions instructed ministers not to church any 'lewd' or unmarried woman, unless 'she do openly acknowledge her fault before the congregation accordingly and show herself to be very penitent'. Whitgift's articles for the diocese of Worcester in 1577 enquired,

whether any minister hath used the form of thanksgiving or churching of any woman after childbirth, being unlawfully begotten with child, otherwise than in form of a penitent person, viz: in a white sheet, and that be done upon a Sunday or holy day, or else take a sufficient caution that she shall not depart the parish before she hath performed such penance.[79]

This particular concern became less prominent in seventeenth-century visitations, and may often have lapsed in practice; but the vicar of Knaresdale, Northumberland, was cited in 1611 'for churching two women being fornicators'. Thomas Knight of Swavesey, Cambridgeshire, reported to Bishop Wren in 1638 that he never churched 'any begotten with child in adultery or fornication' until he 'received order to purify or give thanks for them'. And as late as 1715, Thomas Tanner advised Dr Charlett of Oxford, 'you were right not to use the office of churching to any persons so notoriously guilty of incontinence till she has made satisfaction to the congregation by doing penance'.[80] This would seem to suggest that 'green' women, including the small minority who bore bastards, normally looked forward to fulfilling their thanksgiving. Threatening to withhold the ceremony would be a toothless sanction if it was an unpopular imposition to which women submitted reluctantly.

Decent Veils

One issue which brought together anxieties about Jewishness, popery, and superstition, the lingering stain of purification, and the exercise of ecclesiastical authority, was the wearing of veils. There was nothing in the rubric of the Book of Common Prayer requiring a woman to wear a veil at her churching, and to leading Elizabethan churchmen it was a matter of indifference. When Thomas Cartwright alleged that the customary wearing of a veil smacked of Jewish purification, John Whitgift responded that the veil was the woman's affair, and the puritans were making a fuss over a trifle: 'let the women themselves answer these matters.' On further consideration Whitgift explained that

> this is rather a civil matter and custom of our country, than a ceremony of the church; and the wearing of new gloves (as many at that time, and especially at the time of marriages do) is as much a ceremony as this; for the wearing of the veil first began of that weakness and sickness that nature in that danger doth bring most women unto, thereby to keep them more from the air; and therefore (as I have said) in this country it was taken up as a custom of the people, and not as a ceremony of the church.[81]

In origin, by this argument, the veil was a concession to the woman, not an imposition on her. It was an enclosure and a shelter, rather than penitential garb.

But veils could not be casually disregarded. Radicals objected to the veil at churching, in the same way that they criticized the cross in baptism and the ring in marriage, as unsupportable popish remnants. Making a woman wear a veil, they argued, was much too suggestive of the white garment worn in penance: 'it seemeth to disgrace the blessed estate of marriage and the lawful coupling of man and wife together, when the woman must come . . . like an excommunicate person.'[82] Some godly ministers even refused to church women who came in the traditional costume. At Danbury, Essex, in 1577, Mary Madison and Dorothy Marshall

came to the church to be churched or give thanks for their safe delivery, having kerchiefs over their heads according to the use; and for that they had the same kerchiefs on their heads, the curate would not suffer them to give thanks, and thereby went home without thanksgiving; and they being further examined whether they did wear them for any superstition, [said they did not] but for warmth.

The court ordered them to return to church next Sunday to give thanks. 'And likewise . . . Mr. Dent the curate was [ad]monished, that hereafter he shall not refuse any honest woman to give thanks, coming to the church aforesaid, they being examined that they do not wear the same for any superstition.'[83]

The matter was revived in the seventeenth century, and the grounds of the argument expanded. Rather than reproaching women for adhering to traditional costume, a new generation of ministers criticized them if they omitted it. The Jacobean bishop Thomas Morton defended the veil as a matter of ceremony and discipline, and claimed 'that it signified subjection to superior power'. The veil marked its wearer's place in the hierarchies of clergy and laity, men and women, husbands and wives. John Burges agreed that 'a moral duty was professed by [the veil] just as modesty and shamefastness, gravity and care of not offending, are professed by all apparel of modest honest fashion'. Had not Saints Paul and Chrysostom written that it was *natural* for a woman to be covered? William Ames concluded that the veil was 'but a civil order of decency, used as well out of God's worship as in it'. Puritans should not object to it, no more than ceremonialists should insist on it, for the veil was simply an item of 'women's proper apparel', instituted by custom and 'appropriated unto God's worship'.[84] But puritans could be at odds with themselves if their reading of St Paul led them to favour veils for women when their objection to popish remnants led them to reject them.

A more practical argument was that the woman to be churched should 'have a veil or habit distinct from others, that so it may be known for whom thanks is then particularly given'. The veil was to be the distinguishing costume for the central participant in this rite of passage. Bishop Richard Montague expressed this most clearly in his visitation articles for the diocese of Norwich in 1638 when he asked if the woman 'came to church in her ordinary habit and wearing apparel, or with a fair veil dependent from her head to her shoulders and back, that she may be distinguished from her accompanying neighbours, and that such as take notice of it be thereby put in mind for her and with her, to give God thanks for her deliverance?'[85] The Restoration bishop Anthony Sparrow amplified the argument that

the woman that is to be churched is to have a veil; and good reason, for it is as St. Paul says [1 Corinthians 2], every woman when she prays in public ought to have a veil or covering on her head, in token of her modesty and subjection; then is it much more, when she is to sit in a more eminent place of the church, near to the holy table, apart from the rest of her sex, in the public view, ought she to have such a veil or covering.[86]

Elizabethan and early Jacobean bishops made no mention of veils in their visitation articles, and few took action over what women wore for their churching. Discipline was haphazard, and the traditional headgear became a matter of discretion and custom, and perhaps even widespread neglect. The veil was a 'trifling matter' or 'a thing indifferent',[87] at worst a low-grade irritation. Proceedings were dropped against two Lincolnshire men in 1607 for permitting their wives to be churched without veils. An Essex woman protested in 1614, 'that none but whores did wear veils, and that a harlot or a whore was the inventor of it', though this did not prevent her from performing her thanksgiving.[88] But from the later years of James's reign the veil emerged as a controversial test of conformity and discipline. High ceremonialists of the 1620s and 1630s advanced a notion of reverential decorum that they were prepared to enforce through their courts. A matter of taste became a matter of policy; religious externals became pressing administrative concerns, less about purification than politics.

Bishop John Howson of Oxford enquired in 1619 whether women came 'in decent sort to give God thanks for their delivery'. In 1620 Samuel Harsnett of Norwich was among the first bishops to enquire specifically whether ministers 'admit any to the performance of that holy action that do not come having a decent veil upon their heads, matronlike, as hath been accustomed heretofore'. John Cosin, as archdeacon of the East Riding in 1627, asked whether churching was 'done publicly and reverently in the church, the woman coming in that decent and grave attire which hath been accustomed, and the minister attending in his surplice?'[89]

Cosin envisioned a ceremony at the edge of the sacred enclosure, with the priest in his vestment inside, officiating, and the woman in her veil outside, giving thanks and making her offering. This represented more a vision of vestiarian propriety and sacerdotal order than a reinstatement of popish purification, but on either ground it was distasteful to puritans. Laudians may have supported popular traditions, games, and merriments, so long as they remained outside the sacred arena, the churchyard and service time; but they could be hostile or insensitive to local customs, including seating arrangements and apparel for churching, that clashed with their notions of religious decorum. Ministers who conducted churchings from their reading seat instead of at the altar, and women who sat rather than kneeled or wore hats instead of veils, might now find themselves subject to episcopal discipline.[90]

By the 1630s the high ceremonialists had again made the veil a crucial part of churching, and refocused the ceremony on the woman at the high altar instead of the more comfortable custom of churching in pews.[91] Matthew Wren as bishop of Norwich in 1636 issued 'particular orders, directions, and remembrances' 'that the woman to be churched come and kneel at a side near the communion table without the rail, being veiled according to the custom, and not covered with a hat; or otherwise not to be churched but presented at the next generals'. Two years later at Ely, Wren enquired, 'Doth any married woman within your parish, after child-birth neglect to come to church according to the Book of Common Prayer to give thanks to God for her safe deliverance, veiled in a decent manner, as hath been anciently accustomed?' Juxon's articles for London in 1640 showed similar concerns, and the questions were repeated verbatim in many visitation articles after the Restoration.[92]

The new episcopal policy was intended to promote gravity and decorum. Instead it generated friction. Women who were perfectly content to be churched according to the directions in the prayer book now found themselves at odds with the church if they neglected to wear a veil. Samuel Harsnett's requirements at Norwich produced resentment and resistance, and led to a complex legal process involving the consistory court, Chancery, and King's Bench.

At his visitation in 1620, Harsnett insisted that all candidates for churching wear 'a decent veil upon their heads'. He warned offenders, and took action against such churchwardens as 'presented not the names of the women churched without a veil'.[93] Among those who took exception to this new policy were Thomas and Elizabeth Shipden. Thomas Shipden was a prominent citizen of Norwich, recently made sheriff and alderman. His wife also came from the Norwich civic élite. Their son was born in January 1621, and was baptized in the parish of St Saviour's without incident. The problem arose when Elizabeth went to give thanks without wearing a veil. What happened next can be reconstructed from *Les Reports de Sir Gefrey Palmer* (1678), reporting Shipden versus Dr Redman, chancellor of Norwich, in Trinity term 1622, in the King's Bench.

Elizabeth Shipden was cited for refusing to wear a white veil, and was subsequently excommunicated. The bishop's chancellor sought a writ *de excommunicato capiendo* in Chancery, which Shipden countered by seeking a prohibition in King's Bench. Elizabeth Shipden claimed that there was neither custom nor canon, nor any law of England, that required her to wear a veil at her churching. It was, rather, an ecclesiastical innovation, an alien intrusion, perhaps even a praemunire. Because this was a novel case that threatened to establish precedent, the judges sought the advice of the archbishop of Canterbury before deciding the issue. Archbishop Abbot convened a committee of six bishops, who happened to be in London, and their report certified that it was the ancient custom of the Church of England that women should come veiled to be churched. And on this basis the prohibition was denied, and the Shipdens lost their case.[94] Thomas Shipden later emerged as a leader of the puritan faction at Norwich, becoming mayor in 1631; it is possible that the issue of his wife's churching hardened him as an activist.[95]

A similar problem involving less prominent people arose at Abingdon, Berkshire, in 1635. Following the new ecclesiastical insistence on proper ceremonial costume, the archdeaconry court cited Mary Meales for not wearing 'a kerchief when she went to church to give thanks for her safe delivery of childbirth'. In her defence the mother answered that 'it hath not been the ancient custom in the said parish of St. Helen's in Abingdon so to do'. The authorities insisted that it *was* the custom, if not in the past then certainly in the future, for women to wear veils or kerchiefs at their churchings. Mary Meales was given no further punishment, once she had admitted her error, but was made to promise 'that in case that she be delivered of a child hereafter she shall go to church to give thanks for her safe deliverance in a kerchief or decent habit according to the custom of the place'.[96] This kind of intervention in local custom may partially explain the swelling unpopularity of episcopacy that burst in the 1640s.

Ecclesiastical court records of Charles I's reign record more collisions over the procedures for churching, most of them minor but irritating. A Norfolk man was disciplined in 1627 'for saying it is not lawful for a woman to come to church after her delivery in a veil to give God thanks'. At Toft in Cambridgeshire in 1638 the churchwardens presented 'the wife of Joseph Anger for coming to church after child-birth not veiled in a decent manner when sermon was near half done; she went not to the communion table'. At Trumpington they cited Janet, wife of William Ames (not the puritan casuist), for 'coming to church to be churched without a veil', but she certified that it was all a mistake.[97]

A more serious incident occurred at Wolverhampton, Staffordshire, in 1638, and was referred to the prerogative court of High Commission. William Pinson

together with his wife and her midwife, and other women, went to the church of Wolverhampton that his wife might be churched, but being demanded by the priest why she did not wear a veil, she answered she would not, and being told by the priest that he was commanded by the ordinary not to church any but such as come thither reverently and lowly in their veils, she in the church, after prayers ended, scornfully pulled off her hat and put a table napkin on her head, and put on her hat again, and so departed from the church.[98]

As far as the High Commission was concerned, Pinson was a troublesome puritan, 'a man inconformable . . . to the rites and ceremonies and . . . laws and government of the Church of England'. He was, they claimed, a gadder to sermons and a keeper of conventicles, who discussed religious teaching and expounded the scriptures. The incident in Wolverhampton church would seem to fit this picture. But Pinson's own testimony tells a different story.[99]

He was, he said, a regular churchgoer. While living in Wolverhampton, and 'not otherwise necessarily hindered', he and his wife frequented the parish church, especially to hear sermons by Mr Lee. But when there was no sermon at Wolverhampton, or when Mr Lee preached at Bettanhall, he and his wife sometimes went there or elsewhere but heard 'no unconformable ministers'. (In the margin next to Pinson's 'sometimes' the High Commissioner wrote the word 'often'.) He kept no conventicle, but admitted to conducting family prayers that 'by chance' were sometimes attended by persons of other families. Pinson presents himself as a godly householder, but not a nonconformist. From other sources we learn that he belonged to a faction supporting Richard Lee, a prebendary at Wolverhampton since 1622, against the innovating dean of the college of St Peter, Matthew Wren (1628–35); at Wren's behest, and through Laud's intervention, Lee was suspended in 1635.[100]

Pinson's account shows the churching incident in a different light. He told the court that his wife went to be churched

without a veil *on her head*, as divers others had *there* used to do, *and in such reverent manner as he believes the law requireth*. And *saith* that when Mr. Davis *the curate* . . . spake to her she *put off her hat and did* put on a veil, and put her hat on again. *And the said Mr. Davies refused to church her*, and so she departed unchurched, to her and [his] grief.

(In the margin next to 'veil' the High Commissioner wrote 'napkin'.) In this version, much of it (the words in italics) omitted from the *Calendar of State Papers*, the couple appears less confrontational.[101] It was, rather, the curate who was innovating, following new commandments from Laud and Wren. Mrs Pinson came to church reverently and with her head covered, though not veiled, 'as divers others had there used to do'. She conformed to decency and custom, and to the written letter of the law. It was the minister who blocked the churching, but his parishioner who came before the court. And although Mrs Pinson apparently took the initiative in the confrontation, it was her husband who became answerable to the High Commission.

William Pinson, we learn, was 'an attorney at common law' who had already made an enemy of the curate of Wolverhampton. At one time he had helped a poor man, one Hopkins, to sue Hugh Davis for battery, and assisted in the arrest and humiliation of the minister. As far as Davis was concerned, Pinson was harassing him before the justices and at Quarter Sessions. The curate and the lawyer clearly bore each other a grudge, exacerbated by Davis's public humiliation of Mrs Pinson. The minister may have presented his old adversary to the High Commission as much to hurt an enemy as to uphold the dignity of the clergy and to ensure conformity to the ritual of churching. The Pinsons evidently wanted the thanksgiving, as a public ritual closure to their period of childbearing, but not on the new terms demanded by the ceremonialists. Though charged with being 'inconformable to the rites and ceremonies . . . of the Church of England', William Pinson shared few of the religious objections to churching raised earlier by presbyterians and separatists.[102]

Once again we have a minor incident that took on broader confrontational dimensions; it reminds us that presentments for minor nonconformity could have complicated backgrounds and ramifications; and it contributed to the growth of grievances and the hardening of opinion against the Laudian church. Like Thomas Shipden at Norwich, William Pinson may have been radicalized by this interrupted rite of passage and the attendant affront to his honour; if so, an opportunity arose to revenge himself in 1643 when he testified at Laud's trial.[103]

'Julia's Churching'

The Devonshire clergyman Robert Herrick wrote 'Julia's Churching, or Purification' during the late 1620s or 1630s and published it in his 1648 collection, *Hesperides*. Though superficially simple, the poem embraces many of the issues of ceremony, discipline, and custom that made churching so complex and contested in the reign of Charles I. In its quietly disarming manner, Herrick's verse supports a high ceremonial, sacerdotal version of churching and a patriarchal, possessive, and erotic vision of wifely obligation. This is a highly partisan poem that the puritans who ejected Herrick from his living in 1647 might well have found offensive.[104]

> Put on thy Holy Filletings, and so
> To th'Temple with the sober Midwife go.
> Attended thus (in most solemn wise)
> By those who serve the Child-bed mysteries,
> Burn first thine incense; next, when as thou see'st
> The candid Stole thrown ore the Pious Priest;
> With reverend Curtsies come, and to him bring
> Thy free (and not decurted) offering.
> All Rites well ended, with fair Auspice come
> (As to the breaking of a Bride-cake) home:
> Where ceremonious Hymen shall for thee
> Provide a second Epithalamie.
> She who keeps chastely to her husband's side
> Is not for one, but every night his Bride:
> And stealing still with love, and fear to Bed.
> Brings him not one, but many a Maiden-head.

Julia, of course, is Herrick's idealized woman, a gentlewoman rather than a peasant, imagined here in the bloom of recent motherhood. Safely delivered from childbed, she dutifully prepares for the ceremony of churching 'or purification'. The extra words in the title draw attention to unresolved questions about the meaning and efficacy of the ceremony. Mainstream apologists for the Church of England were careful not to mention 'purification' lest they conceded to the puritans that the service was insufficiently reformed. Country clergymen had no such compunction, especially such ebullient traditionalists as Herrick.[105]

The poet's injunction to Julia, 'put on thy holy filletings', invokes the simmering controversy over veils. Julia will be reverently attired, with ceremonial wrapping of her face and head, appropriate for the central participant in a ritual of purification. She will go to 'the Temple', a self-consciously archaic synonym for the church, a place with classical and Jewish as well as Christian connotations. Attended by 'the sober midwife' and other women who were present at the birth, she will enter this sacred space 'in a most solemn wise', with none of the laughter, gossip, or feminine disorder that misogynist renditions popularly associated with churching.

That 'Julia's churching' is a holy act, not a sisterly outing, is emphasized by the next injunction, 'burn first thine incense'. Incense, as Herrick well knew, was a liturgical accessory beloved by high ceremonialists and excoriated by puritans.[106] Similar controversy attached to ecclesiastical vestments. Herrick's

priest wears not just a surplice, itself an item of contention, but a stole, a ceremonial strip of silk or linen worn over the shoulders. In unreformed practice,
the priest wore a stole when performing exorcisms or conjurations; it was not
required for the churching of women. The word 'priest' itself, though generally acceptable in early Stuart England, has acquired sacerdotal and even
popish connotations. More austere protestants than Herrick preferred the label
'minister'.

Inside the 'temple' the veiled women greets the robed priest with a reverent curtsey, a gesture of submission to his gendered ecclesiastical authority.
He churches her, in John Cosin's manner, relieving and transforming her
condition. Following the prayer-book rubric that 'the woman that cometh to
give her thanks must offer accustomed offerings', Herrick's Julia makes her
'free (and not decurted) offering'. Hers will be no grudging payment of the
usual 4d. or 6d., nor will it fall short of the standard rate. As a 'pious priest'
whose income was augmented by such offerings, the incumbent of Dean
Prior might be forgiven for so instructing his parishioners.

At this point the poem shifts, as the ritual shifted, from sacred to secular
matters. With the ecclesiastical business completed, the social and domestic
business can begin. But instead of dealing with the gossiping, the festivities
of Julia's feminine assembly, Herrick gazes from her husband's point of view.
Instead of the gossips' feast he gives us the image of the bride-cake, and
instead of pausing for food or festivity he brings the woman home. And it
is at home, in private, in her chamber, in bed, that the point of the poem will
be consummated.

'Ceremonious Hymen', the ancient god of marriage, shall 'provide a second Epithalamie', a renewed blessing of the bridal chamber. These classical
references raise us from rural Devonshire to the more courtly heights of the
Renaissance. The final four lines, a celebration of sexual renewal and a hymn
to marital intimacy, appeal not just to Julia but to every married mother. The
wife is restored to her husband, as his bride, his wife, his lover, and companion. At the end of the woman's privileged month, concluding the customary
period of sexual abstinence following childbirth, the marriage bed becomes
a bridal chamber and the woman brings her husband the delights of her
maidenhead. The ceremony of churching has provided her with a kind of
honorary virginity, ready to be deflowered. In the end, in Herrick's vision, it
is the man who is rewarded for the woman's completion of the ritual. This
reading of a minor poem reminds us that many more sources are available
than the sermons, diaries, and church court records; here, in artful distilla-
tion, are many of the elements with which this chapter is concerned.

Churching Continued, 1645–1700

Officially the churching of women came to an end in 1645 when the prayer book was superseded by the Directory of Public Worship. But we know from diaries and family papers that some people, especially royalist gentry, continued to seek out ministers to perform the office, following as closely as possible the Book of Common Prayer. John Greene's children, born in London towards the end of the Civil War, were baptized privately, without the sign of the cross, and their mother was churched 'at lecture' a month after their births. Lady Mary Verney was churched on 4 July 1647, a month after her delivery. Her doctor wrote that she 'is churched and well, but looks ill enough', following a slow recovery. Anthony Blagrave's wife was churched at home in Berkshire in 1652. Thomas Mainwaring recorded in his diary 'that day my wife was churched' on 25 April 1654 and again on 5 June 1656. John Evelyn's wife was regularly 'churched at home' in the 1650s 'by Mr. Owen, whom I always made use of on these occasions, because the parish minister durst not (or perhaps would not) have officiated according to the form and usage of the Church of England, to which I always adhered'. The ceremony invariably concluded with a dinner.[107]

If the ministry refused to provide the service, did the laity resent its omission or seek alternatives? How did members of the Cromwellian élite mark the end of what some people still called 'the childwife's month', and what happened among different religious groups in the towns and villages? We still need to discover the degree to which churching, in some form or other, was perpetuated during the Interregnum, and how far it fell out of popular favour.[108]

Most people lacked the resources commanded by the Evelyns and Verneys, and many may not have shared their attachment to traditional Anglicanism. It is possible that a considerable section was persuaded that churching was unnecessary, and set it aside; but it would be surprising to find such a rapid rejection of long-held beliefs and customs. Accommodating reform to popular pressure, the presbyterian Richard Baxter introduced a new version of the thanksgiving service for the mothers of Kidderminster during the 1650s. 'Every religious woman that was safely delivered, instead of the old feastings and gossipings, if they were able, did keep a day of thanksgiving with some of their neighbours, praising God, and singing psalms, and soberly feasting together.'[109] This, of course, is the minister's view, a self-congratulatory reflection on his own pastoral mediation, rather than a window into womanhood or community norms.

Churching was restored at the Restoration, and soon again became a test of conformity to ecclesiastical discipline.[110] Anglicans insisted that participation in the ceremony signified adherence to law and custom, quite apart from any spiritual benefits that might be thought to accrue from it. This line of argument was especially developed in the second half of the seventeenth century, at a time when the restored Church of England was struggling to maintain its authority, although similar positions were familiar from Luther.[111]

An annual opportunity to preach on the subject of churching occurred each 2 February with the festival of Candlemas, or the Purification of the Blessed Virgin Mary. Mary herself, of course, was 'without the least spot or impurity in the whole business of conception and childbirth', explained the Cambridge churchman Mark Frank, but she none the less went through the Levitical business of purification, and made her customary offering at the temple. If *she* could subject herself to such conformist discipline, so now could Christian mothers follow this 'good example of church duties'.[112] The dean of Chichester, George Stradling, similarly argued that Mary's purification exemplified 'charity, obedience, humility, and gratitude'. 'If she so religiously observed a ceremony which to her was but indifferent, with what care ought we to keep those moral duties of the gospel which require our obedience?' Mary's devotion would serve as an example to all mothers to make their dutiful thanksgiving. It also served to rebuke nonconformists and 'schismatics' in the continuing struggle over religious authority and discipline.[113]

Restoration bishops commonly enquired about churching as they attempted to secure conformity to the Book of Common Prayer, and their visitation questions were often modelled on those of the 1630s. But after 1662 they were more likely to face nonconformist refusal to be churched at all than disputes over adiaphora and externals. Challenged by more fundamental problems of membership and discipline, later Stuart churchmen seem to have abandoned the divisive insistence on veils.

Visitation returns of the 1660s are remarkable, in some dioceses, for the numbers of women presented for refusing to be churched. At Great Dunmow, Essex, in 1664 a dozen women were cited 'for not making (their) public thanksgiving after safe delivery from childbirth'. At least four were dissenters who also refused to have their children baptized, while others were identified as 'poor'. At Wakes Colne, the churchwardens noted, 'some women have neglected public thanksgiving after their child-birth, but we hope they will be persuaded to it'. 'Schismatics' who refused to take part in churching were also found at Maldon, Cold Norton, and Bishops Wickham. At Hillingdon, Uxbridge, and Isleworth in Middlesex there were Quakers and other nonconformists whose wives were never churched, nor their children baptized.

Similar presentments were made in other dioceses—for example, Carlisle, Chichester, Durham, and York.[114] The Yorkshire records identify Quakers, conventiclers, schismatics, dissenters, and recusants among those neglecting their churching. And the same people were often cited and excommunicated for failure to come to communion, baptize their children, or pay the church rate. The Carlisle consistory court records include the citation of Margaret Fell, Elizabeth Fell, and other prominent Quakers in 1663 'for not coming to be churched after their delivery of childbirth'.[115]

Neglect of churching was not always a matter of nonconformist scruples, at least according to testimony given to the courts. At Waltham Magna, Essex, in 1664, several women excused themselves 'by reason of far dwelling from church'. And at Witham the churchwardens reported, 'there are many refuse to come to be churched because of the vicar's scandalous life'. At Abingdon, Berkshire, in 1668 a dispute over seating and custom, not Jewishness or purification, reduced the churching rate; 'women refuse to be churched because they have not their right place, and midwives are excluded . . . from their women, who always used to sit together'.[116] Customary arrangements and female solidarity counted for more than ecclesiastical prescription.

Bishop Henchman of London learnt that at St Ann, Blackfriars, in 1664,

the office for churching of women is very seldom or not at all observed, but . . . our . . . curate [Dr Whitchcott] and others employed by him do take upon them to discharge that office by a bill or bills presented to him or them in the pulpit in behalf of the parties concerned . . . Very few women who have been delivered do make their public thanksgiving as by the rubric in the Book of Common Prayer is required.

A churching of sorts went on, but without the required liturgical placement or trappings. Similarly Mr Swift of Peniston, Lancashire, fell foul of his ordinary in 1682 for 'churching a woman in the pulpit' instead of at the altar. The nonconformist Oliver Heywood was offended on this occasion not so much by the practice of churching as by the authoritarian insistence on strict liturgical form.[117]

Adherence to canonical requirements may have slackened somewhat in the later seventeenth century as some families drifted away from the established church and others sought to domesticate or privatize ecclesiastical ceremonies. We have already noted the rise of private baptism and the lengthening interval between birth and christening. A similar process may have occurred with churching, with ceremonies becoming more secular, perfunctory, or informal. Later Stuart countrymen sometimes talked of 'the welcoming' for a newborn child, a month or so after its birth, emphasizing the familial and festive aspect of churching. The Derbyshire yeoman Leonard Wheatcroft recorded the birth of his daughter on 25 June 1670, adding, 'she was baptised July 23 and my wife churched the same day'; later in 1697 the Wheatcroft family gathered for 'the welcoming' of a newborn kinsman. Wheatcroft comments, 'He was born May 21, 1697. The welcoming was not till July 1. There was we all very merry for two days.'[118]

It is impossible to make any quantitative assessment on the basis of personal papers or church court records, and no source is known that will yield churching rates for the later seventeenth century comparable to those calculated for Elizabethan Salisbury and Jacobean London. An educated guess might be that compliance drifted down to perhaps two-thirds of the population, with enormous local variation. Scattered evidence from the eighteenth and nineteenth centuries points to active churching, and in some districts it is still performed today.[119] Churching continued because women wanted it for religious, cultural, and emotional reasons of their own; custom maintained it, and the established church performed the office in the interests of duty and conformity. After the diminution or exhaustion of post-Reformation controversies the practice seems to have become routine and unremarkable. Most episcopal visitors stopped asking questions about churching by the 1680s, and the issue was allowed to die down.

Multiple Meanings

It is important to stress the multiple meanings of churching, and consider how the ceremony operated differently, or carried different connotations, according to different points of view. Among protestant controversialists—both critics and apologists of the Church of England—there was long discussion about the Jewish aspects of 'purification', and whether it was honourable or dishonourable to God. The debate was academic, theological, and casuistical, and had little bearing on liturgical practice, and impacted only indirectly on the social and cultural experience of women.

Episcopal disciplinarians saw the enforcement of churching as part of the task of securing conformity to the Book of Common Prayer. John Canne claimed that churching 'justified' officials 'in their crooked and unconscionable proceedings',[120] and this was a charge with which the Shipdens and Pinsons would surely have concurred. There was no canon regarding churching, nor was the rubric definitive or clear; but every deliverance from childbearing allowed the church to assert its authority over the laity, and particularly over women.

For the minister who performed the office, churching may have had spiritual or disciplinary connotations, but it was also a supplementary source of income. So whether the clergyman was performing the service for the woman, or imposing it on her, he was also doing it for himself. Parents who failed to make their customary offering—the chrisom cloth or its cash equivalent—were considered as debtors, and could be subject to disciplinary action.

The central actor in churching, of course, was the woman who had recently given birth. What did churching do for her? It involved the church and the community in her recovery from childbearing. It signalled her new status as a mother (after a first birth), or confirmed her status as a breeding woman. The ecclesiastical ceremony and the gossips' feast that followed marked her formal public reappearance after the conventional month of seclusion. The ritual put her on display, as the centre of attention. Normally she would sit to the rear of the church or in a segregated section (although seating plans varied, and some women sat with their husbands), but at her churching she came forward to the most prominent seat or pew by the altar, all eyes upon her.

The ceremony celebrated her survival, and offered the comforts of religion. It recognized her endurance of the pains and the perils of childbearing, and focused on the woman rather than her baby. It was, fundamentally, a thanksgiving. Was it also a purification? Only if she thought herself unclean. Most clergy taught, following Timothy, that the woman was sanctified by childbearing, that the child was the joyful offspring of the marriage bed. If some preachers harped on the curse of Eve or the sinfulness of conception it was to argue that all humankind was corrupt, not simply recently delivered women.[121] In any case, parishioners could take what they wanted from such sermons, and did not necessarily agree with the theological beliefs of their ministers. If the mother shared the superstition that a 'green' woman was out of grace with her neighbours, the ceremony released her from that anxiety, and restored her to her normal condition.

Missing in all of this is the child, who may have been brought to church with the midwife or nurse, and the husband and other male relations. Husbands, it seems, normally accompanied their wives to their churching but took temporarily subordinate positions. The woman had pre-eminence, even if she was not fully in control or 'on top'. In its customary operation it was *her* occasion, even if the church strove repeatedly to make it theirs.

IV

COURTSHIP

FIG. 12   Courtship scene from *The Story of David and Bersheba* in *The Roxburghe Ballads* (London, 1635)

COURTSHIP AND THE MAKING
OF MARRIAGE

This chapter uses evidence from diaries and autobiographies, correspondence and court records, sermons and conduct books, to examine the history
of courtship in Elizabethan and Stuart England. It seeks answers to a wide
range of questions that feed into social, cultural, literary, and demographic
studies. How did people negotiate the change from everyday social interaction to the charged relationship known as 'courtship'? How did they determine they were ready? How did couples choose one another, how did they
come together, and how did they move to the stage of becoming husband
and wife? Who took the initiative and who made the running? Did men and
women simply find themselves attracted to each other and then decide on
marriage, or was marriage their goal from the start? Was 'love' a normal and
necessary part of the process, and how did that differ from 'good will' and
'good liking'? What did the moralists have to say on this matter? What was
expected of couples in their new role of suitors and lovers, and what obstacles lay in their path? To what extent could parents arrange or thwart marriages against their children's wishes? Could young people engage themselves
without parental consent? What was the role of kinsfolk and friends in making
or blocking a match, and what was the part played by intermediaries? Were
women the passive recipients of courtship advances, or were they equal partners to a developing bond?

Once agreement was reached, how was it signalled or celebrated? How
common and how important were handfasting rituals, espousal ceremonies, or
the sealing of matrimonial contracts? What was the social, legal, and religious
significance of these performances, and how did they change over time? What
new privileges or duties befell the contracted couple, on the brink of being
legally married? Could they now intensify their sexual intimacy, anticipating
their morning in church? How much time would pass, and what could go
wrong, between the successful completion of courtship and the couple's new
incarnation as husband and wife?

Serious courtship knew one goal, the achievement of holy matrimony.
Though conducted in accordance with widely understood rules, courtship
was no mere game, no idle dalliance. Toying with affections, or sending fickle

signals about prospective alliances, could be ruinous to all concerned, a source of pain and dishonour. Boys and girls may have played together, walked out together, and fondly exchanged tokens; they may even have teased each other and touched each other's bodies in such games as 'barley break' and 'codpiece kissing'; but once courtship proper commenced the blithe and innocent days of youth were over.[1] Courtship prefigured marriage, and marriage was the business of adults. To the middling sort and the élite, and perhaps through the lower ranks of respectable society, courtship was the acceptable pathway to marriage, a process of selection and bonding that secured a permanent union. By the time they reached their mid-twenties most young people were ready to embark on this perilous passage.[2]

No formal ceremonial process guided the path of courtship. There was no ecclesiastical ritual to adhere to, no standard social script to obey. Yet all over England prospective partners observed the unwritten rules of a deeply patterned activity. Although there were countless circumstances in which men and women could meet, and myriad ways through which their relationship could lead to marriage, the infinite variety of social interaction concealed a remarkably robust framework of expectations. From contact to contract, from good liking to final agreement, most couples passed through a recognizable series of steps.

Amongst the literate and propertied classes, whose lives are best recorded, prospective parties to a wedding engaged in a sequence of enquiries and approaches, rituals and undertakings, before coming to a final matrimonial agreement. Humbler people appear to have acted less formally, with a greater degree of opportunism and independence, but no firm social distinctions can be drawn. Individual cases varied, according to the circumstances and inclinations of those involved, but custom established a social framework within which particular approaches could be judged. When we find Kentish and Derbyshire yeoman, East Anglian and North-Country clergy, rural and metropolitan tradesmen, and gentry all over England from both the sixteenth and seventeenth centuries behaving in a similar manner, it is clear that we are observing the workings of a common culture.

The ritual dance of courtship included mutual familiarization, clarification of intentions, and consideration of prospects. It usually involved the exchange of gifts or tokens, and negotiation of privileges and opportunities, before the sealing of consent. Naturally, the courtship stakes varied according to the wealth, position, and consequence of the parties involved. Depending on the status of the families, the success of a courtship could hinge on dowries (the money or property the wife brings to her husband), portions (the share of an inheritable estate given in marriage), and jointures (the estate reserved for the wife in event of her widowhood). Matchmakers, go-betweens, brokers, and attorneys played their parts, along with the countervailing complexities of calculation and self-interest, goodwill, passion, and love. At every level of society, it seems, the freedom of the couple to conclude their own affairs was counterbalanced by the interests of parents, kinsfolk, and friends. The tension between patriarchal authority and individual choice produced many domestic dramas, as detailed case-studies reveal.

Men with literary pretensions sometimes employed military imagery to describe and to dramatize courtship. Whether the women they won were as passive as their poetry depicted remains a problem for further research. Alexander Niccholes, in *A Discourse of Marriage and Wiving* published in 1615, considers courtship 'a stratagem of war'. Thomas Shipman's poem, 'Right Courtship', penned in 1658, likens courtship to martial combat, with references to siege warfare, bringing to a parley, beating down the bulwarks, and taking the town.[3] Such conceits were especially common in the second half of the seventeenth century, when so many people were familiarized to the vocabulary of war. 'The motions of love are like the motions of war, very slow and uncertain,' opined William Lawrence in 1667 in a letter to his brother about his recent marriage. Lawrence described his courtship of Anne Martin, the daughter of a wealthy apothecary, in terms of sieges and repulses, leading to victory. 'In a word, after the discharge of some sighs, after I had made many assaults upon a white hand, and stormed the blushing bulwarks of her lips, the fortress upon the 24th of September was surrendered, and at night I entered triumphantly into my new possession.'[4] By the middle of the seventeenth century there were handbooks advising lovers how to polish their rhetoric for 'the arts of wooing and complimenting'.[5]

A later seventeenth-century handbook offered similar advice on courtship 'for the use of young batchelors'. Its tone, however, suggests that it was targeted more at those intending seduction rather than matrimony. 'Mistresses are to be attacked like towns, according to their fortifications, situation or garrison, no general rules to be given 'em . . . Some are to be mined, some to be bombed, some won by storm, others by composition, others to be starved into a surrender.' The same publication adopted a more conventional manner for its remarks on the making of matrimony.

To complete a true and happy marriage, are required virtuous inclinations, hearty love, and true liking, so that they may both be of the same mind, and have one and the same interest; and to make this up, there must be suitable agreement in ages, humours, breeding, religion, families, and fortune, which when they concur, we may expect all the satisfaction this world can afford; but when any of these are wanting, marriage but seldom proves comfortable.[6]

FIG. 13 'The Arts of Wooing and Complementing' from Edward Phillips, *The Mysteries of Love and Eloquence* (London, 1658)

Courtship Narratives

A fruitful contribution to this discussion can be made by gathering firsthand reports of early modern courtship and matchmaking. After reading the words of diarists and autobiographers, and straining to hear other voices in the background, we can proceed to a more systematic analysis of the issues. Recovering the courtship strategies of less literate classes will require exploration of more fragmentary sources, including the records of the ecclesiastical courts. The following accounts, in chronological order, have all the biases and shortcomings of retrospective, self-centred, and mostly male narratives, heavily weighted towards the propertied élite, but they include telling details and put flesh on the bones of abstractions. Retelling these stories from a cross-gendered point of view requires an effort of empathy and imagination.

The Elizabethan musician Thomas Whythorne (1528–96) understood the difference between 'wooing' and 'wiving', between flirtatious toying with women on the one hand and serious matrimonial courtship on the other. And Whythorne assumed that the gentle ladies within his orbit could similarly distinguish earnest intentions from merry discourse, the pleasures of the moment from commitments of a lifetime. In Whythorne's account we find him negotiating the rules of courtship as well as the conventions of autobiography. He employed oblique approaches through allies and intermediaries, sought soundings by third parties, and made his addresses to entreat and to sue. Though he does not use the language of warfare and siegecraft, he makes it clear that courtship, for him, required strategies akin to those of the chess-game or the hunt.[7]

At an early stage in his career Whythorne sought the intercessionary help of his employer, an unnamed 'court lady', to win his way to a wife.

I did put her in mind of a young maiden that she had brought up in her house, the which I could like very well to be my wife and if I might have it so. Wherefore I desired to have her good will and furtherance in the matter. To the which my words my gentlewoman said that she, for her part, was willing thereunto. 'But', quoth she, 'the maid is my husband's kinswoman, and therefore he will bestow her where he liketh. And if you would sue to him for his will to have her, I am sure it would be such a troublesome piece of work for you, as it would disquiet you very much. Thus much do I show you for good will', quoth she, 'and therefore, if you will be counselled by me, do you never proceed any further in it.'[8]

Thus was Whythorne advised of his limits.

A few pages further in the autobiography, though perhaps several years later in time, we find Whythorne in hot pursuit of a 'twenty-pound widow' (never identified by name), who led him a merry dance. The musician's dealings with the widow, though ultimately unsatisfactory from Whythorne's point of view, expose several of the protocols and strategies governing courtship in gentle and courtly circles in the later sixteenth century. Whythorne's account of this courtship is constructed to show that it fully followed standard conventions, and that he did everything in his power, by way of speech and gesture, to bring it to a successful end. He was by now a successful professional, approaching middle age, and patently in need of a wife.

Courtship, in these circles, was a collaborative enterprise, in which a man's friends and associates might find a leading role. The courtship of the 'twenty-pound widow' began, Whythorne writes, when a gentle acquaintance 'brake unto me of marriage' and offered 'help' to find a wife. 'How say you if I would help you to a widow, who is come of worshipful parentage and hath twenty pounds a year dowry or jointure, who hath no children and is of years nigh about five or six years younger than yourself?' the prospective go-between asked. Such a catalogue of attributes was irresistible, so Whythorne immediately constituted himself as a suitor. The friend introduced him in this role, and the widow responded as a coquette by greeting him with 'a friendly kiss'. The friend, as third party, broached 'the marriage matter', and Whythorne himself addressed the lady 'for the same purpose'. When she offered 'friendly entertainment' he responded with 'due salutations and ceremonies belonging to a wooer's function'. Each played a practised part in a loosely scripted ritual, each seeking advantage while studiously preserving decorum.[9]

Apparently satisfied about financial affairs, the reciprocity of material benefits, and their good liking one to another, the couple made plans for their marriage. The widow agreed 'to forsake all her other suitors' and to take Thomas Whythorne as her husband. They underwent no formal ceremony of espousal, but on the basis of conditional promises, first made through intermediaries and then repeated face to face, they appeared to be contracted. Whythorne says he 'gave unto her a token of goodwill and she received it', symbolically signalling her acceptance.[10]

Then, inexplicably, it all went wrong. Two days later, Whythorne writes, 'she fetched the token which . . . I had given unto her. And she would have delivered it unto me again, but I would not receive it.' The handling and disposition of the token marked the development and deterioration of the relationship. Whythorne could not understand why the widow's interest had cooled, or what he had done wrong. 'I found my widow so strange as though she had never made me any such faithful promise.' Were they legally contracted to each other, and bound by law and custom to proceed to holy matrimony? Whythorne himself had doubts, conceding that the widow's word 'was no such contract in matrimony as should farther bind your conscience than a friendly promise, without the plighting of our troths the one to another. And yet I, for my part, thought that I should not need to have done it till we met at the church for that purpose.'[11]

Whythorne's dispute with his widow did not lead to any challenge at law, but rather to rueful reflections in an artful autobiography. It reveals, however, the looseness, uncertainty, and risk inherent in marriage negotiations, and the danger of conducting this business without the counsel and witness of friends and relations. If interested parties at Whythorne's social level should question whether or not their matrimonial contract was binding, is it any wonder that couples throughout the social spectrum should be puzzled by the complexities of the law? Whythorne might think that he was party to a contract *de futuri*, but the widow claimed that her promise was none 'but she might break it again upon cause'. There had been no contract, she insisted, only foolish talk. Eventually, Whythorne admitted defeat, retrieved his tokens, and went away to lick his wounds.[12]

Eligible gentle bachelors had little need to initiate wooing expeditions, if autobiographical accounts can be believed. Courtship came looking for them. Simon Forman, the Elizabethan magus, boasted that he was 'offered a wife many times between Easter and Whitsuntide [in 1590] and had the sight and choice of four or five maids and widows'. Forman says he 'went . . . a wooing' several times over the next few years before settling on a gentleman's daughter. Knowing that a lover should look the part, Forman invested in 'much apparel' in preparation for his courtship.[13]

Sir William Ashcombe recalled several proposals from his time as a student at the Inns of Court, when he was 'solicited' or 'importuned' towards matrimony. In 1608, he writes, 'I was much importuned to marry my Lady Garrard's daughter of Dorney by Windsor, mistress Martha Garrard, a fine gentlewoman. I saw her and no more.' In the following year, 'I was importuned to see a brave spirited gentlewoman named mistress Kate Howard, being one of the two daughters and heirs of the Viscount Bindon's brother. I saw her not far from Bath, was earnestly solicited to proceed; being half afraid of the greatness of her spirit I did not; she was since more worthily bestowed and she was most worthy so to be.' And in 1610, 'I was wished unto a fine gentlewoman. I saw her; upon further acquaintance I disliked, and did not proceed.' Ashcombe's autobiography highlights the steps in the dance of courtship which blended individual initiative and outside intervention: suggestion and invitation, viewing and contact, assessment and decision whether or not to proceed. Eventually, Ashcombe writes, 'I seeing so much wickedness in the world, and so much casualty among men, thought good to choose

out a companion for me in an honest course and took a wife.' This was in
1613, when Ashcombe was aged 22. His account adds an interesting dimension to the view of marriage as a moral prophylactic, but gives no information about how it was achieved.[14]

Following an exchange of letters to establish the groundwork, Phineas
Pett, the naval shipwright, accompanied his son Peter on a courtship journey
from Surrey to Suffolk in the spring of 1633. Peter, it seems, had initiated the
courtship, but could not complete it without help from his elders. Both sides
were on their best behaviour, and both involved other family members and
advisers in the affair. From their lodgings at the Crown at Woodbridge, the
Petts 'went to visit Mrs. Cole and her daughters, with whom', Pett senior
relates, 'we had large discourse about the match . . . and found our proposi-
tions entertained'. The elder Pett took 'great liking to the maid' and endorsed
his son's good judgement. On the second day of the visit, a Sunday, the Petts
dined and supped at Mrs Cole's house, and on the Monday, Pett writes,

we invited mother and daughters and Mr. Fleming [their lawyer] to dine with us at
our inn, whither came to us divers of our friends to whom we gave the best entertainment the place could afford. In the afternoon we had private conferences together,
and concluded the match and contracted the parties with free consent on both sides;
we supped this night at Mrs. Cole's.

This round of dining and visiting, with its treating and greeting and hospitality and munificence, produced mutually satisfactory results. Within just three
days the business was settled, leaving the couple to prepare for their wedding
the following September.[15]

John Hayne, a merchant of Exeter, set his sights upon Susan Henley of
Winsham, Somerset, and set out to win her in 1634. He made repeated journeys to Winsham, over thirty-five miles distant, and showered his chosen
one with gifts and tokens. Being an obsessive keeper of financial records,
Hayne enumerated these courtship expenditures, leaving a rare account of
the items that cemented a match within the community of godly merchants
and minor West-Country gentry. Among the first tokens of his esteem, John
Hayne gave Susan Henley a puritan tract, the second edition of Arthur
Hildersham's *Lectures upon the Fourth of John*, which cost him 7s. And, as if
to offset the severity of this improving work, he also gave her 4d. worth of
ribbons. Subsequent gifts included rings, purses, ribbons, bracelets, stockings, and gloves of the sort that any young man might wish to bestow but
only a prosperous merchant could afford. One day he brought her 'two yards
of scarlet kersey' worth 18s., and 'a cabinet bought in Rouen' which cost £3.
More conventional courtship gifts included 'a pair of green silk garters' costing

3s., and 'six pair of ash-colour women's gloves' at 14d. a pair. Hayne was evidently opening his warehouse to her as well as his heart.[16]

At the time of their betrothal, probably in August 1634, John Hayne supplied half of a twenty-shilling piece 'which we brake together', as part of a traditional ritual of engagement. Nor was the spiritual side of their relationship neglected, for Hayne also gave Susan 'a Bible worth 20s.' and 'two sermon books cost[ing] 4s. 6d.' Hayne could not visit Winsham without bringing some material token of his affection, but imagination seemed to fail him over the following months as he carried monotonous consignments of gloves. The marriage in April 1635 occasioned another explosion of ribbons and favours before the couple settled down to the discipline of godly housekeeping.[17]

John Greene's London diary records the progress of the match between his sister Margaret and Mr Edward Bysshe. Both came from legal families attached to Lincoln's Inn. On 12 June 1635 'Bysshe went to our house and saw my sister and liked her and she liked him.' The parties were agreeable to each other, but could not proceed towards marriage without parental approval. It was not until mid-August that the marriage was 'resolved on' and 'concluded' by Greene's mother, and then in October the match was 'almost off again'. Whatever the difficulties they were soon overcome, and the wedding took place on 5 November 1635 amidst the usual entertainments of that memorable day.[18]

When the London merchant Thomas Barrow sought to marry Katherine Oxinden in March 1636 her uncle, Sir James Oxinden, wrote to her brother Henry to assure him that family honour would be preserved. This would be no hasty match between land and trade; all the protocols of gentle courtship would be observed. 'You shall find me very careful for my niece Katherine's good,' wrote Sir James.

If he [the suitor] shall come hither I shall tell him that a business of this nature is first to be treated of by friends, and that if his father will give way to it, he shall be welcome to me, and by that I shall find whether the young man deals really, which as occasion serves I will not fail to acquaint you and my sister. Doubt not but my wife and I will so handle the matter that I hope your sister shall receive no prejudice here, for before I speak with his father I will believe nothing, nor suffer any communication between them.

Before being permitted to pay direct courtship addresses to his young Katherine, Thomas Barrow would have to clear the hurdles of the lady's uncles, aunts, mother, and brother. Evidently he proved successful and Sir James Oxinden was satisfied, for the couple were married before the end of the year.[19]

The Reverend Ralph Josselin's courtship of Jane Constable progressed along the requisite path, from 'first proposal of the match' on New Year's day 1640, through 'mutual promise one to another' on 23 January, and formal 'consents and contract' on 28 September, before their actual marriage on 28 October following. Josselin did little more than date these developments, but thirty years later he discussed the consent, portion, and jointure for the marriage of his daughter Jane.[20]

Sir John Oglander's reluctant acquiescence to the marriage of his daughter Bridget to a husband of whom he disapproved reveals the power of the convention of matrimonial arrangement among the gentry, even in its violation. In 1649, with the traditional order shattered, the royalist gentry debased, and his own fortune and authority undermined, Oglander could not even rule his daughter. In private frustration he set down in his journal the thoughts he would have proclaimed from the roof-top:

know all men that I, Sir John Oglander, do acknowledge that the match between Sir Robert Eaton's son and my daughter Bridget was never with my approbation or good liking. It was her importunity that induced me to give way unto it, and she was resolved to have him whatsoever became of her, and gave me so much under her own hand before marriage. I confess I never liked to Sir Robert or his estate, a swearing, profane man. I beseech God to bless them and to make them happy, which I much doubt . . . The marriage of my last daughter, as I fear she is the worst matched of them all, cost me very dear . . . I pray God bless them, for it is a match of her own making.[21]

When Alice Wandesford, a Yorkshire gentlewoman, reached the age of 25 in 1651, her family considered her ready for marriage. The initiative, as Alice tells it, came not from her but from her widowed mother and from prospective suitors, but the final choice of marriage partner was her own. Several 'persons of very good worth and quality' had solicited Mrs Wandesford on Alice's behalf, and had to be 'disobliged' when William Thornton emerged as the chosen candidate. Alice recalls that 'after the first and second view betwixt us [her mother] closed so far with him that she was willing he should proceed in his suit, if I should see cause to accept'. In her autobiography Alice recalled that she had no urgent wish to change her 'happy and free condition' but was willing to do what seemed best for God, her family, and her friends. Satisfied that 'the gentleman seemed to be a very godly, sober, and discreet person, free from all manner of vice, and of a good conversation', and his estate 'a handsome competency', she agreed to the match. All that was needed to conclude it was completion of 'the treaty of marriage', which was 'earnestly pursued' on the Thornton side and 'discreetly managed' by the widow Wandesford. 'Through God's blessing,' Alice writes, 'this treaty was brought to a period to the satisfaction of each party,' with agreement on the jointure and portion. At the time of her wedding, in December 1651, Alice was preoccupied with the domestic and sexual demands of her 'new estate', but in later years fulfilment of the legal settlement became her 'grand concern'.[22]

The most remarkable of all seventeenth-century courtship narratives, remarkable for its length and detail as well as the relatively humble social status of its author, was written by the Derbyshire yeoman Leonard Wheatcroft (1627–1707).[23] Wheatcroft memorialized in writing his courtship of Elizabeth Hawley, which lasted from June 1655 until their wedding in May 1657. Typically, it began with a suggestion from a mutual friend. 'I had some intelligence of a young maid that would be there [at the summer wakes] by one of her relations, who told me she was very fortunate, besides beautiful [and] lovely.' Wheatcroft's interest was aroused, even before he met her. Having planted the seed, the relation established his role as a go-between and carried similar information about Wheatcroft to his kinswoman.

Deciding at the age of 30 to 'go a-wooing', Leonard Wheatcroft pursued his lady with letters of love. These missives were somewhat overwritten efforts, modelled on conventional romantic literature. 'Friends' acted as couriers and postmen. Elizabeth had the sense not to reply at first (it is not even clear that she knew how to write), and then sent responses that were tantalizingly non-committal.

Not until the following year did Leonard and Elizabeth develop a face-to-face intimacy. With her parents' permission, Leonard escorted Elizabeth to the summer wakes, some several miles distant, and their 'walking out' together included hand-holding, kisses, and embraces. Wheatcroft was firmly established in the Hawley household as a suitor, and used the long summer evenings to solidify his amorous relationship. The sexual temperature increased as Leonard was permitted to stay overnight at her house and at her uncle's, and she was allowed to stay over with him. But it was not until the couple was 'made sure' and a date set for their wedding that they intensified their physical intimacy. Elizabeth came to visit him during the spring of 1657, Leonard recalls, 'and for joy we so happily met together, we embraced each other all that night and the night after'. This may have been 'bundling' (a term no English contemporaries used),[24] but the author represents no part of his courtship as unchaste or improper. On the morning of his wedding Wheatcroft could write of 'leaping forth of my virgin's bed', although this may have been a figure of speech rather than an accurate account of his condition.

Meanwhile, in counterpoint to the developing relationship between Leonard and Elizabeth, their respective families and 'friends' worked out the financial aspect of the match. It was not easy. Fatherless and independent, Leonard spoke for himself, but still gathered friends to support him. Elizabeth's father and uncles represented the other family's interests. Negotiations stalled, Wheatcroft recalled, over the feoffment and portion, and the men 'departed to their several homes, suspecting all was ended'. Leonard's ardour, however, was not easily crushed. Casting himself as the resourceful and persistent lover, he pursued all avenues and rained petitions on Elizabeth's father, uncles, and cousins.

Wheatcroft's courtship, like many others, extended over many months and was subject to reversals and hindrances. His memoir, an artful and self-conscious narrative, represents it as a romantic and dramatic quest. 'How many times I went a-wooing you shall find so many slashes upon an ash tree at Winter town end, and how many miles I travelled for her sake was 440 and odd.' Eventually, in October 1656, under pressure from one of the uncles, Elizabeth's father gave his consent. 'Then did I give him many thanks,' Leonard writes, 'and for joy sent for some strong beer that we might more rejoice. Then did we walk to her father's house, and kindly did I salute her, telling her what her father said, to which she also agreed. And being very merry for that day, at night we departed, and I came home again.' Only from this point, it seems, could the couple consider themselves properly betrothed. But there was no formal ceremony of espousal, no ritual handfasting or exchange of promises, and certainly no immediate retirement to bed. Having recovered from his drinking, Leonard 'made it known in the church of Ashover for three sabbaths together' in the Commonwealth-era equivalency of banns.

There would be no rushing into this marriage, however, until the financial details were fully resolved. The courtship that commenced in the summer of 1655, that was 'made sure' in the autumn of 1656, was not ready for matrimony until the spring of 1657. The wedding was planned for 'Wednesday in Whitsun week', but as late as Easter Elizabeth's father found fault with the details of the jointure, and 'would not seal till his counsel had viewed them over'. Leonard intimated that he might have to go to Jamaica, and no doubt the question arose whether Elizabeth might be pregnant. Hard bargaining was a way of life among these North Country yeomen, but eventually agreement was complete. As soon as Elizabeth's father delivered a down payment of her portion, the invitations went out for the wedding.

Samuel Woodford (son of the puritan steward of Northampton whose pre-Civil War diary we have already encountered) was a student at the Inner Temple at the end of the Cromwellian protectorate when, in his words, he 'fell in love' with his cousin Elizabeth Pike. He 'wrote several times to her and had once an answer', but it came to nothing. A short while later he met Alice Beale at a friend's house in London, with altogether better success. 'By little and little coming better acquainted with her', Woodford writes,

continual converse bred an entire affection in me to her, and finding in her whatever I desired in a wife I gave over myself to her love, having often and often at the throne of grace begged the assistance of the Almighty and his direction. I loved her and after some soliciting it, found she had an inclination to me, and nothing stood in the way but money, yet this love made me pass over and, without my friends' advice I promised her to make her my wife.[25]

Having decided on a wife without consulting his mother or his uncle, Woodford agonized whether he had offended God by neglecting this family duty. He was aged about 24 at this time, his father had died a few years earlier, and he had already accumulated debts. Young Samuel berates himself, 'I was to blame to do it without their knowledge I humbly confess it . . . oh Lord pardon that sin and let it not hinder thy blessing from descending down upon us.' Several months of haggling and heart-searching were required before Woodford's relations would agree to his marriage to the woman he subsequently refered to as 'my dear and loving wife'.[26]

In a less anguished discourse, the Sussex clergyman Giles Moore wrote with cautious optimism to his colleague Mr Crayford in 1671 regarding a match proposed between his favourite niece Martha and the Reverend Crayford's son. 'If the young man could fancy her with this advowson, and that well stocked within and without doors with all kind of necessaries, together also with my library when I left this world, I should not (with her own consent thereto given, which she hath no reason to deny) judge her amiss bestowed.' The match was not to be, however, though whether because the terms were inadequate or liking and consent withheld we cannot tell. Two years later the Moores concluded a successful alliance with another neighbouring clerical family. This time Martha was to marry John Citizen, the rector of Streat. In August 1673, Moore writes, 'Mr. Citizen and I went together to Justice Stapely, and so the next day again, with all the writings and our instructions for drawing up the articles between us concerning Mat's marriage with him.' The wedding took place a month later. By way of a portion Moore gave Citizen the advowson of East Aldrington, valued at £160.[27]

In January 1676 the Sussex merchant Samuel Jeake 'resolved to seek mistress Weeks in marriage'. He was aged 23 at the time, just beginning his mercantile career, and pursuing astrological enthusiasms in the Cinque Port of Rye. His target, Mary Weeks, lived with her parents at Westfield, eight miles distant. Jeake's diary for the next few years traces the quickening and dampening of his hopes in that direction. We learn from this drama about the protocols of provincial courtship, the continuing importance of family counsel, persistence in the face of minimal encouragement, and the thwarting of individual initiative.[28]

The opening stages of this courtship were excruciatingly slow. On 20 March 1676 Jeake 'spoke to John Weeks about my intentions of seeking his sister in marriage'. Almost two months passed before Jeake again had 'some conference with John Weeks and by him his sister's answer'. The answer could not have been completely discouraging, for that same day in May he 'wrote her a letter' which was carried by her brother. The summer passed without progress and it was September before Jeake 'rode to Robertsbridge Fair to get opportunity to speak to Mary Weeks, but could not and came home about eight p.m.'[29]

Thwarted by elder members of the Weeks family, Jeake opened his mind to other matrimonial possibilities. In January 1677, he writes, 'Mr. Jenkins offered his advice to my cousin to speak for my marriage with mistress Ann File, which my cousin told me of.' Again Jeake was slow to move, but on 11 June he 'rode to Appledore Fair to meet with Mr. George Jenkins, and thence to his house with him to see mistress Ann File'. The following day he made his addresses, but they were no more successful than before. All hopes were dashed the following month when Jeake received 'a letter from Mr. Jenkins that he had spoken to Mrs. File and her daughter but refused'.[30]

Jeake then renewed his pursuit of Mary Weeks, and sought help from his cousin in forwarding the match. Emboldened by his kinsman's support, Jeake went to Westfield in March 1678 and 'spake to Mary Weeks' mother for her consent to seek her daughter in marriage'. He also 'spoke to her cousin, but had no encouragement from either, only liberty to speak to her, which [he] did about eleven a.m.' Mary's news was not without comfort for though 'her mother had that day bid her deny me', she herself would have 'given me her consent'. In an attempt to move things forward he 'rode to Battle market' on 9 April 'to speak to Mr. Weeks and his son about the premises, but he desired me to forbear any further applications'.[31]

It is not clear whether the Weeks family objected to Jeake's income, politics, religion, or social position, or found some defect in his character or bearing. Perhaps they feared alliance with a self-taught millenarian astrologer who made his living as a tradesman. Jeake might have been more successful had he had his father to speak for him, or if he commanded more of a fortune, or if he had not been so weird. In his own opinion Jeake was most desirable, but he was still in need of a wife.

Faint heart never won fair lady, so again, six weeks later, Jeake sought out

Mr Weeks at Bodiam Fair. 'He with much importunity and unwillingly granted me leave to mention it once more to his daughter,' but again the suit was rejected. Nothing more could be done until December of the following year when Jeake learnt that old Mrs Weeks was dead and that his principal opponent was removed. Accordingly, just before Christmas 1679 Jeake 'rode to Westfield to see if [he] might be admitted as suitor to Mary Weeks after her mother's death, but her cousin refused'. Mary Weeks herself offered 'no inclination' so finally, after three frustrating years, Jeake accepted defeat and turned his attention elsewhere.[32]

Jeake's next matrimonial quest, beginning in 1680, was altogether more successful. Learning from his previous efforts he went first to the mother of his intended, a neighbouring householder in Rye, and then with her support embraced the rest of the family. Jeake's diary unfolds the progress of the courtship from first contact through negotiation of jointure and portion, to contract and formal betrothal, and eventual marriage and 'devirgination', all accompanied by astrological notes and figurations. 'By my marriage,' Jeake writes, 'I came into actual possession of about £800 of my wife's portion, and the remainder was paid me gradually in 1681.'[33]

Ralph Thoresby, a Yorkshire gentleman, recalled his disappointment at the failure of his first serious attempt at courtship, despite his attempt to play by the rules. In 1684, he writes, 'being now twenty six years of age, I was solicited to change my condition, and was particularly recommended to mistress Mary Cholmley, eldest daughter of Richard Cholmley of Sprustey, esquire, to whom I made my applications, finding the young lady lovely, pious and prudent, and withal a considerable fortune'. Having been pointed in her direction, and having sized her up, Thoresby was prepared to fall in love with her. He continued,

I was courteously entertained by the whole family, and after some time all matters were agreed upon, and the very day of the marriage appointed. Yet all came to nothing, by the interposition of a member of parliament whose estate preponderated mine, to whom afterwards she was married in pure obedience to her parents . . . This unexpected disappointment was to the mutual grief and sorrow of myself and the lady of my affections, and we parted not without many tears on both sides.

Mary Cholmley *could* have refused to marry the MP, and *might* have held out for Thoresby, but she was under considerable pressure to advance her family's ambitions.[34]

As always, there were plenty more fish in the sea, and the eligible Ralph Thoresby soon found himself facing a wealth of matrimonial choices. He reports that he 'was very solicitous for divine directions, and prayed fervently for guidance . . . and it pleased God to answer'. Within a year of his loss of Mary Cholmley he married Anna Sykes, daughter of the senior lord of the manor of Leeds.[35]

John Evelyn's diary exposes the matchmaking efforts of more of the gentry and minor aristocracy over the later seventeenth century. Parents and agents usually made the running, while the young people were left to sort out their ambitions and emotions. In February 1667, Evelyn records, 'my lord of Carlisle treated with me for the proposal of marriage between his eldest son and my niece Anne Evelyn'. This was an honour to the Evelyns but it came to nothing, perhaps because Anne was only 14 years old. The following year it was Lord Ashley's turn to show interest in Anne Evelyn. On 27 November 1668 Evelyn 'dined at my Lord Ashley's . . . where the match of my niece was proposed for his only son, in which my assistance was desired for my lord'. This too came to naught. She was eventually married to William Montague, attorney-general to the Queen, in June 1670.[36]

In August 1677 Evelyn went to London 'to meet with one [unnamed] about a proposal of a match for my son', then aged 22. More fruitful negotiations commenced in November 1679 when Evelyn met Sir John Stonehouse 'with whom I was treating a marriage between my son and his daughter in law'. Soon after Christmas Evelyn gave him 'a particular of the settlement on my son, who now made his address to the young lady his daughter in law'. Success seemed assured, so in January 1680 Evelyn 'went to counsel for the settling my estate on my son, now in treaty about a marriage with my Lady Stonehouse's daughter'. And in February 'were the writings for the settling jointure and other contracts of marriage of my son finished and sealed at Whitehall . . . The lady was to bring five thousand pounds in consideration of a settlement of five hundred pounds a year present maintenance, which was likewise to be her jointure, and five hundred pounds after mine and my wife's decease.' The wedding took place on 24 February 1680, three months after the initial overtures.[37]

In March 1680, barely a week after his son's wedding, Evelyn was again involved in matchmaking for members of his family. On 3 March, he writes, 'I dined at Lord Mayor's in order to the meeting my Lady Beckford, whose daughter, a rich heiress, I had recommended to my brother of Wotton for his only son.' The couple married almost a year later in February 1681, 'her portion eight thousand pounds'. Also in 1681 John Evelyn acted as go-between for Lord Spencer, son of the Countess of Sunderland, and Jane Fox, daughter of Sir Stephen Fox. In this case Evelyn disapproved of the proposed match, judging Spencer to be 'extravagant' and inclined to vice. 'However,' he adds, 'so earnest and importunate was the countess that I would use my interest and break it to him, that I was overcome, and did accordingly promise it . . . My lady, now that I had broken the ice, continues to conjure my assistance, and that I would not leave it in this posture.'[38]

Next in line for this treatment was Evelyn's daughter Mary, aged 19 in 1685. The diarist writes, 'there were now no less than four gentlemen of quality offering to treat with me about marriage; and I freely gave her her own choice, knowing she was discreet'. What none of them knew was that she was ill, and sadly their efforts would be wasted; Mary Evelyn died in March 1685. Another daughter, Elizabeth Evelyn, would have none of the treaties and memoranda of agreement arranged for her contempories. In July 1685 she eloped to a secret marriage with a nephew of the surveyor of the navy, 'he being in no condition sortable to hers'. John Evelyn altered his will to cut her out, but this fatherly precaution was unnecessary for she died of smallpox a month after her wedding.[39]

Nor was this the end of John Evelyn's marriage matters, for in March 1686 'came Sir Giles Gerrard to treat with me about his son's marrying my daughter Susanna'. Too many difficulties lay in the way, Evelyn writes, 'so as we did not proceed to any conclusion'. But Susanna remained to be disposed, so, when 'proposals of a marriage by Mr. Draper with my daughter Susanna' came in 1693 John Evelyn reports he 'embraced' them and settled on her a generous portion. Finally, in his old age, Evelyn took an active interest in his grandson's courtship negotiations, noting when the marriage was proposed, concluded, settled, and engrossed.[40]

A cautionary tale is told by Elizabeth Freke, one of the most wide-ranging but least recognized female diarists of the seventeenth century, about the courtship of her son Ralph. Elizabeth was the wife of Percy Freke, the English sheriff of Cork, who during the 1690s promoted the match of their son with Lady Alice Moore, eldest daughter of the Earl of Drogheda. Elizabeth Freke thought it too ambitious. 'With a portion of three thousand pounds presently laid down, she was a fine lady and very handsome, and nothing to be objected but her quality, which I thought too much for a gentleman.' Despite these misgivings the couple were introduced. Young Ralph Freke was aged 20, his prospective bride about 15. They spent a season in each other's company in Dublin in 1695, she 'kindly' receiving her suitor and he 'mightily fancying the young lady'. Indeed, it seems the boy was smitten, and his love for young Alice ruined the Freke family's bargaining power.[41]

In Mrs Freke's view, the other family 'found my son so taken with the young lady that they would have made us their servants in being paymasters to the young couple . . . They found my son's inclination so far fixed towards this lady that they resolved to bring me to any terms.' Here, explicity, was a warning against the infusion of affection into matrimonial negotiations. Elizabeth Freke refused to expedite this match which she thought ill-judged from the beginning. 'I cared not to be frightened out of my money, nor my son either,' she wrote in her journal. 'They thought my son's affections engaged, yet to my great concern and my son's trouble off went this great match, which I foresaw would be ruinous to us, though my son was bitterly angry with me for it.' With matters at an impasse, 'Mr. Freke and my son went again to Dublin to finish this great match or break it quite off; which after about three weeks stay and attendance it was broke quite off.'[42]

Broken-hearted, Ralph Freke refused other 'great matches' and 'good offers' in London and elsewhere, but 'none would he see'. Eventually, 'without the sight of any good fortune . . . and begged by his father to see several proposed', he took a bride in Ireland without informing his parents. Elizabeth Freke, who herself had married unwisely, berated herself for this lapse. 'My dear and only son never so much as asked my blessing or consent in this match, for which I have and do forgive him, and beg of God to do the like in forgiving of him too, and wish him better fortune than I, who married without my dear father's consent.' And as an afterthought, too late for action, she mused in her journal, 'perhaps I might have opposed this match'. Ralph Freke's bride was Eliza Mead, eldest daughter of Sir John Mead, who brought with her £300 a year in land or £4,000 if the land were sold; this was a decent sum, but not the fortune the Frekes had wished.[43]

Finally, we have Nicholas Blundell, the catholic lord of the manor at Crosby, Lancashire, who kept a detailed diary of his courtship and marriage with Frances Langdale early in Queen Anne's reign. Religious and financial matters had a higher priority for Blundell than personal attraction, for he had never set eyes upon the young woman before opening negotiations. Blundell was aged 33, his prospective bride 17. What mattered most was that they both came from landed recusant families. During February 1703 Blundell studied the Langdale pedigree in preparation for his planned alliance. He opened negotiations in March by writing to Lord Langdale, by way of 'cousin Eyre the lawyer', to express his interest in his lordship's younger daughter. In April Blundell 'received a letter from Lord Langdale' and was encouraged to embark on his courtship in earnest. On 12 April 1703 he had a black coat made in Liverpool, equipped himself with an expensive new wig (costing £12), and the next day set out 'for my journey' to Hatherop, Gloucestershire.[44]

After four nights on the road Blundell arrived safely and 'found the family all there, and also my Lord Langdale'. The next few days were spent in 'discourse', mostly about money, and in meeting people who were likely to become kin. On 19 April, Blundell writes, 'I discoursed Lord Langdale in his chamber and Lady Webb in the dining room. I made my first address to mistress Frances Langdale.' The entry on 21 April—'Lady Webb discoursed me in the garden; I discoursed mistress Langdale in the kitchen garden'— suggests that negotiations were going well. Their success was declared the following night at dinner. The diarist writes, 'I discoursed of cattle and sheep, etc. Lady Dowager Webb read the Heads of Agreement of Marriage to be between mistress Frances Langdale and me, Nicholas Blundell, in presence of Lord Langdale and Sir John Webb.'[45] This amounted to an engagement, a public declaration of intent; but there is no trace of a formal espousal, none of the ceremonial handfasting and pledging that might have been common a century before.

It remained now for the lawyers to cast these agreements into binding form. Accordingly, on 23 April, 'Mr. Trinder the lawyer came to Hatherop for instructions to draw Articles of Marriage', which he drafted the following day. On 25 April: 'Mr. Trinder brought to Hatherop the heads of Articles of Marriage, fairly transcribed, which were agreed to by Lord Langdale, Lady Webb and myself.' Young Frances Langdale played no part in these dealings, except to assent to her marriage, and her reward came on 28 April when Blundell presented her with a diamond ring, value 14s.[46]

After spending just over two weeks in the company of his future wife and family, Blundell set off to London to solidify the legal and financial arrangements. On 12 May, he writes, 'I dined at the Blue Posts in Devereux Court with cousin Henry Eyre and Mr. Trinder; we examined things relating to my marriage.' Satisfied, Blundell returned to Hatherop to behave like a future bridegroom. On 17 May he 'walked with mistress Frances Langdale to Fairford. Morris dancers came to Hatherop.' And a few days later on 20 May, 'the lords and ladies of May came to dance at Hatherop', investing the aristocratic house with the seasonal festivities of 'merry England'.[47]

The lawyers were not yet finished, however, and the dance on the green did not distract from more serious capering indoors. There were more expenses paid for 'drawing up writings at London' and for transcribing the marriage articles in duplicate. Frances's dowry was £2,000 in two instalments, her jointure £200 a year if she was widowed, with a further £100 a year from her grandmother Webb. Blundell wanted some of the money up front, and on 30 May recorded, 'much intercession made to my Lord Langdale to make him sign a single draft to me for the payment of the second thousand pound'. This was a tense week, but by 5 June the 'foul draft of marriage deed' was ready, and could be sent back to London to be engrossed. Lawyers for both families examined the marriage deeds on 12 June, and in a formal ceremony on 15 June, 'Lord Langdale, Lady Webb, Sir John Webb, etc. heard the marriage deeds read; we all at Hatherop concerned therein subscribed them before four witnesses.' Nothing now stood in the way, and the parties could be married. The ceremony was performed quietly on 17 June by a catholic priest, using a wedding ring that cost Nicholas Blundell £1. 5s. And two days after his wedding the new-married man went fishing.[48]

Blundell's diary was a record of transactions and expenses, not an intimate outpouring, so it would be unreasonable to expect him to display more of the emotional content of his courtship. But everything in his account conforms to the pattern of cool calculation notoriously depicted by Lawrence Stone.[49] Whether Blundell was typical or unusual for men of his class at the start of the eighteenth century hardly matters. He was certainly not alone in focusing on the outward forms of courtship and the legal and financial aspects of marriage.

Making a Match

Good marriages, everyone knew, were made in heaven.[50] But bringing suitable people together sometimes required human effort and ingenuity. Diaries and autobiographies reveal that prospective couples were often prompted or assisted by parents or friends who acted as brokers or matchmakers. The role of the courtship intermediary was a classic of the English Renaissance stage.[51] A few more examples from correspondence will show how this worked among the late Elizabethan gentry.

When the young Cheshire gentleman John Bruen came down from Oxford in 1579 at the age of 19, 'being now for ripeness of years and maturity of age fit for marriage, his father considering he was the first born of his strength, the choicest plant of his stock, and chiefest branch of his vine, began to cast about where he might bestow him, seat him and set him in the inheritance of the lord'. Sponsored arrangements and parental direction led John Bruen to get married in 1580, though not, his biographer insisted, without the couple's mutual consent.[52]

The matchmaking process is more explicitly revealed in a letter from the Earl of Essex promoting the marriage of Richard Bagot's son Anthony. Essex wrote to the elder Bagot in 1594,

Being glad to do anything that might be for your son's good and preferment, I did lately write my letters unto Mr. Weston and solicited a motion of marriage with mistress Lowe, a kinsman [sic] of his. The gentleman hath very willingly hearkened unto it, and the gentlewoman well accepted of the motion, and conceiveth well of your son. It remaineth that you deal fatherly with him for the better effecting of this match to his good, which is now the principal point whereupon the conclusion resteth.[53]

At stake here were courtly interests, the building and binding of a network of interest within the Essex alliance, but similar explorations were conducted throughout the gentle élite. The crucial ingredients were solicitation and hearkening, well-conceiving and acceptance, with parents and intermediaries working closely with the parties concerned. No marriage could go forward without mutual consent, but consent could be developed by kinsmanlike counsel and fatherly approbation.

A later letter in the Bagot collection shows the extended kindred at work again in promoting a motion for marriage. Sir William Kniveton promised in 1612 to help Walter Bagot's son fulfil his matrimonial ambitions, 'though I yet know him not, I will do my best endeavour to further in that good course whereunto you now intend him'. Kniveton assured his cousin, 'that as both our nearness of blood and your worthiness do deserve, so will I not fail to do any good office of a kinsman and friend to you and any of yours'.[54] The fruits of this kind of solicitude are shown in Thomas Ridgeway's satisfied remark to Sir Percival Willoughby in July 1610, that 'your Francis and my Cassandra are hail fellow well met already, that they like and love well', and that soon would be a wedding to be 'solemnly and substantially performed'.[55]

At a less lofty social level, Henry Best described how courtships began among the yeomanry and minor gentry of Yorkshire in the reign of Charles I.

Usually the young man's father, or he himself, writes to the father of the maid, to know if he shall be welcome to the house, if he shall have his furtherance if he come in such a way, or how he liketh of the notion; then if he pretend any excuse, only thanking him for his good will, then that is as good as denial. If the motion be well thought of and embraced, then the young man goeth perhaps twice, to see how the maid standeth affected; then if he see that she be tractable, and that her inclination is towards him, then the third time that he visiteth, he perhaps giveth her a ten shilling piece of gold, or a ring of that price.

After that, until it was time to draw up dowers and jointures, the young people were left to themselves.

They visit usually every three weeks or a month, and are usually half a year, or very near, from the first going to the conclusion. So soon as the young folks are agreed and contracted, then the father of the maid carrieth her over to the young man's house to see how they like of all, and there doth the young man's father meet them to treat of a dower, and likewise of a jointure or feoffment for the woman; and then do they also appoint and set down the day of marriage, which may perhaps be about a fortnight or three weeks after.[56]

In Henry Best's idealized world, preparations for marriage began with negotiations among men. Matrimonial engagement was a patriarchal matter concerning 'the young man's father' and 'the father of the maid', although in practice the couple may well have already established contact. Best's observation that the business usually began with a letter indicates the narrowness of his social gaze, in a culture where no more than a third of the male population possessed full active literacy. His 10s. courtship gifts would cost a month's income to an ordinary working man. In writing this description *c.*1642 Best may have been remembering his own marriage a quarter of a century earlier, but as the father of eight children he may have wished to put on record a nostalgic and conservative account that would educate and discipline his offspring.[57]

The father's role was to facilitate, not to impose. Though sometimes conceived as alliances between families, gentry marriages were not all heartlessly commercial or mere dynastic arrangements. Their success turned on 'good will' and 'good liking', and the maid herself had to be courted and won. The procedure included cues to minimize embarrassment and mechanisms to avoid dishonour. The young man's responsibility was to make visits, offer gifts, and to bring his prospective bride to agreement. The woman had the option of being more or less tractable, of offering or withholding affection, of generally signalling her inclinations. The woman's role was passive, but not entirely powerless. Agreement and contract between the couple opened the way for legal and financial agreements between their families. This was an extended social dance involving go-betweens and private moments, courtship and gift-giving, as Henry Best put it, 'from the first going to the conclusion'.[58]

Most people dispensed with formal introductions. In town and country alike, there were plentiful opportunites for young men and women to meet and to mingle without parental supervision. Below the level of the élite a huge number of men and women in their twenties lived away from home as servants or apprentices, and not suprisingly many of them fell in love. Parish games and regional fairs provided endless opportunities for frolic. Church court records reveal 'youth playing at Stoolball' in the churchyard on a sabbath afternoon in 1596, 'divers youth of the parish playing at leapfrog' on a Sunday evening in 1624, and young men and women dancing in a cornfield during time of evening prayer in 1633.[59] Any such activity could lead to courtship. The church court records mention dozens of cases where courtship began in the fields or the streets and grew to fruition in workshops or barns. Social historians are discovering that the freedom of young people to meet their own partners, conduct their own courtships, and make their own decisions about marriage, was especially pronounced among ordinary folk who were not constrained by the burdens of property or an exaggerated sense of honour.[60]

Choice and Consent

Early modern moralists observed that the selection of a marriage partner was one of the most important decisions in life. Careful choice of one's yoke-fellow promised lasting rewards. Critics agreed that a choice based on worldly advantage might miscarry, whereas happiness would more likely follow from a choice based on character. Passionate emotion, however, was a dangerous foundation, as was any that failed to take account of background, reputation, and economic resources.

The Elizabethan poet William Vaughan contrasted 'the matrimony of love' in which 'an honest man and an honest woman are linked together by God for the propagation of mankind', to 'the matrimony of toil, and that which is most common in this last rotten world', in which 'men choose wives, not by their ears, that is for their good report, but by the fingers, to wit for their large dowries', or for other carnal reasons.[61] Fit choice, thought the Jacobean preacher William Whately, made all the difference between the wedlock of 'briars and thorns' and the marriage of 'virtue and godliness'. Whately's advice was typical, urging 'an equal yoke-fellow . . . of due proportion in state, birth, age, education and the like, not much under nor much over, but fit and correspondent'. A proper choice of partner, religious writers concurred, preferred 'inward goodness' over 'outward goods', grace and virtue over beauty and wealth.[62] This applied as much to the children of husbandmen and artisans as to the offspring of the élite.

Ballads and popular expressions summarized the conventional literature of advice. 'Matching in marriage must be with equality', said one proverb. 'Like blood, like good, and like age make the happiest marriage', said a second. 'Equals to equals, good to good', was another aphorism of the age. Shakespeare's Sir Toby Belch observed a similar wisdom in his niece Olivia, 'She'll not match above her degree, neither in estate, years, nor wit.' This was a discussion of marriage horizons, endorsing the conventional practice of social endogamy. Marriages that overstretched these horizons were thought to risk trouble. 'He that marries for wealth sells his liberty', said one proverb. 'A great dowry is a bed full of brambles', warned another. 'The match is marred where minds do not agree', warned a seventeenth-century ballad. Disparity in age, a marriage of winter and spring, was another recipe for strife.[63] Although there were always exceptions, the vast majority of couples heeded this advice. People naturally found their spouses within the social circles they inhabited, and were drawn to partners of comparable wealth and temperament. Most English brides belonged to the same occupational or status clusters as their bridegrooms, and the men were, on average, just a few years older than the women.[64]

If there was little in the way of degree and estate to differentiate prospective partners, the choice came down to questions of character and personal attraction. If it was reasonable for a man to consider 'the age, portion, quality, beauty, etc. of such a maid or widow' when contemplating marriage, it was just as natural for a discriminating woman to avow, 'I shall not settle my affections on any till I see some goodness in a man to induce me to it.'[65] It would be foolhardy to enter into marriage without adequate financial resources, but equally foolish without confidence in the other party's honest dealing.

On the brink of independent adulthood, men and women in their twenties conventionally involved their parents and close relations in the process that led to their marriage. The matter was of such 'weight and consequence', according to popular opinion, that 'a man should ask counsel of all the world'.[66] However, as all manner of evidence makes clear, the protocols of parent–child relations in this regard were extremely fluid. The rules were flexible and contradictory. Parents had an interest in their offspring and were supported by godly sermonists and commentators who brandished the fifth commandment. Yet parents who bullied their children into matrimony were judged to be 'unnatural and cruel'.[67] It was a father's duty to assist his children to the most suitable and advantageous marriage. But parental authority was neither arbitrary nor absolute, and often crumbled in the face of youthful independence. In any case, as many as 50 per cent of young people were fatherless by the time they first came to be married.[68]

Conventionally, out of love and duty, in deference to age and authority, and no doubt with an eye to inheritance prospects, many young people took note of their elders' opinions. But they were not strictly beholden to their parents for matrimonial consent. No man or woman could lawfully be forced to a wedding, nor could they be prevented from marrying where they list so long as they were free from the impediments of affinity and consanguinity, pre-contract, or insufficient age. It was a fundamental tenet of the church that 'marriage ought to be free and uncompelled', and a marriage contract could be invalidated if there was evidence of compulsion.[69] Though surrounded by interested kinsfolk and friends, English men and women were free in principle to choose their marriage partners themselves. Parental approval was advisable and negotiable, but individual consent was the *sine qua non*. A host of legal, literary, and personal writings show this principle at work.[70]

The courtship narratives show parents acting as facilitators and prompters, helping to make or improve a match and sometimes to bring it to a halt. Their main role was at the beginning of the process, to screen suitable suitors, and at its conclusion, to draw up agreements on behalf of a newly contracted couple. Most of the time they seem to have left the courting couple alone. Men whose fathers had died, like Leonard Wheatcroft, had greater freedom of action but were deprived of the asset of fatherly advice; fatherless women, like Alice Wandesford, came under the protection of mothers, uncles, and friends. Widows and widowers contemplating remarriage could do pretty much as they pleased. Samuel Woodford, we have seen, felt deeply guilty after committing himself to marriage without his family's consent; though dependent on his mother and uncle for financial support, he was not obliged to defer to them in the choice of a marriage partner.

A few more examples will show the flexibility and tension of patriarchal relations in the second half of the seventeenth century. Though in his twenties and already ordained as a minister, Isaac Archer promised his father in 1663 that he would not match himself without parental consent. This, the two men agreed, was 'a part of that honour due to a father' according to the fifth commandment. Yet four years later Isaac Archer took a bride without even informing his father, an action which drew upon him 'a chiding letter'.[71] Another later Stuart clergyman, Thomas Brockbank, averred that he was 'in no haste for a wife', but past the age of 28 he consulted his father about possible matches. The senior Brockbank's advice was 'let God be your guide', but he was no doubt gratified by the courtesy of his son's enquiry. Shortly after, when a suitable prospect presented herself, Brockbank assured his father, 'I . . . shall not engage myself too far till you please to let me know your mind, and whether you expect a portion. If she please you not I shall seek out some other.'[72]

Thomas Jolly, a nonconformist minister, coaxed his son out of an unsuitable match that threatened to subvert his strong religious principles, and then congratulated the young man on his 'self denial'. Later in 1686 when his son took a godly wife Thomas Jolly found satisfaction in it being 'his own choice and my consent'. By contrast, when Samuel Jeake, at the age of 28, sought his father's consent for his intended marriage the elder Jeake sought no part in the negotiations, and gave his son 'consent to proceed as I pleased'.[73]

Bridget Oglander, we have seen, married against her father's advice and entered 'a match of her own making'. So too did Elizabeth Freke, who attributed many of the 'troubles' in her unhappy married life to 'my disobedience in marrying as I did, without my dear father's knowledge'. Hers was a sorry tale, which began with a squalid private wedding in Covent Garden church

in November 1671. She married Percy Freke 'without my dear father's consent or knowledge, in a most dreadful rainy day, a presage of all my sorrows
and misfortunes'. To make up for this unfortunate beginning, from which
there was no turning back, Elizabeth's father took the extraordinary step of
seeing the couple remarried in public at St Margaret's, Westminster, the
following summer, with himself 'giving' the bride. It did not appear to be a
joyous occasion.[74]

Even more unhappy was Richard Kidder, the late seventeenth-century
bishop of Bath and Wells, who was deeply distressed when the physician
Claver Morris courted his daughter without first obtaining his permission.
The bishop thought he had put an end to it, through fatherly counsel, yet the
courtship proceeded 'not only without the knowledge, but against the express
will of her father'. Eventually, writes Kidder, he 'submitted' to the match and
consented to allow the marriage, though he warned his future son-in-law
'that he would not oblige himself to do so much for a child that chose for
herself, as one that in that affair should be governed by him'. Here was free
choice in action, as well as the explicit sanction against it. This is a story with
a sting in the tail, for Kidder was further wounded and his family dishonoured
when Morris rejected the terms of the settlement and married someone else.[75]

Matrimonial causes before the ecclesiastical courts throw remarkable fresh
light on this subject. We do not have to believe every assertion by complain-
ants or witnesses, any more than we trust the words of diarists and autobiographers, but they help to supplement our picture of intergenerational
independence, deference, bargaining, and stipulation.

A Durham case from 1571 concerns the courtship of Thomas Soley, who
made his initial addresses to Agnes Smith through the agency of her mother
and her mother's kinsman. With permission from the elders, Thomas and
Agnes then met and 'talked together of matrimony to be had betwixt them
two'. Agreeing that he might make a suitable son-in-law, Agnes's mother
invited Thomas to visit again, 'and in the mean time she told him she would
talk with her friends and give the said Thomas an answer'. Two sets of negotiations were taking place in parallel, the one between Thomas and Agnes, the
other between their families, allies, and friends. So well did the relationship
develop that Thomas and Agnes were left alone in the house on midsummer day while everyone else went to the fair. The couple then agreed to be
married, handfasted and, Thomas said, 'he kissed her and put a ring on her
finger'.[76]

This story would not have come before the courts, and so entered written
history, had not Agnes allegedly been pre-contracted to another suitor three
years earlier. It emerged that one William Headley of Woodside was betrothed

to Agnes Smith, and therefore she was not free to marry Thomas. A stream
of witnesses came forth to testify to their role as observers and facilitators of
Agnes's previous courtship. John Simpson, a husbandman (and kinsman to
William Headley), testified that 'about harvest time this two years ago [he]
carried a bowed groat and a bowed two-pence as tokens' from William to
Agnes. Edward Simpson, his brother, said that he was in a meadow close in
Ebchester west field early in the evening on Easter Monday to join in witnessing a handfasting. Having witnessed the ritual exchange of coin and ring
the deponent 'thought in his conscience that they two were man and wife
before God and could have no other'. One interpretation of this testimony
is that plans were in hand for Agnes to marry William when a better prospect
came into view.[77]

Simon Johnson, a 20-year-old scissor-maker from the parish of St Martin-
in-the-Fields, told the London consistory court a remarkable story in 1632,
explaining the background to his clandestine marriage. Johnson's tale has
many of the ingredients of a classic courtship narrative, including passion,
subterfuge, and the problem of securing consent, but it is unusual to hear
this from one of such lowly status. A significant feature of this story was that
Johnson was too young to marry without his father's permission. The young
man told the court that 'for the space of a twelve month or thereabouts [he]
was a suitor unto Mary Elliot, daughter of Thomas Elliot of Walthamstow,
in the way of marriage, and obtained her consent and her friends' for the said
marriage'. His own family, however, denied him support. He 'was often forbidden by his father to go to the said Elliot's house, and by him told that the
said Mary was an unfitting match for him, and therefore was much persuaded by his said father and mother to forsake the said Mary and leave her
company'. In a strict patriarchal culture this would have been the end of the
matter, but Johnson was a man of determination and initiative, willing to defy
his parents. He told the court,

that notwithstanding the premises, he . . . did frequent the said Mary's company in
the night seasons, and lay out of his said father's house divers night together in the
said Elliot's house and with his knowledge. Being demanded by whose instigation
and persuasion he did forsake his father's house and so frequent the said Mary's
company to his father's great dislike, he answered that it was his mere affection unto
the said Mary, and that the said Mary's father and friends did bid him do what he
would, it should all be one to them.

After six months of intimacy, having obtained Mary's 'goodwill . . . to be married unto him', but still unable to secure his father's consent, Johnson took
his lady to the Fleet, where they went through a clandestine but legally binding
wedding.[78]

Nothing is known of the respective wealth and standing of the two house-holds, but it would appear that the match was more favourable to the Elliots than to the Johnsons. One can appreciate the senior Johnson's concern not to ally himself with a family that showed such disregard for the safety and honour of a daughter. Mary corroborated Simon Johnson's story, emphasiz-ing that his visits had been 'with her said father's good will and liking' but 'against his father's good will and contrary to his command, and without his privity or knowledge'. After the marriage became public, she continued, 'her friends did much desire a reconciliation between her husband's father and friends, but could not come to any'. The concern of the church, of course, was the violation of ecclesiastical discipline in the clandestine marriage, not the young man's disregard for parental authority. There is no mention, in this record, of any prenuptial pregnancy, and no hint that those hours together 'in the night seasons' were especially immoral.[79]

Joan Harris of Woodford-iuxta-Thrapston, Northamptonshire, attempted to deflect the attentions of Nicholas Harding, who asked for her hand in marriage in 1623, by referring the matter to her parents. She told him, she said, 'that if he would acquaint her father and mother with that suit and could obtain their goodwill therein that she might happily entertain his said treaty, and that unless he would and could do so she would not enter into any treaty with him of any kind'. Evidently these people were free to come and go without parental supervision, but Joan in her testimony attempted to suggest that Nicholas was not welcome.[80]

Another Jacobean countrywoman strove more energetically with her father on her lover's behalf. Elizabeth Hopper of County Durham had already made a private contract of marriage to Robert Taler, but her father wanted her to marry someone else. 'Setting her down upon her knees [she] said unto her father, good father give me I pray you leave to make my own choice of my husband, albeit I never get a groatsworth of your goods', to which her father replied, 'I am willing thou satisfieth thine own mind.' Elizabeth and Robert were forthwith handfasted before witnesses but their marriage was prevented by the other man's alleged pre-contract.[81]

Mutual Love and Good Liking

Courtship narratives can be combined with other sources to illuminate the problem of love. Scholars disagree whether human emotions have remained constant over the centuries, or whether such passions as love, grief, and anger, are conditioned by changing historical circumstances. A judicious position might be that while the emotions themselves are enduring marks of human sensibility, the manner in which they are expressed and the language used to describe them are socially and culturally conditioned. Certainly in the literature of the ancient world and in the discourses of Tudor and Stuart England we find traces of emotional behaviour similar to our own. Diaries and letters, as well as plays and poems, reveal people whose emotional lives we think we can understand. But the same sources also show modes of behaviour and styles of expression that seem cold and remote, with emotions that appear stilted, artificial, or even absent. This is especially true of the discourse of love.

What place did love have in courtship and marriage? It seems to have been fundamental. Notwithstanding the sometimes strained formality of the opening moves and the calculation of material advantages, love seems to have been a common and expected ingredient in the majority of matches. Couples grew to love each other, before or after marriage, and either persuaded themselves that they were 'in love' or worked to develop a loving relationship. Rather than being surprised to find people falling in love or continuing in love, as some historians of early modern England have indicated, we should, perhaps, be surprised that anyone should think they did not. The notion, recklessly set forth by Lawrence Stone, that early modern marriage was barren of love, has been thoroughly rejected by studies of diaries, letters, ballads, and church court cases.[82]

Proverbial wisdom carried contradictory messages about the place of love in marriage. 'Love should make marriage, and not marriage love', was one common saying repeated on the late Elizabethan stage. The fashion, however, according to popular lore, was 'to marry first, and love after by leisure'. 'Love is potent, but money is omnipotent', was a much-quoted saying, to set alongside the witticism, 'he who marries for love and no money, hath good nights but sorry days'.[83] The conventional advice of the age, that placed a higher value on character than on fortune, urged people towards love but steered them away from lust.

The foundation of marriage, according to the influential domestic adviser William Gouge, was 'reciprocal affection' between the intending parties. Parents and kinsmen should make their suggestions, of course, and the courtship should develop with the counsel and approval of 'wise and understanding friends'. But without 'mutual liking', Gouge insisted, the marriage should not proceed. Not until 'mutual liking' was established should the couple move on to the next stage. Ideally the couple should then come to love each other, though not lustfully, for 'mutual love and good liking of each other is as glue'.[84] This was a recipe for companionate marriage, not romantic love, but it was neither as revolutionary nor as 'modern' as some historians have suggested. What else would one expect from a Jacobean puritan pastor? Robert

Cleaver offered similar wisdom: 'to the end that marriages may be perpetual, loving and delightful betwixt the parties, there must and ought to be knitting of hearts before striking of hands'. Thomas Gataker told parents that they could not make their childern 'link hearts as they list', for 'love cannot be constrained'. 'Love', wrote the Commonwealth-era counsellor Thomas Hilder, 'is the sap, bud and blossom from whence all other matrimonial duties do spring.'[85]

Despite an understandable reticence about representing complex emotions on paper, a considerable number of diarists and autobiographers mentioned their experience of love. The musician Thomas Whythorne confessed to 'loving' his 'twenty pound widow', a love that was not reciprocated.[86] Phineas Pett, the London shipwright, reports, 'I first fell in love with my now wife . . . about St. James's tide' in 1597. Though busy working to refit the *Elizabeth Jonas* at Limehouse, Pett records, 'I did not neglect my wooing, having taken such a liking to the maiden that I determined resolutely, by God's help, either match with her or never to marry any.' This determination bore good fruit, for the couple became husband and wife the following May. Thirty years later, after a long and productive marriage, Ann Pett died, 'leaving behind a disconsolate husband and a sad family', so Phineas Pett laments. Pett's account of his emotional life may be dutiful and conventional, but it is also indicative of vitality, authenticity, and warmth.[87]

The godly William Whiteway of Dorchester also knew the pangs of love. At the age of 20 he crafted a poem that referred to 'discontented thoughts' and 'pain and grief' that could not be overcome 'Until I see change in Aristo's carriage | And be assured to have my love in marriage.' Whiteway's bride was Eleanor Parkins, to whom he referred as 'my best beloved'. When they married in 1620 Whiteway gave her a ring with the Latin inscription *Congugii firmi, et casti sum pignus amoris* (I am the pledge of a steadfast marriage and of chaste love). Whiteway's expression may have been schooled by provincial Renaissance letters, but his emotions belong to the human mainstream. Though his diary is otherwise reticent on emotional matters it is clear that love was an active force in the making of this puritan businessman's marriage.[88]

The Derbyshire yeoman Leonard Wheatcroft also knew, from experience as well as from reading, that love was 'both a friend, a foe, a heaven, a hell'. The 'joy' he recalled in embracing his prospective bride was one of those glimpses of heaven. Samuel Woodford 'fell in love' with one woman, then was so overwhelmed by love for another that he promised to marry her despite financial and familial objections. Elizabeth's Freke's son Ralph went too far, allowing his affections to run ahead of his prudence. The Lancashire minister, Thomas Brockbank, also discovered the transformative power of love. At first, when casting around for a wife, he weighed the usual factors of suitability, portions, and parental consent. But when he finally discovered Elizabeth Whittingham she awakened affections he barely knew were possible. In passionate letters and verses Brockbank confided, 'my melting heart is so distracted'. Though prepared to marry for social convenience or financial advantage, Brockbank was one who lost neither of these while discovering the torments and pleasures of love.[89]

Gifts and Tokens

Whether driven by love or scripted by social convention, courtship required the giving and acceptance of presents and tokens. Coins, rings, ribbons, gloves, girdles, and similar knick-knacks did the trick. Such gifts, usually passed by hand from the man to the woman, signalled the intimate strengthening of their bond. Their monetary value mattered less than their symbolism. Further gifts, most commonly a ring, changed hands when the couple was contracted, betrothed, or 'made sure'.[90]

The Batchelars Banquet, that relentlessly cynical, misogynist, and satiric entertainment first set forth in English in 1603, purports to advise a young woman how to entice her gallant into marriage by coquettish playing of the gift game. 'Look that you give him good entertainment, and show him good countenance.' If he offers 'a ring, or girdle, or any such thing, at the first refuse it, yet kindly and with thanks; but if he urge it on you twice or thrice, take it, telling him, sith that he will needs bestow it on you, you will wear if for his sake'. In no time the fool will be trapped and contracted.[91]

We have seen how John Hayne, the Exeter merchant, observed these protocols in showering his beloved with gifts. Henry Best set forth an overformal version of the lover's duty among the Yorkshire yeomanry and gentry. 'The third time that he visiteth, he perhaps giveth her a ten shilling piece of gold, or a ring of that price; or perhaps a twenty shilling piece, or a ring of that price; then the next time, or next after that, a pair of gloves of 6s. 8d. or 10s. a pair; and after that, each other time, some conceited toy or novelty of less value.'[92]

Courtship gifts of this sort, though not necessarily of such high value, are frequently mentioned in the course of disputes over frustrated, questionable, or clandestine marriages. They were taken to demonstrate the progress of courtship and to corroborate other evidence of matrimonial intent. According to the ecclesiastical lawyer Henry Swinburne, 'love gifts and tokens . . . as bracelets, chains, jewels, and namely the ring' were 'often used for the very *arrabo* or assured pledge of a perfect promise'. But it was no easy matter to determine whether the proferring and acceptance of a gift was in jest or in earnest, whether it should be understood as a token of goodwill or as a sign of matrimonial consent. A gift could be coercive as well as affectionate, its symbolism open to flexible construction. Much depended on 'the manner of delivery and acceptance' as well as the accompanying words and gestures.[93]

Richard Thornton and Margery Peg exchanged gifts as well as kisses in the course of their courtship in Elizabethan Leicestershire. When Richard asked if Margery would have him, she gave Richard a coin saying, 'I give you this shilling . . . on condition that I will marry you and be your wedded wife.' In exchange for the shilling Richard 'taking a pair of gloves lapped in paper out of his sleeve, said unto her as followeth: Margery, I give you this which is lapped in this paper on the same condition, if you will take it; who answered that she would take it whatsoever it was.' The exchange was complete, each passage being accompanied by a gift, and the contract was made. To Richard it was a clear sign of her acceptance that 'Margery did then and there presently receive and accept of the said gloves, and after they kissed each other.' Though there were no witnesses it soon became 'the common fame . . . that the said Richard Thornton and Margery Peg are contracted together in marriage and have plighted their troths to each other'.[94]

Rosa Clarke of Burton, Leicestershire, was also said to have responded graciously to the gift of a betrothal ring in 1590, exclaiming 'it was as fit for her as if it were made for her finger, or as if her finger had been in the place where it was made'. When a woman pulled a ring from Thomas Wawton's finger and 'put it upon her own', and when she accepted from him a pair of gloves, the church court could take this as evidence that the lovers were on the way to becoming husband and wife.[95] The proffering and accepting of courtship gifts were signs of serious matrimonial intentions.

Elizabeth Yealand of Middleton-in-Teesdale told the Durham court in 1605 about her role as a courtship go-between and courier of gifts. On one occasion she

was entreated by Agnes Newbie to go an errand for her to James Handley, to signify her commendations verbally to him and to deliver him a ring of silver and a race [i.e. a root] of ginger, of which she had bit off a piece, willing [her] to tell him that for her sake it would content him to bite off another piece of the same ginger.

James, by return, sent four apples, which Agnes 'very kindly received'. Two French gold crowns, an enamelled gold ring and a packet of Agnes's hair also passed between the couple, to supplement these delicacies, leading James, not unreasonably, to believe that Agnes was willing to marry him.[96]

A gift, however, could be misconstrued or retrospectively robbed of its symbolism. In denying any contract of marriage with Margery Wormley, Edmund Hodgson of Cockerton insisted 'that there was never any tokens given nor sent to [him] by or from the said Margery, no not so much as a handkerchief'. His only gift to Margery that might be construed as a courtship present was simply 'an old groat, upon friendship, but as no token'.[97] William Wright, a party to an Oxfordshire matrimonial suit in 1583, protested that he never promised marriage to Margaret Townsend, 'neither did he ever give her any tokens of goodwill to any such intent to marry her, but sayeth that he hath given her, as he thinketh, a pair of gloves for a fairing or some such trifle'. Samuel Flint, another Oxfordshire man, in 1584 acknowledged giving Anne Blanch of Hocknorton 'a girdle and a pair of gloves in token of goodwill, but not upon any promise of marriage'. With similar ingenuousness he denied making any contract 'per verba de presenti' and denied all charges of carnal copulation.[98]

That gifts were not simple items of value but potentially complex signifiers of promise and obligation is shown in Joan Harris's circumspect handling of the courtship ring that Nicholas Harris attempted to give her in 1623. On one of his visits to her house in Northamptonshire, which Joan insisted she did not encourage, Nicholas

brought a ring with him which he offered to leave with her as gift from himself, and [Joan] divers times refused to receive any such thing of him . . . After many denials made by her to take it, the said Nicholas vowing and protesting that he did not give it thereby to bind her any way unto him, [she] at his great importunity or rather enforcement took it of him.

She tried several times to return the ring, Joan said, but 'Nicholas refused to take it again. And thereupon [she] conceiving it not fit for her to keep the said ring and not to give unto him something in recompense thereof sent unto him in like manner a ring of small price, which he received as she believeth.' A cynic might say that Joan's reluctance to accept the ring was only to increase her suitor's ardour, while her reciprocation of the gift was an indisputable sign that she was willing to join in matrimony. This seems to have been the view of the court. Her testimony appeared in the course of a bitter suit, after she tried and failed to extract herself from her contract for marriage.[99]

Although English court records contain plentiful testimony about the handling and exchange of tokens, they are generally silent on the application of love magic, a familiar topic in continental depositions. This does not mean that English lovers eschewed the use of divinations, bindings, and other supernatural aids in the course of their courtship, only that evidence of such practices is very hard to find.[100] It remains an open question whether all those gloves, girdles, garters, and ribbons, those bent or broken coins and rings, that bitten root of ginger, were simply commodities to mark the progress of courtship, or whether they were construed to bind or coerce the party to whom they were given. For courtship gifts carried connotations of sexual and domestic intimacy, and may have been intended to enhance or to quicken the condition to which they referred.

ESPOUSALS, BETROTHALS, AND CONTRACTS

Cementing an Engagement

Courtship reached its climax when a couple agreed to marry. How they expressed that agreement, how much publicity they gave to it, what degree of formality was involved, and whether it was legally binding, were matters of lively controversy. While untold numbers proceeded toward matrimony on the strength of a private or informal agreement, others marked their contract with public and ceremonial pledges. The ritual performance of contracting, though encouraged by religious advisers, apparently fell from favour during the early seventeenth century. This chapter deals with the making of contracts which transformed the 'good will' of two parties into a solemn matrimonial bond. It examines religious argument alongside social practice, and concludes by considering the sexual behaviour of newly contracted couples.

Contracts could be expressed in *verba de presenti*, making an immediate and indissoluble commitment expressed by the words 'I do'; *verba de futuro*, a promise of future action expressed by the words 'I will'; or conditionally, such as 'when I inherit my land' or 'if your mother will provide us a house'. All manner of disputes could arise, and an extensive body of matrimonial law addressed the ambiguities, insufficiencies, and irregularities of poorly worded, inadequately witnessed, or contested contracts. Formal espousal, when properly performed, was designed to avoid these embarrassments.[1]

'Every marriage before it be knit should be contracted', advised the Elizabethan lecturer Henry Smith. Rather than rushing headlong into matrimony a couple should pause 'between the contract and the marriage . . . for their affection to settle in'. Like other godly ministers, Smith approved of the ceremony that added solemnity to the business of courtship and marriage. He envisaged an event that marked an agreement, a ritual performance that solidified the covenant between the couple. Smith's *Preparative to Marriage* of 1591 was based on words 'spoken at a contract' where he himself had been the master of ceremonies.[2]

Contracting marked the successful conclusion of courtship, the transition from wooing to wiving. It was known by a variety of terms in different parts

FIG. 14   The betrothal ceremony from *A Pleasant New Ballad of Tobias* in *The Roxburghe Ballads* (London, *c.*1640)

of the country. In his pastoral work in Cambridgeshire Richard Greenham called it 'contracting' and 'handfasting'. In his *Treatise of a Contract before Marriage*, published posthumously in London in 1599, he wrote of 'spousage' and 'betrothing' whereby a couple was 'affianced'. Greenham advised his parishioners to reflect on the solemnity of 'espousage' which, he argued, was 'especially . . . commended by the chosen people of God'. Mary, for example, 'was affianced unto Joseph before the solemnization of their marriage'.[3] Daniel Rogers, a seventeenth-century admirer of Greenham, deemed 'espousals, betrothings, assurings, contractings, affirmings (for they are all one) to be very solemn matters'. The puritan counsellors Dod and Cleaver similarly described how a couple might 'espouse, affiance or betroth' themselves one to another. The London minister Matthew Griffith preferred the term 'a marriage-desiring promise', though, he wrote, 'the more ignorant people call it, making themselves sure'. The Oxfordshire preacher William Whately similarly wrote of the 'covenant' of 'espousal or betrothment, which they call, making sure'.[4] In some parts the term was 'trothplighting', which caught its essential feature of pledging. The word 'handfasting', which called attention to the ritual action, was more commonly used in the north.

Whatever its name, at the core of the procedure lay a ritualized expression of consent. Various forms of utterance would do the job, but most were modelled on the exchange in the ceremony of marriage. Some contracting couples actually used a prayer book for reference or secured the services of a priest to lead them through the words. Richard Greenham preferred a simplified version of the traditional recitation of plighting of troths, a form that his more godly parishioners may have followed. 'Their hands being joined', the man says to the woman, 'I, R., do promise to thee, F., that I will be thine husband, which I will confirm by public manner, in pledge whereof I give thee mine hand. In like manner doth the woman to the man. Then after prayer the parties are dismissed.' This was a binding promise of future performance, so long as the parties were of age to enter into it, were not barred by consanguinity or affinity, and were not precontracted to anyone else. There was no backing out, for 'although it be a degree under marriage, yet it is more than a determined purpose, yea more than a simple promise'. This ceremony, Greenham advised, should be conducted 'without all such levity as of other is used'.[5]

The Jacobean domestic adviser William Gouge also favoured formal premarital contracting. Basing his analysis on scripture, with a nod of approval to Rebecca, Gouge set forth the 'three steps or degrees' by which marriageable parties should proceed unto matrimony. First came 'a mutual liking', then 'an actual contract'; and finally 'a public solemnization of marriage'. The contract was the link between courtship and matrimony. Gouge recognized, as did Greenham, that a fair proportion of his contemporaries failed to observe the letter or the spirit of these proceedings; but the process gained in dignity by being ritually structured. 'It addeth much to the honour of marriage, that it should be deliberately and advisedly, step after step, by one degree after another, consummated and made up.'[6]

According to Gouge, 'when both parties have manifested a mutual liking each to other, and upon mature deliberation and good advice do conceive one to be a fit match for another, it is requisite that a joint consent and absolute promise of marrying one another before sufficient witnesses be made. This rightly made is a contract.' Gouge then described, in outline, the process that often appears in more detail in the spousals litigation of the ecclesiastical courts. In front of witnesses, the couple took each other hand in hand and recited the essential formula, binding each other to marriage. The man, 'taking the woman by the hand, should say, "I, A. take thee, B. to my espoused wife, and do faithfully promise to marry thee in times meet and convenient."' Then the woman, 'again taking the man by the hand, should say, "I B. take thee A. to my espoused husband, and do faithfully promise to yield to be married to thee in time meet and convenient."'[7] The gendering of initiative and authority is captured by the man's promise to marry, the woman's to yield to be married. The ritual solemnity of the contract is enhanced by the joining and loosing of hands.

The contract, wrote Gouge, was 'the beginning of marriage'. It transformed the couple into 'espoused man and wife in the time present' and bound them to marry one another 'afterwards' *per verba de futuro*. Assuming no prior contract, and no impediment of competence, age, consanguinity, or affinity, nobody could come between them. Gouge was no lawyer, and had little interest in the complexities of spousals litigation, but he noted, 'a lawful contract knitteth so firm a knot as cannot be broken'.[8]

The Caroline minister Matthew Griffith, no puritan, also approved of marriage contracts because 'they bind the surer, and the ground for future marriage is better laid'. Contracting allowed due consideration of possible impediments, helped avoid clandestine marriage and suits in ecclesiastical courts, and gave the couple pause so that 'for common honesty's sake, they might not rush like brute beasts into the marriage bed'.[9] Daniel Rogers likewise thought the 'private, mutual, free, unconditional promise' made between two persons to marry each other, should be followed by 'a more solemn and open binding expression of this former promise made, that it may be ratified and strengthened, as becometh a business of so great consequence'. To gather friends as spectators, to have the ceremony conducted by a person of 'gravity and experience' such as himself, and to hear the prayers, acclamations, and thanksgivings of the witnesses at a formal contracting, would secure a firm foundation for matrimony.[10]

A formal ceremony of contracting served to promote commensality and conviviality, and helped to bond the couple into the support system of neighbours and kin. Among other advantages, the procedure provided an opportunity for the parties to reflect on their faith and for the minister to instruct them in their duties. How commonly this ideal was met is hard to tell. In practice, as we shall see, the line was blurred between tacit agreement and public performance. 'Privy contracts', though legally just as binding as those cemented by a formal ceremony of espousal, could create a store of problems for the individuals and their families.[11]

The operative word in this battery of counsel was 'should'. There was no legal or religious requirement for a couple who agreed on marriage to do anything but go to a priest. So long as the banns were read or a licence obtained, and there were no impediments to their joining together, a couple could go directly from courtship to marriage with no intervening ceremony. As Gouge and his colleagues well knew, neither law nor religion required marriage contracts, and a huge number of couples dispensed with them, moving directly to church or to bed. However much godly ministers promoted the advantages of contracts or espousals they could not gainsay the fact that 'marriage may stand as real and firm, in point of substance without it as with it'.[12]

Since there was no registration of contracts there is no way of telling how many couples observed or ignored this stage in the making of marriage. Formal contracting was optional, and a sequence of voices lamented that the ceremony was suffering neglect. Already, in the late Elizabethan period, Richard Greenham had hinted that the custom was falling out of favour. William Gouge too found it 'much neglected' in late Jacobean London. Though contracting was 'an ancient custom . . . meet and requisite', too many of his contemporaries thought it 'needless, and utterly neglect it'.[13]

On the other hand, Gouge noted, some families celebrated espousals with more festivity than the actual wedding, proceeding thereafter as if the parties were truly married. 'Many make it a very marriage, and thereupon have a greater solemnity at their contract than at their marriage.' Miles Coverdale, translating Heinrich Bullinger, had made a similar observation in the sixteenth century, 'in some places there is such a manner, well worthy to be rebuked, that at the handfasting there is made a great feast and superfluous banquet' and the couple then esteem each other as spouse, 'though as yet it be not done in church nor in the street'.[14]

The religious writers hint at a range of behaviour but provide no clue to its social or demographic incidence. The courtship narratives are often ambivalent or laconic. Many couples dispensed with formal espousals or handfastings, while others, as late as the 1680s, joined in formal betrothals under the supervision of attorneys. William Whiteway is remarkable among diarists for tracing the matrimonial path approved by the Jacobean puritan preachers. Months of courtship bore fruit when Whiteway's match with Eleanor Parkins was 'concluded' on 6 April 1620. This marked the moment when the parties reached agreement on the principal matters of concern. But it took another month, until 4 May, before the couple were formally 'betrothed'. Whiteway's betrothal was a semi-public ceremony, hosted by the father of the bride-to-be, conducted by the formidable Dorchester minister John White, in the presence of representatives of both families. Now the

FIG. 15   A betrothal ceremony. Detail from the monthly table for June, printed before the order for morning prayer in *The Holy Byble* (London, 1575)

couple were formally contracted. The process culminated six weeks later on 14 June when William and Eleanor were married 'by Mr. John White in the church of the Holy Trinity in Dorchester, in the presence of the greatest part of the town'.[15]

The church court records show that some contracted couples failed to get married, and that others felt licensed by their contract to act as husband and wife. At present we do not know how closely custom followed prescription, how these patterns varied geographically, or how they changed over time. It might be reasonable to expect that people of the middling and upper sort went in for contracts, especially the more responsible among them, for all the good reasons that Gouge adduces. It might equally be true that contracting prevailed most among humbler rural folk who adhered to an older tradition. It is ironic to find puritan reformers of manners championing a custom that many of them lamented was suffering from neglect. The ritual appears to have been in decline from the end of the sixteenth century, and was rare in the later Stuart era, but, like many cultural practices, it was capable of being revived. In part, the picture of decline may be a product of the decline of the ecclesiastical courts, whose records are less rich in the post-Restoration era. The late Tudor ceremony of contracting, which so often featured the raising of cups at a table, appears to have mutated into the seventeenth-century conclusion of agreements among lawyers around a desk.[16]

Handfasting was conducted with ritual solemnity in the Elizabethan north, though even there the ceremony seemed to decline from the early seventeenth century. Plentiful testimony before the church courts of York and Durham from the 1570s to the 1620s describes the ingredients of handfasting, the holding and releasing of hands, the plighting of troths, kissing, drinking, and the ritual exchange of betrothal rings. The evidence relates to matrimonial contracts that were subsequently challenged, but there is no reason to suspect that these rituals were in any way abnormal. Though couples could pledge themselves in private, the preferred formula had them 'contract true, pure and lawful matrimony together, by words of the time present apt for that purpose, before honest and credible witnesses'. Sometimes a priest, a neighbour, or an elder kinsman presided over the ceremony, rehearsed the words, and prompted the parties how to behave.[17]

William Laborn, a Durham husbandman, told the diocesan court in 1573 that he went 'with many more neighbours . . . to record the handfasting' of Janet Ferry and Martin High one Sunday evening after service. The ceremony took place at Janet's father's house over dinner and was directed by 'one Lancelot Ettes, a very elderly man', identified by another witness as Janet's grandfather. This was a multi-generational gathering of kinsfolk, neighbours, and friends. First the old man asked each party

whether they two were free from all promise and might plight their faith and truth the one to the other. And the said Martin and Janet answered that they were. And thereupon, at the bidding of the said Lancelot, the said Martin and Janet did willingly take hands together, and either of them two did plight their faith and truth to the other as man and wife before God, after the country manner, as freely as ever [William Laborn] hath done at the church door, which hath been twice married.[18]

Similar testimony comes from Michael Myers, a Durham yeoman, who accompanied Henry Aire to John Ridley's house at Wasterley one Sunday evening in 1603 'to be present at the making up of a marriage betwixt [Henry Aire] and Jane Ridley. And the said John Ridley of his own cost bestowed a good dinner upon them and many other substantial friends of both the said parties come thither to that purpose.' One of the purposes of this feast was for the menfolk to make a final determination and public declaration of the economic terms of the match. Henry Aire displayed a satisfactory patent of his worth, and John Ridley promised to give his future son-in-law fourteen head of cattle and sixty sheep. This business concluded, they sent for the women, who were apparently enjoying their own feast in a separate room.

John Ridley addressed his daughter saying, 'Henry Aire and I are agreed what portion of goods I shall give him in matrimony with thee if thee be content, to whom she then answered that she was well content and that no man pleased her better, and thereupon she craved her said father's blessing'. Although she may have been awed by her father's authority and intimidated by the gathering of men, none of them could say that she entered into marriage without her own consent. 'Which done', the testimony continues, the priest John Smith 'took both the parties by their hands and joined the same together after the manner of handfasting and they kissed each other'.[19]

Another Durham deposition reports the vital words in a handfasting performed in 1620 'with a willing and free consent, in the presence and with good liking of witnesses'. George taking Cicely by the hand,

did contract himself to her saying, here I George take thou Cicely to my handfast wife refusing all other women for thy sake, and thereto I plight thee my troth; which done, the said Cicely took the said George by the hand and said unto him, and here I Cicely do take thee George to my handfast husband refusing all other men for thy sake, and thereto I plight thee my troth; and then they kissed each other and the said George with further corroboration of that their contract put a gold or gilded ring upon the said Cicely's finger.[20]

Despite some misgivings, Joan Harris consented to marry Nicholas Harding at Woodford, Northamptonshire, in 1623. Their rector, Hugh Lloyd, agreed 'to be present at a contract of matrimony' held in the great parlour of Sir Rowland St John's house where Harding was employed. The minister's role was to join with Sir Rowland in providing a reputable witness, and to discourse a little on 'what a contract of matrimony was'. That done, the couple 'was made sure and did contract themselves together' using the customary hand-holding and formula *per verba de presenti*. Joan's father, who had not been present when this contracting took place, subsequently claimed that his daughter had been tricked into the match by Harding's misrepresentations of his worth, but the archdeaconry court let it stand and directed the couple to solemnize their marriage *in facie ecclesiae*.[21]

Like most of the evidence from ecclesiastical court records, we only learn about these ceremonies when something subsequently went wrong. A few more examples follow. After a year and a half of courtship, with goodwill and consent on both sides, William Mead and Margaret Rame of Great Waltham, Essex, were ready to plight their troth. The contract was made in Margaret's mother's house in 1577 with the older woman as the only witness. She told the court that William took Margaret by the hand, saying 'I do here now take you to be my wife, and I do give you here my faith and troth; she the said Margaret holding him still by the hand answering, and here I do likewise give you my faith and troth, and do promise to be your wife.' This was a simple handfasting ceremony, with words of spousals *de presenti*. The couple now considered themselves 'lawful man and wife before God', but they still made plans for a public wedding in church. Only on the third calling of the banns did one Nicholas Satch block the marriage by claim of pre-contract.[22]

Elizabeth Jennings apparently made a conditional contract with John Townsend of Oxford one summer afternoon in 1582 in the romantic circumstances of a boat ride on the river. John asked Elizabeth 'whether she would be content to love him above all others. And she answered that she could be content and would, so that he would make such provision that he would have her away from her father and mother at Michaelmas.' The witnesses were the two men who rowed the boat. Elizabeth, however, had already made a similar promise to 'one of London', and when her parents heard of her commitment to Townsend her mother said, 'daughter, I think this is not the first nor second but the third'.[23]

Finally, Francis Beedale, gentleman, of Catworth, Huntingdonshire, and Sara Stacie of Castle Bytham, Lincolnshire, entered into a formal contract of spousals *per verba de presenti* in 1604, borrowing the words from the marriage ceremony in the Book of Common Prayer. A witness reported that

the said Francis Beedale taking the said Sara her hand into his hand said, I Francis take thee Sara to be my wedded wife, to have and to hold, for better for worse, for richer for poorer, in sickness and in health, to love and to cherish, till death us depart, according to God's holy ordinance, and thereto I plight thee my troth. Then they parted their hands and the said Sara taking and holding the said Francis his hand in her hand said, I Sara take thee Francis to my wedded husband, to have and to hold from this day forward, for better for worse, for richer for poorer, in sickness and in health, to love and to cherish and to obey till death us depart, according to God's holy ordinance, and thereto I give the my troth.

The Lincoln diocesan court agreed that this was a binding contract, despite one partner's subsequent change of mind, and ordered the couple to proceed forthwith to a public solemnization of matrimony.[24] Though irrevocably tied to each other, the parties were not yet married in the eyes of the church or the law.

The introduction to Henry Swinburne's *Treatise of Spousals, or Matrimonial Contracts*, published in 1686 more than half a century after its author's death, admits that 'some men may imagine that spousals are now in great measure worn out of use'. Although the underlying law remained unchanged, the book speaks more to the social and ecclesiastical practices of the Elizabethan and Jacobean periods than to the somewhat different climate of the later seventeenth century.[25] Public espousals had faded out of fashion, the church courts had less authority to enforce them, and the ceremonial energy that went into contracting was focused on the wedding day itself.

There are many signs, however, that ritual contracting had not disappeared. The late seventeenth-century *Ladies Dictionary* recognized a standard series of steps in which matrimonial contract followed 'liking, courtship, and settling of love'. Discussing the 'nuptial promise', the dictionary commented, 'though in law it is not an oath, yet so solemn a protestation before God and those present as witnesses is as binding, and ought to be as religiously observed . . . Marriage without a pre-engagement or contract looks so odd, that it appears more like the coupling of irrational than rational creatures.'[26]

That handfasting had not died out in Restoration England is demonstrated by testimony from the Diocese of Lincoln in 1664. Edward Bee of Hough-on-the-Hill, Lincolnshire, had courted Sara Moore of Barnby-in-the-Willows, Nottinghamshire, showering her with gifts of gloves, gold pieces, and a ring to win her hand. Eventually,

after some discourse of love and affection had between them in the way of marriage, the said Edward Bee taking the said Sara by her right hand said to her, I Edward will have you Sara to my wife and none other, and she the said Sara then holding the said Edward by the right hand replied and said, I Sara will have you Edward to my husband and none other, or words to that effect, and so drew their hands and kissed each other with mutual love and affection.

This was a contract *de futuro*, as shown by the repeated verb 'will' instead of 'do'. The words were vague but the actions were precise. Edward's witnesses supported his claim to matrimony after Sara attempted to change her mind.[27]

Contracting may have been in decline, but some godly ministers still considered it an integral step towards marriage. When the Yorkshire divine Oliver Heywood planned to marry Elizabeth Angier, daughter of a prominent presbyterian, 'they were contracted in the close of a solemn day of fasting and prayer, in his study, by Mr. Nathaniel Rathband', and were married 'about a month after that'.[28] Samuel Jeake, the nonconformist astrologer-merchant, was also 'betrothed or contracted' in a traditional ceremony at Rye, Sussex, in July 1680. First 'the writings concerning the marriage' were sealed, settling the financial terms, and then, in the presence of parents, friends, and lawyers, the couple recited the words of a formal espousal *de futuro*. Jeake records, 'taking her by the right hand I said, "I Samuel take thee Elizabeth to be my betrothed wife, and promise to make thee my wedded wife in time convenient, in token whereof is this our holding by the hand." Then loosing my hand, she took me by the right hand, repeating the same words *mutatis mutandis*.' Identical words could have been spoken a hundred years earlier.[29]

Carnal Knowledge

Though many contracted couples considered themselves 'married in the eyes of God' they were not yet entitled to live together as husband and wife. As we shall see in the following chapters, strong social and religious pressures combined to ensure that marriage was incomplete until it was solemnized in church. None the less, it was widely thought acceptable for a couple who had been 'made sure' by contract to progress from kissing and fondling to full sexual intercourse. In the eyes of the law such premarital 'incontinence' was fornication, and might be punished if discovered. But a powerful cultural current permitted betrothed couples to risk each other's chastity in anticipation of matrimony. This section attempts to review these competing strains and to consider the excuses made by unhappy lovers whose courtship intimacy brought them into trouble.

Religious reformers deplored the practice of couples going to bed before they had gone to church. Coverdale's sixteenth-century treatise on *The Christen State of Matrymonye* rebuked those 'handfasted persons' who were 'brought and laid together, yea, certain weeks afore they go to the church'. The Elizabethan puritan Richard Greenham charged contracted couples 'to keep themselves chaste until the marriage be sanctified by the public prayers of the church; for otherwise many marriages have been punished of the Lord for the uncleanness that hath been committed betwixt the contract and the marriage'. William Gouge called it 'an unwarrantable and dishonest practice' for couples to 'take liberties after a contract to know their spouse, as if they were married'. Daniel Rogers likewise counselled contracted couples 'from audacious enterprises one against the other's chastity'.[30] A later Stuart treatise set limits on the behaviour of 'the victorious wooer' who had won consent to be married. 'For now he has free access; he may kiss and play above board as much as he pleases; only there's a little shame and fear which cannot be forgotten, because they have not yet been at church.' But it was hard to escape the truth of popular wisdom, that 'courting and wooing bring dallying and doing'.[31]

Moralists were consistently hostile to sexual intercourse in advance of marriage, but not every couple heeded their advice. Analysis of parish registers shows some 20 to 30 per cent of all brides bearing children within the first eight months of marriage. The illegitimate birth rate was low—around 2 to 4 per cent—and was mostly associated with broken betrothals. Falling bastardy rates and lower bridal pregancy during the reign of Charles I suggests a shift in the moral climate or more effective control.[32] A reasonable guess might be that half the couples who contracted to be married engaged in sexual congress; no more than half were still virgins before their wedding night.

The Elizabethan Thomas Whythorne is remarkable among autobiographers for giving voice to his sexual feelings on the brink of marriage. His relationship with his prospective bride, the elusive 'twenty pound widow', did not permit premarital intimacy. Combining courtliness and diffidence, Whythorne reconciled himself to be patient. 'I promise you so I was stiff,' he records in his autobiography.

But yet, considering that the time was not like to be long to the wedding day; and also that the market was like to last all the year long; and I loving her, meant not to attempt any dishonesty unto her, for a sinful act it had been, till we had been married, and we should have provoked God's heavy displeasure and wrath to have alighted upon us for our wickedness.

Moral and religious arguments sustained his continence, yet Whythorne wondered whether his hesitancy in this regard was one of the reasons that his engagement to the widow foundered. Widows, after all, were said to be notorious for their sexual appetites.[33]

The Jacobean poet Samuel Rowlands offers one young woman's dreamlike account of espousal followed by sexual initiation. Delight soon gave way to tears as she found herself with an unwanted pregnancy and a damaged reputation.

> Methought I went a journey out of town
> And with a proper man I was made sure;
> As sure as death, methought we were assured,
> And all things for the business were procured.
>
> We did agree, and faith and troth did plight,
> And he gave me, and I gave him a ring,
> To do as Mistress Bride will do at night,
> And I protest methought he did the thing . . .
>
> Forsooth (in sadness) I was big with child,
> And had a belly (marry God forbid),
> Then fell a weeping, but he laughed and smiled,
> And boldly said, we'll stand to what we did.
> Fie, fie (quoth I) whoever stands I fall,
> Farewell my credit, maidenhead and all.[34]

This, of course, is literary creation, but it was modelled on hundreds of real-life experiences.

Over and over again the church courts heard aggrieved or delinquent parties explain that they initiated sexual relations in anticipation of holy matrimony, but only after they were contracted or 'made sure'. Countless couples told the same old story, attempting to legitimize their sexual activity by claiming they were 'contracted together' or already 'asked in church'.[35] Invariably, it was the man who pressed for sexual relations, the woman who was left in the lurch. These are the voices behind the poem, and behind the demographers' figures for prenuptial pregnancy and rates of illegitimacy.

A distressed John Baker told the London commissary court in 1590 how his daughter yielded to the desires of 'one George Tompson who did beget his daughter with child'. Tompson, he said, 'did intend to marry her and thereupon did give her a gold ring, which moved his daughter to yield to him the use of her body'. The ring was important, not for its monetary value but for what it signified by way of security and promise. Before the matrimonial promise could be fulfilled, however, 'the said Tompson died', leaving the woman to bear an illegitimate child.[36]

Jane Meade of Dunmow, Essex, told a similar story in 1594, explaining her unwanted pregnancy by reference to an unfulfilled contract and a premature death. The only reason she allowed her lover 'to have the use of her body', she said, was that she was 'betrothed and contracted unto him in matrimony'. She then moved to Whitechapel, on the outskirts of London, to stay with an aunt and was there delivered of a child. The fact that she did not identify her dead lover, and the clerk left a blank for his name, may suggest to sceptics that Jane Meade was not telling the entire truth.[37]

Edward Jones and Elizabeth Turner 'fell in love' while serving together under the dean of Westminster in 1602 and 'did contract matrimony together'. By Elizabeth's account it was not until they had gone so far as to provide 'apparel and diet' for the day of their wedding that 'he had knowledge of her body and did beget her with child. Whereupon the said Jones, perceiving that charge was coming on, as it seemed, or for some other cause which she knoweth not, hath absented himself and by report is gone to Ruthin in Wales, by reason whereof the marriage is deferred and the child is born.' However, Elizabeth persisted, 'she expecteth the return of the said Jones very shortly to marry her'. John Symons and Elizabeth Playster similarly pledged themselves before adequate witnesses at Kidlington, Oxfordshire, in 1606, using the proper form of hand-holding and an acceptable form of words. The only reason we know about this otherwise unexceptional contract is that after they had 'carnal knowledge' John 'went away' leaving Elizabeth to cope with an illegitimate pregnancy.[38]

Stories of this sort are legion. William Mason and Mary Warren of Whitechapel 'did . . . lie together and had carnal knowledge one of the other's bodies' as soon as the banns were called in church in 1595. William Coulborne of Barford and Isabel Lee of Bloxham lay together at an Oxfordshire ale-house soon after making their contract in 1606. Alice Johnson and Philip Orme of Cheshire went straight to bed together in 1626 after making their contract *per verba de presenti*. Another north-countryman proposed to take his betrothed to bed 'in confirmation of their former contract'.[39] Rose Arnold of Scraptoft, Leicestershire, lamented that it was only on Francis Lane's false promise 'to make me his wife, I granted unto him the loss of my chastity'. John and Joan Chapman of Stepney began carnal relations in the interval between 'being contracted in matrimony' and being 'lawfully married' in 1622.[40]

Lawrence Lambert of London and Elizabeth his intended wife contracted themselves to be married in 1622 'before divers notable witnesses'. Elizabeth told the court that 'after such their contract and not before they had carnal ease and knowledge of each other's body and she the said Elizabeth was unlawfully begot with child by the said Lawrence'. At this time Lawrence's master 'on the sudden took a voyage beyond the seas and took with him the said Lawrence', leaving Elizabeth to deliver a bastard. Fortunately this story did not end as sadly it might, for Lawrence eventually returned to marry Elizabeth and give legitimacy to their child. Another bastard-bearer, Mary Adams of Ealing, Middlesex, told the court in 1629 that George Dash, the father of her child,

was a long time a suitor to her . . . in the way of marriage, and did divers and sundry times promise to marry her, and in that respect, being ill advised, through the great and earnest importunity of the said George, she . . . yielded . . . and did (in hope that he would according to his promise shortly marry with her) suffer the said George to have the carnal knowledge of her body.[41]

Rather than depicting a lusty peasantry given to sexual abandon, testimony of this sort points to a code of honour which valued chastity and reputation.[42] Virginity was supposed to be prized until marriage, and might only be yielded when marriage seemed imminent and secure. Restraint, decency, honour, and respect were desirable qualities in a partner, to be nourished by keeping appetites under control. 'The better sort', including autobiographers and diarists, were more likely to conform to the moral imperatives, and less willing to hazard their worth by anticipating matrimony. If they did engage in unchaste practices they failed to tell us.

Courtship, we have seen, occupied a liminal time between youth and adulthood, between the single and the married state. Single people prepared to become part of a couple, and previously married people prepared to enter that state again. In addition to its primary purpose of finding and securing a partner for marriage, courtship provided opportunities for people to achieve or consolidate their social identity. Just as important as the negotiation of portions and jointures was the negotiation of status, relationships, privileges, and prospects. Both before and after reaching consent, the process of court-ship allowed the man and woman, their friends and relations, to discover each other's character and resources, and to prepare for their future engage-ments as kin. The courting couple may have initiated sexual relations, even to the point of 'incontinency', but it was all preparation for the pleasures and obligations of marriage.

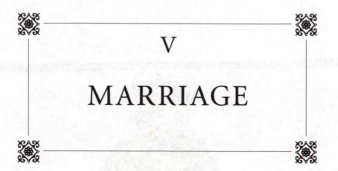

V

MARRIAGE

FIG. 16 The bride and her escorts. From Samuel Rowlands, *The Bride* (London, 1617). This print was made from the reprint done in Boston, Mass. in 1905

HOLY MATRIMONY

Most of the adult population of Tudor and Stuart England embarked on the adventure of marriage. More than 90 per cent of those reaching adulthood in the sixteenth century would marry, and more than 80 per cent in the seventeenth century. Some would marry several times, combining the lottery of widowhood or widowerhood with the practice of serial monogamy. The mean age of first marriage varied little from around 27 or 28 for men and 25 or 26 for women. These facts are firmly established by historical demography, and should no longer be surprising or controversial. They go some way to explaining the moderate population growth of the seventeenth century and the husbanding of resources that fuelled a developing economy. The demographers who first established these figures remarked on the late age of marriage and at the high proportion who never married, but none the less recognized that marriage was the norm.[1]

Marriage was both a ritual process of transformation and an enduring state of affairs. The word 'marriage' had two meanings, referring both to an event and to a condition; it signified the special ceremonial occasion at the entry into holy matrimony, and also the lifelong relationship between a married couple. The word 'wedding' had more popular connotations referring both to the ceremony whereby matrimony was solemnized and to the secular festivities that accompanied the celebration. A wedding (literally, a pledging together) might take several minutes to perform, and hours or days to celebrate, but it ushered in a lifetime commitment to the state of holy wedlock. This section is primarily concerned with marriage as a ritual process, a series of events that transformed single individuals into a lawfully wedded pair.

Contemporaries drew on an extensive vocabulary to discuss the complexity of marriage. The Cambridge lawyer Thomas Eden, speaking in Parliament in 1628, distinguished its various elements and components: 'There is *nuptiae* and *matrimonium*, usually confounded together; but *nuptiae* is the ceremony, *matrimonium* the substance.' Popular writers referred to the taking of 'nuptial vows' in the course of 'Hymen's rites' and the entry into 'holy wedlock' that sealed the couple's commitment to the 'conjugal estate'. Poets employed the language of epithalamiums, while common folk talked of 'knitting together' or 'tying the knot'. The end result, according to one's point of view, ranged from admission to the state of married bliss to unrelieved entanglement in lob's pound.[2]

The early Stuart moral counsellor Matthew Griffith set forth a useful scheme for analysing the ritual components of matrimony, giving separate consideration to its 'antecedents, concomitants, and consequents'. The antecedents, which we have already considered, were 'choice' and 'contract'. Under this heading fell the tortured process of selection, courtship, and agreement between the parties, discussed in Chapters 10 and 11. The concomitants of marriage included the service of solemnization and the secular celebration, requiring 'the parent to give the bride, the priest to bless them' and 'the friends to rejoice with them'. And its consequents were cohabitation and communion, the establishment and continuance of a dutiful Christian household.[3]

The following discussion expands on Griffith's scheme to explore some of the 'concomitants' of marriage in early modern England. It focuses on the social and religious meaning of the wedding ceremony and its ritual and festive accompaniments. Rather than treating marriage as primarily a demographic phenomenon or a moral condition, or as an economic activity or a battle of the sexes, I intend to examine the significance of marriage as a moment in the life cycle. My aim is to understand the entry into marriage within the routines and frictions of domestic and community life, and to consider its conduct or performance within a contested religious culture. Marriage, in this analysis, was a social process with both public and private dimensions. It involved a series of ritual actions with strong legal, cultural, and religious connotations that take us to the heart of Tudor and Stuart society. Though normally uncontroversial, the concomitants of marriage were also subject to difficulties, deviations, and problems exposing the strains and stresses of early modern England.

Transformations

Like other life-cycle ceremonies, the solemnization of matrimony signalled important changes for those who took part. The ritual marked the passage from one state to another. At its completion the parties were no longer as they were before. Similar transitions were associated with the prayer-book ceremonies of baptism, churching, and burial. In baptism, as we have seen, an infant was transformed into a Christian, with community membership, a name, and the prospect of salvation. Through churching a newly delivered mother was restored to her household duties and her husband's bed, and perhaps also purified of any lingering taint of childbirth. And funeral ritual likewise worked to detach a dead person from the world of the living and to rearrange social relationships among the survivors. These were powerful ceremonies with potent cultural consequences. The ritual was not merely performed, but performed to solemn effect.[4] Contemporary observers were clearly aware that their life-cycle rituals involved transformation, and this awareness was particularly acute in the case of marriage.

Marriage assigned new privileges, advantages, and obligations. It redefined social and sexual roles, rearranged patriarchal obligations, and conferred new duties of status, authority, and dependency. The process of ceremony converted men into householders and women into housekeepers. It made lads into masters and maids into dames. Through marriage their relationship to domestic authority became transformed. As single and dependent persons they had followed orders, but as married householders they issued instructions. Marriage for a man meant autonomy, mastery, responsibility, and the prospect of fathering a lineage. Marriage for a woman was, perhaps, the major defining moment of her life, determining her social, domestic, and reproductive future. As the London puritan counsellor William Gouge observed of the ceremony of marriage, 'by it men and women are made husbands and wives. It is the only lawful means to make them fathers and mothers. It is the ordinary means to make them masters and mistresses.'[5] The domestic conduct books that proliferated at this time attempted to teach the couples who had gone through this transformation how to deal with their spouses, servants, and offspring.[6] Most would agree with the Jacobean poet Patrick Hannay that 'in human actions, none is of more consequence than marriage'.[7]

A married couple could hire servants, raise children, and exercise the powers of patriarchy. Their authority proceeded from their condition. A husband was expected to govern his wife and household, and the wife was supposed to command those beneath her through a mediated extension of patriarchal power. Each gained status that could be exercised in the public arena as well as the private domain. As married men, male householders became eligible for local office, as jurymen, reeves, or wardens. Their entry into matrimony alerted neighbours that they were also ready for community responsibilities, including the payment of assessments and taxes. It may be significant, in this regard, that the word 'husband' originally implied mastery and control and that a 'husbandman' extended this control to work on the land; the appellation 'yeoman', indicating a prosperous independent farmer, was originally reserved for freeholders who were married.[8]

Women too gained respect and recognition outside the house as well as at home by the process of putting on a wedding ring. As wives and matrons they were privileged to attend the lyings in and gossipings from which single women were excluded, and as married women they accompanied newly delivered mothers to their churching. The reputation and credit they accumulated was strongly associated with housewifely accomplishments and matronly honour.[9]

In myriad ways, marriage signified a passage into adulthood, a mark of social maturity. It was, by all accounts, 'a solemn change' fraught with profound consequences. The married state carried moral and religious obligations that were not normally expected of single persons. Married people were held to a higher standard of probity and sobriety befitting those heading their 'little commonwealth'. With honesty, credit, and esteem to worry about, husbands and wives occupied a different moral world than that of bachelors and maids.[10] Unlike young single people, who were often permitted considerable leeway, married couples were expected to attend church regularly. In parishes that arranged church seating by family group according to the status of the husband, the newly established household was visually and physically made manifest. In others that maintained a degree of gender segregation, a newly wed woman moved from the company of daughters, maids, and servants to more privileged seating 'among married wives'.[11] In either case, parishioners who married experienced a changed relationship with their neighbours and fellows, and perhaps with their minister and with God. They were held to higher standards of respectability and became responsible for the conduct of their partners and dependants.

In the words of the wedding service, marriage joined husband and wife together 'for better for worse, for richer for poorer, in sickness and in health' until death they did part.[12] It transformed a courting couple into a wedded pair, bound together for the rest of their lives to perform their 'marriage duties'. Some of the immediate effects of this transformation are revealed in William Lilly's account of his passage from servant to master in 1627 when his mistress accepted his proposal of marriage. In Lilly's account of this process his intended, already twice widowed, 'accepted lovingly; and next day at dinner made me sit down at dinner with my hat on my head, and said she intended to make me her husband'.[13] These outward signs of posture, position, seating, and dress announced the transformation to the rest of the household, though in this case the widow remained in control until the marriage was completed. The poet Robert Herrick saw a comparable transformation when household servants reacted to the 'fragrant bride' who was to become their 'dainty mistress'. 'The aged point out, this is she, who now must sway | The house (love shield her) with her yea and nay.' In another poem Herrick traces the change from 'youngling' bride to thrifty housewife, a change that affected her social, sexual, and economic condition.[14]

Marriage was not to be entered into 'unadvisedly, lightly or wantonly', so the prayer book warned. There was no gainsaying the priest's solemn injunction, derived from the gospel, 'those whom God hath joined together, let no man put asunder'.[15] Matrimony was final, till death them did part. Humorists underscored this point by describing marriage as a perilous journey, or by comparing the ceremony at the altar to the ceremony at the gallows. According to a Jacobean characterization of 'a plain country bridegroom' the young man 'shakes hands with everyone he meets as if he were now preparing for a condemned man's voyage'. Another early Stuart author teased that 'our gallant friend is gone to church [on his wedding day] as martyrs to the fire'.[16]

Marriage was a permanent commitment with no turning back. Nobody said it would be an easy row to hoe. When wedding guests wished 'many joys' and 'much happiness' to friends and relations who were about to be married they also knew that matrimony could be a trail of tears. Marriage was 'for better or worse', not necessarily happy ever after. The wedding that committed a couple to domestic duties could also set them on the path to 'household wranglings'. What was supposed to be a matter of honour and blessing could degenerate into disturbance and distraction, the honey turn to gall. Even the official homily on marriage acknowledged 'how few matrimonies there be without chidings, brawlings, tauntings, repentings, bitter curses and fightings'. Though marriage partners were supposed to be 'meet heads and helpers for each other' they could too easily discover in each other 'a riotous and spend-thrifty husband, or [a] waspish and untoward wife'.[17] One of the purposes of the courtship process was to obviate such discoveries.

Popular proverbs and aphorisms, heavily freighted with misogyny, present marriage as the bachelor's ruin; it was the end of a young man's freedom, a condition to be entered with regret. Satirists never tired of jibing that marriage marked the young man's entry into 'the perplexing pond, or rather pound, of wedlock and housekeeping'. Alehouse wits and compilers of commonplace books shared such sayings as 'winter and wedlock tame both man and beast', 'wedlock is padlock', and 'a married man turns his staff into a stake', able to roam no more.[18] Popular playwrights of the early seventeenth century also depicted marriage as the end of youthful freedom and the beginning of adult cares and responsibilities.[19] Young men who had pursued a career of prodigality were supposed to be cured or reformed by the discipline of marriage. Comedic dramatists assumed young men would rise to the occasion and embrace their domestic responsibilities, in the same way that the wayward Prince Hal took on the awesome responsibilities of the throne as Henry V.

Marriage entailed licensed sexual activity and led to lawful procreation. It made of two bodies one flesh. Sexual intercourse outside of marriage was fornication, but within marriage it was pleasing to the Lord, so long as it did not run to excess.[20] Children born out of wedlock were bastards, but those born in marriage were lawful offspring and potential heirs. Single people were supposed to remain continent, but married couples were supposed to make love. The amorous play and fickle flirtation of youth gave way to the sworn commitment and sexual constancy of matrimonial maturity. There would be no more 'codpiece-kissing', no more playing of flirtatious or rowdy games. 'She must no more a Maying', wrote Herrick of his newly married Lady, and farewell to 'those wanton reaks y'ave had at barley-breaks'.[21] Marriage partners made 'the constant nuptial vow' in the sight of God and his church, and promised to forsake all others. The 'marriage duty', so delicately euphemized by William Gouge, was a lifetime of sexual constancy and sexual congress. Church and community strove to maintain this bond by sanctioning adulterers and other sexual offenders.[22]

Samuel Rowlands's early seventeenth-century poem *The Bride* captures many of these transformative effects of marriage. While attempting to adopt a woman's voice, the poet expresses patriarchal satisfaction that his Bride's interests, status, sexuality, title, and even her costume are transformed. *The Bride* delights in the end of 'chaste youth' when the maid becomes maid no more. A company of virgin bridesmaids choruses to the bride, 'we are your fellows' and will accompany you to church; but 'no longer than the wedding day | You hold with us, but turn to t'other side.' Then from that 'other side', the married state, the new-made wife addresses her former companions: 'I am your better now by ring and hat, | No more plain Rose, but Mistress you know what.' The poem asserts that 'marriage life's beyond the single crew', and ventures to suggest that marriage completes a woman's social and sexual identity: 'Unperfect female, living odd you are, | Never true even, till you match and pair.'[23] Wedding guests often drew ribald attention to this aspect of sexual initiation when they drank healths to the bride and groom, competed for the bridal garter, and escorted the newly wed couple to bed. Examples are given in Chapter 16.

A less artful and more instructive comment on the transformations associated with marriage appears in the correspondence between Thomas Ridgeway and Sir Percival and Lady Willoughby in 1610. Though these sentiments belong to the gentry, they point to a widespead appreciation that ritual made all the difference. In a letter anticipating his daughter's wedding, Thomas Ridgeway endorsed the opinion that 'none . . . be properly in the world till they be married, before which time they only go but about the world'. As with Rowland's Bride, the idea seems to be that until one is married one is socially incomplete. On this occasion the Willoughbys, resident in England, could not attend their son Francis's wedding in Dublin, so Ridgeway, the father of the bride, reported the completion of the nuptial activities in two charming letters dated 'Gunpowder day' 1610. Ridgeway's letter to Lady Willoughby begins by discussing social, sexual, and kinship relationships, all of which were transformed by the event. 'Your daughter Cassandra lives, and yet she is a married, nay a bedded wife; your son Francis hath lain with a wench, and yet deemeth it no fault.' Ridgeway then described how young Francis Willoughby acquitted himself on his wedding day:

He plighted his faith to his wife in the public congregation, cheerfully; had her given to him by the viceroy, honestly; was led down to the marriage by two fair virgins, gracefully; armed up again by two great ladies, gravely; kissed the sword and kneeled at his knighting, devoutly; waited at his wedding dinner, with many of us more, diligently and hungrily; danced with his bride, civilly; was well wished unto by many great lords and ladies and other good friends, heartily; graced by maskings, feastings, fireworks and presents, plentifully; was ungartered, unpointed, not disappointed, and went to bed, and rose again, comfortably and contentedly; and so good morrow Sir Francis Willoughby once again, and beware of any more mothers in law.[24]

For Francis Willoughby the day saw a remarkable multiple initiation as husband, kinsman, and knight.

On the same day Ridgeway wrote to Sir Percival, man to man, a more businesslike letter.

We have now thanks be to God according to your constant consent and all persons' good liking, solemnized the well-pleasing marriage between your honest Francis and our spark Cassandra, in as good sort as the time and place could possibly permit . . . The bride and bridegroom were bedded, as hard as the world goes, about four in the morning, when all that long day's solemnities were near their period.[25]

Religious ceremony followed by social festivity and sexual consumation made Francis and Cassandra man and wife; the process established them as an independent married couple; and their union rearranged relationships between the Willoughbys and Ridgeways, giving their elders new sons and daughters as well the promise of grandchildren, and binding the two branches of the family together as allies and kin.

Similar remarks, usually more succinct, are scattered through seventeenth-century plays, diaries, and correspondence. 'Tomorrow I shall change my title for your son, soon as the holy rites shall make me the happy husband to your daughter,' said Beauford to his future father-in-law in James Shirley's play *The Wedding*. The diarist Ralph Thoresby equated marriage with a change of condition and Alice Thornton acknowledged it as 'this greatest change of my life'. Charles Allestree, the vicar of Daventry, Northamptonshire, congratulated his niece on 'the alteration of your condition' when she married in 1679, and wished her 'as many joys and as much happiness in your new change of life as ever any woman in that state enjoyed'. Conventional observations of this sort reveal the contemporary consciousness that marriage was not just a ritual of the church but also a complex social and emotional passage. Newly weds who emerged from the nupital ritual were rightly said to be 'starting their world'.[26] Notwithstanding the example of Queen Elizabeth, the spousal culture of post-Reformation England contrasted sharply with the late medieval privileging of virginity and the single life.[27]

Problems and Questions

Like other rites of passage in early modern England, marriage came freighted with a host of potential problems. Most weddings took place without discord, in a spirit of harmony and consensus, but a number of unresolved issues cast shadows over the ceremony and the institution. Churchmen, lawyers, controversialists, and creative writers explored a wide range of troublesome issues that affected the lives of ordinary men and women.

The problems and questions were manifold. Who was entitled to be married and who was restricted? What social, cultural, or legal conventions governed matrimonial choice, and how was that choice constrained by limitations of consanguinity and affinity, age and parental consent? Could any cohabiting couple set up together as man and wife, or was marriage incomplete without formal ecclesiastical solemnization? How common, and how acceptable, were informal consensual unions that eschewed all public ritual? Assuming that weddings belonged in church, in which part of the church should the ceremony be conducted—in the porch, the nave, or before the altar? Before what assembly, during which times of day or year, and with how much publicity should the wedding ceremony be performed? Why were some marriages considered 'clandestine', and why was this a problem? What complications might follow if the proper protocols were not observed?

How was the wedding service to be performed, by whom, in what spirit, and with what social and religious understandings? What was the ceremony supposed to achieve? Should the parties proceed by banns or by licence, and how much advance notice should they give to the community and to the priest? What were the social and legal consequences of private, hasty or irregular ceremonies? Should the priest marry the couple with a ring, as required by the prayer book, and why was the wedding ring so controversial? Should the bride's father or guardian 'give' her in marriage, and should the husband promise to 'worship' his wife with his body? In sum, was the English prayer-book form for the solemnization of matrimony pleasing to God, as conformists insisted, or was it, as the separatist John Canne charged, more 'petty juggling trash' derived from the popish mass book?[28]

Contemporaries concerned themselves with this range of questions, to which we can add several others. How did the secular festivity of the wedding day cohere with its religious solemnity? How did the secular and the sacred elements of marriage intertwine? What degree of merrymaking was appropriate, what customary activities might be performed, and when did they shade into excess? Were second and subsequent marriages celebrated in the same way as first weddings? What do English matrimonial practices reveal about the roles and relationships of clergy and laity, men and women, neighbours and kin? How much did they vary from gentry to common people, from village to town, from region to region, and how did they change over time? What do they show about customary behaviour, religious discipline, nonconformity, and the shifting social and cultural stresses of Tudor and Stuart England? This catalogue of questions, like questions about other life-cycle passages, points yet again to areas of conflict, irresolution, and unease.

Religious controversialists addressed many aspects of marriage, though without the embattled fervour and confrontational intensity that more commonly characterized their discussions of baptism and churching. Radicals found fault with important details of the authorized wedding service, while apologists for the Church of England defended 'the many ceremonies' associated with holy matrimony. High ceremonialists exacerbated tensions by upholding the ancient calendar of prohibited seasons and by insisting that marriage be performed at the altar rails, to be followed by holy communion. Though puritans often criticized 'the time wherein the liberty of marriage is restrained . . . giving of the woman either by the father or by some friend . . . the custom of laying down money by the bridegroom upon the book . . . the ring . . . the words the bridegroom speaketh of worshipping with the body . . . [and] receiving the sacrament at that time (now in these days out of use)', the purpose of these procedures, as the Oxford minister John Day explained in 1614, was 'to intimate unto us of what dignity marriage is'. The celebrated London puritan William Gouge wrote approvingly of the 'religious consecration' and 'civil celebration' of marriage, each with their liturgical and customary elements.[29] Contemporary moralists, like modern social historians, sought ways to comment on the nature, purpose, meaning, significance, manner, and conduct of early modern marriage.

Discussion of marriage occurred in services and sermons, pamphlets and tracts, household manuals and conduct books, poetry, plays, letters, diaries, and court cases. Each source reveals a different facet or dimension. But most conversations on the subject went unrecorded. Far fewer devotional prayers and meditations survive on marriage than on childbirth and death, perhaps because the subject was less controversial. No more than hints remain of what was said at betrothal ceremonies and wedding dinners. It is tantalizing to learn that Ambrose Westrop, the early Stuart vicar of Great Totham, Essex, was 'a talkative, maggoty person' whose chief topic was marriage, about which he was more merry than a clergyman should be; but it is frustrating to the historian that no details of his discourse on this subject survive.[30]

God's Weddings

'Holy matrimony', so the prayer book insisted, was 'an honourable estate, instituted of God in Paradise in the time of man's innocency, signifying unto us the mystical union that is betwixt Christ and his church; which holy estate Christ adorned and beautified with his presence and first miracle that he wrought in Cana of Galilee, and is commended of St. Paul to be honourable among all men'. Created by God, blessed by his son, praised by his apostle, and invested with mystic significance, marriage was therefore, 'not to be enterprised or taken in hand unadvisedy, lightly or wantonly, to satisfy men's carnal lusts and appetites, like brute beasts that have no understanding; but reverently, discreetly, advisedly, soberly, and in the fear of God'.[31]

These opening remarks from 'the form of solemnization of matrimony' in the Book of Common Prayer reflect the determination of the church to impose religious solemnity on an undertaking that was often coloured by secular concerns. Contrasting frivolity with sobriety, and brute bestiality with Christian civilization, the words of the wedding ceremony advanced the campaign for the reformation of manners as well as the reformation of religion. Working against age-old customs of laxity and informality, the reformed Church of England demanded that all couples married in accordance with its set form of service. In hand with the tightening of its ecclesiastical monopoly, the Edwardian and Elizabethan church promoted marriage as the fulfilment of divine ordinances, and weddings as spiritual and devotional events.

Marriage was not a sacrament of the Church of England, as it had been under Roman Catholicism, but it retained strong sacramental elements. When Tudor and Stuart churchmen preached on the subject of matrimony they echoed the commendations of the service book and praised marriage as a condition crafted in heaven. Miles Coverdale's English popularization of Heinrich Bullinger's treatise on matrimony (frequently reprinted between 1541 and 1575) claimed that 'it is God himself that knitteth the knot of marriage'. The protestant James Calfhill explained in 1565 that though no longer a holy sacrament, marriage was still 'an holy ordinance of God'. God was present in the making of marriage, in the binding of 'holy wedlock' and in the blessings of the religious service. 'Take God with thee in wooing, invite him to thy wedding,' was typical advice from the Jacobean preacher Thomas Gataker. Devout couples prayed for God's continuing presence in 'the Christian state of matrimony'.[32]

To Richard Greenham, the painstaking Elizabethan minister of Dry Drayton, Cambridgeshire, marriage was performed in the service of God, in the sight and in the fear of the Lord. Daniel Rogers echoed these sentiments a generation later in his lengthy treatise on 'matrimonial honour'. To the Jacobean puritan William Gouge, author of *Of Domesticall Duties* (three editions published 1622–34), Christian marriage was 'an honourable estate' for all to enter. For Matthew Griffith, author of the competing handbook, *Bethel; or A Forme for Families* (1633), 'marriage is not only a civil and politic, but also a divine and spiritual conjunction'. Envisaging the Caroline ideal of the settled kingdom as well as the settled domestic union, Griffith saw God's blessing descending upon the Christian married state.[33]

Pious sentiments like these united all but the most radical strands of opinion. A few incautious Laudians of the 1630s still considered marriage to be a sacrament, or so their enemies claimed, but such papistical opinions put them outside the Anglican mainstream. Laud's chaplain William Heywood allegedly approved of the hallowing of the ring in the 'sacrament' of marriage. Edward Shephard, the vicar of Great Maplestead, Essex (instituted 1639, sequestered 1644) allegedly taught in catechizing that marriage was one of the 'seven sacraments', and his eccentricity apparently extended to a belief in purgatory. But Thomas Bedford, preaching at Paul's Cross in 1638 with Laudian approval, went out of his way to insist that matrimony, though consecrated, was 'no proper sacrament' since it did not signify Christ's passion or confer the grace of justification.[34] Equally isolated were radicals who believed that marriage was no business of the church at all, but was rather a matter for civil society.

From moderate puritans to high ceremonialists, the general view held that marriage belonged to God and should be celebrated with solemnity in his church. John Donne put it well, in a wedding semon of 1621, when he balanced the civil and religious aspects of matrimony. 'As marriage is a civil contract, it must be done so in public, as that it may have the testimony of men. As marriage is a religious contract, it must be so done as it may have the benediction of the priest.' The church was the ideal place for public witness, and God's minister the ideal person to conduct the ceremony. Custom, convenience, law, and religion all drew marriage into the orbit of the church. Without public testimony and religious benediction, said Donne, it 'is but regulated adultery, it is not marriage'.[35]

Even the presbyterian Directory of Public Worship of 1645 declared that 'such as marry are to marry in the lord' with 'the blessing of God upon them'. When the revolutionary regime instituted secular weddings in 1653, freeing the ceremony from ecclesiastical ministration, it went against deep-rooted custom. The Reverend John Gauden was one of many who insisted on the 'sanctity' as well as the 'civility' of Christian marriage. A conservative gentleman spoke for many when he protested that marriage was still 'a thing sacred and to be sanctified', notwithstanding the change in the law. 'The whole Trinity hath conspired together to set a crown of glory upon the head of matrimony,' enthused the preacher William Secker in 1658.[36] Lay opinion is hard to gauge but seems generally to have supported the view that marriage was incomplete without clerical ministration.[37]

What was matrimony for? Drawing on biblical teachings, the Book of Common Prayer was quite explicit in its list of 'the causes for which matrimony was ordained'. Elizabethan and Stuart ministers reiterated these three reasons every time they performed the ceremony:

One was, the procreation of children, to be brought up in the fear and nurture of the lord and praise of God. Secondly, it was ordained for a remedy against sin and to avoid fornication, that such persons as have not the gift of continency might marry and keep themselves undefiled members of Christ's body. Thirdly, for the mutual society, help and comfort that the one ought to have of the other, both in prosperity and adversity.

These aims were repeated in countless wedding sermons, including John Donne's sermon at the marriage of Margaret Washington in May 1621.[38]

William Gouge and Matthew Griffith, one a puritan the other a Caroline conformist, agreed that marriage was the foundation of the family. The purpose of marriage, wrote Gouge, was the 'procreation of children . . . that the world might be increased . . . with a legitimate brood'. 'The end of marriage is issue,' Griffith concurred. Gouge also endorsed the notion, derived from St Paul, that marriage was a lawful way to channel sexual energy—especially male sexual energy—to prevent 'inward burning and outward pollution' and 'to avoid fornication'. Griffith too agreed that marriage was a way to avoid 'uncleanness' and sexual danger, a danger that he went on to describe with unusual taxonomic precision:

If it be with a married woman, it is called adultery; if with a single woman, it is called fornication; if with one's cousin, it is called incest; if with either married or single it be done by violence, it is called a rape; if it be the sin of Onan, it is called pollution; if between man and man, it is called sodomitry, etc. But call it what you will, and be it what it can, marriage is a lawful and useful way for avoiding it.

Marriage, from this perspective, was a sexual safety valve, an alternative to sin, as well as an honourable and delightful estate to be entered for its own more positive merits.[39] Isaac Archer, the young vicar of Chippenham, Cambridgeshire, seems to have recognized this when he wrote in his diary soon after his wedding in 1667, 'by marriage all my former youthful desires were cured, and extravagant thoughts ceased. I found it a remedy.' Mrs Archer's thoughts on the subject remain unknown.[40]

The ideal of companionate marriage based on 'mutual society, help and comfort' was enshrined in the prayer book from its inception and was not the invention of seventeenth-century puritans or eighteenth-century modernizers. Puritans, however, were more likely to promote this ideal in their writings. One of the purposes of marriage, wrote William Gouge, was the 'mutual good . . . comfort and happiness' of the parties. Gouge's more conservative contemporary Matthew Griffith stressed the importance in marriage of cohabitation, communion, and enjoyment of the blessings of the Lord.[41]

Religious and secular authors alike used images of yokes, knots, and bonds in discussions of matrimony. The familiar image of a yoke was especially powerful, evoking a device that secured harmony and balance between two forces while combining their effort to a common end. 'Conjugal' relations were those that came together under the yoke of matrimony. For the mid-Tudor reformer Miles Coverdale, marriage was a 'conjugium, a joining or yoking together, like as two oxen are coupled under one yoke . . . but it must also be such a coupling together as cometh from God, and is not contrary to his word and will'. The Jacobean puritan Gouge similarly saw marriage as a bond, a yoking, a knitting together, in which the couple were joined and 'glued' and bound together into one flesh. Each became 'an helpmeet' or 'yoke-fellow' to the other. To Daniel Rogers in 1642, 'the yoke is easy and the burden is light' if both partners were joined and balanced in matrimonial honour. To Richard Meggot, preaching in 1655, the yoking together of husband and wife secured 'a reciprocal and relative interest in each other's actions'. St Paul's injunction to the Corinthians, 'be ye not unequally yoked with unbelievers', gave force to dozens of puritan marriage sermons.[42] A gratified husband, like Oliver Heywood in 1667, could declare himself 'abundantly satisfied in my gracious yoke-fellow'. The legal and commercial language of seals and bonds provided a comparable vocabulary for dealing with marriage. When Hannah Woolley wrote in Charles II's reign that 'marriage is an holy and inviolable bond' she was merely repeating conventional opinion.[43]

PROHIBITIONS AND IMPEDIMENTS

Forbidden Seasons

Unlike most other mammals who adhere to a seasonal calendar of mating and gestation, humans bond together and may be sexually active at any time of the year. It may be true, as poets claimed, that in the spring a young man's fancy turns to love; indeed, some moralists believed the spring to be the most dangerous season for sexual misconduct.[1] But there is no natural biological imperative for humans to form couples or get married at any one particular time of the year rather than another. Marriage is a cultural event, to be scheduled according to social convenience and whim. Unlike the vital events of birth and death, which few people are able to control, the timing of marriage is susceptible to planning and choice.

Against this readiness for marriage at any convenient time the early modern church maintained a religious calendar prohibiting marriage during many holy seasons of the year. This ecclesiastical calendar developed in the Middle Ages to separate times of ribald festivity from times of religious devotion, and it survived intact beyond the Reformation. Indeed, while the Roman Catholic Church reformed its calendar and loosened traditional restrictions at the Council of Trent in 1563 the protestant Church of England, uniquely and perversely, sustained the full set of prohibitions.[2] The principal closed seasons were Lent, a time of penitential austerity in readiness for Easter and mourning for the fall of man; Rogationtide and Trinity in the late spring, reserved for prayer and fasting in preparation for Ascension; and Advent, before Christmas, designated as a time for spiritual rather than carnal joy. This complex ecclesiastical calendar was further complicated by the movement of the date of Easter, to which many of the forbidden seasons were tied. Strict adherence to this matrimonial timetable required not only awareness of the seasonal prohibitions, but also correct information about which days in any given year they applied.

Printed almanacs conveniently reminded readers of 'forbidden times' when marriage was not allowed.

Marriage comes in on the 13 of January, and by Septuagesima Sunday it is out again; until the octaves of Easter, or day after Low Sunday, at which time it comes in again, and goes no more out till Rogation Sunday, for *Rogamen vetitat*; from whence it is forbidden again until Trinity Sunday, [then in until Advent] when it goes out and comes not in again until St. Hilary, or 13 of January next after,

whereupon the whole cycle began again.[3] The nuptial calendar was as confusing as the rules of cricket. Altogether the Church of England marked 144 days as unsuitable for marriage ceremonies, covering close to 40 per cent of the year. The following verse, inscribed in the parish register of Everton, Nottinghamshire, served as a mnemonic device for the minister and congregation, advising them when they could and could not marry.

> Advent marriage doth deny
> But Hilary gives thee liberty.
> Septuagesima says thee nay,
> Eight days from Easter says you may.
> Rogation bids thee to contain
> But Trinity sets thee free again.[4]

As the church lawyer Edmund Gibson pointed out in his *Codex Juris Ecclesiastici Anglicani* of 1713, the prohibited times were nowhere 'expressed or plainly supposed in our constitutions or canons', yet they were deeply embedded in ecclesiastical culture and practice.[5] In the post-Reformation period, under Elizabeth and the early Stuarts, they were also profoundly controversial. Puritan reformers ridiculed the prohibited seasons as unsupportable popish remnants and sought to have them quashed; disciplinarians, traditionalists, and high ceremonialists cherished the rhythms of the Anglican religious calendar and attempted to maintain their dignity. Meanwhile, an increasing number of people ignored them. Strains produced by the English marriage calendar provide yet another gauge of the cultural and religious tension in early modern society.

At the heart of the problem, from a critical point of view, was the apparent hypocrisy, inconsistency, and greed of the church in selling licences to overcome obstacles that had no grounding in scripture or law. Marriage was not absolutely forbidden during the designated prohibited periods but could readily be facilitated by purchasing a licence from episcopal officials. Many observers believed that the calendar regulating marriage had nothing to do with holiness and a lot to do with money. The customary prohibition 'that from three weeks before Lent till the octaves of Easter, from Advent to Twelfth tide, and for three weeks before midsummer, there shall be no marrying at all, without a dispensation', was, in James Calfhill's opinion, 'the milch cow that yieldeth so large a meal of spiritual extortion'.[6] Puritans and radicals continued to berate the Church of England for the peculiarities of its marriage calendar.

This pernicious system, exclaimed the separatist John Canne, was devised by the popes 'for filthy lucre's sake'. According to Anthony Gilby, the practice of forbidding marriage at certain times, and then selling licences to grant permission to evade the restriction, was another of those 'hundred points of popery yet remaining, which deformeth the English reformation'. Fearing the introduction of similar absurdities into Scotland in the reign of James I and VI, the presbyterian David Calderwood ridiculed the English church for its 'forbidden times to marry in, yea, more than the papists have . . . amounting in all to a third part of a year; as if marriage, which is called honourable, did profane these holy times . . . Notwithstanding of these forbidden times, they may get a dispensation for some money, and then it shall be lawful enough; for money hath a great virtue in it.'[7]

Early Elizabethan protestants chided the catholics for their 'tyrannous and impious' laws regarding marriage, and hoped that the Church of England would drop its own seasonal restrictions. Convocation took up the matter of prohibited seasons on several occasions and Parliament came close to abolishing them. Discussions on the subject in 1562 and 1575 were inconclusive. In 1584 the lower house passed a bill 'giving liberty to marry at all times of the year without restraint', but it went no further, possibly quashed by the Queen. It was hardly a burning issue, but it clearly displayed the conservatism of the English reformed church.[8]

The records of episcopal administration show strains between bishops who were charged with enforcing the matrimonial calendar and local clergy who were sometimes inclined to ignore it. Bishop Barnes of Durham admonished his clergy in 1577 'that you do not solemnize matrimony between any persons from the first Sunday in Lent until the first Sunday after Easter'. The curate of Meeching, Sussex, was cited in 1583 'for solemnizing matrimony last Lent', and the curates of Charlbury and Chadlington, Oxfordshire, were cited in 1584 for celebrating marriages in Advent. When charged in 1587 'that he married one John Wollston in the time exempted, viz. upon Shrove Monday, without license', the vicar of Bursted Magna, Essex, explained 'that the banns was full asked, and therefore he committed the same ignorantly, and not upon any contempt'. When Hugh Prichard of Frome Canon, Herefordshire, was married in 1588, following banns but out of season, he explained, 'that he did not know it was in time prohibited'. The real offender, Bishop Westfaling decided, was the incumbent vicar who performed the ceremony rather then the ignorant layman who was irregularly married.[9] Records of this sort are common in the Elizabethan period but relatively rare in the regimes that followed.

An exhaustive study of parish registers shows a strong correlation between the seasonal pattern of marriages and the main periods of ecclesiastical restriction during the sixteenth century. This distinctive seasonality, showing strong aversion to marriage in Lent and also a pronounced shortfall during Advent, generally prevailed through the first three decades of the seventeenth century. The Lenten restriction lasted longest, as countryfolk took warning from the proverb, 'marry in Lent, you'll surely repent'. Charting monthly marriage tallies from 404 parish registers, Wrigley and Schofield report 'a chasm in March', the month approximating Lent. March weddings were extremely rare in the Elizabethan period and unusual through most of the Stuart era. As might be expected, the Interregnum saw a softening of the observance of Lent, and the Restoration a modest recovery. March weddings were still relatively uncommon in the eighteenth century and remained below average in the nineteenth. (Against an index of 100 representing parity, the score for March in the period 1540–99 was 8, for 1600–49 22, for 1650–99 43, and for 1700–49 48. These figures contrast with the peak month of November, with scores of 201, 165, 135, and 125 respectively.) Statistical evidence suggests that the Lenten prohibition endured but was subject to gradual erosion over time. December marriages, approximating Advent, similarly remained low until the middle of the seventeenth century, but gained in popularity thereafter. (The December indices were 41 in 1540–99, 48 in 1600–49, 72 in 1650–99, and 97 in 1700–49.) Elizabethans also avoided marrying during Rogationtide, but their seventeenth-century successors increasingly ignored this prohibition.[10]

Liturgical constraints on the timing of marriage were offset by the seasonal requirements of agricultural production. In order to devote more resources to nuptial festivity, people commonly chose to get married during seasons of relative abundance and in times of respite from their working regime. In arable areas this normally produced a surge of weddings after harvest, around Michaelmas (29 September) in southern England and closer to Martinmas (11 November) further north. In pastoral regions the peaks came after spring lambing or calving. Economic factors associated with the terms of servants' contracts produced more local and regional variations, and these became more distinct as rural economic specialization increased in the later seventeenth and eighteenth centuries. The old religious calendar was not repealed but became attenuated, and operated with diminishing force. Advanced urban areas like London, which depended less on agricultural rhythms, saw a gradually flattening pattern, with marriages becoming more evenly distributed throughout the year.[11] But marriages during Lent, Rogationtide, and Advent were still technically prohibited, and required a special licence from the church.

The evidence of parish registers reveals that the Advent prohibition was widely disregarded, and Rogationtide made little difference to the timing of marriages after the sixteenth century; only the Lenten season was generally diligently observed. Perhaps the matter would have mouldered, with the church authorities winking at people who quietly ignored the ancient prohibitions, had not issues of discipline and ceremony returned to the national religious agenda in the 1620s and 1630s. Historians of this period continue to argue about the nature of religious controversy and the question of innovation in the early Stuart church. Were the puritans undermining the established order by eroding the ceremonial trappings of the prayer book and dispensing with canonical requirements such as the wearing of surplices and the use of the sign of the cross? Or were the ceremonialists and Arminians the ones who destabilized a broadly consensual Jacobean church by insisting on new stand-ards of devotional decorum and strict adherence to long-relaxed or even non-canonical regulations? The debate over the calendar for marriages provides us some further purchase on this problem.[12]

The Jacobean puritan William Gouge had little use for the traditional cal-endar and paid it no attention in his discussion of domestical duties. None the less, like ceremonial churchmen at the opposite end of the religious spec-trum, Gouge believed that certain times were 'unseasonable' or inappropriate for weddings. Instead of calendrical holy seasons, however, Gouge thought weddings should yield time to the more solemn moments of sabbatarian and domestic regimes, 'as on the Lord's day, or in time of mourning'. Other-wise, all seasons belonged to the Lord and all were equally appropriate for weddings. An examination of the marriage register in the London parish of St Ann, Blackfriars (where Gouge was preacher from 1608, lecturer from 1611, and rector from 1621 to 1653) finds that February was the most popular month for weddings and that March marriages were generally avoided, but the differences were less extreme than the national average; otherwise marriage registrations were spread throughout the year. Though this pattern may indic-ate the suppressed seasonality of a metropolitan parish, it may also reflect the reformist teaching of the minister.[13]

Under the influence of protestant reformers, communities throughout England had silently begun to adjust and override the official calendar of prohibited periods, saving Lent, allowing people to marry whenever they thought best. Against this laxity, which to some ecclesiastics smacked of irreverence, ceremonialists like John Cosin insisted on strict adherence to the ecclesiastical calendar and avoidance of marriage in 'times prohibited, that is to say, in Advent, Lent, and in the Rogations, without a licence first obtained from the archbishop or his chancellor'. From their point of view such mar-riages were disrespectful of the christological calendar, as well as disorderly and disobedient. Lenten weddings were unheard of in Cosin's parish of

Brancepeth, County Durham, and weddings in the other prohibited periods extremely rare.[14] In practice, of course, the ceremonialists never controlled enough dioceses or archdeaconries to ensure widespread compliance with these prohibitions, nor were they always averse to parishioners outstepping them by obtaining a licence. But to political and religious opponents their position smelt of imperious sacerdotalism, if not downright popery. In this as, in so many other areas, the ceremonialist insistence on dignity and discipline invited a vigorous challenge.

Outraged by John Cosin's reverential enthusiasm for the full-blown liturgical calendar and his insistence on strict observation of the prohibited seasons for matrimony, the London puritan minister Henry Burton argued in 1628 against the 'difference between the times sacred, and common'. These seasonal restrictions, Burton charged, 'lurked among some rubbish of Romish relics, and so escaped the shipping away with other of Rome's trinkets'. Though not set forth in the Book of Common Prayer they were none the less embodied in the ecclesiastical calendar and were commonly reiterated in almanacs. Burton demanded:

Where doth God's sacred word suspend or prohibit any times from sacred and solemn nuptial rites? . . . And is not the prohibiting of marriage for certain times in the year (and those no small times neither, as encroaching upon above a third part of the year) . . . a branch of that very forbidding of marriage, which the apostle calleth a doctrine of devils? [1 Timothy 4] . . . This ten weeks limitation from marriage falls unhappily (if we go according to the course of nature's rules) upon the most dangerous season of the year, the spring time, wherein the blood and spirits are most stirring. But our author [John Cosin] takes order for that, he will have them well macerated and mortified, tempered and tamed with nine weeks fast . . . What times fitter for solemnizing the rites of marriage, than times of festivity and joy? . . . Alas, poor marriage, art thou now become so unclean, unholy, as to be shut out from holy times?[15]

In that same year, 1628, the House of Commons again came close to passing a bill 'to take away the prohibited times for matrimony' and to allow 'free liberty to marry in any season of the year'. Detailed reports allow us to reconstruct parts of this lively and thoughtful debate. Speaking against the ecclesiastical prohibitions and the episcopal licences sold to surmount them, William Coryton observed, 'these licences are plain remnants of popery. I desire they may be swept away.' His colleague Sir Robert Harley called the prohibition 'a remnant of superstition, not swept out with the rest . . . If we continue such a branch of popery, to deny that which God has made lawful, how much do we connive at that which God prohibits.' Ignatius Jordan, speaking in the same vein expostulated, 'if it pleases God to forbid no time, neither I hope need we'.[16]

On the other side, more cautious lawyers like William Sherland accepted the traditional 'constitutions for marriage' as 'counsels of mature deliberation and ancient marks of our church' which 'ought to be preserved'. Sherland was one of the leaders of the parliamentary attack on Arminianism, but on this issue he stood with the religious conservatives. His colleague, the Cambridge lawyer Thomas Eden, similarly defended the traditional calendar because he thought the merriments of marriages unseemly during 'times of devotion and mortification'. Eden's justification would seem to have allied him, in part, with William Gouge, but his call for strict devotion to the liturgical calendar and more austere observance of Lent put him here in the camp of John Cosin. The bill was reported and engrossed, but died without becoming law.[17]

Amid so many other ecclesiastical controversies the prohibition of certain seasons for marriage was a relatively minor concern. If it threatened to affect them, intending couples could circumvent the restriction or wait it out. The argument between puritans and ceremonialists, summarized in the debate between Burton and Cosin, was more about ideology than practice. Most administrators of the 1630s chose not to press the matter, while opponents found it as easy to evade as to complain. Neither William Laud, Richard Montague nor Matthew Wren drew attention to the matrimonial calendar in their visitation articles, except for safeguarding Lent, though they were deeply committed to litugical propriety and discipline in other regards. The issue was more significant for what it represented than for its impact on people's lives. When William Smith and his wife of Tilney All Saints, Norfolk, were married in 1627 'upon Whitsun Monday last without licence or banns being asked', the bishop of Norwich seemed more concerned that their arrangements were irregular than that they married during a prohibited season. Similarly when Ralph Thornebury and Margaret his wife of Stoke Lyne, Oxfordshire, were 'married upon Shrove Monday last at a time prohibited, without licence' in 1630, the court paid less attention to what they had done than to what they had omitted.[18]

In 1645, attempting to settle the matter once and for all, the presbyterian authors of the Directory of Public Worship allowed marriage to take place 'at any time of the year, except on a day of public humiliation', though preferably not on the Lord's day. Seasonal patterns in the 1650s show some flattening of the profile, as people took advantage of this relaxation, but the continuing general avoidance of marriage during Lent points to a deep-rooted popular conservatism.[19]

The old liturgical calendar came back with the restored Church of England in 1660, but enforcement of the prohibited periods was haphazard and ineffective. The vicar of Hillingdon, Middlesex, had a difficult time with his parishioner John Allen, who 'neglecting to be married in due time, when marriage was out, went to Harefield, a lawless church, in a prohibited time', and then had the affrontery to refuse the minister his fee. Allen was by no means a nonconformist, but like many parishioners of the early 1660s saw no merit in the calendar of prohibited times or the mercenary hypocrisy of its enforcement. The minister of Tasley in the diocese of Hereford himself violated the offical calendar by performing a marriage in his parish church on 21 April 1663 (Easter Tuesday) 'which some say is a time prohibited; but neither the canon nor the late book of common prayer doth make any mention of such prohibited times; however, if there be any error therein, it is an error of ignorance, not of wilfulness;' and he promised 'to be careful for the future not to offend in the like'.[20]

Demographic indices from the later seventeenth century show gradual attenuation of the aversion to marriage during Lent and increasing disregard of the other prohibited periods. Only the most scrupulous Anglicans still cared. One of them, John Evelyn, confided his disquiet to his diary in 1680 when his son was scheduled to be married in Lent. 'I would fain have had the marriage deferred till after the Lent; but several accidents requiring it now, it was left to the disposal of her friends, and their convenience.' The marriage took place on Shrove Tuesday, on the eve of Lent, and strictly within the ancient prohibited period.[21]

Banns and Licences

In normal practice, before anyone could be married, 'the banns must be asked three several Sundays or holy-days, in the time of service, the people being present, after the accustomed manner'. These obligations were set forth in the Book of Common Prayer and repeated in the canons of 1604.[22] As the Elizabethan commentator William Vaughan explained, 'the priest is bound openly in the church to ask the banns, to wit, whether any man can allege a reason wherefore they that are about to be married may not lawfully come together; which being done, and no exception made, they then are joined in the holy links of matrimony'.[23]

Episcopal visitors frequently enquired whether any had 'married solemnly, the banns not first lawfully asked'. Elizabethan churchmen insisted that marriage be brought firmly under ecclesiastical control, and their concerns were echoed by their early Stuart successors. Archbishop Grindal instructed the clergy of York in 1571 not to marry any persons 'without the banns be thrice, on three several Sundays or holy days, first openly asked, without any impediment or forbidding'. Virtually the same words appear in Bishop Laud's visitation articles of 1628 and Bishop Montague's of 1638.[24] Even Princess Elizabeth, the daughter of James I, was 'asked three times in the church . . . in St. Margaret's, Westminster', before her wedding to the Count Palatine Frederick in 1613.[25]

The publication of the banns gave neighbours notice of an impending wedding and encourged them to speed any preparations; it announced to the community at large that agreement had been reached between parties to a match. In some parts of England a peal of bells, known as a 'spurring peal', accompanied the first publication of the banns of marriage, to signify that from this time forward the intended couple began to gallop.[26] Public calling of the banns also gave the community a chance to consider whether there was any cause of impediment that might prevent the couple from joining together as husband and wife. If either of the parties was suspected already to be married or precontracted to another, now was the time to object. If the couple fell within the prohibited degrees of consanguinity or affinity, or were believed to be disqualified by reason of age or lack of parental consent, the public calling of the banns invited these objections to be heard.

The banns were a safety device to prevent those who were ineligible from attempting the passage into matrimony. Puritans and traditionalists alike acknowledged their utility. The godly family counsellor William Gouge recognized the advantage of waiting three weeks or more from the making of a marriage contract to the performance of the ceremony; the pause allowed for the thrice reading of banns in church and also allowed time for the couple 'to provide all things fit for their dwelling together'.[27] The Scottish presbyterian system similarly required advance public notice of marriages, 'to the intent that if any person have interest or title to either of the parties, they may have sufficient time to make their challenge'. So too did the short-lived Directory of Public Worship adopted in England in 1645. During the revolutionary Protectorate a public reading of the wedding banns in the market-place was supposed to replace the customary publication in church, but ecclesiastical declaration continued. At Boston, Lincolnshire (said to be a puritan stronghold), 314 banns were declared in the market between 1656 and 1658 compared to 151 published in church.[28]

Church court records capture some of the drama of a challenge to the banns of marriage, though they barely hint at the heartbreak and embarrassment that some irregularities entailed. William Mead and Margaret Rame were ready to be married at Great Waltham, Essex, in 1577 after the banns were asked openly in church on two successive Sundays. But on the third Sunday 'they were forbidden by Nicholas Satch, who claimed marriage' to

Margaret by virtue of an alleged pre-contract. Agnes Neville 'did forbid the banns' of marriage between George Hien and Margaret Jenkins of Banbury, Oxfordshire, in 1583 on the grounds that George 'had once carnal knowledge of her body, for which he was openly punished, but denieth that he ever made promise to Agnes Neville of marriage'. Although Agnes Neville was pregnant, said to be carrying George Hien's child, the court concluded that her challenge was worthless and ordered George's marriage to Margaret to proceed. Agnes's objections to the banns washed a good deal of dirty linen in public, but were not sufficient to block the wedding.[29] The banns were similarly stayed at Burford, Oxfordshire, in 1584 until the authorities were satisfied whether William Pickering, the intended bridegroom, 'were contracted to another in London or not'. And in the same year the rector of Abbess Roding, Essex, was presented for allowing 'a young maid to be married, knowing that she was assured to another, and the banns forbidden by her mother'. Mary Evans of Grays Thurrock, Essex, called out against the banns in church and objected to John Richardson's marriage in 1633 because she was carrying his child, but lacking proof of contract she was unable to stop the wedding.[30]

Legally, pre-contract was a fatal impediment to marriage. If one intending partner was already contracted to another the wedding was not supposed to proceed. And if such a person forgot or concealed a pre-existing contract, the marriage, if solemnized, could be declared invalid. This opened up vast opportunities for claims and counterclaims that filled diocesan registries with reams of documents relating to matrimonial litigation. Because of the ambiguity of words and the uncertainty of memory, the ease with which promises could be misconstrued and the difficulty of proving whether an informally expressed contract was binding, the way was open for disappointed lovers or their families to block a marriage or gain revenge. Some couples may even have 'remembered' a pre-contract in order to invalidate their marriage, in effect to secure a divorce.

Disputes over contracts touched many more people than were affected by prohibitions of marriage based on affinity or kindred. The marriage of William Hickman and Emma Carpenter at Cullingham, Oxfordshire, for example, was solemnized in church by the curate in 1594, after thrice calling of the banns, with many witnesses present; but it was later charged to have been unlawful because the bride 'was contracted to another'.[31] More commonly a 'bigamous' marriage of this sort was prevented by proclaiming the pre-contract at the calling of the banns. Prior sexual relations with another partner were insufficient grounds for objecting to a marriage, unless it could be proved that a contract was involved.

Calling the banns in church did not necessarily guarantee that a wedding would go forward. At Aston-under-Edge, Gloucestershire, the churchwardens complained in 1563 that 'one Robert Spearpoint being thrice lawfully asked in the church to one Anne Elle, has forsaken her and will not marry her, and has gone out of the country'.[32] The Oxford archdeaconry court heard in 1584 that Anthony Payne of Duns Tew 'was asked in the church unto one Ursula Fuller three times . . . and since that time was married unto one Alice Franklin', the marriage taking place in Buckinghamshire, beyond the court's jurisdiction. After the banns were called in church at Swanton Morley, Norfolk, between George Raven and Mary Lincoln in 1597 'he lewdly ran away and married another woman'. In a similar sad unfolding, a woman of Stepney, Middlesex, carrying the child of one William Jones, told a London court in 1605 that 'he promised her marriage, and after the banns there published went and married another woman'.[33]

People who initiated the public process of matrimony by calling for the banns to be read and then for some reason changed their minds were liable to censure by the courts. Nicholas Lynch of Theydon Bois, Essex, was forced to make public confession of his fault in 1584 'for offending almighty God' and for abusing the congregation 'in procuring the banns openly to be asked in the church between him and Joan Roberts, and not proceeding in the marriage'.[34] Lesser problems with banns involved couples who married with only one or two callings, or who had the banns called in one church and then were married in another. William Bates and Eleanor Young 'caused banns of matrimony to be published' in the church at Cotterstock, Northamptonshire, in 1633 but failed to proceed to a wedding. In this case there was no breach or abandonment, but rather neglect to proceed to the next stage of the ceremony. Three months later, the court heard, William and Eleanor 'kept company together, and defereth the solemnization of marriage, to the offence of the parishioners'.[35]

Much more offensive was the behaviour of John Backe of Minster, Derbyshire, who called off his marriage to Elizabeth Lomasse after being publicly 'asked' in church. John and Elizabeth had been courting for three years, and their relationship had progressed to full sexual intimacy. Elizabeth was pregnant at the time that the banns were called, and was confident that John would make her an honest women. However, 'because he could not get her mother's house to dwell in he denied all and everything', and left her with a bastard child that he would not own. Breach of contract and fathering a bastard were, of course, more serious offences than failure to follow through on the banns. Elizabeth presented her case in a suit before the bishop of Lichfield in 1636, in which her midwife and three other women appeared as witnesses on her behalf. Unfortunately, as too often happens in these cases, the outcome is unknown.[36]

The open publication of banns could be dispensed with by purchasing an ecclesiastical licence. One had only to apply to the episcopal authorities—to the bishop's chancellor, commissary, or vicar general, or to the archdeacon or any other competent official—present one's bona fides, and pay the requisite fee of 5s. or 7s. The official granting the licence was supposed to be satisfied that there was no lawful impediment to hinder the marriage, that it overrode no controversy or suit touching contract, and that the marriage had the express consent of a minor's parents or guardians. In the diocese of Norwich the standard formula for a marriage licence included the provision that there was 'no lawful let or impediment by reason of consanguinity or affinity . . . or of precontract, strife or suit in law'. Persons applying for matrimonial licences had to sign allegations and bonds to this effect, designed to reduce the risk of 'fraud and collusion'. As a further safeguard against deceit the canons stipulated that licences should be granted 'unto such persons only as be of good state and quality, and that upon good caution and security taken'.[37] But everyone knew that the system was open to abuse.

Because of the extra cost and effort involved in securing a licence, the decision to seek this form of authorization for marriage was more prevalent among the more prosperous sectors of the population. The names of the poor and the humble are conspicuously absent from surviving registers of marriage licences, but some of the middling sort and many members of the upper classes thought it worth their while.[38] In some jurisdictions more than a fifth of all marriages were performed by licence, a proportion that may have doubled in the later seventeenth century with the decline of parish discipline. Daniel Rogers, writing in 1642, thought the 'humour and vanity' of persons 'of fashion and wealth' made them 'itch as they do after private marryings', without publication of banns. During William Gouge's incumbency at St Ann, Blackfriars, between 1623 and 1634 when this information is recorded, 56 per cent of all marriages were by licence, rising to 89 per cent during Lent.[39]

An ecclesiastical licence allowed a couple to marry in haste, when time was of the essence; it allowed them to marry during religious seasons when matrimony was otherwise prohibited; it permitted them to marry in a parish away from home, in the church or chapel of their choice; and it secured them a degree of privacy, removed from the scrutiny of kinsfolk or neighbours that came with the publication of banns. Some families may have preferred a quiet marriage by licence to a highly publicized wedding with banns because it spared them the expense of hospitality to a ravenous assembly of guests. The privacy and flexibility afforded by marriage by licence contributed further to the cultural separation of the élite from routine parochial activities, a pattern also seen in their baptisms and funerals.

Marriages performed by licence were not supposed to be secret or clandestine, but were supposed to take place in the home church or chapel of one of the parties, during the canonical hours of eight to twelve in the morning. Sometimes the licence was valid 'in any church within the diocese' or came with particular conditions such as 'after one publication of banns only'.[40] Forged and fraudulent licences exacerbated the problem of irregular or illegal marriages and further brought the system into disrepute. John Bassforth married Anne Turner at Eyam, Derbyshire, in 1590 with a licence that he claimed was issued 'by word of mouth without writing' from one of the Earl of Shrewsbury's chaplains. John Smalley of Ragdale, Leicestershire, paid 11s. for a questionable licence, that the parish clerk obtained with neither oath nor bond, for his hurried wedding in 1634. Reversing the usual order of proceeding, John and Alice Shuffleworth of Thorneton, Yorkshire, 'sent for a licence after they married' clandestinely in 1640. Richard Morris, the enterprising curate of Bettws, Herefordshire, married a couple in 1673 'with a licence of his own forging . . . for which he demanded and received 13s.' His colleague and contemporary John Edwards of Mossbury ran a similar racket, procuring 'a false and forged note' for a clandestine marriage, 'pretending it to be a licence and procuring fees for the same'.[41] The legality of licences became a point of contention in many of the hundreds of cases involving clandestine marriage.

Although most licences to marry were beyond reproach, an unknown number were used to facilitate unions that would not otherwise have been permitted. Despite the safeguards of the licensing procedure, the system was notorious for its opportunities for dissimulation and deceit. Members of the propertied classes became alarmed that unsuitable suitors were snapping up heiresses without respect for contracts and that ambitious ne'er-do-wells were marrying their daughters in violation of parental wishes. Ecclesiastical officials took note of these concerns in 1614 when they ordered the archdeacon of St Albans to be more careful in the issue of licences, for 'by this means many men are robbed of their children, yea, and many children are utterly undone, being married to persons of ill quality by colour of licences granted by the archdeacons and officials'. The controversial Laudian canons of 1640 sought to limit the granting of marriage licences to applicants who lived within the particular licensing jurisdiction, or who had dwelt there for a least one month. But the entire system of episcopacy collapsed in the revolution before this minor reform could be implemented.[42]

Marriage by licence became increasingly common in the later seventeenth century, especially among the gentle and commercial élites. It became a public scandal that licences could be obtained so easily, without due enquiry into the parties' background and circumstances. According to Humphrey Prideaux in 1691, 'the good orders of the church have been so far neglected in all these particulars, and the corruption of officers in our ecclesiastical courts, for the sake of gain, hath run so high, that everything is done contrary to them in this matter'.[43] Marriages performed by licence still required an officiating minister, and still had to be solemnized solemnly in church.

The late seventeenth-century observer Henri Misson noted the fashion for marriages that were private, though not strictly clandestine. 'To proclaim banns is a thing nobody now cares to have done; very few are willing to have their affairs declared to all the world in a public place, when for a guinea they may do it snug and without noise.' Then on the wedding day the parties

go early in the morning with a licence in their pocket and call up Mr. Curate and his clerk, tell him their business, are married with a low voice and the doors shut, tip the minister a guinea and the clerk a crown, steal softly out one one way and the other another either on foot or in coaches, go different ways to some tavern at a distance from their own lodgings or to the house of some trusty friend, there have a good dinner, and return home at night as quietly as lambs.[44]

The problem of clandestine weddings will be discussed at length in a later section.

Impediments

Though most people expected, at some time in their lives, to get married, their behaviour was constrained by a variety of legal, social, religious, and demographic factors. Although by law nobody could be forced to marry, an unknown number may have gone to the altar under some degree of duress. We cannot gauge how many young women were pressured to marry by their parents, or how many young men felt similar obligations. Most couples, apparently, entered into wedlock through their own volition, even if at the same time they satisfied the hopes of parents and kinsmen. In the course of the service the minister asked each partner whether they gave their free consent, and few couples baulked at this perilous question.

A marriage might be challenged, however, if the parties were not fully entitled to join together as man and wife. They needed to be of marriageable age, at least 14 for a boy and 12 for a girl, and if under 21 should have the consent of parents or guardians; they could not be married if they fell within the forbidden degrees of consanguinity or affinity; and their union might be void if either party was legally precontracted to another. In some godly parishes the minister might threaten to refuse to solemnize holy matrimony if the couple were spiritually unprepared, for example if they could not recite their catechism. And some communities appear to have attempted to block the intended marriage of desperately poor people whose families seemed likely to become a burden to the parish.[45] These last two restrictions had no grounding in law, but reflected the view that marriage was a solemn undertaking replete with social and economic obligations.

In England a male was legally old enough to be married at the age of 14, a female at the age of 12, but teenage marriages were extremely rare. Most couples waited until their mid-to-late twenties. Canon 100 of the canons of 1604 repeated the rule that 'no children under the age of one and twenty years complete shall contract themselves, or marry, without the consent of their parents, or of their guardians and governors if their parents be deceased'. Relatively few marriages took place between couples so young, but occasionally problems arose when a minor sought to marry without consent, or when consent was withheld or ignored. Bishops sometimes addressed this matter in their visitation enquiries and cited offenders before the ecclesiastical courts.[46]

In the Diocese of Chichester in 1579 Bishop Curteys learned that 'William George of the age of sixteen years hath contracted himself with one Joan Yerrish without the consent of his nighest kinsmen or others his friends in the house of his master Edward Markwork.' At Selsey, Sussex, Thomas Gooden and Agnes Man were 'contracted without the consent of the woman's father'. And John Wingham and Bridget Ford were 'contracted privily without consent of the parents of the said Bridget and as they say without their good will'.[47] In these cases the young couple had advertised their intended union, and the courts attempted to forestall any problem before they entered the state of matrimony. In other cases, however, the couple lied about their lack of consent, or procured a priest to marry them clandestinely despite the lack of parental permission.

Once a couple was married, albeit irregularly, there was little that the authorities or the aggrieved families could do. The church might impose sanctions of chastisement or penance, but could not undo a marriage that was otherwise adequately performed. Runaway lovers sometimes took advantage of this flexibility. For example, it was alleged before the High Commission in 1624 that one Robert Marshe of York 'did by fraudulent and unlawful means allure and entice one Anne Metham, sole daughter to Guy Metham of the city of York, gentleman, a young girl of the age of 15 or 16, from her said father' without his consent, and with the help of accomplices stole her away to Selby 'to get her secretly married there'. Though the circumstances were highly irregular, and possibly illegal, Guy Metham would have to adjust to the reality of having Robert Marshe for a son-in-law, provided it could be shown that Anne herself had given her consent.[48]

Prohibited Degrees

Near the beginning of Elizabeth's reign the Church of England set forth its 'table of kindred and affinity' specifying which relations by blood or by marriage a person was prohibited from marrying. Based on medieval precedents, promulgated by Archbishop Parker in 1560, and then further modified for general adoption in 1563, the table laid out a revised codification of the ancient restrictions on incest.[49] Every church was required to display this table, and its restrictions were vigorously enforced. The table identified a total of thirty relationships which barred marriage for either sex, ranging from grandparents, parents, siblings, and offspring to the siblings and spouses of such kin. It may have seemed obvious that a man could not marry such consanguinal relations as his mother, sister, or daughter; but marriage to such affinal relations as his father's brother's wife, his wife's sister, or his brother's son's wife were also regarded as incestuous. Marriage was prohibited between nephews and nieces, aunts and uncles, but there were no explicit restrictions on marriage between cousins. The tables said nothing about marriage to a parent's sibling's child.[50]

The Jacobean canons reiterated that

No person shall marry within the degrees prohibited by the laws of God, and expressed in a table set forth by authority in the year of our Lord God 1563. And all marriages so made and contracted shall be adjudged incestuous and unlawful, and consequently shall be dissolved as void from the beginning, and the parties so married shall by course of law be separated. And the aforesaid table shall be in every church publicly set up and fixed at the charge of the parish.

The presbyterian Directory of Public Worship, which briefly supplanted the prayer book in 1645, simply forbade marriage between those 'within the degrees of consanguinity or affinity prohibited by God'.[51]

Reading the records of episcopal administration one might think that the table of degrees of kindred and affinity was almost as important to some bishops as the table of the ten commandments. Episcopal visitors routinely asked whether any had married within the degrees 'of consanguinity or affinity prohibited', and checked to see that the printed table listing those degrees was properly installed. In the Diocese of York in 1571 Edmund Grindal issued injunctions to his clergy to observe the table of prohibited degrees, 'lately appointed to be affixed in your parish church', and to read it twice yearly to their parishioners, for their better knowledge and understanding. William

Laud's visitation articles for the Diocese of London in 1628 asked, 'whether have any in your parish been married within the prohibited degrees forbidden by law, and expressed in a certain table published by authority in anno 1563? If yea, then you shall present their names. And whether have you the said table publicly set up in your church, and fastened to some convenient place?'[52] Even today a modern version of this table is commonly posted inside the parish church porch.

Bishops repeatedly expressed frustration when parishes were inadequately equipped in this regard. In his visitation of the Diocese of Chichester in 1579 Richard Curteys asked specifically whether each parish had the tables of degrees of consanguinity, and found dozens of parishes wanting. The churchwardens of Warming confessed that 'we have not as yet the table of degrees for consanguinity', implying that they had not yet laid out the necessary money. But at Singleton they reported, 'we had one of the same tables but now he is worn out', perhaps from intensive use, and at Stedham they promised to have one 'shortly'. Most of the parishes in the Diocese of Ely had the table in 1570, but in the Diocese of Norwich in 1597 as many as 10 per cent of the parishes were wanting. The matrimonial tables were still missing in various parishes of the Diocese of Norwich in 1627, and also within the Diocese of Lincoln in 1634. A later bishop of Chichester in 1636 found that a quarter of his parishes could not display the table of kindred and affinity, and it was missing from dozens of Nottinghamshire parishes in 1638.[53] Post-Restoration authorities were no more successful in securing the proper display of the table in every parish.[54]

From the point of view of many local churchwardens, the table, though required by the authorities, was not of the highest priority. To obtain a copy would cost them a couple of pennies, for it was not bound or printed with the Book of Common Prayer. Some parishes in the reign of Charles I went to the other extreme and paid for an elaborate frame to mount their table of prohibited degrees of matrimony. This was in keeping with the ceremonialist aesthetic that put covers on fonts, carpets on communion stools, cloths over pulpits, and furnishings over altars; it reflected concern for the beauty of holiness and the reverential separation of religious accoutrements, but it had nothing directly to do with attitudes to marriage.[55]

Actual cases of matrimonial incest were rare, for most people understood that they were not to marry their close relations. Among the few to be cited for offending against the prohibited degree was Eustace Wiseman of St Gregory's, Norwich, cited in 1620, 'for that contrary to the laws of the land he married with his first wife's sister's daughter'. Another Norwich citizen, William Mallet, a glover of St Andrew's, took for his second wife one Anne Fuller, 'own sister by the father's side to Elizabeth Fuller alias Mallet, late wife of the said William'. In this case disciplinary action extended to the episcopal officials who had made the mistake of granting Mallet a licence for his incestuous marriage. In 1631 the ecclesiastical High Commission imposed a humiliating public penance and levied the enormous fine of £12,000 on Sir Giles Alington for marrying Dorothy Dalton, his half-sister's daughter.[56]

Religious Restrictions

Although there was no religious test for marriage, some ministers used their control of the ceremony as a last opportunity to instruct young people in the fundamentals of the protestant religion before they set up as independent householders. Parents were supposed to have implanted this knowledge, in co-operation with parish officials, but not all families lived up to these responsibilities. Edmund Grindal, the reforming archbishop of York, went well beyond law and custom when he instructed his clergy in 1571, 'ye shall not marry any persons, or ask the banns of marriage between any persons which before were single, unless they can say the catechism by heart, and will recite the same before you before the asking of the banns'.[57]

Richard Greenham's pronouncement, in the late Elizabethan period, that 'marriage is holy unto them only whose hearts are sanctified by faith in his name', implied that the minister could withhold it from those he considered less robust Christians. Godly ministers may sometimes have attempted to impose such a test, but it could not be sustained in law. Nor were puritan clergy alone in erecting religious knowledge as another hurdle, or its absence as an impediment to marriage. In his Yorkshire visitation in 1627 the ceremonialist John Cosin asked similarly whether any were married 'that cannot yet say their Catechism', and in his unfulfilled plans for the revision of the prayer book in 1661 Cosin made 'want of . . . instruction in the catechism, and of confirmation', a basis for denying marriage.[58] Only if one or both of the parties was excommunicated could they be prevented from saying their vows in church.[59]

CLANDESTINE AND
IRREGULAR MARRIAGES

The great majority of marriages in Elizabethan and early Stuart England took place under ecclesiastical auspices. The early Church of England was largely successful in its campaign to control the ceremonies of family formation. Until it was fragmented by the seventeenth-century revolutions, and before it was undermined by later waves of nonconformity and irreligion, the established church held effective sway over marriage. This does not mean that every wedding followed the protocols of banns or licences, or that every ceremony observed the niceties of custom and law. But it does reflect a widespread understanding that unsolemnized contracts were inadequate and mere consensual unions were improper. Unchurched marriages based on simple consent may have met the minimum requirements of the law, but they were severely deficient in social and cultural terms. The vast majority of couples in early modern England acknowledged the importance of religious ritual in establishing conjugal unions, and accepted the role of the clergy in the solemnization of holy matrimony. Even so-called clandestine weddings were usually solemnized by an ordained minister using the words of the Book of Common Prayer in a consecrated building in the presence of lawful witnesses. Despite irregularities and defects, which bulk disproportionately large among the legal records of the period, most weddings were conducted in accordance with the wishes of the church.[1]

The period between 1560 and 1640 may have been unique in this regard. In contrast with the more casually made consensual marriages of medieval times, and the increasing irregularity and concubinage alleged for the late seventeenth and eighteenth centuries, the age of Queen Elizabeth and the early Stuarts stands out as a period of exceptional cultural discipline. Legal, social, moral, and religious pressures brought all but the most marginal or the most reckless into line and into church. The ecclesiastical authorities were vigorously opposed to concubinage or unlawful cohabitation, and under Elizabeth and the early Stuarts were generally effective in enforcing their will. Members of the laity, especially those with property or reputations at stake, also accepted the obligation of a public ecclesiastical ceremony. The registration of marriages in parish registers, started in 1538, secured a documentary record of the liturgical event.[2]

It is true, as many historians have indicated, that marriage in early modern England involved a considerable degree of flexibility. The law of spousals and matrimony was notoriously ambiguous and complex, allowing a wide range of uncertainty and dispute.[3] Ecclesiastical law and common law sometimes pulled in competing directions, and matrimonial litigation bogged down in a morass of anomalies and contradictions. But during the century following the Reformation, the church succeeded in convincing its members that matrimony was a public as well as a private activity, requiring a religious rite of passage. Duty to one's family, parents, offspring, neighbours, governors, and God required one to marry in ways that would not be subject to question. Religious solemnization became the norm. There is very little evidence from this period to support the notion that couples commonly flouted ecclesiastical authority, or that the provisions of the Book of Common Prayer concerning holy matrimony were widely ignored.

Confusion has set in because some scholars have failed to differentiate late medieval legal principle from early modern social practice, and have mistaken 'clandestine' and irregular marriages for informal unions that rested on mere consent. This chapter sets out to review the problem of 'clandestine' marriages in Tudor and Stuart England, and to show that despite obvious technical defects they were, for the most part, conformable to social and legal expectations.

In principle, a marriage existed if the man and the woman committed themselves to each other by words of consent expressed in the present tense. It would be enough to say, 'I, N. *do* take thee, N, to be my wedded wife/ husband.' A marriage was technically made valid in law by this contract or spousals *per verba de presenti*, providing there were no overriding impediments. A contract *de futuro*, made in the future tense (such as, 'I *will* marry you'), became immediately binding if followed by sexual intercourse. Such was the core of medieval law, that was not changed in England until Lord Hardwicke's Marriage Act of 1753.[4] In practice, however, such simple, private, secular commitments were treated as seriously deficient. Even if they took place with some degree of formality, in the presence of witnesses, with ritual handfasting and exchange of gifts, and even if the parties thereafter called each other 'husband' and 'wife', the mere expression of spousal consent no longer satisfied the mainstream expectations of early protestant England. Even though mutual consent remained at the core of the contract, a wedding was insufficient if not conducted by a priest. In the course of the sixteenth century the majority of the population conformed to the view that marriage was incomplete without ecclesiastical solemnization. Court cases differentiated espousals and pre-contract from actual marriage, while considerations of the binding legitimacy of a marital union turned less on whether each party had expressed consent, and more on whether their marriage had been performed by a minister in a church.[5]

Canonical Hours

Weddings belonged to God, but they also belonged to the community. They were supposed to take place in open church, in public view, at times when witnesses could easily observe the proceedings. Ideally, they were part of the public life of the parish, to be shared with the same congregation who witnessed baptisms and churchings. The ecclesiastical canons of 1604 reiterated the convention that marriage could be solemnized 'only between the hours of eight and twelve in the forenoon'.[6] Couples who were joined outside of these hours were, technically, guilty of an irregularity, and their marriage may have been considered 'clandestine'. Samuel Pepys may have been justifiably anxious that 'the canonical hour would be past' before the ring and licence arrived for an Essex wedding he attended in 1665.[7]

The requirement that weddings took place in daylight, within canonical hours, was one way to safeguard against deception. When Elizabethan bishops (such as Matthew Parker in 1560, John Aylmer in 1577, and Herbert Westfaling in 1586) enquired 'whether any minister have married any in times forbidden by the ecclesiastical laws', they were more concerned to prevent irregular, clandestine, or incestuous marriages from being conducted at night than to enforce the old prohibited seasons of Advent, Lent, and Rogationtide. Bishop Thomas Cooper of Lincoln made this clear in 1574 when he asked whether any in his diocese 'were joined in matrimony at unseasonable time, to wit, at night, or in the morning before clear light'.[8] Clerical disciplinarians of the 1620s and 1630s sought similarly to enforce these regulations through visitations. John Cosin enquired specifically of his parishes in the archdeaconry of the East Riding in 1627 whether any were married 'in a private house, or secretly in a corner, out of the face of the church and congregation, or before the hour of eight, or after the hour of twelve in the forenoon'. Bishops Laud, Montague, and Wren used similar phrasing in their visitations from 1628 to 1638.[9]

Most weddings took place during canonical hours. The morning service could then be followed by an afternoon of feasting and revels. But some couples had reasons to avoid this publicity, and local visitation records point to a host of irregularities in scheduling. The archdeacon of Nottingham, for example, heard of clandestine marriages being performed 'before sun rising . . . in the morning a little before day . . . about four in the morning' and at other times that would evade the normal public scrutiny such as 'about nine of the clock at night . . . late in the evening . . . in the night time by candle light'. Most of these weddings were solemnized in church, employing the words of the Book of Common Prayer. It was their circumstances rather than their conduct that made them irregular. The vicar of Greasley, Nottinghamshire, faced censure and suspension for marrying Mr Lancelot Rollston and Margaret Ashe in his parish church on the Wednesday before Whit Sunday, 1594, 'about four of the morning'. In 1588 a Kentish couple, Thomas Hunt and Jane Jetter, were married by the vicar of Boughton at two o'clock in the morning. It is tempting to imagine them attending to their nuptials after a hard night with the Armada beacons. Another accommodating clergyman, the minister of Elkesley, Yorkshire, married Thomas Lilliman and Thomasine Stringer in the pre-dawn darkness 'between six and seven o'clock in the morning' on 18 January 1602, 'without banns asking' and without the priest knowing whether the bride's father gave his consent. The minister of Brampton Bryan, Worcestershire, was another who performed similar ceremonies in a private house at seven one morning in 1617.[10] Late night or pre-dawn weddings were notoriously presumed to be clandestine; besides being conducted during irregular hours they often violated other conventions regarding banns, licences, or consent. The fact that they were performed by a minister and followed the form of the marriage service did not mitigate the offence.

Clandestine Weddings

Puritans and conformists alike agreed that weddings belonged in church. Only the most extreme sectarians called for civil rather than ecclesiastical marriage, and only briefly in the 1650s did they have their way.[11] The church was the ceremonial centre of the parish, a place of public witness as well as religious worship, and the minister was the accepted master of ceremonies. Social, cultural, and legal conventions called for the ceremony to be performed in the church in view of the bride and bridegroom's kinsfolk, friends, and neighbours. As the puritan William Gouge explained in the 1620s, 'a religious consecration of marriage is performed by the blessing of a public minister of the word in the open face of the church in the day time'.[12] When the presbyterian John Angier was married 'very publicly in Manchester church in the heat of the wars' in 1643 the ceremony was marked by no less than two sermons. 'Nor was the solemnity in his marriage any fruit of vain glory or ostentation,' remarked Angier's eulogist, 'but upon consideration it was his settled judgement and advice that marriage should be publicly solemnized.'[13] The church wedding was not just a ceremony but a lesson. Weddings that took place at night-time, in secret, in deserted churches or even in private houses, clearly fell short of these ideal conditions.

It is impossible to gauge how many weddings took place in clandestine or irregular circumstances. Probably the overall proportion was low, before the later seventeenth century, except in the shadiest parts of London.[14] None the less, offences against propriety and discipline in this regard provided a considerable amount of business for the ecclesiastical courts. The visitation returns, presentments, act books, and cause papers of almost every ecclesiastical jurisdiction are thick with references to clandestine marriages. Sometimes the courts themselves initiated proceedings *ex officio,* to investigate or punish offenders. More commonly such cases began with an aggrieved party—often an angry kinsman or thwarted lover—who opened affairs that others preferred to keep closed.

One of the dangers of clandestine marriage was that the person performing the ceremony might turn out to lack the essential credentials of religious ordination. In that case the marriage was a sham. An early Elizabethan case is instructive in this regard. John Bradshaw of Nottingham claimed to have been married to Katherine Burdock in 1569 'in the house of a certain John Harrison of Ilkeston, Derbyshire, by Cuthbert Bee, clerk, curate of Dale Abbey'. It later turned out that Bee was a reader, not a curate, and that he was not in holy orders. This was a useful discovery for Bradshaw, who could now assert that 'he was not lawfully married to Katherine Burdock', and that his subsequent citation for bigamy was therefore without merit. After first siding with Katherine the judge reversed himself, on the evidence that Bee was a layman, and ordered Bradshaw to have nothing more to do with poor Katherine, 'but to live with . . . Joan Godbehear as his wife'. A similar cloud of uncertainty hung over the marriage of Richard Needham and Isabel Dob who were joined in matrimony in 1602 by one Francis Marples, 'a minister as he thinketh'.[15]

This particular problem harkened back to an earlier debate about the necessity of marriage by a priest. The notion had not entirely disappeared that anyone could make a marriage, provided there was goodwill, commitment, and consent. John Bale, a vigorous protestant reformer of the mid-Tudor period, had argued that though matrimony was a holy state, it was not made holy by priestly action or by solemnization at clerical hands. The Elizabethan puritan minister Richard Greenham, 'being asked whether the solemnization of marriage in a public assembly after an holy and faithful conjunction used privately were necessary or no, answered it was necessary *non ad essentiam sed ad sanctimoniam conjugii*'. Greenham's disciple, the Reverend Daniel Rogers, avowed that though some of the reformed churches had instituted civil marriage, 'the practice of our church to do it by the minister is every way most convenient'. The publicity of ministerial solemnization 'makes the matter more solemn [and] awes the parties much more', though it did not, by itself, make them any more married. A private discussion among Jacobean churchmen came dangerously close to giving up the ship. At one session of Bishop Neile's visitation of the Diocese of Lincoln in 1614 the clerical table talk was 'whether a lay-man might tie the knot of matrimony. It was defended that *factum valet, quanquam fieri non debet*.'[16] It was not surprising, then, that some members of the laity should think that they could arrange their own weddings as they pleased, in defiance of ecclesiastical regulations. This argument was captured by mid-seventeenth century radicals who, for a few years, converted marriage into a secular affair. But it was shot down by moderates like John Gauden, who insisted that marriage belonged in Christ's church.[17]

The mainstream position of the church remained that marriage required a minister. No lay parish clerk, schoolmaster, or magistrate could lawfully preside. The majority of men and women appear to have endorsed the view that an essential step towards a wedding was to send to a priest. It was vital to ensure that anyone conducting the ceremony was properly ordained, not just to preserve the dignity and authority of the church, but also to safeguard innocent parties against fraud, fornication, and bastardy. The best way to do this was to have the wedding lawfully celebrated in church, during canonical hours, as a matter of public record, by a minister who was known to all concerned.

Marriages that took place in private chambers or inns, in meadows or barns, in dead of night with absence of witnesses, risked a store of grief to the parties involved, especially if the minister performing the ceremony was a stranger. William Emerson was made to do penance in the Diocese of Durham in 1635 after confessing 'that he was married in a barn of his own at Barmeton . . . and that the marriage was made by a stranger with whom he was not acquainted, neither did he know whether he had any lawful ordination or not'.[18] The parties to this clandestine ceremony had violated liturgical propriety and ecclesiastical discipline, but the marriage was 'made' and could not be undone unless it had ignored insuperable legal impediments or the stranger turned out to lack ordination.

Despite strenuous efforts by the Church of England to bring marriage within 'eccesiastical cognizance' and to ensure that all couples recited their vows in church, a number of weddings took place in private houses, ale-houses, and other secular settings. Nottinghamshire court records from the 1590s mention weddings performed in a room of 'the Swan' in Mansfield, 'in a barn in Warsop in the night time by candle', and even outdoors 'in a meadow in the parish of Sandiacre . . . before sun rising'. Thomas Horsely of Durham confessed in 1635 that he too 'was married in an open field'. Oxford diocesan officials in 1631 investigated a marriage that allegedly took place at ten o'clock at night in a private house at Chadlington. A marriage at East Retford, Nottinghamshire, in 1632, performed by the vicar of Habblestrope, took place in the house of John Wilson but, the householder assured the court, 'contrary to his knowledge or consent'. Another marriage 'at a private house' was reported in the Diocese of Chichester in 1636.[19]

Such marriages evaded the public scrutiny provided by banns and the administrative vetting associated with licences, and escaped the church's control of the ceremony. Catholic recusants may have been among those who favoured hugger-mugger weddings, in order to avoid the protestant liturgy. Among the 'manifold enormities' in the county of Lancashire in 1590, a group of godly ministers alleged that 'divers [were] married in private houses without any banns asked, or any intelligence thereof given to the minister'. Many of these clandestine marriages, they suspected, were performed by 'massing priests' whose activities helped to keep the old religion alive.[20] Others involved in midnight weddings included runaway lovers and alehouse-haunters, who were more concerned with secrecy and speed than with fulfilling their religious obligations. For some it was an advantage that clandestine weddings avoided the expenditure as well as the public display of matrimonial festivity.

For poor, humble, and marginal people the alehouse served as a social centre, an alternative focus of communal life to the parish church. Frequenters of alehouses were not necessarily bad Christians, but some seem to have valued the approval of drinking companions over the official ceremonies of the church. There must have been many like Jane Minors, the Essex woman who drank and caroused instead of attending to her churching in 1597 and said it was but a ceremony.[21] The informal betrothals and irregular ceremonies that took place in alehouses were, by their nature, undocumented. But occasionally they left traces in the records. Alehouse weddings were highly offensive to ecclesiastical decorum, but they offered convenience and conviviality to some less reputable sectors of the population. Real or mock weddings in an alehouse were usually followed by a not-so-mock consummation.[22]

It is important to point out that even participants in alehouse weddings used words of marriage from the prayer book, and usually attempted to obtain the services of a priest. Even disreputable couples knew that marriage required more than simply saying the words of espousal and declaring themselves married in the eyes of God. In 1621, for example, the curate of Minsterworth, Gloucestershire, reported that he was drinking at a local alehouse when a couple asked him to marry them, there and then. After haggling over the fee he agreed, and 'having neither book nor candle, the said Mr. Jones took them by the hands and joined their hands together'. It was left to the courts to decide whether this irregular union satisfied the requirements of the law. In 1632 the London commissary court ordered William Money and his wife to perform public penance in Whitechapel church 'for being married in an alehouse in Southwark'. Ecclesiastical strictures in this case extended to the wedding guests who were cited 'for being present when Money and Mary his wife were married in an alehouse in Southwark'. Despite the impropriety of the setting, there was no question that the couple were legally married. The court was content to recognize 'Mary his wife' rather than 'his pretended wife'.[23]

A case from the archdeaconry of Oxford describes how, after drinking in an alehouse until about eleven or twelve at night on Lady Day 1637, Richard Dodwell and friends went into the church at Biddlesden, on the Oxfordshire–Northamptonshire border, where Richard was solemnly, if somewhat tipsily, married to his wife Elizabeth.[24] From the point of view of the ecclesiastical court, this was disorderly and irreverent conduct, and a patently clandestine marriage; but the participants saw nothing wrong in their behaviour. Indeed, had they not made concessions to respectability by performing the ceremony in the church?

Alcohol was also involved in 1634 when Richard Harbort of Churchill, Oxfordshire, claimed he was tricked into marrying Mary Maunder in William Price's house while drunk. Price pressed Mary upon him, procured a minister, Mr Belcher, to perform the ceremony, and lubricated it with alcohol. Still, no doubt, recalling his hangover, Harbort told the court that 'coming unto Price's house they did force drink upon him and Mr. Belcher the curate, that they were both much in drink, otherwise he believeth he should not have been wrought over to marry him'. Mary subsequently confessed to her new husband 'that the said Price did persuade her to marry [Harbort] promising her if she would so do he would free her from all trouble'. It seems likely that Mary was Price's former lover, by this time pregnant, and marrying her to the besotted Harbort was a way for Price to get her off his hands. To complete the trick they needed the services of a priest, who they likewise plied with drink.[25]

Couples who married clandestinely, even if sober, could not be certain that their partner was free from prior matrimonial entanglements, or whether they were hiding an impediment. Nor could they be completely certain that they had been truly and legally married at all. At least one of the weddings conducted in 'a warren or cony-keeper's house' in late Elizabethan Nottinghamshire violated the prohibited degrees of matrimony by linking Richard Scartcliff to his deceased wife's sister. Another clandestine marriage, conducted 'in a chamber' in Nottingham in 1592, was performed by an intimidated minister serving under duress. That, at least, is what he told the investigating court. Charles Ainsworth, rector of Bulwell, reported that he was 'sent for by Lady Manners, and at his coming she took him aside and required him to do it and the door was straight shut to them and he dared not to do it for fear', and so married Lady Theodosia Manners to William Bradwell. After performing the clandestine and, as it turned out, bigamous marriage between Thomas Silvester of Ecclesfield, Yorkshire, and Anne Silvester 'his pretended wife' in 1635, the minister, Henry Taylor of Wath, protested that he thought Silvester's first wife 'was dead of childbirth, as he was informed'.[26]

Reports of clandestine marriages like these echo the passions and subterfuges presented dramatically on the Elizabethan and Jacobean stage. The theme of desperate lovers circumventing family restrictions was enacted in real life as well as in the commercial theatre. Late one night at Thornhill, Yorkshire, in 1624, for example, Ann Cookson, a gentleman's daughter, was married to Thomas Edmunds 'betwixt the hours of eleven and twelve or thereabouts in an inner court within the house of Lady Anne Saville, widow . . . there being no candle or light that [the minister] could see to read'. The couple had no parental consent, no banns or licence, and no witnesses to the ceremony, but apart from these deficiences they claimed that their marriage was conducted 'according to the words of the Book of Common Prayer'.[27] Despite being highly irregular and clandestine, it was not easy to rule that the marriage was invalid. Reform of the licensing system would not help in cases like this where the parties were driven by their passions.

Gentle and aristocratic correspondence also sheds light on the practice of clandestine marriage. Richard Rugely, a nephew of Baron Lumley, created problems for several branches of his family when he and his bride married secretly in 1589. Lord Lumley reported to Richard Bagot, Rugely's godfather, 'the young couple have with more speed than was meet coupled themselves together in marriage without the consent and privity of their parents, to the utter subversion and undoing of the young couple'. Faced with a *fait accompli*, the elders would have to retrieve the situation and put together a package of jointures and sureties that should have been settled before the couple slipped off to church.[28]

A generation later in 1622 Walter Bagot could not believe that his ward, Humphrey Okeover, had married the daughter of Sir Oliver Cheney with neither consent nor due ceremony. Bagot wanted to keep the young man in his custody, and had hoped to match him with his own daughter, but Okeover, 'after some speeches betwixt me and Sir Oliver, told us that he thought neither of us could in right keep or detain him, for that he was married, and that to Sir Oliver's daughter. Sir Oliver protested he was ignorant in the matter, which I believe.' Even when a friend of Okeover's confirmed that this marriage had taken place, and 'named the place and persons present', the elders remained unconvinced. Only after diligent enquiry 'whether the young gent or Sir Oliver's daughter were from home in the forenoon any day' and learning that 'they were married at a church . . . at nine or ten of the clock, which could hardly be done without notice taken', did Bagot accept that his ward was irrevocably married. Begrudgingly he concluded, 'if it were done I think it was concealed'.[29]

Unbeneficed priests were more likely than incumbent rectors or vicars to risk performing marriages at irregular times or in clandestine circumstances or in blatant disregard of parental consent. Some made quite a trade of it, risking ecclesiastical censure while lining their purses. Private fees for clandestine weddings ranged from 5s. to 15s., several times the normal ecclesiastical charges. Anthony Benet, a minister who 'had not the cure of souls', charged 6s. 8d. for marrying Daniel Hallam and Agnes Ashforth in Skegby church, Nottinghamshire, during the second week of Lent, 1595. John Smalley of Ragdale, Leicestershire, paid 11s. for a questionable licence, that the parish clerk obtained with neither oath nor bond, for his hurried wedding in 1634.[30]

So-called 'lawless' churches specialized in clandestine weddings. As soon as one was suppressed, it seems, another would take its place to accommodate the continuing need for secrecy and speed. Couples would find their way to such churches, and make private arrangements to be married. The archdeacon of Northamptonshire asserted his authority against 'lawless' churches in the late 1580s. The bishop of Lincoln cracked down on the practice at Risby, Lincolnshire, where until 1603 scores of marriages were conducted without banns or licence 'at unlawful and inconvenient times'. Until disciplined by the bishop of Oxford in 1607, Oliver Edwards, the curate at Brackley, Northamptonshire, ran another 'lawless' church, conducting irregular weddings 'in the night or about two of the clock in the morning' or 'upon the Sunday before Whit Sunday in the morning between three and four of the clock . . . without any banns or licence'.[31]

Ecclesiastical officials noted Kinoulton, Nottinghamshire, as a popular venue for clandestine marriages in the 1620s and Keam chapel, Leicestershire, as 'a lawless place where they used to have clandestine marriages' in the 1630s. Robert Ward of Huddersfield, Yorkshire, was suspended for three years in 1631 for solemnizing 'divers clandestine and unlawful marriages between divers persons, being none of his parishioners, nor having any licence withal before obtained, contrary to the law and canons of the church of England'. A few years later the court disciplined 'George Buck, an old man who maketh many clandestine marriages' in Yorkshire.[32] Leading churchmen of the reign of Charles I were especially hostile to clandestine marriages that undermined ceremonial reverence and disparaged ecclesiastical authority, but they were no more effective than their Elizabethan and Jacobean predecessors in preventing them.

Chadshunt, Warwickshire, was another 'lawless' church of the 1630s where William Baker, the curate, was notorious for his quick and easy weddings. Walter Fifield, an Oxfordshire man, confessed in 1633 that

he was married to Anne Gifford his now wife upon the first day of March last was twelvemonths [during Lent] at the church of Chadshunt, Warwickshire, by William Baker the curate of that church without any licence that he knoweth of, other than that the said Mr. Baker did tell him that he had sufficient authority to marry them; and [Fifield] understanding by common report that he did usually marry such as came to him to that purpose went thither to be married.

Fifield paid Baker the exhorbitant sum of 13s. for his services. The offending minister lay outside the bishop of Oxford's jurisdiction and so could not be prosecuted, but the court ordered Fifield and his wife to perform public penance in their home parish of Cropredy.[33]

The same authorities were reluctant to accept that Isabel Humphreys, a young woman of Oxford, was truly married to Elias Birch, a recent graduate of Exeter College. Isabel, the court charged, was 'begotten with child unlawfully, viz. out of wedlock', but she protested that she and her husband were married in Buddlesdon chapel in Buckinghamshire 'by one Mr. Thomas Taylor minister there' on 29 April 1633, 'the said chapel being a lawless church'. The marriage, Isabel said, took place with neither banns or licence, but otherwise followed proper form and was attended by her mother and other witnesses. Normally such testimony would demonstrate that there really had been a wedding, and would remove the charge of bastard-bearing. But in this case the court did not credit Isabel as being Elias's wife or *uxor*. Although details are missing it seems likely that the guardians of the 20-year-old Elias Birch were trying to extract him from an unsuitable match, that he had already departed home to Shropshire where his father was a priest, and that the Oxford diocesan authorities, many of them themselves associated with Oxford colleges, chose to side with one of their own.[34]

People flocked to churches or chapels in peculiar or exempt jurisdictions where they knew they could obtain a speedy solemnization of matrimony with few questions asked. The precincts of the Tower of London was one such place that long resisted the disciplinary efforts of the Church of England. In 1630 diocesan authorities cited John and Martha Tinsley of Whitechapel 'for being married in the Tower of London clandestinely, without lawful licence or banns of matrimony first published'. The minister, Richard Allen, and several of the wedding guests were also cited. But their punishment was little more than a caution. In the same year the London consistory court cited Humphrey Bailey and Susan his wife of St Giles in the Fields, 'for being married clandestinely in the Tower of London'. Susan testified that they, 'not knowing of any danger that would befall them, did, by persuasion of a friend, procure themselves to be married in the Tower of London', and conceded that the marriage was performed 'without either banns first published or any licence obtained'.[35] Archbishop Laud attempted to suppress the trade in clandestine weddings at the Tower, only to see the market boom in other exempt jurisdictions.

'Fleet' marriages, performed within the 'rules' or precincts of the old Fleet prison in London, were also notoriously flexible, disorderly, and clandestine.[36] Simon Johnson, a young scissor-maker of St Martins in the Fields, Middlesex, and Mary Elliot, his sweetheart of Walthamstow, Essex, resorted to a Fleet wedding in 1632 after their request for a licence was rejected for lack of the bride's father's consent. Under subsequent examination, Simon said that they

went to the Fleet to one that was minister in the Fleet, and desired him to marry them; who demanded of [him] their licence; to which he replied he could get none, nor had any. But notwithstanding, the said minister took [him] and the said Mary into a [illegible] room of the said Fleet, and there married them according to the Book of Common Prayer and the orders and ceremonies of the Church of England in the presence of two strangers which the minister brought in and none other.

Mary's testimony was much the same, but took pains to emphasize that the ceremony was performed 'with a ring as is prescribed by the Church of England'.[37] Though willing to do penance for a clandestine marriage, she was careful to dissociate herself from any hint of sexual impropriety or religious nonconformity.

Participants in clandestine marriages sometimes offered elaborate explanations to excuse their actions. The vicar of Spelsbury, Oxfordshire, admitted to marrying Richard Fletcher and Dorothy Hanwell without banns or licence in 1593, but he said that 'he did it at the earnest suit of them and some friends, not knowing the danger of the law'. Richard Smith, the curate of Selby, Yorkshire, who married the under-age heiress Anne Metham to Robert Marshe in 1624 in highly irregular circumstances, argued before the High Commission that since Selby was a peculiar (an exempt juridisdiction) he was entitled to marry anyone. Unfortunately he could not recall the names of the ecclesiastical officials who had given him this information, which proved to be erroneous. The court, for its part, insisted that the curate had done wrong, 'to the grief of the parents of the said Anne, the contempt of the laws in that case provided, and the scandal of the godly and the evil example of others'. Smith's testimony sheds remarkable light on the process by which clandestine marriages might be accomplished. He told the court that the runaway couple arrived in Selby early in the afternoon on 14 February. This, as everybody knew, was St Valentine's day, an appropriately romantic occasion for an elopement. At first, when their messengers entreated him to come to their inn, Smith affected to be sick; 'yet afterwards, being much importuned to go thither', he agreed to join the young lovers for supper. Over the meal they discussed various aspects of their intended marriage, including the generous offer of 12s. 4d. to the curate as a fee for performing the ceremony. Smith told the court that a servant informed him that the girl's father gave his consent and 'was well pleased to that match', and therefore he saw no objection to marrying them the next morning in Selby church in the presence of various witnesses.[38]

Simply being present at a clandestine marriage could get one into trouble, though in practice the courts rarely proceded harshly against mere witnesses. Elizabeth Peryn of Walthamstow, Essex, who was cited in October 1622 'for being present at the solemnization of a clandestine marriage between Thomas Reading and Annie Robinson', attempted to distance herself from the offence. She explained,

that about six weeks since, in an evening, she . . . seeing torch light in the church at Walthamstow, went in there to see what was there doing, and being there she saw and heard one Thomas Reading and Anne Robinson married together . . . by Mr. Leonard Taylor, curate of that church, and they were there married together without any banns asked or licence obtained.

The wedding took place outside the approved hours, without the required publicity or permission, but it was otherwise properly conducted by the local minister using the Book of Common Prayer. A London couple accused of 'being present at a clandestine marriage' of a mariner in 1630 answered that they did not know it was clandestine, for they believed the banns had been published.[39]

Even respectable clergymen could offend in this regard, sometimes stretching the credulity of the courts. When Richard Wright, the minister of Wargrave, Berkshire, married a fellow minister, the vicar of Shiplake, in 1634, he told the Oxford archdeaconry court, 'he then did think that Mr. Haddon had obtained a licence for the celebrating of the said marriage, but now believeth that he had no licence'. The timing and circumstances of the ceremony gave further indication that this was a clandestine marriage, for it took place between five and six o'clock on a Monday morning, with none but the couple, the minister, and the parish clerk in attendance. The parish clerk acknowledged to the court that they had neither banns nor licence.[40]

'Living Together as Man and Wife'

If a couple could not demonstrate that they had been lawfully married, how were their neighbours to know whether they lawfully cohabited, or whether they dwelt in fornication? Without a witnessed record of the solemnization of matrimony, who could adjudge rights of inheritance or the legitimacy of offspring, and who could tell good housekeeping from sin? Parties to clandestine marriages put themselves and their families at risk, but lawfully married couples might also arouse suspicion if they moved to a parish where their history was not known. Migrant couples, newly arrived from some distance, might readily be accepted as man and wife, but rumour or misbehaviour could call their status into question.

In the course of its campaign to bring marriage firmly under ecclesiastical control, the Elizabethan church frequently investigated claims like those brought before the dean of York in 1570 that 'William Butler alias Fisher and Margaret Cook liveth together as man and wife offensively and not married.'[41] The offence, of course, was against ecclesiastical propriety, social order, and domestic decorum. In addition to enjoining penance, the courts would either separate the couple who were living in sin or force them to solemnize their marriage. The publicity and punishment were designed to deter other couples from cohabiting without marriage. In 1575 the churchwardens of Giggleswick, Yorkshire, informed the bishop that 'Hugh Clapham and Ellen his wife do keep house together, and it is not known whether they be married or not.' In this case the couple responded that they were, indeed, married, though clandestinely, and the banns had not been asked. John Wilson and Janet Clough of Halifax, Yorkshire, were similarly cited in 1598 'for keeping house together as man and wife, and hath had a child together, their marriage unknown'.[42] Early Stuart courts continued to cite offenders 'for living together as man and wife, it is not known whether they be married or no'.[43]

Few couples could escape this scrutiny as long as the courts maintained their vigilance and their neighbours were willing to complain.

Once the seed of suspicion was planted it fell to those accused to demonstrate the legality of their union. Couples who considered themselves married in the eyes of God, because of their own private contract, were hard-pressed to prove it to a sceptical court or congregation. Participants in clandestine marriages were especially vulnerable, but even those who had gone through lawful public ceremonies might have difficulty documenting their wedding if they were strangers to a district. Reference to parish registers provided the surest way to prove that a marriage had been performed, but certification of this information required a combination of good record-keeping, document retrieval, co-operation, literacy, and luck. The process of verification and documentation generated hundreds of certificates, based on register entries, stating the names of the parties and the officiating minister, the place and date of their wedding, whether it was performed by banns or licence, and sometimes the names of witnesses.

Phillip Curtis of Henley assured the Oxford archdeaconry court in 1584 that he had been married in London the previous year, 'and promiseth he will bring a sufficient certificate of the said marriage . . . at the next visitation'. A document of this sort, signed by the pastor of Morborne, Huntingdonshire, and certifying that Joan Lightfoot 'was married by licence at Yarwell, Northamptonshire, last November according to law', satisfied a court in the Diocese of Lincoln in 1593. Similar proof came more than 200 miles from Surrey to Yorkshire in 1615 when the minister and chuchwardens of St Saviour's, Southwark, certified in writing 'that having duly searched the register book of our aforesaid parish church, we do evidently find therein that John Robinson and Christine Miles were married together' on 8 September 1610.[44] Any doubt whether John and Christine were husband and wife could safely be put to rest.

In 1620, after several years of harbouring suspicions, the churchwardens of St Giles in the Fields, Middlesex, presented that William Temperson and Elizabeth Martin did 'live incontinently together . . . as they were man and wife these five years, and that it is thought that they were never married'. It is not known what mischance brought the couple to the attention of the authorities, but William defended himself with vigour, saying, 'that he and the said Elizabeth Martin have lived together in St. Giles parish these five years, and before that at Marlborough in Wiltshire ten years and more, and have all this while lived together as lawful man and wife, and were and are commonly accounted, reputed and taken for lawful man and wife'. At first sight this appears to be a description and justification of a common-law marriage. But William went on to assert that his was no mere consensual union. He and Elizabeth had been truly married in church as well as in public estimation, although there was some doubt about the documentation.

He further sayeth that above fifteen years since banns of matrimony were published between them in Marlborough church aforesaid three several times . . . but he sayeth they were married together in Prescot church which is a quarter of a mile off Marlborough. And he sent thither for a certificate of his marriage, and had answer that the church book was by a mischance burnt, and by reason thereof he could not have any certificate of his marriage.

In support of this claim William produced a witness, his brother, John Temperson, 'who, as he sayeth, was present at his marriage and knoweth the premisses to be true'. At length the court was satisfied, and William and his wife were dismissed.[45]

Couples who had gone through clandestine weddings in the house of 'one Jarvis Neville, a minister who dwelleth and keepeth a school in Holborn,' London, in the early 1630s, could not clearly demonstrate that they were married, and could not therefore attest to the legitimacy of their children. Stephen Potter and Anne Moore of Wapping, Middlesex, thought that they were married at Neville's hands, but the wardens of their parish reportedly made 'diligent search and find no such matter'. Similarly challenged in 1639 to prove that they were legally married, Henry and Sara Norton who lived together as man and wife in the teeming warrens of Stepney, Middlesex, alleged 'that they were married together about eight years since in Yorkshire, and humbly desireth a convenient time to prove the same by a certificate out of the church book'.[46]Once again, the outcome of the case, the respectability of the couple, and the inheritance rights of their children turned on 'diligent search' in distant parish documents.

Unaccompanied women, whether spinsters, wives, or widows, attracted deep suspicion if they were pregnant or brought to bed in childbirth while travelling away from home. As we have seen in our discussion of childbirth, such women might well be treated as harlots and their babies as bastards if they could not satify the authorities that they were married. Once again, documentation made all the difference. A lone woman who gave birth in a victualling house in St Sepulchre's, London, in 1620 was able to satisfy the court of her married status by obtaining a written certificate that she 'was married to one James Lingard in the parish church of St. Mary Islington by Mr. John Shrigley, curate there'. Not so fortunate was the woman brought to bed in the house of Nicholas Matthews of St Botolph, Aldgate, in 1627, who 'having no certificate of her marriage', fled unchurched and unpunished after her baby was born.[47] A Worcestershire woman, Abigail Johnson, was ordered to bring proof of her marriage after being 'delivered of a child incontinently begotten' in 1637. In this case she was able to show that she had been married to one William Coldicott of Shipston, by licence from the bishop of Worcester, some three or four weeks before the baby was born. Exonerated of the crime of bearing a bastard, she still had to perform penance for her admitted premarital fornication.[48]

After the Restoration

The problem of clandestine marriage became more acute in the later decades of the seventeenth century. Banns or licences were required again after 1660, as the legal, liturgical, and administrative apparatus of the Church of England was cranked back into life. But the interruptions and confusions of the revolutionary era had so weakened the authority of the Church of England that dissenters and others questioned the necessity of matrimony at the hands of an Anglican priest. The church courts had no effective sanction against nonconformists like John and Elizabeth Chapman of Edmonton, Middlesex, who were cited in 1669 'for being married without banns or licence'. Post-Restoration sectaries, according to their enemies, 'despise[d] the solemnity and rites of marriage, relying upon each other's bare words and godly meanings'.[49] Quakers in particular reverted to the medieval practice of unsolemnized matrimony by common consent. William Banbury and Elizabeth Hensam, for example, were cited in the Diocese of Worcester in 1682 'for cohabiting together, being suspected of incontinency, it being reported that they were married according to the Quaker usage at the house of Thomas Cooke, where they had a supper and invited sixty people of their own opinion'.[50]

At the same time the middling and upper classes were placing a higher value on privacy, and sought to separate their ritual practices from those of the common people. Religious conformists among the élite, as well as those who leaned towards nonconformity or catholicism, increasingly chose to be married privately by licence, or, if necessary, clandestinely. Samuel Jeake's marriage in 1681, like William Westmacott's the previous year, may have been typical in being performed quietly, by licence, on a weekday morning, with just two guests and the minister and sexton in attendance. Jeakes notes in his diary, 'we going through in the day time, yet so much incognito, that there was no concourse or notice taken either of our going or coming'.[51] By 1690, the French visitor Henri Misson observed, 'persons of quality, and many others who imitate them, have lately taken up the custom of being married very late at night in their chamber, and very often at some country house'. Public weddings, he believed, had become a rarity, for 'the ordinary ones . . . are generally incognito'. One effect of this trend, according to Misson, was uncertainty about who was really married. 'People are amazed to see women brought to bed of legitimate children, without having heard a word of the father.'[52]

The restored Church of England did its best to safeguard matrimonial discipline, but the effect was uneven. Irregular weddings in alehouses and private houses became increasingly common, as did clandestine weddings conducted in out-of-the-way churches. When asked by the diocesan court at Oxford in 1662 whether or not he was married, Giles Titmarsh of Chipping Norton answered, 'yea'. But 'being interrogated in what church he was married, he answered, in God's church', and refused all further information.[53] Such an answer would have been unacceptable a quarter of a century earlier.

After John and Mary Cornelius of Sandford, Oxfordshire, were married in January 1662 'without licence procured or banns published', they were cited before the diocesan court. Cornelius apologized, saying

he was then misled thereto by the example of others and the common error of that time. But as far as this his fact is against the ecclesiastical law and rule of church government, he is sorry therefore and submitteth himself. Whereupon the [judge] pronounced that he had made a clandestine marriage, and therefore according to the penalty of the common law, he and his said wife were both *ipso facto* excommunicated. But looking upon the ingenuity of his confession, he did suspend the denouncing of the same, but monished him to prove his said marriage by the fourth day of October next.

The marriage, Cornelius said, had been performed in St Bartholemew's hospital, London, 'by Mr. Hill, Dr. Smith's curate of Hambledon' and it would not be too difficult to obtain a certificate to that effect.[54]

It became something of a standard excuse in the post-Restoration period for the parties to a clandestine marriage to say that they 'hoped that they had not thereby broken or transgressed any law'. Francis Higgins of Burford told the court that his marriage in 1662, without banns or licence, 'was ignorantly done by him and he was misled by the common practice of these late licentious times'. Robert and Elizabeth Butcher similarly apologized after marrying clandestinely at Leafield, Oxfordshire, in the summer of 1665. Their minister, Daniel Cowley of Astall, had assured them 'that the said marriage was lawfully performed'. Cowley allegedly told Butcher 'that so as he would give him ten shillings, which, as he said, was the fee of a licence, he would secure him against any trouble that might accrue to him thereby'. Trouble enough followed, however, for the authorities first doubted whether Butcher was lawfully married, and then prosecuted him for his clandestine wedding. More than twenty people were present at the solemnization, but because it lacked banns or licence it violated ecclesiastical law.[55]

Charged with making a clandestine marriage in 1665, William Walker of Oxford protested that his wedding to Mary Edwards had been solemnized by Mr Daniel Whitby of Trinity College in the nearby church of Binsey; 'supposing it to be a privileged place, and that it might be done lawfully there without either banns or licence; alleging that the said Mr. Whitby had made diligent enquiry before the solemnization of the said marriage whether he might lawfully do it there or not, and was fully satisfied that he could'. In this case the court dismissed him with a censure.[56]

Testimony about another clandestine marriage in Oxfordshire in 1668 provides unusual information about its conduct, but also reveals some of the uncertainties that could ensue. William Goldley of Sarsden told the Oxford diocesan court that 'about a fortnight since Michaelmas last past upon a Sunday after the ending of evening service', he saw Thomas Hicks and Anne Watts enter the church, followed by

a certain person who had the Book of Common Prayer in his hand, and as soon as they were entered into the chancel he saw Thomas Hicks and Anne Watts holding each the other by the hand; the said person read in the said common prayer book the usual words of marriage in the form set down and expressed in the said book; and the said Thomas and Anne making some answer, but what the very words were he remembereth not; nor doth he know whether or no the said person that read the said words of marriage . . . were a minister in holy orders, or whether he had any licence so to do, or what his name is.[57]

Citations for clandestine marriage appear commonly in diocesan court books throughout the reign of Charles II, but attempts at enforcement had only modest effect. Episcopal visitors insisted that 'marriages [be] legally and decently solemnized' but their efforts were undermined by the twin scourges of scrupulous dissent and disorderly disrespect. Officials in the Diocese of York made fitful attempts to police matrimony, citing couples like John and Mary Thompson of Ledsham 'for living together as man and wife without evidence of lawful marriage', and Matthew Morley and Susan Bell of Sowerby 'for not giving an account of their marriage and for refusing to show a certificate by whom, when or where they were married'.[58] Not surprisingly, historical demographers find rates of defective marriage registration in the Restoration period more than twice as high as under the early Stuarts. The problem would worsen before it was addressed by Lord Hardwicke's marriage act of 1753.[59]

One final example deserves mention for its entanglement of social, domestic, legal, and religious issues. John Wren, a servant to the bishop of Durham, was married to Margaret Morpeth in 1671 before witnesses, 'in a private house in Newcastle upon Tyne about eight of the clock in the night, by a certain person who were in canonical apparel, according to the form and ceremony prescribed in the book of common prayer'. This clandestine marriage would have been unexceptional if Wren had not previously been married to Margaret's mother, also named Margaret Morpeth, thereby drawing down a charge of incest. Wren insisted that he and the late Margaret, senior, had never been married, and therefore he was free to marry Margaret's daughter. But witnesses testified to Wren's husbandly expression of grief at the elder Margaret's death, his donning of mourning garb that proclaimed a spousal relationship, and his claiming of the deceased's goods and chattels and discharging of her debts. One witness told the court that Wren had remarked 'that he had lost the best wife and the best bedfellow that ever man had'. Several witnesses recalled the ceremony in Thomas Masham's house in Durham in 1670 when Wren and Margaret senior were married 'in the great dining room' by a popish priest 'according to the rites and ceremonies used in the church of Rome'. But the deceased Margaret's sister, aunt to the new and perhaps incestuous bride, testified that this popish ceremony was only for a contract, not a wedding.[60]

NUPTIAL VOWS

The Solemnization of Matrimony

Whether public or private, grand or quiet, most early modern weddings followed the set form of service laid out in the Book of Common Prayer. Even clandestine weddings adhered as close as possible to the words in the book. This chapter examines the order for the solemnization of matrimony, paying particular attention to those elements that remained controversial under Queen Elizabeth and the early Stuarts.

Pre-Reformation weddings customarily began at the church porch, on the threshold of God's building, rather than at the altar, in the centre of the sacred space.[1] This was the point of entry where the sacred and secular domains intersected, an especially appropriate place to inaugurate the spiritual and social conditions of holy matrimony. Of his worthy wife of Bath, Chaucer noted, 'husbands at the church door she had five'. But high social rank could override this convention. According to an early Tudor etiquette book, an earl's son or daughter could be married inside the church at the choir door, just below the chancel; a knight's wedding might take place 'within the church or chapel door'; but those 'of a lower degree' like the wife of Bath were 'to be married without the church door', though perhaps under the shelter of the porch.[2] A version of this custom prevailed in seventeenth-century France, where the proxy marriage between Charles I and Henrietta Maria in 1625 took place at the door of Notre Dame, not within its aisles or chapels. Protestant England, by contrast, placed marriage indoors at the devotional centre of the church. However, the custom of paying a bride's dower at the church porch on the day of her wedding is said to have continued well into the seventeenth century, even though the actual marriage took place inside.[3]

The early Tudor wedding ceremony, which was substantially modified by the Reformation, can be reconstructed from late medieval missals. According to the Sarum Missal, widely used in southern England, the service began 'before the door of the church, or in the face of the church, in the presence of God, and the priest, and the people. The man should stand on the right hand of the woman, and the woman on the left hand of the man, the reason being that she was formed out of the rib in the left side of Adam.'[4] The priest then recited the banns, asking three times if there were any impediment to the intended marriage. This was the last public opportunity for anyone to object on the grounds of pre-contract, consanguinity, or affinity, or to prevent the marriage of minors who lacked parental consent. At this point the priest could ask about the woman's dower, which might then be publicly displayed and exchanged.

Addressing the man and the woman, the priest asked each if they were willing to proceed with the ceremony, to which the expected answer was, 'I will'. The woman was 'given' in marriage by her father or by an adult male friend, in a silent but potent symbolic transfer of authority. With the priest as mediator, and family members and friends as witnesses, the couple took careful hold of each other by the hand in a recapitulation of the ceremony of betrothal. This was no mere casual touching, talking, or gesturing, but rather a solemn scripted ritual freighted with protocols and promises. The directions of the Sarum Missal are remarkably specific about how the parties were to conduct themselves. 'If she be a maid, let her have her hand uncovered; if she be a widow, covered; and let the man . . . hold her by the right hand in his right hand.' Properly positioned with hands appropriately clasped, the man should say to the woman, 'I, N. take thee N. to my wedded wife, to have and to hold from this day forth, for better for worse, for richer for poorer, in sickness and in health, till death us depart, if holy church will it ordain, and thereto I plight thee my troth.' The man then withdrew his hand, and the woman took it again while she made her somewhat more expansive recitation of the marriage vows. 'I, N. take thee N. to my wedded husband, to have and to hold from this day forth, for richer for poorer, in sickness and in health, to be bonair and buxom [i.e. courteous and kind], in bed and at board, till death us depart, if holy church will it ordain, and thereto I plight thee my troth.'[5]

Then came the business with the ring, that later protestant reformers found so offensive. The man was supposed to lay the ring, along with a monetary offering, upon a dish or book, and the priest was supposed to bless it, 'that she who shall wear it may be armed with the strength of heavenly defence, and that it may be profitable unto her eterrnal salvation'. Blessed by the priest and sprinkled with holy water, the ring then passed from the bridegroom to his bride. The liturgical directions for handling the ring are again remarkably precise.

The man shall take it in his right hand with his three principal fingers, holding the right hand of the bride with his left hand, and shall say after the priest, 'With this ring I thee wed and this gold and silver I thee give; and with my body I thee worship, and with all my worldly cattle I thee honour.' Then shall the bridegroom place the ring upon the thumb of the bride, saying, *in the name of the Father*; then upon the second finger, saying, *and of the Son*; then upon the third finger, saying, *and of the Holy Ghost*; then upon the fourth finger, saying, *Amen*, and there let him leave it . . . because in that finger there is a certain vein, which runs from thence as far as the heart.

Thus the first stage of the wedding ceremony was accomplished, with all the theatricality of performers, action, script, and props.[6]

At this point the wedding party could move inside, from the threshold of the church as far as the step before the altar, for a nuptial mass and blessing. Prayers and benedictions reminded everyone that matrimony was a sacrament of the church. In traditional Catholic practice, 'when there was a marriage before mass, the parties kneeled together, and had a fine linen cloth, called the care cloth, laid over their heads during the time of mass, till they received the benediction and then were dismissed'.[7] Folklorists have conjectured that the bridal canopy or pall was originally intended to deceive demons and to protect the couple from the evil eye at this particularly vulnerable moment. But its practical purpose, like the aristocratic canopy or cloth of estate, was to ensure that the central participants remained the visual focus of attention.[8] Finally, with all prayers done, 'the bridegroom shall receive the pax from the priest and convey it to the bride, kissing her'. And, in the interest of probity and decorum, the instructions continued, 'neither the bridegroom nor the bride are to kiss anyone else'.[9]

The protestant Church of England drew on these ceremonies of late medieval catholicism to produce a reformed and standard procedure for the solemnization of holy matrimony. As they did with the other life-cycle offices of baptism, churching, and burial, the Edwardian and Elizabethan prayer books followed the old form of service while introducing major modifications. Although puritan critics might disagree, mainstream observers could concur with William Vaughan, who wrote of matrimony in Elizabethan England, 'superstitious ceremonies there are none'.[10]

For a start, the wedding group brushed straight through the church porch to come 'into the body of the church with their friends and neighbours'. The ceremony was to be performed in public, in the heart of the parish church. Prefaced by a homily on the 'honourable estate' of matrimony and a review of the godly purposes for which marriage was ordained, the service was designed for the benefit of auditors and witnesses as well as for the couple about to be joined. The service was supposed to be performed in the face of the full congregation, and to be integrated into the routines of parochial worship. There was no instruction how the parties should position themselves by reference to the rib of Adam, though by custom the man continued to stand on the right.[11]

The minister then asked, 'if any man can show just cause, why they may not lawfully be joined together, let him now speak, or else hereafter for ever hold his peace'. Bride and groom too were charged to disclose any impediments to the solemnization that was about to take place. This was a dramatic moment, that was normally followed by a thankful silence. Hearing no objection, the minister proceeded to ask the couple whether each would take the other as man and wife, 'forsaking all other . . . as long as you both shall live'. Each would answer, 'I will', in a public expression of consent. The minister's next question, 'who giveth this woman to be married unto this man?' required no verbal response, but in dumbshow 'the minister receiving the woman at her father or friend's hands, shall cause the man to take the woman by the right hand, and so either to give their troth to other'. There followed a recitation of vows, a joining and loosing of hands, the giving of a ring, a further joining of hands, and the recitation of prayers and blessings, before the couple could leave the church as husband and wife. The entire ceremony would take from ten to twenty minutes, unless followed by a sermon or communion.[12]

Giving the Bride

The ritual 'giving' of the bride was, and still is, one of the more controversial aspects of the wedding ceremony. Feminists have criticized it as a symbolic treatment of woman as chattel, being passed like property from father to husband. The bride, in this reading, is passive and dependent; she is acted upon, and is literally handed over from her natal to her conjugal family, from one patriarchal domain to another. The rubric makes clear, however, that, when the bride is 'given', she is given to be married; she is given to God; she is handed from her father (or his representative) not directly to her husband but to God, through his minister, the priest. The priest makes no further bestowal, though the woman's final conveyance to her husband may be readily construed.[13] For a father or guardian to 'give' the bride was also a tacit and public demonstration of his consent for her to be married. It signalled permission rather than possession.

The late Elizabethan apologist for the Church of England Richard Hooker approved 'the delivering up of the woman, either by her father or some other', as an ancient custom with a strongly gendered message. 'It putteth women in mind of a duty whereunto the very imbecility of their nature and sex doth bind them, namely, to be always directed, guided and ordered by others.' The moderate puritan minister Richard Greenham similarly approved of the father's giving of the bride. It was, he thought, 'a laudable custom in the church and a tolerable ceremony . . . both to show his authority over her and to witness his consent in bestowing her'. The Jacobean minister Roger Hacket advised the bride, at the point in the service when 'it shall be asked, who gives this maiden unto wife, cause not thy aged father to withhold his hand, but cause him rather to step forth with joy, and before God and his church, to perform for thee that blessed work'. The Restoration churchman Anthony Sparrow reiterated Hooker's remarks, adding, 'it is a decent custom. For it cannot be thought fit, that a woman whose chiefest ornament is modesty and shamefastness, should offer herself before the congregation to marriage to any person, but should rather be led by the hand of another, and given by him.'[14] Nothing in the record indicates that women felt abused by this rubric, but the very fact that Anglican apologists thought it necessary to justify it suggests that they faced an undocumented groundswell of objection.

The next stage of the ceremony was the handfasting, the taking and loosening of hands and the plighting of troths. This was word-for-word the same as the old Catholic ceremony except that the marriage was sealed 'according to God's holy ordinance' instead of 'if holy church will it ordain', and the woman no longer promised to be 'bonair and buxom in bed and at board'. The man said aloud, 'I, N. take thee N. to my wedded wife, to have and to hold from this day forward, for better, for worse, for richer, for poorer, in sickness and in health, to love and to cherish, till death us depart.' The woman said much the same, adding the significant promise 'to obey'.[15]

A simplified ring ceremony followed, in which 'the man shall give unto the woman a ring, laying the same upon the book with the accustomed duty to the priest and clerk. And the priest taking the ring, shall deliver it unto the man, to put it upon the fourth finger of the woman's left hand.' There was to be no blessing or sprinkling of the ring, no ritual placing of it on successive fingers, just a simple promise of the man to the woman: 'With this ring I thee wed; with my body I thee worship; and with all my worldly goods I thee endow.'[16] The majority of English protestants grew to appreciate this ceremony, but, as we shall see, a principled minority viewed the retention of the ring in marriage as an intolerable remnant of popery. Some puritans also claimed that the husband's promise to 'worship' his wife with his body was akin to superstitious pagan idolatry.[17]

The complete solemnization of matrimony involved a composite series of actions and utterances whereby the couple proceeded to their new and irrevocable condition; there was no single phrase or act that marked or secured their transition. Strictly speaking, the couple married themselves, or secured their marriage before God and the congregation, by performing the critical words and gestures: the minister's task was simply to preside and to pray, and to conduct the ceremony according to the Book of Common Prayer. To the common observer, however, it might appear that the couple was married by priestly action. The effective part of the ritual was complete when the minister made his forbidding injunction, 'those whom God hath joined together, let no man put asunder'.[18]

The minister's next task was to proclaim the marriage to the people.

Forasmuch as N. and N. have consented together in holy wedlock, and have witnessed the same before God and this company, and have therefore given and pledged their troth either to other, and have declared the same by the giving and receiving of a ring, and by joining of hands: I pronounce that they be man and wife together.

Active verbs advanced the ritual, whereby the couple had 'consented' and 'witnessed', 'given and pledged' and 'declared' by their actions and speech. Finally came blessings and prayers, and psalms of rejoicing. The service was supposed to conclude with communion and a sermon, but in practice these were often omitted. There was no official kissing in church, as there had been under the Sarum Missal, but customs of this sort were hard to obliterate as the ceremony moved quickly from religious to secular celebration.[19]

Most English protestants accepted this service, and many came to cherish its simplicity and beauty. Even mainstream puritans found it decent and acceptable, setting aside their misgivings about the ring. William Gouge, the puritan rector of St Ann's, Blackfriars, London, read the marriage service hundreds of times a year under James I and Charles I, as did most of his clerical associates and colleagues. Commenting on 'the form of consecrating marriage, which is prescribed in our liturgy or common prayer book', Gouge remarked that it

doth so distinctly, perspicuously and fully set down whatsoever is to be observed and done by the parties to be married, their parents, or other governors, and the minister that joineth them together, that I can add nothing thereunto. There are declared the grounds, ends, and uses of marriage. There open proclamation is made whether any can except against the intended marriage. There each party is solemnly charged, that if either of them do know any impediment, why they may not lawfully be married, to disclose it. There also each party is openly demanded if freely and willingly they will take one another for man and wife. There the duties of married persons are declared, and they severally asked whether they will subject themselves thereto or no. All which being openly professed, the parent or some in his stead is called forth to give the bride to the bridegroom. Then they two actually taking each other to be man and wife, and testifying the same by express words, and by mutual pledges, the minister in God's name joineth them together, pronounceth them to be lawful husband and wife, and by prayer craveth God's blessing upon the action, and upon their persons. Thus is the marriage consecrated, and they two made one flesh, that is, lawfully joined together by the inviolable bond of marriage.[20]

Gouge set forth a puritan conformist view of marriage with enough subtlety to gloss the ceremony as a public witnessing rather than a sacramental action.

The Ring in Marriage

In early modern England, as today, it was customary to place the wedding ring on the fourth finger of the bride's left hand. The Book of Common Prayer included no particular directions in that regard, but folk practice preserved and justified the traditional placement on the woman's ring finger. The old Latin missals had explained that 'a certain vein . . . runs from thence as far as the heart', and even in the seventeenth century popular opinion still held that 'that a particular vessel, nerve, vein or artery' connected the woman's ring finger to her heart. Simple anatomy would prove this wrong, but the whimsical notion persisted. Citing a more practical reason, the scholar-physician Thomas Browne observed that the left hand was less actively employed than the right, and therefore a ring in that position was less likely to incur or receive damage.[21]

Apologists for the ring went to some lengths to explain the antiquity, the propriety, and the symbolic benefits of its use in marriage. The view espoused in the fifteenth-century religious manual *Dives and Pauper*, that 'the ring is round about and hath no end, in token that their love should be endless, and nothing depart them but death alone', found many echoes within the reformed Church of England. Richard Hooker endorsed the use of the ring on these grounds, as 'an especial pledge of faith and fidelity, nothing more fit to serve as a token of our purposed endless continuance in that which we never ought to revoke'. It signified 'the perfect unity and indissoluable conjunction' of the married couple, 'that their mutual love and hearty affection should roundly flow from one to the other', wrote the ecclesiastical lawyer Henry Swinburne, though he could not explain why only the women wore one.[22]

The puritan Daniel Rogers, who may have been uneasy about the ritual exchange of the ring in marriage, none the less used the image of 'the marriage ring . . . beset with may rich jewels' to teach the virtues of honourable marriage: the jewels in the ring signified 'humility . . . peace . . . purity . . . [and] righteousness'. Another seventeenth-century writer similarly observed that 'sober and knowing men have ever approved of the ring as the fittest and most significant pledge for the binding of that perpetual contract of reciprocal faith and affection that is between man and wife'. The 'fit' of the wedding ring could be taken to symbolize the fit between husband and wife.[23]

Some commentators elaborated this simple symbolism. In Matthew Griffith's view, 'the husband presently puts the ring upon his wife's finger, that she may likewise understand, that her heart is shut up, and sealed from love, or thought in that kind, of any other man'. The Elizabethan minister Henry Smith explained 'the first use of the ring in weddings' to represent the fit of husband to wife, 'for if it be straighter than the finger it will pinch, and if it be wider than the finger it will fall off; but if it be fit, it neither pincheth nor slippeth'. In courtly practice, by contrast, it was a gallant conceit to find the bride's fingers too small for the ring, interpreting this as a tribute to her feminine daintiness. 'Her finger was so small, the ring | Would not stay on, which they did bring,' wrote Sir John Suckling of the 1638 marriage between Lord John Lovelace and Lady Anne Wentworth.[24]

Most writers agreed that the ring was a token of love and commitment, a symbol of closure and eternity. It also served as a tag, a mark of ownership, and a visible advertisement of a woman's married state. The ring was a material symbol of the change from maidenhood to wifedom, and its transfer during the marriage service was, except for sedulous puritans, as crucial as the crown in coronation. As the Jacobean poet Samuel Rowlands remarks in 'The Bride', 'with wedding rings, be wives of credit known'. The Stuart scholar John Aubrey knew that wedding rings were of ancient origin, probably Roman, and their antiquity helped to validate their use. Some antiquarians have also suggested that the ring represented an ancient bride price, given by the man to the woman as a symbol of purchase as well as a token of commitment. In folk belief a wedding ring was empowered to conquer disease and to frustrate devils, and could be employed as part of the housewife's domestic medical armoury. Although, in protestant practice, they were no longer hallowed, that did not prevent people from treating wedding rings as if they were invested with sacred power.[25]

Rings, like everything else, could be simple or elaborate, modest or expensive. Elizabeth Polsted's wedding ring cost 4s. in 1567, with an extra 9d. spent on added gold.[26] Little is known of the rings used in common village weddings, but they were most likely unostentatious. There was no reason that the same ring given in courtship should not also be employed in the course of the wedding ceremony. People of wealth and sentiment also used the ring itself for didactic or declaratory purposes. The ring that transformed Grace Sherrington into Lady Grace Mildmay carried the inscription *Maneat inviolata fides.* The court musician Thomas Whythorne commissioned a ring for his prospective bride in 1569 with the words, 'The eye doth find, the heart doth choose, and love doth bind till death doth loose.' The godly William Whiteway of Dorchester gave a wedding a ring with the Latin inscription

Congugii firmi, et casti sum pignis amoris to his bride in 1620, though it is not entirely clear that he gave it to her in the course of the service of solemnization. Though renowned as a puritan, John White, the formidable minister of Dorchester who married them, was not necessarily averse to the use of the ring.[27]

The giving of the ring was one of the most dramatic elements in the wedding service. To ignorant people it might easily appear that the ring made the marriage, just as they might erroneously believe that the sign of the cross was the operational action in baptism. In the old catholic service the priest sprinkled the ring with holy water and consecrated it with prayer; in the reformed English ceremony the act of laying the ring on the service book before putting on to the woman's hand might still be interpreted as an act of hallowing. Reformers did not want to be told that this was simply the most convenient place to put it, but feared that it might be ignorantly interpreted as a sympathetic application of the book's sacred power. As late as 1590 in some parts of Lancashire critics claimed that traditionalist clergy continued the catholic practice of 'transposing the ring from finger to finger at the several names of the father, the son, and the holy ghost', and 'laying down and giving a large portion of money, as an endowment of the woman' in the course of the wedding ceremony.[28]

From mid-Tudor to mid-Stuart times, godly critics alleged that the ring was 'superfluous, if not superstitious' and sought to have it removed. Reformers objected that the ceremony with the ring was one of the unfortunate 'traces of the church of antichrist' still contaminating the Church of England.[29] The authors of the presbyterian *Admonition to the Parliament* of 1572 (probably John Field and Thomas Wilcox) agreed with other Elizabethan puritans that 'the use of the ring in marriage is foolish', and listed it among their catalogue of remaining popish abuses. 'As for matrimony,' they wrote:

that also hath corruptions too many. It was wont to be counted a sacrament, and therefore they use yet a sacramental sign, to which they attribute the virtue of wedlock. I mean the wedding ring, which they foully abuse and daily withal, in taking it up, and laying it down. In putting it on, they abuse the name of the Trinity; they make the new married man, according to the popish form, to make an idol of his wife, saying: with this ring I thee wed, with my body I thee worship, etc.

The separatist Henry Barrow, writing in 1590, similarly disparaged the prayer-book ceremony which 'teacheth the man to wed his wife with a ring, in the name of the Father, the Son, and the Holy Ghost, which ring must before, by the man be laid upon the service book, together with his offering unto the priest and clerk. The book serveth instead of holy water to hallow the ring,' thereby perpetuating popish superstition. Barrow noted that 'the reformed and better sort of priests will not marry with the ring', but defiant nonconformity earned them only censure and reproof.[30]

The puritan Millenary Petition of 1603 ('millenary' because it claimed a thousand signatures) sought to remove the prayer book's insistence on the ring in marriage. So did the learned puritans at the Hampton Court Conference in 1604. But 'the king confessed that he was married withall, and added that he thought they would prove to be scarce well married who are not married with a ring'. James's utterance, effectively 'no ring, no marriage', was made on the same day as his more famous judgement, 'no bishop, no king'. Against so staunch a royal supporter of the established rubric the nonconformists stood no chance, although this did not diminish their objections.[31]

The Lincolnshire nonconformists of 1605 complained, among other things, of the retention of the ring and its placement on the book in the official service of matrimony. Robert Parker's *Scholasticall Discourse Against Symbolizing with Antichrist in Ceremonies* (1607) included the ring in marriage among the heathenish survivals contaminating the Church of England. Scottish protestants, who used no ring in their ceremonies, feared that the English practice might be imposed on them. The Jacobean presbyterian David Calderwood criticized the ring as a profanation and pollution. Continuing the attack from his exile in Amsterdam, the early Stuart separatist John Canne charged that the use of the ring in marriage was 'a popish and idolatrous practice'.[32]

Puritans in the parishes were not necessarily so outspoken or confrontational, nor were they necessarily consistent in their actions or objections. Despite the extremists' proclivity to conflict, most clergy and laity inclined more often towards accommodation than collision. In practice, moderate nonconformists downplayed or quietly omitted the business with the ring as circumstances permitted. Only occasionally did it get them into trouble.

Visitation returns and court books reveal a scatter of low-grade nonconformity that was only partially responsive to episcopal discipline. An Essex couple, Ralph and Elizabeth Barnes, were married in 1585 'without the ring, required by the book'. Edward Beale and his wife of Banbury, Oxfordshire, were presented in 1614 'for not bringing a ring to be married'. Robert Smart, the moderate puritan vicar of Preston Capes, Northamptonshire, compounded his problem with the authorities in 1591 by continuing some of the practices of his radical predecessor John Elliston and not marrying with the ring. John Norris of Leicester spoke evil of the ring in marriage, and was presented for this fault in Archbishop Laud's visitation in 1634.[33] On the other hand, participants in clandestine marriages were often eager to assert their general religious conformity, despite their lapse of discipline, by insisting that their ceremony followed the form of the prayer book and included the gift of a ring. When Godfrey Britland married Ann Watson in a private chamber in Mansfield, Nottinghamshire, in 1602, for example, it was considered a matter of importance that he gave his bride a golden ring.[34]

Moderate puritans like Richard Greenham of Dry Drayton, Cambridgeshire,

refused not the ring in marriage *if it were offered*, but took it using these words, to teach the man to say to his spouse, I promise to be thy faithful husband and to keep my body proper unto thee and to make thee partake of all my worldly substance. In token whereof I give thee this ring and with a pure and sincere heart I marry thee.[35]

This was a remarkably free adaptation from the Book of Common Prayer. Similar unofficial modifications may have been common in the parishes of Elizabethan and Jacobean England. The London minister William Gouge made absolutely no mention of wedding rings in his book *Of Domesticall Duties*. Acceptance of the ring could be implied, as somehow within 'the form . . . which is prescribed' and according to the rubric of 'whatsoever is to be observed and done'. But Gouge's omission of any reference to the controversial wedding ring may also reflect a pastoral practice in which he quietly dispensed with the ring for any who scrupled against it.[36]

Faced with local laxity and puritan indiscipline, late Elizabethan and early Stuart bishops frequently enquired whether all clergy used 'the ring in marriage, and the sign of the cross in baptism'. The two disputed items frequently went together as symptoms of nonconformist irregularity, and both were susceptible to fudging. Ceremonialist disciplinarians of the reign of Charles I were especially determined to go by the book and to punish those who did not. In this, as in so many things, they turned a long-standing disagreement into a test of loyalty and discipline. Archdeacon Cosin of the East Riding of Yorkshire asked in his visitation of 1627 whether any minister solemnizing matrimony used 'any other manner, words or form than is in the Book of Common Prayer appointed'. In particular Cosin wanted to make sure that no marriages took place 'without a ring, and without using the ceremony thereunto belonging'. Bishop Wren expressed like concerns in his visitation of Ely in 1638, and Montague of Norwich asked similarly in the same year, 'are any married without a ring, joining of hands, or the fees laid down upon the book?'[37] It seems less likely that such disorderly practices were on the rise than that these prelates sought to see all vestiges of irregularity firmly suppressed. Strict conformity showed respect for authority, besides any ritual benefits that may have accrued. The same ceremonialists also expected the newly joined couple to kneel before the altar, and to begin their married life with holy communion as the Tudor prayer books had intended. When the marriage produced offspring the children were to be baptized at the font with the sign of the cross, and later the mother in her veil was to kneel at the rail for her churching. Here was a package of propriety and discipline that honoured God and the King; yet those very demands persuaded others that the reformed religion was in danger.

Conformist churchwardens, of course, took pleasure in reporting the diligent orthodoxy of their ministers. In response to Matthew Wren's enquiries of 1638 the wardens of St Edward's, Cambridge, wrote that their Mr Pelsant performed everything by the book.

He hath not solemnized the marriage of any person under the age of twenty-one years without the consent of their governors, or married any which do not audibly answer all things appointed by the liturgy, or any without a ring or at times prohibited or without the banns first published three several Sundays or holy-days in service time in the churches of their abode, except they brought him a licence from the bishop of his chancellor so to do; and he begins in the body of the church and then goes up to the table as is appointed, and our minister after matrimony doth read that which the church hath appointed then to be read.[38]

Here at least the bishop could congratulate himself that all was well.

With the collapse of episcopal discipline after 1640 ministers could choose to omit the ring if they wished, and as puritans gained power they attempted to restrict the use of the ring by others. After the introduction of the Directory of Public Worship in 1645, which required weddings to be conducted in church but explicitly 'without any further ceremony', continued use of the ring could be interpreted as a token of malignancy, just as neglect of the ring a few years earlier had indicated nonconformity. When Richard Venn, the sequestered vicar of Offerton, Devon, officiated at a wedding in Broadhembury vicarage in 1649, in defiance of puritan policy, the parish register noted that it was celebrated *cum annulo*. Though weddings were removed from ecclesiastical control in the 1650s the revolution did not necessarily put an end to the giving and receiving of wedding rings.[39]

Presbyterians at the Savoy Conference in 1661, seeking accommodation with the restored Church of England, 'desired that this ceremony of the ring in marriage may be left indifferent, to be used or forborn' according to individual discretion. The bishops' rejection of this request was followed by the Act of Uniformity of 1662, which drove hundreds of nonconformist clergy out of the church.[40] Like their early Stuart predecessors, Restoration-era bishops and archdeacons sought full conformity to the prayer book and to the canons of 1604, with varying degrees of success.[41] Given the removal of dissenting ministers, and the popularity of the wedding ring among the people, this may have been one area where ecclesiastical discipline and popular approval coincided.

The Accustomed Duty

Marriages brought money to the minister and his clerk. The scale of fees
varied from place to place, ranging from several pennies to several shillings.
People paid more to be married at unusual times, or on days when the minister was not otherwise conducting services. Weddings in the London parish
of St Olave, Hart Street, cost 3s. 4d. on 'Sunday or holiday at service time',
but twice that amount 'afore service time or upon a working day'. Elsewhere
in London the fees for private weddings were 'as the parties can agree with
the parson'. The Exeter merchant John Hayne gave 10s. to the minister who
married him in 1635 and 7s. more 'to his clerk and the ringers'. Poorer couples
paid much less, and sometimes the fees were forgiven. The Oxford diocesan
court recorded in 1633 that it was the custom in the parish of Cropredy 'for
persons married by banns to pay to the vicar 12d. and to the clerk 4d. for the
marriage and 2d. for making the banns'. A table of fees in the London parish
of St Bennet Paulswharf reserved 5s. to the minister and 20d. to the clerk for
each marriage by banns. At Bury St Edmunds, Suffolk, in 1665 the curate earned
a shilling for publishing the banns and 2s. 6d. at the wedding, or 5s. for a
marriage by licence. His clerk earned a shilling each time. A note of 'customs
of the parish' at St John the Baptist's church, Oxford, in 1687 recorded that
'the chaplain's dues for marrying are 5s.'[42]

Fees might be agreed in advance, but they were normally handed over in
the course of the service by laying the money on the minister's book. This was
'the accustomed duty' specified in the Book of Common Prayer. The money
became an integral ingredient of the ceremony, and therefore a potential
source of friction. Couples were supposed to pay a fee to their parish priest,
even if another minister performed the ceremony.

Strictly speaking these payments for weddings were 'offerings', not fees,
but refusal to pay caused trouble.[43] Among the charges disgruntled parishioners of Ellington, Huntingdonshire, levelled against their vicar, Anthony
Armitage, in 1602 was his wrangling over fees for weddings. He 'would not
marry one Francis Morley, having a licence, unless he would give him 10s. for
his pains'. In the end they agreed on a fee of 5s., but the wedding had to be
performed by Armitage's brother. John Glass, a curate at Stepney, was presented in 1605 'for taking unreasonable bribes for marriages, and for asking
and marrying them for parishioners which are not parishioners'.[44] Caroline
clergymen seem to have been more aggressive in demanding their fees for the
solemnization of matrimony, while some of their parishioners resisted paying
their dues. A baker, a carpenter, and other London artisans faced prosecution
in 1630 for not paying their 'marriage duties'. John Cock, another baker of

the parish of St Leonard, Foster Lane, was presented to the London church court in 1639 'for not paying 8s. 6d. for marriage due to the parson and clerk'. Mr Richard Cartwright of Cropredy, Oxfordshire, was cited in 1633 because he 'oweth to the vicar and clerk their duties for his marriage'.[45]

Similar difficulties contributed to the frictions of parish life in the second half of the seventeenth century. Charles Allestree, vicar of Daventry, wrote to a fellow minister late in Charles II's reign regarding an error which led to him being cheated of his fee. Marrying two strangers by licence, Allestree writes,

I forgot to take the caution which the rubric directs of having my dues laid upon the book with the ring, so that, after I had finished the whole, I saw no pence stirring, and then, to correct the oversight, I was forced to intimate to the bridegroom that there were some fees due to the officers of the church, meaning myself, you may be sure, in the first place, for one. But he impudently replied, 'I'll not give you one farthing sir, for you have married me to the damnedest whore in Christendom.'

To protect himself for the future, Allestree resolved: 'I will never marry any strangers again without having my dues paid beforehand, or in the midst of the office, as the calendar prescribed.' Similarly aggrieved, Thomas Brockbank, curate of Colton, Lancashire, threatened action in the spiritual courts in 1699 against a parishioner who owed him 5s. as his 'wedding dues'.[46] Was this too high a price for legitimating a union and securing the legal and spiritual advantages of holy matrimony?

WEDDING CELEBRATIONS

Marriages were festive as well as sacred occasions. Indeed, the English population at large appears to have invested more cultural energy in the social than in the religious aspects of weddings. Whereas the ecclesiastical solemnization took place in a matter of minutes, the nuptial cheer could go on for hours or even days. Even the most scrupulously austere religious authors accepted some secular rejoicing at weddings, while being careful to criticize festive excess. Had not Christ himself graced the wedding at Cana and contributed to the revels by turning the water into wine? It was impossible to gainsay this example, which was remembered in each reading of 'the form of solemnization of matrimony'.[1]

Since wedding festivity lay outside the area of ecclesiastical cognizance and rarely concerned the ecclesiastical courts, our reconstruction of this aspect of the life cycle depends on diaries, correspondence, and commentaries, and on popular literary texts.[2] This chapter examines 'Hymen's revels' and the rituals of 'nuptial cheer' that brought the 'concomitants' of marriage to a conclusion.

Festive Excess

For their own polemical purposes, sixteenth-century reformers exaggerated the wantonness, excess, and irreligion that commonly prevailed at weddings. 'The devil hath crept in here also,' wrote Miles Coverdale (adapting Heinrich Bullinger), 'and though he cannot make the ordinance of going to the church to be utterly committed and despised, yet is he thus mighty, and can bring it to pass that the ordinance is nothing regarded but blemished with all matter of lightness.' This complaint, of course, was a hostile caricature by an early protestant reformer of manners, but many of its features could be found in later and more sympathetic accounts of weddings. Eating, drinking, dancing, music, jesting, and sexual innuendo remained standard accompaniments to the rituals of holy matrimony, despite godly disapproval of these 'unmannerly and froward customs'.[3]

According to Coverdale, the wedding day began with 'superfluous eating and drinking'. The ritual would be celebrated with food, dress, and noise.

FIG. 17   A married couple from the frontispiece to Louis de Gaya's, *Matrimonial Customs* (London, 1687)

Even before going to church 'the wedding people' became mildly intoxicated. Many consented to go to church 'only because of custom', and were 'half drunk, some altogether', before the preaching and prayer.

Such folks also do come unto the church with all manner of pomp and pride, and gorgeousness of raiment and jewels. They come with a great noise of basins and drums, wherewith they trouble the whole church and hinder them in particulars pertaining to God. They come into the lord's house as if it were into an house of merchandize, to lay forth their wares, and offer to sell themselves unto vice and wickedness. And even as they come to the church, so go they from the church again light, nice, in shameful pomp and vain wantonness.[4]

With their church duty done, the wedding party accelerated their irreverent abandon.

After the banquet and feast there beginneth a vain, mad and unmannerly fashion. For the bride must be brought into an open dancing place. Then is there such a running, leaping and flinging among them, then is there such a lifting up and discovering of the damsels' clothes and of other women's apparel, that a man might think all these dancers had cast all shame behind them, and were become stark mad and out of their wits, and that they were sworn to the devil's dance. Then must the poor bride keep foot with all dancers and refuse none, how scabbed, foul, drunken, rude and shameless soever he be. Then must she oft times hear and see much wickedness and many an uncomely word. And that noise and rumbling endureth even till supper. As for supper, look how much shameless and drunken the evening is more than the morning, so much the more vice, excess, and misnurture is used at the supper. After supper must they begin to pipe and dance again of anew. And though the young persons, being weary of the babbling noise and inconvenience, come once toward their rest, yet can they have no quietness. For a man shall find unmannerly and restless people that will go to their chamber door, and there sing vicious and naughty ballads, that the devil may have his whole triumph now to the uttermost.[5]

The Elizabethan puritan *Admonition to the Parliament* expressed similar outrage at the disorderly mingling of the sacred and the secular at weddings. The authors complained 'that women contrary to the rule of the apostles, come and are suffered to come bare headed, with bagpipes and fiddlers before them, to disturb the congregation, and that they must come in at the great door of the church, or else all is marred'. And in their second edition they added that, 'with divers other heathenish toys in sundry countries, as carrying of wheat sheaves on their heads, and casting of corn, with a number of such like . . . they make rather a May game of marriage than a holy institution of God'.[6] The polemical point of these observations was to associate the half-reformed Book of Common Prayer with the excesses of popish traditionalism and rustic superstition. Protestant zealots implied that the festive delights of the wedding day were incompatible with devout solemnization, whereas ordinary folk saw wedding cheer as the natural joyful accompaniment to the priestly business in church.

A chorus of Elizabethan and Jacobean divines criticized the 'gluttony and drunkenness, and strife, and envy, and chambering, and wantonness' at otherwise laudable festive occasions, though that did not stop them attending. William Bradshaw compared the 'laughing and scoffing' of contemporary weddings with the modesty and sobriety of more honourable Christian celebrations. Alas, not only 'profane swaggerers' offended, in Bradshaw's view, but also 'those, many times, that have the reputation of civil honest men, yea of professors of religion'. Thomas Gataker agreed that wedding guests too often succumbed to 'looseness and lewdness' and too easily fell into 'filthy discourse and obscene songs'.[7] Even God's ministers were known to loosen their collars.

More moderate voices, even those of Jacobean puritans, acknowledged a positive role for 'nuptial cheer', and went so far as to say that the festive celebration of marriage added to the honour and distinction of the occasion. Under this heading William Gouge included 'all those lawful customs that are used for the setting forth of the outward solemnity thereof, as meeting of friends, accompanying the bridegroom and bride both to and from the church, putting on best apparel, feasting, with other tokens of joy, for which we have express warrant out of God's word'. In Gouge's view there was no reason for godly families to forswear the customary festivities of weddings, so long as they were not 'unlawfully abused'. The problem was not custom but excess. Moderate and decent enjoyment was encouraged, disorderly abuse condemned. Cakes and ale would be relished, 'gluttony and drunkenness' abhorred. The 'mirth and joy' of the occasion would be marked by 'witty questions' rather than 'unchaste songs'.[8] Outside the church as well as within, the ideal wedding celebration would demonstrate cheerful sobriety, Christian edification, neighbourly affection, and remembrance of the poor.

Matthew Griffith, writing in 1633, also recognized the rejoicing and feasting of friends as a normal concomitant of marriage. Such activity was lawful in itself, though unfortunately prone to abuse. By no means a puritan, Griffith shared the puritan aversion to godless excess. Wedding feasts, he regretted, were notorious for their bawdy jests, devilish ditties, and alcoholic excess, where 'feasting mirth' slid too easily into 'riot, luxury and pride'. But such merriment might be moderated if the festivity was tied to a religious solemnization, and the priest himself was present as a guest.[9] In practice, it was common for the priest who tied the knot to raise a glass, and for clergy and laity to join in offering blessings and drinking healths.

A wide range of critical and satiric writing repeated the puritan accusation that weddings were more memorable for their 'heathenish' customs than for the taking of sacred vows. Marriages, according to the late Elizabethan *Batchelars Banquet*, were occasions for 'gadding' and 'wantoning', feasting, dancing, drinking, and flirtation. On the 'nuptial day', wrote the Jacobean Richard Brathwaite, the bride and her guests formed 'a frolic gamesome crew'.[10] Clerical reformers repeatedly complained that wedding parties interrupted church services and disturbed normal devotions by their 'unseasonable' and 'tumultuous' coming and going. 'By bringing the parties to and from the church with piping, and spending the whole sabbath in dancing', they distracted other parishioners from both morning and afternoon services.[11] One exasperated minister at Kendal, Westmorland, attempted to control this unseemly exhuberance by order in 1601:

whereas many young persons and others, void of all reverence and civil behaviour, have been and are accustomed to stand upon the stall and seats to gaze about them in the time of any wedding or marriage . . . it is enjoined that none shall use any unreverent gestures or behaviour but quietly keep their places . . . at the time of any wedding or otherwise.[12]

But participants in these rites of passage were often in no mood for the discipline of religious decorum.

Church court records occasionally permit glimpses of the rowdier side of popular behaviour. Charged with allowing dancing in his house during service time in 1572, Robert Browne of Leyton, Essex, explained 'that it was a wedding day, and that he could not rule the youth'. Overcome by the permissive licentiousness of social ritual, the householder's patriarchal authority was temporarily set aside. Henry Gray of Southweald, Essex, was cited for practising his dancing during sermon time and for 'dancing the morris home' with the bridegroom after a wedding service in 1604. He was, indeed, making 'rather a May game of marriage than a holy institution of God'. Remarkably, when John Wilkins, the parish clerk of Whitstable, Kent, was cited in 1599 'for going about the street in women's apparel' he excused himself by saying 'that at a marriage in a merriment he did disguise himself in his wife's apparel to make some mirth to the company'.[13]

Thomas Moulder, his wife (formerly widow Burnell), and friends, of Ealing, Middlesex, were cited 'for keeping disorder and disturbing the parish in time of divine service on the sabbath day' in October 1613. Moulder's explanation throws unusual light on social and festive practices among the poor. He told the court 'that on a sabbath day about three weeks ago he was married, and divers of his friends and others of his acquaintance came to solemnize the same; who in the afternoon at service time made orders as is usual at marriages, which was to tipple at the aforesaid widdow Burnell's house'. Moulder acknowledged that the drinking went on all afternoon, following the ecclesiastical solemnization, but promised that he would 'take warning by this to avoid the like fault hereafter'.[14]

Alcohol was frequently responsible for turning reputable good cheer into disorderly excess. In 1635 a wedding celebration among the clergy and gentry of Durham—those models of sobriety and good order—degenerated into a violent brawl as wine and ill-humour did their work. After John Falder, clerk, and Jane Forster were married the guests retired to a tavern in Alnwick to drink wine and take tobacco. The bride's kinsman Thomas Forster, esquire, and the groom's friend, Robert Stephenson, clerk, were drinking together, when Forster allegedly blew smoke in Stephenson's face. Goodwill rapidly turned to recrimination, and angry words led to bloody faces.[15] Another wedding in 1635 descended into disorder even before the bridal party had left the church. Edward Cumberland of Rayleigh, Essex, was cited 'for offering violence unto John Riggs, pulling off his garters and behaving . . . in a very irreverent and uncivil manner in the church of Rayleigh, at the communion table, upon the 12th of September'. Cumberland acknowledged his fault, 'that he did pull the bridegroom's garter off at the communion table', but suggested that it was simply a lark, the sort of thing one did at weddings.[16] Disciplined ceremonialists and puritan reformers alike would be offended by this raucous irreverence in the midst of solemn ceremonies, at the sacred heart of the church. Neither would have much sympathy for Richard Peacock, the vicar of Swaffham Prior, Cambridgeshire, who allegedly got so drunk at one wedding in 1641 that he could not recite evening prayers.[17]

Hymen's Revels

Compared with the records of ecclesiastical courts and the misgivings of religious reformers, literary sources offer a much more benign, indulgent, and approving view of nuptial festivity. Though prone to sentimental idealization and often self-consciously archaic, imaginative representations shed valuable light on social and cultural processes. The following section contributes to the reconstruction of matrimonial ritual by reference to Thomas Deloney's account of Jack of Newbury, the popular 'Ballad of Arthur of Bradley', the ballad of 'The Winchester Wedding', and the wedding poetry of Robert Herrick and Sir John Suckling. It makes no claim to literary criticism, but rather intends to harness this material for the purpose of historical analysis.

Writing in the 1590s for an audience of gentlefolk, citizens, and literate artisans, Thomas Deloney immortalized the exploits of the early Tudor tycoon Jack of Newbury. Little is said about the conduct of Jack's first wedding to a wealthy widow, but his second wedding, to a former servant, is lovingly described. 'The marriage day being appointed, all things were prepared meet for the wedding, and royal cheer ordained.' Jack, as bridegroom, wore his finest clothes and wedding shoes, but the focus of attention was his bride, her 'head attired with a biliment of gold'. Jack of Newbury's bride was led to church

according to the manner in those days ... between two sweet boys, with bride laces
and rosemary tied about their silken sleeves ... There was a fair bride cup of silver
and gilt carried before her, wherein was a goodly branch of rosemary gilded very fair,
hung about with silken ribbons of all colours; next was a great noise of musicians
that played all the way before her; after her came all the chiefest maidens of the
country, some bearing bride cakes, and some garlands of wheat finely gilded, and so
she passed into the church.[18]

Deloney skips over the religious service, as is usual in this kind of account,
to dwell on the social comcomitants of the ceremony. 'The marriage being
solemnized,' he continues, 'home they came in order as before, and to dinner
they went, where was no want of good cheer, no lack of melody.' Jack's nuptial festivities, in Deloney's account, did not end on the wedding night, for
'this wedding endured ten days, to the great relief of the poor; and in the end
the bride's father and mother came to pay their daughter's portion; which
when the bridegroom had received, he gave them great thanks' and gifts in
exchange. Finally, 'the bride kneeled down and did her duty to her parents;
who weeping for very joy, departed'.[19]

This, of course, is a nostalgic and idyllic account, extolling the virtues
of harmony, hospitality, and largesse. Many would have considered these
virtues in short supply in the stressed economy of the late Elizabethan era
when Deloney's *Pleasant History* was first published. Yet Deloney's depiction of a grand early Tudor wedding—'according to the manner in those
days'—includes customary elements that would still have been recognizable
to later audiences. Most brides wore head-dresses, even if they did not sport
biliments of gold. Bridal veils, however, were rare before the nineteenth century and bridal accoutrements had little in common with the showy confec-
tions of twentieth-century 'classic' white weddings.[20] Bride-laces, bride-cups,
bride-cakes, and garlands had not gone out of fashion in the Elizabethan or
Jacobean eras. And the other main features of Jack of Newbury's wedding—
the bridal procession, the noise of musicians, and sumptuous dining—are
attested in dozens of seventeenth-century descriptions.

'The Ballad of Arthur of Bradley', a traditional entertainment collected in
An Antidote Against Melancholy in 1661, cheerfully sets forth the principal
festive elements of a traditional country wedding. Replete with jollity, plenty,
music, dance, and the promise of sexual fulfilment, the nuptial festivity became the epitome of merry England.[21] Ignoring the religious ceremony, the
energy of the ballad is entirely invested in the secular activities of movement,
noise, food, and licentiousness.

The wedding party is piped to church by 'Peirce the piper, | His cheeks as
big as a mitre, | Piping among the swains | That danced on yonder plains.'
A vibrant turnout of young people escorts the bridal pair.

The chief youths of the parish
Came dancing of the morris,
With country lasses trouncing,
And lusty lads bouncing,
Dancing with music pride
And every one his wench by his side.

Returned from church, the revellers tackled their feast of beef and mustard, furmity, mince pies, and custard. 'But when that dinner was ended | The Maidens they were befriended.' Now it was time for the serious business of promiscuous kissing and sexual jesting, with music, dancing, and 'mirth and merry glee'. Samuel Pepys and the king himself would surely have enjoyed themselves if invited.

Then 'gan the sun decline,
And everyone thought it time
To go unto his home,
And leave the bridegroom alone.
To 't, to 't quoth lusty Ned,
We'll see them both in bed;
For I will jeopard a joint
But I will get his codpiece point . . .

And thus the day was spent
And no man homeward went,
That there was such crowding and thrusting
That some were in danger of bursting,
To see them go to bed.
For all the skill they had,
He was got to his bride,
And laid him close by her side,
They got his points and garters,
And cut them in pieces like quarters . . .
And then did they foot it and toss it
Till the cook had brought up the posset,
The bride-pie was brought forth,
A thing of mickle worth,
And so all at the bed side
Took leave of Arthur and his bride.

Another ballad in this style, 'The Winchester Wedding', first printed in 1670, similarly celebrates the pleasures of nuptial celebrations.[22] Here too were processions of lads and lasses, attended by fiddlers, escorting the couple home. Here too was abundant food, memorable good cheer, and the sexual frisson of games with garters and stockings. As in the ballad of Arthur of

Bradley, the religious solemnization is taken for granted and the focus moves at once to the secular festivities. Larger than life, the event at Winchester was 'a wedding, the like was never seen', though many of its features were conventional. There were musicians galore in attendance, 'for all the whole country came in'.

> The bridegroom came out to meet 'em,
> Afraid the dinner was spoiled,
> And usher'd them in to treat 'em,
> With bak'd, and roast and boil'd.
> The lads were frolic and jolly,
> For each had a lass by his side;
> But Willy was melancholy,
> For he had a mind to the bride.

The Winchester wedding supper, like Arthur of Bradley's, concluded with health-drinking, dancing, and games involving intimate items of costume. It was not only the bridal couple who were encouraged towards erotic arousal, for the young wedding guests too were sexually charged. One imagines the crowd, slightly tipsy, pulling at points and laces and loosening each other's clothes. Of fifty maids in attendance, the ballad suggests, scarce five were still maids at the evening's end.

> And now for throwing the stocking,
> The bride away was led;
> The bridegroom, got drunk, was knocking
> For candles to light them to bed . . .
>
> And now the warm game begins,
> The critical minute was come,
> And chatting, and billing and kissing,
> Went merrily round the room . . .
>
> Sukey that danc'd with the cushion
> An hour from the room had been gone,
> And Barnaby knew by her blushing
> That some other dance had been done.

These ballads, of course, were artful creations, saturated with nostalgia; they contributed to a vision of bucolic harmony, and were more intended to amuse than to inform. We might think of them as the verse equivalent of the social sketches made famous by Hogarth in the eighteenth century, or certain modern cinema productions, mingling affectionate comedy and gentle social criticism. Some of these verses may even have been recited at weddings, both to entertain the company and to prepare them for the festive routines that would follow.[23] Despite their caricature quality, these accounts reveal a range of rituals that are but hinted at in many other sources. Even if the depictions of Jack of Newbury, Arthur of Bradley, and his ilk are archaic, exaggerated, or mildly satiric, their performances and accessories would have been immediately recognizable to Elizabethan and Stuart audiences.

The cavalier poet Sir John Suckling drew on this tradition when he composed his 'Ballad upon a Wedding' in 1638. Written to honour the marriage of Lord John Lovelace and Lady Anne Wentworth, it construes these conventional aristocratic nuptials as 'the rarest things . . . without compare'.[24] The procession to the church, 'forty at least, in pairs', supported the young man who was 'going to make an end of all his wooing'. Relishing her role, the blushing bride appeared to say to her lover, 'I will do what I list today, And you shall do 't at night.' Even the parson was stirred by her beauty. 'Just in the nick the cook knocked thrice', and thoughts of the bedroom gave way to 'the business of the kitchen'. The party sat to dinner, with a hurried grace, before round after round of health-drinking. 'Now hats fly off, and youths carouse', and the feasting, dancing, and drinking continued until late in the day. The bridal pair enjoyed centre-stage. 'O' th' sudden up they rise and dance; | Then sit again and sigh, and glance; | Then dance again and kiss.' Eventually, it was time to withdraw. 'By this time all were stol'n aside | To counsel and undress the bride.' The couple were readied for bed, with lively assistance from the guests. 'But just as Heav'ns would have to cross it, | In came the bridemaids with the posset.' Heartened and stimulated by this traditional drink, husband and wife were finally left to each other. 'At length, the candle's out; and now | All that they had not done they do.' The entire poem, like the nuptial festivity itself, builds to this sexual consummation.

Robert Herrick's wedding verses, slightly earlier than Suckling's, also dwell on the social and sexual elements of 'Hymen's revels'. Though written by a minister of the church, they focus on dressing, feasting, and bedding rather than the religious solemnization of matrimony. Herrick's 'Nuptial verse to Mistress Elizabeth Lee, now Lady Tracy', captures the erotic elements in a single couplet, 'Despatch your dressing then; and quickly wed: | Then feast, and coy't a little; then to bed.'[25] Another Herrick epithalamium, addressed 'to Sir Thomas Southwell and his Lady', looks forward with mild prurience to 'the act', the sexual completion of 'these holy bridal rites', and has the refrain, 'Then away, come Hymen guide | To the bed the bashful Bride.'[26] The poet-priest blesses the couple:

> O! give them active heat
> And mosture, both complete:
> Fit organs for increase
> To keep and to release

> That, which may the honour'd stem
> Circle with a diadem.

Herrick's 'Nuptial Song, or Epithalamie, on Sir Clipseby Crew and his Lady' has as its central motif the adornment, disrobing, and defloration of the bride.[27] At the beginning the bride appears like 'emergent Venus', finely attired and richly perfumed, her head 'with marjoram crowned'. Virgin brides-maids shower flowers and sprinkle the bridal pair with wheat as they pro-ceed from the church ('the shrine of holy saints') to the wedding feast. By the middle of the poem the couple are in bed, after a semi-public ceremonial dis-robing. The young men and women of the wedding party crowd around to catch the ribbons and laces that held the couple's clothes together, and Herrick urges the bride,

> Quickly, quickly then prepare,
> And let the young men and the bride-maids share
> Your garters, and their joints
> Encircle with the bride-groom points.

The bride has 'green hopes', signifying freshness but also alluding to the 'green' condition of newly delivered motherhood. Her marriage bed is an erotically encoded bower, ideal for defloration.

> Strip her of spring-time, tender-whimpring maids,
> Now autumn's come, when all those flowery aids
> Of her delays must end; dispose
> That *lady-smock*, that *pansy*, and that *rose*
> Neatly apart;
> But for *prick-madam*, and for *gentle-heart*;
> And soft *maidens-blush*, the Bride
> Makes holy these, all others lay aside:
> Then strip her, or unto her
> Let come, who dares undo her.

Lady-smocks were a kind of wild watercress, prick-madam was a house leek used in salads, gentle-heart may have been heart's-ease, a kind of pansy, and maidens-blush may have been a rose. Herrick appears to have chosen these plants for their suggestive names rather than their floral or pharmacological virtues.[28]

The Reverend Robert Herrick, a guest at the wedding supper, imagines himself performing yet one more ministerial task. 'If needs we must, for cere-mony's sake, | Bless a sack posset; luck go with it.' All are on edge in anticipa-tion of Sir Clipseby's manly performance of his marriage duty.

But since it must be done, despatch, and sow
Up in a sheet your Bride, and what if so
It be with rock, or walls of brass,
Ye tower her up, as *Danae* was;
Think you that this,
Or hell itself a powerful bulwark is?
I tell yee no; but like a
Bold bolt of thunder he will make his way,
And rend the cloud, and throw
The sheet about, like flakes of snow.[29]

Wedding Gear

The literary depiction of wedding festivity tended to be deeply conservative, self-consciously antique, and mildly lascivious. But many of the elements of 'Hymen's revels' described in the poems and ballads can also be traced in more conventional historical sources. Diaries, letters, court records, and sermons allude to the clothing, ornaments, entertainments, feasting and sexual titillation customarily associated with weddings. This section attempts to gather and discuss these notations.

There is hardly an account of a Tudor or Stuart wedding that does not draw attention to the bride's or bridegroom's costume, or to the wedding guests who were tricked out in nuptial knots and ribbons.[30] Even today published reports of weddings tend to focus on what the participants wore rather than how they behaved. Wealthy couples spent lavishly on their nuptial attire, and even the poorest attempted to look their best. New shoes and fresh clothes were considered appropriate wear for a ceremony of new beginnings. The Elizabethan puritan Henry Smith attempted to turn this custom to godly use observing that 'Christ showeth that before parties married they were wont to put on fair and new garments, which were called wedding garments, a warning unto all which put on wedding garments to put on truth and holiness too.' 'For when a man putteth on fair clothes,' said Smith, 'he maketh himself fair too.' The Stuart preacher John Gauden wrote similarly on behalf of 'comely adornings', arguing against the austerity of the 1650s that 'it would seem very grievous to bridegrooms and brides, to be denied the use of their best clothes, their richest ornaments and jewels, which God permits and scripture alludes to'.[31]

Not only the bridal couple but their friends and attendants favoured wedding clothes, new gowns or fresh costumes. As soon as the parties had named the day, according to the Yorkshireman Henry Best in 1641, 'they get made

the wedding clothes, and make provision against the wedding dinner'. Following this custom, as soon as he had finalized the terms for his marriage in
1657, the Derbyshire yeoman, Leonard Wheatcroft, 'took notice for wedding
apparel'. Wheatcroft and his love 'went to a market not far distant, where we
did provide ourselves of apparel both linen and wool', so that they would
look their best. John Greene's wedding in 1643 was a quieter affair, shadowed
by the crisis of civil war, though this did not prevent the couple from purchasing wedding clothes, or their fathers, both lawyers, from appearing in
full scarlet robes.[32]

Joyce Jeffries's account books *c.*1640 reveal that she spent £20 on a wedding dress for her goddaughter, Elizabeth Acton. Margaret Harlakenden, a
neighbour of the Essex clergyman Ralph Josselin, 'laid out £120 at London,
about wedding clothes, her father being exceeding angry . . . for her vanity'.
This shopping spree took place a month before Margaret's wedding in 1657.
The wedding suit that the Lancashire gentleman Nicholas Blundell wore at
his marriage at the end of the Stuart era was trimmed with expensive gloves,
silver buttons, and scarlet stockings. Blundell acquired it a week before the
ceremony and sported it at special pre-wedding dinners as well as on the day
of solemnization.[33] Gentle families spent lavishly because their honour was
invested in their costume. Their collective sartorial effort helped to separate
the nuptial celebration from ordinary daily routines. Less privileged celebrants
had to make do with fresh laundry and ornamental ribbons to express their
good will.

Elizabethan and Stuart reports concur in associating marriages with bride-
knots, gloves, and favours. Trinkets and ornaments of the kind that courting
couples gave each other to cement their affection were also worn at weddings
and distributed to friends and kinsfolk as tokens of affinity or mementoes of
the occasion.[34] According to Henry Best it was customary for marriage partners

to buy gloves to give to each of their friends a pair on that day; the man should be at
cost for them; but sometimes the man gives gloves to the men, and the women to the
women, or else he to her friends and she to his; they give them that morning when
they are almost ready to go to church to be married.

Custom preferred the bride herself to go bare-handed; only widows and married women were expected to wear gloves.[35] Guests at gentle weddings came
to expect a gift of gloves, and even associates who had not attended the ceremony might receive a pair as a token, a symbolic extension of the hand of
friendship. After marrying quietly at a 'private' wedding in 1680, John Verney
distributed lace-trimmed gloves and other favours to an intimate circle of
friends. Verney singled out 'one of my wife's wedding garters for master Ralph,

as one of her bridemen', and added 'these tokens of a wedding I desire them to wear for my sake'.[36]

A later seventeenth-century observer, Henri Misson, commented that the custom of wedding guests accepting bridal ribbons 'to be worn by the guests upon their arms' was followed by all social classes in England, even nobles, whereas in the France of Louis XIV it was confined to peasants. Similar ribbons were given as favours to friends and relations who did not attend the wedding, along with buttons and gloves, according to purse and fashion.[37]

References to wedding gear are scattered through account books and diaries. We learn that the three daughters of a London scrivener, married in a remarkable triple wedding in 1560, were not only adorned with 'chains, pearls and stones' but also appropriately 'garnished with laces, gilt and fine flowers'. The Exeter merchant John Hayne laid out £5. 13s. for ribbons, favours, points, and roses at his wedding in 1635. This decorative custom prevailed even during wartime, even among families who could barely afford it. Ralph Josselin frowned at the excess expenditure on fripperies at a wedding he attended in 1644 when 'a poor man gave curious ribbons to all, gloves to the women and to the ringers'. Leonard Wheatcroft would not be denied the accoutrements of festivity at his marriage in 1657, when he equipped the bell-ringers with 'flying colours tied to the wrist or hand'. Wheatcroft's guests competed for wedding favours—scarlet, crimson, dark blue, and light blue ribbons—and wore them as garters or in their hats. The 'bride-garters' were a much admired trophy for whoever managed to catch them. Wedding garters were traditionally blue, the colour associated with the Virgin Mary, but could also be white or red. One young guest at a Northamptonshire wedding in 1671 reportedly 'lost his ribbon and burst into tears'.[38]

Bridal Flowers

Depending on their seasonal availability, fresh flowers served as wedding ornaments and nosegays, as sprigs and bouquets to be worn or carried, and as decorations for the church, the table, and the bed. They brought colour and delight to the nuptial ceremony, and further emphasized the marriage as a special festive occasion. Floral garlands, according to early Tudor commentary, betokened 'the gladness and the dignity of the sacrament'.[39] A full bouquet was offered in the poetic floral tribute to the princess bride Elizabeth Stuart in 1613:

> With Costmary, and sweet Angelica.
> With Spyknard, Margerom, and Pimpernel,
> Strawberry leaves, Savory, and Eglantine

With Endive, Holy-thistle, Sops in wine,
Smallage, Balm, Germander, Basil and Lily,
The Pink, the Flower-de-luce and Daffadilly,
The Gilliflower, Carnation, white and red.
With various spots and stains enamelled,
The Purple Violet, Paunce, and Hearts-ease,
And every flower that smell, or sight, can please.
The yellow Marigold, the sun's own flower,
Pagle, and Pink, that deck fair Flora's Bower,
The Daisy, Cowslip, Wall-flower, Columbine,
With the broad-leaves late cropped from Bachus' vine,
Besides a thousand other fragrant posies
Of Woodbine, Rosemary, and sundry Roses.[40]

Among gentry collections the Verney family papers evoke the gaity of a young aristocratic bride dancing her way through a flower-filled house in 1657, as 'servants waited on her and the music followed her' to her wedding. Along the way the party was greeted by 'women with garlands'. 'This is a day for roses and violets', announced the preacher at a London wedding in June 1655. Other commentators describe the wedding table strewn with floral 'rose cake . . . bone-lace, and Coventry blue', the bride adorned with 'ginger, rosemary and ribbons', and the groom with 'a sprig of willow in his hat'.[41] Daisies and violets, pansies and roses, were more colourful, more aromatic, and more common at weddings than Herrick's suggestive bouquet of prick-madam, lady-smock, gentle-heart, and maidens-blush. Evergreen rosemary and myrtle would substitute in colder months for spring and summer blossoms.

According to early modern lore, the myrtle was 'dedicated by the poets to Venus, and consecrated to wedlock'. The rose too, a symbol of secrecy and silence, was thought to be especially suitable for brides. Elizabethan observers knew as well as twentieth-century theorists that floral arrangements at weddings united nature and culture to promote the liminal *communitas* of the rite of passage. 'At bride-ales the house and chambers were wont to be strewed with these odiferous and sweet herbs, to signify that in wedlock all pensive wrangling strife, jarring variance and discord ought to be utterly excluded and abandoned, and that in place thereof all mirth, pleasantness, cheerfulness, mildness, quietness and love should be maintained.'[42] Nor was the church neglectful when it came to construing meanings. The Jacobean preacher Roger Hacket, rector of North Crawley, Buckinghamshire, saluted the 'ancient and laudable custom . . . to grace the married couple with divers presents'. His own 'marriage present', in the form of a sermon, invoked the properties of flowers in the wedding bouquet—primroses, maiden's blush, violets, and rosemary—to recommend obedience, mild patience, and faithfulness to the wife, and wisdom, love, and loyalty to the husband.[43] Who is to say that the bridal nosegay was not an instrument of patriarchal domination?

Giving and Bidding

William Vaughan described the practice among literate Elizabethans of sending written invitations to a wedding. 'In some shires, when the marriage day approacheth, the parents of the betrothed couple do certain days before the wedding write letters to invite all their friends to the marriage, whom they desire to have present.'[44] In most cases the publication of banns would serve as notice, to be supplemented by word of mouth among neighbours. The Derbyshire yeoman Leonard Wheatcroft spread news of his impending marriage in 1657 through a network of markets, inns, and relations, and 'did invite many to our wedding, who did promise to come in their own person'. Others were 'bid' through intermediaries to join in this 'nuptial feast'.[45] Close family members would be expected to attend, along with neighbours and friends. Only in the case of clandestine weddings, where speed and secrecy were of the essence, would broad attendance be curtailed.

Though the bridal couple or their kinsfolk were expected to provide hospitality, they were also accustomed to receive wedding presents. Weddings were occasions of reciprocal giving and receiving, in a culture that calibrated the honour as well as the intrinsic worth of a gift. Presents could be financial, material, consumable, or symbolic. Parents or guardians might present the bride's dowry, or some representation of it, in the course of the wedding service or at the reception. Wealthy relations might give money or silverware. Neighbours might bring food or drink for the feast. Guests at a Surrey gentry wedding in 1567 contributed, swans, capons, partridges, woodcocks, and other birds, hares, does, hinds, and other game, fish, sweetmeats, puddings, cheeses, spices, and wine, to keep the party going. In recognition of their relationship to a seigneurial family, when Lord Desmond's daughter married Lady Gawdy's son in 1657, 'all the country sent her in presents, she had four brace of bucks and fish and fruits and all good things', as subfeudal tokens of esteem and respect. When Edward Bysshe married Margaret Greene at Lincoln's Inn in 1635, according to the bride's brother, 'favours cost 2s. 2d. a piece. They had a little plate given them.' Samuel Pepys 'bespake three or four dozen bottles of wine' for a cousin's marriage in 1660, and never went to a wedding without taking a gift.[46]

A minister might contribute his fee or offer the gift of a sermon before taking his place at the wedding banquet, as did Giles Moore, the Restoration-era rector of Horsted Keynes, Sussex. As an act of charity to his parishioners,

Moore sometimes forgave them their wedding fees, or returned the money
to them twofold. To help those 'newly married to begin the world'—a telling
phrase—Moore would sometimes give a few shillings to a newly married
couple. Sometimes he would treat the fiddlers at a wedding and pay for the
cost of a sugar loaf. On special occasions he might offer a silver spoon. One
such wedding spoon cost him 9s. 6d. in 1658, another cost 3s. 6d. in 1670. When
two of his former servants 'married away' in 1676, Giles Moore not only
performed the ceremony 'gratis', but also covered their wedding expenses.
His largesse included 'fiddlers . . . a large cake, all their fuel and free use of
my house and stables for two days, with a quart of white wine with recipes,
being in all not less than 40s. or one year's wages'. Moore contributed 9s. 4d.
for sack and meat for his niece's wedding in 1673, where, as usual for those
who could afford it, the celebration went on for a second day after the ecclesiastical ceremony.[47]

William Vaughan described the shower of money that often helped a young
couple to set up their household.

Afterwards, the marriage day being come, the invited guests do assemble together,
and at the very instant of the marriage do cast their presents, which they do bestow
upon the new married folks, into a basin, dish, or cup, which standeth upon the table
in the church, ready prepared for that purpose. But this custom is only put in use
amongst them which stand in need.[48]

Traditionalists thought nothing amiss in collecting the wedding cash (like
parish assessments) upon the communion table, though high ceremonialist
churchmen bristled at this act of profanation.[49]

Traditional sixteenth-century bride-ales raised funds by brewing and bak-
ing to supply the needs of the wedding. Parish accounts sometimes record
such payments as 6d. 'for bread and wine for three weddings' at Tallaton,
Devon, in 1595, or 2d. 'for bread and wine against a wedding' at the same
place in 1601. These refreshments allowed the parish clerk and bell-ringers to
join in the festivity. Bid-ales invited neighbours to drink in honour of the
wedding, 'and then for all guests to contribute to the house-keepers'. Far
from preventing indigents from getting married, parishioners at Hackney,
Middlesex, organized collections at the church door in 1663 to help the poorest newly weds to set up their households.[50]

The guests at Leonard Wheatcroft's wedding brought money with them to
the reception. Though the families of the bride and groom provided basic
refreshments, the guests who were 'bid' were expected to augment the repast
by contributing 'shots' or shares at their own expense. Funds raised in this
way more than covered the initial costs of the feasting, much to Wheatcroft's

satisfaction. On the second day of celebration, Wheatcroft noted, 'much moneys was taken that day'. Newly arrived wedding guests 'laid their shots' or 'gave us their shots freely', so that 'for eleven days together we got eleven shot dinners'. Wheatcroft recorded these contributions in his account book, commenting, 'I thought all very well bestowed, as did their moneys, and what I did gain by the feast was sufficient, for which I give all my friends many thanks, and shall be ready to congratulate them in the like manner.'[51] This festive circulation of resources contributed to Wheatcroft's local honour and reputation as well as to the financing of the feast.

Traditionally, a public wedding, like a public funeral, was an occasion for the central participants to distribute doles to the poor. At weddings, in particular, the bridal party was expected to share its goodwill. Documented reports of this practice are rare, but the substantial amount of £3 was distributed to the poor at a wedding at All Hallows, Barking, Essex, in 1654. A gentleman who was married in the same church on Easter Tuesday, 1661, gave 6s. to the poor. The late seventeenth-century *Ladies Dictionary* depicts newly weds passing from the church through 'the congratulating crowd' bestowing charitable largesse on the poor. At the same time the new bride might also be expected to give 'ball money' to her old playfellows, to symbolize her separation from the world of unmarried maids.[52]

Bridal Processions

Literary accounts of traditional grand weddings describe the festive procession that escorted the couple to and from the church. A cavalcade of dancers, prancers, and musicians added to the honour of the participants and to the delight of the occasion, and singled out the ceremony as a significant rite of passage. By the later seventeenth century, however, the great bridal processions of the kind that supported Jack of Newbury and Arthur of Bradley were increasingly rare. As the *Ladies Dictionary* of 1694 observed, after describing some ancient processional traditions, 'we find that custom is laid aside, and the matter is managed with less ceremony and more decency; the good natured bride not expecting such fantastical attendance'. The new-found taste for privacy and decorum worked against festive processions. The post-Restoration urban élite would go to their nuptials by coach, 'environed with a throng of starers and gapers', and might even 'sneak to church by themselves [and] sneak to a taven by themselves', to avoid all 'pomp and public ceremony'.[53] For the rest of the population, on most occasions, the wedding party and guests simply turned up for the service; in many villages, where weddings were attached to routine worship, the congregation was already assembled in church.

Henry Best provides a mid-seventeenth-century account of the business of going to a wedding among the middling sort.

So soon at the bride is [at]tired, and that they are ready to go forth, the bridegroom comes, and takes her by the hand, and sayeth, 'Mistress, I hope you are willing,' or else kisseth her before them, and then followeth her father out of the doors; then one of the bridegroom his men ushereth the bride and goes foremost; and the rest of the young men usher each of them a maid to church.[54]

There was no need for morris dancers or fiddlers to accompany the procession.

No doubt there continued to be celebrated weddings with large and formal turnouts. But the later Stuart gentry preferred equestrian escorts or lines of coaches to the bouncing lads and lasses of the ballad tradition. 'Six score horse of the gentlemen and yeomen' escorted the aristocratic Gawdy-Desmond wedding party on the final three miles of their ride home to Debenham in 1657. Twelve riders on horseback accompanied the bridegroom at a North-amptonshire gentry wedding in 1672. After Ralph Thoresby married Anna Sykes in February 1685, in what was supposed to be a quiet ceremony, Thoresby writes, 'notwithstanding our designed privacy, we were met at our return to Leeds by about 300 horse'. This large equestrian attendance was an appropriate honour for the son-in-law and daughter of the lord of the manor.[55]

Entertainment on the way back from church might include running at the quintain, 'a game of sport still in request at marriages in some parts of this nation, especially in Shropshire', according to a later Stuart account. 'A quintain . . . is set fast in the ground of the highway where the bride and bridegroom are to pass, and poles are provided with which the young men run a tilt on horseback; and he that breaks most poles, and shows most activity, wins the garland.' Guests at Leonard Wheatcroft's country wedding in 1657 engaged in rustic 'tournaments' of this sort, broke spears riding at quintains, and played antique games of chivalry as if they were champions of Henry VIII or Edward III rather than Derbyshire yeomen under Oliver Cromwell.[56] Wheatcroft was deliberately modelling his wedding festivity (and his narrative) on the nuptial ballad tradition, and may have gone further than usual in providing traditional entertainments. Most wedding groups were probably too impatient to return to the food and drink to dally over rustic sports.

Ever attentive to deviance and disorder, church court records reveal that weddings could be targets for derision as well as good cheer. Thomas Bred of Coddington, Oxfordshire, confessed in 1599 'that at such time as Thomas Paxton was to be married he was set on by Mrs. Boskyn and Mrs. Jackson to carry a garland to the church and to blow a horn in the middle of the street'.

The noise and display drew attention to the wedding, though not in the manner that respectable families would have wished. Mocking the usual floral accoutrements of the bridal procession, William Gilchrist of West Ham, Essex, allegedly spoilt a wedding in the summer of 1602 by taunting gestures. 'He the said Gilchrist, in derision of holy matrimony, got a bough hanged with ropes ends and beset with nettles and other weeds, and carried the same in the street and churchyard before the bride, to the great offence of the congregation.'[57] Unfortunately the evidence is insufficient to gauge whether Gilchrist was drunk or simple-minded, whether he was driven by anger as a suitor spurned, or whether his bouquet of nettles was intended to comment on the chastity or character of the bride. Another possibility is that Gilchrist's obstacle belonged to a tradition of jesting, pranking, and barring the way, comparable to the modern Anglo-American practice of tying tin cans or shoes to the rear of a newly married couple's car.

Edward Row's behaviour at the marriage of Thomas Brock and Rebecca Foster at Thorrock Parva, Essex, in 1605, is easier to understand. Row 'did fasten a pair of horns upon the churchyard gate . . . and being rebuked for the same afterwards did avow that he did it, and if it were to do again he would do it'. Horns were the standard symbol for cuckoldry and incontinence, and their display announced that the bride was notorious for her sexual misconduct. Robert Brooke of Arlington, Sussex, was similarly charged with disorderly behaviour in 1639 'for wearing a great pair of horns upon his head in the churchyard when Henry Hall and his wife were going to be married, showing thereby that the said Hall was like to be a cuckold'.[58] Often used to comment on discordant relationships *within* marriage, the charivari tradition was here used to publicize irregularities at its beginning.

Actions of Piety and Mirth

Wedding feasts were ideally occasions of amity and *communitas*, appropriate to rituals of separation and incorporation.[59] No nuptial festivity would be complete without convivial distribution of food and drink, as the business with the ring gave way to 'the business of the kitchen'. It would not do to start married life hungry, or to fail to offer hospitality to guests. Clandestine weddings, by their nature, were low-key and discreet, but they too were usually followed by dining and drinking at an inn. Participants in public weddings, the minister often included, retired to the table or the tavern. If the wedding was performed within canonical hours, between eight and twelve of the forenoon, the rest of the day could be spent in feasting. The quality and range of refreshments varied with the ability of families to provide them, and the menu also varied with seasonal conditions. Late summer weddings could turn harvest abundance into spreads of breads and pastries. Autumn weddings would find more fresh-killed livestock for serving of meats—roast, baked, or boiled.

Traditionalists might insist on the preparation of such delicacies as a 'bride cake'. The antiquarian John Aubrey recalled seeing 'the bride and bridegroom kiss over the bride cakes at the table; it was about the latter end of dinner; and the cakes were laid one upon another, like the picture of the sewbread in the old Bible'. This custom may have faded by the time Aubrey wrote in the later seventeenth century, for he locates it 'before the civil wars . . . according to the custom then'. Other sources refer to the continuation of 'confarreation . . . a ceremony used at the solemnization of a marriage, in token of most firm conjunction between man and wife, with a cake of wheat or barley; this ceremony is still retained in part with us, by that which we call the bride cake, used at weddings'.[60] It was customary at wedding dinners for the bridegroom to serve the bride, an inversion of the household etiquette that would prevail for the rest of their married career. In a Civil-War era pamphlet mocking 'the new fashion of marriage' among artisanclass conventiclers, 'our young holy sister waited at the table on her bridegroom', in ostentatious violation of the former fashion.[61]

Diaries and letters permit glimpses of wedding festivity, mostly among the middling and upper classes. The London diarist Henry Machyn observed a citizen's wedding in 1559 which offered 'a bride cup and wafers and hippocras [spiced wine] and muscadel plenty to everybody', before proceeding 'unto Mr. Blackwell's place to breakfast, and after a great dinner'. At Sir Philip Herbert's wedding at court in 1604, 'there was none of our accustomed forms omitted, of bride-cakes, sops in wine, giving of gloves, laces and points . . . and at night there was sewing into the sheet, casting of the bride's left hose, and twenty other petty sorceries'. Dudley Carleton, who provides this account, seemed both satisfied and amused that the check-list of customary actions had been accomplished.[62]

William Carnsew and his circle of Cornish gentry enjoyed 'good cheer' and 'great feasting' at each other's weddings in the 1570s. Two of the wedding celebrations Carnsew attended in September 1576 continued for a second day. Phineas Pett's wedding to Ann Nichols in May 1598 involved relatively modest entertainment and feasting. Pett recalled, 'I kept my wedding at my own charge at my new dwelling house in Limehouse, accompanied with my brothers and sisters, my wife's parents, and divers of her friends and kindred.' The celebrations could not last too long, for there was urgent shipwright's work to be done on the river. A generation later, however, when Pett hosted the wedding of his son's widow to a fellow shipwright in 1631, the marriage feast lasted 'from Thursday till Monday'. And in 1637 when the shipwright's daughter married a former apprentice, the couple were 'accompanied with the best sort of our neighbours, who were entertained in the garden under a long tent, set up for that purpose, where they ate, dined and supped' from morning till night.[63]

Puritan discipline would not stand in the way of wedding festivities, even under the exigiencies of war or during the allegedly austere days of the Cromwellian protectorate. Most good Christians knew the difference between festivity and excess. Of his marriage in London in 1643 John Greene writes,

the wedding was kept at my father's house in the Old Jewry very privately, none but brothers and sisters and a friend or two more were at it. My wife expected an ague upon Sunday and Tuesday, and for that reason it was done on Monday, the Wednesday after being fast day. On Tuesday, the day after my wedding, we went to the Mermaid in Bread Street to dance and to be merry, where music met us.[64]

When the godly Oliver Heywood married the devout Elizabeth Angier in April 1655 they were joined by 'a numerous congregation in the chapel . . . and then feasted above an hundred persons of several ranks, ages and sexes'. Ralph Josselin similarly noted with approval that on 15 December 1657, 'Mistress Margaret Harlakenden married to Mr. John Eldred, her father kept the wedding three days, with much bounty; it was an action mixed with piety and mirth.'[65]

Leonard Wheatcroft's wedding, also solemnized during the protectorate, was, by his own account, a celebration of festive abundance. It snowed meat and drink at his table, like Chaucer's franklin's, as Wheatcroft and his friends mounted a triumph of conviviality, hospitality, and display. Wheatcroft clearly took pleasure in his role of host.

The guests being all invited in several parishes, it was then my care to provide all necessaries for their entertainment . . . so coming home again I set very many at work, the butcher for one, who dressed me against that time and while the wedding did last thirty five head of wares. As for beer, it was brewed before to the value of eight quarters of malt, with many more needful qualities to the value of £62 9s. 9d.[66]

Wheatcroft's wedding was to be no meagre affair, but a memorable Whitsuntide occasion to make Derbyshire sing. The catalogue of preparation and consumption recalled (and was no doubt intended to recall) the great wedding feasts of popular literature, like those of Jack of Newbury and Arthur of Bradley. Leonard of Ashover would take his place besides these semilegendary heroes. 'The wedding days did last long. For eleven days together

there was eleven dinners got. All was shot dinners. And there was break-
fasted, dined and supped to the value of 200 persons, and I had one cook or
two all the while.' At the main wedding dinner 'fourteen tables sat full at one
time', and the guests took turns at two or three sittings for breakfast and
dinner on the morrow. 'The next day being Friday was the bride-pie eaten,
at which dinner was above twenty two mess; almost all of these were women.'
And for more than a week guests kept arriving from outlying villages to
extend their goodwill and to share in the bounty. This wedding, like many
throughout the period, was filled with the sound of music with 'merry bells'
at church in the morning, 'merrily played' music for the dancers and diners
in the afternoon, and 'pleasant lessons and choice tunes' to end the evening.[67]

Restoration-era weddings perpetuated many of the traditional customs,
adapted as needed to the conventions of polite society. It is no surprise to
find the 'Ballad of Arthur of Bradley' and 'The Winchester Wedding' printed
at this time.[68] The dissenting preacher Oliver Heywood described a North-
Country wedding in 1678 where 'all at the marriage give the 2d. a piece to the
music, then the pipers go with the bridegroom and bride to invite guests for
the second day'. The wedding feast for a London alderman's son at Drapers'
Hall in 1675 went on for three days. After a long afternoon of festivities at a
naval purveyor's wedding in 1666, Samuel Pepys wrote appreciatively of 'a
good dinner, and what was best, good music. After dinner the young women
went to dance.'[69]

Edward Verney likewise enjoyed himself at a neighbouring gentleman's
wedding in 1675, not least because all the customary arrangements were
observed. 'We saw Sir Richard and his fine lady wedded, and flung the stocking, and then left them to themselves' in bed. The retirement of the bridal
couple barely affected the intensity of merrymaking, for 'after that we had
music, feasting, drinking, revelling, dancing and kissing; it was two of the
clock this morning before we got home'. Ralph Thoresby enjoyed much the
same at a Yorkshire wedding in 1682 attended by 'a vast company of men and
women'. On the second day of festivities the bride's grandmother, a Quaker,
felt moved to warn everyone 'that Satan might not get advantage by our
carnal mirth'. A few years later Thoresby wrote approvingly of another wedding supper, 'which was the more suitable, because without the usual vanities'. Charles Allestree remarked on the refinement of his niece's wedding in
1679, as if such decorum was uncommon. 'There was nothing of ribaldry, or
scurrility, no unmannerly satire to spoil the contenture of it, but a spirit of
wit and fineness of thought shined through all parts of it.'[70]

The French visitor Henri Misson, whose observations of late seventeenth-
century England are so valuable, recognized many of the social, regional, and

religious variables in marriage customs. Weddings, he commented, 'generally vary according to the several customs of the countries, the rank or quality of the persons, and their different religions. The Presbyterians profess so great a strictness, and such a mighty reservedness, that their weddings are commonly very plain and very quiet.' At weddings of the middling sort, unless held quietly in private,

they invite a number of friends and relations; every one puts on new clothes, and dresses finer than ordinary; the men lead the women, they get into coaches, and so go in procession, and are married in full day at church. After feasting and dancing, and having made merry that day and the next, they take a trip into the country, and there divert themselves very pleasantly.[71]

Nonconformist weddings were not necessarily as austere as Misson imagined. Though Oliver Heywood's remarriage in 1667 was, reportedly, 'a very solemn business', conducted at Salford chapel 'in a decent manner' in the presence of 'under twenty persons of the nearest relations', his guests would not be denied good eating. Heywood was by this time a prominent dissenter and a model to Lancashire nonconformists. A few years later Heywood was disturbed, though not so upset as some brother dissenters, at the worldly excess of a 'marriage dinner' in 1678. The couple, though nonconformists, 'made such a public business of it, inviting twenty mess [i.e. eighty dinner guests], keeping two days of feasting, had fiddlers' and pipers, and made 'a sad compliance with the vain corrupt customs of the world'. What especially disgusted the staunch nonconformists was that Mr Ashburn, the Anglican minister who 'refused to marry them', none the less invited himself to the feast.[72]

Misson marked what he took to be a new feature of the later seventeenth century, the fashion among 'persons of quality and many others who imitate them' of marrying quietly, privately, or clandestinely, away from the public gaze. The Frenchman's observation accords with other developments at this time, like the taste for private christenings and night-time funerals. Many of the élite were detaching themselves from the culture of neighbourliness and display, preferring quiet, private, and select solemnities to the public extravaganzas of the sort that Leonard Wheatcroft praised for their 'mirth and melody'. John Verney's wedding in London in May 1680 was described as 'private', for example, but only to indicate that attendance was limited to close family members. There was certainly nothing clandestine about it, although the celebration was modest by gentry standards. Having concluded the religious formalities in church, the party adjourned to the Rummer in Queen Street for a dinner costing £3. 17s.[73]

Possets and Stockings

In life as in literature, weddings could be sexually charged occasions for guests as well as the newly weds. The wealthy widow who first married Jack of Newbury boasted she would 'take him down in his wedding shoes, and would try his patience in the prime of his lustiness'. In John Stephens's Jacobean characterization of 'a plain country bride' whose 'best commendation is to be kissed often', the woman can hardly wait 'to loose her garters quickly, that she may lose her maidenhead likewise'.[74] The kissing often began in church, at the conclusion of the wedding service, and built in intensity till evening. Mild sexual teasing and buffeting were normal parts of wedding behaviour in the fen-edge parish of Dry Drayton, Cambridgeshire, notwithstanding the earlier reform efforts of Richard Greenham and the ceremonialist discipline of Bishop Matthew Wren. The churchwardens assured Wren in 1662 that 'to our knowledge nothing is said or done more than is befitting, unless that there be pulling of ribbons or such like things for the bride and bridegroom. But who so did we know not, but hereafter will take better notice'.[75]

No marriage was complete without consummation.[76] Bridal couples and wedding guests alike knew that the time was rapidly approaching for the completion of 'the act'. In reality, of course, a large proportion of brides may already have lost their virginity, and some 20 per cent were already pregnant; but the fiction was maintained that the wedding night was the time for defloration. Given the double standard, it seems reasonable to assume that a higher proportion of bridegrooms were already sexually initiated, though not necessarily competent or experienced. Bulstrode Whitelock's wedding night in 1630 was a disaster for bride and groom when 'expecting marriage joys' they 'met with strange discomforts'. By contrast, a note of triumph appears in the Sussex merchant Samuel Jeake's entry in his diary for his wedding night in 1681, 'devirgination'.[77]

To help them to their happiness, and to help establish plausible evidence of their consummation, wedding parties conventionally escorted the bridal couple to bed. Notoriously, the air was filled with sexual jokes and commendations. The bed itself might be flower-strewn, 'decked with ribbons and scented with violets and essence of jasmine', if anyone had taken the trouble, and in older times under Roman Catholicism the bed itself would have been blessed or sprinkled with holy water.[78]

By custom, at this point, the couple consumed a specially prepared drink, like the strengthening caudle given to newly delivered mothers. The 'sack posset', made of fortified wine and spices, was supposed to relax the woman and embolden the man. According to Samuel Pepys, the sack was to make him lusty, the sugar to make him kind. Arthur of Bradley, Sir John Lovelace, and Sir Clipseby Crew each shared this drink with their bride. When Oliver Cromwell threw sack posset over the women's dresses at his daughter's wedding in 1646, his action was interpreted as a ribald jest.[79]

An associated tradition was 'throwing the stocking', which was a prelude to the sight of four bare legs in a bed.[80] If the wedding party followed custom, when they crowded into the bridal chamber, they played a rowdy game with the bride's and bridegroom's hose. Such was the practice at some courtly and gentry weddings, as well as in popular ballads. Unlike the modern divination practice, in which the woman who catches the bridal bouquet is thought next in line for the altar, the stockings were thrown at, not by, the married couple. 'And after it comes the bride-groom who when he was in bed, the stocking being mentioned, the bride must sit up to have it thrown at her nose, that the bachelors may know by him that first hits it, who is to be married next'.[81]

When it came to the bedding of the bride, the traveller Henri Misson so outdid himself as an ethnographic reporter that his late Stuart description deserves to be given at length.

When bed-time is come the bride-men pull off the bride's garters, which she had before untied that they might hang down and so prevent a curious hand coming too near her knee. This done, and the garters being fastened to the hats of the gallants, the bride-maids carry the bride into the bed chamber, where they undress her and lay her in bed. The bridegroom, who by the help of his friends is undressed in some other room, comes in his night-gown as soon as possible to his spouse, who is surrounded by mother, aunt, sisters, and friends, and without any further ceremony gets into bed. Some of the women run away, others remain, and the moment afterwards they are all got together again. The bride-men take the bride's stockings, and the bride-maids the bridegroom's; both sit down at the bed's feet and fling the stockings over their heads, endeavouring to direct them so as that they may fall upon the married couple. If the man's stockings, thrown by the maids, fall upon the bridegroom's head, it is a sign she will quickly be married herself; and the same prognostic holds good of the woman's stockings thrown by the man. Oftentimes these young people engage with one another upon the success of the stockings, though they themselves look upon it to be nothing but sport. While some amuse themselves agreeably with these little follies, others are preparing a good posset, which is a kind of caudle, a potion made up of milk, wine, yolks of eggs, sugar, cinnamon, nutmeg, etc.. This they present to the young couple, who swallow it down as fast as they can to get rid of so troublesome company; the bridegroom prays, scolds, entreats them to be gone, and the bride says ne'er a word, but thinks the more. If they obstinately continue to retard the accomplishment of their wishes, the bridegroom jumps up in his shirt, which frightens the women and puts them to flight. The men follow them, and the bridegroom returns to the bride.[82]

Not until these rituals were accomplished would the couple be left in peace. And even then they might be interrupted by drums and fiddles, and the noise of drunken laughter, which might greet them again in the morning. Leonard Wheatcroft's wedding guests put the couple to bed 'with no small ado', and had to be chased from the room, the bridegroom writes, 'so that none might seem to hinder or molest us from our nearer unitings'. Next morning, awakened by music from 'our bed of pleasure', the dutiful Leonard sought a blessing from Elizabeth's father, 'who was then made my father-in-law, for I had lain with his daughter'. Noting the omission of this ritual at a 'private' wedding in 1667, Samuel Pepys commented, 'there was no music in the morning to call up our new-married people, which is very mean methinks, and is as if they had married like dog and bitch'.[83] As Pepys's observation suggests, Hymen's revels were loosely scripted, with nothing to enforce them but the tyrannies, sanctions, and vagaries of custom.

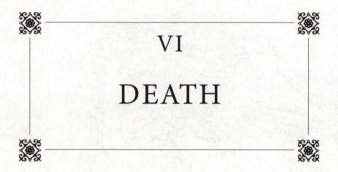

VI

DEATH

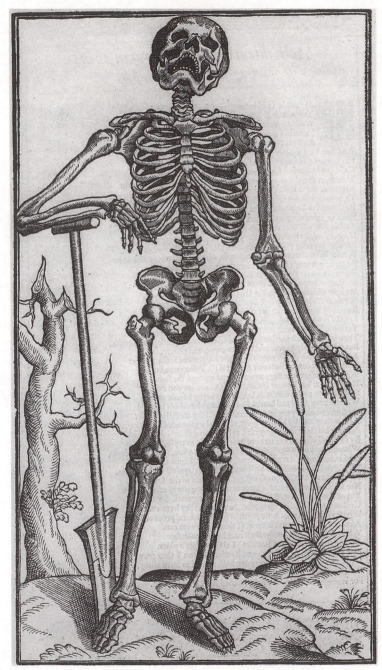

FIG. 18   Death. John Banister, *The Historie of Man* (1578)

DEATH COMES FOR ALL

Death has two histories, one the cosmic account of its origins in sin and its conquest by Christ's redemption, the other the more mundane story of how humans coped with mortality. The first story affected the second, for death and interment were meaningless in Christian England if shorn of their religious significance. Beliefs about the fate of the body and the destiny of the soul had complex consequences for religious liturgy and cultural practice. Changes in the theology of salvation produced profound alterations in attitudes to death and led to radical revision of the conduct of funerals and burials. Though the inevitability of death was untoppled, its meaning, performance, and trappings were all subject to question in the generations following the reformation. How to handle the mortal body, how to gauge the disposition of the soul, and how to navigate the journey from this world to the next, were issues that exercised moral and religious counsellors as well as men and women of every social class.

This section investigates the social and religious understanding of death in the sixteenth and seventeenth centuries.[1] It moves from theology through liturgy to secular social activity. Topics for consideration include the separation of body and soul, and the tension between traditional and reformist modes of burial. Later chapters deal in detail with the cultural practice of funerals in protestant England, the ritual interment of bodies, memory, memorials, and the problematic relationship of neighbourliness between the living and the dead. Death and burial are treated here in relation to the customs and tensions of a complex society, rather than as indicators of 'a growing sense of individualism'.[2] The evidence reveals diversity and dialogue within a continuing contested conversation about religious and secular solemnities, rather than a simple linear progression from medieval to modern.

Some elementary definitions are in order. 'Dying' was the process of sloughing of one's mortal coil, a process thought to begin at birth that accelerated in the final stages of illness or decrepitude. 'Death' was the extinction of the flame of life, the moment when most Christians thought the soul departed the body. 'Funerals' were the social and ceremonial observances performed to honour or accompany a body that was about to be buried, and could extend to include posthumous commemorative activities. 'Burial' included the religious service for burial and the final interment in the ground. Some writers also mentioned 'exequies' and 'obsequies', referring to the secular processional and commemorative activities of funerals. Their language became more florid or more archaic whenever they tried to associate the customs of Tudor or Stuart England to those of the ancient classical or biblical worlds.

Death was omnipresent in early modern England, its reminders everywhere. 'For to what end serve so many funerals of all sorts, old, young, rich, poor, noble, and base? To what end so many graves and sepulchres in the place of burial, so many dry bones cast out of the graves, but to set forth visibly before our eyes the mortal state of mankind?' asked the Suffolk preacher Robert Pricke in a Jacobean sermon. 'He that sees every churchyard swell with the waves and billows of graves, can think it no extraordinary thing to die,' observed a more celebrated Jacobean preacher, John Donne.[3] Adults and children, laity and clergy, all lived in close proximity with the dead and dying, and assembled for frequent worship amidst the tombs and monuments of neighbours who had gone before.

Death had 'a thousand doors to let out life . . . a thousand ways to guide us to our graves'. It came through 'sickness . . . through an external bad air, or some internal distemper of blood, by the sword, or by the infection of other men, or the sting or fury of wild beasts, by dead palsies, by miscarryings or unfortunate child-births, or by any other means or mischance', wrote the godly merchant James Cole.[4] 'We are full of holes and breaches,' wrote the London preacher Sampson Price. 'Some we see come to their graves by apoplexies, lethargies, dead palsies, some by sudden blows, some as a wasted candle goes out naturally.'[5] Nor did this begin to exhaust the catalogue of causes sometimes summarized in the bills of mortality. In the plague year of 1665, for example, in addition to the 68,000 in London allegedly felled by the pestilence, hundreds died of flux and ague, consumption and 'tissick', griping in the guts, and 'rising of the lights'. Death-rates normally fluctuated around 25 per 1,000 with mortality of 35 per 1,000, or even higher in the worst of seasons.[6] (This compares to death-rates of 8 to 12 per 1,000 in the modern industrial West.)

Death, Christians learnt, was not part of God's original plan for humankind, but came about as the consequence of sin. In the words of the layman James Cole, death was 'begot of the devil, brought into the world by sin, born in Paradise, the midwife Eve, the nurse Adam'.[7] Once established, its appetite was insatiable, and death set out to consume all flesh. Typically, in these discussions, death was personified as a ruthless adversary, 'a terrible enemy and a very cruel tyrant', if not reified as 'a heavy and fearful thing'. Contemporary woodcuts and engravings picture death as a walking skeleton, sometimes equipped with his lethal arrow or holding a spade to dig the grave.[8] 'Whatsoever death be, it is certainly a state and condition common to all the posterity and generation of Adam,' warned the Jacobean preacher Robert Pricke. 'All men must die, and none can avoid the stroke of death.'[9] In James Cole's maritime turn of phrase, 'death is our last port, unto it we are all bound, and at it everyone must arrive . . . Old, young, rich, poor, honest, dishonest, all tread that path.'[10]

Proverbial wisdom knew that 'death keeps no calendar'. His was not a visit one could plan. All were born to die, and 'even in our swathe-clouts [swaddling clothes] death may ask his due'. An early Stuart ballad asked the timeless question,

> Can you dance the shaking of the sheets,
> A dance that every one must do?
> Can you trim it up with dainty sweets,
> And every thing as longs thereto?
> Make ready then your winding sheet,
> And see how you can bestir your feet,
> For death is the man that all must meet.[11]

It was a commonplace of early modern preaching, as it had been before the Reformation, that people should be to be ready for death at all times. Nor should they resist it for, as John Donne reiterated, 'it is a rebellious thing not to be content to die'.[12] Preferring the language of estate management to the vocabulary of Christian theology, Robert Hegge, an Oxford academic, counselled Henry Oxinden in 1629 on 'these common crosses of mortality' that all men bore: 'In this world we are but tenants-at-will and no man has a lease of his life for term of years.' The great landlord in the sky would call us all in, as he had just called Oxinden's father.[13] What would follow when the lease fell due was not addressed in this particular discussion.

Human beings, alone of all creatures, were thought capable of contemplating their end. But only the most dissolute, tied to 'the pleasures of this world . . . think no more of death than the brute beast that is without understanding'. Anyone who lived 'as if they should never die, and as if hell were but a gull and a fable', would suffer the anger and jealousy of the Lord. Unfortunately there is no telling whether such atheistic beliefs were widespread, for most of our sources come from the devout and reputable élite.[14] Most writers agreed that death was loathsome, his visage grim. It was commonly observed that 'the greater, yea the better part of men do fear death'.[15] Yet countless tracts and sermons challenged the natural fear of dying by

FIG. 19 'As thou art, I once was | As I am, thou shalt be'. Deathbed scene from Christopher Sutton, *Disce Mori: Learne to Die* (London, 1601)

asserting that none should fear death if buoyed by Christian faith. The medieval refrain, *timor mortis conturbat me*, still echoed in the sixteenth and seventeenth centuries but its fearful sentiment was drowned out by countless promises of death as liberation.

Body and Soul

St Augustine taught that life was death and death was life, and this inverted notion found many English exponents in the sixteenth and seventeenth cen-

FIG. 20 'As death leaveth thee | So shall judgment find thee'. Resurrection scene from Christopher Sutton, *Disce Mori: Learne to Die* (London, 1601)

turies.[16] The faithful in Christian England were conditioned to expect a happier life beyond the painful passages of dying, on the other side of this present vale of tears. For catholics, eternal bliss came after the pains of purgatory; for protestants, the passage of the soul to heaven could take place in an instant so long as it belonged to one of the elect. It is hard to judge which religion allowed the greatest degree of equanimity.

Like the catholic missals, the protestant Order for the Burial of the Dead was full of references to living and rising, resurrection and life, felicity and joy. Didactic verses expressed similar messages: 'And fear not death, pale ugly though he be | Thou art in thrall, he comes to set thee free.'[17] The Book of Common Prayer no longer spoke of the departed going to Abraham's bosom, but this comfortable notion persisted in popular culture and in sermons.[18] A constant flow of religious comfort assured believers that their fear of death was baseless. Every death was a beginning as well as an end, 'a passage to eternal bliss'. The angel comes 'to lead me out of prison into liberty . . . from this vale of tears into eternal bliss', the dying man assured himself in Samuel Hieron's *Help Unto Devotion*. 'The death of Christ is the death of death' was a reassuring aphorism, so death, where is thy sting?[19]

'The day of our death is better than the day of our birth,' preached Thomas Playfere in an often-reproduced sermon of 1595. 'For when we are born we are mortal, but when we are dead we are immortal. And we are alive in the womb to die in the world, but we are dead in the grave to live in heaven.'[20] A barrage of Christian teaching neatly united the begining and end of human life and promoted the spiritual benefits of dying. 'We have a winding sheet in our mother's womb', John Donne preached before the King in 1630, 'and we come into the world wound up in that winding sheet, for we come to seek a grave.' It was a popular pulpit conceit to say that 'birth and death are twins'.[21]

Central to these discussions was the theory of the separation of body and soul. According to orthodox belief, body and soul became unhinged at the moment of death and went their separate ways. Kissed by God, the soul was the animating principle. The body was merely a vehicle or an encumbrance. At death the immortal soul flew off on its mysterious journey, while the material human husk began the process of decomposition.[22]

Uncounselled by protestant wisdom, the despairing Claudio in Shakespeare's *Measure for Measure* reflects on this crisis of separation. Understandably attached to the lively sensations of the body, he imagined a wandering soul that was sensitive to heat and cold. This was barely a Christian notion, that must have sent shudders through more orthodox members of Shakespeare's audience.

> Ay, but to die, and go we know not where;
> To lie in cold obstruction and to rot;
> This sensible warm motion to become
> A kneaded clod; and the delighted spirit
> To bathe in fiery floods, or to reside
> In thrilling region of thick-ribbed ice;
> To be imprisoned in the viewless winds
> And blown with restless violence round about
> The pendant world.[23]

The Bedfordshire puritan preacher Thomas Adams explained more ponderously in a sermon of 1613, 'corporeal death is the departure of the soul from the body, whereby the body is left dead, without action, motion, sense. For the life of the body is the union of the soul with it.' However, Adams explained, 'our death is . . . not a perishing but a parting . . . The soul is not lost to the body, but only sent before it to joy . . . Death cannot be eventually hurtful to the good, for it no sooner takes away the temporal life but Christ gives eternal life in the room of it.'[24] The court instructor Patrick Scot dressed this complex theology in familiar terms when he reminded the young Prince Charles in 1621 that 'the body of man is but a ruinous cottage wherein the soul of man is imprisoned'.[25] The imprisoned soul would be released by death to rise to its home in heavenly grandeur.

Another Jacobean minister, Robert Pricke, preaching at the burial of Sir Edward and Lady Lewkenor in Suffolk, contrasted the body's present corruption with its future resurrection in glory. This was a common theme in seventeenth-century funeral sermons.

The body lieth in the grave senseless and without motion, even as a block of stone . . . the majesty and beauty of the face and whole body departeth, and a pale, deformed, and ugly form succeeds . . . the body putrifieth and rotteth, and from thence proceeds a most horrible and stinking savour, and in the end is wholy turned to dust.

But ultimately, unlike the corpses of carrion, the bodies of the faithful shall be 'quickened and raised up, their souls restored to them again, and there withal the qualities of their bodies shall be changed from their former worse to a better renewed estate; to wit, from mortal to immortal, from corruption to incorruption, from earthly to heavenly, from weak to strong, from base to glorious'. With this in mind, Pricke continued,

it ministreth comfort to them that bestow and lay up the dead bodies of their friends in the graves; for why? they know they do not yield or deliver them up to destruction, but lay them up, as it were in soft beds, to the end that they may sleep quietly till they be awakened by the sound of the last Trumpet.[26]

The reference to 'sleep' was not just an evasive euphemism for death, but part of a complex eschatological theology. It was comforting and commonplace to think of churchyards and sepulchres as 'the dormitories of Christians'.[27] One of the most charming expositions of this notion came in an address by Matthew Wren when he consecrated a churchyard in Herefordshire in 1635. The churchyard, said the bishop, was 'a dormitory or place for Christians to sleep in . . . because they lying in their graves expect to be raised again at the last day by the voice of the archangel, as they which lie in their beds are raised in the dawning of the day by the cock's crowing'. This dormitory was a silent community, he noted, filled with 'those which in their life time like neighbours assembled together in one place, as members of the same body, might after death lie together in one place, expecting the same resurrection'. Linking the ceremonies of life and death, baptism and burial, Wren thought it fitting that the inhabitants of the graveyard 'lie as near the place as might be where they were first initiated into the church'.[28] We will return to this theme in our final chapter.

Under Roman Catholicism, people generally believed that the soul went first to purgatory, where it suffered in proportion to its lifetime accumulation of sins. The duration and intensity of these torments could be offset not only by the individual's devotional acts and religious good works while on earth, but also by the intercessionary prayers of the community of departed saints and living Christians after the person died. Eventually, at the day of judgement, the fortunate soul with its newly reconstituted body would be received into heaven or consigned to limitless hell. An important contingent belief was that the fate of the soul could be tempered, its passage to salvation improved or quickened, by prayer and ritual action. Hence the incantations at the burial of the body, and at various times thereafter; hence the business of month-minds, year-minds, obits, trentals, and chantry prayers; and hence, too, the early protestant claim that the old catholic service was so much mindless babbling to escape the imagined terrors of purgatory.[29]

Protestants jettisoned the notion of purgatory, claiming that it lacked scriptural foundation. To believe in purgatory, preached Edwin Sandys in 1574, was vain, perilous, and injurious.[30] This was a shift of enormous significance, affecting the dying person's preparations for the afterlife and the social relationship between the living and the dead. There was no painful waiting, no uncomfortable holding in purgatory, and of course, no purpose at all in prayers for the dead. As Robert Pricke said in a funeral sermon of 1608,

the soul after death . . . doth not wander up and down from place to place, nor yet remaineth in a third place, as papists and pagans have dreamed . . . but . . . it returneth unto God that gave. . . . The souls of everyone shall immediately after death appear before God their creator and judge . . . So that the souls of them that have believed in the Lord Jesus Christ, and obeyed the will of his heavenly father, do presently meet with the Lord Jesus in Paradise, are gathered into the bosom of Abraham, do enjoy unspeakable happiness and glory. But contrariwise, the souls of such infidels as have contemned Christ and his gospel, and have showed themselves disobedient, they do forthwith and without stay pass into a place of torments.[31]

The merchant James Cole concurred in 1629, 'concerning a mid-way mansion, or fiery prison, which some have endeavoured to settle by the way, there to purge and purify the blessed souls some certain years before their ascension in to heaven, we find nothing at all in holy writ'.[32]

There were now only two realms beyond the earth, the realms of salvation and damnation, heaven and hell. Neither was accessible to intercessionary effort; in the one case all prayer for the dead was superfluous, in the other it was hopeless and forlorn. Protestants believed, for the most part, that salvation was only achieved by the exercise of faith or by the inscrutable will of God. Good works during life had limited efficacy, and prayers after death had no effect at all on one's destiny, and could easily be regarded as superstitious. Calvinists were especially strict in this regard, with their awesome doctrine of predestination, but even Arminians, who came to dominate the Church of England in the seventeenth century, found no sound basis for intercessionary prayers for the dead.[33] As far as most English protestants were concerned, God's judgements existed outside of time, so the soul of the dead went at once to its reward.

Despite important disagreement over details, protestants and catholics concurred that when human history came to an end with Christ's descent in glory, the bodies of the just would be made new again, resurrected to their prime condition. Christians believed, and most still believe, in the end of the world, a second coming of Christ, his final judgement at doomsday, and the resurrection of the bodies of the dead to rejoin those souls that were saved for everlasting life. This set of notions was reiterated in the creed, in the articles of religion, and in the words of the service for the burial of the dead. It was a familiar, comforting, and internally coherent set of concepts, which guided much of the ritual and religious activity at early modern funerals.

Early modern protestants taught that the bodies of Christians, 'which have been the temples of the holy ghost, and in whom God did dwell and inhabit through faith',[34] were destined to rise again at the general resurrection. The reconstituted body would come in handy at that time and for all eternity to provide accommodation for the redeemed soul. As William Perkins explained, 'the body must rise again out of the earth, that it may be made a perpetual mansion for the soul to dwell in. The bodies of the faithful are the temples of the holy Ghost, and therefore must rise again to glory.'[35] John Donne drew on this tradition in 1627 when he preached over the remains of Lady Danvers, 'that body, which was the tabernacle of a holy soul and a temple of the holy ghost . . . shall have her last expectation satisfied, and dwell bodily with that righteousness, in these new heavens and new earth forever'. A generation later Samuel Clarke preached that Jesus 'takes care of all the bones, yea, of the very dust of his saints, that none of it shall be wanting when he comes to raise their bodies again at the last day. Our bodies, even whilst they are in the grave, are members of Christ, and therefore its no marvel, though he takes such care of them'.[36]

Christians could comfort themselves that the separation caused by death was temporary. It was a commonplace of protestant funeral preaching that 'the godly deceased are not lost forever but left for a time, not gone away from us, but sent to God before us'.[37] Since death was the portal to everlasting life there was no need to weep heavily on behalf of those who had gone. 'Our friends yet live,' insisted James Cole. 'Although our loving parents, husbands, wives, and children or friends are departed out of this world, yet for all that they be not therefore dead, but alive, yea they may still be called ours. And what greater comfort or reason then can we have to stay or stop our mourning than this?' John Donne likewise assured his listeners at St Paul's in 1627, 'the dead and we are now all in one church, and at the resurrection shall be all in one choir'.[38]

Diarists and correspondents repeatedly reassured themselves that the loved ones they had lost had gone to a better place. Solid Calvinists who believed in the mystery of predestination none the less expressed confidence that their kinsfolk were among the elect. For the Worcestershire businesswoman Joyce Jeffries, her sister, who died in 1640, was now 'a saint in heaven'.[39] Alice Thornton's sister Danby, who died after childbirth in 1645, 'delivered up her soul into the hands of her saviour, sweetly falling asleep in the lord'.[40] Isabella Twysden similarly took comfort in 1649, 'my good father left this world and went to God'.[41] John Brockbank's mother was understandably distressed at her son's death in 1687, but his father, a minister, took comfort in his belief that God had taken a life 'which he did but lend us for a time'. John's grandfather, a layman, wrote with a bleaker sense of loss of the young man, 'removed into that dark pit of the grave where we shall never see him with these bodily eyes again'.[42]

The pain of losing a child or a loved companion was alleviated by the prospect of eventual reunion in heaven. Disciplined but distraught when he buried his son in 1648, the Reverend Ralph Josselin wrote, 'thy bones rest out of my sight, but thy soul liveth in thy and my God's sight, and soul and body shall assuredly arise to enjoy God, and these mine eyes shall see it'. When he buried his daughter Mary two years later, Josselin reminded himself that her 'soul being with Jesus it rests there till the resurrection'.[43] Isaac Archer similarly hoped that he would meet those children that God had taken from him 'at the resurrection of the just'.[44] There may be an element of desperate wishing in all these formulations, shading into pious resignation and disciplined hope. Ordinary lay Christians appear to have shared these hopes, though the evidence for popular piety is scarce.

Though materially dead, the body deserved reverential treatment both in respect for what it had been and for what it would become. At the very least it warranted a decent funeral. When the priest committed the body to the earth, remarked Anthony Sparrow, it was 'not as a lost and perished carcase, but as having in it a seed of eternity', with hope of glorious resurrection.[45] One could not just dispose of dead bodies like carrion. Human decency and Christian honour demanded more reverent disposal. Indeed, it was a source of pride in some quarters that God's people did not handle human cadavers 'as we be wont to carry forth dead horses or dead swine', nor buried their dead like dogs.[46] If a funeral was rushed or mishandled it was likely to be complained of that the party had been treated like a beast. Human remains deserved reverential respect, both with regard to their prior station in life, and because they had been vessels of the soul and were destined to rise again. The trick, according to reformers, was to maintain the proper level of respect without allowing it to grow into sumptuous pomp or superstitious ritual. One exception was suicides, who forfeited the right of Christian burial; another, less clear-cut, applied in certain circumstances to people who died while excommunicated.[47]

Once buried, a body could not be exhumed without official permission. On the road to decomposition, and patiently awaiting the general resurrection, it belonged to no one. It lay, now, in God's freehold, and was subject to ecclesiastical cognizance if removed or abused.[48] For these reasons, as well as the demands of social convenience and decorum, the burial ground in the churchyard was supposed to be kept in a reverent manner. As we shall see in a later chapter, ideal standards were hard to maintain, and some graveyards fell foul of foraging animals and criminal activity, remodelling, misuse, and neglect.

Ars Moriendi

Refined and devoted Christians cultivated the art of dying. Many would wish it were said of them that nothing so became them in their life as the leaving of it. Only the godless or thoughtless refused to take death seriously. As the Jacobean Robert Hill wrote in *The Pathway to Prayer and Pietie*, 'it is the art of all arts, and science of all sciences, to learn to die'. Life was a preparation, and death its culmination. Far from fading with the Reformation, the medieval *ars moriendi* or art of dying enjoyed a lively revival under Elizabeth and the early Stuarts.[49] James Cole advocated a lifetime of preparation 'to die well'. So too did Sampson Price, who preached that 'the greatest work we have to do is to die well'.[50] Robert Herrick was one of many poets to contemplate 'a good death', writing, 'For truth I may this sentence tell, | No man dies ill, that liveth well.' From Thomas Becon's *Sick Man's Salve* (1561) through Christopher Sutton's *Disce Mori* (1600) to Jeremy Taylor's *Rule and Exercises of Holy Dying* (1651), a spate of publications offered guidance on preparation for dying and the performance of death.[51] Morbid thoughts were part of religious consciousness, rising and swelling with the great religious movements of the age.

Since medical cures were often ineffective, the victims of illness or accident faced days of pain in which to contemplate their impending mortality. Fortunately, they would rarely face it in isolation. Ideally, according to Christian counsel, the deathbed would be attended by ministers and friends, neighbours and kin, who would share godly comfort and bear witness to a satisfactory passing. If blessed by God, the fortunate Christian would be fully articulate to the end. It was a 'multiplied misery', according to John Donne, to be so tormented by sickness that one could not 'enjoy death', or to face the ordeal alone.[52] Children as well as adults were watched for signs of fortitude and grace, and their silences as well as utterances were weighed for spiritual significance. Men and women who were sufficiently well-loved or well-placed might then deserve a funeral euology, in which the manner of their dying attracted as much attention as the achievements of their life. Sudden death or death while sleeping forestalled the assembly of comforting witnesses, but could be interpreted as God taking the soul directly to its reward.

Exemplary Christian biography featuring the 'holy life and happy death' of one or another worthy contributed to a popular genre of seventeenth-century writing. Accounts of the life and death of men like John Bruen and John Angier could be considered as protestant versions of the instructive lives of saints.[53] All included edifying deathbed scenes. Pious women were likewise held up as exemplars, among them the renowned Elizabeth Joceline, for whom 'the course of her life was a perpetual meditation on death', and whose death in childbed in 1622 gave 'comfortable testimony of her godly resolution'.[54] By contrast, it was a scandal in 1629 when Mr Spod, lecturer at Uxbridge, Middlesex, refused to pray with two parishioners who were dying, 'the one because she could not give an absolute answer of her faith, the other because he had been of lewd and dissolute life'.[55]

Common cultural practice turned each rite of passage into a social and collective event. Like the birthroom where women gathered to witness the entry into life, the sickroom was an arena of action where people watched and waited for a mortal life to expire. Called by messengers or summoned by bells, a cluster of neighbours, helpers, relations, and prospective heirs might gather to attend the deathbed or wait in an adjacent room. 'The bell rung

FIG. 21 Deathbed scene. Detail from *The crie of the poore for the death of the Right Honourable Earle of Huntingdon* (London, 1596)

out, my friends came in', sang the 'dead man' in a popular seventeenth-century ballad.[56] When Oliver Heywood's son lay sick in 1667, 'neighbours were called in to see him die, but God restored him'.[57] In John Brockbank's last illness in 1687, his father wrote, 'he grew worse, so that night he was like to die, and we called in neighbours'. Neighbours and kin came together to share in the experience, to provide mutual comfort, and to witness the passing with heartfelt prayers, kisses, and farewells. Describing the event to his younger son who was studying at Oxford, Brockbank senior commented, 'he made the most sweet and comfortable end of any dying person that ever I took notice of'. The bereaved parents and friends sought solace in the exemplary manner of John Brockbanks's parting and in his clear demonstration of Christian faith.[58] Thomas Brockbank, who now became heir to the estate, could reflect that his brother lived up to the highest deathbed expectations.

More moving scenes of deathbed intimacy and social performance appear in seventeenth-century diaries. Robert Woodford, for example, reports that he and his mother joined other godly neighbours to watch and pray while Mr Freeman died at Cranford, Northamptonshire, in August 1637. Woodford writes, 'my mother closed his eyes at his departure', and all attended his burial two days later.[59] Ralph Josselin described similar observances at the deaths of his young children. On 21 February 1648 he writes,

this day my dear babe Ralph quietly fell asleep, and is at rest with the lord . . . We looked on it as a dying child three or four days . . . it died quietly without shrieks or sobs or sad groans, it breathed out the soul with nine gasps and died . . . Mrs. King and Mr. Harlakenden of the priory closed up each of them one of his eyes when it died; it died upwards, first in the feet and then in the head, and yet wonderful sweetly and quietly.[60]

William Johnson, a fellow of Clare College, Cambridge, registered strong satisfaction in his final exchange with his 'dear pupil Mr. Searle' in August 1661. The young man

made a confession of faith answering affirmatively to every article of the Apostle's creed. When I asked him if he was in charity and forgave all the world, he answered, Aye, all, all . . . When I told him I doubted not but God would raise him up again he answered, O take me up. He blessed God and had a steadfast faith in his saviour.

Johnson told Searle of another friend who, when dying, 'had thought he saw the devil at the bed's feet but he could spit in his face'. Searle answered, 'that he thanked God he saw no such thing, but if he did he could spit in his face, he was not afraid of him'. Almost delirious as he passed away, Searle told his tutor, 'he had been twice in heaven since his sickness', and when assured 'we should meet in heaven, had answered, that we should be joyful indeed'. This was an exemplary Christian death as well as exemplary deathbed counselling, and a remarkable glimpse of the student–teacher relationship *in loco parentis*.[61]

Besides being the centre of a moral theatre, the deathbed was also the place from which to finalize domestic and financial arrangements and perhaps to give instructions for burial. Dying, advised the puritan counsellor William Gouge, provided parents the opportunity to bestow on their children their memorable 'last blessing'. Doing this right was part of the script for a parent's good death. 'Let parents therefore, as they commend their own souls into God's hand, so commend their children into God's grace and blessing,' advised the premier handbook of domestical duties.[62]

It was time now, in James Cole's words, for a dying man 'to strive to end all quarrels and suits with his adversaries, to reveal all doubtful things to his friends, and besides to make a plain and lawful partition of his goods by his last will'.[63] Only those with property to dispose of or minor children to safeguard had the need to make a will, but the document could also be used to express religious beliefs. Comparison of dates reveals that as many as half of the wills proved in early modern courts were drawn up shortly before death, when the testator was convinced of his imminent parting. Nuncupative wills, expressed verbally rather than in writing, were also accompaniments to the deathbed scene.[64]

Grief

Despite the conceit that death entailed release, and despite the powerful hope that the departed had gone ahead to heaven, immediate survivors often experienced convulsions of grief. The Josselins and Brockbanks, for example, despite their Christian courage, had heartfelt pain when their loved ones died. To grieve was to cope, to register one's loss, and to work through the rift of separation. Grief helped bereaved survivors to adjust to altered conditions through the emotional processes of distress and release. Grief was, perhaps, a necessary form of self-indulgence, benefiting not the dead but the people left behind.

Historians once advanced the notion that people in the past did not love each other and were coldly unemotional in the face of a death in their family. But the bulk of the evidence indicates that love, pain, and grief were deeply rooted and widely experienced in early modern England. Even with death all around them, with mortality rates that a modern society might find numbing, the people of Stuart England displayed intense emotions when a child, a spouse, or a parent died. Nor did trust in providence and confidence in the resurrection prevent the welling of tears in their eyes.[65] Grieving spouses made up a high proportion of Richard Napier's practice as a healer of mental afflictions in the early Stuart South Midlands. Expressions of grief were common in the seventeenth-century iconography of death. One could even die of grief, as noted in the London bill of mortality for 1665 when forty-six deaths were attributed to that cause.[66]

Grief was both a natural and a cultural phenomenon. It was something people felt, but also something they performed. Failure to grieve might be seen as cold and heartless, while excess grief displayed weakness and lack of control. The subject easily lent itself to the Aristotelian discourse of balance and moderation. Thomas Playfere, in his sermon of 1595, judged weeping to be permissible so long as it was not immoderate.[67] Reminded that Jesus himself had wept, early Stuart writers judged weeping to be appropriate at funerals, so long as it was done with moderation.[68] It was natural to grieve for the dead, wrote John Weever, 'for as God hath made us living, so he has made us loving creatures'. 'We bewail our children, as fruits not yet ripe, too soon plucked from the tree,' observed James Cole in his godly treatise *Of Death*. 'It is fit,' wrote Samuel Clarke, 'that the body, when its sown in corruption, should be watered with the tears of them that plant it in the earth,' for 'to be without natural affections is an heathenish sin'.[69]

Diaries and letters make it impossible to assert that people were not immensely moved by the death of those close to them. Robert Woodford prayed heartily that his week-old child would live, and reported deep 'affliction' when the infant died in August 1640.[70] Ralph Josselin's and Isaac Archer's reactions to similar circumstances have already been documented. 'It was the saddest day of [his] life when his dear wife died,' Bulstrode Whitelock wrote in 1649. Even two weeks later, amidst the distractions of his legal career, he was unable to 'remove his grief or stop his tears'. John Evelyn registered 'great grief and affliction' at the loss of children and grandchildren, and his wife was reportedly 'disconsolate' at the death of her father in 1683. The dissenter Henry Newcome expressed 'pain and grief' at the loss of his son Daniel in 1683. 'My heart is so incurably pierced with grief,' wrote Edmund Verney in similar circumstances in 1686. After the death of their 3-year-old grandson, Elizabeth Freke records, both grandparents were 'in an extreme melancholy for the fatal loss of this our dear babe'.[71]

Oliver Heywood in June 1674 attended the funeral of 'Joshua Stansfield's wife who died in childbirth . . . and the child with her, whom I saw laid in one coffin, the child in her arms, as though it were asleep, an affecting sight, sad for relations'. Ralph Thoresby was 'not able to refrain from tears' at a much-loved gentleman's funeral in Nottinghamshire in 1681, an occasion that stimulated mournful introspection. The Reverend Thomas Jolly was likewise struck by grief and a feeling of 'sinking' when his 'loving wife' died in 1675. 'I thought my soul should never forget that distress', he confided to his notebook. At her burial, he wrote, 'I felt [the] suitableness of the 39th Psalm to my case, and verses 7 [and] 8 were more especially spoken to me.' These were the words in the Order for the Burial of the Dead asking, 'Lord, what is my hope: truly my hope is even in thee.'[72]

Grieving, for the most part, was brief and cathartic, but some people cultivated and dwelt on their sorrow. The pious Robert Woodford grew mournful on the anniversary of his father's passing. On 2 June 1639 he wrote, 'this day three years my father was buried. Lord fit me for death. Let it not come unawares or unwelcome to me for the lord's sake.' Ralph Thoresby, who lost his father in 1679, also kept up an annual meditation, surrounded by his father's papers and memorabilia. In October 1680, on the first anniversary, Thoresby wrote that he spilled 'rivers of tears' for his loss. Six years later he writes, 'upon the annual return day of my dearest father's death I was, as usual, overwhelmed with sorrow', and reread 'the sermon preached upon that mournful occasion'.[73] Woodford and Thoresby may have taken patriarchal sentiment beyond the call of duty, but it was hard to relinquish loved ones who were still emotionally bonded to the living. Deprived of the catholic remedy of prayers for the dead, these self-conscious protestants harnessed the process of grief to the art of living and dying.

Against this emotional transcript we have contrasting testimony from people like John Weever, a promoter of elaborate funerals, who thought that people did not grieve enough. Writing in 1631 he observed,

we in these days do not weep and mourn at the departure of the dead so much nor so long as in Christian duty we ought. For husbands can bury their wives, and wives their husbands, with a few counterfeit tears, and a sour visage masked and painted over with dissimulation; contracting second marriages before they have worn out their mourning garments, and sometimes before their cope-mates be cold in their graves.[74]

William Blundell wrote in his commonplace book in Restoration Lancashire, 'Soon cry, soon dry. See how mourning and tears are commended at funerals, as it were for fashion's sake and to satisfy others.'[75] No doubt there was much shallow and sentimental weeping, especially among shallow and cultivated people, but that did not offset the intensity of painful and authentic grief. Discussion of the ritual process of mourning is reserved for a later chapter.

RITUAL AND REFORMATION

One of the most profound effects of the protestant elimination of purgatory was to shrink the community of souls and to sever the relationship between the dead and the living. Though their bodies remained in the churchyard, the souls of departed protestants were now thought to be beyond the reach of intercessionary prayer. There was much less sacramental action under the reformed religion, much less commemorative ritual. Most of the ritual precautionary or intercessionary activity of traditional catholic burials was abrogated or undermined in the course of the Reformation. Trentals, masses, dirges, and prayers for the dead were resolutely set aside.[1] This does not mean that reformed practices took widespread or immediate root with the adoption of the Book of Common Prayer, but the new theology provided both moderate and zealous protestants with a standard against which local practices could be judged. This chapter returns to the records of religious controversy and ecclesiastical administration to examine the vectors of criticism and discipline in the wake of the disappearance of purgatory.

The Order for Burial of the Dead

In the old catholic service the priest wished the soul Godspeed on its journey while sprinkling and censing the body: 'Almighty and everlasting God, we humbly entreat thy mercy, that thou wouldest commend the soul of thy servant, for whose body we perform the due office of burial, to be laid in the bosom of thy patriarch Abraham; that, when the day of recognition shall arrive, he may be raised up, at thy bidding, among the saints of thy elect.'[2] A version of this survived in the first English prayer book of 1549, without holy water or incense, but reference to commendation of the soul was excised in 1552 and was never officially reinstated in the ceremonies of the Church of England. The soul went immediately to its reward, and had no need to be entrusted, commended, or committed.

The protestant revolution radically revised the conceptual geography of salvation. The 1549 service asked that the soul might escape 'the gates of hell, and pains of eternal darkness', and instead 'dwell in the region of light, with

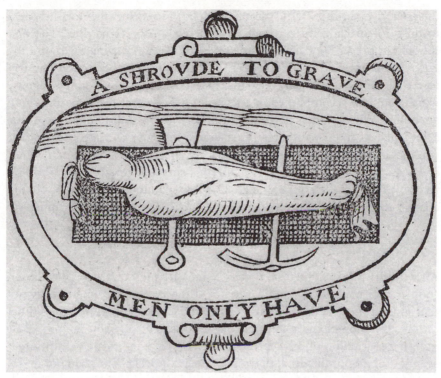

FIG. 22 'A shroud to grave men only have'. Detail from the *Map of Mortalitie* (London, 1604)

Abraham, Isaac, and Jacob, in the place where is no weeping, sorrow, nor heaviness', while awaiting the general resurrection. The priest commended the soul to God in hope that, 'when the judgement shall come', it 'may be found acceptable'. The second Edwardian and Elizabethan prayer books, by contrast, asserted that the souls of the elect lived immediately in the Lord, 'delivered from the burden of the flesh . . . in joy and felicity'. Instead of petitioning God for good favour, the reformed prayer book rejoiced 'that it hath pleased thee to deliver this N. our brother, out of the miseries of this sinful world'.[3]

Both Tudor versions of the Order for the Burial of the Dead required the priest or minister to meet the corpse at the church stile (the entry to the churchyard) and accompany it into the church or towards the grave. It was a matter of discretion, more likely associated with the deceased's social position than the minister's religious sensibilities, whether the ceremony took place inside the church or outside in the churchyard. Both versions of the service included the drama of casting earth on the corpse committed to the ground, and the powerful incantation, 'earth to earth, ashes to ashes, dust to dust, in sure and certain hope of resurrection to eternal life'. The first Edwardian prayer book assigned the priest the task of casting earth into the grave, but in 1552 and in all subsequent versions this symbolic action was performed 'by some standing by'. In either case, it was a service of simple dignity, which could be accomplished in a few minutes without overexposing those attending to the weather. There was little here for radicals to object to or for ceremonialists to embellish, and it generated little of the heated debate that continued around matrimony, baptism, and churching. Puritans sometimes baulked at the words in the service offering 'sure and certain hope of resurrection to eternal life', but moderate Calvinists contended that hope sprang eternal; anyone could hope, though God alone could make the determination.

Persistent Tradition

After the first flurries of reform under Henry VIII and Edward VI, the Marian counter-reformation once again promoted the customary funeral activities that most Tudor families seemed to prefer. Seeking to enforce traditional catholic ceremonies and to crack down on dissidents, Bishop Bonner asked in his 1554 visitation of the Diocese of London whether anyone 'murmured' against 'burying of the dead, praying for them, especially in saying of dirges and commendations'.[4] Murmurs of this sort were no doubt bruited abroad, but in the mid-sixteenth century they were drowned out by enthusiasm for customary ceremonies. The old order was both familiar and comforting. Few people, besides protestant enthusiasts, were convinced of the absence of purgatory at this time, and gentles and commoners alike persisted in their demand for comprehensive funeral rituals.

Prayer for the dead was such a deeply engrained practice in mid-Tudor England that it took several decades of preaching and discipline to draw it to a close. Some people believed that the soul still lingered in the vicinity of the body during the first thirty days after burial, a liminal situation requiring great ritual caution. During the Elizabethan period, especially in the early part of the reign, some testators contined to provide for this 'triginal' period by ordering a black cover for their coffin or grave during this month's mind, or arranging for another service, dole, and funeral feast when it came to an end. Though repudiated by the Reformation, the traditional month-mind and year-mind had a customary half-life in many parts of England as far apart as Lancashire and Essex. Provisions for obits and month-minds and prayers for all Christian souls were not uncommon in wills of the 1550s, 1560s, and 1570s, though heirs and executors were increasingly hard-pressed to carry them out.[5]

Elizabethan reformers worked hard to erode this deep-seated conservatism. Determined to suppress all superstition and to extirpate 'all hypocrisy, enormities and abuses' in religious worship, the new regime reimposed the protestant services of the 1552 Book of Common Prayer, and attempted to enforce uniformity through the disciplinary apparatus of the church.[6] It was a slow and painful process, not completed in many areas until the second half of Elizabeth's reign.[7]

Ecclesiastical records reveal the range and development of episcopal concerns. By specifying practices that they wished to see eliminated the reformers drew attention to a pattern of devotional activity that belonged to the discredited catholic regime. Once again, we are forced to work with fragments and the evidence is often more tantalizing than complete. Investigators in the Diocese of Canterbury in 1560 were horrified to find crosses being borne at the burial of mother Cosen at Willesborough, Kent, acccompanying her body on its journey to the church. Almost a decade later when Archbishop Parker visited the diocese in 1569 he still sought to curtail bequests and annuities supporting 'obits, dirges, trentals, or any such like use, now by the laws of this realm not permitted'.[8] This was not so much a blanket condemnation of the rejected past as a continuing disciplinary engagement with the remnants of a deeply held faith.

James Pilkington, bishop of Durham from 1561 to 1576, spent much of his energy criticizing popish beliefs and practices that still persisted in early Elizabethan England. In his own rules for funerals (published posthumously in 1585) Pilkington insisted

that no superstition should be committed in them, wherein the papists infinitely offend; as in masses, dirges, trentals, singing, ringing, holy water, hallowed places, years's days and month-minds, crosses, pardon letters to be buried with them, mourners, *de profundis* by every lad that could say it, dealing of money solemnly for the dead, watching of the corpse, bell and banner, with many more that I could reckon.[9]

Bishop Richard Barnes, Pilkington's successor at Durham, continued to reform the diocese, enjoining in 1577 'that no communions or commemorations (as some call them) be said for the dead, or at any burials of the dead; or anniversaries or months minds be used for the dead, nor any superfluous ringing at burials, nor any superfluous ringings on All Saints day at night or the day following, of old superstitiously called All Souls day'.[10] All of these practices were outlawed by the Reformation, but they were not necessarily eliminated from English religious culture.

Nicholas Robinson, the reforming bishop of Bangor, similarly worked hard to eradicate 'disordered services and vain ceremonies' in Elizabethan Wales.

Robinson acted firmly in 1570 when word came from Beaumaris that 'two curates and three clerks of that parish, with three singing boys, were in their surplices in the house of Lewis Roberts . . . singing of certain psalms over his dead corpse, when also is certain wax candles were lit upon the hearse'. This was blatant popery that had to be crushed with vigour. Employing the combined authority of episcopacy, mayoralty, and magistracy, the bishop 'forbade all prayers and ceremonies over the dead not authorized by law'. He preached 'against such faithless prayers' and forced the offenders to perform public penance, 'to stay the ignorant from other relics of fond superstition'. Civic officials assured him that 'the disorder which was committed was done of mere ignorance and a foolish custom there used, and that the like should never by god's grace be attempted in that town'. The bishop in turn was able to reassure the council in London that godly reformation was in hand.[11]

In much the same vein Archbishop Grindal attempted to impose protestant discipline in the province of York 1571, insisting that 'no month-minds or yearly commemorations of the dead, nor any other superstitious ceremonies be observed or used which tend either to the maintenance of prayer for the dead or of the popish purgatory'. Funeral processions would be prohibited from pausing at crosses along the route, and burial services would no longer resound with 'superfluous or superstitious ringing'.[12] Marmaduke Middleton likewise sought to extinguish the old catholic customs from the Diocese of St David's, asking in 1583, 'whether at the burial of the dead they use any lights, tapers or trindles, or use any superstitious means either at crosses, stiles, the church door; or otherwise set up any crosses of wood in the church or churchyard about the graves of the dead'.[13] These articles and strictures would not have been necessary if protestantism had already triumphed. Scattered evidence suggests that traditional unreformed practices persisted through much of the north and west, as well as closer to London, though by the 1580s they seem to have been in sharp decline.

Traditional catholic funeral practices continued in Lancashire well into the late sixteenth century, according to the region's more progressive preachers who claimed to be scandalized by these 'manifold enormities'. Their summary of 'manifold popish superstition used in the burial of the dead' reveals activist outrage at unreformed activities and points to a local culture in the midst of an uncomfortable transition.

1. Some use the popish rites of burial towards the dead corpse at home, as it were burying it before it come to the church.

2. After they have set forth the corpse in their houses all garnished with crosses, and set round about with tapers and candles burning night and day, till it be carried to the church. All which time the neighbours use to visit the corpse, and there

everyone to say a *Pater noster* or *De profundis* for the soul; the bells all the while being rung many a solemn peal. After which they are made partakers of the dead man's dole of banquet of charity.

3. Thus all things being accomplished in right popish order at home, at length they carry the corpse towards the church all garnished with crosses, which they set down by the way at every cross, and there all of them devoutly on their knees make prayers for the dead.

4. And when in this superstitious sort they have brought the corpse to the church, some with haste prevent the minister, and bury the corpse themselves, because they will not be partakers of the service said at the burial; some overtreat the minister to omit the service, and sometimes obtain their purpose; and when the minister is ready to accomplish the order of service appointed for the burial, many of these that come with the corpse will depart; for recusants refuse not to bring it to the church, though they will not partake the service of the church.

5. Then, concerning those that remain with the corpse till it be buried, when they have set down the corpse in the church they bend themselves to their private prayer with crossing and knocking themselves, all kneeling round about the corpse neglecting the public service then in hand. And when the corpse is ready to be put into the grave, some by kissing the dead corpse, others by wailing the dead with more than heathenish outcries, others with open invocations for the dead, and another sort with jangling the bells, so disturb the whole action, that the minister is oft compelled to let pass that part of the service appointed for the burial of the dead and to withdraw himself from their tumultuous assembly.

6. After which burial, at their banquet in the alehouse they often have a *Pater noster* for the dead.

7. All the day and night after the burial they use to have excessive ringing for the dead, as also at the twelve months day after, which they call a minning [reminding] day. All which time of ringing, their use is to have their private devotions at home for the soul of the dead. But while the party lieth sick, they will never require to have the bell knolled, no, not at the point of death; whereby the people should be stirred up to prayer in due time; neither will any almost at that time desire to have the minister to come to him for comfort and instruction.[14]

There is no firm evidence that unreformed practices of this sort were truly widespread. Rather than flaunting their catholicism, it appears that the Lancashire traditionalists by 1590 had to work around the edges of the new official religion, sustaining their belief in purgatory through subterfuge or informal domestic devotions. Conservatives clashed with conformists in the course of rites of passage, and some parish services were disrupted; but the times were against them and eventually the catholics retreated indoors. Recusant funerals were likely to be held at untoward hours, or performed quietly with grudging acquiescence by local authorities.[15] A picture emerges of a hybrid religious culture, in which reformed and unreformed elements intermingled while being pressured towards conformity. Power and authority lay with the protestants, and the balanced tipped their way almost year by year.

The godly reformation, however, was never complete. Traditionalists continued to keep up some of the older customs, demonstrating to puritans that popery ever beckoned. Quasi-catholic ceremonies continued in Lancashire, though not without contest and challenge. At Ribchester in 1639 Robert Abbott was disciplined for accompanying the corpse of a suspected recusant 'in a superstitious manner'. The citation charged that

there was a cross towel laid over her corpse upon the bier, and she was set down at stone and wooden crosses by the way; and you did at the same cross in a superstitious manner take off your hat and kneeled down and prayed. And many people which saw you do think that you did worship and pray unto the crosses.

Here, thought the authorities, was a case of those 'manifest enormities' catalogued fifty years earlier, with a body 'garnished with crosses' and the mourners stooping to pray at crosses along the way. But Abbot had a different tale to tell, deflecting charges of religious irregularity. 'A towel was laid along the corpse,' he said, 'and another less towel was pinned over it to keep the long one from flying off, and not in any superstitious sort. And the corpse was set down at the crosses, and he amongst others took off his hat and said the Lord's Prayer.' The trouble, by his account, lay in personal clashes between him and the newly appointed vicar, not in deeply engrained divisions over funeral solemnities. If this was a mixture of sophistry, casuistry, and ingenuousness, it may be symptomatic of how such issues were negotiated in everyday local practice.[16]

Traditional ways of thinking and acting lingered for several generations, though increasingly reduced to the status of folk practices and superstitions. Writing after the Restoration, John Aubrey recalled traditional funeral customs from his West Country boyhood in the reign of Charles I. 'I heard 'em tell that in the old time, they used to put a penny in the dead person's mouth to give to St. Peter, and I think that they did do so in Wales and in the north country.' And in Yorkshire, he added, 'to this day, they continue the custom of watching and sitting up all night till the body is interred', while the watchers entertained themselves with conversation and prayers, card games, drink, and tobacco.[17] Aubrey's contemporary, the Yorkshire minister Joshua Stopford, believed that sprinkling the dead with holy water to drive away evil spirits, carrying candles or torches in the procession to the church, pausing with the body at holy stations, and casting flowers or herbs into the grave with the corpses, were all popish practices derived from heathen customs, though some of them continued in post-Restoration England.[18] The belief in ghosts and unquiet spirits may be related to the incomplete eradication of purgatory from popular consciousness, long after its elimination from the official protestant religion.[19]

Puritan Criticism

From the time of Elizabeth to beyond the Restoration, protestant activists continued to object to residual practices that revealed the failure of thoroughgoing reform. Some went well beyond the bishops in the virulence and zeal of their concerns. Puritan controversialists found less to argue about in the Order for Burial of the Dead than in many other services in the Book of Common Prayer, but that did not stop them finding fault with unreformed burial customs. Their main area of complaint concerned traditional cultural activities that preceded the actual interment of the body, but the formal religious burial service also drew godly criticism.

The 'view of popish abuses yet remaining in the English church', attached to the 1572 *Admonition to the Parliament*, catalogued a variety of practices that puritans could find offensive.

They appoint a prescript kind of service to bury the dead, and that which is the duty of every Christian they tie alone to the minister, whereby prayer for the dead is maintained . . . We say nothing of the threefold peal because that is rather licensed by Injunction than commanded in their book; nor of their strange mourning by changing their garments, which if it be not hypocritical, yet it is superstitious and heathenish, because it is used only of custom; nor of burial sermons, which are put in place of trentals, whereout spring many abuses, and therefore in the best reformed churches are removed. As for the superstitions used both in country and city, for the place of burial, which way they must lie, how they must be fetched to church, the minister meeting them at church stile with surplice, with a company of greedy clerks, that a cross white or black must be set upon the dead corpse, that bread must be given to the poor, and offerings in burial time used, and cakes sent abroad to friends, because these are rather used by custom and superstition than by the authority of the book.[20]

Blended together here were traditional catholic practices that the Church of England no longer sanctioned and elements of the official rubric of the Book of Common Prayer that presbyterians thought hearkened back to Rome. The *Admonition* served as a puritan manifesto, but not one to which all subsequent puritans adhered.

The separatist Henry Barrow renewed the charges in 1590, similarly ridiculing the burial practices of Elizabethan protestantism and confusing them with unreformed catholicism:

the priest meeting the corpse at the church stile in white array, his ministering vesture, with solemn song, or else reading aloud certain of their fragments of Scripture, and so carry the corpse either to the grave, made in their holy cemetery and hallowed churchyard, or else, if he be a rich man, carry his body into the church; each where his dirge and trental is read over him after they have taken off the holy covering cloth, and the linen crosses wherewith the corpse is dressed, until it come into the churchyard or church into that holy ground, lest sprights in the mean time should carry it away . . . If he be a man of wealth, that he make his grave with the rich in the church, he shall then pay accordingly; for that ground is much more precious and holy than the churchyard, having been consecrate and all to be sprinkled with holy water; there he shall be sure to lie dry, his grave being cut east and west, and he so laid that he may rise with his face into the east . . . But if he be of any great degree or but stepped into the genty, then he hath accordingly his mourners, yea, his heralds peradventure, carrying his coat armour and streamers before him with solemn ado, and pitching them over his tomb, as if Duke Hector, or Ajax, or Sir Launcelot were buried.[21]

The whole business was nonsense, Barrow argued, completely lacking in scriptural foundation. 'I never read in all the practice or epistles of the Apostles, that it belonged to any minister of the church, as by office, to bury the dead.' Nor was there any justification for burying in the church or churchyard. But such was the extent of superstition and ignorance, Barrow thought, that 'if they be not buried there, and that by the priest, with his book, then are they buried like dogs, say the common people'.[22] Where, Barrow asked his enemies in a later publication, did you learn 'to make burial of your dead an ecclesiastical action? . . . Where learned you to bury in your hallowed churches and churchyards, as though you had not fields and grounds to bury in?' Where did the church of England learn such things as ritual words and action, 'if not of the pope?'[23]

Barrow had few followers in Elizabethan or Jacobean England but Amsterdam exiles and Scottish Presbyterians repeated his criticisms. Determined nonconformists rehashed the litany of the presbyterian *Admonition*, and separatists continued to argue for burial with 'gravity and sobriety' but 'without either singing or reading' or 'any ceremonies of praying or preaching'.[24] Radicals sometimes argued 'that the children of God may bury their dead without the presence of a minister', claiming that 'in the primitive church the dead were buried by their friends, and burial was not a function of the minister until the time of popery'.[25] They wanted burial without funerals, interment without ceremony. But opportunities to put these preferences into practice were severely limited before the revolutionary breakdown of the 1640s and 1650s. Despite the intermittent stream of puritan criticism, there was no distinctive 'puritan way of death' in Elizabethan or early Stuart England.[26]

Instances of lay burial were rare. The authorities were quick to react if they heard of interment without a priest. The post-Reformation Church of England was adamant that burial required the service of a minister, just as it insisted that a parson was essential to the performance of baptism or the solemnization of matrimony. Attempting to preserve both liturgical dignity and clerical monopoly, bishops often asked in their visitations 'whether your clerk doth meddle with any thing above his office, as churching of women, burying the dead, reading of prayers, or such like'.[27] Burial belonged to priestcraft, no matter how much lay, familial, or heraldic investment governed the secular ceremonies of funerals. It was the minister's task, and none but his, to read over the body and to offer the prayers that accompanied its burial in the ground. Only the most radical of puritans dissented from this view, and held that anyone could take it on himself to bury his kinsfolk or friends.

In one egregious case the archdeacon of Essex faced defiant radicalism when he learned that a maid servant of the puritan Quarles family had been buried at Romford in 1589, 'without any ceremony, and not according to the communion book'. Clustered around the open grave, one of the diggers asked 'who should bury her', to which John Leech replied, 'all we here present'. Leech, a nonconformist schoolmaster and a constant thorn in the side of the authorities, conducted a makeshift burial service of his own and 'threw the earth on her and covered her' himself, an action that led to his excommunication.[28] Also in Essex, in 1607, William Bird was 'much complained upon for burying the dead, being a mere lay man . . . he hath buried many dead bodies in the parish of Coggeshall but hath not read the form of burial set forth in the Book of Common Prayer, neither was there any minister present'.[29] Bird's offence was deeply troubling to the ecclesiastical authorities, but it was not one they had to deal with often.

In another episode in London in 1636 the wife of Francis Jessop of St Katherine Creechurch demanded to bury her daughter 'without the observance of the order of church burial, declaring herself that they could bury without a minister; and her friends which accompanied the corpse to the grave, so soon as the minister began the form of church burial, left the corpse and went away'. This was a serious sign of sectarian disorder, and an affront to the dignity and authority of the church. It was also a threat to clerical income, for Jessop also refused to pay the 'duties belonging to the minister, the parish and the clerk, being commanded'.[30] The radicals made their protest, akin to that of the Lancashire papists in 1590, and then retreated and allowed the minister to get on with his job.

More common were cases explaining irregular burial in terms of contingent necessity. Bodies had to be buried promptly, but sometimes no minister was available to perform the ceremony. If the parson was absent or indisposed it could happen that a corpse could arrive at the church and no ordained minister found to read the service. Epidemic disease could overload the system, and the priest himself might be afflicted during outbreaks of plague or other crises of mortality. On such occasions parishioners had no alternative but to undertake the task themselves, either dispensing with the religious ceremony altogether or making their own best attempt at it. The parish clerk or sexton, or some other layman associated with the office, might do his best to replicate the service. It was then up to the authorities to distinguish the improvisations of urgent necessity from radical puritan objections to burial at the hands of a priest.

The ways in which parishioners handled these crises, and how they dealt with subsequent ecclesiastical enquiries, can be glimpsed through the veil of the visitation records. The parishioners of Abthorpe, Northamptonshire, for example, explained in 1573 that they had no curate and therefore no services, and so 'for want of a priest they have been compelled to bury the dead bodies themselves'. After the minister died of plague in 1604 the parish clerk of St Botolph Aldgate, London, took over part of his duties in burying the dead. It was as if his former association with the minister lent him the authority that could only be properly supplied by ordination. Similarly at Selsey, Sussex, in 1625, because the minister was non-resident, 'divers corpses have of necessity been buried by our parish clerk'.[31] There was not much the authorities could do after the fact, except to issue reprimands and order that it not happen again.

Sometimes the minister was available but failed to provide the necessary priestly ceremony. When charged with irregular conduct in 1593, the minister of Norton Mandeville, Essex, explained that 'he did not go to the grave according to the Book of Common Prayer, by reason of a great wind, and he not being well durst not go into the danger of taking cold by the air'. Although this excuse sounds plausible, the suspicion lingers that the minister's sensible precaution was a cover for clerical recalcitrance. Similar suspicions accompanied the report from Broxted, Essex, in 1605 that Ralph Bugge's daughter was buried on Candlemas day, 'after evening prayer was done', not 'orderly and lawfully according to the king's book of common prayer', but 'undecently without knell or any bell ringing or tolling, or without the reading of the divine service belonging to the burial'. At first glance this looks like another case of puritan nonconformity, and indeed that may be part of the truth. But the court accepted a much simpler explanation. Witnesses explained that the vicar could not get back in to the locked church to get the new prayer book because his sexton had gone home with the keys. Under examination the sexton said that he did not know there was to be a burial that day, and by the time he returned with the keys he found the corpse already 'laid in the ground and the grave in covering, and Mr. White [the vicar] reading the order of burial at the grave out of the old service book that Mr. White kept with him in his own house'.[32] In this case, the urgent necessity of concluding the burial took priority over the niceties of liturgical correctness. This fragment of testimony is also instructive about relations between sextons and ministers, the locking of churches, and the transition between the Elizabethan and Jacobean Books of Common Prayer.

In another case from this period, Anthony Armitage, the puritan vicar of Ellington, Huntingdonshire, was charged with multiple irregularities, including some related to burials. 'The said Mr. Armitage will not at any time meet the corpse at the churchyard gate,' claimed his enemies, though the church-warden testified he did so 'sometimes'. Once he refused to bury two children, 'but appointed the clerk of the parish to put them into the earth, very unreverently and undutifully, contrary to the order of the Book of Common Prayer'. On another occasion, despite being given due warning, he went off to Huntingdon on the day appointed for the burial of Mary Hale, wife of Giles Hale, 'and came not home till very near night, and the corpse being brought to the church stayed there two hours and the whole parish also, and yet when the said Mr. Armitage came he would not say any prayers till the corpse was brought out of the church, insomuch that he could scarce see to read prayers'.[33] The records tell just one side of this story, from a community divided between orthodox, godly, and traditionalist factions. It cannot be claimed that the minister was opposed in principle to burying the dead, though his pastoral schedule left some parishioners wanting.

Not surprisingly, puritan ministers who were uncomfortable wearing the surplice and were slack about signing with the cross in baptism were also prone to nonconformity in other areas. Visitation records bristle with vicars who rejected the surplice, fudged the prayer book, failed to meet the funeral procession, or refused to allow the dead to be brought inside the church.[34] Lay puritans often supported these ministers but rarely took initiatives themselves of the kind we have seen at baptisms and churchings. Most moderate puritans within the Church of England swallowed their discontent and accommodated themselves to approved prayer-book practices. Some may have cavilled about the surplice—'a popish massing garment'—and argued that the priestly vestment rather demeaned than distinguished the religious ceremony.[35] Some were uneasy about bringing a dead body into church and were watchful for signs of superstition. But otherwise most ministers adhered to the words and the rubric of the Book of Common Prayer and most layfolk took comfort from their services. By the time of James I progressive incumbents were much more inclined to use the occasion of funerals for godly instruction than to object to the ceremony on principle.

Some early reformers also argued against funeral sermons. It is hard to imagine that a puritan was ever against preaching, but until the end of the sixteenth century there were radicals complaining that funeral sermons were akin to masses or obits because they insinuated prayers for the dead. Thomas Cartwright charged that preaching at funerals 'was better used among the Athenians than amongst Christians', since the practice was devoid of scriptural warrant and was notoriously subject to superstition. The *Admonition* of 1572, which Cartwright helped write, listed 'burial sermons, which are put in place of trentals' among its catalogue of abuses. John Whitgift answered that 'there is as much difference betwixt our sermons and the papistical masses and trentals, as there is betwixt cold and hot, black and white, light and darkness, lies and truth, heaven and hell'.[36] Bishop Pilkington recognized that protestants disagreed 'whether burial sermons are to be suffered and used', but to him it was a matter of indifference. 'And if they have too many burial sermons in the city, God grant us some more in the country.'[37]

Most moderate protestants welcomed them, and some could not hear enough. Puritans soon realized that their objections were ill-founded, and that far more spiritual mileage could be obtained by preaching funeral sermons than by agitating against them. Funeral sermons were vehicles for expounding true doctrine, and provided occasions to prepare listeners for death. Leading protestants were among the most distinguished preachers of funeral sermons in the 1560s and 1570s.[38] Late Elizabethan puritans took to their pulpit with gusto, preparing for the great age of funeral sermons in the seventeenth century. The hundreds of funeral sermons that were published represent a fraction of the thousands that were delivered.[39]

Most ordinary burials passed without sermons, the simple service at the graveside being thought sufficient. But to more prominent parishioners, especially members of the clergy and gentry, a funeral was incomplete without a sermon. In many cases such sermons included a eulogy of the deceased, praising his or her virtues and achievements within a Christian frame of reference. The Jacobean preacher Robert Hill took pains to caution that 'they are not for the bare commendation of the dead, but for the instruction and consolation of them that are alive'.[40] But later in the seventeenth century John Dunton complained that 'funeral sermons have generally been rather for ostentation and vainglory than for profit'.[41] Sermons could legitimately be preached in honour of a person's memory, not for the sake of the soul.[42] In

1641 the London Laudian Edward Finch acknowledged that he charged 20s. for a funeral sermon for 'the most able sort', and half that amount or even nothing at all for 'those of an inferior rank' who 'were desireous to bury their friend in a fashionable way, being the last duty or office of live they could perform for them'.[43] Both puritans and conformists preached at Stuart funerals, and neither associated their work with superstitious popish practice.

Ceremonial Discipline

Like every other area of parish business, the burial of the dead could be subject to principled disagreements, clerical shortcomings, and lapses by members of the laity. Not surprisingly, the frictions of orthodoxy and dissent and the ordinary interactions of everyday life extended to the ceremonies of funerals and the solemnities of the burial service. The absence or intransigence of a priest was by no means the only source of indiscipline. Ceremonialists cringed when the ceremony was profaned, and when godly order was subverted by rowdiness or irreverence.

Minor lapses of discipline during funeral solemnities brought several layfolk before the ecclesiastical courts. Urged on by another young man, John Howet of Flintham, Nottinghamshire, 'being at the funeral sermon of Mr Hotofte' in 1608, 'did sew women's clothes together', and caused a disturbance when they rose. Charged with 'laughing in the church' at Tredington, Worcestershire, in 1633, Alice Richardson said she meant no offence, but 'she did smile in modest sort upon occasion of some commendatory words delivered then by the preacher of him whose funeral sermon was then preached'.[44] These were indiscretions that bored young servants might make on any formal occasion.

More serious was the affront to good order at Kingston, Herefordshire, in 1588 when Margaret Price pursued Richard Jones to the grave with a stream of scolding invective. The archdeacon had to admonish her 'for cursing and using most uncharitable words against the corpse of one deceased'. Funerals were similarly disrupted at King's Sutton, Oxfordshire, in the reign of James I, when instead of solemnity and prayer the corpse was attended by railing words and antic fury. Anne Chapman, well known locally as a scold, intercepted a burial party in 1617 and railed against the priest. According to the citation,

whereas the minister was attentive and waited at the church stile to meet a corpse and according to the form set down in the Book of Common Prayer to bury it, she contemptuously raging, blasphemously swearing by the lord's wounds and blood, to his great grief and the congregation's, disturbed him as he was reading divine service at the grave. She caused the men to carry the corpse from the grave, and swore that unless he would come into the church and read prayers to it she would bury him alive.

Two years later in the same parish the churchwardens presented Humphrey Justice

for disquieting the minister being present in the churchyard attending to bury a corpse; the grave being made and the corpse being coming near to the church stile, the said Justice came like a mad man to the grave and scrabbled in the the earth with his hands and feet into the grave and filled the grave half full of mould, do what the minister could to resist him, and because the minister did resist him for filling the grave, the corpse being at hand, the said Humphrey shouldered him and abused him until the clerk came to stay his fury.[45]

These two incidents were abusive to the clergy, disruptive of established ritual, and offensive to the rest of the community. But the perpetrators apparently thought they were standing up for right. Anne Chapman wanted the minister to read prayers inside the church, Humphrey Justice wanted to stop the corpse from being buried in that particular place. It seems possible that, notwithstanding their verbal violence and intemperance, the scolds of King's Sutton were pursuing a veiled liturgical agenda.

The business of bishops changed substantially between the beginning of Elizabeth's reign and the time of Charles I. Reforming administrators of the earlier period worked hard to eradicate superstition and to purge their parishes of popish practices. Their primary task was to secure the transformation from a catholic to a protestant religious culture while guarding against the errors of sectarian excess. Later bishops, by contrast, sought to hold the line against further reform and to secure allegiance to a uniform Church of England. Some even wanted to beautify and elaborate its services. Although episcopal administration was always subject to the variables of personality, energy, and circumstance, the bench of 1635 had markedly different goals from its counterpart of sixty years earlier. While a previous generation of prelates targeted popish beliefs and practices, their Caroline successors seemed more troubled by protestant indiscipline and irregular adherence to the ceremonial requirements of the church.

Ceremonialists of the reign of Charles I added nothing new to the funeral service but insisted on 'the full form, manner and rites prescribed' in the Book of Common Prayer. The minister in his surplice should meet the corpse at the church stile or entrance to the churchyard, 'saying or singing that which is appointed until they come to the grave'. The corpse should be interred 'in decent manner . . . with the lessons and prayers for that purpose ordained'. Thus John Cosin in Yorkshire in 1627.[46] William Laud in 1628

asked whether any minister in the Diocese of London had 'at any time refused or delayed to bury any corpse that hath been brought to the church or
churchyard, convenient warning having been given', and whether 'he buried
any in Christian burial which ought not to be so interred'. Bishop Montague
of Norwich asked much the same.[47] Ceremonialist insistence on liturgical propriety and decorum helps explain the bishop's outrage at disturbances in the
London parish of St Bartholemew the Great in 1630 when funeral services
were brought to a halt. The offender was cited, 'for profaning their church
and causing a tumult there by serving a writ in time of burying a dead corpse'.[48]

To avoid association with prayers for the dead, earlier reformers had
excised the commendation of the soul at burial and reduced the practice
of commemoration of the departed. But both were defended and sometimes
ostentatiously revived by several conservative clergy of the early seventeenth
century. Richard Field, the Jacobean dean of Gloucester, argued that 'prayer
for the resurrection, public acquittal in the day of judgment, and perfect
consummation and bliss of them that are fallen asleep in the sleep of death,
is an apostolical tradition, and so proved by the rule of St. Augustine'. Oxford
and Cambridge colleges, he observed, still had services for commendation of
the dead, and there was nothing wrong with the practice so long as it did not
imply a belief in purgatory or pretend to relieve the souls of the damned.[49]
Commendation of the soul was, strictly, an entrusting or committing it to
God, but it might be seen to verge on popery if it hinted that God could be
moved or the condition of the soul alleviated by intercessionary prayer.
Though arguably compatible with protestant belief in the absence of purgatory, commendation sat awkwardly with the stricter Calvinist theology
of predestination. Bishop Richard Montague of Norwich went so far in 1638
as to recommend 'prayer, praise, thanksgiving, for the living and the dead,
by way of commemoration, that the righteous may be had in everlasting
remembrance, God be glorified in and for them, and the living incited to
follow them'. Such prayers, Montague argued, offered no benefit to the souls
departed but were simply intended to praise God and to edify the living; they
also healed the rift in the community of Christians, associating the quick and
the dead.[50] But puritans would readily seize on this as yet another sign of
creeping catholicism. The godly William Whiteway was scandalized in 1634
to hear that an Oxford preacher had prayed for the dead, and was further
upset that the man was not punished. Here was one more symptom for those
that believed that the Caroline church was back-sliding towards papism.
Another was John Cosin's remark that while puritans deemed prayer for
the dead 'popish and superstitious', he for his part esteemed it 'pious and
Christian . . . our prayers for them then will not be in vain'.[51]

The War on Pomp

Long before the Reformation, reformers debated the advantages and disadvantages of lavish funerals. Neither modesty nor ostentation were products of the early modern era. Even before there were puritans there were moralists and critics who wished to reduce the elaborations of pomp. *Dives and Pauper,* a much-reproduced devotional dialogue of the late medieval period, argued against simple burial such as 'men hold it a great perfection nowadays'. From the popular standpoint, funereal asceticism was counterproductive. Frugal funerals denied everybody the enjoyment of a spectacle, short-changed the poor by limiting the distribution of alms, and, worst of all to traditional catholics, offended 'all the souls that be in purgatory, that should be relieved by masses singing'. The rich man Dives asks, 'What sayest thou of them that will no solemnity in their burying, but be put in earth anon, and that that should be spent about the burying of them, they bid that it should be given to the poor folks, as blind and lame?' To which Pauper not unreasonably replies that he prefers the 'great doles' that come with elaborate funerals.[52]

Many of the traditional practices involved in accompanying and burying a body survived the Reformation because they were unencumbered by theological or liturgical considerations. So long as there were no superstitious candles or crosses, and no suggestion that the soul of the dead might benefit from the handling or treatment of the body, the social and material conduct of funerals was of little concern to the church. Neither the abnegation of purgatory nor the simplification of religious ritual required the reduction of funeral pomp. Indeed, expenditure on display and consumption may have increased in the post-Reformation era as mourners invested their energy in those aspects and trappings of burial that did not fall within ecclesiastical cognizance. Early modern culture was not only highly ritualized but ritually creative, supporting a blend of continuity, adaption, and reinvention in this as in so many other areas.

The reformation of religion, however, went hand in hand with the reformation of manners. Along with their attacks on the errors of papism, English protestant reformers urged propriety and decency in social and religious rituals. Notions of seemliness accompanied Calvinist soteriology in many Elizabethan and Jacobean discussions of death. 'Sumptuous and costly burials are not to be commended, neither do they profit either body or soul, but only set forth a vain, foolish and boasting pomp,' wrote the influential Tudor reformer Thomas Becon.[53] It was a common cry among godly activists that 'we ought . . . to bury our dead decently, comely and honestly', without the vanity or error of pomp. Though 'gorgeous and costly funerals' could still be justified in terms of status, dignity, and honour, they attracted criticism from reformers who associated the ceremonial elaborations of mourning with the unacceptable horrors of pomp.[54] Reformers used the authority of St Augustine to point out the vanity of pomp and to argue that funerals 'are rather for the comfort of the living than for the aid and help of the dead'.[55] Perhaps they recalled the words of baptism and catechism, which demanded Christians 'should forsake the devil in all his works and pomps, the vanities of the wicked world, and all the sinful lusts of the flesh'.[56]

Moderate protestants sought a balance between sumptuousness and simplicity, seeking on the one hand to show due respect for the departed, on the other to avoid superstitious ostentation and excess. James Pilkington, the first Elizabethan bishop of Durham, promoted 'that comely order which Christian charity requireth', and recommended no more than a quiet funeral procession made up of comforting friends. Englishmen, he urged, should 'avoid great cost and sumptuousness, as shrines, tombs, tapers, torches, candles, mourning coats, feastings, etc., which do no good to the dead and are too chargeable and unprofitable to their friends'. Yet people with money and families concerned with status continued to spend heavily on funerals, and even Bishop Pilkington was forced to acknowledge the propriety of socially differentiated mourning.

If civil policy add some solemnity to princes and noblemen, as their coat, armour, flag, sword, head-piece and recognizance, I dare not utterly condemn it; and yet would wish it more moderately used than many times it is. As there was difference in them while they lived, from the common sort and state, so there may be in their burials for policy's sake, but not for religion or holiness at all.

In his own will of 1571 Pilkington asked 'to be buried with as few popish ceremonies as may be, or vain cost', but he probably anticipated that notwithstanding he would be buried with the dignity and splendour appropriate to his rank as a spiritual lord. He was buried at Bishop Auckland, where he died in January 1576, but four months later his remains were removed for more ceremonial interment before the high altar in Durham cathedral.[57]

Archbishop Grindal likewise willed that he be buried 'without any solemn hearse or funeral pomp', although as archbishop of Canterbury he realized that it would be necessary for the heralds to be 'reasonably compounded withal, and satisfied for their accustomed fees in such cases'.[58] Archbishop Sandys of York requested to be buried 'neither in superstitious nor superfluous manner', but 'decently and conveniently brought to ground, as appertaineth to a Christian, a servant of almighty God, and a man of my calling'.[59]

Further insight into protestant sensibility can be gained through analysis of wills in which Elizabethan gentlemen gave directions for their funerals. Though some testators at the beginning of Elizabeth's reign desired traditional catholic ceremonies, and others requested elaborate and expensive cortèges and monuments, there was a steady demand among gentle will-makers 'to be buried in decent manner' or 'to be comely and decently buried' or to leave matters in the hands of their executors.

Robert Camocke of Layer Marney, Essex, was one of dozens who wanted only 'to be buried honestly'. It became a refrain in some gentle wills that the burial be performed 'without any pomp'. Robert Bradbury requested in 1577 'to be buried in the chancel of Littlebury church besides my ancestors decently without pomp'. In 1589 George Scott of Hatfield Broadoak asked for burial 'without any pomp or great ado'. This did not rule out bells and mourning dress, processions, doles, feasts, or monuments, but put these customary observances under the constraint of moderation. John Barnaby of Inworth requested 'to be buried without pomp', and then gave instructions which embraced all the ritual elements of an Elizabethan gentleman's funeral.[60]

'Without pomp' was an ambiguous formulation. On the one hand it signified the same as 'decency', allowing no more display than was appropriate to one's rank, but not stinting on expense lest that invite reproach. It could be a conventional proclamation against excess, against vanity and ostentation, rather than a call for funerary simplicity. But funerals 'without pomp' could also imply puritan associations, especially when the phrase was given extra emphasis or coupled with the adjective 'vain'. George Medley, esquire, in his will of 1561 desired to be buried 'without pomp, pride or vain superstition'. His son Henry Medley willed similarly in 1577, 'my body I commit to the earth without any vain pomp or ceremony'. The elder Medley requested 'a sermon at my burial by a learned man of good conversation', while his son asked for burial 'only with a sermon of some godly man'. Rowland Eliot similarly seems to have been a staunch protestant, of the kind that one is tempted to call puritan, on the basis of his instruction 'to be buried without vain pomp or superstitiousness by the grave of my father in Bishops Stortford church'. Eliot was a gentleman of Farnham, Essex, who died in 1576.[61]

In these cases the funeral requests and the language in which they are couched imply a strict religious position, although aversion to pomp is not, by itself, a sure token of puritanism. The gentlemen who signalled an aversion to pomp were more likely to request a sermon, less likely to issue detailed instructions about mourning garments, but otherwise there was no apparent austerity in their preparations and no consistent pattern. The late Elizabethan antiquary Francis Tate, an upholder of 'accustomed solemnities' appropriate to rank and condition, argued for 'reverence and comeliness' at funerals without their 'turning into pomp and superstitious vanity', but it would be hard to think of him as any kind of puritan. Nor were early Stuart testators who sought interment 'without worldly vain pomp' necessarily in conflict with the established Church of England.[62]

'Burial is a testimony of the love and reverence we bear to the deceased', wrote the Cambridge Calvinist William Perkins in 1600, and 'ought to be solemnized after an honest and civil manner'. A Christian funeral, in Perkins's opinion, should be 'agreeable to the nature and credit as well of those which remain alive, as them which are dead'. Those taking part were advised to follow these three prescriptions:

Concerning the living, they must see that their mourning be moderate, and such as may well express their affection and love for the departed . . . They must avoid superstition, and not surmise that funeral ceremonies are available to the dead . . . They ought to take heed of superstitious pomp and solemnities. For of all ostentations of pride, that is most foolish, to be boasting of a loathsome and a deformed corpse.[63]

The prescription was clear, but in practice it was hard to judge the line between moderation and excess.

Throughout the early Stuart period a chorus of puritan counsellors reiterated that funerals should be conducted with decency and honour, though not with ceremonial ostentation. A dead Christian deserved to be buried 'in religious sort', advised the Jacobean preacher Robert Hill, though more with regard to social propriety than for any contingent benefits. 'Burials are in some sort civil, human, and politic things,' advised his colleague Thomas Sparke, but that did not remove them from the auspices of the ministry or the venue of the church.[64]

The puritan family counsellor William Gouge advised, 'it is the duty of children to bring the bodies of their parents deceased [for burial] with such decency and honour as may be answerable to the place and reputation wherein they lived'. But disregarding such decency, Gouge lamented, some worldly children thought only of themselves as inheritors and neglected their duty to the dead. Shame on them! 'So soon as their parent's breath is out of their body, they so busy themselves about the goods which they have left behind them, as their corpse is ready to stink before care be taken for the burial of it.' As to the style of the funeral, Gouge urged a middle way between 'overlavish and prodigal sumptuousness' on the one hand, and 'too base and private a manner' on the other.[65]

Even royal funerals were supposed to adhere to these guidelines. The Jacobean court author Patrick Scot urged a robust British reticence in regard to mourning and burial, and warned against the 'conceited fooleries' of continental practice.

> I do only allow of such honourable burial of princes as is observed amongst Christians, and which is rather accompanied and condoled with the presence and tears of all good subjects; sermons, funeral orations and alms (thereby inciting the succeeding posterity to imitate the virtues of the deceased prince), than defaced by superstitious rites or prodigal profusion of superfluous and unprofitable charge.[66]

As is readily evident, these cautions and injunctions were not always followed. Indeed, by the mid-seventeenth century there was a resurgence of funeral elaboration among the gentle and prosperous classes that left traditional strictures against pomp in the shade.

Revolution and Restoration

The presbyterian Directory for the Public Worship of God, adopted by Parliament in 1645, required burial of the dead 'without any ceremony' and explained why this reformation of religion was necessary.

> Because the customs of kneeling down and praying by or towards the dead corpse, and other usages in the place where it lies before it be carried to burial, are superstitious; and for that praying, reading, and singing, both in going to and at the grave, have been grossly abused, are in no way beneficial to the dead, and have proved many ways hurtful to the living, therefore let all such things be laid aside.

Instead, the Directory recommended, 'the Christian friends which accompany the dead body' might 'apply themselves to meditations and conferences suitable to the occasion', and the minister, '*if he be present,* may put them in remembrance of their duty'.[67]

The revolutionary regime allowed broad discretion to the parties involved, and permitted a wide variety of practices. In any case, it lacked the disciplinary machinery to secure any kind of uniformity. Radicals could bury as they wished, while conservatives could continue as before. The secular furnishers of funerals thrived in this period, even while the religious service was in flux.[68] Despite the restrictions of the revolution, John Evelyn was able to give his mother-in-law Lady Browne a traditional religious funeral in October 1652.

> We carried her in an hearse to Deptford, and interred her in the church near Sir Richard's relations . . . accompanied with many coaches of friends, and other persons of quality; with all decent ceremony, and according to the church office, which I obtained might be permitted, after it had not been used in that church of seven years before, to the great satisfaction of that innumerable multitude who were there.[69]

Richard Culmer, the radical minister of Thanet, Kent, faced recurrent trouble with more conservative parishioners when he refused to conduct graveside services, preferring instead to preach sermons in church after the corpse was interred. 'He would not be chaplain to the worms, to say grace to them before they go to dinner,' explained Culmer's son in his defence. The traditional practice, he said, pandered only to 'popish, ignorant and superstitious people, as if some good came to the dead by the minister's speaking over the dead at the grave'. Not so, replied his opponents, whose usual answer was, 'if we can have nothing at the grave, we will have nothing in the church'.[70] A less bitter confrontation took place in Lancashire in 1659 over similar issues when, Henry Newcome records, 'we had some small contests with some upon occasion of burying the dead'. The point of contention was whether to first take the body into the church, or to proceed directly to the grave, not whether a minister should be involved.[71] Though burial was unhinged from formal liturgy and freed from priestly ministration, most families continued to use their parish burying grounds and clung to elements of tradition.

At the Savoy Conference in 1661, when presbyterians and Anglicans briefly and fruitlessly sought areas of common ground, the reformers asked for minor modification to the order for burial in the Book of Common Prayer. 'We desire it may be expessed in the rubric that the prayers and exhortations here used are not for the benefit of the dead, but only for the instruction and comfort of the living.' And they asked for discretion to perform the entire service inside the church, rather than at the graveside, 'for the preventing of these inconveniences which many times both ministers and people are exposed unto by standing in the open air'. Neither request was granted. The only substantial change made in the burial service, at the request of the ceremonialist John Cosin, was to assert in the rubric that it was 'not to be used for any that die unbaptized, or excommunicate, or have laid violent hands upon themselves'.[72]

Restoration bishops faced the compound problem of enforcing lay and clerical conformity while trying to keep parishioners from abandoning the Church of England. A common visitation query of the 1660s was whether the minister performed the burial service 'decently and gravely, not swerving from the form prescribed by the church in the common prayer book' or 'without any addition, omission or alteration of the same'. Earlier visitations had asked whether the minister ever refused to bury anybody; but episcopal visitors after 1662 were more concerned that the laity might refuse to be buried according to the standardized rites of the church.[73]

Private interment, lay burial, and improvised ceremonies that flourished alongside more traditional practices during the 1640s and 1650s were once again outlawed with the passage of the Act of Uniformity. But radical dissenters, Quakers, and Roman Catholics had all developed burial practices of their own beyond the purview of the Church of England. Anglican authorities knew what was happening but were usually unable to prevent it. In Buckinghamshire, for example, Matthew Haines of Burnham was presented in 1662, 'for refusing to bury his child' in the proper place. William Natkins was cited in the same visitation 'for burying of a child contrary to the forms of the Church of England, that is without a minister, in the churchyard of Wing'. And Edward Andrew of Olney was in trouble for burying his wife in private ground.[74] William Canon of Ellisfield in the Diocese of Oxford was another nonconformist who admitted 'he doth not approve of the common prayer'. When his mother died in 1662 the parish clerk refused to call the minister on his behalf, so Canon simply undertook the task himself and buried his mother 'without church prayers or a minister'. Two years earlier this would have been unexceptional practice; now it was an ecclesiastical offence.[75]

The bishop of London collected more information about irregular burial practices in his visitation of 1664. At Burnham in Essex he found a group of so-called Anabaptists and Quakers who had been excommunicated for refusing to pay their parish rates and then charged with 'not burying their dead according to the rites of the church of England'. At the same time, he learnt, 'several persons called Quakers have taken in a piece of land in Halstead, and do bury their dead in the same, slighting the church'. Individual parishioners were cited for burying in private ground or for failure to follow the rites of the Church of England, but few of them turned up to answer the charges and excommunication had lost its sting.[76]

Likewise, the 'very great sectaries' of Hillingdon, Middlesex, refused to bring their dead wives into the church. In the same parish two children of William Prince of Uxbridge were 'buried very irregularly', the vicar noted in 1664, 'without my knowledge, till the business was done, and without the office of burial'. Here as elsewhere it seems that the nonconformists continued to use the parochial burying ground in the churchyard, treating it as common property, but otherwise distanced themselves from the rituals of the Church of England. At Isleworth, however, the sectaries buried their kinsfolk in open fields. Thomas Glace, a yeoman of Burnham, Essex, was cited by the archdeacon in 1684 as an anabaptist who had 'a burying place in his garden'.[77]

Quakers 'would not bury at the church' and this refusal caused them endless trouble. The churchwardens of Warbleton, Sussex, put diocesan officials on the track of a Quaker burying ground in 1674. When the Yorkshire

Quakers interred one of their own 'at Sowerby Street, the Quakers' burying place', in September 1678, the Anglican minister sent two men to take the names of everyone present. The observers saw the burial party retire to Joshua Smith's house, and on this information the local magistrate charged it as a conventicle. The minister, Dr Hook, told the nonconformist Oliver Heywood that he had not *persecuted* the Quakers, but prosecuted them 'out of principles of conscience, for I cannot endure that Christian people should be buried like a dog; they had as good have hanged a stone about her neck and thrown her into Calder'.[78]

Some leading dissenters maintained cordial relations with the Church of England clergy, and this served them well when it came time to bury their dead. For separation from the church did not necessarily entail separation from the community of the Christian dead. Henry Newcome, a Lancashire presbyterian, consulted with 'Mr. Pilkington, the vicar' in April 1663 about arrangements for burying the former nonconformist minister and schoolmaster Mr Hiat. The body would be interred in the churchyard at Croston, but without the full prayer-book ceremony. Newcome writes, 'we had much ado about his burial, but Mr. Pilkington at last went his way, and so he was buried without ceremony or book'. Another friend preached a good sermon.[79]

But accommodation was not always the order of the day. A funeral party at Charleton, Wiltshire, one Sunday in 1668 waited at the churchyard gate for the minister, as they were supposed to, but after he failed to appear they carried the body directly into the church and laid it in the pre-dug grave. When the minister eventually arrived he ordered them to retrace their steps and to take the body back to the gate, saying 'there I am to meet you'. This the parishioners refused to do. The ensuing argument benefited no one, only adding to the accumulated animosity between the pastor and his flock. The body lay exposed in the open grave all through evening prayers, and the minister then left the church without reading the Order for the Burial of the Dead.[80]

A hostile priest could not only refuse to perform the burial service for a religious opponent, but lock up the prayer book and surplice to frustrate the efforts of neighbouring ministers who might be more accommodating. This is what John White of Avebury, Wiltshire, did at the end of the Stuart era to thwart the burial of Richard Bayly, who was not only a presbyterian but also owed him tithes. In another petty collision, when the vicar of Avebury, Wiltshire, refused to bury a late Stuart dissenter his parishioners took matters into their own hands but unfortunately (or more likely deliberately) buried Walter Alexander 'with his head pointing in the wrong direction'.[81]

As in earlier periods, some parishioners pleaded necessity when charged with conducting irregular burials. Because of the absence and negligence of their minister, the churchwardens of Kerdford, Sussex, explained in 1664, 'we have had dead corpses to be buried and have been brought to the church and have been set down for three or four days together before he came to administer burial'. The parishioners of Westport, Wiltshire, justified burying a neighbour without informing the minister in 1673, because 'the body . . . being an aged diseased person, was so offensive . . . that it could not be kept any longer from burial, being kept from about midnight till sunset'. Similar problems occurred at Berrow, Worcestershire, where the churchwardens reported in 1690, 'We had a dead corpse to be buried and nobody to bury her. We had a corpse lie in our church all night, and have been forced to have a minister out of another county.'[82] These minor lapses into nonconformity were the product of contingency and caprice, and are not necessarily to be explained by reference to religious dissent.

Disorders marred some post-Restoration funerals, but no worse than in earlier periods. Jane Collingwood, a catholic mother in Cumberland, was cited by the bishop of Durham in 1665 'for snatching at the common prayer book in Mr. Tallentire's hand, to tear it up, while he was about to bury her son'. Her violent disruption of the ceremony seems to have been compounded by grief at her loss and unrestrained hostility to the service of the Church of England.[83] Much more serious was the riot at the Countess of Strafford's funeral at York in January 1686. Despite an honour guard of soldiers, 'the rabble or rout of ordinary people' assaulted the hearse and tore off the escutcheons by force. Several people were injured as the fighting continued inside York Minster, which was also 'plundered' of its black cloth and escutcheons. The target of this attack was Anne Stanley, daughter of the seventh Earl of Derby and wife of the second Earl of Strafford. The mob behaviour may have been conditioned by the recent repeal of the Edict of Nantes in France and by fears that James II was about to abolish the Test Act, but it is hard to disentangle rowdy opportunism from protestant fundamentalism.[84]

FUNERALS AND BURIALS

Funeral ritual, it has been shrewdly observed, 'was not so much a question of dealing with a corpse as of reaffirming the secular and spiritual order by means of a corpse'.[1] In England, as elsewhere, the practicalities involved in preparing a body for burial and transporting it to a grave were matters of routine necessity, but many parts of the process were also ritualized and freighted with social and religious meaning. This chapter examines the material accoutrements of funerals and the ordinary business of burials. It follows the corpse from the deathbed to the church, from the burial service to its final resting place, and traces the contingent behaviour of family members, neighbours, and friends from the onset of death to the completion of mourning.

Much of this business was uncontentious and unremarkable; it was usually undocumented, and therefore hard for the historian to recover. But occasional entries in diaries and account books, sermons and devotional writings, commentaries and church court records, can be made to reveal the ordinary patterns and costs as well as controversies and complications. Each of these fragments helps us to recover obscure and neglected aspects of our past. The discourse of death and burial, like discussions of childbirth and marriage, sheds light on customary conditions and illuminates the strains and cross-currents of sixteenth- and seventeenth-century society and culture. Like so much of the material discussed in this book, it operated at the intersection of social and religious obligations where, in the words of the Elizabethan Thomas Playfere, 'the duties of love' met 'the comforts of faith'.[2]

For Whom the Bell Tolls

Parish bells tolled when a person was dying, then signalled that someone was dead, and often rang again at the time of their burial. Sometimes the bells sounded for hours on end, ringing both day and night.[3] Their purpose was to show respect, to alert the community, to summon attendants to the bedside or the graveside, to bring comfort to the living and the dying, and to assist the parting person by prompting neighbours to their prayers. Catholic

Within the image: *Tim: Cap: 4. v. 7.*
I have fought a good fight
I have finished my course
I have kept the faith.

I was in Prison, and ye came unto me
I was sick, and ye visited me: *Matt: 25. 36.*

resurgam.

FIG. 23   A shrouded corpse. Detail from the title verso of Daniel Featley, *The Dippers Dipt* (7th edn., London, 1660)

traditionalists believed that the bells helped to sanctify the soul in passing, and superstitious villagers may also have thought that the sound of the sacred bells would ward off evil spirits that might otherwise molest the vulnerable soul. Not surprisingly, there were disagreements about the purpose and propriety of bells in the post-Reformation discourse on dying, death, and interment.

The custom of tolling continued after the Reformation, though no longer, officially, associated with belief that the ringing was beneficial to the dead person's soul. Edward VI's commissioners ordered communities to 'abstain from such unmeasurable ringing for dead persons at their burials', to ring with one bell only 'at such time as sick persons lieth in extreme danger of death', and to ring only 'moderately' at funerals.[4] The Elizabethan religious 'Advertisements' ordered the church bell to be tolled 'when any Christian body is in passing . . . and after the time of passing, to ring no more but one short peal, and one before the burial, and another short peal after the burial'.

Edmund Grindal in 1571 approved the tolling of the passing bell 'to move the people to pray for the sick person', but was hostile to ringing after anyone had died. 'One short peal' would suffice at funerals, he advised the province of York; anything more would be 'superfluous or superstitious'.[5]

William Chaderton of Lincoln was one of several Jacobean bishops who asked in their visitations, 'whether doth your clerk or sexton, when any is passing out of this life, neglect to toll a bell, having notice thereof; or the party being dead, doth he suffer any more ringing than one short peal, and before his burial one, and after the same another?'[6] The aim was not to eliminate the passing bell or the funeral knell but to rid them of superstition and to reduce them to moderation. If there was to be ringing, it should focus on the moment of dying rather than the time of interment. Puritan activists excoriated the 'solemn peals' and 'excessive ringing' of funeral ceremonies, but encouraged the tolling 'at the point of death, whereby the people should be stirred up to prayer at due time'.[7] John Donne found it necessary to expostulate against the godly critics who disapproved of bells at funerals because the practice had been abused or because the 'ringing hath been said to drive away evil spirits'. The ringing was valuable, he countered, because it 'brings the congregation together and unites God and his people'.[8]

Perhaps the most eloquent disquisition on passing bells from within the reformed protestant tradition came from Thomas Adams, a Jacobean preacher in Bedfordshire:

It is a custom not unworthy of approbation, when a lanquishing Christian draws near to his end, to toll a heavy bell for him. Set aside the prejudice of superstition and the ridiculous conceits of some old wives, whose wits are more decrepit than their bodies, and I see not why reasons may not be given to prove it, though not a necessary, yet an allowed ceremony.[9]

Adams was fully aware of folk beliefs about the supernatural efficacy of bells, and also alert to more radical puritan criticism, but as an earnest parish pastor he sought to accommodate custom and good churchmanship.

One of the virtues of the passing bell, wrote Adams, was that 'it puts into the sick man a sense of mortality . . . Thus with a kind of Divinity, it gives him the ghostly counsel to remit the care of his carcase, and to admit the cure of his conscience'. Furthermore, the sound of the bell

excites the hearers to pray for the sick . . . The bell, like a speedy messenger, runs from house to house, from ear to ear, on thy soul's errand, and begs the assistance of their prayers . . . As the bell hath often rung thee into the temple on earth, so now it rings thee unto the church in heaven, from the militant to the triumphant place.[10]

In a bravery of wit, a severely ill Jacobean gentleman is said to have heard the passing bell and called out from his sick bed, 'Tell me, master doctor, is yonder music for my dancing?' He might have been answered by John Donne's memorable injunction, 'never send to know for whom the bell tolls, it tolls for thee'.[11]

The records of ecclesiastical administration reveal enormous local variation in bell-ringing practices. This should not be surprising, given the diversity of post-Reformation opinion, the variety of bell-tower equipment, differences in social status, and the need for somebody to pay the ringers. At Hollingbourne, Kent, it was reported in 1562, 'they use three peals in ringing at burials', which was excessive but not illegal. The passing bell was a customary courtesy, but at Kettlewell, Yorkshire, in 1575 Archbishop Grindal was offended to learn that 'the bell is not tolled to move the people to pray for the sick' when someone was dying. 'Faithful professors' in Lancashire around 1590 complained that traditionalists in that region 'have excessive ringing for the dead . . . . But while the party lieth sick, they will never require to have the bell knolled, no, not at the point of death.'[12] All was well, however, at Cropredy, Oxfordshire, where the churchwardens reported in 1619, 'the bell is usually for the most part tolled when any are passing out of this life'. Notified of a death at Holton, Oxfordshire, in 1631 the bell-ringers 'rang two or three peals for Mrs. Horseman', who happened to be excommunicated, and consumed 'a bottle of drink and a little loaf of bread brought them to the church' by the dead woman's maid.[13]

Most parishioners expected ringing as part of their due, and were upset when the practice was curtailed by religious objection or parochial friction. The church encouraged the tolling of the passing bell and attempted to limit the ringing at funerals, but much was left to local discretion. William Reade, a later minister at Cropredy, Oxfordshire, offended some parishioners in 1632 'when he denied the ringing of a peal for the death of Margery Winter, widow of Bourton'. In 1633 Ambrose Robinson of Long Preston, Yorkshire, caused friction of another kind when he put 'sand and gravel into the bell stocks while certain of the parish were ringing for the burial of a corpse'. Whether this was done out of prankish humour, vindictiveness, or hostility to the practice of ringing, is not recorded.[14] Joyce Jeffries was content to pay 3s. 6d. for ringing five peals at the burial of her cousin about 1640 and nobody is known to have objected. The catholic squire William Blundell was buried at the end of the Stuart period with 4s. worth of ringing.[15]

Ringing for the dead contributed to the aural environment of seventeenth-century England, alongside the regular ringing for worship and the celebratory and commemorative peals of the protestant dynastic calendar. To maintain propriety, and perhaps in the interest of peace and quiet, the authorities at Wells cathedral in 1612 limited the duration of ringing for the dead to half an hour. In 1676 the common council of Nottingham tried to limit tolling to fifteen minutes. Tolling for the dead continued at parliamentarian Cambridge during the Civil War, but only between the hours of four in the morning and ten at night. The bells of Bilney, Norfolk, tolled for two days for the burial of Elizabeth Freke's grandson in 1705, and for five days at the funeral of her husband in 1706.[16]

Restoration churchmen encouraged the ringing of tolls for the dying, knells for the dead, and subdued peals on the occasion of burials. The bells helped to rehabilitate the ceremonies and customs of the restored Church of England. Strict dissenters had already ceased to listen. Bishop Robert Sanderson of Lincoln promoted the traditional practice of ringing when he asked in his visitation of 1662, 'when any person is passing out of this life, doth [the sexton] upon notice given him thereof toll a bell, as hath been accustomed, that the neighbours may thereby be warned to recommend the dying person to the grace and favour of God'. This 'tolling of a passing bell for any that are dying', explained Bishop Humphrey Henchman of London in 1664, was to 'admonish' the living that they might thereby 'meditate of their own death, and to commend the other's weak condition to the mercy of God'.[17] Low church and dissenting clergy 'condemned that heathenish practice of ringing bells so soon as ever funeral solemnities are performed', and thought the joyous sound of the peal improper at such times of sadness.[18] Others allowed that joyful ringing was appropriate, to celebrate the passing of the soul to a better world.

Winding and Watching

While theologians and churchmen discussed the disposition of the soul, associates of the deceased faced the immediate problem of dealing with the body. Death was rarely sanitary, and often left a detritus of disfigurement. Even those who died a 'good death' could leave behind a cadaver defiled with sweat and vomit, urine and excrement, or pus and blood. Rigor mortis, corruption, and putrefaction would surely follow. It was therefore a matter of urgent practical necessity to prepare the dead body for burial and to transport it promptly from the deathbed to the grave. The work included washing, winding, and watching before taking the body to the church. In exceptional cases, if thought necessary and affordable, a surgeon might be engaged to open a body to investigate its organs to determine the cause of death, or to undertake the gruesome task of embalming.[19]

Usually no more than two or three days passed between the death of a person and the burial of a corpse. In a group of Yorkshire parishes in the mid-Stuart period, where exact dates can be checked, 95 per cent of all bodies were buried within two days of death; 41 per cent were buried on the day the person died. In the wealthy London parish of St Mary Woolnoth in the second half of the seventeenth century, over 70 per cent were buried within three days, and close to 90 per cent by the fourth day.[20] Infectious or badly soiled bodies were buried as soon as possible. The ground was rarely so hard that a grave could not be dug, or the weather so cold that burial could be delayed. Even in rocky or waterlogged areas, a grave could be made in reasonably short time, for the health and convenience of all who remained above ground.

One Christopher, a cobbler of Dagenham, Essex, was buried in 1606 within four hours of his dying. We know about this because someone complained that he was buried in haste, 'without any tolling of a bell, or any duty done by the minister'. Faced with another urgent interment, the Mayor of Coventry allowed Lady Archer's man to buy links for a night-time burial in December 1655, despite it being the sabbath, because her son had 'died last night of the pox and could not be kept longer than this night'.[21]

Women who bled to death during childbirth, or succumbed to puerperal fever or other childbed complications, were commonly buried within twenty-four hours. After Sir William Ashcombe's sister died in childbirth in 1620 'of the purples, as it is thought', interment was quickly arranged and the still-born child was 'buried with her the same night'. The rushed burial of Isabel Fieldsend of Waddington, Lincolnshire, in 1635, so upset her friends that one of them protested that the poor woman 'was buried like a dog'. This appeal to human decency, we have seen, was a common concern. The visitation court was reassured, however, that 'the said Isabel was buried by a lawful minister in the parish church there in the night time before eleven o'clock, because she died in childbed and could not be kept up'.[22] The gentle Ellen Angier was buried a day after she died of puerperal fever in 1642. The body of Margaret Godolphin, by contrast, was preserved enough for a journey from London to Cornwall in 1678. Whenever the entourage stopped, 'the corpse was ordered to be taken out of the hearse and decently placed in the house, with tapers about it, and her servants attending, every night all the way'.[23]

Too long a delay caused obvious problems. The vicar of Raynham, Essex, was charged with negligence in 1624 for permitting a body 'this summer to lie three days unburied after it was dead until it did stink'. The body of Mrs Horseman of Wheatley, an Oxfordshire recusant, lay on a table in her parlour for several days in January 1631 until 'she began to smell so strong that they could not endure her in the house; whereupon on Monday night they drew her corpse in her coffin out into the garden and the next morning drew her into the parlour again, and continued this course until Wednesday'. Arrived at Brampton, Huntingdonshire, for his Uncle Robert's funeral in July 1661, Samuel Pepys found 'my uncle's corpse in a coffin, standing upon joint-stools in the chimney in the hall; but it begun to smell, and so I caused it to be set forth in the yard all night and watched by several men'.[24]

Apart from prompt burial, the only way to avoid such problems was to attempt some kind of embalming or to sheathe the body in lead. These were expensive remedies, available only to the rich. But only the rich had an interest in postponing burial until all social or ceremonial arrangements were complete. Aristocratic corpses were commonly embalmed to allow time for the appropriate heraldic preparations, and wrapped or coffined in lead for transport and interment. The protocols of status dictated that they be buried in a place and a manner appropriate to their rank.[25]

The custom of 'watching' a corpse, that is, sitting up all night in the company of the dead body, was practised by rich and poor with varying degrees of diligence. Not every corpse was so attended, but the custom certainly continued long after the Reformation. Writing in 1600, Francis Tate described how the body was 'laid forth, as they term it, upon a floor in some chamber, covered with a sheet, and candles set burning over it on a table day and night, and the body continually attended or watched'. However, he added, 'the custom of burning candles be now grown into disuse, being thought superstitious'.[26] The evidence is sparse, but it seems that northerners kept watch more often and with a higher degree of ritual activity, and some areas shared in the Celtic custom of wakes. The custom continued among the common people long after it was abandoned by the élite. John Aubrey reported in the later seventeenth century the custom in Yorkshire of 'watching and sitting all night till the body is interred', while drinking beer, taking tobacco, and sometimes engaging in 'mimical plays and sports'.[27] By the early eighteenth century the Newcastle antiquarian Henry Bourne could distinguish 'that watching of the vulgar, which is a scene of sport and drinking and lewdness', from the 'modern' custom in politer society 'of locking up the corpse in a room, and leaving it there alone'.[28]

'Watching', at one level, secured yet another mark of respect to the deceased and his or her family, and provided a final period of intimate attendance before the body was publicly laid to rest. One practical benefit was to safeguard the corpse from tampering; another was to have someone on hand in case the body unexpectedly revived. For people who believed that the soul or spirit was not fully detached, and might in some way hover or linger during that liminal interval between death and interment, the experience of watching could be full of terrors. Reformers chastised superstitious watchers who thought they saw visions or engaged in divinations while sitting with a body at night. Similarly they disapproved of wakes and games, in which drinking and merriment distracted from solemn meditation on death. Praying *with* the dead was an admirable activity, so long as it did not degenerate into prayers *for* the dead. Candles were permissible to lighten the dark, so long as no devotional significance was attached to them and they were not arranged with crosses.

Generally the practice of watching was unremarked, but a few vignettes throw light on the darkness. After Queen Elizabeth died at Richmond in 1603 her body was brought by barge to Whitehall and laid in the drawing chamber, 'where it was watched all night by several lords and ladies'. Courtiers and aristocrats came and went, to mark the passing of an era. Lady Anne Clifford recalled that her mother was among those who sat with the dead queen 'two or three nights', but she herself, aged 13 at the time, 'was held too young'. Sixteen years later Lady Anne herself took part in the overnight watching of the body of another queen. When James's Queen Anne died in 1619 her corpse was taken from Hampton Court to Denmark House and was watched by respectful courtiers.[29]

A testamentary case from Newcastle upon Tyne in 1625 provides another glimpse of the overnight watching much lower down the social scale. Mary Foster, the wife of a gentleman, testified that, 'upon the very same night that Dorothy Stowe departed this life and very shortly after her death, divers of her friends and neighbours being come into the place where she was lying, as the fashion is, to keep company and watch with her, and they being set down at a table and eating bread and cheese' Cuthbert Atkinson, one of Dorothy's former servants, claimed that she owed him money and began speculating about what might appear in her will. The church court had no interest in the business of watching and only recorded this information incidentally; its main concern was that Cuthbert might have falsified his mistress's will.[30]

Francis Tate describes the next stage in the mortuary process, as practised at the end of the sixteenth century. 'The appointed day for the funeral being near, the body is wrapped up with flowers and herbs in a fair sheet, and this we call winding a corpse.'[31] Rosemary was favoured as an evergreen herb with an agreeably pungent smell. It usually fell to family members to prepare a body for burial, but specialists were available to assist with all or part of the process. Neighbouring women and female servants were most commonly employed to clean and dress a corpse. Midwives sometimes took charge of this business, as adept at laying out as lying in. Winding a corpse in cloth had points in common with swaddling a child, so it was perhaps fitting that the same people who straightened the limbs of newborn babies at their entry to this world should clean them and wrap them at their exit.

Poor women were often employed to sit by someone dying, to watch by the corpse, and to clean it and prepare it for burial. The menial and gendered quality of this work is shown in payments for 'watching' and 'washing' and for 'laying out' and 'winding' the deceased that commonly appear in household and parochial accounts. After Sir Nicholas Bacon died in 1579 his executors paid 13s. 4d. 'to two women for laying forth of the body', and £1. 6s. 8d. 'to four women for trimming and laying forth the body besides the apparel'. At the opposite end of the social scale, the overseers for the poor at Ashby de la Zouch, Leicestershire, assigned women to Ruth Farmer's deathbed in 1630, paying 4d. to 'two women that sat up with her the night she died', and 6d. to 'them that were at the winding her'.[32]

Lord William Howard's accounts at Naworth Castle, Durham, in 1633 recorded contributions towards the funerals of servants and retainers, including 5s. 'for a winding sheet for Richard Wilkinson with the sore face', and 2s. 6d. 'for making a grave for Alice Smelter'. Later in the reign of Charles I, for the burial of her recently departed cousin, the West-Country gentlewoman Joyce Jeffries paid 5s. for 'the shroud being five yards and a half of white calico', 3s. more for 'tape to wind about it', and 6d. 'for helping to shroud and dress the corpse'.[33] In 1689 the Somerset physician Claver Morris spent 19s. on a shroud for his wife. Burying his sister at the very end of the Stuart era, the Sussex lawyer Timothy Burrell paid £1. 6s. 'for crepe and worsted for the shroud' and 8s. more 'for making it'.[34] By the end of the seventeenth century the élite were more likely to depart in tailored grave clothes than a traditionally wound shroud. The winding sheet gave way to 'a white [flannel] shirt [and] a clean cap, with their toes tied with a black ribbon', but the principle of decent apparelling remained the same.[35]

Even recipients of parish relief could rest assured that they would be afforded adequate solemnity and suitable dress. Payments for paupers' funerals show how deep-rooted was the concern for decent burial. At Castle Donnington, Leicestershire, in 1598 the churchwardens paid 8d. 'for a sheet to bury a poor woman', 3d. 'for winding the said poor woman', and 2d. 'for making of her grave'. At Ashby de la Zouch in 1626 the overseers spent 16d. 'for a sheet for Hawfield's wife' and similar amounts for grave clothes for other indigents. When 'old Huntwick' died in 1631 they spent 2d. for making his grave and 2d. more 'for ringing Huntwick's passing peal'.[36] Later in the century in 1676 the churchwardens of St Nicholas, Durham, paid 3s. 6d. 'for a winding sheet for Mary Sidebottom, by Mr. Major's order'. The parish accounts of St Mary

Coslany, Norwich, show payments for the burial of a vagrant in 1682, including 3s. 'paid for winding the stranger that died at the woolpack' and 3s. more for 'the bearers that carried him and the women that did bind him'. Even a vagrant stranger deserved Christian charity and the elements of a proper funeral. In this case the parish also paid 2s. 6d. 'for bell ringing, grave making, and chiming'.[37]

No one was lowered to the grave without some sort of covering. It was a point of human dignity to observe that only animals were buried naked. A winding sheet or burial shroud was the minimal equipment for the properly outfitted corpse, though none but the wealthy could look forward to decomposing in their own wooden box. 'A shroud to grave men only have', intoned the *Map of Mortalitie*. This early Stuart broadside featured sketches of skulls and bones and lines of Christian exhortation alongside a drawing of a shrouded corpse with the pick-axe and shovel used to dig the grave.[38] Shrouded portraits and memorial effigies enjoyed a minor vogue in seventeenth-century England. John Donne's final portrait shows him resting in a neatly tied shroud, and his post-mortem statue renders the late medieval cadaver monument in fashionable baroque form. The Reverend Daniel Featley, who died in 1645, likewise appears in a posthumous publication attired in his shroud and surrounded by inspirational verses.[39] Some devout Christians kept their shrouds in readiness, as a reminder of their end. Elizabeth Joceline, we have seen, laid out her winding sheet as she lay in for childbirth. Judge James Whitelock followed his wife's death in 1631 with preparation for his own. 'When the servants took out a winding sheet for her dead body, he caused them to lay forth the fellow of that sheet to wrap his own dead body in.'[40] Dead babies, by tradition, were wrapped for burial in the chrisom sheet prepared for their christening, and women who died in childbirth were sometimes interred with stillborn or neonatal infants wrapped in their arms.

Jacobean sensibility regarding burial attire is revealed in a parish register entry from Poynings, Sussex, where on 18 April 1608

was buried John Skerry, a poor man that died in the place stable, and being brought half naked with his face bare, the parson would not bury him so, but first he gave a sheet and caused him to be sacked therein, and they buried him more Christian like, being much grieved to see him brought so unto the grave.[41]

Unlike the hearse cloth that could be used again and again, the shroud itself was an intimate item that was usually used but once. A bed sheet would suffice—either the linen the party died in or a better piece from the household stock—though shrouds could be bought for pennies or shillings. That common shrouds had value is shown by another Jacobean case in which a felon, William Haines, was found guilty at the Lent assizes at Leicester, for entering a churchyard at night, digging up the graves of three men and a woman, stripping the shrouds or winding sheets from the dead bodies, and attempting to bury them again. Since the bodies had been consigned to the earth, interred in God's ground, there was some legal uncertainty about the ownership of the shrouds.[42]

Another extraordinary story preserved in the parish register of Malpas, Cheshire, concerns one Richard Dawson who in 1625,

being sick of the plague and perceiving he must die at that time arose out of his bed and made his grave, and caused his nephew John Dawson to cast straw into the grave, which was not far from his house, and went and lay him down in the said grave, and caused clothes to be laid upon [him], and so departed out of this world. This he did because he was a strong man and heavier than his said nephew and another wench which were able to bury.

It is not known whether straw was a normal cushioning for corpses or a concession to the dying man's need for comfort. Nor do we know how serious epidemics disrupted normal patterns of care for the dying and treatment of the dead. Attentive to social protocols, Richard Dawson took pains to ensure that clothes 'were laid upon him' and he could die with his honour intact.[43]

Similarly aware of customary procedures, though by no means in such desperate distress, the fastidious Margaret Verney left detailed instructions in her will of 1639 regarding her post-mortem *toilette*. 'Let no stranger wind me, nor do not let me be stripped, but put me a clean smock over me . . . and let my face be hid, and do you stay in the room and see me wound and laid in the first coffin, which must be wood if I do not die of any infectious disease.' The whole ensemble was then to be wrapped in lead and buried in the family tomb.[44]

Linen shrouds fell out of use in the later seventeenth century after legislation of the reign of Charles II required all bodies to be buried in wool. This was a concession to the wool industry, and it led to a change in the documentation of burials as well as a shift in their wardrobe. A typical certificate of compliance states that

we, Francis Norris and Anne Stoneaxe of the hamlet of Westwick, do make oath, that Matthew Lynto of Westwick, buried 13 October 1678, was not put in, wrapped up, or wound up or buried in any shirt, shift, sheet, or shroud made or mingled with flax, hemp, silk, hair, gold or silver, or other than what is made of sheeps' wool only; nor in any coffin lined or faced with any cloth, stuff or any other thing whatsoever made or mingled with flax, hemp, silk, hair, gold or silver, or any other material but sheeps' wool only.[45]

Families who wished to use more costly materials could evade the provisions
of the act by paying a suitable fine. Funeral undertakers of the later Stuart
period provided a varied range of grave clothes and ornaments, to under-
score the point that men and women, though naked when they came into
this world, at their leaving it would be suitably attired.

Furnishings and Equipment

From the time of their departure for the church until they were finally set in
the ground, most bodies rested on biers or similar equipment that belonged
to the local community. A bier was a frame with handles designed for supporting and transporting a body, easily constructed by a local carpenter. It
would normally be kept at the back of the church, and reserved for the ritual
transportation of the dead. The sight of his cousin Kirkard's wife in 1638,
'laid upon her bier at her door ready to be carried to burial', prompted the
Northamptonshire puritan Robert Woodford to pray, 'Lord make me mind-
ful of my mortality and prepare me for eternity, for the lord's sake.' A few
years later when Ellen Angier was buried in Yorkshire in 1642, 'three gentlemen and Mr. Horrocks her kinsman, a grave minister, of their own accord,
took hold on the bier and brought her to the grave', thereby demonstrating
their respect for this godly woman.[46] For present purposes, the specificity of
these observation is more interesting than their religious sentiments. In each
case we are permitted a glimpse of a corpse at rest and the means of its
movement from one place to another.

Most parishes provided a wooden bier for carrying or supporting the corpse.
Some would also loan or rent a mortuary cloth or pall, just as London livery
companies and organizations of city yeomen provided hearse cloths and similar trappings for the funerals of their members.[47] A pall, sometimes described
as a bier cloth or mortuary cloth, was draped or held over the bier or coffin.
A hearse was originally a frame to hold candles and decorations that stood
over the body in the course of the service, but gradually the word was used
for the whole ensemble that transported a corpse to a grave. Hearse cloths
were similar to palls, though more likely lain across a coffin than lifted above
it. Churchwardens' accounts occasionally mention the provision or repair of
equipment of this sort, and episcopal visitors sometimes included it in their
range of enquiries. The parishioners of Pittington, Durham, for example,
paid 17d. 'for a new bier' in 1592. The bishop of Norwich learnt that the 'blue
bier cloth' belonging to the parish of Runton, Norfolk, had been detained in
private hands by someone from Cromer in 1597. At Chester in 1600 a merchant's wife gave to Holy Trinity church 'a calico sheet of three breadths,

with laces through it, to be lent to cover the body of poor people on the bier'.
In 1611 the Chester churchwardens paid a carpenter a shilling for remaking
the bier.[48]

Thorough ecclesiastical visitors of the 1630s asked specifically whether the
necessary funeral items were present and correct. Most parishes in the Diocese of Chichester in 1636 could report their ownership of serviceable biers,
but almost one out of ten were lacking and others were defective. Upmander,
Sussex, had 'no bier to carry the dead to church', while at Merston 'the bier
whereon they carry the dead to church is like a ladder'. At Heaton, Nottinghamshire, in 1638 the archdeacon noted, 'the bier for carrying the corpse to
the church is not sufficient'. At Berrington, Shropshire, in 1639, two parishioners were cited 'for breaking the bier which the parish bought for to carry
the dead corpse'. It seems that rather than using the equipment for its proper
purpose they had been larking about, offending against the Caroline culture
of holiness.[49]

Post-Restoration surveys also checked on cloths, biers, and hearses and
ordered parishes to purchase them if missing. The churchwardens of Amersham, Buckinghamshire, were not alone in 1662 in acknowledging, 'we have as
yet no hearse cloth for the burial of the dead, but we will speedily provide
one'. Dozens of other parishes were similarly deficient. At Barking, Essex, in
1664, the churchwardens reported, 'we have an hearse cloth but no bier'.
Wakes Colne had a bier but no hearse cloth. At Kelvedon, 'we have no black
hearse cloth for the burial of the dead'. Wennington lacked both items.[50] One
bier built in response to Restoration enquiries survives at South Creake,
Norfolk, dated 1663.[51]

Parochial inventories sometimes included coffins. A coffin was a container,
similar to a coffer, and not necessarily reserved for burials. Bringing together
the material and spiritual aspects of funerals, the Jacobean preacher Thomas
Adams remarked, 'our graves shall be coffins to our bodies, as our bodies
have been coffins to our souls'.[52] Many parishes provided a reusable wooden
coffin for a shrouded body to lie in for the duration of the funeral ceremony.
The churchwardens of St Alphage, London, paid 5s. for such a coffin in 1569.
The parishioners of St Oswald, Durham, repaired their parish coffin in 1614,
and had it remade in 1666 at a cost of 14s.[53] The mid-Stuart equipment at
Easingwold, Yorkshire, with oaken boards and iron rings, is believed to be
the only complete parish coffin of this period to survive.[54]

People of rank preferred their own personal coffins, and would not be
seen dead in the common parish box. Carpenters and plumbers would
furnish a gentleman's coffin, plain or grand depending on purse and position, and their work became more elaborate as the seventeenth century

Guli: Vaughan sculp:

ET SINE BUSTO IACEO SEPULTUS.

Fig. 24 A coffined corpse from *The Lamentable Estate and Distressed Case of the Deceased Sr. William Dick* (London, 1657)

progressed. In their funeral customs as in so many other cultural activit-ies, the élite contrived to distinguish themselves from the masses. Only the most privileged corpses enjoyed the kind of lead coffin costing £5. 9s. 11d. commissioned for Sir Nicholas Bacon in 1579 or the nested lined and sealed coffins, 'two of wood and one of lead', that were the containers of choice for the later Stuart gentry. Margaret Verney's specification of a double coffin of wood and lead reflected the funeral practices of her family, class, and time. Her grandson Ralph, who died in 1686, was likewise 'put up into three coffins, two of wood and one of lead', before interment at Middle Claydon, Buckinghamshire.[55]

Though few seventeenth-century coffins survive, the records of the period contain occasional reference to their price. Sir Gawen Hervey's coffin for his burial in Essex in 1627 cost 12s. 6d. The coffin commissioned for Thomas Crosfield's sister-in-law's funeral at Spennithorne, Yorkshire, in 1653 cost 6s. 2d. Thomas Pepys's coffin in 1664, as noted by his brother the diarist, cost £1. 9s. Sir William Davenant's coffin in 1668 was built of walnut and, Sir John Denham said, ' 'twas the finest coffin that ever he saw'.[56] Young William Fitzwilliam's coffin in 1699 was 'covered with velvet and lined with lead and quilted with silk within', necessitating payment of a fine to avoid the statutory provision for burial in wool. The Lancashire catholic William Blundell was buried in 1702 in 'a plain black coffin' that cost 10s. Timothy Burrell's accounts show more lavish provision for his sister's funeral in Sussex in 1708, including £2. 2s. 'for making and nailing the coffin', 11s. 'for baize to line it', and a further £1. 6s. for 'cloth to cover it'.[57]

In exceptional circumstances a parish notable might arrange to be buried in a recycled medieval stone coffin. In his capacity of parish clerk of Ashover, Derbyshire, the later Stuart yeoman Leonard Wheatcroft laid claim to an ancient stone coffin in which he intended to be buried. Wheatcroft planned to be carried to church in his winding sheet, temporarily ensconced in the reusable parish coffin, borne on twelve wooden staves that he dyed black for that purpose. He would then be transferred to his improvised sarcophagus where he would await the general resurrection. Opportunities of this sort were rare, but a leading parishioner of Balsham, Cambridgeshire, reputedly a member of the 'family of love', also secured burial in a medieval stone coffin.[58]

Funeral Processions

The passage from the place of death to the place of burial was no ordinary journey. For the corpse it was a one-way transit from domestic to sacred space, from the deathbed to the dormitory of Christians. For the accompanying kinsfolk, neighbours, and friends it was an occasion for respectful mourning and also for social display. For the poor who expected some distribution of dole, as well as for merchandizers of funerary ornaments, it could also be an opportunity for profit. Mourners could transport the dead body in whatever manner they pleased—on their shoulders, on a cart, or on

FIG. 25 The bride's burial, with women coffin bearers, from *Two Unfortunate Lovers* (London, 1621)

a sumptuous funeral hearse—though a bier was normally employed. It could be moved with quiety dignity or lavish expense. The corpse could be carried simply and silently, with little more ceremony than carting a load of wood, or it could be the centre-piece of an honourable cortège, amidst an ostentatious demonstration of wealth and power. As John Dunton observed in the late seventeenth century, 'nothing of this concerns the dead . . . it is all one whether they be carried forth in a chariot or a wooden bier'.[59] It mattered little to religion how the body came to church, so long as it was moved without superstition; rather, the transportation of the dead was a civil affair, balancing the estate and circumstance of the deceased with the social and cultural concerns of the living.

Carrying the corpse was an act of intimacy, sometimes delegated to poor people or servants. Pallbearers, however, at funerals of the middling and upper classes, were drawn from the principal mourners and close associates of the deceased. Hefting the bier or carrying the coffin required strength as well as dignity, while holding the pall was invested with honour and respect. Married women or maids held the pall at the funerals of one of their gender, while their menfolk carried the weight of the corpse. There is no evidence that women were excluded from the ritual. Writing of gentry funerals at the end of the Elizabethan era, Francis Tate observed, 'the corpse is taken up and carried either by poor people chosen out for that purpose, or by the servants of him that is dead . . . his kinsfolk and familiar friends follow after in black gowns and hoods'.[60]

Elizabethan wills suggest that carrying a corpse was a menial task to be performed for pay rather than a mark of honourable fellowship and peer respect. William Fitche, esquire, of Little Canfield, Essex, allowed 'to everyone that shall bear me to church to be buried 2s.' in his will of 1577. William Beriff, an Essex merchant who made his will the same year, provided a shilling each 'to eight poor men to carry me to church'. William Hearde, an Essex yeoman, left 'to six labourers of the ancientest of Rainham six new caps of the price of 20d. apiece for their pains to carry my body to the church' in 1592.[61] Funeral processions in London and in other Elizabethan towns were often led by members of the poor who were dressed in mourning livery and paid and fed for their services.[62]

Seventeenth-century records show wide variation in these intimate social relationships around the body, but preserved the distinction between physical labour and social respect. The puritan Robert Woodford was as sensitive as any to the social nuances of placement and wrote, after a funeral in 1639, 'I was a little melancholy to see . . . others take place before me on purpose, yet I laboured to keep down my base proud spirit.'[63] The occasion offered an opportunity to practise puritan self-discipline, even if the melancholy was caused by a social snub rather than the presence of mortality. Funeral managers usually ensured that the pallbearers held equivalent social rank to the deceased, but occasionally great men condescended to honour their inferiors. John Evelyn 'with three knights' held up the pall at the funeral of the master shipwright Jonas Shish in 1680 because, though not even a gentleman, in Evelyn's words, 'he was worthy of it'. Arranging for the burial of William Fitzwilliam in 1699 his father, Lord Fitzwilliam, advised his steward, 'the coffin is very heavy, being lined with lead, therefore you must appoint eight strong men to carry it'. The six pallbearers, by contrast, were privileged kinsmen and gentlemen, arranged by rank from the head to the feet.[64]

Most funeral journeys were short, going no further than the nearest parish church. But people of high social station often required burial in a place of honour some distance from where they died. Bishop Matthew Wren, for example, died in London but was carried back to Cambridge for a magnificent burial in 1667. Attended by parsons and gentlemen, 'the hearse coach hung round with his escutcheons' entered the city on 25 April. Coffined in lead, the bishop's body lay in state in the University Schools until 11 May, magnificently furnished with heraldic trappings, black cloth, and tapers. Poor scholars in mourning gowns stood watch, while visitors of all sorts came to pay their respects. Finally, a grand cortège led to Pembroke Hall, where Wren was interred in the chapel that he himself had built and consecrated.[65]

Margaret Godolphin's body was carried ceremoniously from London to Cornwall for burial in 1678 'in an hearse with six horses, and two other coaches of as many, and with about thirty people of her relations and servants'. Elizabeth Freke's 'dear sister Choutt, being embalmed in London where she died, was carried down to Hollingbourne in Kent' for burial in a family plot in 1675. Some years later her grandson, accidentally killed by a pistol shot in London, was carried up to Norfolk 'to be here interred'. Elizabeth paid 'the hearse man' £6 'for bringing of him'.[66]

It was customary in Stuart funeral processions for mourners to carry sprigs of greenery, such as ivy, laurel, or rosemary. For some these evergreens were 'an emblem of the soul's immortality', but they also served as a nosegay, and perhaps as a counter to the smell of putrefaction.[67]

Mourning Black

If grief was an emotion to which people might legitimately succumb, mourning was a practice in which many more could publicly participate. Though closely linked, the one was rooted in inward feeling, the other a matter of outward display. Discussion continued in Elizabethan and Stuart England about the propriety and protocols of mourning, in particular who should mourn, how to mourn, and for how long mourning should be observed. Since money and leisure were required for large-scale mourning, the practices that were debated belonged mostly to the privileged classes. Ordinary people may have grieved, and may have made gestures towards mourning, but only the wealthy could afford the acres of black cloth that went into mourning cloaks and gowns, hangings, draperies, and covers, or the gifts of rings and gloves they showered on funeral guests. Participants in common funerals wore their everyday costume, and returned in short order to the routine concerns of their lives.

Moderate mourning was acceptable, thought the Elizabethan reformer James Pilkington, so long as 'it be not too much, and seem to grudge at God's doings in taking our friends from us'. Two or three days was sufficient, a week at the utmost. The puritan Thomas Cartwright conceded that it was 'lawful to lament the dead', so long as the mourning was not 'immoderate' and did not extend to superstitious pomp.[68] Extended mourning, paced by periodic intervals, might seem to mimic the old catholic practice of month's minds and year's days, but seventeenth-century fashion appeared not to be troubled by this. By the end of the Stuart era it was not thought improper to observe formal mourning for a year, though full compliance with this evolving etiquette was rare. A principal mourner could just as easily appear in mourning apparel after a brief withdrawal from the world, and then get on with his life. When his father-in-law died in 1683 John Evelyn wrote, 'I went not to church, obeying the custom of keeping at home till the ceremonies of the funeral were over'.[69]

The death of Samuel Pepys's mother in 1667 occasioned the first stage of mourning, with the usual intensity of black robes, hoods, scarves, and gloves. Six weeks later the 'second mourning' began, in which Pepy's wife could display her elegant black dress tastefully trimmed with siver lace. Decked out in fashionable black, occupied with oysters and claret, and immersed in agreeable conversation, Samuel Pepys, was not too selfish to observe, after burying his brother in 1664, 'how the world makes nothing of the memory of a man an hour after he is dead'.[70]

Moralists repeatedly complained of perfunctory mourning, and even more of the speedy remarriage of widows and widowers. John Dunton wrote:

We in these days do not weep and mourn at the departure of the dead so much nor so long as in Christian duty we ought. For husbands can bury their wives and wives their husbands with a few counterfeit tears and a sour visage masked and painted over with dissimulation, contracting second marriages before they have worn out their mourning garments, and sometimes before their cope-mates be cold in their graves.[71]

The most obvious sign of mourning was costume; a mourner was easily identified by apparel or accessories of black. Puritan agitators mocked the black costumes as hypocritical and superstitious, but John Whitgift claimed to 'see not why the wearing of mourning apparel should not be profitable to put a man in mind of his own mortality'. Donning black mourning robes had custom and antiquity to recommend it, added Whitgift, though 'it is no matter of religion, but of civility and order. If any man put religion in it, then no doubt it is superstitious.'[72] In his widely read treatise on *The Meane in Mourning*, the Elizabethan Thomas Playfere commented,

in respect to us which are alive, it is a very charitable custom, yea it is a very honourable custom, to give mourning cloaks or gowns. But in respect of them that are dead it is altogether needless. For what need we wear black cloaks in sign of sorrow, seeing (as it is in Revelation) they wear long white robes in token of triumph.[73]

Continuing this conversation into the seventeenth century, the Jacobean preacher Robert Hill justified mourning customs (and costumes) with the following six points.

1. By it we keep a memory of our friend.
2. We are drawn to some humiliations.
3. We are put in mind of our own mortality.
4. It argues His love that bestows it upon us.
5. By this means many poor are clothed.
6. It is but a legacy of the dead to the living.[74]

Mourning gear helped to distinguish funeral participants from mere onlookers, and the quality and amount of black cloth served further to identify those most intimately associated with the deceased. Aristocratic funerals featured blackness in abundance. Perhaps the principal beneficiaries were the clothiers, drapers, and dyers who supplied the black fabric, and the poor who had the use of it when mourning was done. The black cloth provided for Sir Nicholas Bacon's funeral in 1579 must have stimulated the economy of the city of London, for the Lord Keeper's executors accounted for £648. 11s. 5d. 'paid for blacks at the funeral', all carefully listed by yardage and recipient. Similar expenses at the Earl of Sussex's funeral in Essex in 1583 reached £437. 6s. 8d.[75]

Reference to mourning gear abounds in the wills, accounts, and correspondence of the Elizabethan gentry. Thomas Meade, an Essex justice of the peace who died in 1585, specified that

there shall be bestowed at my burial and funeral one hundred pounds at the least to buy black cloth and other things, and every one of my serving men shall have a black coat; and a gown of black cloth to my brethren and their wives, my wife's daughters and their husbands, my sister Swanne and her husband, my brother Turpyn and his wife, my aunt Bendyshe, and Elizabeth wife of John Wrighte.

His neighbour Thomas Colshill, esquire, whose will was dated 1593, assigned

to my son Stanhope and his wife each a mourning gown to be worn at my funeral, two of his men that shall wait on him at my funeral each a black coat, two of his servants a black coat, my brother Crafford and my sister his wife, my cousin Manwood and his wife and my cousin Francis Smithe, each a mourning gown.

Robert Bradbury of Littlebury provided 'each a mourning gown' to an uncle, an aunt, two brothers, and three cousins.[76] Bequests of this sort reveal the role that relations were expected to play in funeral rituals, and show the range of effective kinship extending beyond the immediate nuclear family at least to uncles and cousins. All were distinguished by their mourning black.

Wearing black was a mark of dependency as well as respect. George Scott of Chigwell, Essex, by his will dated 1588, put his servants into black coats for his funeral and ordered 'two and a half yards of black cloth to make them a cloak' for two of his nephews. Edward Hubbard, esquire, ordered 'twelve black frieze coats at my burial' for a dozen poor mourners, and 'to every manservant that I have black coats being at my burial and such mourning gowns as my executor shall think fit'. Edward Thursby allowed 13s. 4d. to each of his farmers and tenants (he named eighteen) 'to buy so much black cloth as shall make each a mourning coat, to accompany my corpse' at his burial in 1602.[77] His worship would bow out amidst a host of appropriately liveried servants and dependants. The last service they could do their master was to show up at his funeral in mournful costume.

William Saunders, another Elizabethan gentleman, expected most of his relations to attend his father's funeral in July 1585. Announcing by letter, 'the day appointed for the solemnizing of the funeral is tomorrow seven-night', he sent 'blacks' to his uncle and aunt, apologizing that they were not so good or so fine as they might wish or deserve. Sending black cloth or clothing signalled the death of a significant kinsman, and identified the wearers or recipients as principal mourners. Saunders also invited 'my uncle Dairell and mine aunt, my cousin Thomas Dairell and his wife, my cousin Richard Ingolsby and his wife, my cousin Walter Bagot and his wife, and my brother Tiringham, and do verily look for all their coming'. All would be mournfully attired. The funeral would gather the kin in an expensive but select tribute to one of their number. In this case it was not open to all-comers. Saunders asked his uncle, 'I pray you conceal the funeral day. Welford House is but small of receipt, and our company will be great, especially if the day be known.' The letter continues, 'I purposed to have bestowed black upon my uncle Beaumont and my cousin Henry and his wife, to have invited them hither, but God hath disappointed me by shortening my uncle's days.' More blacks would have to be provided for Uncle Beaumont's funeral, 'to which they will all, no doubt, be invited in turn'.[78]

Almost identical concerns can be found in diaries and correspondence of the seventeenth century. Black garb and mourning trinkets distinguished the principal mourners and demonstrated that they were exhibiting respect. Sir Gawen Hervey's widow wore black pins, black ribbons, black stocking, and a black 'tier' or ruffle at the burial of her husband in 1627. The Exeter merchant John Hayne dressed his infant daughters in black taffeta hoods and coats, and even their nurse wore mourning garb, at their grandfather's funeral in 1638.[79] A sea of blackness, black wall hangings, black bed furnishings, black saddlery and trim, almost overwhelmed the family home in Buckinghamshire after the death of Dame Margaret Verney in 1641. Katherine Wyvill's funeral in Yorkshire in 1653, in a clerical family, was dignified by sixty-one yards of black ribbon costing £2. 1s. 9d.[80] Samuel Pepys 'got a pair of shoes blacked on the soles' in readiness for his brother's funeral in 1664, so his mourning ensemble would be perfect, even when kneeling. The mournful costume did not necessarily induce a mournful spirit, however, for Pepys enjoyed 'a pleasant *rancontre* of a lady in mourning' at another funeral in 1669.[81]

William Lawrence attended a city merchant's funeral in 1675 in which the house became 'the house of mourning . . . The hall and parlour were hung with black cloth and escutcheons. There were about a hundred persons invited by tickets, and rings given . . . The hearse was adorned with escutcheons and attended by a train of thirty-two coaches, and there he was entered.'[82] Ralph Thoresby similarly described 'the funeral of lawyer Bathurst's brother' in 1681,

who was interred with the greatest state has been known in this town; near one hundred torches carried in state; the room hung with black, and escutcheons and tapers; so was the pulpit; a velvet pall, hung with escutcheons, and carried by the chief gentry, who had gloves and scarves; all the company had gloves, with sack and biscuits. Mr. Benson preached at nine at night, from Job 19: 26–27.[83]

A few years later Ralph Verney expressed approval at the mourning provisions at another gentry funeral. 'Sir Richard Pigott was buried very honourably . . . and at a considerable charge, with two new mourning coaches and a hearse, one of which coaches and the hearse had six horses apiece.' All were accessorized in black. 'We that bore up the pall had rings, scarves, hat-bands, chamois gloves of the best fashion, and sarsenet escutcheons delivered to us; the rest of the gentry had rings, all the servants gloves.'[84]

Similar mourning gear embellished the funeral of William Fitzwilliam, a young aristocrat who died in 1699. There were black gowns and black staves for the attendants, mourning suits for the chief mourners, mourning gloves, and mourning hatbands. The church too was swathed in black; mourning cloth covered the pulpit for several Sundays after the service, and the 'baize and escutcheons' that hung in the chancel were supposed to stay up a whole year. Lord Fitzwilliam of Milton, who made these arrangements, set limits on the supply of gloves. 'I have ordered some gloves to be sent down, that if any gentleman in the neighbourhood comes in to the funeral, or the tenants, they may each have a pair of gloves, but I do not mean to give to all the mob that are not my tenants.'[85] Claver Morris, a West-Country physician, spent almost £50 on his wife's funeral in 1689, and almost £12 more on her tombstone. The greatest expense was on mourning gifts, £14. 11s. on gloves and £8. 15s. on rings. Morris memorialized his wife and consoled himself for his loss by wearing 'a pair of buttons with my wife's hair set in gold'.[86]

The visual coding of mourning gear became an issue in a testamentary case in the reign of Charles II. John Wren, a gentleman-servant to the bishop

of Durham, 'put himself into mourning apparel' and expressed suitable husbandly grief at the death of his wife, or supposed wife, Margaret in 1673. 'With
weeping and great lamentation', Wren declared 'that he had lost a dear and
loving wife . . . the best wife and the best bedfellow that ever man had'. The
case turned on whether the couple were truly married and whether John was
therefore entitled to inherit Margaret's goods. His public display of mourning, however heartfelt, was clearly intended to establish his claim to the status
of husband and widower, a claim undermined by the irregularity or clandes-
tinity of their marriage. Various witnesses alleged that John had discharged
Margaret's debts after her death, and presumed that therefore he must have
been her husband. His public parade in the costume of a mourning husband
was intended to clinch the matter.[87]

Doles and Dinners

By tradition, the funerals of the middling and upper sort provided opportunities for deeds of charity and acts of largesse. Funerals of the gentry and
those who emulated them often included distribution of dole to the poor,
though few appoached the vast sum of £193. 6s. 8d. 'given to the poor' at the
funeral of Sir Nicholas Bacon in 1579.[88] 'Funeral doles were an ancient custom,' wrote Anthony Sparrow in his mid-Stuart *Rationale Upon the Book
of Common Prayer*, and were approved of by society, church, and state. But
changing views on charity and hardening attitudes to the poor altered the
scale and manner of distribution. Wealthy testators of the sixteenth century
commonly requested that a portion of their charity be distributed in dole at
their funerals in the form of money, food, and beer, and this could cause
scenes of confusion. Their counterparts in the seventeenth century were more
likely to limit their charitable giving and to reserve the refreshments for their
friends.[89]

Traditionally the dole was given to 'the poor', who defined themselves by
their willingness to accept it. The funeral bell could be a summons to dinner
at the cost of watching a stranger buried. The dole attracted large numbers
to gentry funerals, large numbers being interpreted as a mark of respect. It
was an act of deference to take the dead man's money as well as a Christian
obligation to provide it. From the point of view of the poor, these occasions
provided a useful diet supplement, and a bonus of 'relief and charity'. They
were open to all-comers, either residents of specific parishes or, as Bartholemew
Averel of Southminster, Essex, specified in his will of 1562, 'the poor walking
people that resort to my burial'.[90]

The funeral philanthropy of Elizabethan gentlemen may be seen in a sample of wills from Essex. Though John Barnaby, a gentleman of Inworth, requested 'to be buried without pomp', he none the less expected a large attendance at his funeral. In his will of 1563 Barnaby provided for a cash dole to the poor, 'if they be forty score or more, which I trow will not be, and to have bread, cheese or other victual and good drink sufficient and plenty in the church or some other meet place there'. The better class of mourners, 'such priests and clerks with the most rich and substantial persons of the parish where I shall be buried and other substantial men that then be there', were to be treated to superior refreshments, 'a dinner together with meat and drink and victuals in some convenient house or mine own, and the poor specially well refreshed with some things as bread, drink, and cheese'.[91] Major funerals like this often ended with two feasts, a dinner for the up-scale participants and a rowdier picnic for the poor.

Francis Jobson in 1572 left 'to the poor people coming to my burial in the church of St. Giles near Colchester ten pounds at the rate of 2d. apiece', a sum that would satisfy 1,200 applicants. More often the dole was reserved for seventy or eighty 'poor people' of a particular parish, with a further distribution at the 'month day' for as long as that custom still survived.[92] The executors handed out the money to the crowd, sometimes with the assistance of the overseers of the poor.

Thomas Franck, esquire, of Hatfield Broad Oak, was remarkably precise when he allocated £6. 13s. 4d. to the poor in his will of 1573, 'to be thankful and give praise to God for the departing of my soul'. Providing this money was a final and dramatic demonstration of the landowner's ability to distribute alms, and a last deed of charity that might possibly affect his prospect of salvation. Strict protestant reformers frowned on such glosses, but they were hard-pressed to counter the popular appeal of the dole. William Fitch of Little Canfield left 'to the poor people coming to my burial four pounds in meat, drink, and money' in 1579. The following year Wistan Browne of South Weald ordered, 'at the day of my funerals dole be given to the poor people, viz. 6d. apiece to so many of them as will hold up their hands to take it, besides sufficient meat, bread and drink to every of them'.[93]

It was hard to get through a funeral without drinking. 'Grief is thirsty, and must drink', quipped the poet Thomas Shipman.[94] Mourners who assembled to escort the body to the church were customarily fortified with beer, wine, or spirits. Later, when the ritual interment was complete, the guests regrouped around a table laden with meat and drink. Neighbours and followers who were not directly involved in the mourning might be satisfied with a token refreshment, a cake or biscuit or a sip of ale. 'It is a commendable custom', wrote James Cole, 'that after any burial the nearest friends return to the funeral house to comfort those that survive'.[95] Conviviality, a coming together of the living, marked the conclusion of the burial service and a return to normal life. The feast allowed mourners to discharge the solemn tension of the funeral and to reassert the warm-blooded vitality of survivors. Sometimes the good fellowship went too far, in the eyes of censorious observers, so that 'the house of mourning is turned into the house of mirth and feasting' and drunken funeral guests 'become more like beasts than men'.[96]

Even more than christening feasts and nuptial dinners, Elizabethan funeral meals were semi-public occasions. William Saunders may have gone against custom in 1585 when he attempted to keep his father's funeral small and quiet so as not to overwhelm the household resources. A great company was expected, but even more would be bound to descend on the dole and refreshments if the event was exposed to widespread publicity.[97]

More in accord with tradition, the great baronial funeral of the Earl of Shrewsbury in 1560 featured 320 messes (i.e. 1,280 individual servings) available 'to all manner of people who seemed honest'. The venison dishes alone accounted for fifty does and twenty-nine red deer. The leftovers were given to the poor, who had 'bread and drink great plenty as well as the customary dole of cash'.[98] At a humbler level, Robert Gaywood of Maldon, Essex, arranged dinners for the clergy at his funeral, and made provision in his will of 1559 for general refreshments for his neighbours. 'There be provided at my burial a half seam of wheat to be baked into bread, two barrels of beer, and a half wey of cheese . . . and every of the bailiffs, aldermen and head burgesses at service in the parish church at my month's day shall have their dinners.' His contemporary, John Stanton, left 'to the poverty and other at my burial five bushels of wheat to be made into bread and as much cheese and drink as is needful . . . and like money at my month day called the trigintal day'. John Coult of Heydon left strict instructions in 1561,

I ordain at my burial a solemn drinking to be made by my executors, i.e. three fat sheep, three barrels of beer, and six dozen of bread, to be provided for my poor and rich neighbours that will come to it. At my month's day another drinking to be provided, i.e. one barrel of beer, two dozen of bread, and two cheeses the price 16d.[99]

Also following custom, Henry Rolfe, a gentleman of Kelveden Hatch, Essex, made elaborate provisions for general feasting in his will of 1602, specifying,

a bullock of the price of three pounds shall be bought and distributed by the discretion of my executor, with ten bushels of wheat and six barrels of beer, among the poor of the parishes (Kelveden and seven neighbours), or eight pounds at their discretion, provided that such persons as shall be at my funerals and be troublesome shall have no part.[100]

It appears that in this case the feast came some time after the interment, as a memorial dole rather than part of the burial ritual. A cash disbursement could take its place if the executors thought fit, and those who had made nuisances of themselves at the actual funeral could be excluded. This is a rare hint that gentlemen's funerals were not always decent and orderly, but that some rowdiness could intervene. Rolfe's posthumous instruction to his executors was his last attempt to impose order, a mild gesture from the grave towards the reformation of manners.

Diaries and accounts of the seventeenth century show the custom of funeral dining continuing, though rarely with tables for all-comers. Most were select occasions, restricted to family and friends or associates and dependants. Guests at Stuart funerals often contributed to the store of meat and drink, just as they helped to supply the table at weddings, establishing reciprocity with the family of the host. The Exeter merchant John Hayne contributed a brace of capons and a gallon of Mallaga sack to his father-in-law's funeral refreshments in 1638. When the Essex clergyman Ralph Josselin 'heard Tom Humfrey was dead' in 1657 he 'sent down six dozen of cakes for his burial'.[101]

Attendance at gentry funeral dinners was increasingly by invitation only. Vast amounts of food and drink were consumed, though by a restricted range of stomachs. 'Forty mess provided for', observed the Lancashire squire Nicholas Assheton at his cousin's funeral feast in 1617, where most of the guests were fellow landowners and tenants. Sweetmeats to the value of £3. 17s., seven dozen cakes, seven and three-quarter gallons of claret, and almost six gallons of sack helped see Sir Gawen Hervey to his grave in 1627.[102] The usual 'funeral circumstances' for Oxford's academic gentry and clergy included distribution of refreshments, alms, and rosemary, and when the Warden of All Souls was buried in 1636 more than £100 was spent on cakes and wine. At Katherine Wyvill's Yorkshire funeral in 1653, her Oxford kinsman recorded, the dinner of mutton and beef, bread, and cheese cost £4. 3s. 6d., and another 9s. 1½d. was spent on currants, raisins, ginger, cinnamon, cloves, and spices.[103] Samuel Pepys 'fell to a barrel of oysters, cake and cheese', after burying his brother in 1664. He had 'bid' or invited 120 guests but 'many more' came, 'nearer one hundred and fifty. Their service was six biscuits apiece and what they pleased of burnt claret.' The claret cost £2. 2s. 6d., while biscuits ran to £4. 11s.[104] Five hundred 'boxes of banquet . . . to the value of about 5s. a box' were distributed to the clerical and academic guests at Matthew Wren's funeral in 1667. 'We had burnt wine and biscuits in great plenty, all the servants had burnt wine and biscuits,' wrote Ralph Verney with pleasure after attending the funeral of Sir Richard Piggott in 1685.[105]

The custom of providing an open table at funeral feasts had not disappeared, though uninvited Stuart funeral-goers were less well supplied than their Tudor predecessors. Mourners in search of alcohol might have to pay for their own. After the formal drinking at the funeral of Richard Boocock at Stump Cross, Yorkshire, in 1676, 'a company of fellows would needs drink 2d. a piece', and the nonconformist preacher Oliver Heywood joined them briefly, but did not imbibe. 'I did not appear so much as I ought against their vain way of drinking shots,' he wrote, 'though I did say something to dissuade them from their intemperance.'[106]

Roger Lowe, a diary-keeping mercer's apprentice in Restoration Lancashire, sought out funerals for their company, conviviality, and conversation, and judged them by the liberality of their refreshments. The normal provision included wine and biscuits, but sometimes the hospitality fell short. Lowe and a companion quit one funeral in 1665 'somewhat hungry and angry', and wet their whistles at an alehouse. At a Sunday funeral in 1666, he writes, 'we had buried the corpse and expected according to custom to have some refreshment, and were a company of neighbours together round about a table'. Expectations fell short, however, when 'the doctor comes and prohibits the filling of any drink till after prayers; so I came home with Thomas Harrison and . . . we were disappointed'.[107]

Experienced funeral-goers expected ritual provision appropriate to the deceased's social position, and were quick to notice signs of meanness or inadequacy. Sour comments about cheap funerals indicate the high social value placed on appropriate display. They also point to normative expectations. Samuel Pepys, for example, was disappointed at the turnout for his aunt Kite's funeral in September 1661, commenting, 'besides us and my uncle Fenner's family there was none of any quality, but poor rascally people'. Pepys was also dismissive of arrangements for the burial of Sir Robert Slingsby in October 1661. 'Pretending that the corpse stinks, they will bury it tonight privately, and so will unbespeak all their guests, and there shall be no funeral.' In Pepys's view both Sir Robert and his friends were short-changed by this modest ritual.[108]

William Dugdale tells of a mean funeral in 1660, in which the dead woman's husband served as both undertaker and parson. When the physician Fisher Dilke's wife died, says Dugdale,

he first stripped his barn wall to make her a coffin, then bargained with the clerk for a groat to make a grave in the churchyard to save eightpence for one in the church. This done, he speaketh about eight of his neighbours to meet at his house for bearers, for whom he provided three twopenny cakes and bottle of claret; and some being come he read a chapter of Job to them, till all were there ready; when, having distributed the cake and wine among them, they took up the corpse, he following them to the grave. Then, putting himself in the parson's place, none being there, the corpse being laid in the grave and a spade of mould cast thereon, he said, 'Ashes to ashes, dust to dust,' adding, 'Lord now lettest thy servant depart in peace, for mine eyes have seen thy salvation,' and so returned home.

This may seem, to some, like a modest and dignified ceremony, in which a grieving husband performed his duty to God and to his departed wife. But to Dugdale it was symptomatic of a society gone wrong. The improvised simplicity of this funeral, its lack of pomp and preparation, the husband's usurpation of the priestly function, and the absence of a structured service, may all have accorded with the wishes of the deceased Mrs Dilke, reportedly 'a frequenter of conventicles', but to a conservative herald like Dugdale they were all developments to lament.[109]

Alderman Samuel Newton of Cambridge, another connoisseur of good funerals, observed with distaste the mean provision for the burial of the wife of a colleague in 1665. Though this was 'a great funeral' with a sermon and interment in the chancel of Great St Mary's church, it was performed with 'but little solemnity' and 'small order'. There were 'no gloves, nor ribbons', refreshments were limited to 'one cup of claret, one cup of Ipocras ... sugar cakes, two rolls', and for 'the best sort, only two mackeroons'. A mourner could go home hungry and thirsty![110]

In 1672 another observer reported that Mr Cornelius Bee was buried at St Bartholemew's 'without sermon, wine or wafers, only gloves and rosemary'. In 1673, when

Mrs. Brigs of Boyston was buried, the invited guests waited in that house most of them five hours, and had nothing but a bit of cake, draught of wine, piece of rosemary, and pair of gloves, contrary to the custom of our country, which did not please our people; they had given them notice to come at ten o'clock, had the sermon at three.[111]

In October 1681, Ralph Josselin recorded, 'the good old Lady Honeywood buried; not a glove, ribbon, scutcheon, wine, beer, biscuit given at her burial, but a little mourning to servants; the servants carried her, six persons with scarves and gloves bore up the pall'. Josselin, assuredly, was not complaining, but the lack of customary provision was something he felt to be remarkable.[112] Thomas Idle's funeral at Holbeck, Nottinghamshire, in 1680 was almost ruined by the pressures of the crowd, 'such vast multitudes, what bidden and what unbidden, that abundance of confusion must unavoidably happen'. The diarist Ralph Thoresby, Idle's nephew, commented, 'of 130 dozen cakes not one left'.[113]

It was to avoid such scenes that some high-ranking families arranged relatively simple funeral ceremonies that were sometimes described as 'private'. Noting that 'Sir Clement Fisher . . . was privately buried at Packington' in April 1683, William Dugdale meant that the funeral was carried out without the assistance of the heralds.[114] It was neither indecent nor clandestine, but avoided the cost and fuss of knightly honour. The scale and honour of the event was less than Sir Clement's dignity might have deserved. After Sir Ralph Verney died in 1696 his family planned to invite forty or fifty neighbouring gentry to his funeral, but on reading his will they found that he too had asked 'to be buried privately and with as little pomp as may be'. After 'serious thought', evaluating their own social needs against the old man's peculiar directions, his heirs decided 'to bury him publicly', though with the minimum of pomp. Not surprisingly, the funeral was mobbed.[115]

The Triumph of Pomp

Though death was the great leveller, survivors ensured that gradations of honour and status were carefully observed. Some élite families, as we have seen, were almost obsessive in this regard. Varying degrees of care and ornament attested to a person's rank or standing, and the pomp or grandeur of funeral accoutrements demonstrated that the social identity of the deceased had not been entirely extinguished. Family members registered to themselves and to all who saw them that their conduct was commensurate with their loss. Lady Sussex, for example, who had just lost her husband, expressed the common sentiment of her class when she told Ralph Verney in 1643, 'I would not neglect anything for his burial that may express my love and value of him; it will cost a great deal of money, but I must not be failing in my last service to him.'[116] Adjusted for economic resources, these obligations of love, value, and service were felt across the social spectrum. When an Oxford sergeant at law was killed in 1627, Thomas Crosfield noted, he was buried 'with due respect and pomp, attended with solemnities answerable to his profession'.[117]

The protestant reformation had little impact on the *scale* of élite funerals, only stripping them of crosses and silencing the singing of dirges. Even the reformers who frowned on 'pomp' understood the social benefits of a well-furnished funeral procession. Advanced opinion in Elizabethan England had frowned on pomp, but the leaders of seventeenth-century society took pains to ensure that their funerals were performed with the highest degree of honour and respect. Though attuned to the debate about 'pomp', the sponsors of lavish funerals insisted that elaborate ceremonials were not incompatible with spiritual austerity. Some historians have discerned 'a notable reduction in the number of opulent funerals' towards the end of the sixteenth century and a 'new insistence on economy' among the aristocracy of the early seventeenth century, but the evidence for this is anecdotal rather than statistical.[118] Gentle and aristocratic funerals in the later Stuart period could be as sumptuous as any seen in the sixteenth century. Whereas Tudor élite funerals had been designed to attract crowds and to marshal the various ranks of society, including trains of poor people and dependants, the polite and gentle classes of the Stuart era seemed more interested in impressing each other. Grand families continued to insist on grand funerals, but they were increasingly likely to restrict the guest-list, and increasingly inclined to conduct the burial at night. Lit by links and flaming torches, the nocturnal procession added drama to the occasion, while keeping the vulgar at bay.[119]

Whereas sixteenth-century reformers used the authority of St Augustine to point out the vanity of pomp and to argue repeatedly that funerals 'are rather for the comfort of the living than for the aid and help of the dead',[120] early Stuart conservatives used similar words to encourage a return to more elaborate ceremonies. John Weever led the campaign in the early years of Charles I. 'Now howsoever the procuration of funerals, the manner of burial, the pomp of obsequies, be rather comforts to the living than helps to the dead; and although all these ceremonies be despised by our parents on their deathbeds, yet they should not be neglected by us their children or nearest kindred, upon their interments.' As a good protestant, Weever knew perfectly well that there was nothing to be done for the soul of the departed; but as an advocate of armorial dignity he recognized the wealth of social opportunities that an elaborate funeral presented. Weever exaggerated when he claimed that 'funerals, in any expensive way here with us, are now accounted but as fruitless vanity, insomuch that almost all the ceremonial rites of obsequies heretofore used are altogether laid aside'.[121] One had only to look at expensive funerals for the aristocracy and gentry to see that the taste for pomp was well supplied.

In death as in life, the aristocratic and armigerous classes sustained their dominant position by means of elaborate display. Their funerals were often noteworthy public events, and their burials often marked by ornate memorials or tombs. Although heraldic funerals may have lost ground in the Stuart period, and faced local competition from unofficial suppliers of escutcheons, the heralds continued to offer their services to an élite that was sensitive to status and reputation. It was important, for social hierarchy and self-esteem, that funerals expressed the 'difference of personages in the carriage of their dead bodies to the place of sepulchre, according to their state and dignity'. It may have been sufficient for ordinary mortals to be carried simply by their

FIG. 26 A heraldic funeral procession. Detail from *A Funerall Elegie upon the deplorable and much lamented death of . . . Robert Devereux* (London, 1646)

friends or servants, but a rich man's corpse deserved to be drawn in a carriage, befitting his rank and resources.[122] Gentle funerals accordingly had all the trappings of an elaborate linear theatre, a social ballet choreographed with mourners and marchers, biers and hearses, escutcheons, banners, and palls. Mourning garb, mourning gifts, and the proper provison of refreshment added to the expense of the performance. The costs could rise to strain family funds, but the investment paid off in terms of dignity, honour, and reputation.

If a decision was made to involve the College of Arms in the management of a funeral the executors lost control of the process and surrendered to the arcane demands of heraldic protocol. It might take several weeks for the banners, pennons, and escutcheons to be properly assembled, and several hours for them to make their way to the church. William Dugdale's specifications 'for a funeral proceeding' in 1675 would not have been out of place a century before. The heraldic procession would consist of

two conductors with black staves; poor men in gowns; servants to gentlemen, esquires, knights, etc.; the standard; servants of the defunct; gentlemen, and gentlemen of the kindred; doctors of physic; divines and doctors of divinity; esquires, knights and baronets; noblemen's younger sons; noblemen; a trumpet; the guidon [a flag] the mourning horse; the minister who buries the corpse; the pennon [another flag]; the helm, crest, gantlet and spurs; the sword and target; the coat of arms; the corpse [borne by] men in gowns; the pall supported by two baronets.[123]

Sir Jeffrey Palmer's funeral was celebrated at Carlton, Northamptonshire, in this manner in 1670, 'with great pomp . . . the heralds and many of the nobility and judges attending him to the grave'.[124]

With or without the heralds, the ingredients of a decent funeral among the later Stuart élite included advanced advertisement, preferably by printed ticket or invitation; principal mourners who were clearly people of 'quality'; 'a great good company' rather than a promiscuous 'rabble'; mourning gear all round, not forgetting blackened soles of the shoes; ribbons and hatbands for all guests and 'white gloves' and 'good rings' for those more nearly connected. It also required suitable hearses and pallbearers, coaches and escutcheons, torches and candles. And it concluded with a fine sermon, preferably brief; interment in a fashionable church, according to the rubric of the Church of England; flowing claret and mountains of biscuits.[125] Dissenters too supported each other by performing 'solemn funerals' with 'multitudes of people' and 'great lamentation'. In the 1670s the nonconformist Oliver Heywood often preached at such gatherings, which invariably concluded with eating and drinking.[126]

John Evelyn's diary includes many appreciative remarks about later Stuart funeral practices. In 1675 he attended the funeral of the poet Abraham Cowley, whose body was 'conducted to Westminster Abbey in an hearse with six horses, and all funebral [sic] decency, near an hundred coaches of noble men and persons of quality following'. Evelyn was similarly satisfied with the funeral of Sir Richard Browne in 1683, which was solemnized 'with as much decency as the dignity of the person, and our relation, required'. Guests included the bishop of Rochester, several noblemen and knights, and all the fraternity of the Trinity Company, of which the deceased had been master.[127]

Evelyn also took note that the funeral of his nephew and namesake in 1691 was done 'very decently, and ordered by the heralds . . . a very great appearance of the country being there'. This time the diarist was chief mourner. Six other gentlemen held up the pall. This was an afternoon funeral with 'an innumerable concourse of coaches and people accompanying the ceremony'. Likewise, when his brother George Evelyn was buried in 1699 it was done, the diarist reports, 'with extraordinary solemnity, rather as a nobleman than a private gentleman. There were, I computed, above 2,000 people at the funeral, all the gentlemen of the county doing him that last honour.' It even made the press, the *Postboy* reporting that George Evelyn, esquire, was 'interred with great state at Wotton in Surrey'.[128] On each occasion Evelyn registered the solemnity and decency of the event and the size and quality of the turnout, as if these social manifestations served as mitigation for the loss of a loved one or a friend.

Elizabeth Freke, an indefatigable cataloguer of social slights and successes, also understood the value of outward appearances and the importance of proper form to the maintenance of gentry authority. After the unfortunate death of her grandson in 1705, she remarks, 'I buried him very handsomely;

he had an appearance of about two hundred of my neighbours at his funeral, all which attended from Sunday one o'clock till ten at night, and so from Monday ten o'clock till eight at night. I kept his passing bell going them two days till he was entered.'[129] This generous turnout was not for the boy, who was almost unknown to the neighbours in Norfolk, but for the family in the great house and for the estate they represented.

This was just a rehearsal for the funeral of Percy Freke at Bilney, Norfolk, in the summer of 1706. Elizabeth Freke's marriage had not been happy, but at the end she gave her husband a funeral 'suitable to his quality and desert'. Percy Freke, esquire, had died of asthma and dropsy at Swaffham and was transported the dozen miles to Bilney accompanied by gentry, tenants, and neighbours. For five days he lay in a double leaded coffin, with 'all the bells in the seven parishes tolling'. Then on Friday, 7 June, Elizabeth writes,

I did inter my dear husband in the vault under Bilney chancel. I gave him a gentle-man's burial, and had all the gentry and neighbours in the country of my twenty-five years acquaintance to attend it, by me invited, and several hundreds I did not know; with eight gentlemen to carry him and eight more to carry up the pall. All had rings, gloves, scarves, and hatbands, with wine, cakes and ale, whatever they would drink.

The final tally, important for keeping score, was 'an appearance . . . of above seven hundred people at his funeral'. Elizabeth, triumphant in widow's weeds, distributed rings and mourning suits, and treated herself to a 'a little mourn-ing coach' with 'mourning harnesses'.[130]

By the late seventeenth century the English were said to be famous for cheap weddings and lavish funerals. Urban patrician funerals in particular were renowned for their 'magnificent obsequies' with printed invitations, costly mourning gear, flambeaux-lit processions, and distribution of gloves and rings.[131] Funerals at Durham took so much time, and their drinking so much toll, that the later Stuart authorities attempted to regulate the practice. In 1687 the city council ordered that whoever 'invites to a funeral shall within two hours after the time invited carry the said corpse from the said house to the church or chapel where the said person is to be interred'. Regulation had limited effect, however, for in 1696 the council observed, 'people have stayed at such funerals two or three hours or more . . . neglecting their own neces-sary occasion and business'. Henceforth, they ordered, 'no longer time shall be allowed for the gathering together at the funeral house and serving the people there than two hours'. And to accomplish this they set up a system of signals and timekeepers, with fines for offenders, the proceeds going to the poor.[132]

Henri Misson, the French-Swiss observer of William III's England, claimed to be particularly interested in 'middling people, among whom the customs of a nation are most truly to be learned'. We have already benefited from his comments on christenings and weddings. Misson's detailed descriptions of funeral practices among the city merchants and gentry have the flavour of ethnographic reports by early colonial explorers, and compare well to Ned Ward's facetious depiction of baptisms. Once again, Misson's remarks are worth reporting at length.[133]

First, Misson says, the dead body was washed, shaved if a man, and dressed in woollen cloth according to law, before being laid in a coffin. Coffins by this time had become *de rigueur* among the patrician classes. 'That the body may lie the softer, some put a layer of bran, about four inches thick, at the bottom of the coffin', as if the corpse was fastidious about its comfort or to prevent it rolling about. Then, just to be sure, 'they let it lie three or four days in this condition, which time they allow as well to give the dead person an opportunity of coming to life again, if his soul has not quite left his body, as to prepare mourning and the ceremonies of the funeral'. During this time the principal mourners send out invitations, 'sometimes they have printed tickets', for relations and associates to pay their last respects.

The day of burial began at the home of the deceased, where the body in its open coffin lay 'upon two stools, in a room, where all that please may go and see it'. By this time, Misson noted,

the relations and chief mourners are in a chamber apart, with their more intimate friends, and the rest of the guests are disperesed in several rooms about the house. When they are ready to set out, they nail up the coffin, and a servant presents the company with sprigs of rosemary. Everyone takes a sprig, and carries it in his hand, till the body is put in the grave, at which time they all throw their sprigs in after it.

Rosemary was the herb of remembrance, of course, but its sharp odour may also have offset putrescent smells from the corpse. Misson evokes a poignant scene, with the mourners scattering nosegays in the grave as the earth clods down on the coffin. 'Before they set out, and after they return, it is usual to present the guests with something to drink, either red or white wine boiled with sugar and cinnamon, or some other such liquour. Everyone drinks two or three cups.'

On its way to the place of interment the coffin was draped by a mortuary cloth or pall. 'The parish always has three or four mortuary cloths of different prices' which could be hired for the solemn occasion. The attendants, too, were decorated, even if they did not wear formal mourning costume. 'They generally give black or white gloves, and black crepe hatbands to those that carry the pall; sometimes also white silk scarves.' Beadles led the procession, to be followed by the officiating clergy, then the body and its ensemble, the relations in close mourning, and finally 'all the guests two and two'. The body was either carried into church, there to rest upon trestles for the duration of service and sermon, or taken directly to the grave site for an outdoor service in the churchyard. There it was 'interred, in the presence of the guests who are round the grave, and do not leave it till the earth is thrown in upon it. Then they return home in the same order that they came, and each drinks two or three glasses more before he goes home.'

THE GEOGRAPHY OF INTERMENT

When all funeral ceremonies were completed and the burial service done, the living departed for refreshments and the dead were left in the ground. The bodies began to decompose, and would only be quickened, so Christians believed, by the angel's trumpet at the general resurrection. The dead, however, were not forgotten. Their presence was recalled through the mounds in the churchyard or through markers and memorials inside the church. They lived on in memory, and as a fading physical presence in the community's sacred space. This chapter examines the material history of burial and the cultural geography of interment. It is concerned with the making of graves and the administration of churchyards, the erection of memorials and the specification of tombs. As in every other chapter, its aim is to transcend mere antiquarian description and to probe the social and religious ligaments of complex cultural processes. A useful start can be made by looking at the flow of money.

Fees and Dues

Strictly, there was no fee for Christian burial. In principle, any person could be buried by the minister without charge in the churchyard of the parish where they died. But in practice, death entailed a variety of expenses and custom required payment of fees to the church. Oftentimes this meant no more than unofficial tipping of coins to ministers, sextons, and parish clerks. But many parishes turned these voluntary payments into a standard scale of charges. As the historian of ecclesiastical law Richard Burn coyly observes, 'albeit the clergy may not demand anything for burial, yet the laity may be compelled to observe pious and laudable customs'.[1] Most people paid their fees without demur, but disagreements over payments for burials left a trail of recrimination.

Critics both before and after the Reformation attacked these clerical exactions.[2] Hunne's case, a scandal encompassing heresy and murder, began with a dispute about mortuary fees in the early years of Henry VIII. The rector of Whitechapel claimed his right to the winding sheet in which Hunne's child was brought to burial, and the father refused to deliver it. Hunne's supporters claimed the unreformed church was grasping and insensitive in its demand for payments associated with burials, and the matter was taken up by the so-called Reformation Parliament.[3]

'Mortuaries, in some places called corpse presents,' were restricted by the legislation of 1530 but were still subject to dispute a century later. Only men dying possessed of goods valued at £6. 13s. 4d. or more were required to pay mortuary fees, and then only when constrained to do so by local custom. The fee was assessed on a sliding scale from 3s. 4d. to 10s., based on movable wealth, but might also be subject to negotiation. In practice it was hard to distinguish the mortuary, which was 'a right settled on the church upon the decease of a member of it', from the corpse present, 'a voluntary oblation usually made at funerals'. Some ministers insisted on their fees, even when a parishioner who died was carried away for burial elsewhere.[4]

Disputes about mortuary fees continued long into the seventeenth century. Anne Atkinson, the widow of Thomas Atkinson of Tollerton, Yorkshire, refused to pay a mortuary fee in 1627. The minister, Hugh Bethell, insisted that the fee was due because Thomas had 'goods and chattels at the time of his death to the value or worth of twenty pounds', but his widow insisted that she 'hath not paid the same, for that she is not bound by law thereunto'. At Aldborough, Yorkshire, in 1664 the vicar demanded 10s. as a mortuary fee on the death of Edward Thompson, but Thompson's widow argued that the amount due was only 6s. 8d. In this case the dispute was not whether mortuary fees should be demanded, but who should receive them and how they should be calculated.[5]

Catholic or protestant, puritan or conformist, the clergy of the sixteenth and seventeenth centuries were notorious for their exaction of fees. When children died under popery, claimed Barnaby Googe in 1570, 'Their parents for their funerals constrained are to pay, | Lest of the popish tyranny should any part decay.' James Pilkington, the reforming bishop of Durham, complained that 'the papists . . . are thieves also in picking poor men's purses' for preferential places of interment.[6]

Few wrote with such vehemence on this subject as Katherine Chidley, who fulminated in 1641 against the 'petty dues' and oppressive exactions of the Church of England clergy. Chidley charged that some ministers refused to bury without a fee. To have a child buried in London, she reported, 'it will cost the poorest parent seven or eight shillings'. And even 'to Bedlam, which is the cheapest place that I know, ye when all things else is discharged, even as bearers' wages, gravediggers' wages, and the ground paid for also, yet they must be constrained to have a twelve-penny priest, to say something over the grave, and he will grudge it if he have not more than a shilling'. We have already heard Katherine Chidley on churching; here she spoke with the anger of a bereaved parent, as well as a notorious sectarian.[7]

The fees of 'casualties' for performing a variety of tasks and services provided a boost to parish funds and a supplement to meagre clerical incomes. In the London parish of St James Garlickhithe in the 1630s burial fees added £5 a year to the parish coffers, five times the proceeds of weddings. At St Botolph Aldgate in 1638 the priest collected 'the casualties of burials, weddings and churchings, the chiefest of which being burials, I may say, if people do not die I cannot live'. Eight burials at Great St Mary's, Cambridge in 1633 netted the parish £2. 1s. 8d.[8]

Clergymen sometimes overstepped the mark by refusing to bury unless they were paid in advance. John Glass, one of the curates of Stepney, Middlesex, 'refused to bury some for whom none would undertake to pay the vicar's duties', and was cited for this before the bishop of London's commissary in 1604. Parishioners at Launsing, Sussex, complained in 1624 that 'Mr. Robinson our vicar . . . doth . . . raise a new custom upon the parish of 5d. for burying the dead, which was never demanded nor known of before his time.'[9] The Laudian minister of Wicken, Cambridgeshire, Robert Grimmer, allegedly refused to bury parishioners who had not paid their tithes, and also levied a fine against someone for not taking off his hat when passing a funeral. Locked in battle with parishioners, his contemporary Edward Finch of Christ Church, London, denied that he shut the church door and would not suffer the ground to be broken, and kept one corpse unburied from Monday till Saturday, 'until his undue exactions had been satisfied'.[10]

Some of the better organized parishes attempted to standardize the schedule by displaying a set table of fees. Maidstone, Kent, had a scale that provided 'that the richer sort of parishioners, who contributed to parish duties, at their death should be buried in one churchyard, and the poorer sort in another'.[11] In the London parish of St Bennet Paulswharf in the reign of Charles I the minimum fee for burial was almost 2s., rising to over a pound for interment inside the church.

> Burials in the church:
> To the parish for the great bell knoll, 6s. 8d.
> To the parish for breaking the ground, 6s. 8d.
> To the parson, 6s. 8d.
> To the clerk, 2s.
> To the sexton for making the grave, 2s.
>
> Burials in the churchyard:
> In a coffin, to the parson, 2s.
> In a shroud, to the parson, 12d.

In a coffin, to the clerk, 6d.
In a shroud, to the clerk, 6d.
To the gravemaker for a man, 6d.
To the gravemaker for a child, 4d.[12]

The church court records include dozens of references to refusals and arrears. The basic fee for burial at St Margaret's, Canterbury, in 1573 was only '2d. for an old body and a penny for a child', but even this modest scale led to grumbles in 1573. More substantial sums were at stake at Flixton, Cheshire, in 1596 when Leonard Ashall was deficient 3s. 4d. for burial fees. In the same year, diocesan visitors heard, John Rawden of York 'refuseth to pay for his wife's burial in the church'. And two years later James Parker of Blaidburne, Yorkshire refused to pay 2s. 'for his father and mother's graves in the church, being an accustomed duty'.[13] Most of these tussles were with people of means, who buried their dead *inside* the church.

In the large and unruly parish of Stepney, Middlesex, Agnes Betson refused to pay the 15d. demanded for the burial of her child in 1605, 'but scornfully scoffing made answer she would pay when she got a good husband'. Her neighbour widow Richardson at the same time refused to pay 'for the burial of her husband, according to their table, the sum of 2s. 10d.' Thomas Strath of Buttercrambe, Yorkshire, likewise fell foul of the archdeacon of Cleveland in 1632 'for not paying for the burial of his wife in the church according to custom'. When Thomas Biggins of Waltham Cross, Middlesex, was cited in 1639 'for not paying accustomed duties' for the burial of his servant, the court reminded him what those duties were: 12d. to the curate, 6d. to the parish clerk, and 1s. 10d. to the sexton, a total of 3s. 4d.[14] Paupers would be buried at the cost of the parish, but substantial householders were expected to pay their share.

After the Restoration it became increasingly difficult for the church to collect its traditional fees, especially from parishioners who baulked at its services. The vicar of Hillingdon, Middlesex, despaired in 1664 of 'several mortuaries here unpaid, and not only so but denied'. A dispute at Lambourne, Essex, in 1665 turned on differential fees for burying 'inhabitants' and 'strangers'. The parish charged £2 for breaking the ground in the church and 6s. 8d. for 'the minister's duty for officiating at the burial in the chancel', but doubled these sums for non-parishioners.[15]

A table of fees at Bury St Edmunds, Suffolk, in 1665 allowed the minister 1s. for every burial in the churchyard and 2s. for burial inside the church. The parish clerk got 4d. at churchyard burials and 1s. at burials in the church, while the sexton earned a variety of fees: 1s. for making a grave for anyone buried in a coffin, 4s. for interment and resetting the stones in the church, 2s.

for ringing the great bell or 1s. for ringing the small bell for an hour 'at any one's departure', and reduced fees for those receiving poor relief. At Merton College, Oxford, serving the parish of St John the Baptist, the chaplain in 1687 earned 5s. for burying in the churchyard, 10s. for burying in the chapel, and 5s. even if a dead parishioner was buried elsewhere.[16]

Places of Honour

Late medieval catholics sought association with sanctity by arranging their burials in particular parts of the churchyard, or inside the church in close proximity to a favoured altar or devotional image.[17] The Reformation under-cut the religious reasons for such preferences but did not eliminate the prac-tice of selective placement in the ground. The Elizabethan and Stuart élite continued to use their churches as mausoleums, though rather to assert the lineage and status of the living than to acquire any posthumous merit for the dead.

Not surprisingly, early Elizabethan protestants argued against the notion 'that one earth or ground is holier than another' and that there were advan-tages, 'either to the body or to the soul', in particular locations for interment. 'Wheresoever we be buried, we are buried in the Lord's earth,' wrote the Anglo-French minister John Veron, so the burial ground 'hath no need of the blessing of our priests for to be made holy'. James Pilkington, the first Elizabethan bishop of Durham, agreed. It was part of popish wickedness, he wrote, to teach 'that one place is more holy than another to be buried in, as in the church rather than in the churchyard, and near the high altar rather than in the body of the church'. Inside or out, 'the place of burial needeth no bishop's blessing nor popish hallowing; but every comely place is holy enough, so it be reserved for that use only'.[18] Any consecrated earth would do, though for most people the choice was restricted to their parish church or churchyard.

Indoors or outdoors, the deciding factor was social rank. Many of the gentry and members of the élite who occupied the best pews and who dom-inated parish life demanded to be buried in prominent positions. Wealthy families gathered their dead into multi-generational burial zones and found satisfaction in contemplating their achievements of lineage and service. The embittered Elizabeth Freke, for example, took pleasure in enumerating her deceased relations, 'near three score of them, in Hollingbourne chancel' in Kent. She saw a perverted kind of justice when John Hull, her enemy who had cheated her of her house in Ireland, died penniless under James II and was buried 'in the open part of the church of Rathbarry amongst the common

Irish, to his eternal infamy'.[19] To her and others like her, the place and manner of burial involved keeping and settling scores.

Preferential placement was a matter of honour. Just as parishioners squabbled over seats in the church, so they sometimes argued about final resting places. Ellis Parry of St Mary Aldermanbury was so upset when 'a woman that takes the alms of the parish' was 'buried in the church hard by his . . . wife' in 1621 that he fell to blows with the parish clerk, who he held responsible for this affront to his honour, 'and did strike him on the head and face with a book'. Parry apologized, and had to accept what to him was an irregular and undignified intrusion.[20]

Protestants knew that no spiritual advantage attached to being buried in one piece of holy ground rather than another, but proximity to the altar and location within the chancel or aisle still mattered for social reasons. Premium placement, with appropriate memorial masonry, would demonstrate to posterity the position one held in this world. Instructions about the final disposition of the body in a sample of Elizabethan gentry wills reveal a hierarchy of social, familial, and religious concerns. While requesting interment within a particular church, more often in the chancel than the aisle, these testators displayed a stronger preference for burial alongside other members of their families than for burial adjacent to spiritually potent parts of the church.

Elizabethan gentle testators often requested burial alongside a departed spouse or in close proximity to other members of their family, so that they might enjoy the resurrection in familiar company. John Ive's desire, 'to be buried in Boxted church near to the place where my wife lieth', was a common formulation. Wistan Browne, esquire, willed in 1580 that he 'be buried in the chancel of South Weald church near the body of Mary my late dear and virtuous wife, one of the daughters of Sir Edward Capell, knight, there buried'. To be publicly united with her in death was a mark not only of the bond of affection between husband and wife but also a constant reminder of the link between the Brownes and the higher ranking Capells.[21] No rotation of pews would ever dislodge Wistan Browne from his prominent position.

Remarriage apparently posed no problem for the prospect of spousal reunion in heaven. Double widowers like George Scott of Chigwell wished for burial 'between my two wives'. Lady Margaret Curson, twice a widow, arranged to lie 'in St. Peter's church, Ipswich, by the late Lord Curson and the Lady his first wife', rather than next to her more recently departed husband Sir Edward Green. She would rest until judgement day in the company of her higher ranking first husband, even though she shared that ground as his second wife. Gentle widows conventionally requested burial alongside their late husbands.[22]

Other requests which indicate the desire for eternal reunion included 'to be buried in North Ockendon church besides my mother', 'to be buried in Writtle church as near as possible to my father', and 'where my grandfather is buried'. Once the family had established its spot there was a strong incentive to stay in that part of the church rather than seek a better position. Some gentlemen planned their burial 'in the usual place where my ancestors have been buried', rather than next to a particular spouse or family member. Hercules Mewtas, esquire, arranged for interment 'in West Ham church where my mother, brother and kindred lie', while Henry Harleston wanted 'to be buried in South Ockendon amongst my friends departed'.[23] In all these cases the mortal remains would lie in proximity to those of the previously departed, whose affection, reputation, or family connection was considered important. The kinsmanlike intimacy and solidarity that was supposedly one of the lineaments of gentle society would continue beyond death. It is significant, however, that most of these requests specified placement alongside members of the testator's lineal or nuclear family rather than his lateral or extended kin.

Some aristocratic families were united in death more closely, more publicly, and certainly more permanently than they ever were in life. The cluster of family tombs was a striking reminder of power, continuity, and cohesion. The Essex Darcys of St Osyth, for example, dominated their local community in death as in life, through strategic interment in the parish church. Lady Elizabeth Darcy willed in 1564 that she 'be buried at St. Osyth church by my honourable lord and husband the Lord Darcy'. Her son, Sir John Darcy, arranged in 1581 to be buried alongside his parents and next to his late wife, and he paid for 'convenient tombs' to be erected for all of them, 'meet for our estates and degrees'.[24]

Thomas Radcliffe, Earl of Sussex, specified not that he be buried near his ancestors but that they be reburied near him. He built a chapel with monuments at Boreham parish church, and ordered in 1583 that 'the corpse of my Lord my grandfather and my Lady my grandmother, my Lord my father and my lady my mother shall be removed and brought thither and buried in the vault of the chapel, and myself also when it shall please God to call me to be buried in the same place'. Three generations of Radcliffe Earls would be gathered together in a monument to aristocratic power and the family name.[25]

According to ecclesiastical law, 'no person may be buried in the church, or in any part of it, without the consent of the incumbent', because normally, 'the soil and freehold of the church is only in the parson and in none other'. Anyone wanting to bury inside the church required ministerial permission and would have to pay a substantial fee to the sexton and churchwardens, 'by reason the parish is at the charge of repairing the floor'.[26] Many wealthy families assumed this privilege, and felt themselves entitled to distinguished funereal placement. The Jacobean minister Robert Hill advised his readers to avoid 'the fond conceit of many, who think it a great blessing to be buried in a church, especially if it be in the chancel, near the altar'.[27] But burial in these privileged places was one of the ways the Tudor and Stuart élite defined themselves, apart from the common herd in the churchyard outside.

Interment inside the church was disruptive as well as expensive. Churches were used almost daily for prayers and special services, and routine worship could not have been improved by the presence of workmen's tools and open tombs. Uncovered graves inside the church were as common as ill-tended churchyards without, and too many families failed to finish the job or to pay all the necessary fees. A distinctive smell in early modern churches must have been the odour of human decomposition, not always masked by the scent of floral garlands and incense that the reformers were seeking to abolish. Bishop Middleton of St David's ordered his clergy in 1583 to 'permit no corpses to be buried within their parish church or chapel, for that by their general burying there great infection doth ensue, except those of the best sort of the parish; and they do pay ten shillings towards the repairing of the church or chapel'. The problem was malodorous air rather than contagion, and it evidently did not apply to 'the best sort', defined by their willingness to pay.[28]

The cost of removing and replacing masonry for interment inside the church restricted the practice to the wealthiest families. Interment in the chancel or aisle cost from 5–15s., quite apart from the costs of memorials and the furnishing of a tomb. At Great St Mary's, Cambridge, in 1578 a Mr Burwell paid 6s. 8d. 'for breaking the ground in the church for his wife', 2s. of which went toward setting stones and 'mending the church pavement'.[29] Receipts of this sort appear commonly in churchwardens' records. The income from such services provided a supplement to parish funds which could then be used to offset the cost of burying the poor.

'When the ground is broken for burials,' asked Bishop Montague in his visitation of the Diocese of Norwich in 1638, 'is it again renewed, levelled, paved? If not, by whose default is it?'[30] Members of the gentry could be as remiss in this regard as their less affluent neighbours, as shown by the church court records. Mr Edward Chambers of Oxfordshire, for example, buried his child in 1611 in the aisle of King's Sutton church but failed to pay the fee or to repair the pavement. Edmund Hunt of Norfolk, buried his wife in Aylsham church in 1619, but a year later he still had not covered her grave. Offenders at All Saints, King's Lynn, were similarly cited in 1629 'for breaking the pavement in the church for graves and not covering it again'.[31]

Ezekiel Brent of Tredington, Worcestershire, was cited in 1633 'for burying in the chancel and not repairing again the pavement . . . He ought to have paid the 6s. 8d. to the parson for his leave to bury there.' This did not mean that the workmen left a gaping hole or that human remains were in view, but they had not finished the job by restoring the paved flooring of the church. Conditions were less salubrious at Edlington, Lincolnshire, in 1636 where the floor in the church was said to be so 'decayed' that 'the corpse of one of Mr. Clipham's daughters there buried lieth above the ground, to the great and grievous annoyance of all the parishioners assembling to hear divine service'.[32] This was not only a nuisance and an offence but also, in ceremonialist eyes, an affront to 'the beauty of holiness'.

Mid-century revolutions did not remove the incentive for powerful people to be buried in the most favoured interior positions. Though the prayer-book Order for the Burial of the Dead was proscribed, the secular ceremonies of funerals and the process of gentle interment went on much as before. In 1657 the churchwardens of Houghton-le-Spring, Durham, attempted to limit the disruption caused by burials in church, while allowing the leading families to continue their practice. They ruled that 'none be suffered to break the ground within the church to bury their dead, but such as have been accustomed, and with the licence of the churchwardens'. Only established families would have this privilege, and none without paying their fees in advance: 3s. 4d. for burying an adult and 20d. for interring a child. At the same time, while caught with the regulatory mood, they specified that the sexton should 'dig and make every grave within the church a yard and a half deep at least', and to 'keep the spades and shovels for the making graves for that use and no other'.[33]

'Is it a matter of any moment in what place we lay the bodies of our deceased friends?' asked the author of the late Stuart treatise, *A Mourning-Ring*. Husband and wife would surely meet again at the resurrection, 'at what distance soever [their] graves shall be made' from each other, and their 'souls shall not enjoy the less felicity for the remoter distance and separation of the bodies'. From a religious point of view it mattered little where a body was placed, so long as it lay in consecrated ground. But social and familial considerations of duty, honour, and convenience could not be lightly ignored. At the end of the seventeenth century, as a hundred years earlier, by custom, 'the corpse is interred in the chancel, if it was the body of a rich and honourable man, or churchyard, if it was the body of a mean and ordinary person'.[34]

Sir Richard Browne, John Evelyn's father-in-law, was unusual in taking offence in 1683 at what he called the novel custom of burying everybody within the body of the church and chancel, as a favour heretofore granted only to martyrs and great princes, this excess of making churches charnel houses being of ill and irreverent example, and prejudicial to the health of the living besides the continual disturbance of the pavement and seats, the ground sinking as the carcases consume, and several other undecencies.

There was in fact nothing 'novel' about this practice, though its popularity may have grown along with the greater numbers and higher pretensions of the gentry of the later seventeenth century. To the consternation of some kinsmen, Browne elected to be buried in 1683 not inside the church at Deptford, as befit his social rank, but rather, 'in the churchyard under the south east window of the chancel, joining to the burying places of his ancestors'.[35] Precise choice of location was still important, as it had been several generations before.

The Dormitories of Christians

John Donne's evocation of the churchyard, swelling 'with the waves and billows of graves',[36] reminds us that the vast majority of Christians were buried in consecrated ground *outside* the church, and that their graves were unmarked except for disturbances of the earth. The bodies decayed anonymously, interred in the freehold of the lord. The preparation and maintenance of this sacred space posed problems for many communities.

Church of England ministers insisted that bodies could only be buried in consecrated ground. Christians would be gathered together within the sacred enclosure, completing their bond of association between the dead and the living. That tradition had continued for more than a thousand years and was unbroken by the protestant reformation. Unless they forfeited that right by suicide or irreversible excommunication, everyone could look forward to burial in the churchyard or inside the church. Unbaptized babies, we have seen, were often given the benefit of the doubt and buried alongside their parents or siblings, while recusants and offenders who died while excommunicated were usually afforded a churchyard burial, even if they were denied a formal religious service.[37]

Catholics and nonconformists usually secured burial in the churchyard, regarding the place as belonging to God and his people in general rather than exclusively to the adherents of the established church. Some dramatic scenes were reported as catholics forced the issue against ministerial objection, though most places saw neighbourliness triumph over sectarianism.[38] For catholics in the contested areas of Jacobean Lancashire, recalled William Blundell, the churches in all parts denied them burial; some were laid in the fields, some in gardens, and others in highways as it chanced. One of these, as I have heard it credibly reported, being interred in a common lane, was pulled out by the hogs and used accordingly. Hereupon, to prevent the like for the future, there was a part of the demesne of Crosby enclosed by my grandfather Blundell for the decent burial of such poor catholics as were otherwise likely to want it.

For his pains, this earlier Blundell 'was grievously fined for making this new churchyard', but between 1611 and 1686 it served to bury 'above one hundred lay catholics and a dozen or fourteen priests'.[39] Baptists and Quakers made similar private provision for their dead in the second half of the seventeenth century, and had a similar uneasy stand-off with the authorities.[40]

Churchyard graves were supposed to be six feet deep, oriented east and west, with the body buried face up to greet the angel at the resurrection dawn. Dead parishioners would be oriented in their graves in the same direction they had sat or knelt in church. It was a gross violation, more often imagined than practised, to bury a human 'face downward' or 'with his head pointing in the wrong direction'. By tradition the south side of the churchyard was preferable to the north, and burial near the building better than burial near the fence or ditch.[41] In crowded spaces the gravediggers might be forced to make exceptions, and they often encountered the remains of previous burials. Fresh bodies were superimposed on those who had gone before, and in some parishes, archaeologists have learnt, they were stacked as many as five deep. City parishes often maintained charnel-houses for the bones of their previously buried dead, but country parishes usually had plenty of room.[42] The graves were rarely distinguished by markers or headstones, so the identity of the deceased was soon submerged.

It was the sexton's job to prepare the grave, though any able-bodied man could help with the digging. The bell-ringers were sometimes recruited for this task. Little is heard on this subject before the 1630s, when Laudian bishops included questions about graves in their comprehensive visitation enquiries. Bishop Matthew Wren reminded those responsible to make graves six feet deep in parishes throughout his Diocese of Ely. At Littleport, Cambridgeshire, in 1638 the churchwardens presented their sexton, John Wright, 'for that he doth not make the graves six foot deep'.[43] In his defence the sexton might have argued that the ground was waterlogged, and that it was difficult to dig the required depth in fen country; gravediggers in highland parishes faced similar problems when their spades hit solid rock. Environmental circumstances might be mentioned in mitigation of a minor ecclesiastical offence.

Bishop Richard Montague of Norwich was even more specific in his visitation of 1638 when he asked, of the graves in the churchyard,

be they conveniently covered, made seven foot deep, kept from scraping of dogs, rooting up of hogs, fouling and polluting otherwise, as the resting places of Christians dead? . . . Is the grave made east and west, is the body buried with the head to the west, is the grave digged seven foot deep, and being made up and buried, preserved from violation?[44]

The standard answer was *omnia bene*—all well—for the question served more as a reminder than an invigilation.

Fastidious Caroline ceremonialists were not alone in their horror of pollution or violation. Their Elizabethan and Jacobean predecessors had struggled to maintain the decency and salubrity of churchyards which were used for a wide range of activities besides Christian burial. Many parishioners regarded their churchyard as public space, available for games and gatherings, or grazing and other business. Churchyards were supposed to be fenced, to demarcate the sanctified soil and to ward off roaming cattle, but fences and ditches were easily breached. The churchyard stile, specified in the prayer book as the place where the minister should meet the corpse, was supposed to be the animal-proof entrance to this haven, but stiles and lich-gates were not always secure. Problems with pigs and dogs were endemic, and larger animals occasionally foraged in the well-fertilized ground, with or without the collusion of their owners.

At Brook, Kent, it was reported in 1573, 'the churchyard lieth open, whereby swine and other cattle come in and dig up the graves . . . It hath been presented divers times and no reformation had.' Oxfordshire officials were offended in 1584 to find that the churchwardens of Southstock allowed 'dancing in the churchyard and digging thereof with swine'.[45] Samuel Theed of Wingrave, Buckinghamshire, was admonished by the archdeaconry court in 1623, 'for that his hogs spoil and deface the churchyard'. His neighbour Henry Smith of Hulcot fell foul of the rector in 1627, 'for breaking down the churchyard mounds or pales to make way for his hogs and sheep to annoy the churchyard'. In the same year at Saddington, Lincolnshire, the churchyard fence was broken, it was reported, 'so that cattle and hogs came into the same and rooted up the graves of dead bodies there interred'. 'The churchyard wants fencing' was a familiar finding in parish surveys throughout the land.[46]

Episcopal visitation articles express many of the concerns about the 'annoyance' or violation of churchyards. Bishop Chaderton of Lincoln asked in 1598 whether every churchyard was 'well fenced and cleanly kept'. He particularly wanted to know whether any churchyard 'be abused or profaned by any unlawful or unseemly act, game or exercise, as by lords of misrule, summer lords or ladies, pipers, rush-bearers, morris dancers, pedlars, bowlers, bear-wards, and such like'.[47] Bishop Montague's questions for the Diocese of Norwich in 1638 enquired similarly but at greater length,

If you have a several churchyard, is it well enclosed and fenced with mounds, ditches, hedges, walls, pales or the like; if otherwise, by whose default is it? . . . Though the surface of the soil and the grass there growing, if any such be, are the minister's, yet it being consecrated ground, is not to be profaned by feeding and dunging of cattle. Is it therefore all or in part at any time, let or hired out to be employed for pinfolds of sheep, stalls for oxen or horses, booths or standings for chapmen, at any time of any fair or market, nor to dry clothes there, tanned leather or the like? For, of the base-court of the Temple, said our Saviour, have these things hence. Much less is it to be unhallowed with dancings, morrises, meetings at Easter, drinkings, Whitsun ales, midsummer merriments or the like, stool ball, football, wrestlings, wasters or boys' sports. If such abuse hath been committed, say by whom, whose procurement, countenance or abetting. Is your churchyard or any part thereof, made a laystall or dunghill, or be any such impious nuisances laid near unto the pale or mounds thereof, let the offenders be named upon enquiry and presented? Hath any neighbouring *quidam* or great man, encroached upon any part of the churchyard, enclosing it to his garden, hop-yard, stableyard or so, present him or them so transgressing? Be there any houses fronting or abetting your churchyard, the dwellers wherein do annoy, soil and profane the churchyard by washing of bucks, emptying of sinks, chamber-pots or the like, by easing of nature either way within that place, or under and against the church walls?[48]

In fact, all of these things went on from time to time, and ecclesiastical officials were sore-pressed to bring irregularities to a halt. Burials took place amidst a variety of other business, and the 'dormitory of Christians' had sometimes the flavour of a barnyard or a country fair.

Encroachment by neighbouring property owners also threatened the sanctity of the final resting place. Three cases from Nottinghamshire in the reign of Charles I may be considered typical. Mr Christopher Haslam of Newark admitted enclosing part of the churchyard in 1628, but claimed in mitigation that his 'private use' of the area was better than 'the indecency' of allowing it to lie open to 'filthiness and excrements'. Justifying his own establishment of a garden, building a barn, and installing a kiln in the churchyard of Sutton Bonnington, the rector, Thomas Savage, explained in 1635 that the ground was sufficiently 'large and spacious to receive all and singular the bodies of parishioners that are or happily shall be hereafter there interred'. As to the area of his encroachment, it had 'not within the memory of man been employed for the burial of the dead, some one, two or three, and those still- or dead-born, as was reported, excepted'. John Rogers, a gentleman of Clayworth who had driven a cart-way through the churchyard, explained in 1639 'that he cannot possibly bring his hay any other way to his barn than over part of the churchyard, and that time out of memory of man there hath not been any body buried in that part of the said churchyard'. In the first case Mr Haslam was ordered to undo his enclosure; in the second the rector's garden was allowed to stand 'for his better housekeeping and maintenance of hospitality'; and Mr Rogers, the offender in the third case, was dismissed with a warning.[49]

Shortage of ground in urban areas left some graveyards at the mercy of neighbouring enterprises. Overflows from bleaching processes in the Norwich textile industry violated the sanctity of city churchyards as well as creating environmental hazards. John Grimley of St Leonard's, Shoreditch, was cited in 1630 'for encroaching on the churchyard and carrying away dead men's bodies'. Similar problems continued in the second half of the century when Nicholas Ogden of St Botolph Aldgate was cited in 1664 'for making a sink into the churchyard, and throwing soap suds into the graves of the dead'.[50]

Post-Restoration visitations found some churchyards violated by roaming animals and graves 'digged up by swine'. The archdeacon of Buckinghamshire heard in 1662 that at Drayton Beauchamp, 'the churchyard lieth ruinous and out of repair' and the churchwarden 'knoweth not who to present, for that he is not certain whose tombs they are [that] are out of repair'. At Fawley, Buckinghamshire, in 1662 the archdeacon found the churchyard delapidated, the parishioners no longer maintaining their mounds 'as by custom they ought'. At Datchet too the churchyard mounds were out of repair, though the churchwardens assured the court, 'they intend to amend them as soon as possibly they can'.[51] Neglect and abuse were perennial problems, perhaps accentuated by the late unhappy troubles, but the scale of the problem may be exaggerated by the nature of the records. Most parishes throughout the period endeavoured to maintain their burial grounds, in the same way they kept up the fabric of their church. Keeping an orderly churchyard showed respect for the community of Christians and was not merely a matter of satisfying the present ecclesiastical regime.

Markers and Memorials

Though personal identity was extinguished by death, an individual's name and achievements could long endure among the living. If they did not we would have no history. Gentle and aristocratic families used plaques and statuary to commemorate their departed, but ordinary people were soon lost to memory. In most cases, as we have noted, the individuality of the deceased dissolved, becoming blended in the churchyard with the community of departed Christians. Even a plain wooden marker was unusual. It was considered noteworthy in 1606 when Humphrey Vincent of Northolt, Middlesex, promised to 'lay a plank upon his father's grave because it was his will upon his deathbed, and he took order with the carpenter to make it convenient'.[52] Families of the middling sort sometimes erected ephemeral memorials of perishable material, and tidy-minded bishops sought to have them removed. 'Is your churchyard pestered and cloyed with frames of wood, piles of brick, or stones laid over the grave?' asked Matthew Wren of the Diocese of Ely in 1638.[53] Permanent outdoor headstones were rare before the eighteenth century, even for the gentry, who were especially protective of their status and reputation.

Memorial monuments inside the church were another matter. Though most of the bodies interred beneath aisles and chancels had no distinctive monument, armigerous and aristocratic families vied with each other to commission elaborate and permanent reminders of their lineage, status, and power. The artistic energy and cultural investment that an earlier age had devoted to representations of the saints now proclaimed the social position of great secular families. The gentry who trooped to church in style and sat in the most privilged pews could view the likenesses and read the inscriptions commemorating members of their kindred and their class.[54]

Family groupings were the most frequently requested subjects for monumental masons. Thomas Mildmay, esquire, a wealthy and well-connected member of the Essex gentry community, specified in his will of 1566,

my executors shall bestow upon a comely tomb or monument of hard stone, to be set up and builded by, near or within the church wall of Chelmsford adjoining to the place where Avice my late wife lieth buried, forty pounds within short time after my decease, in which shall be engraven my arms and the arms of my wife together with the pictures of us both and fifteen children, the one half men children and the other half women children, as a remembrance to our children and friends left behind us, without any pomp or glory or other respect.

William Fitch of Little Canfield, in his will of 1577, wanted

a convenient and fair marble stone engraved with the arms and the pictures of myself, my wife and children and with such superscriptions as shall seem best to my executors, and the stone to be laid over my corpse for a perpetual remembrance as well of the day of my death as of the names of my wife and children.

John Hayes of Rettendon arranged for 'a marble stone and superscription thereupon, with my image, my wife's and my children, to be laid on my grave'.[55] The gentlemen who requested such memorials projected themselves as husbands and fathers, as heads of households, rather than as mere individuals. With their heraldic arms representing the past, and their progeny pointing to the future, the dead man took a crucial place in the maintenance of gentle dynastic continuity. Styles would evolve from the time of Elizabeth to the age of Queen Anne, but their public memorial purpose remained unchanged.

Though some critical voices were raised against the 'great cost and sumptuousness' of funeral monuments and the 'ambition' and 'pride' they betrayed, the majority of commentators accepted them as proper to the social order. John Donne was worried not that 'sumptuous monuments in the church' might misrepresent the social order, but that they claimed too much for insincere Christians. It was pride, not virtue, when 'such as have given nothing at all to any pious uses . . . have given large annuities, perpetuities, for new painting their tombs, or for new flags and scutcheons, every certain number of years'.[56] The jurist Edward Coke approved the erection of 'tombs, sepulchres or monuments' as 'the last work of charity that can be done for the deceased', so long as they did not hinder the celebration of divine service. The Jacobean preacher Robert Hill endorsed the erection of memorial monuments that distinguished 'betwixt person and person; for, though all die alike, yet all must not be alike buried'.[57]

The antiquarian John Weever similarly approved of funeral monuments that maintained social differentiation, but worried that vulgar wealth could rise above ancient distinction. 'Sepulchres should be made according to the quality and degree of the person deceased, that by the tomb everyone might be discerned of what rank he was living,' wrote Weever. This was not always possible, for the early Stuart period was a slippery time for social hierarchy, its ceremonies as confusing as its costumes. 'In these times,' he continued, 'more honour is attributed to a rich quondam tradesman or griping usurer, than is given to the greatest potentate entombed in Westminster.'[58] In conservative eyes, a grand funeral monument would be fitting for a lord, but similar ostentation for a jumped-up commoner might be seen as a sign of unseemly vanity.

Another concern, almosty entirely unheeded, was that elaborate tombs might stimulate excessive respect for the dead, especially if they incorporated sculpted likenesses. The Caroline divine Edmund Gurnay warned that lively representations of the deceased undermined the message of mortality, dust to dust, until the resurrection. 'To set forth those bodies in such pompous

and glorious manner while they are under the doom of corruption and dissolution in the grave, is little less than a kind of resistance unto mortality, and
reluctation against that great decree.'[59]

More down to earth was the concern in some parishes, especially those
home to powerful gentry and aristocrats, that funeral monuments would
obstruct the sightlines in church and block the traffic in the aisles. Bishop
Matthew Wren addressed this problem in his visitation of the Diocese of Ely
in 1638 when he enquired about oversize tombs or unfit monuments. Wren
also found it necessary to regulate the ephemeral memorials of funerals
that sometimes sprouted in early modern chuches. In 1638 he asked, 'are any
other mean toys and childish gew-gaws, such as the fonder sort of people
prepare at some burials, suffered to be fastened up in your church at anyone's pleasure? Or any garlands and other ordinary funeral ensigns to hang,
where they hinder the prospect, or until they grow foul and dusty, withered
and rotten?'[60] Unlike the puritans who protested garlands because of their
alleged pagan floral associations, ceremonialists intent on promoting the
beauty of holiness opposed them because of the mess they created in the
church as they wilted and decayed. The note of exasperation in the bishop's
query suggests that he lacked sympathy with established tradition and set
the decorum of God's dwelling above the customary needs of the bereaved.
(Flowers and garlands were traditionally carried before the corpse of young
girl or an unmarried woman, then hung in the church above the place where
she sat.[61])

Diaries and correspondence of the seventeenth century show the interest
that gentle families took in their funeral monuments. Two months after
Henry Pettit's burial in the church at Denton, Kent, in 1625 his family was
still discussing designs for 'a grave stone' with inscription and coats of arms.
At issue was which branches of this armigerous family should be represented
on Pettit's funeral monument. Sir William Slingsby arranged for his own
tomb to be 'packed up in two great sugar chests' for transportation across
Yorkshire in 1634, 'to be laid in the chapel where my father's tomb lieth'.[62]
Claver Morris, a West-Country gentleman-physician, gave public testimony
of his love for 'one of the best and kindest of wives' when he commissioned
her tomb in 1689. Morris paid £9. 8s. 6d. to a monumental mason in London
'for a black marble tombstone of six and a half feet long and three and a
quarter feet broad, with arms, mantling, and cress embossed, and inscription
cut', £1. 6s. 6d. more for transporting it 'by land and sea' to Somerset, and
4s. 'for laying it' on his wife's grave in Manston church. This work was
completed in 1694, almost five years after Grace Morris had died. About the
same time Elizabeth Freke could survey with pride the 'very fine monument

. . . of black and white marble, to the value of about two hundred pounds' erected for her sister Lady Norton in the chancel at Hollingbourne, Kent.[63]

Funeral monuments were designed for posterity, but they sometimes fell into disrepair. Families that maintained their local connections might be expected to care for the tombs of their ancestors, but social and demographic change left some gentle monuments untended. At Warley Parva, Essex, in 1685, for example, the archdeacon found 'my Lady Strutt's monument on the south side of the chancel is ready to fall down, if the heirs of the estate do not repair it, it will fall down'.[64] Secular monuments in churches rarely attracted the attention of iconoclasts, even in the heady 1640s, but bishops sometimes enquired about their condition in visitations. Richard Montague of Norwich asked in 1638, 'have any monuments or tombs of the dead in your church or churchyard been cast down, defaced, ruined? . . . Have any leaden or brazen inscriptions upon grave stones been defaced, purloined, sold, by whom?'[65] Most English churchgoers followed the example of ancient Rome, cited by Patrick Scot, where 'the least defacing of sepulchres of the dead, or touch or reproach, hath been holden an offence of higher quality than the ruination of the houses of the living'.[66] Though sometimes less perfect or less permanent than intended, material memorials, like ritual processes, bound kinsfolk and community to each other, and sustained continuity between the living and the dead.

CONCLUSION

Over the course of the sixteenth and seventeenth centuries the English population weathered fluctuations in fertility, nuptiality, and mortality to grow from three to five millions. Across this period, despite dislocations, depressions, and readjustments, the economy diversified and prospered. The apparatus of the state expanded in reach and scope, against the background of political and dynastic turmoil, war and revolution, familiar to students of Tudor and Stuart England. Changes in religion rearranged relationships between England and Rome, church and state, clergy and laity, and between devout parishioners and their God. Within this framework people of all sorts struggled to cope with the everyday realities of birth, marriage, and death. Though national events commanded attention, they were often overlain by the joys and worries of childbearing, the emotional strains of courtship and marriage, and the fears and ravages of death.

This study has shown how people negotiated the complex demands of custom, authority, and religion at critical moments in the life cycle. One conclusion, confirmed in every chapter, is that ritual was crucial to English social life. Ritual observance of stages in the life cycle gave meaning and structure to routine occurrences, assigned people roles and status, marked their transitions, and helped bond participants within social and familial groups. Ritual, indeed, did most of the things that social anthropologists say it did, both before and after the Reformation. Whether rooted in custom or scripted and scrutinized by religion, ritual activity helped to remind people of what they had in common. Participants performed their parts for a variety of reasons— to express conformity with tradition, to demonstrate respect for authority, to display their engagement with kinship and community, to procure spiritual blessings, or to offset sin. If they fell short in their ritual obligations, through open objection or simple neglect, clerical officials and neighbours had means and incentive to put them right.

Some ritual business, like that set forth in the Book of Common Prayer, helped to inscribe an English protestant identity, a unique relationship to God that was rooted in ancient Christianity but purged of the errors of Rome. Protestants could pride themselves on their accomplishment of rituals they thought most pleasing to the Lord. Standard liturgical performance reminded people of their Christian heritage and their reformed Christian faith. Other ritual activities, like the ceremonies associated with childbirth and the secular accompaniments to baptisms, weddings, and funerals, drew on this religious background for assistance, comfort, and understanding. Whether raising a glass or raising a prayer, God was never far from hand.

The rituals of birth, marriage, and death also assured people of their common humanity. It was frequently remarked that life-cycle rituals helped distinguish Christians from animals, and that without them they risked behaving like beasts. Midwifery and gossip gave babies the beginnings of their social identity; baptism and godparentage confirmed it. The woman's month of sexual abstinence before churching was said to be one of the differences 'betwixt reasonable creatures and beasts'.[1] Courtship and marriage was no mere rutting and coupling, but an elaborate social dance with formal embellishments, exchanges, and public consents. Holy matrimony, everyone knew, was 'not to be enterprised or taken in hand unadvisedy, lightly or wantonly, to satisfy men's carnal lusts and appetites, like brute beasts that have no understanding; but reverently, discreetly, advisedly, soberly, and in the fear of God'.[2] Death, emphatically, was not extinction, and corpses maintained their dignity after the departure of the soul. Only the worst of sinners thought 'no more of death than the brute beast that is without understanding', for it was given to humans alone to contemplate their end. Dealing with death was another mark of species distinction, for only animals were buried without cladding and ceremony. God's people, his spokesmen assured themselves, did not handle human cadavers 'as we be wont to carry forth dead horses or dead swine', nor bury their dead like dogs.[3]

Ritual required an audience. Its performance demanded witnesses or auditors to verify that the words and actions had been performed, and that they had been done properly. The audience could be intimate and select in a private chamber or open to all in the face of the congregation or in view of the street. Ritual markers of the life cycle were subject to scrutiny by family and friends, neighbours and associates, and even by officers of the church and state. For the business of the household was also the business of the wider community. The political and religious concerns of central government impacted on social life, while the ritual, reproductive, and domestic arrangements of the family deeply concerned both the polity and the church. As cases that came within ecclesiastical cognizance demonstrate, any distinction between public and private spheres is slippery and unstable, for the two domains intermeshed.

A central argument of this book is that parish disagreements and local disputes about the meaning and conduct of life-cycle rituals reflect the unresolved problem of England's adoption of protestantism. The Reformation, however slow and fitful that may have been in England, had effects that were profoundly traumatic. From the mid-sixteenth century to the mid-seventeenth, the secular and ecclesiastical governments asked men and women, laity and clergy, to abandon long-held beliefs about salvation and to give up traditional modes of devotion, to conform themselves to a national protestant church. At the same time, with varying degrees of intensity, a goodly minority thought reform had not gone far enough and either pressed for the elimination of popish remnants from the Book of Common Prayer or sought to remove them from their own religious practice. The complex crises of the revolutionary era compounded and exacerbated these problems, which were still reverberating in the stunned and riven religious culture of the later seventeenth century.

Despite the adoption of protestantism, with its denials of sacramental efficacy, the spiritual and social drama of the life cycle remained freighted with religious meaning and graced with elaborate ceremony. I have attempted to show how these ceremonies were politicized, and how they turned customary routine performance into tests of conformity and discipline. I make no claim to have found the key to puritan sensibility or to have exposed the liturgical origins of the British Civil Wars; but it seems clear that strains could become fractures, and anxiety could grow into anguish, with divisive social consequences, if demands for uniformity were pressed too hard. By examining the fall-out of these issues at both the parochial and the episcopal level, by attending to the theological and ecclesiastical discourse on ritual and its liturgical and disciplinary accompaniments, we may be able to calibrate some of the changes in religious culture across our period, and show how people resisted or accepted the strictures of the established church or accommodated themselves to ecclesiastical authority.

The Church of England was never a monolith and spoke with multiple voices. It accommodated not only a swirl of theological perspectives—Lutheran, Zwinglian, Calvinist, Arminian—but was home to a host of differing personalities. Its members could be cautious or reckless, lazy or zealous, affable or angry, and so on. If it achieved, at times, a moderate practical tolerance, that was partly due to its inability to enforce uniform discipline and partly a matter of taste. The system of ecclesiastical justice depended on the willingness of churchwardens or incumbents to present offenders, of church court judges to pursue them, and on those cited to appear and confess; its goal, most often, was reconciliation rather than punishment, as shown in dozens of the cases mentioned here. Though capable of wielding the rod, most Christian administrators were averse to confrontation. Most recognized that insistence on full compliance with every rule and rubric might be counterproductive. The Church of England, through much of its history, sought the preservation of harmony, or at least the framework and semblance of harmony, rather than sharp polarization. Collisions were usually local affairs, of short-lived intensity, and rarely stretched to the point of schism.

The evidence assembled here points to the wide diversity of experience within early modern society and culture. Despite its central government and ecclesiastical hierarchy, despite acts of uniformity and disciplinary injunctions, the Tudor and Stuart regime, in practice, exhibited a broad and flexible tolerance for a range of variant behaviour. Life-cycle rituals responded as much to custom and tradition, local needs and popular unruliness, as to the strictures and interpretations of the church. None the less, changes in theology, and in the organization and activity of religion, affected generations of lay people in early modern England, in the family, the parish, and the street. High-level developments in theology and faith, on such topics as predestination and the efficacy of baptism, were not confined to convocation or the universities but impacted, in myriad ways, on ordinary social experience. Although we might, a priori, expect this to be true, the personal, local, and diocesan records show something of how this worked out.

If you believed or were taught, for example, that baptism was absolutely essential to salvation, you would clutch at any straw, including emergency baptism by a midwife, to ensure that each child was covered. If, on the other hand, you accepted baptism as a sign, or simply as a ritual of initiation, and trusted God's inscrutable judgement to govern the fate of the soul, then baptism would be less urgent and the informal intervention by women in the birthroom would be redundant. If, at the same time, you accepted that sacramental business belonged exclusively to priests, as both presbyterians and sacerdotalists insisted, you would not mourn the passing of a tradition that left some baptisms in lay and female hands.

Similarly, if you valued tradition and accepted authority you might be content to observe baptisms around the old font, following the rubric of the Book of Common Prayer. If you were persuaded that beauty and ornament were pleasing to God, as ceremonialists taught in the 1620s and 1630s, you might even be willing to contribute to the painting or gilding of the font and its cover, alongside other additions to the beauty of holiness. If, on the other hand, you believed that fonts were papistical, and that baptism was better administered by a priest with a basin, you might approve of ministerial flexibility and independence, and be alarmed when your pastor, a bastion of godliness, was cited or suspended by an increasingly intolerant regime.

So too with items like the sign of the cross, the use of the ring in marriage, and the veiled solemnities of churching. If you thought these elements vital, as some countryfolk evidently did, you would feel short-changed if they were omitted, the sacrament or ceremony flawed or incomplete. If you believed, with the mainstream Church of England, that the sign was adiaphora—theologically indifferent—but was kept up by tradition and discipline, you might recognize it as part of the priestly business in the ceremony. If, however, you found the sign offensive, as a blatant popish remnant, you might request it to be omitted and your minister might be willing to agree. Ministers who served their parish, wore the surplice, stood by the font, and followed the words in the prayer book did not, on the surface, look like puritans, but their bishops might punish them, and their parishioners take sides, if indiscipline or ambivalence in this regard became a matter for the courts. On these issues and many others, such as the ancillary protocols of churching and the meeting of corpses at the church stile, we see much of the flexibility of the earlier era fading as hard-line Caroline churchmen began to identify their mildly nonconformist colleagues as 'sectarians'.

We can trace many changes over time, from the time of Henry VIII to the time of William III, but every reign accommodated more diversity than historians have usually recognized. Notwithstanding the Act of Uniformity and the machinery of episcopal visitation, the Elizabethan regime was willing to wink at many things. This was partly a shrewd recognition of reality, since the country was divided and some would say half-reformed. But there was also an accommodating principle at work, voiced by bishops from Parker to Whitgift to Sandys, that absolute conformity and liturgical precision were not worth striving for, so long as popery and superstition were not encouraged.

The Jacobean regime too, notwithstanding its new church canons and improved episcopal machinery, was unwilling to push for more than outward conformity. The King himself, and many of his bishops, placed a high premium on 'peace' and local concord. Although they explained, in the canons, why the sign of the cross was important and why other ceremonies had to be maintained, they did little in practice to ensure that every minister conformed. Historians still argue whether there was a Calvinist consensus or a Jacobean consensus in the religious culture of this time, but when looking at rites of passage we see a thousand flowers bloom.

In Charles's reign, however, the blossoms began to fade, the thorns became more exposed. Again, historians disagree whether the 1630s was a time of order and harmony, or whether the country was gripped by conflicts that would lead to Civil War. The major issues, of course, concerned Parliament and ship-money, finance and law. But Charles's promotion of controversial Arminians, and their insistence on strict ceremonial precision, substituted disciplinary intransigence for a long tradition of negotiation and accommodation. By ensuring that priests alone performed the life-cycle offices, and only in the authorized locations; by demanding an end to slackness or subterfuge associated with liturgical gestures like the sign of the cross; by insisting that fonts and altars be covered and upgraded and approached with reverence; by requiring that women be churched in dignified form, kneeling at the altar and attired with a veil; by a strict interpretation of the marriage calendar and insistence on clerical fees; by these and a dozen similar impositions of authority, the Caroline regime promoted its vision of order, but in so doing tore the culture apart.

For most of this period, and even in many places in the 1630s, liturgical discipline could be contingent, variable, and adjustable, so long as nobody brought it to the attention of the authorities, and so long as the authorities themselves were reluctant to act. Scrupulous lay puritans with strong opinions about sacramental practice sought ministers to accommodate them, if not in their own parish then elsewhere. Such people clearly intended to remain loyal to the Church of England, if only the church could be Christian-like and flexible in its discipline. Only when agreement broke down, foundering on unshifting principle, or when intransigent authorities exercised their power, would strains become fractures and wounds begin to fester.

It comes as no surprise, then, that reformers and revolutionaries of the 1640s and 1650s altered the rules for the rituals associated with birth, marriage, and death; that baptismal fonts were such a common target for iconoclasts or that derision of the old order involved mock baptism of cats and horses and other crude inversions of Anglican ceremony; or that marriage and burial were temporarily cut loose from their ecclesiastical moorings. Rites of passage were always critical events in the lives of each family and individual, but they also touched the key points (or hot buttons) of religious and cultural discourse, and provided occasions and formulae for articulating anxieties and complaints. That remained true in the aftermath of the mid-century turmoils, when a somewhat exhausted religious culture attempted to work with the fragments of authority, tradition, irreligion, and dissent within an increasingly secular society.

Anglican ritual was restored in the final forty years of the seventeenth century, but not without problems and objections. The immediate task of the post-Restoration church was to undo the damage of the previous two decades, to repair the disciplinary framework of episcopacy and to reinvigorate parochial liturgical routines. Most parishes settled down to the customary round of baptisms, weddings, and burials, no longer divided over adiaphora. Dissenters negotiated their own ceremonial proceedings, and their relationships with their conformist neighbours were usually more cordial than contentious.

Increasingly, the evidence suggests, later Stuart families and communities invested their energies in activities that were not directly controlled by the church. Baptisms became blended with christening parties, and amongst the gentle and metropolitan élite the minister was more often invited to the house than the baby taken to the font. Old-fashioned handfastings fell out of favour, to be replaced by businesslike dinners among parties to a contract. Weddings still followed the words in the prayer book, but increasing numbers, notoriously, were conducted privily or in clandestine circumstances. The formal business with the ring was often overshadowed by the celebratory drinking of healths and other nuptial merriments. Funerals, too, could be more memorable for their food and their finery than for words of spiritual assurance. The later Stuart period saw the creative elaboration of funeral ritual and the emergence of professional undertakers. In all these areas clergymen seem to have been relegated to the role of functionaries rather than sacerdotal masters of ceremonies.

Ritual activities that once concerned the whole community became increasingly the preserve of particular central participants. The life-cycle ceremonies in the prayer book were still supposed to be performed in open church, on days of worship, with the entire congregation present. Many country parishes no doubt strove to adhere to these protocols. But the evidence strongly indicates that the later Stuart élite worked hard to distance itself from the common routines of ordinary people. While customary culture occupied the church and the churchyard, the alehouse, the green and the street, the privileged classes withdrew into private parlours or shuttered chambers. Women of wealth and position attended childbirth events by invitation rather than by common custom. Their baptisms, by preference, took place indoors, at home, with delicate refreshments. Their weddings were quieter and unpublicized, by licence rather than banns, their transport more often in closed coaches than open procession, and their entertainments more polite and select. The post-Restoration gentry, and those who followed them, favoured funerals at night, with lines of coaches and flaming torches; and though their furnishings were lavish and their refreshments expensive, these ceremonial activities were not free for all-comers, as had been customary under the Tudors, but were increasingly confined to those with tickets. The evidence confirms the view that the classes of later Stuart England were drawing further apart. It suggests, in ways that further research may elaborate, that rituals that worked to bind communities together could also be instruments of cultural polarization.

A work of this scale follows many lines of enquiry and suggests avenues for future research. Among topics that call out for more study three have particular urgency. As I mentioned at the outset, and have alluded to from time to time, the local variations and regional patterns of English cultural history need thorough investigation. We need to know whether it is reasonable or audacious, or simply wrong-headed, to treat early modern England as a single cultural area. We need, too, to know much more about the peculiarity, or typicality, of the English conduct of the life cycle. While some historians work fruitfully with microscopes, others with a larger compass may begin to compare the social, cultural, and religious experience of the English to that of their neighbours in Scotland, in continental Europe, and in the colonies of British America. Finally, it is worth remarking how little is know about the social and cultural history of families and communities in the period 1640–60. This, from some perspectives, is the most intensively studied period in English history, and certainly the most controversial. Yet so much of the attention has focused on politics and ideas, on religious and constitutional innovations, on the King, Parliament and the army, that common rites of passage are obscured. We need more research on the social history of revolutionary England to show how ordinary experiences were adjusted to the demands of extraordinary times.

Notes

INTRODUCTION

1. Arnold Van Gennep, *The Rites of Passage* (Chicago, 1960, from French of 1908).
2. William Keatinge Clay (ed.), *Liturgical Services: Liturgies and Occasional Forms of Prayer Set Forth in the Reign of Queen Elizabeth* (Parker Society; Cambridge, 1847), 36.
3. Keith Thomas, *Religion and the Decline of Magic* (New York, 1971), 38; Natalie Zemon Davis, *Society and Culture in Early Modern France* (Stanford, Calif., 1975), 145.
4. William Gouge, *Of Domesticall Duties* (1622; STC 12119), 210.
5. Van Gennep, *Rites of Passage*; Victor Turner, *Dramas, Fields, and Metaphors: Symbolic Action in Human Society* (Ithaca, New York, 1974); John J. MacAllon (ed.), *Rite, Drama, Festival, Spectacle* (Philadelphia, 1984); Ronald L. Grimes, *Research in Ritual Studies: A Programmatic Essay and Bibliography* (Metuchen, NJ, 1985); David I. Kertzer, *Rituals, Politics and Power* (New Haven, 1988); Catherine Bell, *Ritual Theory, Ritual Practice* (New York, 1992).
6. Peter Laslett, 'The Wrong Way Through the Telescope: A Note on Literary Evidence in Sociology and Historical Sociology', *British Journal of Sociology*, 27 (1976), 319–42 . I have benefited, as have many others, from such works as Leah Marcus, *The Politics of Mirth: Jonson, Herrick, Milton, Marvell, and the Defense of Old Holiday Pastimes* (Chicago, 1986), and Kevin Sharpe and Steven N. Zwicker (eds.), *Politics of Discourse: The Literature and History of Seventeenth-Century England* (Berkeley and Los Angeles, 1987).
7. A. W. Pollard and G. R. Redgrave, *A Short Title Catalogue of Books Printed in England, Ireland, Scotland and of English Books Printed Abroad, 1475–1640* (revised edn., 2 vols., 1976–86).
8. Cf. David Underdown, 'Regional Cultures? Local Variations in Popular Culture during the Early Modern Period', in Tim Harris (ed.), *Popular Culture in England, c.1500–1850* (New York, 1995), 28–47.

CHAPTER 1

1. Patricia Crawford, 'The Construction and Experience of Maternity in Seventeenth-Century England', in Valerie Fildes (ed.), *Women as Mothers in Pre-Industrial England* (1990), 3–38; Linda Pollock, 'Embarking on a Rough Passage: The Experience of Pregnancy in Early Modern Society', ibid. 39–67; Adrian Wilson, 'The Ceremony of Childbirth and its Interpretation', ibid. 68–107; Adrian Wilson, 'Participant or Patient? Seventeenth Century Childbirth from the Mother's Point of View', in Roy Porter (ed.), *Patients and Practitioners: Lay Perceptions of Medicine in Pre-Industrial Society* (Cambridge, 1986), 129–44; Audrey Eccles, *Obstetrics*

and Gynaecology in Tudor and Stuart England (Kent, Ohio, 1982). See also R. V. Schnucker, 'The English Puritans and Pregnancy, Delivery and Breast Feeding', *History of Childhood Quarterly*, 1 (1974), 637–58. For a provocative literary analysis of the humoral economy of childbearing, see Gail Kern Paster, *The Body Embarrassed: Drama and the Disciplines of Shame in Early Modern England* (Ithaca, New York, 1993), esp. 166–208. Valuable French studies include Jacques Gélis, *History of Childbirth: Fertility, Pregnancy and Birth in Early Modern Europe* (Cambridge, 1991; publ. Paris, 1984, as *L'Arbre et le fruit*), and Mireille Laget, *Naissances: L'Accouchement avant l'âge de la clinique* (Paris, 1982). For a modern cross cultural analysis, see Karen Erickson Paige and Jeffery M. Paige, *The Politics of Reproductive Ritual* (Berkeley and Los Angeles, 1981).

2. Christopher Hooke, *The Child-birth or Womans Lecture* (1590; STC 13702), sigs. B3^v, D^v.

3. Gen. 3: 16; 1 Tim. 2: 15; Richard Adams, 'How may Child-Bearing Women be Most Encouraged?', in Samuel Annesley (ed.), *A Continuation of Morning-Exercise Questions and Cases of Conscience* (1683), 662.

4. Richard Hooker, 'Of the Laws of Ecclesiastical Politie', in *The Works of that Learned and Judicious Divine, Mr. Richard Hooker* (1723), 268, 209; Robert Hill, *The Pathway to Prayer and Pietie* (1610; STC 13473), 415; Hooke, *The Child-birth or Womans Lecture*, sig. B2^v; William Hinde, *A Faithful Remonstrance of the Holy Life and Happy Death of Iohn Bruen of Bruen-Stapleford* (1641), 3. For similar notions see also John Cosin, 'A Thanksgiving after Childbirth', in P. G. Stanwood (ed.), *John Cosin: A Collection of Private Devotions* (Oxford, 1967), 288; George R. Potter and Evelyn M. Simpson (eds.), *The Sermons of John Donne*, 10 vols. (Berkeley and Los Angeles, 1962), v. 198; Thomas Adams, *The Workes of Thomas Adams* (1629; STC 104), 1134; Stephen Charnock, 'A Discourse for the Comfort of Child-bearing Women', in his *A Supplement to the Several Discourses upon Various Divine Subjects* (1683), 76–86; Annesley (ed.), *Continuation of Morning-Exercise Questions*, 663, 646.

5. Elizabeth Joceline, *The Mothers Legacie, to her Vnborne Childe* (1624; STC 14624), 1; Elizabeth Clinton, *The Covntesse of Lincolnes Nvrserie* (1622, STC 5432), 19, 20; Ernest Axon (ed.), *Oliver Heywood's Life of John Angier of Denton* (Chetham Society; Manchester, 1937), 124; Alice Thornton, *The Autobiography of Mrs. Alice Thornton* (Surtees Society; Durham, 1875), 84; E. S. de Beer (ed.), *The Diary of John Evelyn*, 6 vols. (Oxford, 1955), iii. 368.

6. Hooke, *The Child-birth or Womans Lecture*, sigs. B2^v–B3; Crawford, 'The Construction and Experience of Maternity', 19; *A Thanksgiving for the Queenes Maiesties Safe Deliverance* (1605; STC 16535), sig. A2^v. The phrase derives from the Bible, Judges 9: 9 and 13.

7. Jane Sharp, *The Midwives Book: Or the Whole Art of Midwifery Discovered* (1671), 18, 33; *The Problemes of Aristotle* (1597; STC 764); Alan Macfarlane, *The Family Life of Ralph Josselin: A Seventeenth-Century Clergyman. An Essay in Historical Anthropology* (Cambridge, 1970), 83; Gélis, *History of Childbirth*, 36; Paster, *Body Embarrassed*, 166–84.

8. William Keatinge Clay (ed.), *Liturgical Services: Liturgies and Occasional Forms of Prayer Set Forth in the Reign of Queen Elizabeth* (Cambridge, 1847), 217.

9. Ibid. 199; *Articles Whereupon it was agreed by the Archbishoppes and Bishoppes of both provinces and the whole cleargie* (1571; STC 10036a), no. 9.

10. John Milton, Sonnet 19, in H. C. Beeching (ed.), *The Poetical Works of John Milton* (Oxford, 1900), 86; Daniel Featley, *Ancilla Pietatis: or, The Hand-Maid to Private Devotion* (1626; STC 10725), 498; Daniel Featley, *Clavis Mystica: A Key Opening Divers Difficult and Mysterious Texts of Holy Scripture* (1636; STC 10730), 207; Sampson Price, *The Two Twins of Birth and Death* (1624; STC 20334); 8–14; Folger Shakespeare Library, Ms. V.a. 436, 'Nehemiah Wallington, Writing Book 1654', 1.

11. Potter and Simpson (eds.), *Sermons of John Donne*, v. 171–2. Within this one paragraph Donne cites Psalms 51: 5, Job 14: 4, Ephesians 2: 3, Psalms 5: 6, and Proverbs 30: 12. According to Donne, baptism did not completely eradicate the stains of original sin, ibid. ii. 166. See below for an extended discussion of the cleansing efficacy of the sacrament of baptism.

12. For a preview, see *Certaine Questions by Way of Conference betwixt a Chauncelor and a Kinswoman of His Concerning Churching of Women* (Middleburg?, 1601: STC 20557); David Cressy, 'Purification, Thanksgiving and the Churching of Women in Post-Reformation England', *Past and Present*, 141 (1993), 106–46.

13. Thomas Pierce, *A Collection of Sermons upon Several Occasions* (Oxford, 1671), 274; Edward Sparke, *Scintilla Altaris: Primitive Devotion in the Feasts and Fasts of the Church of England* (6th edn., 1678), 391; George Stradling, *Sermons and Discourses upon Several Occasions* (1692), 90.

14. John Day, *Day's Festivals or, Twelve of His Sermons* (Oxford, 1615; STC 6426), 236–7; John White, *The First Century of Scandalous, Malignant Priests* (1643), 50; Harold Smith, *The Ecclesiastical History of Essex Under the Long Parliament and Commonwealth* (Colchester, 1932), 111, 171.

15. Charles Severn (ed.), *Diary of the Rev. John Ward . . . 1648 to 1679* (1839), 102; R. C. Latham and W. Matthews (eds.), *The Diary of Samuel Pepys*, 9 vols. (Berkeley and Los Angeles, 1970–6), iii. 91.

16. Beryl Rowland, *Medieval Woman's Guide to Health: The First English Gynecological Handbook* (Kent, Ohio, 1981), 31; David Cressy, 'De la Fiction dans les Archives? Ou le Monstre de 1569', *Annales E.S.C.* 48 (1993), 1314.

17. Pollock, 'Embarking on a Rough Passage', 52; John Parkinson, *Paradisi In Sole, Paradisus Terrestris: A Garden of all sorts of pleasant flowers* (1629; STC 19300), 40, 199, 274; John Gerarde, *The Herball or General Historie of Plantes* (1636; STC 11752); Leonard Sowerby, *The Ladies Dispensatory* (1652).

18. Robert Parker Sorlien (ed.), *The Diary of John Manningham of the Middle Temple, 1602–1603* (Hanover, NH, 1976), 82; John Pechey, *Some Observations Made upon the Maldiva Nut: Shewing Its Admirable Virtue in giving an Easie, Safe and Speedy Delivery to Women in Child-bed* (1694).

19. Keith Thomas, *Religion and the Decline of Magic* (New York, 1971), 28, 31, 34, 73; James Gairdner (ed.), *Letters and Papers, Foreign and Domestic, of the Reign of Henry VIII*, x (1887), 138–43; W. H. Frere and W. M. Kennedy (eds.), *Visitation*

Articles and Injunctions of the Period of the Reformation, 3 vols. (1910), ii. 59; Percival Price, *Bells and Man* (New York, 1983), 111; Gélis, *History of Childbirth*, 69–75, 116–18; Rowland, *Medieval Woman's Guide to Health*, 33.

20. Frederick E. Warren (tr.), *The Sarum Missal in English*, 2 vols. (1913), ii. 161–4; John Bale, *A Declaration of Edmonde Bonners articles concerning the cleargye of London dyocese* (1561; STC 1289), fo. 61; Gélis, *History of Childbirth*, 69.

21. Thornton, *Autobiography*, 145; de Beer (ed.), *Diary of John Evelyn*, iv. 150, v. 190.

22. Philip Caraman (tr.), *John Gerard. The Autobiography of an Elizabethan* (1951), 20. Margo Todd is studying the 'lost sacrament' of unction among the 17th-cent. protestant ministry.

23. Frere and Kennedy (eds.), *Visitation Articles and Injunctions of the Period of the Reformation*, ii. 59; *The Injunctions and other Ecclesiastical Proceedings of Richard Barnes, Bishop of Durham, from 1577 to 1587* (Surtees Society; Durham, 1850), 18; John Strype, *Annals of the Reformation*, 3 vols. (Oxford, 1824), i. 243; *The Book of Oaths* (1689), 162. See below for the practice of midwives.

24. John Rylands Library, Manchester, Ms. 524, 'The Acts and Speeches of Richard Greenham', fo. 35^v.

25. Crawford, 'The Construction and Experience of Maternity', 22; Sharp, *Midwives Book*, 182–3.

26. Nicholas Culpeper, *A Directory for Midwives* (1651), 150–3; William Sermon, *The Ladies Companion, Or the English Midwife* (1671), 96; Rowland, *Medieval Woman's Guide to Health*, 33–4; Thomas, *Decline of Magic*, 189–90.

27. Thomas Bentley, *The Monvment of Matrones: conteining seuen seuerall Lamps of Virginitie* (1582; STC 1892–3), 'The Fift Lampe', 95–156. See also Colin B. Atkinson and William P. Stoneman, '"These Griping Greefes and Pinching Pangs": Attitudes to Childbirth in Thomas Bentley's *The Monument of Matrones* (1582)', *Sixteenth Century Journal*, 21 (1990), 193–203; Charlotte F. Otten, 'Women's Prayers in Childbirth in Sixteenth-Century England', *Women and Language*, 16 (1993), 18–21.

28. Hill, *Pathway to Prayer and Pietie*, 411–13, qu. 411; Samuel Hieron, *A Helpe vnto Deuotion* (1612; STC 13407), 270–81; Featley, *Ancilla Pietatis*, 492–514, qu. 492.

29. Stanwood (ed.), *John Cosin: A Collection of Private Devotions*, 287–8; Samuel Rowlands, 'Godly Prayers', in *Heavens Glory, Seeke It* (1628; STC 21383), 228–31; George Wither, *Halelviah* (1641), 76–8.

30. John Oliver, *A Present for Teeming Women. Or, Scripture-Directions for Women with Child, how to prepare for the hour of Travel* (1663), title-page, sigs. A2, A3. Another edn., entitled *A Present to be Given to Teeming Women: By their Husbands or Friends*, was published in 1669.

31. Pollock, 'Embarking on a Rough Passage', 48; British Library, Egerton Ms. 607, 'Devotional pieces by Elizabeth Countess of Bridgewater', fos. 22^v, 27, 31.

32. New College, Oxford, Ms. 9502, 'Robert Woodforde's Diary'.

33. Alan Macfarlane (ed.), *The Diary of Ralph Josselin 1616–1683* (1976), 50, 325, 403, 415; Macfarlane, *Family Life of Ralph Josselin*, 84.

34. Annesley (ed.), *A Continuation of Morning-Exercise Questions*, 658, 662.

35. Thomas Heywood (ed.), *The Diary of the Rev. Henry Newcome, from September 30, 1661, to September 29, 1663* (Chetham Society; Manchester, 1849), 30; Richard Parkinson (ed.), *The Autobiography of Henry Newcome, M.A.* (Chetham Society; Manchester, 1852), 303; J. Horsfall Turner (ed.), *The Rev. Oliver Heywood, B.A. 1630–1702: His Autobiography, Diaries, Anecdote and Event Books*, 4 vols. (Brighouse, 1882–5), ii. 63, 73, 101, 222, iii. 155.

36. *Prayers Appointed to be vsed in the Church at Morning and Evening Prayer by every Minister, For the Queenes safe deliverance* (1605; STC 16534), sigs. A2, A3ᵛ; *Thankesgiving for the Queenes Maiesties safe deliverance* (1605; STC 16535); *A Thankesgiuing and Prayer for the safe Child-bearing of the Queenes Maiestie* (1629, 1631; STC 16548.3, STC 16549.5). H. R. Wilton Hall, *Records of the Old Archdeaconry of St. Albans: A Calendar of Papers A.D. 1575 to A.D. 1637* (St Albans, 1908), 127, records the distribution and reading of these prayers.

37. Hooke, *The Child-birth or Womans Lecture*, sig. D; *Prayers and Thanksgiving to bee used by all the Kings Maiesties loving Subiects For the happy deliverance of his Maiestie, the Queene, Prince, and states of Parliament, from the most Traiterous and bloody intended Massacre by Gunpowder, the fift of November, 1605* (1605; STC 16494). For the cultural politics of these anniversaries, see David Cressy, *Bonfires and Bells: National Memory and the Protestant Calendar in Elizabethan and Stuart England* (1989).

38. Annesley (ed.), *A Continuation of Morning-Exercise Questions*, 662.

39. Leland H. Carlson (ed.), *The Writings of Henry Barrow 1587–1590* (1962), 463; William Gouge, *Of Domesticall Duties* (3rd edn., 1634; STC 12121), 405.

40. e.g. Bentley, *Monvment*, 'the fift lampe', 122; Hooke, *Child-birth Lecture*, sigs. D3–D3ᵛ; Hill, *Pathway to Prayer*, 415; 'Devotional Pieces by Elizabeth Countess of Bridgewater', fo. 30.

41. 'The Diary of Richard Rogers', in M. M. Knappen (ed.), *Two Elizabethan Puritan Diaries* (1933; repr. Gloucester, Mass., 1966), 73–4, 76.

42. Macfarlane (ed.), *Diary of Ralph Josselin*, 50, 325, 415, 502; Macfarlane, *Family Life of Ralph Josselin*, 82–5.

43. Matthew Storey (ed.), *Two East Anglian Diaries, 1641–1729; Isaac Archer and William Coe* (Woodbridge, Suffolk, 1994), 125, 139.

44. F. R. Raines (ed.), *The Journal of Nicholas Assheton* (Chetham Society; Manchester, 1848), 81; Axon (ed.), *Oliver Heywood's Life of John Angier*, 124–6.

45. De Beer (ed.), *Diary of John Evelyn*, iv. 150.

46. Joceline, *Mothers Legacie, to her Vnborne Childe*, sig. A5. 'The Approbation' was written by Thomas Goad, rector of Hadleigh, Suffolk. Mrs Joceline's story was retold in Annesley (ed.), *A Continuation of Morning-Exercise Questions*, 654, and in N.H., *The Ladies Dictionary* (1694), 143. *The Mothers Legacy* was reprinted in 1625, 1635, 1684, and in its centenary year 1724.

47. Jacques Guillemeau, *Child-Birth, or The Happy Deliverie of Women* (1612; STC 12496), 86.

48. Roger Schofield, 'Did the Mothers Really Die? Three Centuries of Maternal

Mortality in "The World We Have Lost" ', in Lloyd Bonfield, Richard M. Smith, and Keith Wrightson (eds.), *The World We Have Gained: Histories of Population and Social Structure* (Oxford, 1986), 231–60; see Antonia Fraser, *The Weaker Vessel* (New York, 1984), 59–80; Irvine Loudon, *Death in Childbirth: An International Study of Maternal Care and Maternal Mortality 1800–1950* (Oxford, 1992), 158–62; Adrian Wilson, 'The Perils of Early Modern Procreation: Childbirth With or Without Fear?', *British Journal for Eighteenth-Century Studies*, 16 (1993), 1–19.

49. Cambridge University Library, Additional Ms. 8499. References are to the recently published Storey (ed.), *Two East Anglian Diaries*.

50. Ibid. 117.

51. Ibid. 118–19.

52. Ibid. 125–6.

53. Ibid. 139.

54. Ibid. 145, 150–1.

55. Ibid. 153.

56. Ibid. 154–5.

57. Ibid. 155, 156, 157.

58. Ibid. 157, 159, 160.

59. Ibid. 163, 164.

60. Ibid. 165.

61. Ibid. 170, 171.

CHAPTER 2

1. Eucharius Roesslin, *The Birth of Man-Kinde; Otherwise Named The Womans Book* (tr. Thomas Raynold, 1626; STC 21163), 92; William Gouge, *Of Domesticall Duties* (3rd edn., 1634), 404; John Oliver, *A Present to be Given to Teeming Women. By their Husbands or Friends* (1669), 153.

2. Much of this literature is surveyed in Audrey Eccles, *Obstetrics and Gynaecology in Tudor and Stuart England* (Kent, Ohio, 1982). See also Jean Donnison, *Midwives and Medical Men: A History of the Struggle for the Control of Childbirth* (1977).

3. For the literacy of midwives see David Harley, 'Provincial Midwives in England: Lancashire and Cheshire, 1660–1760', in Hilary Marland (ed.), *The Art of Midwifery: Early Modern Midwives in Europe* (1993), 34. Female illiteracy is discussed in David Cressy, *Literacy and the Social Order: Reading and Writing in Tudor and Stuart England* (Cambridge, 1980).

4. John Pechey, *The Compleat Midwife's Practice Enlarged* (5th edn., 1698), sig. A2. Pechey's phrase, of course, is redolent of self-advertisement.

5. Roesslin, *Birth of Man-Kinde*; Jacques Guillemeau, *Child-Birth Or, The Happy Deliverie of Women* (1612; STC 12496); Jacob Rueff, *The Expert Midwife* (1637; STC 21442).

6. Guillemeau, *Child-Birth*, Huntington Library, rare book 87312, facing title-page.

7. John Sadler, *The Sicke Womans Private Looking-Glasse* (1636; STC 21544); John Oliver, *A Present for Teeming Women* (1663).

8. Nicholas Culpeper, *A Directory for Midwives: Or, A Guide for Women, In their Conception, Bearing, and Suckling their Children* (1651); Richard Bunworth, *The Doctoresse: A plain and easie method of curing those diseases which are peculiar to women* (1656); Philip Barrough, *The Method of Physick* (1652); A.M., *A Rich Closet of Physical Secrets* (1652), 1.

9. Nicholas Fonteyn (Fontanus), *The Womans Doctour* (1652), frontispiece; William Harvey, *Anatomical Exercitations, Concerning the Generation of Living Creatures* (1653).

10. Jane Sharp, *The Midwives Book. Or the Whole Art of Midwifery Discovered. Directing Childbearing Women how to behave themselves in the Conception, Breeding, Bearing, and Nursing of Children* (1671); William Sermon, *The Ladies Companion, or the English Midwife* (1671); Francis Mauriceau, *The Diseases of Women with Child* (1672, 1683); Francis Mauriceau, *The Accomplisht Midwife* (1673); W.M., *The Queens Closet Opened* (1674); Hannah Woolley, *The Gentlewoman's Companion* (1675).

11. Percival Willughby, *Observations in Midwifery*, ed. Henry Blenkinsop (Warwick, 1863); *The English Midwife Enlarged* (1682); John Pechey, *A General Treatise of the Diseases of Maids, Big-Bellied Women, Child-bed Women, and Widows* (1696); id., *Compleat Midwife's Practice Enlarged*; Robert Barret, *A Companion for Midwives, Child-Bearing Women, and Nurses* (1699).

12. See Patricia Crawford, 'Sexual Knowledge in England, 1500–1750', in Roy Porter and Mikulas Teich (eds.), *Sexual Knowledge, Sexual Science: The History of Attitudes to Sexuality* (Cambridge, 1994), 82–106, esp. 93–4; Gail Paster, *The Body Embarrassed: Drama and the Disciplines of Shame in Early Modern England* (Ithaca, New York, 1993), 186–8.

13. Roesslin, *Birth of Man-Kinde*, 3, 12, 16; *The Problemes of Aristotle* (1597; STC 764); John Banister, *The Historie of Man, sucked from the sappe of the most approued Anathomistes* (1578; STC 1359), fo. 88ᵛ.

14. Helkiah Crooke, *Microcosmographia: A Description of the Body of Man* (2nd edn., 1631; STC 6063), 197, 257; Eccles, *Obstetrics and Gynaecology in Tudor and Stuart England*, 13; Sharp, *Midwives Book*, 5; James Wolveridge, *Speculum Matricis Hybernicum; or, The Irish Midwives Handmaid* (1670), 'the author to his book'. The address 'to the reader' in Bunworth's *Doctoresse* similarly avows the author's desire to be 'somewhat indulgent' to the 'modesty' of 'the female sex' in 'avoiding all obscenity' in his treatment of intimate matters.

15. N.H., *The Ladies Dictionary, Being a General Entertainment for the Fair-Sex* (1694), 123.

16. N.H., *Ladies Dictionary*, 123; Guillemeau, *Child-Birth*, 2–8; Rueff, *Expert Midwife*, 181–92; Culpeper, *Directory for Midwives*, 125–8; Sermon, *Ladies Companion*, 16–21; Wolveridge, *Speculum Matricis Hybernicum*, 95.

17. Guillemeau, *Child-Birth*, 2–3; Sermon, *Ladies Companion*, 16; Mauriceau, *Diseases of Women with Child*, 23–4; Robert Parker Sorlien (ed.), *The Diary of John Manningham of the Middle Temple, 1602–1603* (Hanover, NH, 1976), 189. The Lancashire squire William Blundell observed in the 1660s that 'very many barren

wives do strongly fancy themselves to be with child, that they do even send for the midwife as being ready to bring forth, when yet there is no conception', T. Ellison Gibson (ed.), *Crosby Records: A Cavalier's Note Book . . . of William Blundell* (1880), 157. Cf. similar accounts of servants who commenced labour yet claimed not to know they were pregnant.

18. Guillemeau, *Child-Birth*, 2–8; Stephen Blancard, *A Physical Dictionary* (1684), 52; Sermon, *Ladies Companion*, 16–21; N.H., *Ladies Dictionary*, 123–4; Barret, *Companion for Midwives*, 64–5; Sadler, *Sicke Womans Private Looking-Glasse*, 144–6; Sharp, *Midwives Book*, 102–5; Wolveridge, *Speculum Matricis Hybernicum*, 95–9; James Primrose, *Popular Errours. Or the Errours of the People in Physick* (1651), 78; Jacques Gélis, *History of Childbirth: Fertility, Pregnancy and Birth in Early Modern Europe* (Cambridge, 1991), 46–9.

19. Sharp, *Midwives Book*, 102; Alan Macfarlane (ed.), *The Diary of Ralph Josselin 1616–1683* (1976), 89; Matthew Storey (ed.), *Two East Anglian Diaries, 1641–1729: Isaac Archer and William Coe* (Woodbridge, Suffolk, 1994), 153, 163; Huntington Library, Hastings Irish Papers, HA 15618; Crooke, *Microcosmographia*, 336; Eccles, *Obstetrics and Gynaecology in Tudor and Stuart England*, 44–5; Gélis, *History of Childbirth*, 61–5.

20. Roesslin, *Birth of Man-Kinde*, 89; *Problemes of Aristotle*; Culpeper, *Directory for Midwives*, 129–30; Sermon, *Ladies Companion*, 20; N.H., *Ladies Dictionary*, 123–5, 141; Sadler, *Sicke Womans Private Looking-Glasse*, 147; Sharp, *Midwives Book*, 105; Wolveridge, *Speculum Matricis Hybernicum*, 99, Gélis, *History of Childbirth*, 89–90. For the preference for a male child see Christopher Hooke, *The Child-birth or Womans Lecture* (1590; STC 13702), sigs. A3^v, A4^v, B2, and Storey (ed.), *Two East Anglian Diaries*, 118, 139, 155.

21. Mauriceau, *Diseases of Women with Child*, 43–7; Primrose, *Popular Errours*, 47, 76.

22. Keith Thomas, *Religion and the Decline of Magic* (New York, 1971), 283–385, esp. 316–17; Bernard Capp, *Astrology and the Popular Press* (1979).

23. Culpeper, *Directory for Midwives*, 62–71; Henry W. Robinson and Walter Adams (eds.), *The Diary of Robert Hooke . . . 1672–1680* (1935), 10.

24. Charles Severn (ed.), *Diary of the Rev. John Ward . . . 1648 to 1679* (1839), 104–5.

25. Mauriceau, *Diseases of Women with Child*, 57–8, 287; Barret, *Companion for Midwives*, 37; Linda A. Pollock, 'Embarking on a Rough Passage: The Experience of Pregnancy in Early Modern England', in Valerie Fildes (ed.), *Women as Mothers in Pre-Industrial England* (London, 1990), 39–67.

26. William Gouge, *Of Domesticall Dvties* (1622; STC 12119), 506. Cf. id., *Of Domesticall Duties* (3rd edn., 1634; STC 12121), 405.

27. Gouge, *Of Domesticall Dvties*, 505; Oliver, *Present for Teeming Women*, 41.

28. E. S. de Beer (ed.), *The Diary of John Evelyn*, 6 vols. (Oxford, 1955), iii. 368; Joseph Hunter (ed.), *The Diary of Ralph Thoresby . . . 1677–1724*, 2 vols. (1830), i. 190.

29. Rueff, *Expert Midwife*, 58; Wolveridge, *Speculum Matricis Hybernicum*, 17; Oliver, *Present for Teeming Women*, 29–30.

30. George R. Potter and Evelyn M. Simpson (eds.), *The Sermons of John Donne*, 10

vols. (Berkeley and Los Angeles, 1962), v. 172; Beryl Rowland, *Medieval Woman's Guide to Health: The First English Gynecological Handbook* (Kent, Ohio, 1981), 36; Angus McLaren, *Reproductive Rituals: The Perception of Fertility in England from the Sixteenth to the Nineteenth Centuries* (1984), 107–9; Pollock, 'Embarking on a Rough Passage', 44. See also Barbara Duden, *Disembodying Women: Perspectives on Pregnancy and the Unborn* (Cambridge, Mass., 1993), 79–82.

31. Ernest Axon (ed.), *Oliver Heywood's Life of John Angier of Denton* (Manchester, 1937), 124; Storey (ed.), *Two East Anglian Diaries*, 153–4; John Gough Nichols (ed.), *The Diary of Henry Machyn, Citizen and Merchant-Taylor of London . . . 1550 to . . . 1563* (Camden Society; 1848), 76; *A Thankesgiuing and Prayer for the safe Child-bearing of the Queenes Maiestie* (1629, STC 16548.3); *A Form, or Order of Thanksgiving, and Prayer . . . upon Occasion of the Queen's being with Child* (1688). The prayers for Mary of Modena sought to 'defend her from all dangers and evil accidents, that what she has conceived may be happily brought forth', and prayed a 'watchful providence' to 'grant her an easy and happy deliverance'.

32. Gouge, *Of Domesticall Dvties*, 506; Sadler, *Sicke Womans Private Looking-Glasse*, 155–64; Culpeper, *Directory for Midwives*, 146; A.M., *Rich Closet of Physical Secrets*, 1; N.H., *Ladies Dictionary*, 66–7; Gélis, *History of Childbirth*, 83.

33. Rueff, *Expert Midwife*, 68, 58–9; Barret, *Companion for Midwives*, 65–6; Pechey, *Compleat Midwife's Practice Enlarged*, 64–9.

34. Wolveridge, *Speculum Matricis Hybernicum*, 111; Severn (ed.), *Diary of the Rev. John Ward*, 255.

35. Andrew Boorde, *The Breviary of Health, for all maner of sickenesses and diseases the which may be in man or woman* (1552; STC 3374), fo. 8; Guillemeau, *Child-Birth*, 23; Pechey, *Compleat Midwife's Practice Enlarged*, 65–7; Gélis, *History of Childbirth*, 85; Thomas Browne, *Pseudodoxia Epidemica: or, Enquiries into Very Many Received Tenents and Commonly Presumed Truths* (2nd edn., 1650), 173.

36. Thomas, *Religion and the Decline of Magic*, 188; Gélis, *History of Childbirth*, 53–70, 97; Enid Porter, *Cambridgeshire Customs and Folklore* (1969), 10–14.

37. John Parkinson, *Paradisi In Sole, Paradisus Terrestris. A Garden of all sorts of pleasant flowers* (1629; STC 19300), 40, 274, 478; John Gerarde, *The Herball or Generall Historie of Plantes* (1636; STC 11752), 766, 1455, 1517.

38. Sharp, *Midwives Book*, 181–2, 206–10; Culpeper, *Directory for Midwives*, 150. See also Woolley, *Gentlewoman's Companion*; W.M., *Queens Closet Opened*, 84, 113, 116, 124.

39. William H. James, 'The Incidence of Spontaneous Abortion', *Population Studies*, 24 (1970), 241–5; John Bongaarts, 'Why Birth Rates are so Low', *Population and Development Review*, 1 (1975), 289–96.

40. New College, Oxford, Ms. 9502, 'Robert Woodforde's Diary'; Axon (ed.), *Oliver Heywood's Life of John Angier*, 124; Macfarlane (ed.), *The Diary of Ralph Josselin*, 50, 199; Alice Thornton, *The Autobiography of Mrs. Alice Thornton* (Surtees Society; Durham, 1875), 49; Buckinghamshire Record Office, D/A/V3, fo. 10. See also Pollock, 'Embarking on a Rough Passage', 49–53.

41. Boorde, *The Breviary of Health*, fo. 8; Crooke, *Microcosmographia*, 333; Fonteyn, *Womans Doctour*, 195; McLaren, *Reproductive Rituals*, 108–11.

42. Norfolk Record Office, C/S3/23 A; S. D. Amussen, 'Gender, family and the social order, 1560–1725', in Anthony Fletcher and John Stevenson (eds.), *Order and Disorder in Early Modern England* (Cambridge, 1985), 211; Susan Amussen, *An Ordered Society: Gender and Class in Early Modern England* (Oxford, 1988), 114–15.

43. John M. Riddle, 'Oral Contraceptives and Early-Term Abortifacients during Classical Antiquity and the Middle Ages', *Past and Present*, 132 (1991), 3–32; John M. Riddle, *Contraception and Abortion from the Ancient World to the Renaissance* (Cambridge, Mass., 1992); Edward Shorter, *A History of Women's Bodies* (New York, 1982), 177–224; Eccles, *Obstetrics and Gynaecology in Tudor and Stuart England*, 67–70; McLaren, *Reproductive Rituals*, 89–112. For the transfer of this knowledge to the New World see Cornelia Hughes Dayton, 'Taking the Trade: Abortion and Gender Relations in an Eighteenth-Century New England Village', *William and Mary Quarterly*, 48 (1991), 19–49.

44. Ben Jonson, *Epicoene, or The Silent Woman* (1620; STC 14764), Act 4, scene 2; Linda Pollock, *With Faith and Physic: The Life of a Tudor Gentlewoman. Lady Grace Mildmay 1552–1620* (1993), 135; Pollock, 'Embarking on a Rough Passage', 53–9.

45. Rueff, *Expert Midwife*, 59; N.H., *The Ladies Dictionary* (1694), 144.

46. *The examination and confession of certaine Wytches at Chensforde* (1566), in Barbara Rosen (ed.) *Witchcraft in England, 1558–1618* (Amherst, Mass., 1991), 73–5; Public Record Office, SP 12/130, fo. 128; SP 12/131, no. 26.1; Porter, *Cambridgeshire Customs*, 11; Riddle, *Contraception and Abortion*, 156; Shorter, *History of Women's Bodies*, 183–6. Graham Swift's novel *Waterland* (1983) includes a graphic account of a botched abortion in the mid-20th cent. fenland.

47. John Addy, *Sin and Society in the Seventeenth Century* (1989), 139; Berkshire Record Office, D/A2/c74, fo. 479. For similar cases from Somerset and Essex, see G. R. Quaife, *Wanton Wenches and Wayward Wives: Peasants and Illicit Sex in Early Seventeenth Century England* (1979), 118–20; Alan Macfarlane, 'Illegitimacy and Illegitimates in English History', in Peter Laslett, Karla Oosterveen, and Richard M. Smith (eds.), *Bastardy and its Comparative History* (Cambridge, Mass., 1980), 76–7.

48. Essex Record Office, T/A 4651, Colchester Book of Examinations and Recognisances, 1619–1645. Downes and her associates were charged with infanticide.

49. Rueff, *Expert Midwife*, 60; Oliver, *A Present to be Given to Teeming Women*, 25.

50. Bunworth, *Doctoresse*, 10–19; Barrough, *Method of Physick*, 186; Martin Ingram, *Church Courts, Sex and Marriage in England, 1570–1640* (Cambridge, 1987), 159.

51. Boorde, *The Breviary of Health*, fos. 8, 55ᵛ, 127; Culpeper, *Directory for Midwives*, 95–6; Sharp, *Midwives Book*, 221–4, 261; Rueff, *Expert Midwife*, 61. See also Wolveridge, *Speculum Matricis Hybernicum*, 106–7.

52. Parkinson, *Paradisi In Sole*, 289, 335, 453, 456, 479, 491; Leonard Sowerby, *The Ladies Dispensatory, Containing the Natures, Vertues, and Qualities of all Herbs* (1652), 146–53, 158–6; Gerarde, *Herball*, 60, 79, 694, 833, 845–6, 909, 1014, 1104, 1121, 1246, 1428.

53. Richard Adams, 'How may Child-Bearing Women be Most Encouraged?', in Samuel Annesley (ed.), *A Continuation of Morning-Exercise Questions and Cases of Conscience* (1683), 661, 649; Oliver, *Present for Teeming Women*, sig. A4ᵛ.

54. John Canne, *A Necessity of Separation from the Church of England* (Amsterdam, 1634; STC 4574), 110; John Rylands Library, Manchester, Ms. 524, 'The Acts and Speeches of Richard Greenham', fo. 35ᵛ.

55. Sharp, *Midwives Book*, 187; Barret, *Companion for Midwives*, 6; Margaret Cavendish (Duchess of Newcastle), *CCXI Sociable Letters* (1664), 95. See also A. Marsh, *The Ten Pleasures of Marriage* (1682), 105–6, for a satiric male perspective on the abundance and complexity of childbed linen.

56. Guillemeau, *Child-Birth*, 87–8; Rueff, *Expert Midwife*, 79–80; Roesslin, *Birth of Man-kinde*, 100, 107; Crooke, *Microcosmographia*, 269; Sermon, *Ladies Companion*, 94–5; Sharp, *Midwives Book*, 204; Barret, *Companion for Midwives*, 8; Wolveridge, *Speculum Matricis Hybernicum*, 27; Pechey, *General Treatise of the Diseases of Maids*, 125–6; Pechey, *Compleat Midwife's Practice Enlarged*, 109; English Midwife Enlarged, 36; Marsh, *Ten Pleasures of Marriage*, 111; M. Halsey Thomas (ed.), *The Diary of Samuel Sewall 1674–1729*, 2 vols. (New York, 1973), i. 41. See also Adrian Wilson, 'The Ceremony of Childbirth and its Interpretation', in Valerie Fildes (ed.), *Women as Mothers in Pre-Industrial England* (1990), 74, for the variety of birthing techniques.

57. Guillemeau, *Child-Birth*, 87; Sermon, *Ladies Companion*, 93; Gélis, *History of Childbirth*, 119.

58. Guillemeau, *Child-Birth*, 190; 'As for Deliverance of a Queen', in *A Collection of Ordinances and Regulations for the Government of the Royal Household, Made in Divers Reigns* (1790), 125.

59. Fonteyn, *Womans Doctour*, 200; Gélis, *History of Childbirth*, 97; Adrian Wilson, 'Participant or Patient? Seventeenth Century Childbirth from the Mother's Point of View', in Roy Porter (ed.), *Patients and Practitioners: Lay Perceptions of Medicine in Pre-Industrial Society* (Cambridge, 1986), 134–5; Wilson, 'Ceremony of Childbirth', 73, 82.

60. Pollock, 'Embarking on a Rough Passage', 51.

61. W. G. Perrin (ed.), *The Autobiography of Phineas Pett* (Navy Records Society; 1918), 17.

62. F. W. Bennitt (ed.), 'The Diary of Isabella, Wife of Sir Roger Twysden, Baronet, of Royden Hall, East Peckham, 1645–1651', *Archaeologia Cantiana*, 51 (1939–40), 117, 121; de Beer (ed.), *Diary of John Evelyn*, iv. 282; Charles Kerry, 'Leonard Wheatcroft of Ashover', *Journal of the Derbyshire Archaeology and Natural History Society*, 21 (1899), 50.

CHAPTER 3

1. Adrian Wilson, 'The Ceremony of Childbirth and its Interpretation', in Valerie Fildes (ed.), *Women as Mothers in Pre-Industrial England* (1990), 39–67; Gail Paster,

The Body Embarrassed: Drama and the Disciplines of Shame in Early Modern England (Ithaca, New York, 1993), 185.

2. John Jones, *The Arte and Science of Preserving Bodie and Soul* (1579; STC 14724), 31–2; Robert Barret, *A Companion for Midwives, Child-Bearing Women, and Nurses* (1699), 7; Samuel Hieron, *A Helpe vnto Deuotion* (1612; STC 13407), 276–7.

3. *Oxford English Dictionary*, vi. 699–700.

4. F. P. Wilson (ed.), *The Batchelars Banquet* (Oxford, 1929), 21–2. The work is sometimes attributed to Thomas Dekker. See also A. Marsh, *The Ten Pleasures of Marriage* (1682), 111; *The Pleasures of Matrimony* (1688), 129–30; and Jacques Gélis, *History of Childbirth: Fertility, Pregnancy and Birth in Early Modern Europe* (Cambridge, 1991), 100, on 'les Caquets de l'accouchée' in 17th-cent. France; John Brand, *Observations on Popular Antiquities*, 2 vols. (1813), ii. 1–6.

5. J. Charles Cox, *The Parish Registers of England* (1910), 57; British Library, Lansdowne Ms. 101, fos. 20–3; Folger Shakespeare Library, Bagot Ms. L.a. 258; 'As for Deliverance of a Queen', in *A Collection of Ordinances and Regulations for the Government of the Royal Household, Made in Divers Reigns* (1790), 125–6.

6. C. W. Foster, *The State of the Church in the Reigns of Elizabeth and James I as Illustrated by Documents Relating to the Diocese of Lincoln* (Lincoln Record Society; Lincoln, 1926), xcvi; *Strange Newes out of Kent, of a Monstrous and misshapen Child, borne in Olde Sandwich* (1609; STC 14934), sigs. A4ᵛ, B; Oxfordshire Archives, Archdeaconry, c. 12, fo. 75ᵛ.

7. Alice Thornton, *The Autobiography of Mrs. Alice Thornton* (Surtees Society; Durham, 1875), 141; Mary Carbery (ed.), *Mrs. Elizabeth Freke Her Diary 1671 to 1714* (Cork, 1913), 25.

8. Dorothy M. Meads (ed.), *Diary of Lady Margaret Hoby 1599–1605* (1930), 63, 184, 195; New College, Oxford, Ms. 9502, 'Robert Woodforde's Diary'.

9. British Library, Lansdowne Ms. 101, fo. 25; Charles Severn (ed.), *Diary of the Rev. John Ward . . . 1648 to 1679* (1839), 102; Alan Macfarlane (ed.), *The Diary of Ralph Josselin 1616–1683* (1976), 12, 111, 165.

10. Thomas Heywood (ed.), *The Diary of the Rev. Henry Newcome, from September 30, 1661, to September 29, 1663* (Chetham Society; Manchester, 1849), 62, 155.

11. Useful studies include Thomas G. Benedek, 'The Changing Relationship between Midwives and Physicians during the Renaissance', *Bulletin of the History of Medicine*, 51 (1977), 550–64; Jean Donnison, *Midwives and Medical Men: A History of the Struggle for the Control of Childbirth* (2nd edn., 1988); Hilary Marland (ed.), *The Art of Midwifery: Early Modern Midwives in Europe* (1993). See also Alice Clark, *Working Life of Women in the Seventeenth Century* (1919, repr. 1982), 265–85.

12. Thomas Rogers Forbes, *The Midwife and the Witch* (New Haven and London, 1966), 112–32; Lawrence Stone, *The Family, Sex and Marriage in England 1500–1800* (abridged edn., New York, 1979), 64.

13. Barbara Ehrenreich and Deirdre English, *Witches, Midwives and Nurses: A History of Women Healers* (Old Westbury, New York, 1973 and later edns.), 6, 13, 15;

Barbara G. Walker, *The Crone: Women of Age, Wisdom and Power* (San Francisco, 1985), 128; Robert A. Erickson, *Mother Midnight: Birth, Sex, and Fate in Eighteenth-Century Fiction* (New York, 1986), x. For a thorough assault on this type of gullibility, see Ronald Hutton, *The Pagan Religions of the Ancient British Isles: Their Nature and Legacy* (Oxford, 1991).

14. Clive Holmes, 'Popular Culture? Witches, Magistrates, and Divines in Early Modern England', in Steven L. Kaplan (ed.), *Understanding Popular Culture* (Berlin, 1984), 98–9. Christina Larner, *Witchcraft and Religion: The Politics of Popular Belief* (Oxford, 1984), 149–52, considers the view that the witch-hunts were 'an attempt by the emergent male medical profession to eliminate competition from female healers'. For a devastating critique of widely held opinions, see David Harley, 'Historians as Demonologists: The Myth of the Midwife-Witch', *Social History of Medicine*, 3 (1990), 1–26.

15. Some of the confusion may be traced to the claim by Elizabeth Cellier, a catholic court midwife under James II, that ancient midwives in Hebrew, Egyptian, Athenian, and British traditions were devotees of female deities. Elizabeth Cellier, *To Dr. —, An Answer to his Queries concerning the Colledg of Midwives* (1688). Cf. Ann Barbeau Gardiner, 'Elizabeth Cellier in 1688 on Envious Doctors and Heroic Midwives Ancient and Modern', *Eighteenth-Century Life*, 14 (1990), 24–34; and Helen King, 'The Politick Midwife: Models of Midwifery in the Work of Elizabeth Cellier', in Marland (ed.), *Art of Midwifery*, 115–30. Harley's historiographical review, tracing the baneful influence of Margaret Murray in this regard, is most convincing, 'Historians as Demonologists', 18–20.

16. Claude Jenkins (ed.), 'An Unpublished Record of Archbishop Parker's Visitation in 1573', *Archaeologia Cantiana*, 29 (1911), 291; PRO SP 12/131, no. 26.1. See also the Oxfordshire midwife who searched the body of the pregnant Joan Cary in 1631, in Oxfordshire Archives, Diocesan Papers, c. 2, fo. 101; G. R. Quaife, *Wanton Wenches and Wayward Wives: Peasants and Illicit Sex in early Seventeenth Century England* (1979), 89; David Harley, 'Provincial Midwives in England: Lancashire and Cheshire, 1660–1760', in Marland (ed.), *Art of Midwifery*, 36–9.

17. See, however, *The Wicked Midwife, the cruell Mother, and the harmlesse Daughter* (c.1640; STC 17915.7); *The Murderous Midwife, with her Roasted Punishement* (1673). The latter refers to an infanticide scandal in France.

18. *A Declaration of a Strange and Wonderfull Monster* (1646), 7; Norfolk Record Office, Norwich, TES/1, 7; Harley, 'Provincial Midwives in England', 31–2, 42; Lichfield Record Office, Transcript 51/69, 'Bishop Lloyd's Survey of Eccleshall, 1693–98', 18, 32; Doreen Evenden, 'Mothers and their Midwives in Seventeenth-Century London', in Marland (ed.), *Art of Midwifery*, 9–26.

19. Contrast the views of Hilda Smith, 'Gynecology and Ideology in Seventeenth-Century England', in Berenice A. Carroll (ed.), *Liberating Women's History: Theoretical and Critical Essays* (Urbana, Ill., 1976), 97–114, and Barbara Brandon Schnorrenberg, 'Is Childbirth any Place for a Woman? The Decline of Midwifery in Eighteenth-Century England', *Studies in Eighteenth-Century Culture*, 10 (1981),

393–408. See also Adrian Wilson, *The Making of Man-midwifery: Childbirth in England, 1660–1770* (1995).

20. *The Mid-wives Just Petition* (1643), sig. A2ᵛ; *The Mid-wives Just Complaint* (1646), sig. A2ᵛ; Ned Ward, *The London-Spy* (1703), 404; Erickson, *Mother Midnight*, x.

21. For baptism by midwives, see below, Ch. 5.

22. Marsh, *Ten Pleasures of Marriage*, 130.

23. Thomas Bentley, *The Monument of Matrons* (1582; STC 1893), 'The Fift Lampe', 134; Jacob Rueff, *The Expert Midwife* (1637; STC 21442), 44, 78, 81.

24. John Pechey, *The Compleat Midwife's Practice Enlarged* (5th edn., 1698), 113.

25. Jane Sharp, *The Midwives Book. Or the Whole Art of Midwifery Discovered: Directing Childbearing Women how to behave themselves in the Conception, Breeding, Bearing, and Nursing of Children* (1671), 198–9; Rueff, *Expert Midwife*, 78. Comparable advice appeared in Eucharius Roesslin, *The Birth of Man-Kinde; Otherwise Named The Womans Book* (1626; STC 21163), 97, 121–2; Jacques Guillemeau, *Child-Birth Or, The Happy Deliverie of Women* (1612; STC 12496), 195–6; A.M., *A Rich Closet of Physical Secrets* (1652), 14–17; Nicholas Fonteyn, *The Womans Doctour* (1652), 201; James Wolveridge, *Speculum Matricis Hybernicum; or, The Irish Midwives Handmaid* (1670), 28; Pechey, *Compleat Midwife's Practice Enlarged*, 124, 128.

26. Guillemeau, *Child-Birth*, 86; William Sermon, *The Ladies Companion, or the English Midwife* (1671), 6; Nicholas Culpeper, *A Directory for Midwives: Or, A Guide for Women, In their Conception, Bearing, and Suckling their Children* (1651), 160, 172; Francis Mauriceau, *The Diseases of Women with Child* (1683) 'the translator to the reader'; Pechey, *Compleat Midwife's Practice Enlarged*, sig. A3, 107–8; Barret, *Companion for Midwives*, 10–14.

27. Helkiah Crooke, *Microcosmographia: A Description of the Body of Man* (2nd edn., 1631; STC 6063), 269; Sermon, *Ladies Companion*, 5. See also Wolveridge, *Speculum Matricis Hybernicum*, 29; Pechey, *Compleat Midwife's Practice Enlarged*, 107.

28. Sharp, *Midwives Book*, 3; Harley, 'Provincial Midwives in England', 29.

29. *Statutes of the Realm*, 3 Henry VIII, c. 11; Andrew Boorde, *The Breviary of Health, for all maner of sickenesses and diseases the which may be in man or woman* (1552), bk. 2, fo. 15ᵛ; Elizabeth Cellier, *To Dr. — An Answer to his Queries, concerning the Colledg of Midwives* (1688), 6; John R. Guy, 'The Episcopal Licensing of Physicians, Surgeons and Midwives', *Bulletin of the History of Medicine*, 56 (1982), 528–42.

30. Norfolk Record Office, VIS/8, Table of Fees, 1687; Harley, 'Provincial Midwives in England', 30.

31. W. H. Frere and W. M. Kennedy (eds.), *Visitation Articles and Injunctions of the Period of the Reformation*, 3 vols. (1910), ii. 58–9.

32. John Bale, *A Declaration of Edmonde Bonners articles concerning the cleargye of London dyocese* (1561; STC 1289), fos. 61, 64ᵛ.

33. John Strype, *Annals of the Reformation*, 3 vols. (Oxford, 1824), i. 243.

34. *The Book of Oaths* (1689), 161–4.

35. Guildhall Library, MS. 9057/1, fo. 2ᵛ; Oxfordshire Archives, Diocesan Papers, c. 18, fos. 143, 148. See also Lincolnshire Archives, Vj 27, fos. 5, 34, 36, 38, 47, 48.

36. *Articles to be enquired of within the Dioces of Winchester, in the Metropolitical visitation* (1590; STC 10355), no. 46; 'Articles to be Enquired of Within the Dioces of London . . . 1628' in *The Works of . . . William Laud, D.D.*, 7 vols. (Oxford 1853), v. 417. Cf. Archbishop Grindal's articles of 1576 in William Nicholson (ed.), *The Remains of Edmund Grindal* (Parker Society; Cambridge, 1843), 174.

37. West Sussex Record Office, Diocese of Chichester, Churchwarden's Presentment, Ep 1/23/5.

38. Ibid.

39. e.g. Norfolk Record Office, TES/3; Guildhall Library, Ms. 10,116; Canterbury Cathedral Archives, L.P.L. vx 1a/11; Forbes, *Midwife and the Witch*, 150–5 and pls. 1–8 following p. 144; Cheshire Record Office, Chester, EDC 5 1663/16.

40. F. R. Raines (ed.), *The Derby Household Books* (Chetham Society; Manchester, 1853), 42; Alison D. Wall (ed.), *Two Elizabethan Women: Correspondence of Joan and Maria Thynne 1575–1611* (Wiltshire Record Society; Devizes, 1983), 6; Dorothy Gardiner (ed.), *The Oxinden Letters 1607–1642* (1933), 24.

41. Michael Drayton, 'The Moone-Calfe', in J. William Hebel (ed.), *The Works of Michael Drayton*, 5 vols. (Oxford, 1961), iii. 166. In this poem the world itself is in labour, in need of midwife and gossips.

42. New College, Oxford, Ms. 9502, 'Robert Woodforde's Diary'.

43. E. M. Symonds (ed.), 'The Diary of John Greene (1635–57)', *English Historical Review*, 43 (1928), 599.

44. Macfarlane (ed.), *The Diary of Ralph Josselin*, 50.

45. Ibid. 415.

46. Carbery (ed.), *Mrs. Elizabeth Freke Her Diary*, 24–5.

47. Patricia Crawford, 'The Construction and Experience of Maternity in Seventeenth-Century England', in Valerie Fildes (ed.), *Women as Mothers in Pre-Industrial England* (1990), 21; *Strange Newes out of Kent*, sig. B2; T. N. Brushfield (ed.), 'The Financial Diary of a Citizen of Exeter, 1631–43', *Reports and Transactions of the Devonshire Association*, 33 (1901), 206, 207, 211.

48. British Library, Egerton Ms. 3054, fo. 25; R. G. Griffiths, 'Joyce Jeffreys of Ham Castle: A Seventeenth-Century Business Gentlewoman', *Transactions of the Worcestershire Archaeological Society*, 11 (1935), 2; Ruth Bird (ed.), *The Journal of Giles Moore* (Lewes, 1971), 78, 336.

49. Bodleian Library, Rawlinson Ms. D 1141, fo. 27ᵛ; Harley, 'Provincial Midwives in England', 33–4.

50. Alan MacFarlane, 'Illegitimacy and Illegitimates in English History', in Peter Laslett, Karla Oosterveen, and Richard M. Smith (eds.), *Bastardy and its Comparative History* (Cambridge, Mass., 1980), 71–85; David Levine and Keith Wrightson, 'The Social Context of Illegitimacy in Early modern England', ibid. 158–75; Keith Wrightson, 'The Nadir of English Illegitimacy in the Seventeenth Century', ibid. 176–91; Martin Ingram, *Church Courts, Sex and Marriage in England, 1570–1640* (Cambridge, 1987), 158, 166, 276–7.

51. Quaife, *Wanton Wenches and Wayward Wives*, 90–1; Levine and Wrightson, 'Social Context of Illegitimacy', table 5.4, 164. For more on sexual behaviour during courtship, see below, Ch. 11.

52. Macfarlane, 'Illegitimacy and Illegitimates', 73–6, 84–5; Wrightson, 'Nadir of English Illegitimacy', 177. The evidence of creative literature, still largely unexamined by historians, may prove particularly fruitful in this regard.

53. William Lambard, *Eirenarcha, Or the Office of the Iustices of Peace . . . enlarged* (1610; STC 15172), 350, 357; Ferdinando Pulton (ed.), *A Kalender, Or Table, Comprehending the effect of all the Statutes* (1612; STC 9549), fos. 139–139ᵛ; John Cordy Jeaffreson (ed.), *Middlesex County Records*, 4 vols. (1886–92), *passim*; Staffordshire Record Office, Q/SO 4, Quarter Sessions Order Book, 1631–1639, Q/SR/231, Quarter Sessions Rolls, 1637/8.

54. British Library, Lansdowne Ms. 101, fos. 21–33. Agnes Bowker's story is told in full in David Cressy, 'De la Fiction dans les Archives? Ou le Monstre de 1569', *Annales E.S.C.* 48 (1993), 1309–29.

55. Public Record Office, SP 12/123, fo. 70; SP 12/131, no. 26.1. 'Dragon water' was most likely derived from dracunculus, dragonwort, or 'dragon', a garden or pond plant, which when distilled 'hath virtue against the pestilence or any pestilential fever or poison' but also 'scoureth and cleaneth mightily' and is 'hurtful to women newly conceived with child'. John Gerarde, *The Herball or Generall Historie of Plantes* (1636; STC 11752), 60, 831–3, 845, 1130.

56. Lincolnshire Archives, Diocesan Court Papers, CP 68/2, no. 15.

57. *Statutes of the Realm*, 21 Jac. I, c. 27, 1624; Keith Wrightson, 'Infanticide in Earlier Seventeenth-Century England', *Local Population Studies*, 15 (1975), 10–22; J. A. Sharpe, *Early Modern England: A Social History 1550–1760* (1987), 45–6; Peter C. Hoffer and N. E. H. Hull, *Murdering Mothers: Infanticide in England and New England 1558–1803* (New York, 1981).

58. Jenkins (ed.), 'An Unpublished Record of Archbishop Parker's Visitation', 291.

59. Richard Brome, *A Joviall Crew: or, The Merry Beggars* (1652), sig. F2.

60. British Library, Additional Ms. 33,410, fo. 80.

61. Guildhall Library, Ms. 9064/18, fo. 32ᵛ; Ms. 9064/20, fo. 167ᵛ; Greater London Record Office, DL/C 316, fo. 42ᵛ; *William Whiteway of Dorchester His Diary 1618 to 1635* (Dorset Record Society; Dorchester, 1991), 151.

62. Thomas Heywood, *The Wise Woman of Hogsdon* (1638; STC 13370), Act 3, scene 2. The play was written *c.*1604.

63. Guildhall Library, Ms. 9064/17, fo. 33; Ms. 9064/21, fos. 80ᵛ, 152ᵛ; Ms. 9064/19, fo. 34; Ms. 9064/20, fo. 134. Cf. Quaife, *Wanton Wenches and Wayward Wives*, 103, on 'places that made a business of caring for the pregnant spinster and supervising her travail'.

64. Guildhall Library, Ms. 9064/13, fo. 30; Ms. 9064/15, fo. 186.

65. Oxfordshire Archives, Diocesan Papers, c. 18, fos. 52, 54ᵛ, 84ᵛ; Guildhall Library, Ms. 9064/16, fo. 74.

66. Oxfordshire Archives, Diocesan Papers, c. 16, fos. 72–72ᵛ; Lichfield Record Office, B/C/5, 'Lomasse v. Backe'.

CHAPTER 4

1. William Sermon, *The Ladies Companion, or the English Midwife* (1671), 108.
2. John Jones, *The Arte and Science of Preserving Bodie and Soul* (1579; STC 14724), 35; Jane Sharp, *The Midwives Book. Or the Whole Art of Midwifery Discovered. Directing Childbearing Women how to behave themselves in the Conception, Breeding, Bearing, and Nursing of Children* (1671), 375. See also Jacob Rueff, *The Expert Midwife* (1637; STC 21442), 82; Thomas Browne, *Pseudodoxia Epidemica: or, Enquiries into Very Many Received Tenents and Commonly Presumed Truths* (1650), 202; Nicholas Culpeper, *A Directory for Midwives: Or, A Guide for Women, In their Conception, Bearing, and Suckling their Children* (1651), 172–80; Philip Barrough, *The Method of Physick* (1652), 204; Richard Bunworth, *The Doctoresse: A plain and easie method of curing those diseases which are peculiar to women* (1656), 60; James Wolveridge, *Speculum Matricis Hybernicum; or, The Irish Midwives Handmaid* (1670), 30; W.M., *The Queens Closet Opened* (1674), 156; John Pechey, *A General Treatise of the Diseases of Maids, Big-Bellied Women, Child-bed Women, and Widows* (1696), 128–9; id., *The Compleat Midwife's Practice Enlarged* (5th edn., 1698), 113; Robert Barret, *A Companion for Midwives, Child-Bearing Women, and Nurses* (1699), 12–14.
3. Sharp, *Midwives Book*, 212, 373; Helkiah Crooke, *Microcosmographia: A Description of the Body of Man* (2nd edn., 1631; STC 6063), 210; Culpeper, *Directory for Midwives*, 174–5; Thomas Lupton, *A Thousand Notable Things of Sundrie Sorts* (1631; STC 16961), 13. See also Heather Dubrow, 'Navel Battles: Interpreting Renaissance Gynecological Manuals,' *ANQ* 5 (1992), 67–71.
4. Eucharius Roesslin, *The Birth of Man-Kinde; Otherwise Named The Womans Booke* (1626; STC 21163), 154; Rueff, *Expert Midwife*, 192; Culpeper, *Directory for Midwives*, 175; Sharp, *Midwives Book*, 214–15.
5. Wolveridge, *Speculum Matricis Hybernicum*, 30; Roesslin, *Birth of Man-Kinde*, 155; John Geninges, *The Life and Death of Mr. E. Geninges* (St Omer, 1614; STC 11728), 14.
6. Jones, *Arte and Science of Preserving Bodie and Soul*, 32; Rueff, *Expert Midwife*, 94; Roesslin, *Birth of Man-Kinde*, 154; Pechey, *Compleat Midwife's Practice Enlarged*, 120; Barret, *Companion for Midwives*, 14.
7. Rueff, *Expert Midwife*, 97.
8. Jacques Gélis, *History of Childbirth: Fertility, Pregnancy and Birth in Early Modern Europe* (Cambridge, 1991), 195, 204; Enid Porter, *Cambridgeshire Customs and Folklore* (1969), 15.
9. Jones, *Arte and Science of Preserving Bodie and Soul*, 35, 156.
10. Henry Smith, *A Preparative to Marriage. The Summe whereof was spoken at a contract and inlarged after* (1591; STC 22686), 79; William Gouge, *Of Domesticall Dvties* (1622; STC 12119), 507.
11. Sharp, *Midwives Book*, 372–3; William Keatinge Clay (ed.), *Liturgical Services. Liturgies and Occasional Forms of Prayer Set Forth in the Reign of Queen Elizabeth* (Cambridge, 1847), 237.

12. Sharp, *Midwives Book*, 230; Nicholas Fonteyn, *The Womans Doctour* (1652), 216; Wolveridge, *Speculum Matricis Hybernicum*, 31; John Day, *Day's Festivals or, Twelve of His Sermons* (Oxford, 1615; STC 6426), 236.

13. Harry Oxorn, *Human Labor and Birth* (5th edn., 1986), 865.

14. Jacques Guillemeau, *Child-Birth Or, The Happy Deliverie of Women* (1612; STC 12496), 102–3; Fonteyn, *Womans Doctour*, 216; Wolveridge, *Speculum Matricis Hybernicum*, 126–9; *Of Physical Secrets* (1652), 17; Sharp, *Midwives Book*, 229; James Primrose, *Popular Errours: Or the Errours of the People in Physick* (1651), 177–8. Primrose's book was first published in Latin in 1638.

15. Oxorn, *Human Labor and Birth*, 865–6.

16. Sharp, *Midwives Book*, 233–4; Wolveridge, *Speculum Matricis Hybernicum*, 115; A.M., *Rich Closet*, 16.

17. See below, Ch. 9.

18. Guillemeau, *Child-Birth*, 103, 194; Sermon, *Ladies Companion*, 111.

19. Rupert H. Morris, *Chester in the Plantagenet and Tudor Reigns* (Chester, 1893), 336; Mary Bateson (ed.), *Records of the Borough of Leicester . . . 1509–1603* (Cambridge, 1905), 122; Richard S. Ferguson (ed.), *A Boke off Recorde or Register . . . of Kirkbiekendall . . . 1575* (Kendal, 1892), 89–90. The primary target of this regulation was gossips' feasts at churchings.

20. Robert Hill, *The Pathway to Prayer and Pietie* (1610; STC 13473), 412.

21. F. P. Wilson (ed.), *The Batchelars Banquet* (Oxford, 1929), 68, 22.

22. Margaret Cavendish (Duchess of Newcastle), *Playes* (1662), 401; ead., *CCXI Sociable Letters* (1664), 96–7; *The Pleasures of Matrimony* (1688), 127–8. For ballads in this vein see J. A. Sharpe, 'Plebeian Marriage in Stuart England: Some Evidence from Popular Literature', *Transactions of the Royal Historical Society*, 5th ser. 36 (1986), 81.

23. Henry Parrot, *The Gossips Greeting* (1620; STC 19331); Michael Drayton, 'The Moone-Calfe', in J. William Hebel (ed.), *The Works of Michael Drayton*, 5 vols. (Oxford, 1961), iii. 166–202. See also Samuel Rowlands, *A Whole Crew of Kind Gossips all met to be Merry* (1609; STC 21413); *The Gossips Feast or Morral Tales* (1647); *The Gossips Meeting. Or, The Merry Market Women of Taunton* (c.1674).

24. Guillemeau, *Child-Birth*, 199, 221.

25. N.H., *The Ladies Dictionary* (1694), 235; Wilson (ed.), *Batchelars Banquet*, 29, 31.

26. Quoted in Diana O'Hara, ' "Ruled by My Friends": Aspects of Marriage in the Diocese of Canterbury, c.1540–1570', *Continuity and Change*, 6 (1991), 31.

27. Guildhall Library, Ms. 9064/18, fos. 31ᵛ–32ᵛ; Oxfordshire Archives, Archdeaconry Papers, c. 12, fos. 75–75ᵛ. For an extended analysis of this case see David Cressy, 'Gender Trouble and Cross-Dressing in Early Modern England', *Journal of British Studies* (1996).

28. F. R. Raines (ed.), *The Journal of Nicholas Assheton* (Chetham Society; Manchester, 1848), 19, 84; Richard Parkinson (ed.), *The Autobiography of Henry Newcome, M.A.* (Chetham Society; Manchester, 1852), 63–4.

29. Frances Parthenope Verney (ed.), *Memoirs of the Verney Family During the Civil*

War, 2 vols. (1892), ii. 268; Edmund Hobhouse (ed.), *The Diary of a West Country Physician. AD 1684–1726* (1935), 57; E. S. de Beer (ed.), *The Diary of John Evelyn*, 6 vols. (Oxford, 1955), iv. 587, 591.

30. Valerie A. Fildes, *Breasts, Bottles and Babies: A History of Infant Feeding* (Edinburgh, 1986), 98–133, 152–63; ead., *Wet Nursing: A History from Antiquity to the Present* (Oxford, 1988), 79–100; Marylyn Salmon, 'The Cultural Significance of Breastfeeding and Infant Care in Early Modern England and America', *Journal of Social History*, 28 (1994), 247–69; David Harley, 'From Providence to Nature: The Moral Theology and Godly Practice of Maternal Breast-feeding in Stuart England', *Bulletin of the History of Medicine*, 69 (1995), 198–223.

31. John Sadler, *The Sicke Womans Private Looking-Glasse* (1636; STC 21544), 10; Roesslin, *Birth of Man-Kinde*, 73; Stephen Blancard, *A Physical Dictionary* (1684), 52. See also *The Problemes of Aristotle* (1597; STC 764); Primrose, *Popular Errours*, 182; Thomas Moffett, *Health's Improvement* (1655), 119.

32. John Dod and Robert Cleaver, *A Godly Forme of Houshold Gouernment* (1630; STC 5388), sig. P5.

33. Bunworth, *The Doctoresse*, 62–4; Culpeper, *Directory for Midwives*, 203–12; Fonteyn, *Womans Doctour*, 243; W.M., *Queens Closet Opened*, 33, 108; John Gerarde, *The Herball or Generall Historie of Plantes* (1636; STC 11752), 232, 239, 296, 308, 524; Leonard Sowerby, *The Ladies Dispensatory* (1651), 79–81.

34. Roesslin, *Birth of Man-Kinde*, 156–7, 161; A.M., *Rich Closet*, 18; Fildes, *Wet Nursing*, 136.

35. Guillemeau, *Child-Birth*, part 2, 18, 'The Nursing of Children'; Roesslin, *Birth of Man-Kinde*, 161; Charles Severn (ed.), *Diary of the Rev. John Ward . . . 1648 to 1679* (1839), 254. For a personal record of nursing and weaning see *The Autobiography of Mrs. Alice Thornton* (Surtees Society; Durham, 1875), esp. pp. 92, 124, 142, 144, 148, 166.

36. Smith, *Preparative to Marriage*, 77; John Oliver, *A Present for Teeming Women. Or, Scripture-Directions for Women with Child, how to prepare for the hour of Travel* (1663), 17–18; Moffett, *Health's Improvement*, 120; Elizabeth Clinton, *The Covntesse of Lincolnes Nvrserie* (Oxford, 1622; STC 5432), 13.

37. John Knodel, 'Breast Feeding and Population Growth', *Science*, 198 (1977), 111–15; Dorothy McLaren, 'Marital Fertility and Lactation, 1570–1720', in Mary Prior (ed.), *Women in English Society, 1500–1800* (1985), 22–53; Chris Wilson, 'The Proximate Determinants of Marital Fertility in England 1600–1799', in Lloyd Bonfield, Richard M. Smith, and Keith Wrightson (eds.), *The World We Have Gained: Histories of Population and Social Structure* (Oxford, 1986), 225.

38. Clinton, *The Covntesse of Lincolnes Nvrserie*, sig. A2^v, 1–3, 5, 9–11, 14; Harley, 'From Providence to Nature', 205.

39. Dod and Cleaver, *Godly Forme of Houshold Gouernment*, sigs. P4^v–P5; William Gouge, *Of Domesticall Duties* (3rd edn., 1634; STC 12121), 517, 520; Daniel Rogers, *Matrimoniall Honovr: Or, The mutuall Crowne and comfort of godly, loyall, and chaste Marriage* (1642), 279. See also R. V. Schnucker, 'The English Puritans and

Pregnancy, Delivery and Breast Feeding', *History of Childhood Quarterly*, 1 (1974), 637–58.

40. *Autobiography of Mrs. Alice Thornton*, 92; Sharp, *Midwives Book*, 353.

41. Henry Newcome, *The Compleat Mother. or An Earnest Perswasive to all Mothers (especially those of Rank and Quality) to Nurse their own Children* (1695), 2, 6, 48–9, 53, 63, 106–7. Cf. 'The Dissertation of Favorinus, the philosopher, in which he endeavours to persuade a noble lady to nurse the children she had, or should bring forth, with her own, and not with foreign milk', translated by a Northamptonshire gentlewoman in the 1670s, British Library, Additional Ms. 27,440, 'Memoirs of Charles Allestree 1677–1702', fos. 27–9.

42. Roesslin, *Birth of Man-Kinde*, 157. Cf. Moffett, *Health's Improvement*, 126.

43. Sharp, *Midwives Book*, 363–5; *Problemes of Aristotle*; Primrose, *Popular Errours*, 183.

44. Roesslin, *Birth of Man-Kinde*, 160; Jones, *Arte and Science of Preserving Bodie and Soul*, 14; A.M., *Rich Closet*, 19.

45. Lady Newdigate-Newdegate (ed.), *Gossip from a Muniment Room: Being Passages in the Lives of Anne and Mary Fytton 1574 to 1618* (1897), 16, 17, 20.

46. Ibid. 52, 64.

47. Francis Bamford (ed.), *A Royalist's Notebook: The Commonplace Book of Sir John Oglander* (1936), 177; de Beer (ed.), *Diary of John Evelyn*, ii. 6. See also Lady Dorothy Rawden in 1664, 'I have agreed with a nurse . . . it is Higgersons's wife of Ballendart . . . her milk will not be above 16 or 17 weeks old as I think when I shall be brought to bed', Huntington Library, Hastings Irish Papers, HA 15615.

48. New College, Oxford, Ms. 9502, 'Robert Woodforde's Diary'.

49. Ibid.

50. Alan Macfarlane (ed.), *The Diary of Ralph Josselin 1616–1683* (1976), 12, 14, 51; Matthew Storey (ed.), *Two East Anglian Diaries, 1641–1729: Isaac Archer and William Coe* (Woodbridge, Suffolk, 1994), 150; *Autobiography of Mrs. Alice Thornton*, 124.

51. D. J. H. Clifford, *The Diaries of Lady Anne Clifford* (Stroud, 1990), 123.

52. Geninges, *Life and Death of Mr. E. Geninges*, 14–15.

CHAPTER 5

1. Arnold van Gennep, *The Rites of Passage* (Chicago, 1960); W. S. F. Pickering, 'The Persistence of Rites of Passage: Towards an Explanation', *British Journal of Sociology*, 25 (1974), 63–78; Victor Turner, *Dramas, Fields, and Metaphors: Symbolic Action in Human Society* (Ithaca, New York, 1974).

2. Thomas Comber, *A Brief Discourse Upon the Offices of Baptism and Confirmation* (1674), appended to his *A Companion to the Altar* (1675), 358, 411.

3. E. A. Wrigley and R. S. Schofield, *The Population History of England, 1541–1871* (Cambridge, Mass., 1981), 286–90.

4. Richard Hooker, 'Of the Laws of Ecclesiastical Politie', in *The Works of that Learned and Judicious Divine, Mr. Richard Hooker* (1723), 210.

5. William Keatinge Clay (ed.), *Liturgical Services: Liturgies and Occasional Forms*

of Prayer Set Forth in the Reign of Queen Elizabeth (Parker Society; Cambridge, 1847), 206.

6. Wrigley and Schofield, *Population History of England*, 289; B. Midi Berry and R. S. Schofield, 'Age at Baptism in Pre-Industrial England', *Population Studies*, 25 (1971), 453–63.

7. *Articles Whereupon it was agreed by the Archbishoppes and Bishoppes of both provinces and the whole cleargie* (1571; STC 10036a), no. 27; Hooker, 'Of the Laws of Ecclesiastical Politie', 212–20; William Perkins, *A Golden Chaine; or, The Description of Theologie, Containing the Order of the Causes of Saluation and Damnation* (Cambridge, 1600; STC 19646), 110; John Day, *Day's Festivals or, Twelve of His Sermons* (Oxford, 1615; STC 6426), 111; Anthony Sparrow, *A Rationale upon the Book of Common Prayer of the Church of England* (1668), 289.

8. F. D. Price (ed.), *The Commission for Ecclesiastical Causes within the Dioceses of Bristol and Gloucester, 1574* (Bristol and Gloucestershire Archaeological Society; Bristol, 1972), 37, 39, 64, 69–70, 74, 76–8, 106.

9. Ibid. 39–40, 103–4.

10. Ibid. 107–8; *Calendar of State Papers, Domestic, 1581–90*, 32.

11. Norfolk Record Office, Norwich, VIS 5/3/3 *sub* 'Sturston'; W. M. Palmer (ed.), *Episcopal Visitation Returns for Cambridgeshire: Matthew Wren, Bishop of Ely, 1638–1665* (Cambridge, 1930), 20.

12. Examples from the 1620s appear in Norfolk Record Office, VIS 5/3/1 *sub* 'Yaxham'; VIS 6/1, fo. 37.

13. William H. Hale (ed.), *A Series of Precedents and Proceedings in Criminal Causes* (1847), 193, 216; Hilda Johnstone (ed.), *Churchwardens' Presentments (17th Century) Part 1. Archdeaconry of Chichester* (Sussex Record Society; Lewes, 1947–8), 77; Hereford Record Office, Court Books, Box 27/98; Lichfield Record Office, B/V/1/64.

14. Guildhall Library, Ms. 9064/14, fo. 89; J. F. Williams (ed.), *Diocese of Norwich: Bishop Redman's Visitation 1597* (Norfolk Record Society; Norwich, 1946), 74, 103.

15. E. S. de Beer (ed.), *The Diary of John Evelyn*, 6 vols. (Oxford, 1955), v. 190, 194.

16. e.g. Canterbury Cathedral Archives, U3/65/1/1, parish register of Herne, Kent, 14 Sept. 1571: 'A wayfaring woman delivered in the fields by the butts and harboured in Barbone's widow's house, whose child is baptised and called Mark', and 24 Aug. 1573: 'Thomas, an infant fathered upon Mason the butcher, the mother's confession in her travail, baptised'; Staffordshire Record Office, parish register of St Peter, Wolverhampton, 1638: 'Elizabeth, the daughter of the people, was baptised the 14th day of November'.

17. Guildhall Library, Ms. 9064/13, fo. 30; W. J. Sheils (ed.), *Archbishop Grindal's Visitation, 1575: Comperta et Detecta Book* (York, 1977), 54; *The Injunctions and other Ecclesiastical Proceedings of Richard Barnes, Bishop of Durham from 1575 to 1587* (Surtees Society; Durham, 1850), 126.

18. Hereford Record Office, Court Books, Box 18/71; Claude Jenkins (ed.), 'Act Books of the Archdeacon of Taunton, 1623–4', Somerset Record Society, *Collecteana II* (1928), 50; Guildhall Library, Ms. 9583/2, part 5, fo. 1.

19. Colin W. Field, *The State of the Church in Gloucestershire, 1563* (Robertsbridge, Sussex, 1971), 25, 28; *Injunctions*, 139.

20. *Injunctions*, 136–7; Hale (ed.), *A Series of Precedents and Proceedings*, 256; Williams (ed.), *Diocese of Norwich: Bishop Redman's Visitation*, 51.

21. *The Acts of the High Commission Court Within the Diocese of Durham* (Surtees Society; Durham, 1857), 5; Lincolnshire Archives, Court Papers, Box 69/2, no. 26; Somerset Record Office, D.D. Ca. 289, fo. 169; Guildhall Library, Ms. 9583/2, part 3, fos. 124–5.

22. Hooker, 'Of the Laws of Ecclesiastical Politie', 217.

23. Clay (ed.), *Liturgical Services*, 199–205.

24. J. D. C. Fisher, *Christian Initiation: Baptism in the Medieval West* (1963), 172–9; id., *Christian Initiation: The Reformation Period* (1970), 80–4; Joseph Ketley (ed.), *The Two Liturgies, A.D. 1549, and A.D. 1552* (Parker Society; Cambridge, 1844), 106–13, 284–90; William Keeling (ed.), *Liturgiae Britannicae, or The Several Editions of the Book of Common Prayer . . . Arranged to Shew their Respective Variations* (2nd edn., 1851). See also G. W. Bromiley, *Baptism and the Anglican Reformers* (1953); Hughes Oliphant Old, *The Shaping of the Reformed Baptismal Rite in the Sixteenth Century* (Grand Rapids, Mich., 1992).

25. 'An Act for the Uniformity of Common Prayer' (1 Eliz., c. 2), printed in the Book of Common Prayer, Clay (ed.), *Liturgical Services*, 27–32; canon 30 in J. V. Bullard (ed.), *Constitutions and Canons Ecclesiastical* (1934), 260–4.

26. Clay (ed.), *Liturgical Services*, 199–203.

27. Ibid. 203–5.

28. 'An Admonition to the Parliament [1572]' in W. H. Frere and C. E. Douglas (eds.), *Puritan Manifestoes* (1954), 14, 21.

29. Leland H. Carlson (ed.), *The Writings of Henry Barrow 1587–1590* (1962), 432; John Canne, *A Necessity of Separation from the Church of England* (Amsterdam, 1634; STC 4574), 100.

30. Robert Parker, *A Scholastical Discourse Against Symbolizing with Antichrist in Ceremonies* (Amsterdam, 1607; STC 19294), 101, 108. The discussion 'Of Ceremonies' in the Book of Common Prayer explained why certain ritual procedures were retained, Clay (ed.), *Liturgical Services*, 36–8.

31. *Articles Whereupon it was agreed by the Archbishoppes and Bishoppes*, no. 27.

32. Bullard (ed.), *Constitutions and Canons Ecclesiastical*, 251. For tension between the articles of religion and the Book of Common Prayer, see Nicholas Tyacke, *Anti-Calvinists: The Rise of English Arminianism c.1590–1640* (Oxford, 1987), 3.

33. Alexander Nowell, *A Catechisme or First Instruction and Learning of Christian Religion* (1570; STC 18708) fos. 70^v–73. See also Arthur Dent, *A Pastime for Parents* (1612; STC 6624.4), sig. G.

34. Thomas Morton, *A Defence of the Innocencie of the Three Ceremonies of the Church of England* (1618; STC 18179), 228–9; George R. Potter and Evelyn M. Simpson (eds.), *The Sermons of John Donne*, 10 vols. (Berkeley and Los Angeles, 1962), v. 169, viii. 52.

35. Parker, *Scholastical Discourse Against Symbolizing*, 101; William Ames, *A Fresh Suit against Human Ceremonies in Gods Worship* (Rotterdam, 1633; STC 555), 75; Perkins, *Golden Chaine*, 108–9. See also William Perkins, *The Whole Treatise of the Cases of Conscience* (Cambridge, 1608; STC 19670), 108–15.

36. J. Horsfall Turner (ed.), *The Rev. Oliver Heywood, B.A. 1630–1702; His Autobiography, Diaries, Anecdote and Event Books*, 4 vols. (Brighouse, 1882–5), i. 328; iii. 238, 240–7; v. 237; Thomas Heywood (ed.), *The Diary of the Rev. Henry Newcome, from September 30, 1661, to September 29, 1663* (Chetham Society; Manchester, 1849), 23. For the fifty-sixth anniversary of his baptism, see Richard Parkinson (ed.), *The Autobiography of Henry Newcome, M.A.* (Chetham Society; Manchester, 1852), 252.

37. e.g. Richard Baxter, *A Christian Directory: Or, A Summ of Practical Theologie, and Cases of Conscience* (1678), bk. 3, pp. 13, 15, 108–9, 113.

38. George Webb, *Catalogus Protestantium: Or, The Protestants Kalendar* (1624; STC 25161), 52; 'An Admonition to the Parliament', 26. Cf. Robert Charles Hope (ed.), *The Popish Kingdome or reign of Antichrist, written in Latine Verse by Thomas Naogeorgus, and Englyshed by Barnabe Googe* (1880), fo. 30ᵛ.

39. Albert Peel (ed.), *The Second Part of a Register: Being a Calendar of Manuscripts under that title intended for publication by the Puritans about 1593*, 2 vols. (Cambridge, 1915), i. 70; John Aubrey, 'Remains of Gentilisme and Judaisme', in John Buchanan-Brown (ed.), *John Aubrey: Three Prose Works* (Carbondale, Ill., 1972), 167; Peter J. Jagger, *Clouded Witness: Initiation in the Church of England in the Mid-Victorian Period, 1850–1875* (Allison Park, Pa., 1982), 2–7.

40. Hale (ed.), *A Series of Precedents and Proceedings*, 162; John White, *The First Century of Scandalous, Malignant Priests* (1643), 45; Clive Holmes (ed.), *The Suffolk Committees for Scandalous Ministers 1644–1646* (Suffolk Records Society; Ipswich, 1970), 39.

41. George Ornsby (ed.), *The Correspondence of John Cosin*, 2 vols. (Surtees Society; Durham, 1869), i. 113–15; ii. 65. See also John Cosin, *The Works of the Right Reverend Father in God, John Cosin*, 5 vols. (Oxford, 1843–55), v. 136–8.

42. Tyacke, *Anti-Calvinists*, 52, 78, 175–6, 208.

43. *Articles of Enquiry and Direction for the Diocese of Norwich . . . 1638* (1638; STC 10299), sig. Cᵛ; F. W. Moorman (ed.), *The Poetical Works of Robert Herrick* (Oxford, 1921), 396.

44. Day, *Day's Festivals*, 112; Potter and Simpson (eds.), *Sermons of John Donne*, v. 172–3. In a sermon of 1618 Donne considered the idea that original sin remained after baptism, its roots never completely eradicated, ibid. ii. 166.

45. White, *First Century of Scandalous, Malignant Priests*, 1, 3; A. G. Matthews, *Walker Revised. Being a Revision of John Walker's Sufferings of the Clergy during the Grand Rebellion 1642–60* (Oxford, 1948), 356, 362; Anthony Sparrow, *A Rationale upon the Book of Common Prayer of the Church of England* (1668; 1st publ. 1655), 286.

46. Peel (ed.), *Second Part of a Register*, i. 300. See also *An Abridgement of that Book which the Ministers of Lincoln Diocess delivered to his Maiestie upon the first of December last, 1605* (1605; STC 15646), 72.

47. Perkins, *Golden Chaine*, 107; William Gouge, *Of Domesticall Duties* (3rd edn., 1634; STC 12121), 529; Christopher Dow, *Innovations Unjustly Charged upon the Present Church and State* (1637; STC 7090), 197. For similar disparagement of the sacrament of baptism in the 1640s, see John Cordy Jeaffreson (ed.), *Middlesex County Records*, 4 vols. (1886–92), iii. 92.

48. New College, Oxford, Ms. 9502, 'Robert Woodforde's Diary'.

49. *Injunctions and other Ecclesiastical Proceedings of Richard Barnes*, 18.

50. Hooker, 'Of the Laws of Ecclesiastical Politie', 209.

51. Edward Cardwell, *A History of Conferences, and other Proceedings connected with the Revision of the Book of Common Prayer* (3rd edn., Oxford, 1849), 174–6. See also *An Abridgement of that Book which the Ministers of Lincoln Diocess delivered to his Maiestie*, 26.

52. Hale (ed.), *A Series of Precedents and Proceedings*, 183; Walter C. Renshaw, 'Notes from the Act Books of the Archdeaconry Court of Lewes', *Sussex Archaeological Collections*, 49 (1906), 53; Lincolnshire Archives, Court Papers 69/1, 23 (1602); Johnstone (ed.), *Churchwardens' Presentments (17th Century) Part I*, 62.

53. Bullard (ed.), *Constitutions and Canons Ecclesiastical*, 285 (canon 69); *Articles to be Enqvired of within the Dioces of London* (1607; STC 10257), no. 8.

54. Peel (ed.), *Second Part of a Register*, ii. 45.

55. Helena Hajzyk, 'The Church in Lincolnshire c.1595–1640', Ph.D. thesis, Cambridge, 1980, p. 253. Visiting his diocese, Lincoln, in 1614, Richard Neile reported, 'our table talk at dinner was whether children dying before baptism might be saved. The affirmative was maintained, and the distinction was alleged, viz.: that baptism was necessary only *ex necessitate praecepti*, and not *ex necessitate medii*,' E. Venables, 'The Primary Visitation of the Diocese of Lincoln by Bishop Neile, A.D. 1614', *Associated Architectural Societies' Reports and Papers*, 16 (1881), 48.

56. White, *First Century of Scandalous, Malignant Priests*, 45, 43, 40.

57. Matthew Storey (ed.), *Two East Anglian Diaries, 1641–1729; Isaac Archer and William Coe* (Woodbridge, Suffolk, 1994), 150.

58. Ibid. 150–1.

59. *Strange Newes out of Kent, of a Monstrous and misshapen Child, borne in Olde Sandwich* (1609; STC 14934), sig. B3^v.

60. Comber, *Brief Discourse Upon the Offices of Baptism and Confirmation*, 363; Baxter, *Christian Directory*, bk. 3, p. 114. Cf. Alice Thornton's hopes for her dead unbaptized babies of 1652 and 1657, *The Autobiography of Mrs. Alice Thornton* (Surtees Society; Durham, 1875), 87, 95.

61. Robert Barret, *A Companion for Midwives, Child-Bearing Women, and Nurses* (1699), 91; Jagger, *Clouded Witness*, 67–71.

62. E. A. Wrigley, 'Births and Baptisms: The Use of Anglican Baptism Registers as a Source of Information about the Numbers of Births in England before the Beginning of Civil Registration', *Population Studies*, 31 (1977), 281–312, esp. tables 7 and 8.

63. Clay (ed.), *Liturgical Services*, 206–9.

64. Fisher, *Christian Initiation: Baptism in the Medieval West*, 176–7; John Bale, *A Declaration of Edmonde Bonners Articles concerning the cleargye of London dyocese* (1561; STC 1289), fos. 69ᵛ–71.

65. W. H. Frere and W. P. M. Kennedy, *Visitation Articles and Injunctions of the Period of the Reformation*, 3 vols. (1910), ii. 23, 50, 58, 292.

66. Bale, *Declaration of Edmonde Bonners Articles*, fos. 69–71; John Ayre (ed.), *The Sermons of Edwin Sandys* (Parker Society; Cambridge, 1842), 433; John Greenwood, *M. Some laid open in his coulers* (1590; STC 12342), 63, 66; Gouge, *Of Domesticall Duties*, 528. See also request in the puritan 'Millenary Petition' of 1604, 'baptism not to be ministered by women', in J. P. Kenyon, *The Stuart Constitution* (Cambridge, 1966), 133.

67. 'An Admonition to the Parliament', 11, 26; John Ayre (ed.), *The Works of John Whitgift*, 3 vols. (Parker Society; Cambridge, 1851–3), ii. 528–9.

68. Carlson (ed.), *The Writings of Henry Barrow 1587–1590*, 420; Peel (ed.), *Second Part of a Register*, i. 280.

69. Hooker, 'Of the Laws of Ecclesiastical Politie', 212–13.

70. Edward Cardwell (ed.), *Documentary Annals of the Reformed Church of England*, 2 vols. (Oxford, 1844), i. 238.

71. *Injunctions and other Ecclesiastical Proceedings of Richard Barnes*, 18. See also Marmaduke Middleton's 1583 articles for the Welsh Diocese of St David's, which expressly forbade baptism by lay men or women, W. P. M. Kennedy, *Elizabethan Episcopal Administration*, 3 vols. (1924), iii. 148.

72. Greenwood, *M. Some laid open in his coulers*, 66–8.

73. J. S. F. Chamberlain, 'Staplehurst Register', *Archaeologia Cantiana*, 28 (1909), 293; J. Charles Cox, *The Parish Registers of England* (1910), 57; John Southerden Burn, *The History of Parish Registers in England* (1862), 88, 89, 94, 133. See also the examination of Elizabeth Gaynsford, midwife, who christened a child 'born in jeopardy of life' in the diocese of Rochester in 1523, in Samuel Denne, 'Evidence of a Lavatory . . . and Observations on Fonts', *Archaeologia*, 11 (1794), 125.

74. West Sussex Record Office, Diocese of Chichester, Churchwarden's Presentment, Ep 1/23/5.

75. Greenwood, *M. Some laid open in his coulers*, 63, 68, 89–90.

76. Clay (ed.), *Liturgical Services*, 206–9; *An Abridgement of that Book which the Ministers of Lincoln Diocess delivered to his Maiestie*, 75; Comber, *Brief Discourse Upon the Offices of Baptism and Confirmation*, 401; Jagger, *Clouded Witness*, 99.

77. Cardwell, *A History of Conferences*, 174–6; Tyacke, *Anti-Calvinists*, 15–18.

78. Francis Procter, *A History of the Book of Common Prayer* (1875), 388; James F. Larkin and Paul L. Hughes (eds.), *Stuart Royal Proclamations*, i. *Royal Proclamations of King James I, 1603–1625* (Oxford, 1973), 74–6; *The Book of Oaths* (1689), 163–4; Comber, *Brief Discourse Upon the Offices of Baptism and Confirmation*, 410.

79. Kenneth Fincham (ed.), *Visitation Articles and Injunctions of the Early Stuart Church*, i (Church of England Record Society; Woodbridge, Suffolk, 1994), 159, 208; *Articles to be Inquired of Within the Dioces of Ely* (1639; STC 10197), no. 6.

80. Guildhall Library, MS 9057/1, fos. 2^v–3.

81. Ornsby (ed.), *The Correspondence of John Cosin*, i. 113–15; Thomas Bedford, *A Treatise of the Sacraments* (1638; STC 1789), 32.

CHAPTER 6

1. William Keatinge Clay (ed.), *Liturgical Services. Liturgies and Occasional Forms of Prayer Set Forth in the Reign of Queen Elizabeth* (Parker Society; Cambridge, 1847), 204.

2. J. D. C. Fisher, *Christian Initiation: Baptism in the Medieval West* (1963), 172–9; J. D. C. Fisher, *Christian Initiation: The Reformation Period* (1970), 80–4.

3. Edward Cardwell, *A History of Conferences, and other Proceedings connected with the Revision of the Book of Common Prayer* (3rd edn., Oxford, 1849), 41; John Ayre (ed.), *The Sermons of Edwin Sandys* (Parker Society; Cambridge, 1842), 433.

4. James Calfhill, *An Answer to John Martiall's Treatise of the Cross*, ed. Richard Gibbings (Parker Society; Cambridge, 1846), 70–6. Cf. Anthony Sparrow, *A Rationale upon the Book of Common Prayer of the Church of England* (1668), 300.

5. Richard Hooker, 'Of the Laws of Ecclesiastical Politie', in *The Works of that Learned and Judicious Divine, Mr. Richard Hooker* (1723), 226–33; Albert Peel (ed.), *The Second Part of a Register: Being a Calendar of Manuscripts under that title intended for publication by the Puritans about 1593*, 2 vols. (Cambridge, 1915), i. 70; *An Abridgement of that Book which the Ministers of Lincoln Diocess delivered to his Maiestie upon the first of December last, 1605* (1605; STC 15646), 40.

6. John Rylands Library, Manchester, Ms. 524, 'The Acts and Speeches of Richard Greenham', fo. 25; David Calderwood, *The Altare of Damascus or The Patern of the English Hierarchie* (1621; STC 4352), 206.

7. Peel (ed.), *The Second Part of a Register*, i. 125; John Ayre (ed.), *The Works of John Whitgift*, 3 vols. (Parker Society; Cambridge, 1851–3), iii. 123.

8. 'An Admonition to the Parliament [1572]' in W. H. Frere and C. E. Douglas (eds.), *Puritan Manifestoes* (1954), 27; Anthony Gilby, *A Pleasaunt Dialogue, Between a Souldior of Barwicke, and an English Chaplaine* (1581; STC 11888), sig. M4^v; Peel (ed.), *Second Part of a Register*, i. 33.

9. J. S. Cockburn (ed.), *Calendar of Assize Records, Surrey Indictments, Elizabeth I* (1979), 324.

10. 'Millenary Petition', in J. P. Kenyon, *The Stuart Constitution* (Cambridge, 1966), 132; Cardwell, *History of Conferences*, 196–9, 210–11.

11. J. V. Bullard (ed.), *Constitutions and Canons Ecclesiastical* (1934), 260–4.

12. Ibid. 264.

13. William Bradshaw, *A Shorte Treatise, Of the Crosse in Baptism* (Amsterdam, 1604; STC 3526), 1, 14; *The Psalmes of David in Meeter* (Edinburgh, 1611; STC 16591), 128–42.

14. Kenyon, *Stuart Constitution*, 127–8; *An Abridgement of that Book which the Ministers of Lincoln Diocess delivered to his Maiestie upon the first of December last*, 70–8.

15. Robert Parker, *A Scholastical Discourse Against Symbolizing with Antichrist in Ceremonies* (Amsterdam, 1607; STC 19294), 1, 5, 65.

16. John Canne, *A Necessity of Separation from the Church of England* (Amsterdam, 1634; STC 4574), 104.

17. 'A Priest to the Temple, or, The Countrey Parson his Character and Rule of Holy Life', in Louis L. Martz (ed.), *George Herbert and Henry Vaughan* (Oxford, 1986), 217–18.

18. Thomas Sparke, *A Brotherly Perswasion to Vnitie, and Vniformitie in Ivdgement* (1607; STC 23020), 22–34; Thomas Morton, *A Defence of the Innocencie of the Three Ceremonies of the Church of England* (1618; STC 18179), 228–9.

19. John Burges, *An Answer Reioyned to that much applauded Pamphlet of a Namelesse Author* (1631; STC 4113), 476–7. For a similar insistance that the Anglican ceremony of baptism had 'not the least jot or tittle' of popery in it, see Thomas Hewardine, *The Countrey-Curate to the Countrey-People* (1701), 12–22.

20. *Articles to bee enquired of by the Church-wardens and sworne-men: In the Ordinary Visitation of the Lord Bishop of Excester* (1599; STC 10204), no. 4; Kenneth Fincham (ed.), *Visitation Articles and Injunctions of the Early Stuart Church*, i (Church of England Record Society; Woodbridge, Suffolk, 1994), 28, 56, 89, 102, 142, 158, 162, 188; George Ornsby (ed.), *The Correspondence of John Cosin*, 2 vols. (Surtees Society; Durham, 1869), i. 114. See also 'Articles to be Enquired of Within the Dioces of London . . . 1628' in *The Works of . . . William Laud, D.D.*, 7 vols. (Oxford 1853), v. 400.

21. Citations sampled from act books and presentments of the dioceses of London, Lincoln, Durham, Norwich, Oxford, Chichester, Bath and Wells, and York.

22. *Certaine Questions by Way of Conference betwixt a Chauncelor and a Kinswoman of His Concerning Churching of Women* (Middleburg?, 1601, STC 20557), 39.

23. R. A. Houlbrooke (ed.), *The Letter Book of John Parkhurst, Bishop of Norwich . . . 1571–5* (Norfolk Record Society; Norwich, 1974–5), 218; H. C. Johnson (ed.), *Wiltshire County Records: Minutes and Proceedings in Sessions 1563 and 1574 to 1592* (Devizes, 1949), 123.

24. Harold Smith, *The Ecclesiastical History of Essex Under the Long Parliament and Commonwealth* (Colchester, 1932), 51–2; Robert von Friedeburg, 'Reformation of Manners and the Social Composition of Offenders in an East Anglian Cloth Village: Earls Colne, Essex, 1531–1642', *Journal of British Studies*, 29 (1990), 354; A. Percival Moore (ed.), 'The Metropolitical Visitation of Archdeacon [sic] Laud', in *Associated Architectural Societies' Reports and Papers*, 29 (1907), 532; Borthwick Institute, York, Cause Papers, H. 2069.

25. Buckinghamshire Record Office, Aylesbury, D/A/C4, fo. 19; Frederick Pollock (ed.), *Table Talk of John Selden* (1927), 9.

26. Borthwick Institute, Cause Papers, H. 2046.5.

27. J. F. Williams (ed.), *Diocese of Norwich: Bishop Redman's Visitation 1597* (Norfolk Record Society; Norwich, 1946), 69.

28. Ibid. 38; C. W. Foster, *The State of the Church in the Reigns of Elizabeth and James*

I as Illustrated by Documents relating to the Diocese of Lincoln (Lincolnshire Record Society; Loncoln, 1926), lxxxi; John Southerden Burn, *The High Commission: Notices of the Court, and its Proceedings* (1865), 55. See also the case of Elizabeth Perkins of Bow, Middlesex, who allegedly helped prevent the minister signing her godchild with the cross in 1601, Guildhall Library, Ms. 9064/14, fo. 120ᵛ.

29. J. Horsfall Turner (ed.), *The Rev. Oliver Heywood, B.A. 1630–1702; His Autobiography, Diaries, Anecdote and Event Books*, 4 vols. (Brighouse, 1882–5), iii. 238, 281, 296.

30. Peel (ed.), *Second Part of a Register*, i. 295; Hereford Record Office, Court Books, Box 18/71; William H. Hale (ed.), *A Series of Precedents and Proceedings in Criminal Causes* (1847), 249; Borthwick Institute, Visitation Court Book, 1633/1, fo. 266.

31. Borthwick Institute, Cause Papers, H. 2432.

32. Guildhall Library, Ms. 9583/2, part 1, fo. 56.

33. 'The Rationale of Ceremony', in Fisher, *Christian Initiation: The Reformation Period*, 80–4; Fisher, *Christian Initiation: Baptism in the Medieval West* (1963), 160, 164, 171–9; Frederick E. Warren (tr.) *The Sarum Missal in English*, 2 vols. (1913), i. 13–14. Much of this derives from Mark 7: 34. On the magical and liturgical uses of salt, see Michel Mollat (ed.), *Le Rôle du sel dans l'histoire* (Paris, 1968), 277–303. For a hostile recapitulation of popish baptismal rites, see William Prynne, *Canterburies Doome* (1646), 295–6.

34. British Library, Additional Ms. 45027, fos. 5–6; Maria Dowling and Joy Shakespeare, 'Religion and Politics in Mid Tudor England through the Eyes of an English Protestant Woman: The Recollections of Rose Hickman', *Bulletin of the Institute of Historical Research*, 55 (1982), 100.

35. Stephen Reed Cattley and George Townsend (eds.), *The Acts and Monuments of John Foxe*, 8 vols. (1837–41), vii. 98–9, 103.

36. Antonia Fraser, *Mary Queen of Scots* (1970), 337.

37. Calfhill, *Answer to John Martiall's Treatise of the Cross*, 17, 213–15.

38. Ibid. 213–15; John Bale, *A Declaration of Edmonde Bonners Articles concerning the cleargye of London dyocese* (1561; STC 1289), fos. 19, 50ᵛ; James Scholefield (ed.), *The Works of James Pilkington* (Parker Society; Cambridge, 1842), 518, 541. See also Robert Charles Hope (ed.), *The Popish Kingdome or reign of Antichrist, written in Latine Verse by Thomas Naogeorgus, and Englyshed by Barnabe Googe* (1880), fo. 31; Ayre (ed.), *Works of John Whitgift*, iii. 87.

39. William Nicholson (ed.), *The Remains of Edmund Grindal* (Parker Society; Cambridge, 1843), 124, 159–60; W. P. M. Kennedy, *Elizabethan Episcopal Administration*, 3 vols. (1924), iii. 148; F. R. Raines (ed.), *A Description of the State, Civil and Ecclesiastical, of the County of Lancaster about the year 1590* (Chetham Society; Manchester, 1875), 7.

40. *An Abridgement of that Book which the Ministers of Lincoln Diocess delivered to his Maiestie upon the first of December last*, 34; Parker, *Scholastical Discourse Against Symbolizing with Antichrist*, 103, 108; William Ames, *A Fresh Suit against Human Ceremonies in Gods Worship* (Rotterdam, 1633; STC 555), 291; Canne, *Necessity of*

Separation, 105; Joshua Stopford, *Pagano-Papismus: Or, an Exact Parallel Betweene Rome-Pagan, and Rome-Christian, in their Doctrines and Ceremonies* (1675), 175.

41. Abraham Darcie, *The Originall of Idolatries: or, The Birth of Heresies* (1624; STC 4747), 27–9.

42. William Gouge, *Of Domesticall Duties* (3rd edn., 1634; STC 12121), 528; Huntington Library, San Marino, rare book 214745.

43. Richard Baxter, *A Christian Directory: Or, A Summ of Practical Theologie, and Cases of Conscience* (1678), bk. 3, p. 123; R. C. Latham and W. Matthews (eds.), *The Diary of Samuel Pepys*, 9 vols. (Berkeley and Los Angeles, 1970–6), vii. 329.

44. Baxter, *Christian Directory*, bk. 3, pp. 123–4.

45. Clay (ed.), *Liturgical Services*, 200; John Day, *Day's Festivals or, Twelve of His Sermons* (Oxford, 1615; STC 6426), 109. See also Daniel Featley, *Clavis Mystica: A Key Opening Divers Difficult and Mysterious Texts of Holy Scripture* (1636; STC 10730), 207; Thomas Comber, *A Brief Discourse Upon the Offices of Baptism and Confirmation* (1674), appended to his *A Companion to the Altar* (1675), 357.

46. William Perkins, *A Golden Chaine; or, The Description of Theologie, Containing the Order of the Causes of Saluation and Damnation* (Cambridge, 1600; STC 19646), 109; Thomas Bedford, *A Treatise of the Sacraments* (1638; STC 1789), 88; Sampson Price, *The Two Twins of Birth and Death* (1624; STC 20334), 17; George R. Potter and Evelyn M. Simpson (eds.), *The Sermons of John Donne*, 10 vols. (Berkeley and Los Angeles, 1962), v. 110, 172. John Cosin concurred that 'in baptism the true and natural element of water is required', but, he added, 'it is not bare water; it is changed, and made the sacrament of regeneration. It is water consecrated', John Cosin, *The Works of the Right Reverend Father in God, John Cosin*, 5 vols. (Oxford, 1843–55), v. 136, 483.

47. John Strype, *Annals of the Reformation*, 3 vols. (Oxford, 1824), i. 243; *Articles of Enquiry and Direction for the Diocese of Norwich . . . 1638* (1638; STC 10299), sig. Cᵛ.

48. Thomas Edwards, *The Third Part of Gangraena* (1646), 6; T. Ellison Gibson (ed.), *Crosby Records. A Cavalier's Note Book . . . of William Blundell* (1880), 113.

49. Edward Cardwell (ed.), *Documentary Annals of the Reformed Church of England*, 2 vols. (Oxford, 1844), i. 157–8.

50. Kennedy, *Elizabethan Episcopal Administration*, iii. 148; Ames, *Fresh Suit against Human Ceremonies*, 249; Clay (ed.), *Liturgical Services*, 203–4.

51. Perkins, *A Golden Chain*, 108; Bedford, *Treatise of the Sacraments*, 23.

52. Gouge, *Of Domesticall Duties*, 58, 529.

53. Mark Frank, *LI Sermons* (1672), 233; Sparrow, *Rationale upon the Book of Common Prayer*, 289; Comber, *Brief Discourse Upon the Offices of Baptism and Confirmation*, 403–4. See also Hewardine, *Countrey-Curate*, 12–25.

54. Ames, *Fresh Suit against Human Ceremonies*, 292, 295, includes criticism of Andrewes. See also Peter Smart, *The Vanitie and Downefall of Superstitious Popish Ceremonies* (Edinburgh, 1628; STC 22643).

55. A popular rationale for using water to test for witchcraft was that 'water, as

the element of baptism, would reject those who had renounced that sacrament by swearing allegiance to the devil', Clive Holmes, 'Popular Culture? Witches, Magistrates, and Divines in Early Modern England', in Steven L. Kaplan (ed.), *Understanding Popular Culture: Europe from the Middle Ages to the Nineteenth Century* (Berlin, 1984), 104. Old women in some rural areas are alleged to have believed that well water used in baptism was especially good for washing the eyes, John Brand, *Observations on Popular Antiquities*, 2 vols. (1813), ii. 264.

56. J. G. Davies, *The Architectural Setting of Baptism* (1962), 91–118.

57. Ayre (ed.), *Works of John Whitgift*, ii. 463.

58. Fisher, *Christian Initiation: Baptism in the Medieval West* (1963), 165–72; Fisher, *Christian Initiation: The Reformation Period*, 84; Warren (tr.), *Sarum Missal in English*, i. 279. For vigorous protestant criticism see Bale, *A Declaration of Edmonde Bonners Articles*, fos. 19, 26.

59. W. H. Frere and W. P. M. Kennedy, *Visitation Articles and Injunctions of the Period of the Reformation*, 3 vols. (1910), ii. 239, 331; Cardwell (ed.), *Documentary Annals*, i. 152.

60. *Aduertisements partly for due order in the publique administration of common praiers* (1565; STC 10028); Cardwell (ed.), *Documentary Annals*, i. 326. See also John Bruce and Thomas Thomason Perowne (eds.), *Correspondence of Matthew Parker* (Parker Society; Cambridge, 1853), 450.

61. Davies, *Architectural Setting*, 93–113; Nigel Yates, *Buildings, Faith, and Worship: The Liturgical Arrangement of Anglican Churches, 1600–1900* (Oxford, 1991), 34–5. See also J. Charles Cox and Alfred Harvey, *English Church Furniture* (1908), 160–239; Francis Bond, *Fonts and Font Covers* (Oxford, 1908). See below, Ch. 8, for baptismal practice during the the revolutionary era.

62. Leland H. Carlson (ed.), *The Writings of Henry Barrow 1590–91* (1966), 84.

63. *Depositions and other Ecclesiastical Proceedings from the Courts of Durham* (Surtees Society; Durham, 1845), 230–1.

64. F. D. Price (ed.), *The Commission for Ecclesiastical Causes Within the Dioceses of Bristol and Gloucester, 1574* (Bristol and Gloucestershire Archaeological Society; Bristol, 1972), 37, 64, 69–78.

65. *The Injunctions and other Ecclesiastical Proceedings of Richard Barnes, Bishop of Durham from 1575 to 1587* (Surtees Society; Durham, 1850), 25; Kennedy, *Elizabethan Episcopal Administration*, iii. 293; *Articles to be Enqvired of, within the Diocesse of Lincolne* (1598; STC 10235), 7.

66. Claude Jenkins (ed.), 'An Unpublished Record of Archbishop Parker's Visitation in 1573', *Archaeologia Cantiana*, 29 (1911), 308–9; Arthur Hussey (ed.), 'Visitations of the Archdeacons of Canterbury', *Archaeologia Cantiana*, 27 (1904), 224. For reasons as yet unknown, the parishioners of Pittington, Durham, paid 2s. 6d. 'for shifting the font' in Jan. 1588, *Churchwardens' Accounts of Pittington and other parishes in the Diocese of Durham* (Surtees Society; Durham, 1888), 27.

67. Williams (ed.), *Diocese of Norwich: Bishop Redman's Visitation*, 31, 117–18, 137, 144.

68. Bullard (ed.), *Constitutions and Canons Ecclesiastical*, 293.

69. *Articles to be Enqvired of within the Dioces of London* (1607; STC 10257), no. 31; *Second Report of the Ritual Commission* (Parliamentary Papers 38; 1867–8), appendix E, p. 474; Fincham (ed.), *Visitation Articles and Injunctions of the Early Stuart Church*, i. 31, 58, 71, 102, 162, 185, 191–2.

70. A. Percival Moore, 'Leicestershire Churches in the Time of Charles I', in Alice Dryden (ed.), *Memorials of Old Leicestershire* (1911), 158; Cambridge University Library, Ms. Mm. 4. 29, 'Act Book, Peculiar of Tredington', fo. 112; Nicholas Tyacke, 'Anglican Attitudes: Some Recent Writings on English Religious History, from the Reformation to the Civil War', *Journal of British Studies*, 35 (1996), 159; Buckinghamshire Record Office, D/A/V 4, fo. 156; R. F. B. Hodgkinson (ed.), 'Extracts from the Act Books of the Archdeacons of Nottingham', *Transactions of the Thoroton Society*, 31 (1928), 131–4.

71. e.g. the churchwardens of St Edmund's, Salisbury, spent 8s. 10d. in 1632 for 'painting and new making the cover of the font', Henry J. F. Swayne (ed.), *Churchwardens' Accounts of S. Edmund and S. Thomas, Sarum, 1443–1702* (Wiltshire Record Society; Salisbury, 1896), 195. The small Berkshire parish of Stanford in the Vale spent 6s. 8d. on masonry work about the font and 16s. for a font cover between 1632 and 1634, Violet M. Howse (ed.), *Stanford in the Vale Churchwardens' Accounts 1552–1725* (Oxford, 1987), 194, 199.

72. Norfolk Record Office, ANW/3/25; J. E. Foster (ed.), *Churchwardens' Accounts of St. Mary the Great, Cambridge, from 1504 to 1635* (Cambridge, 1905), 455–6.

73. West Sussex Record Office, Diocese of Chichester, Church Inspections, Ep 1/26/2.

74. Buckinghamshire Record Office, D/A/V 2, fo. 8ᵛ.

75. Peter Smart, *A Catalogue of Superstitious Innovations in the change of Services and Ceremonies* (1642), 12, 24; Ornsby (ed.), *The Correspondence of John Cosin*, i. 161–99.

76. Smart, *Vanitie and Downefall of Superstitious Popish Ceremonies*; Peter Smart, *A Short Treatise of Altars* (1643), 9. A prebendary at Durham since 1609, Peter Smart was the most outspoken opponent of the innovating ceremonialists. Smart was personally involved in this baptism on 7 Sept., since his wife Susan was one of the godmothers. George J. Armytage (ed.), *The Baptismal, Marriage, and Burial Registers of the Cathedral Church of . . . Durham, 1609–1896* (Harleian Society, 1897), 3.

77. Cambridgeshire Record Office, P26/5/1, St Botolph Churchwardens' Accounts 1600–1646, fos. 180, 192; Richard Culmer, *Cathedral Newes from Canterbury* (1644), 3; Cox and Harvey, *English Church Furniture*, 198; Bond, *Fonts and Font Covers*, 269, 301.

78. Moore (ed.), 'The Metropolitical Visitation of Archdeacon [sic] Laud', 481; Cardwell (ed.), *Documentary Annals*, ii. 255; *Articles of Enquiry and Direction for the Diocese of Norwich . . . 1638*, sig. A4; Ornsby (ed.), *The Correspondence of John Cosin*, i. 114.

79. Moore (ed.), 'The Metropolitical Visitation of Archdeacon [sic] Laud', 517; *Calendar of State Papers Domestic, 1637*, 491; *CSPD 1638–39*, 74.

CHAPTER 7

1. William Gouge, *Of Domesticall Duties* (3rd edn., 1634; STC 12121), 526–7.
2. Joseph Ketley (ed.), *The Two Liturgies, A.D. 1549, and A.D. 1552* (Parker Society; Cambridge, 1844), 113, 290.
3. J. F. Williams (ed.), *Diocese of Norwich: Bishop Redman's Visitation 1597* (Norfolk Record Society; Norwich, 1946), 103, 115–16; William H. Hale (ed.), *A Series of Precedents and Proceedings in Criminal Causes* (1847), 216; Hilda Johnstone (ed.), *Churchwardens' Presentments (17th Century) Part 1: Archdeaconry of Chichester* (Sussex Record Society; Lewes, 1947–8), 2, 114.
4. William Keatinge Clay (ed.), *Liturgical Services. Liturgies and Occasional Forms of Prayer Set Forth in the Reign of Queen Elizabeth* (Parker Society; Cambridge, 1847), 199; J. V. Bullard (ed.), *Constitutions and Canons Ecclesiastical* (1934), 260.
5. John Rylands Library, Manchester, Ms. 524, 'The Acts and Speeches of Richard Greenham', fos. 11^v, 41.
6. W. M. Palmer (ed.), *Episcopal Visitation Returns for Cambridgeshire: Matthew Wren, Bishop of Ely, 1638–1665* (Cambridge, 1930), 46, 55; W. M. Palmer and H. W. Saunders (eds.), *Documents Relating to Cambridgeshire Villages* (Cambridge, 1926), 70; J. E. Foster (ed.), *The Diary of Samuel Newton, Alderman of Cambridge (1662–1717)* (Cambridge, 1890), 41; Henri Misson, *M. Misson's Memoirs and Observations in his Travels over England* (1719), 118.
7. N.H., *The Ladies Dictionary* (1694), 315.
8. John Gough Nichols (ed.), *The Diary of Henry Machyn, Citizen and Merchant-Taylor of London . . . 1550 to . . . 1563* (Camden Society, 1848), 242; James Calfhill, *An Answer to John Martiall's Treatise of the Cross,* ed. Richard Gibbons (Parker Society; Cambridge, 1846), 212; Frederick Pollock (ed.), *Table Talk of John Selden* (1927), 9. See also Richard Baxter, *A Christian Directory: Or, A Summ of Practical Theologie, and Cases of Conscience* (1678), book 3, pp. 114–17.
9. 'An Admonition to the Parliament', in W. H. Frere and C. E. Douglas (eds.), *Puritan Manifestoes* (1954), 14–15, 26–7.
10. John Ayre (ed.), *The Works of John Whitgift,* 3 vols. (Parker Society; Cambridge, 1851–3), i. 130, iii. 118; Anthony Gilby, *A Pleasaunt Dialogue, Between a Souldior of Barwicke, and an English Chaplaine* (1581; STC 11888), sig. M5. The layman Francis Baxter of Beckinghall, Suffolk, wrote to Foxe in 1572 'touching baptising with godfathers and godmothers, for that hath been troublesome unto me and many there be in the country about us that hath been greatly troubled for not using them', British Library, Harleian Ms. 416, fo. 191. (I owe this reference to Tom Freeman.)
11. F. D. Price (ed.), *The Commission for Ecclesiastical Causes Within the Dioceses of Bristol and Gloucester, 1574* (Bristol and Gloucestershire Archaeological Society; Bristol, 1972), 76; 'Acts and Speeches of Richard Greenham', fos. 11^v–12, 32^v, 41; Thomas Comber, *A Brief Discourse Upon the Offices of Baptism and Confirmation* (1674), appended to his *A Companion to the Altar* (1675), 382–3.
12. *William Whiteway of Dorchester His Diary 1618 to 1635* (Dorset Record Society;

Dorchester, 1991), 37, 49, 64, 77, 94, 114, 134. For religious and cultural change in Dorchester see David Underdown, *Fire From Heaven: Life in an English Town in the Seventeenth Century* (New Haven and London, 1992).

13. Gouge, *Of Domesticall Duties*, 529–33; Clay (ed.), *Liturgical Services*, 202.

14. New College, Oxford, Ms. 9502, 'Robert Woodforde's Diary'; *The Autobiography of Mrs. Alice Thornton* (Surtees Society; Durham, 1875), 91, 92, 94, 124, 142, 148, 165.

15. Anthony Sparrow, *A Rationale upon the Book of Common Prayer of the Church of England* (1668), 289. Cf. Thomas Sparke, *A Brotherly Perswasion to Vnitie, and Vniformitie in Ivdgement* (1607; STC 23020), 56–8.

16. Leland H. Carlson (ed.), *The Writings of Henry Barrow 1587–1590* (1962), 419; id. (ed.), *The Writings of Henry Barrow 1590–91* (1966), 87.

17. 'Acts and Speeches of Richard Greenham', fo. 10; Gouge, *Of Domesticall Duties*, 530–3; Guildhall Library, Ms. 4509/1.

18. 'Millenary Petition', in J. P. Kenyon, *The Stuart Constitution* (Cambridge, 1966), 132; Edward Cardwell, *A History of Conferences, and other Proceedings connected with the Revision of the Book of Common Prayer* (3rd edn., Oxford, 1849), 167–212; C. H. Firth and R. S. Rait (eds.), *Acts and Ordinances of the Interregnum, 1642–1660*, 2 vols. (1911), i. 594. See below, Ch. 8, for 'baptism in times of distraction'.

19. Cardwell, *A History of Conferences*, 323, 325, 431.

20. *Aduertisements partly for due order in the publique administration of common praiers* (1565; STC 10028); Cardwell (ed.), *Documentary Annals*, i. 326–7; Bullard (ed.), *Constitutions and Canons Ecclesiastical* (1934), 260.

21. *Articles to be Enqvired of, within the Diocesse of Lincolne* (1598; STC 10235), 7; *Articles to be Inquired of Within the Dioces of Ely* (1638; STC 10197), sect. 2, no. 5; *Second Report of the Ritual Commission* (Parliamentary Papers 38; 1867–8), appendix E, p. 476.

22. George Ornsby (ed.), *The Correspondence of John Cosin*, 2 vols. (Surtees Society; Durham, 1869), i. 114–15; Durham County Record Office, 'Brancepeth Register, 1629–1638'. J. Charles Cox, *The Parish Registers of England* (1910), 50–1, lists registers, mostly from the 16th cent., that record the names of godparents.

23. Hale (ed.), *Series of Precedents and Proceedings*, 193; Williams (ed.), *Diocese of Norwich: Bishop Redman's Visitation*, 74, 128.

24. Bullard (ed.), *Constitutions and Canons Ecclesiastical* (1934), 260; Hale (ed.), *Series of Precedents and Proceedings*, 173; Williams (ed.), *Diocese of Norwich: Bishop Redman's Visitation*, 121; Hereford Record Office, Court Books, Box 18/71.

25. Hale (ed.), *Series of Precedents and Proceedings*, 150; Bodleian Library, Oxford, Ms. Top. Oxon. c. 378, 'Diary of Thomas Wyatt', 315.

26. Williams (ed.), *Diocese of Norwich: Bishop Redman's Visitation*, 129, 158; Sidney A. Peyton (ed.), *The Churchwardens' Presentments in the Oxfordshire Peculiars of Dorchester, Thame and Banbury* (Oxfordshire Record Society; Oxford, 1928), 200.

27. Dorothy M. Meads (ed.), *Diary of Lady Margaret Hoby 1599–1605* (1930), 107, 118, 192, 195, 222.

28. Matthew Storey (ed.), *Two East Anglian Diaries, 1641–1729: Isaac Archer and William Coe* (Woodbridge, Suffolk, 1994), 92.

29. John Bossy, 'Godparenthood: The Fortunes of a Social Institution in Early Modern Christianity', in Kaspar von Greyerz (ed.), *Religion and Society in Early Modern Europe* (1984), 194–201; Louis Haas, 'Boccaccio, Baptismal Kinship and Spiritual Incest', *Renaissance and Reformation*, NS 13 (1989), 343–56.

30. Huntington Library, Ms. HM 30665, 'Memorable Accidents of Sir William Ashcombe, 1591–1625', fo. 7^v. F. R. Raines (ed.), *The Journal of Nicholas Assheton* (Chetham Society; Manchester, 1848), 126; E. S. de Beer (ed.), *The Diary of John Evelyn*, 6 vols. (Oxford, 1955), ii. 5, iv. 238–9, 272, 324, 396, 561.

31. *William Whiteway of Dorchester His Diary*, 37, 64; Foster (ed.), *The Diary of Samuel Newton*, 24; de Beer (ed.), *Diary of John Evelyn*, iv. 129; Somerset Record Office, Taunton, DD/SAS/C/1193, 'John Cannon's Memoirs', 23.

32. James Orchard Halliwell (ed.), *The Autobiography and Personal Diary of Dr. Simon Forman . . . 1552 to 1602* (1849), 18; de Beer (ed.), *Diary of John Evelyn*, iii. 369.

33. Andrew Browning (ed.), *Memoirs of Sir John Reresby* (Glasgow, 1936), 75; British Library, Additional Ms. 27,440, 'Memoirs of Charles Allestree 1677–1702', fo. 52^v.

34. Lady Newdigate-Newdegate (ed.), *Gossip from a Muniment Room: Being Passages in the Lives of Anne and Mary Fytton 1574 to 1618* (1897), 19–20, 46; Folger Shakespeare Library, Ms. L.a. 47; R. C. Latham and W. Matthews (eds.), *The Diary of Samuel Pepys*, 9 vols. (Berkeley and Los Angeles, 1970–6), i. 234.

35. Latham and Matthews (eds.), *Diary of Samuel Pepys*, v. 176, viii. 403.

36. Richard Trappes-Lomax (ed.), *The Diary and Letter Book of the Rev. Thomas Brockbank, 1671–1709* (Chetham Society; Manchester, 1930), 131. Cf. John Birket, *The God-father's Advice to his Son: Shewing the Necessity of performing the Baptismal Vow* (1700).

37. Thomas Shipman recalls the custom of 'the Gossips' giving gilt bowls and spoons, in *Carolina: Or, Loyal Poems* (1683), 113.

38. Folger Shakespeare Library, Ms. L.a. 148; Browning (ed.), *Memoirs of Sir John Reresby*, 53; R. G. Griffiths, 'Joyce Jeffreys of Ham Castle: A Seventeenth-Century Business Gentlewoman,' *Transactions of the Worcestershire Archaeological Society*, 10 (1934), 1–32; 11 (1035), 1–13; 12 (1935), 1–17; British Library, Egerton Ms. 3054, 'Accounts of Joyce Jeffries, 1638–46'.

39. Latham and Matthews (eds.), *Diary of Samuel Pepys*, ii. 109–10, v. 265, viii. 548; Joseph Hunter (ed.), *The Diary of Thomas Cartwright, Bishop of Chester . . . 1686–87* (Camden Society; 1843), 68.

40. Newdigate-Newdegate (ed.), *Gossip from a Muniment Room*, 16, 137; Folger Shakespeare Library, Ms. L.a. 437; Charles Kerry, 'Leonard Wheatcroft of Ashover', *Journal of the Derbyshire Archaeology and Natural History Society*, 21 (1899), 47; Trappes-Lomax (ed.), *Diary and Letter Book of the Rev. Thomas Brockbank*, 13, 29.

41. David Cressy, 'Kinship and Kin Interaction in Early Modern England', *Past and Present*, 113 (1986), 38–69.

42. Folger Shakespeare Library, Ms. L.a. 628; Ms. L.a. 779.

43. F. J. Snell (ed.), 'A Devonshire Yeoman's Diary', *The Antiquary*, 26 (1892), 258; H. J. Morehouse (ed.), *Yorkshire Diaries and Autobiographies in the Seventeenth*

and Eighteenth Centuries (Surtees Society; Durham, 1877), 93, 112; Griffiths, 'Joyce Jeffreys of Ham Castle', *Transactions*, 10 (1934), 22; Robert Willis Blencowe (ed.), 'Extracts from the Journal and Account-Book of Timothy Burrell . . . 1638 to 1714', *Sussex Archaeological Collections*, 3 (1850), 135, 143; Browning (ed.), *Memoirs of Sir John Reresby*, 169–70.

44. F. G. Emmison (ed.), *Elizabethan Life: Wills of Essex Gentry and Yeomen* (Chelmsford, 1980), 132; Wiltshire Record Office, Trowbridge, Consistory Court Wills, G; Cressy, 'Kinship and Kin Interaction', 57, 67. See also Dan Beaver, ' "Sown in Dishonour, Raised in Glory": Death, Ritual and Social Organization in Northern Gloucestershire, 1590–1690', *Social History*, 17 (1992), 412, 417.

45. Clay (ed.), *Liturgical Services*, 211, 203.

46. Daniel Scott Smith, 'Child-Naming Practices as Cultural and Familial Indicators', *Local Population Studies*, 32 (1984), 17–27; id., 'Child-Naming Practices, Kinship Ties, and Change in Family Attitudes in Hingham, Massachusetts, 1641 to 1880', *Journal of Social History*, 18 (1985), 541–66.

47. I owe this information to Will Coster who kindly allowed me to consult his D.Phil. thesis, 'Kinship and Community in Yorkshire, 1500–1700', University of York, 1992, p. 169.

48. Storey (ed.), *Two East Anglian Diaries*, 139, 157, 159.

49. Coster, 'Kinship and Community in Yorkshire', 164–71; Jeremy Boulton, 'The Naming of Children in Seventeenth-Century London', in David Postles (ed.), *Naming, Society and Regional Identity* (forthcoming). I am grateful to Jeremy Boulton for allowing me to see this work before publication.

50. Comber, *A Brief Discourse Upon the Offices of Baptism and Confirmation*, 400; de Beer (ed.), *Diary of John Evelyn*, v. 125. See also Thomas Adams, *The Workes of Tho: Adams, Being the Svmme of His Sermons* (1629; STC 104), 1199.

51. Charles Wareing Bardsley, *Curiosities of Puritan Nomenclature* (1897), 117–28, 138–54; Kenneth Fincham (ed.), *Visitation Articles and Injunctions of the Early Stuart Church*, i (Church of England Record Society; Woodbridge, Suffolk, 1994), 41; 'A Priest to the Temple, or, The Countrey Parson his Character and Rule of Holy Life', in Louis L. Martz (ed.), *George Herbert and Henry Vaughan* (Oxford, 1986), 217–18.

52. G. W. Bromiley, *Baptism and the Anglican Reformers* (1953), 147; Lincolnshire Archives, Court Papers, 69/1, 23.

53. Buckinghamshire Record Office, D/A/V 2, fo. 34; A. G. Matthews, *Walker Revised: Being a Revision of John Walker's Sufferings of the Clergy during the Grand Rebellion 1642–60* (Oxford, 1948), 239; A. Percival Moore (ed.), 'The Metropolitical Visitation of Archdeacon [sic] Laud', in *Associated Architectural Societies' Reports and Papers*, 29 (1907), 523.

54. Lincolnshire Archives, Ch.P/12, 3.

55. Charles Severn, *Diary of the Rev. John Ward . . . 1648 to 1679* (1839), 123–4.

56. Richard Burn, *Ecclesiastical Law*, 4 vols. (1809), i. 320; J. D. C. Fisher, *Christian Initiation: Baptism in the Medieval West* (1963), 174; J. D. C. Fisher, *Christian*

Initiation: The Reformation Period (1970), 83; Edmund R. Nevill (ed.), 'The Chrysom Book of St. Thomas, New Sarum', *Wiltshire Notes and Queries*, 5 (1908), 462–8, 510–14, 561–6; 6 (1911), 19–25, 57–60, 107–10, 208–11, 302–5, 344–8, 391–5, 455–9, 492–8, 547–50; N.H., *The Ladies Dictionary*, 107.

57. Robert Parker, *A Scholastical Discourse Against Symbolizing with Antichrist in Ceremonies* (Amsterdam, 1607; STC 19294), 108.

58. Donald Woodward (ed.), *The Farming and Memorandum Books of Henry Best of Elmswell, 1642* (1984), 200.

59. Ronald Hutton, *The Rise and Fall of Merry England: The Ritual Year 1400–1700* (Oxford, 1994); David Cressy, *Bonfires and Bells: National Memory and the Protestant Calendar in Elizabethan and Stuart England* (1989).

60. Felicity Heal, *Hospitality in Early Modern England* (Oxford, 1990), 80–1, 367–8.

61. William Shakespeare, *Henry VIII*, Act 5, scene 3, ll. 36–7. See below for Pepys, Lawrence, and Ward.

62. Bodleian Library, Ms. Eng. hist. b. 208, 'Orders and Regulations for an Earl's House', fos. 15–19ᵛ.

63. Ibid., fos. 20–2. See also the early Tudor orders 'for the christening of a prince or princess' in *A Collection of Ordinanances and regulations for the Government of the Royal Household, Made in Divers Reigns* (1790), 126.

64. John Southerden Burn, *The History of Parish Registers in England* (1862), 75; F. R. Raines (ed.) *The Derby Household Books* (Chetham Society; Manchester, 1853), 46.

65. Francis Bamford (ed.), *A Royalist's Notebooks: The Commonplace Book of Sir John Oglander* (1936), 184–5, 176–7.

66. John Cordy Jeaffreson (ed.), *Middlesex County Records*, 4 vols. (1886–92), iii. 332; Alan Macfarlane, *The Family Life of Ralph Josselin* (Cambridge, 1970), 89; E. M. Symonds (ed.), 'The Diary of John Greene (1635–57)', *English Historical Review*, 43 (1928), 599; 44 (1929), 109; Margaret M. Verney (ed.), *Memoirs of the Verney Family During the Commonwealth* (1894), 193.

67. F. P. Wilson (ed.), *The Batchelars Banquet* (Oxford, 1929), 21.

68. Margaret Cavendish, *CCXI Sociable Letters* (1664), 96; John Aubrey, 'Remains of Gentilisme and Judaisme', in John Buchanan-Brown (ed.), *John Aubrey: Three Prose Works* (Carbondale, Ill., 1972), 167; Henri Misson, *M. Misson's Memoirs and Observations in his Travels over England* (1719), 35.

69. Mary Carbery (ed.), *Mrs. Elizabeth Freke Her Diary 1671 to 1714* (Cork, 1913), 36.

70. British Library, Additional Ms. 22,084, 'Proceedings against Malignants in Wiltshire, 1646', fo. 7ᵛ; J. Horsfall Turner (ed.), *The Rev. Oliver Heywood, B.A. 1630–1702; His Autobiography, Diaries, Anecdote and Event Books*, 4 vols. (Brighouse, 1882–5), iii. 207.

71. Reuben Bourne, *The Contented Cuckold, or, the Woman's Advocate. A Comedy* (1692), 25; *The Gossips Feast or Morrall Tales* (1647), 1–2.

72. Shipman, *Carolina*, 113.

73. Philip Stubs, *Of Publick Baptism* (1693), 27.

74. Norman Marlow (ed.), *The Diary of Thomas Isham of Lamport (1658–81)* (Farn-

borough, 1971), 115; Kerry, 'Leonard Wheatcroft of Ashover', 44; Trappes-Lomax (ed.), *Diary and Letter Book of the Rev. Thomas Brockbank*, 194.

75. Latham and Matthews (eds.), *Diary of Samuel Pepys*, ii. 109–10.

76. Ibid. ii. 216.

77. Ibid. iv. 82; v. 200, 211; vii. 49; viii. 202.

78. Cavendish, *CCXI Sociable Letters*, 207.

79. G. E. Aylmer (ed.), *The Diary of William Lawrence covering periods between 1662 and 1681* (Beaminster, Dorset, 1961), 13–14.

80. Ned Ward, *The London-Spy, Compleat, in Eighteen Parts* (1703), 393–412.

CHAPTER 8

1. Francis Bond, *Fonts and Font Covers* (Oxford, 1908), 275; Bodleian Library, Rawlinson Ms. D, 158, fos. 43–55. I am grateful to Buchanan Sharp for drawing this record to my attention.

2. *A Strange and Lamentable Accident that happened lately at Mears Ashby in Northamptonshire* (1642), sigs. A2–A4. The best survey of this material is still Christopher Hill, *The World Turned Upside Down: Radical Ideas During the English Revolution* (New York, 1972).

3. Thomas Edwards, *Gangraena: Or a Catalogue and Discovery of many of the Errours, Heresies, Blasphemies and pernicious Practices of the Sectaries of this time* (1646), 28, 67; Thomas Edwards, *The Third Part of Gangraena* (1646), 17–18.

4. C. H. Firth and R. S. Rait (eds.), *Acts and Ordinances of the Interregnum, 1642–1660*, 2 vols. (1911), i. 106, 176, 180, 425, 879.

5. Ibid. i. 582–607.

6. Ibid. i. 594–6.

7. John Morrill, 'The Church in England 1642–1649', in his *The Nature of the English Revolution* (1993), 148–75; Christopher Durston, *The Family in the English Revolution* (Oxford, 1989), 115–21; Richard Culmer, *A Parish Looking-Glasse for Persecutors of Ministers* (1657), 17.

8. J. F. McGregor, 'The Baptists: Fount of All Heresy', in J. F. McGregor and Barry Reay (eds.), *Radical Religion in the English Revolution* (Oxford, 1984), 23–63. For a description of a baptist dipping ceremony at Bourne End river in Hertfordshire in 1646, see *Mercurius Civicus*, 177 (8–15 Oct. 1646), repr. in Joad Raymond (ed.), *Making the News: An Anthology of the Newsbooks of Revolutionary England, 1641–1660* (New York, 1993), 388–90.

9. *Catalogue of the Pamphlets, Books, Newspapers, and Manuscripts Relating to the Civil War, the Commonwealth, and Restoration, Collected by George Thomason, 1640–1661*, 2 vols. (1908).

10. Thomas Lechford, *New Englands Advice to Old England* (1644), sigs. A3ᵛ–A4; David Cressy, 'Books as Totems in Seventeenth-Century England and New England', *The Journal of Library History*, 21 (1986), 92–106.

11. Henry Fishwick (ed.), *The Notebook of the Rev. Thomas Jolly AD 1671–1693* (Chetham Society; Manchester, 1894), 121–2.

12. *Susanna's Apology Against the Elders*, in Elspeth Graham, Hilary Hinds, Elaine Hobby, and Helen Wilcox (eds.), *Her Own Life: Autobiographical Writings by Seventeenth-Century Englishwomen* (1989), 106.

13. John Southerden Burn, *The History of Parish Registers in England* (1862), 92; Morrill, 'The Church in England 1642–1649', 155; Bond, *Fonts and Font Covers*, 275–7.

14. *Churchwardens' Accounts of Pittington and other Parishes in the Diocese of Durham* (Surtees Society; Durham, 1888), 305, 310; J. Charles Cox and Alfred Harvey, *English Church Furniture* (1908), 173–4.

15. E. H. White, *The Journal of William Dowsing* (Ipswich, 1885), 27. See also John Morrill, 'William Dowsing, the Bureaucratic Puritan', in John Morrill, Paul Slack, and Daniel Woolf (eds.), *Public Duty and Private Conscience in Seventeenth-Century England* (Oxford, 1993), 173–203.

16. Francis Bamford (ed.), *A Royalist's Notebooks: The Commonplace Book of Sir John Oglander* (1936), 109; John Spurr, *The Restoration Church of England, 1646–1689* (New Haven and London, 1991), 2; Levi Fox (ed.), 'Diary of Robert Beake Mayor of Coventry, 1655–1656', in *Miscellany I* (Dugdale Society; Oxford, 1977), 114–15.

17. E. M. Symonds (ed.), 'The Diary of John Greene (1635–57)', *English Historical Review*, 43 (1928), 392, 599, 603; 44 (1929), 109.

18. F. W. Bennitt (ed.), 'The Diary of Isabella, Wife of Sir Roger Twysden, Baronet, of Royden Hall, East Peckham, 1645–1651', *Archaeologia Cantiana*, 51 (1939–40), 117, 121, 127, 132.

19. Frances Parthenope Verney (ed.), *Memoirs of the Verney Family During the Civil War*, 2 vols. (1892), ii. 258–60. Born on 3 June, the boy was baptized Ralph on 17 June 1647.

20. *The Autobiography of Mrs. Alice Thornton* (Surtees Society; Durham, 1875), 81, 87, 91, 92, 94; Alice Thornton's *Book of Remembrances*, in Graham, Hinds, Hobby, and Wilcox (eds.), *Her Own Life*, 152–4, 163.

21. E. S. de Beer (ed.), *The Diary of John Evelyn*, 6 vols. (Oxford, 1955), iii. 75, 89, 146–7, 194. Though performed at home, these events were dutifully entered in the parish register of St Nicholas, Deptford.

22. Ibid. ii. 544, 555; iii. 218.

23. Spurr, *Restoration Church of England*, 17; E. A. Wrigley and R. S. Schofield, *The Population History of England, 1541–1871* (Cambridge, Mass., 1981), 19, 27; Durston, *Family in the English Revolution*, 115; Firth and Rait (eds.), *Acts and Ordinances of the Interregnum*, ii. 715–18.

24. John Beadle, *The Journall or Diary of a Thankfull Christian* (1656), 45.

25. Spurr, *Restoration Church of England*; Gordon Rupp, *Religion in England 1688–1791* (Oxford, 1986).

26. John Cordy Jeaffreson (ed.), *Middlesex County Records*, 4 vols. (1886–92), iii. 92, 12; Edwards, *Gangraena*, 28.

27. *Statutes of the Realm*, 14 Car. II, c. 4.

28. Cumbria Record Office, Carlisle, DRC/5/2, fo. 163^v; John H. Pruett, *The Parish*

Clergy under the Later Stuarts: The Leicestershire Experience (Urbana and Chicago, 1978), 24.

29. *A Representation of the State of Christianity in England, and of its Decay and Danger from Sectaries aswel as Papists* (1674), 9–10; Spurr, *Restoration Church of England*, 74, 194; Robert Barret, *A Companion for Midwives, Child-Bearing Women, and Nurses* (1699), 91.

30. Guildhall Library, Ms. 9583/2; E. R. C. Brinkworth (ed.), *Episcopal Visitation Book for the Archdeaconry of Buckingham, 1662* (Buckinghamshire Record Society; Aylesbury, 1947), 67; Oxfordshire Archives, Diocesan, c. 4, fo. 155.

31. Durham University Library, Archives and Special Collections, DDR. II/3, fo. 40ᵛ; Guildhall Library, Ms. 9583/2, part 5, fo. 115; part 6, fo. 145; part 4, fos. 63, 157.

32. Spurr, *Restoration Church of England*, 214–17.

33. Guildhall Library, Ms. 9583/2, part 5, fos. 12–13; part 3, fo. 38ᵛ; Brinkworth (ed.), *Episcopal Visitation Book for the Archdeaconry of Buckingham*, 53; Oxfordshire Archives, Diocesan, c. 4, fos. 1, 13ᵛ, 14, 28, 34, 51ᵛ. See also Charles Jackson (ed.), *The Diary of Abraham de la Pryme* (Surtees Society; Durham, 1870), 151, for the sons of Yorkshire sectarians belatedly coming in to be baptized.

34. R. C. Latham and W. Matthews (eds.), *The Diary of Samuel Pepys*, 9 vols. (Berkeley and Los Angeles, 1970–6), ii. 171.

35. Edward Cardwell, *A History of Conferences, and other Proceedings connected with the Revision of the Book of Common Prayer* (Oxford, 1840), 310–11,

36. Nathaniel Resbury, *The Case of the Cross in Baptism Considered* (1684), 1, 4; Thomas Comber, *A Brief Discourse Upon the Offices of Baptism and Confirmation* (1674), appended to his *A Companion to the Altar* (1675), 406.

37. Comber, *Brief Discourse Upon the Offices of Baptism and Confirmation*, 412; Richard Baxter, *A Christian Directory: Or, A Summ of Practical Theologie, and Cases of Conscience* (1678), book 3, p. 124; Resbury, *Case of the Cross in Baptism*, 38.

38. Cardwell, *History of Conferences*, 429–31; Jackson (ed.), *Diary of Abraham de la Pryme*, 150; Thomas Hewardine, *The Countrey-Curate to the Country-People* (1701), 22. See also Thomas Hewardine, *Some Plain Letters in the defence of Infant Baptism* (1699).

39. Thomas Heywood (ed.), *The Diary of the Rev. Henry Newcome, from September 30, 1661, to September 29, 1663* (Chetham Society; Manchester, 1849), 89.

40. Matthew Storey (ed.), *Two East Anglian Diaries, 1641–1729: Isaac Archer and William Coe* (Woodbridge, Suffolk, 1994), 88–9, 91.

41. Pruett, *Parish Clergy under the Later Stuarts*, 25; J. Horsfall Turner (ed.), *The Rev. Oliver Heywood, B.A. 1630–1702: His Autobiography, Diaries, Anecdote and Event Books*, 4 vols. (Brighouse, 1882–5), ii. 292; Heywood (ed.), *Diary of the Rev. Henry Newcome*, 165, 185.

42. Cardwell, *History of Conferences*, 324, 355, 363.

43. Anthony Sparrow [Bishop of Exeter], *A Rationale upon the Book of Common Prayer of the Church of England* (1668), 299; 'Articles of Visitation and Enquiry Within the Diocese of Lincoln', in Brinkworth (ed.), *Episcopal Visitation Book for*

the Archdeaconry of Buckingham, 86. See also Humphrey Henchman's articles for the Diocese of London in 1664, in *Second Report of the Ritual Commission* (Parliamentary Papers 38; 1867–8), appendix E, pp. 631–3.

44. Guildhall Library, Ms. 9583/2, part 3, fos. 59, 124; part 4, fo. 157; W. M. Palmer (ed.) *Episcopal Visitation Returns for Cambridgeshire: Matthew Wren, Bishop of Ely, 1638–1665* (Cambridge, 1930), 108; I. M. Green, *The Re-Establishment of the Church of England 1660–1663* (Oxford, 1978), 173.

45. *Churchwardens' Accounts of Pittington and other Parishes in the Diocese of Durham*, 327; J. S. Leatherbarrow (ed.), *Churchwardens' Presentments in the Diocese of Worcester, c.1660–1760* (Worcester Historical Society; Worcester, 1977), 7; Borthwick Institute, Cause Papers, H. 2419; Brinkworth (ed.), *Episcopal Visitation Book for the Archdeaconry of Buckingham*, 4; Raymond Richards, *Old Cheshire Churches: A Survey of their History, Fabric and Furniture with Records of the Older Monuments* (1947), 81.

46. Guildhall Library, Mss. 9583/4 and 5, Mss. 9537/19 and 20; Hilda Johnstone (ed.), *Churchwardens' Presentments (17th Century) Part 2. Archdeaconry of Lewes* (Sussex Record Society; Lewes, 1948–9), 18, 29; W. J. Pressey, 'Notes on Visitations in the Archdeaconry of Essex', *Transactions of the Essex Archaeological Society*, 19 (1930), 260–76; 20 (1930–1), 216–42; 21 (1933–4), 306–26; 22 (1936–40), 113–25, 316–29; 23 (1942), 145–64.

47. Henry Bradshaw (ed.), 'Notes on the Episcopal Visitation of the Archdeaconrry of Ely in 1685', *Cambridgeshire Antiquarian Communications*, 3 (1879), 323–62.

48. Burn, *History of Parish Registers*, 90. For earlier problems with the nonconformists of Hillingdon, including refusal to baptize babies in church, see Guildhall Library, Ms. 9583/2, part 6, fos. 72–4.

49. John Gother, *A Discourse of the Use of Images: In Relation to the Church of England and the Church of Rome* (1687), 6. Gother's description does not exactly match the surviving font at St James, attributed to Grinling Gibbons, which has been repositioned at least three times since the reign of James II. An earlier font, now destroyed, was given to the parish of St Anne, Soho, in 1686; F. H. W. Sheppard (ed.), *Survey of London*, xxix. *The Parish of St. James Westminster* (1960), 45.

50. Comber, *Brief Discourse Upon the Offices of Baptism and Confirmation*, 403–4. Similar sentiments appear in Sparrow, *Rationale upon the Book of Common Prayer*, 289; Hewardine, *Countrey-Curate to the Country-People*, 12–25.

51. William Keatinge Clay (ed.), *Liturgical Services. Liturgies and Occasional Forms of Prayer Set Forth in the Reign of Queen Elizabeth* (Parker Society; Cambridge, 1847), 206–9. For criticism of 'slight occasions and frivolous pretences' used to justify private baptism in the 1630s, see Daniel Featley, *Clavis Mystica: A Key Opening Divers Difficult and Mysterious Texts of Holy Scripture* (1636: STC 10730), 214.

52. Leland H. Carlson (ed.), *The Writings of Henry Barrow 1590–91* (1966), 87; William Gouge, *Of Domesticall Duties* (3rd edn., 1634; STC 12121), 529, 533.

53. Kenneth Fincham (ed.), *Visitation Articles and Injunctions of the Early Stuart*

Church, i (Church of England Record Society; Woodbridge, Suffolk, 1994), 38, 42, 58, 111, 159, 196, 208; Sparrow, *Rationale upon the Book of Common Prayer*, 302.

54. De Beer (ed.), *Diary of John Evelyn*, ii. 5.

55. William Sherlock, *A Practical Discourse of Religious Assemblies* (2nd edn., 1682), 290.

56. De Beer (ed.), *Diary of John Evelyn*, iii. 368, 421, 495, 528; iv. 272, 396.

57. Ibid. iv. 49, 129, 561.

58. Latham and Matthews (eds.), *The Diary of Samuel Pepys*, viii. 202; Ned Ward, *The London-Spy, Compleat, in Eighteen Parts* (1703), 393–412.

59. J. E. Foster (ed.), *The Diary of Samuel Newton, Alderman of Cambridge (1662–1717)* (Cambridge, 1890), 41.

60. e.g. the conversion of the public parish commemoration of 5 Nov. into the private 'Gunpowder Treason dinner' at St Botolph without Bishopsgate, Guildhall Library, Mss. 4534, 4525. See also Keith Thomas, 'Cases of Conscience in Seventeenth-Century England', in Morrill, Slack, and Woolf (eds.), *Public Duty and Private Conscience in Seventeenth-Century England*, 53–6; Linda A. Pollock, 'Living on the Stage of the World: The Concept of Privacy among the Elite of Early Modern England', in Adrian Wilson (ed.), *Rethinking Social History: English Society 1570–1920 and its Interpretations* (Manchester, 1993), 78–96.

61. Henry Compton, *Episcopalia: or, Letters . . . to the Clergy of this Diocese* (1686), 3, 6; Spurr, *Restoration Church of England*, 209.

62. Wrigley and Schofield, *Population History of England*, 24–32.

63. Sherlock, *Practical Discourse of Religious Assemblies*, 289–95; Edmund Arwaker, *The Ministration of Public Baptism of Infants to be used in the Church, or A Disswasive from Baptising Children in Private* (1689).

64. Philip Stubs, *Of Publick Baptism* (2nd edn., 1699), 'Postscript', 22–30; Martin Strong, *The Indecency and Unlawfulness of Baptizing Children in Private, Without Necessity, and with the Public Form* (1692).

65. Philip Stubs, *Of Publick Baptism* (1693), 26–7; 'Henry Lord Bishop of London's Judgement concerning Publick Baptism', ibid. (2nd edn.); Strong, *Indecency and Unlawfulness of Baptizing Children in Private*, 19.

66. De Beer (ed.), *Diary of John Evelyn*, iv. 633–4.

67. Ibid. v. 67, 124–5, 373–4.

CHAPTER 9

1. This is a revised and expanded version of my essay, 'Purification, Thanksgiving and the Churching of Women in Post-Reformation England', *Past and Present*, 141 (1993), 106–46. I am grateful to the editors and readers of *Past and Present* for their comments, and to the North American Conference on British Studies for selecting this essay for the 1994 Walter D. Love Prize.

2. See e.g. Patrick Collinson, *The Religion of Protestants: the Church in English Society, 1559–1625* (Oxford, 1982); id., *The Birthpangs of Protestant England: Religious and Cultural Change in the Sixteenth and Seventeenth Centuries* (1988); Julian Davies, *The Caroline Captivity of the Church: Charles I and the Remoulding of*

Anglicanism (Oxford, 1992); Kenneth Fincham (ed.), *The Early Stuart Church, 1603–1642* (1993); Christopher Haigh, *English Reformations: Religion, Politics, and Society under the Tudors* (Oxford, 1993); Peter Lake, *Moderate Puritans and the Elizabethan Church* (Cambridge, 1982); id., *Anglicans and Puritans? Presbyterianism and English Conformist Thought from Whitgift to Hooker* (1988); Nicholas Tyacke, *Anti-Calvinists: The Rise of English Arminianism, c.1590–1640* (2nd edn., Oxford, 1990); id., *The Fortunes of English Puritanism, 1603–1640* (1990). Other works on religion in early modern England are accessible through the notes and bibliographies of these publications.

3. Related issues are addressed in Susan Amussen, *An Ordered Society: Gender and Class in Early Modern England* (Oxford, 1988); Anthony Fletcher and John Stevenson (eds.), *Order and Disorder in Early Modern England* (Cambridge, 1985); Martin Ingram, *Church Courts, Sex and Marriage in England, 1570–1640* (Cambridge, 1987); Barry Reay (ed.), *Popular Culture in Seventeenth-Century England* (1985); and David Underdown, *Revel, Riot and Rebellion: Popular Politics and Culture in England 1603–1660* (Oxford, 1985).

4. Keith Thomas, *Religion and the Decline of Magic* (New York, 1971), 38, 59–61.

5. Jeremy Boulton, *Neighbourhood and Society: A London Suburb in the Seventeenth Century* (Cambridge, 1987), 276–7; Will Coster, 'Purity, Profanity and Puritanism: The Churching of Women, 1500– 1700', in W. J. Sheils and Diana Wood (eds.), *Women in the Church* (Studies in Church History, 27; 1990), 377–87; Alan Macfarlane, *The Family Life of Ralph Josselin* (Cambridge, 1970), 88; Peter Rushton, 'Purification or Social Control? Ideologies of Reproduction and the Churching of Women after Childbirth', in Eva Garamarnikow (ed.), *The Public and the Private* (1983), 118–31; Adrian Wilson, 'Participant or Patient? Seventeenth Century Childbirth from the Mother's Point of View', in Roy Porter (ed.), *Patients and Practitioners: Lay Perceptions of Medicine in Pre-Industrial Society* (Cambridge, 1986), 138–40; Adrian Wilson, 'The Ceremony of Childbirth and its Interpretation', in Valerie Fildes (ed.), *Women as Mothers in Pre-Industrial England: Essays in Memory of Dorothy McLaren* (1990), 84. See also Arnold van Gennep, *The Rites of Passage* (Chicago, 1960), 46–9; Gerald Hammond, *Fleeting Things: English Poets and Poems 1616–1660* (1990), 17, 221; Walter von Arx, 'The Churching of Women after Childbirth: History and Significance', in David Power and Luis Maldonado (eds.), *Liturgy and Human Passage* (New York, 1979), 63–72; and Susan C. Karant-Nunn, 'Churching, a Women's Rite: Ritual Modification in Reformation Germany', conference paper, Wolfenbuttel, June 1991.

6. Coster, 'Purity, Profanity and Puritanism', 384, 378; Patricia Crawford, 'The Construction and Experience of Maternity in Seventeenth-Century England', in Fildes (ed.), *Women as Mothers in Pre-Industrial England*, 5, 25; Edward Shorter, *A History of Women's Bodies* (1983), 286–7. See also Antonia Fraser, *The Weaker Vessel* (New York, 1984), 72; Bonnie S. Anderson and Judith P. Zinsser (eds.), *A History of Their Own: Women in Europe from Prehistory to the Present*, 2 vols. (New York, 1988), i. 80, 147; and Karant-Nunn, 'Churching, a Women's Rite'.

7. Susan Wright, 'Family Life and Society in Sixteenth and Early Seventeenth Century Salisbury', Ph.D. thesis, University of Leicester, 1982, p. 154.

8. Wilson, 'Ceremony of Childbirth', 79, 85–9, 96, original italics; Natalie Zemon Davis, 'Women on Top', in her *Society and Culture in Early Modern France* (Stanford, Calif., 1975), 145, 313.

9. Gail Paster, *The Body Embarrassed: Drama and the Disciplines of Shame in Early Modern England* (Ithaca, New York, 1993), 194–7.

10. F. R. Raines (ed.), *The Derby Household Books* (Chetham Society; Manchester, 1853), 48; Felicity Heal, *Hospitality in Early Modern England* (Oxford, 1990), 81, 353; William H. Hale, *A Series of Precedents and Proceedings in Criminal Causes* (1847), 216; Public Record Office, SP 16/340, no 24, fo. 64.

11. John Gough Nichols (ed.), *The Diary of Henry Machyn, Citizen and Merchant-Taylor of London, A.D. 1550 to A.D. 1563* (Camden Society, 1848), 249, 301.

12. Rupert H. Morris, *Chester in the Plantagenet and Tudor Reigns* (Chester, 1894), 336; Mary Bateson (ed.), *Records of the Borough of Leicester . . . 1509–1603* (Cambridge, 1905), 122; Richard S. Ferguson (ed.), *A Boke off Recorde, or Register . . . of Kirkbiekendall . . . 1575* (Kendal, 1892), 86–91; Heal, *Hospitality*, 366–7, 370.

13. F. P. Wilson (ed.), *The Batchelars Banquet* (Oxford, 1929), 14; Margaret Cavendish, Duchess of Newcastle, *Playes* (1662), 401; Emmanuel van Meteren, 'Nederlandtsche Historie', in Harry Ballam and Roy Lewis (eds.), *The Visitor's Book. England and the English as Others Have Seen Them AD 1500 to 1950* (1950), 36. These observations span a hundred years and point to a deep-rooted cultural practice.

14. Wilson (ed.), *The Batchelars Banquet*, 6, 10, 31, 33–5.

15. Reuben Bourne, *The Contented Cuckold, or, the Woman's Advocate* (1692), 25. See also *The Gossips Feast: or, Morrall Tales* (1647), and *The Gossips Meeting: Or, the Merry Market Women of Taunton* (1674?).

16. The Queen's College, Oxford, Ms. 390, 'The Diary of Thomas Crosfield', entry for 18 Dec. 1626; New College, Oxford, Ms. 9502, 'Robert Woodford's Diary', entry for 10 Sept. 1639, other churching dinners on 3 Sept. 1637 and 13 Sept. 1640; R. C. Latham and W. Matthews (eds.), *The Diary of Samuel Pepys*, 11 vols. (Berkeley and Los Angeles, 1970–83), ii. 146, 185; iii. 259.

17. J. Horsfall Turner (ed.), *The Rev. Oliver Heywood, B.A. 1630–1702: His Autobiography, Diaries, Anecdote and Event Books*, 4 vols. (Brighouse, 1882–5), i. 339; ii. 58, 59, 62, 101, 106, 112; Henry Fishwick (ed.), *The Note Book of the Rev. Thomas Jolly AD 1671–1693* (Chetham Society; Manchester, 1894), 88–9.

18. Robert Herrick, 'Julia's Churching, or Purification', in L. C. Martin (ed.), *The Poetical Works of Robert Herrick* (Oxford, 1956), 286. The poem is discussed later in this chapter.

19. Robert Hill, *The Pathway to Prayer and Pietie* (London, 1610, STC; 13473), 412.

20. Hale, *Series of Precedents*, 167.

21. John Stewkeley to Sir Ralph Verney, 1655, in Margaret M. Verney (ed.), *Memoirs of the Verney Family During the Commonwealth 1650 to 1660* (1894), 229. Stewkeley

wanted male companionship at a time when his house was overrun with women. John Taylor mocked a hypocritical puritan father: 'But 'twas in Gandermonth, his wife lay in | His flesh rebell'd, and tempted him to sin.' *A Swarme of Sectaries and Schismatiques* (1641), 5. Cf. *Oxford English Dictionary*, 2nd edn., s.v. 'gander month' and 'gander moon': the month after a wife's confinement, also, perhaps, an 'allusion to the gander's aimless wandering while the goose is sitting'. Another contemporary meaning of 'gander' was a dull or stupid person, a simpleton or fool, suggesting that the husband was temporarily unmanned.

22. William Gouge, *Of Domesticall Duties* (3rd edn., 1634; STC 12121), 526: William Whately, *A Bride-Bvsh: or, A Direction for Married Persons* (1619; STC 25297), 69.

23. T. N. Brushfield, 'The Financial Diary of a Citizen of Exeter, 1631–43', *Reports and Transactions of the Devonshire Association*, 33 (1901), 209; Wilson, 'Ceremony of Childbirth', 77–8.

24. Examples can be found in Guildhall Library, Ms. 9064/17, fo. 33 and Ms. 9064/18, fo. 5; Oxfordshire Archives, Diocesan Papers, d. 4, fo. 9; c. 16, fo. 17; c. 17, fo. 109ᵛ; and Hilda Johnstone (ed.), *Churchwardens' Presentments (Seventeenth Century), Part 1, Archdeaconry of Chichester* (Sussex Record Society; Lewes, 1947–8), 69.

25. John Tanner, *The Hidden Treasures of the Art of Physick* (1659), 314–15; Patricia Crawford, 'Attitudes to Menstruation in Seventeenth-Century England', *Past and Present*, 91 (1981), 53. See also *Oxford English Dictionary*, s.v. 'green', 10d.

26. George Elwes Corrie (ed.), *Sermons by Hugh Latimer* (Parker Society; Cambridge, 1844), 336; Thomas, *Religion and the Decline of Magic*, 38–9, 612. Cf. Crawford, 'Attitudes to Menstruation', 60–3.

27. F. G. Emmison, *Elizabethan Life: Morals and the Church Courts* (Chelmsford, 1973), 160; Johnstone (ed.), *Churchwardens' Presentments (Seventeenth Century), Part 1*, 90.

28. Herrick, 'Julia's Churching, or Purification'; Hammond, *Fleeting things*, 263.

29. Eucharius Roesslin, *The Birth of Man-Kinde: Otherwise Named the Womans Booke* (1626, STC; 21163), 160; Jacques Guillimeau, *Child-Birth: or, The Happy Deliverie of Women* (1612, STC; 12496), 189, 199, 206, 221; ibid, part 2, *The Nursing of Children*, 18; A.M., *A Rich Closet of Physical Secrets* (1652), 19; John Jones, *The Arte and Science of Preserving Bodie and Soule in Healthe, Wisedom, and Catholike Religion* (1579, STC; 14724), 14; Thomas Browne, *Pseudodoxia Epidemica: Or, Enquiries into Very Many Received Tenents and Commonly Presumed Truths* (1650), 173. For comparable constraints in modern complex societies see Karen Ericksen Paige and Jeffery M. Paige, *The Politics of Reproductive Ritual* (Berkeley and Los Angeles, 1981), 276–7.

30. Chris Wilson, 'The Proximate Determinants of Marital Fertility in England 1600–1799', in Lloyd Bonfield, Richard M. Smith, and Keith Wrightson (eds.), *The World We Have Gained: Histories of Population and Social Structure* (Oxford, 1986), 203–30, discusses fecundability and the duration of the post-partum non-susceptible period.

31. Alan MacFarlane (ed.), *The Diary of Ralph Josselin 1616–1683* (1976), 118; J. J. Bagley (ed.), *The Great Diurnal of Nicholas Blundell of Little Crosby, Lancashire*, i (Record Society of Lancashire and Cheshire; 1968), 69; Wilson, 'Ceremony of Childbirth', 77–8.

32. *Certaine Questions by Way of Conference betwixt a Chauncelor and a Kinswoman of His Concerning Churching of Women* (Middleburg?, 1601; STC 20557), 15–16.

33. Richard Hooker, *The Works of that Learned and Judicious Divine, Mr. Richard Hooker* (1723), 268; *Dives and Pauper* (1534; STC 19214), fo. 229; Roger E. Reynolds, 'Churching of Women', in *Dictionary of the Middle Ages* (New York, 1983), iii. 383; John T. McNeill and Helena M. Gamer, *Medieval Handbooks of Penance* (New York, 1938), 197, 208; William Shakespeare, *The Winter's Tale*, Act 3, scene 2, ll. 103–4.

34. Bodleian Library, Oxford, Tanner Ms. 5, 'Benedictio super mulieres post partum ante ostium ecclesie', 276; *Missale Ad Usum Insignis Ecclesie Sarum* (Rouen, 1519 (STC 16201); Antwerp, 1527 (STC 16207), fo. 43; Antwerp, 1555 (STC 16218), fo. 116); William Maskell, *Monumenta Ritualia Ecclesiae Anglicanae: The Occasional Offices of the Church of England According to the Old Use of Salisbury*, 3 vols. (Oxford, 1882), i. 46–8; *The Sarum Missal in English*, 2 vols. (1913), ii. 164–5.

35. See, however, the 1610 Douai edn. of the Sarum Missal, repr. in Maskell, *Monumenta Ritualia Ecclesiae Anglicanae*, i. 48.

36. Cf. Psalm 51: 7. Hyssop was used to return the sacred vessels from sacramental to secular use; metaphorically, the woman having been the vessel of God's gift of life to a new person, returned to her normal state. I am grateful to John Morrill for this observation.

37. Joseph Ketley (ed.), *The Two Liturgies, A.D. 1549, and A.D. 1552* (Parker Society; Cambridge, 1844), 149, 321–2; W. K. Lowther Clarke and Charles Harris (eds.), *Liturgy and Worship: A Companion to the Prayer Books of the Anglican Communion* (1933), 425–6; William Keatinge Clay (ed.), *Liturgical Services: Liturgies and Occasional Forms of Prayer Set Forth in the Reign of Queen Elizabeth* (Parker Society; Cambridge, 1847), 237–8.

38. Henry Christmas (ed.), *The Works of Nicholas Ridley* (Parker Society; Cambridge, 1841), 534. Cf. the emphasis on thanksgiving in *A Newe Boke Conteyninge An exortacion to the sicke, The sycke mans prayer. A prayer with thanks, at ye purification of women* (1561; STC 3363.3) and the earlier edn. of 1548 (STC 3362).

39. Ketley (ed.), *Two Liturgies*, 149, 321; Robert Horne to Henry Bullinger, in the time of Edward VI, in Hastings Robinson (ed.), *The Zurich Letters (Second Series)* (Parker Society; Cambridge, 1845), 356. As *Kirchgang, relevailles*, or *bendicion de la madre*, churching was practised throughout Christian Europe. Hard-line protestants curtailed it, but various forms of the ceremony continued in Lutheran Germany; Adolph Franz, *Die Kirchlichen Benediktionem im Mittelalter* (Frieburg, 1909); Karant-Nunn, 'Churching, a Women's Rite'.

40. Ketley (ed.), *Two Liturgies*, 149, 321. I am grateful to Diarmaid MacCulloch for discussion of this point.

41. Ibid. 321; Clay (ed.), *Liturgical Services*, 237.

42. Corrie (ed.), *Sermons by Hugh Latimer*, 335–6.

43. Ibid. 336.

44. Edward Cardwell (ed.), *Documentary Annals of the Reformed Church of England*, 2 vols. (Oxford, 1844), i. 165; W. H. Frere and W. M. Kennedy (eds.), *Visitation Articles and Injunctions of the Period of the Reformation*, 3 vols. (1910), ii. 331–59.

45. 'An Admonition to the Parliament', in W. H. Frere and C. E. Douglas (eds.), *Puritan Manifestoes* (1954), 8–39, esp. 28–9. All discussions begin with Leviticus 12: 1–7.

46. Dr Williams's Library, University College, London, Old Loose Papers, 'Certayne Considerations', fos. 47–8; Albert Peel (ed.), *The Seconde Part of a Register*, 2 vols. (Cambridge, 1915), i. 127.

47. Extracts from Thomas Cartwright, *A Replye to an Answere Made of M. Doctor Whitegift* [1573] and *The Second Replie of Thomas Cartwright* [1575], repr. in John Ayre (ed.), *The Works of John Whitgift*, 3 vols. (Parker Society; Cambridge, 1851–3), ii. 557.

48. Peel (ed.), *Seconde Part of a Register*, i. 98.

49. Leland H. Carlson (ed.), *The Writings of Henry Barrow 1587–1590* (1962), 462–4; id. (ed.), *The Writings of Henry Barrow 1590–91* (1966), 77–8.

50. *Certaine Questions Concerning Churching*, 7–8, 12, 18.

51. H. C. Johnson (ed.), *Wiltshire County Records: Minutes of Proceedings in Sessions, 1563 and 1574 to 1592*, 4 vols. (Devizes, 1949), iv. 123.

52. Edward Cardwell, *A History of Conferences and Other Proceedings Connected with the Revision of the Book of Common Prayer* (Oxford, 1840), 201, 334, 362.

53. Clay (ed.), *Liturgical Services*, 237–8; 'Admonition to the Parliament', 29; *Certaine Questions Concerning Churching*, 26; John Milton, *An Apology Against a Pamphlet Call'd A Modest Confutation of the Animadversions upon the Remonstrant against Smectymnuus* [1642], in Harry Morgan Ayres (ed.), *The Works of John Milton: Anti-Prelatical Tracts* (New York, 1931), iii/1. 352; William Keeling (ed.), *Liturgiae Britannicae, or the Several Editions of the Book of Common Prayer . . . Arranged to Shew Their Respective Variations* (2nd edn., 1851), 342–5; *The Book of Common Prayer* (1662).

54. Dr Williams's Library, Old Loose Papers, 'Certayne Considerations', fos. 47–8; Peel (ed.), *The Seconde Part of a Register*, i. 127.

55. Ayre (ed.), *Works of John Whitgift*, ii. 557–9. See also David Calderwood, *Altare Damascenum ceu Politia Ecclesiae Anglicanae* (Amsterdam?, 1623; STC 4353), 884–5.

56. *Certaine Questions Concerning Churching*, 69.

57. W. P. M. Kennedy, *Elizabethan Episcopal Administration*, 3 vols. (1924), ii. 55; iii. 95, 115, 113; [Thomas Cooper], *Injunctions Given by . . . Bishop of Lincolne* (1577; STC 10230); [William Wickham], *Articles to be Enquired of Within the Diocese of Lincoln* (1588; STC 10232); [William Chaderton], *Articles to be Enquired of, Within the Diocese of Lincolne* (Cambridge, 1598; STC 10235).

58. Kennedy, *Elizabethan Episcopal Administration*, iii. 149. Middleton's excessive zeal and peculiar morality led to his deprivation in 1589.

59. George Ornsby (ed.), *The Correspondence of John Cosin*, 2 vols. (Surtees Society; Durham, 1869), i. 120; W. Scott and J. Bliss (eds.), *The Works of . . . William Laud*, 7 vols. (Oxford, 1847–60), v. 403, 409, 416; Cardwell, *Documentary Annals*, ii. 255; [Matthew Wren], *Articles to be Inquired of Within the Diocese of Ely* (1638; STC 10197); [id.], *Articles of Enquiry . . . for the Diocese of Ely* (1662). See also the selection of injunctions and visitation articles, 1561–1730, in *Second Report of the Ritual Commission* (Parliamentary Papers 38; 1867–8), appendix E, pp. 401–682.

60. Examples can be found from 1617 in the Hereford Record Office, Diocesan Court Books, box 18, no. 71; Borthwick Institute, York, Metropolitan Visitation Court Book, 1633, part 1, fo. 191ᵛ; and W. M. Palmer (ed.), *Episcopal Visitation Returns for Cambridgeshire: Matthew Wren, Bishop of Ely, 1638–1665* (Cambridge, 1930), 24. See also the title of Herrick, 'Julia's Churching, or Purification'.

61. Peel (ed.), *The Seconde Part of a Register*, i. 127–8; Anthony Gilby, *A Pleasaunt Dialogue Between a Souldier of Barwicke and an English Chaplaine* (1581, STC 11888), sigs. I4, M4, M5. John Canne, *A Necessity of Separation from the Church of England* (Amsterdam, 1634, STC 4574), 99–100, 244.

62. Wright, 'Family Life and Society in Sixteenth and Early Seventeenth Century Salisbury', 156, 333–5; Edmund R. Nevill (ed.), 'The Chrysom Book of St. Thomas, New Sarum', *Wiltshire Notes and Queries*, 5 (1905–7), 462–8, 510–14, 561–6; 6 (1908–10), 19–25, 57–60, 107–10, 208–11, 302–5, 344–8, 391–5, 455–9, 492–8, 547–50.

63. Boulton, *Neighbourhood and Society*, 276–9. Boulton has since found similarly high churching rates in the parish clerk's notebook of St Botolph's, London. Whether rural areas, or less well-organized parishes, had similar rates has yet to be proved. For comparable evidence from Preston, Lancs., see Coster, 'Purity, Profanity, and Puritanism', 381.

64. J. Charles Cox, *The Parish Registers of England* (1910), 60, 62, 71; Cardwell, *Documentary Annals*, i. 238.

65. Nevill (ed.), 'The Chrysom Book of St. Thomas, New Sarum'; N.H., *The Ladies Dictionary: Being a General Entertainment for the Fair Sex* (1694), 107, s.v. 'chrisome'; T. F. Thisleton-Dyer, *Church-Lore Gleanings* (1892), 147–8; John Cosin, *The Works of the Right Reverend Father in God, John Cosin*, 5 vols. (Oxford, 1843–55), v. 500.

66. Nevill (ed.), 'The Chrysom Book of St. Thomas, New Sarum'; T. C. Dale (ed.), *The Inhabitants of London in 1638* (1931), 18, 26, 70, 75. In the archdeaconry of Sudbury and the town of Bury St Edmunds in the 1660s the minister was supposed receive 6d. and the clerk 3d. 'for churching of every woman', West Suffolk Record Office, Bury St Edmunds, E 14/1/13. In Merton College chapel, formerly the parish church of St John the Baptist, Oxford, the fee for churching had risen to 1s. 6d. by 1687, Alan Bott (ed.), *Baptisms and Marriages at Merton College* (Oxford, 1981), 116.

67. Katherine Chidley, *The Iustification of the Independent Churches of Christ* (1641), 56–7; Norfolk Record Office, Norwich, Hare Ms. 3527b. See also Francis Sadler, *The Exactions and Impositions of Parish Fees Discovered* (1738), 24; and Naylor *v.* Scott, in Robert Lord Raymond, *Reports of Cases Argued and Adjudged in the Courts of King's Bench and Common Pleas* (1743), 1558.

68. G. W. O. Addleshaw and Frederick Etchells, *The Architectural Setting of Anglican Worship* (1948), 84; J. Barmby (ed.), *Churchwardens' Accounts of Pittington and other Parishes in the Diocese of Durham from A.D. 1580 to 1700* (Surtees Society; Durham, 1888), 43, 141, 190, 274; Norfolk Record Office, Y. C39/1, accounts of St Nicholas, Great Yarmouth, 1604; Palmer (ed.), *Episcopal Visitation Returns for Cambridgeshire*, 70; Thisleton-Dyer, *Church-Lore Gleanings*, 190–4.

69. Emmison, *Elizabethan Life: Morals and the Church Courts*, 202; Peel (ed.), *The Second Part of a Register*, ii. 42; Margaret Steig, *Laud's Laboratory: The Diocese of Bath and Wells in the Early Seventeenth Century* (East Brunswick, NJ, 1982), 191.

70. Peel (ed.), *The Second Part of a Register*, i. 292, 295; W. J. Sheils, *The Puritans in the Diocese of Peterborough 1558–1610* (Northamptonshire Record Society; Northampton, 1979), 37–8, 43, 52, 61, 68.

71. Hale, *Series of Precedents and Proceedings*, 193, 216, 206, 225.

72. Emmison, *Elizabethan Life: Morals and the Church Courts*, 161; Hale, *Series of Precedents and Proceedings*, 230. For similar domestic churchings see Arthur J. Willis, *Church Life in Kent: Being Church Court records of the Canterbury Diocese, 1559–1565* (London and Chichester, 1975), 28; J. F. Williams (ed.), *Diocese of Norwich: Bishop Redman's Visitation 1597* (Norfolk Record Society; Norwich, 1946), 51; C. W. Foster, *The State of the Church in the Reigns of Elizabeth and James I as Illustrated by Documents Relating to the Diocese of Lincoln* (Lincoln Record Society; Lincoln, 1926), lxxix; *Certaine Questions Concerning Churching*, 46. Cf. Lawrence Stone, *The Family, Sex and Marriage in England, 1500–1800* (1977), 611 on 'the incongruity of performing a "churching" in a private room'.

73. New College, Oxford, Ms. 9502, 'Robert Woodford's Diary', entries for 3 Sept. 1637, 10 Sept. 1639.

74. Buckinghamshire Record Office, Aylesbury, D/A/V 3, fo. 37^v.

75. Sheils, *Puritans in the Diocese of Peterborough*, 43; Foster, *State of the Church in the Reigns of Elizabeth and James I*, lxxix; Oxfordshire Archives, Diocesan, d. 5, fo. 107^v; Guildhall Library, Ms. 9583/2, part 6, fo. 36.

76. Bedfordshire Record Office, Bedford, Archdeaconry Court, ABC 5, 247. Earlier in 1587, Thomas Smith's wife of Eastbourne, Sussex, 'did say the service that is appointed in the book for the churching of women when the woman came to church [at a time] not appointed by the minister', Walter C. Renshaw, 'Notes from the Act Book of the Archdeaconry Court of Lewes', *Sussex Archaeological Collections*, 49 (1906), 51.

77. Emmison, *Elizabethan Life: Morals and the Church Courts*, 161; Foster, *State of the Church in the Reigns of Elizabeth and James I*, lxxix; Johnstone (ed.), *Churchwardens' Presentments (Seventeenth Century)*, Part 1, 77.

78. Foster, *State of the Church in the Reigns of Elizabeth and James I*, xxxix; Emmison, *Elizabethan Life: Morals and the Church Courts*, 160.

79. William Nicholson (ed.), *The Remains of Edmund Grindal* (Parker Society; Cambridge, 1843), 127; Frere and Kennedy (eds.), *Visitation Articles and Injunctions*, iii. 308, 332; Kennedy, *Elizabethan Episcopal Administration*, ii. 55; iii. 95, 115, 113; Emmison, *Elizabethan Life: Morals and the Church Courts*, 4.

80. Durham University Library, Archives and Special Collections, Diocesan Records, 11/7, fo. 155ᵛ; Palmer (ed.), *Episcopal Visitation Returns for Cambridgeshire*, 24; Bodleian Library, Ballard Ms. 4, fo. 118. See also Cosin, *Works*, v. 499 for the archdeacon's insistence on penance.

81. Ayre (ed.), *Works of John Whitgift*, ii. 557, 563–4, iii. 490.

82. Dr Williams's Library, Old loose Papers, 'Certayne Considerations', fo. 47ᵛ; *Certaine Questions Concerning Churching*, 21.

83. Hale, *Series of Precedents and Proceedings*, 169. The curate was Arthur Dent, later vicar of South Shoebury and a prolific author of godly tracts and sermons.

84. Morton and Burges are both cited in William Ames, *A Fresh Suit Against Human Ceremonies in Gods Worship* (Amsterdam?, 1633; STC 555), 345–9.

85. Anthony Sparrow, *A Rationale Upon the Book of Common Prayer of the Church of England* (1668), 357; *Articles of Enquiry and Direction for the Diocese of Norwich, in the first visitation of the reverend father in God, Richard Mountaigu* (1638; STC 10299), sig. C3.

86. Sparrow, *Rationale Upon the Book of Common Prayer*, 356–7.

87. *Certaine Questions Concerning Churching*, 3, 16; Ayre (ed.), *Works of John Whitgift*, ii. 563–4.

88. Foster, *State of the Church in the Reigns of Elizabeth and James I*, lxxix; Hale, *Series of Precedents and Proceedings*, 237.

89. *Second Report of the Ritual Commission*, appendix E, pp. 480, 485; Ornsby (ed.), *Correspondence of John Cosin*, i. 120.

90. For similar reactions to different issues see Underdown, *Revel, Riot and Rebellion*, esp. 66–8, 77–8, 90, 130, 139–40.

91. Theodore Beale of Ash Bocking and Robert Sugden of Benhall were among the Suffolk clergy later ejected for insisting that women to be churched came up to the rail, A. G. Matthews, *Walker Revised. Being a Revision of John Walker's Sufferings of the Clergy during the Grand Rebellion 1642–60* (Oxford, 1948), 327, 345; Clive Holmes (ed.), *The Suffolk Committees for Scandalous Ministers 1644–1646* (Suffolk Records Society; Ipswich, 1970), 43, 69. See also the problem involving James Bradshaw's insistence on churching at the altar at Chalfont St Peter, Buckinghamshire, in 1639, Bodleian Library, Tanner Ms. 62, fo. 69.

92. Cardwell, *Documentary Annals*, ii. 255; [Matthew Wren], *Articles to be Inquired of Within the Diocese of Ely* (1638; STC 10197), ch. 7, art. 10; *Second Report of the Ritual Commission*, appendix E, p. 591; [Matthew Wren], *Articles of Enquiry . . . for the Diocese of Ely* (1662); [Robert Pory], *Articles to be Enquired of Within the Archdeaconry of Middlesex* (1662).

93. *Second Report of the Ritual Commission,* appendix E, p. 485; Norfolk Record Office, VIS 5/1; Kenneth Fincham, *Prelate as Pastor: The Episcopate of James I* (Oxford, 1990), 282.

94. *Les Reports de Sir Gefrey Palmer* (1678), 296–7. Attempts to learn more about this case have so far proved unsuccessful. I would like to thank John Baker, John Guy, Sybil Jack, John Morrill, and Sheila Lambert for their assistance. The mayor's court records at Norwich show Thomas Shipden setting out for London in Dec. 1622, entrusted with city documents but perhaps also going to battle on his wife's behalf, Norfolk Record Office, Mayor's Court Book, 1615–24, fo. 436.

95. Bodleian Library, Tanner Ms. 68, fo. 147; John T. Evans, *Seventeenth-Century Norwich: Politics, Religion, and Government, 1620–1690* (Oxford, 1979), 93, 97, 113.

96. Berkshire Record Office, Reading, D/A2/c 74, fo. 456ᵛ. See also the dispute at Basingstoke, Hants, in 1636 that was exacerbated by the Laudian vicar's insistence that women to be churched follow the 'ancient custom of the parish' and offer 'a piece of linen cloth which is called a chrisom'. The vicar, Ambrose Webb, refused to church Phillipa East because she brought no chrisom, 'but was ready to have paid Mr. Webb 6d. if he would have accepted of it'. Despite being suspected as a conventicler, Goody East appeared eager to be churched. Public Record Office, SP 16/340, no. 24, fo. 60–1.

97. Norfolk Record Office, VIS 5/3/3, s.v. 'Sturston'; W. M. Palmer and H. W. Saunders (eds.), *Documents Relating to Cambridgeshire Villages* (Cambridge, 1926), 72, 73.

98. *Calendar of State Papers, Domestic, 1637–38,* 382–3.

99. Public Record Office, SP 16/388/41, pieces 1, 2, 3.

100. Ibid.

101. Ibid.

102. Ibid.

103. *Victoria County History . . . Staffordshire,* iii. 327; William Prynne, *Canterburies Doome: or, The First Part of a Compleat History of the Commitment, Charge, Tryall, Condemnnation, Execution of William Laud* (1646), 380–1, 538.

104. Robert Herrick, *Hesperides: or, The Works both Humane and Divine* (1648), 339; Martin (ed.), *Poetical Works of Robert Herrick,* 286.

105. Leah Marcus, *The Politics of Mirth: Jonson, Herrick, Milton, Marvell, and the Defense of Old Holiday Pastimes* (Chicago, 1986), 140–68. I am grateful to Professor Marcus for advice about this poem.

106. *Hierurgia Anglicana: Or Documents and Extracts Illustrative of the Ritual of the Church of England After the Reformation* (1848), 180–4.

107. E. M. Symonds (ed.), 'Diary of John Greene', *English Historical Review,* 43 (1928), 599, 603; Frances Parthenope Verney (ed.), *Memoirs of the Verney Family During the Civil War* (1892), 272; John Spurr, *The Restoration Church of England, 1646–1689* (London and New Haven, 1991), 16; Cheshire Record Office, Chester, DDX 384/1, 'Diary of Thomas Mainwaring', a reference I owe to Geoffrey L.

Hudson; E. S. de Beer (ed.), *The Diary of John Evelyn*, 6 vols. (Oxford, 1955), iii. 76, 90, 146–7, 195.

108. Cf. John Morrill, 'The Church in England, 1642–9', in John Morrill (ed.), *Reactions to the English Civil War* (1982), 89–114, 230–4; Christopher Durston, *The Family in the English Revolution* (Oxford, 1990), 121–2.

109. Richard Baxter, *Reliquiae Baxterianae* (1694), 83; Richard Baxter, 'The Reformed Liturgy: A Thanksgiving for the Deliverance of Women in Childbearing', in *The Practical Works of Richard Baxter*, 4 vols. (Ligonier, Pa., 1990), i. 940–1.

110. The Book of Common Prayer of 1662 substituted Psalms 116 or 127 for Psalm 121 in the churching service, and incorporated minor adjustments to the rubric; see Keeling (ed.), *Liturgiae Britannicae*, 342–5.

111. Thomas Pierce, *A Collection of Sermons on Several Occasions* (Oxford, 1671), 296; Edward Sparke, *Scintilla Altaris: Primitive Devotion in the Feasts and Fasts of the Church of England* (6th edn., 1678), 392.

112. Mark Frank, *LI Sermons* (1672), 226–38; Pierce, *Collection of Sermons*, 261–2, 274–5; Sparke, *Scintilla Altaris*, 384–91.

113. George Stradling, *Sermons and Discourses upon Several Occasions* (1692), 91–101.

114. Guildhall Library, Ms. 9583/2, part 5, fos. 12–13; part 4, fo. 63; part 3, fo. 44, 49, 126ᵛ; part 6, fos. 72, 78.

115. Cumbria Record Office, Carlisle, DRC/5/2, fos. 17ᵛ, 71, 78; Hilda Johnstone (ed.), *Churchwardens' Presentments (Seventeenth Century), Part 2, Archdeaconry of Lewes* (Sussex Record Society; Lewes, 1948–9), 15, 50; Durham University Library, Archives and Special Collections, Diocesan Records II/3, fos. 2, 30ᵛ, 34, 40, 70ᵛ, 73ᵛ; Borthwick Institute, Y V/CB 3, fos. 2, 25ᵛ, 56, 488, 518ᵛ, 541ᵛ, 550ᵛ; Y V/CB/4, fos. 101, 103.

116. Guildhall Library, Ms. 9583/2, part 3, fos. 39, 125; Sidney A. Peyton (ed.), *The Churchwardens' Presentments in the Oxfordshire Peculiars of Dorchester, Thame and Banbury* (Oxfordshire Record Society; Oxford, 1928), xxxiv.

117. Guildhall Library, Ms. 9583/2, part 1, fo. 4ᵛ; Turner (ed.), *Rev. Oliver Heywood*, ii. 292.

118. Charles Kerry, 'Leonard Wheatcroft of Ashover', *Journal of the Derbyshire Archaeological and Natural History Society*, 21 (1899), 33, 53.

119. Rushton, 'Purification or Social Control?', 124–6; Wilson, 'Ceremony of Childbirth', 88–9, 104. For 18th-cent. examples see Claver Morris, *The Diary of a West Country Physician: AD 1684–1726*, ed. Edmund Hobhouse (1935), 57; Francis Griffin Stokes (ed.), *The Bletchley Diary of the Rev. William Cole 1765–67* (1931), 7, 56, 108, 132, 149, 167, 232, 273, and John Beresford (ed.), *The Diary of a Country Parson: The Reverend James Woodforde*, 5 vols. (Oxford, 1926–9), i. 28, 36, 44, 90, 191, 302, 336, 340; ii. 24, 80, 121, 207, 286, 311, 313, 320; iii. 252, 308, 357; iv. 15, 93, 163, 178. For the continuing popularity of churching see Jim Obelkevich, *Religion and Rural Society: South Lindsay 1825–75* (Oxford, 1976), 273–4, and David Clark, *Between Pulpit and Pew: Folk Religion in a North Yorkshire Fishing Village* (Cambridge, 1982), 115, 119, 122–4. Some Church of England clergymen tell me

that churching is entirely forgotten today, but others report its continuation in rural areas from Devon to Durham. The service is still available, on request.

120. Canne, *Necessity of Separation*, 100.

121. 1 Timothy 2: 15 For sermons on this topic see Thomas Adams, *The Workes of Tho: Adams: Being the Summe of His Sermons* (1629; STC 104), 1134; Samuel Annesley (ed.), *A Continuation of Morning-Exercise Questions and Cases of Conscience* (1683), 633–63; Stephen Charnock, *A Supplemental to the Several Discourses Upon Various Divine Subjects* (1683), 76–81. See also John Day, *Day's Festival or, Twelve of His Sermons* (Oxford, 1615; STC 6426), 235–6, and George R. Potter and Evelyn M. Simpson (eds.), *The Sermons of John Donne*, 10 vols. (Berkeley and Los Angeles, 1959), v. 171, 198; Hammond, *Fleeting Things*, 263.

CHAPTER 10

1. Young people's revels in Oxfordshire on St Stephen's night in 1596 included 'codpiece kissing' with the suggestive chant, 'codpiece up and codpiece down, there were but a few in Southly town'. Oxfordshire Archives, Diocesan Papers, d. 5, fo. 50ᵛ. The poet Robert Herrick referred to 'those wanton reaks y'ave had at barley-breaks', a kissing and chasing game thought unsuitable for married adults, in 'An Epithalamie to Sir Thomas Southwell and his Ladie', in F. W. Moorman (ed.), *The Poetical Works of Robert Herrick* (Oxford, 1921), 56. See *The praise of our Country Barly-Brake: Cupids advisement for Young-men to take Vp this loving old sport, Called Barly-Brake* (1680s?), Roxburghe Ballads, i. 344. For the suggestion that 'barley break' could imply copulation, see James T. Hencke, *Courtesans and Cuckolds: A Glossary of Renaissance Dramatic Bawdy (Exclusive of Shakespeare)* (New York, 1979), 13.

2. The mean age of first marriage for men in the period 1600–49 was 28, for women 26, E. A. Wrigley and R. S. Schofield, *The Population History of England 1541–1871* (Cambridge, Mass., 1981), 255, 423–4.

3. Alexander Niccholes, *A Discourse of Marriage and Wiving* (1615; STC 18514), 4; Thomas Shipman, *Carolina: Or, Loyal Poems* (1683), 28.

4. G. E. Aylmer (ed.), *The Diary of William Lawrence Covering Periods Between 1662 and 1681* (Beaminster, 1961), 52.

5. e.g. 'Philomusus', *The Academy of Complements* (1640; STC 19883); *The Card of Courtship: or, The Language of Love* (1653); Edward Phillips, *The Mysteries of Love and Eloquence* (1658).

6. N.H., *The Ladies Dictionary* (1694), 198–9, 323.

7. James M. Osborn (ed.), *The Autobiography of Thomas Whythorne* (Oxford, 1962), 95, 150–71.

8. Ibid. 95.

9. Ibid. 150–2.

10. Ibid. 151–2.

11. Ibid. 153.

12. Ibid. 154–65.

13. James Orchard Halliwell (ed.), *The Autobiography and Personal Diary of Dr. Simon Forman . . . 1552 to 1602* (1849), 21–3, 30.

14. Huntington Library Ms. HM30665, 'Memorable Accidents' (Diary of Sir William Ashcombe, 1591–1625), fos. 3–3ᵛ.

15. W. G. Perrin (ed.), *The Autobiography of Phineas Pett* (Navy Records Society; 1918), 150–4.

16. T. N. Brushfield (ed.), 'The Financial Diary of a Citizen of Exeter, 1631–43', *Reports and Transactions of the Devonshire Association, 33* (1901), 201–4.

17. Ibid. 202–5.

18. E. M. Symonds (ed.), 'The Diary of John Greene (1635–57), *English Historical Review, 43* (1928), 387–9.

19. Dorothy Gardiner (ed.), *The Oxinden Letters 1607–1642* (1933), 111–12. Cf. negotiations for the hand of the widowed Margaret Verney, in Frances Parthenope Verney (ed.), *Memoirs of the Verney Family During the Civil War*, 2 vols. (1882), i. 277–81.

20. Alan Macfarlane (ed.), *The Diary of Ralph Josselin 1616–1683* (1976), 8, 551, 552, 553, 555.

21. Francis Bamford (ed.), *A Royalist's Notebook: The Commonplace Book of Sir John Oglander* (1936), 130.

22. Alice Thornton, *The Autobiography of Mrs. Alice Thornton* (Surtees Society; Durham, 1875), 75–82. See also negotiations for the marriage of her daughter in 1668, ibid. 226–31.

23. George Parfitt and Ralph Houlbrooke (eds.), *The Courtship Narrative of Leonard Wheatcroft, Derbyshire Yeoman* (Reading, 1986), 41–89. Quotations are from pp. 41, 52, 78, 84, 88–9.

24. Lawrence Stone appears to be alone in having 'no doubt that British courting rituals normally involved the habit' of 'bundling'. *Road to Divorce: England 1530–1987* (Oxford, 1990), 61–2. Contrast Eric Josef Carlson, *Marriage and the English Reformation* (Oxford, 1994), 231, 'I have found no examples of the court-ship practice of "bundling"'.

25. Lori Anne Ferrell (ed.), 'An Imperfect Diary of a Life: The 1662 Diary of Samuel Woodforde', *Yale University Library Gazette, 63* (1989), 143–4.

26. Ibid.

27. Ruth Bird (ed.), *The Journal of Giles Moore 1656–1679* (Sussex Record Society; Lewes, 1971), 77, 79–80.

28. Michael Hunter and Annabel Gregory (eds.), *An Astrological Diary of the Seventeenth Century: Samuel Jeake of Rye 1652–1699* (Oxford, 1988), 130.

29. Ibid. 130–2.

30. Ibid. 134–6.

31. Ibid. 138.

32. Ibid. 138, 148–9.

33. Ibid. 149–55.

34. Joseph Hunter (ed.), *The Diary of Ralph Thoresby* . . . *1677–1724*, 2 vols. (1830), i. 176–7.

35. Ibid. i. 179. The wedding was performed by licence in the bride's home parish church at Ledsham.

36. E. S. de Beer (ed.), *The Diary of John Evelyn*, 6 vols. (Oxford, 1955), iii. 475, 519, 551.

37. Ibid. iv. 112, 189, 192, 193, 194.

38. Ibid. iv. 195, 238, 245–7.

39. Ibid. iv. 425, 420, 460–4.

40. Ibid. iv. 502–3; v. 133, 138, 587–8, 602, 605–7.

41. Mary Carbery (ed.), *Mrs. Elizabeth Freke Her Diary 1671 to 1714* (Cork, 1913), 41.

42. Ibid. 41–2.

43. Ibid. 48–9.

44. J. J. Bagley (ed.), *The Great Diurnal of Nicholas Blundell of Little Crosby, Lancashire*, i (Record Society of Lancashire and Cheshire; 1968), 33–4.

45. Ibid. 34.

46. Ibid.

47. Ibid. 35–6. For the revival of Maytide customs see Ronald Hutton, *The Rise and Fall of Merry England: The Ritual Year 1400–1700* (Oxford, 1994).

48. Bagley (ed.), *The Great Diurnal of Nicholas Blundell*, i. 36–7.

49. Lawrence Stone, *The Family, Sex and Marriage in England 1500–1800* (1977). See the discussion below on 'love'.

50. John Ray, *A Collection of English Proverbs* (1670), 47; Morris Palmer Tilley, *A Dictionary of the Proverbs in England in the Sixteenth and Seventeenth Centuries* (Ann Arbor, Mich., 1950), 445.

51. Ann Jennalie Cook, *Making a Match: Courtship in Shakespeare and his Society* (Princeton, 1991), 104–19.

52. William Hinde, *A Faithfull Remonstrance of the Holy Life and happy Death of Iohn Bruen* (1641), 24–5.

53. Folger Shakespeare Library, Ms. L.a. 473.

54. Folger Shakespeare Library, Ms. L.a. 564. For further operation of the kinship system see David Cressy, 'Kinship and Kin Interaction in Early Modern England', *Past and Present*, 113 (1986), 38–69.

55. Huntington Library, Stowe Ms. STB Box 2 (1).

56. Donald Woodward (ed.), *The Farming and Memorandum Books of Henry Best of Elmswell, 1642* (1984), 122–3.

57. For Best's family see ibid., p. lvii.

58. Ibid. 123.

59. Oxfordshire Archives, Diocesan Papers, d. 5, fo. 103; Buckinghamshire Record Office, D/A/C 4, fo. 174^v; Berkshire Record Office, D/A2/c74, fo. 114.

60. Carlson, *Marriage and the English Reformation*, 110; Illana Krausman Ben-Amos, *Adolescence and Youth in Early Modern England* (New Haven and London, 1994), 191–205; Paul Griffith, *Youth and Authority: Formative Experiences in England, 1560–1640* (Oxford, 1996).

61. William Vaughan, *The Golden-grove, moralized in three Bookes* (2nd edn., 1609; STC 24611), bk. 2, ch. 2; George Whetstone, *An Heptameron of Ciuill Discourses* (1582; STC 25337), sigs. E–F.

62. William Whately, *A Care-cloth: Or a Treatise of the Cvmbers and Trovbles of Marriage* (1624; STC 25299), sig. A4, 71–5; Matthew Griffith, *Bethel: Or, a Forme for Families* (1633; STC 12370), 249. See also Thomas Hilder, *Conjugall Counsell: or, Seasonable Advise, both to unmarried, and Married Persons* (1653), 10–45.

63. Ray, *Collection of English Proverbs*, 46–53; Tilley, *Dictionary of the Proverbs in England*, 190, 55; Cook, *Making a Match*, 39; *Twelfth Night*, Act 1, scene 3; J. A. Sharpe, 'Plebeian Marriage in Stuart England: Some Evidence from Popular Literature', *Transactions of the Royal Historical Society*, 5th ser. 36 (1986), 69–90. See also James Obelkevich, 'Proverbs in Social History', in Peter Burke and Roy Porter (eds.), *The Social History of Language* (Cambridge, 1987), 43–72.

64. Viven Brodsky Elliot, 'Mobility and Marriage in Pre-Industrial England', Ph.D. thesis, University of Cambridge, 1979. See also Vivian Brodsky, *Londoners: Migration, Marriage Kinship and Neighbourhood, 1580–1640* (Oxford, 1997).

65. T. Ellison Gibson (ed.), *Crosby Records: A Cavalier's Note Book . . . of William Blundell* (1880), 128; Verney (ed.), *Memoirs of the Verney Family During the Civil War*, i. 278.

66. Tilley, *Dictionary of the Proverbs in England*, 445; Niccholes, *A Discourse of Marriage and Wiving*, 4.

67. Whately, *Care-cloth*, 32–3, 69–70; John Dod and Robert Cleaver, *A Godly Forme of Houshold Gouernment* (1598, 1630 edn.; STC 5388), sig. V5ᵛ; Hilder, *Conjugall Counsell*, 55–63.

68. James E. Smith and Jim Oeppen, 'Estimating Numbers of Kin in Historical England Using Microsimulation', in David S. Rehere and Roger Schofield (eds.), *Old and New Methods in Historical Demography* (Oxford, 1993), 306–8.

69. Miles Coverdale, *The Christen State of Matrymonye, wherein housebandes and wyves maye lerne to kepe house together wyth loue* (1552; STC 4049), fos. 21ᵛ–22 (this was an English rendition of the work of Heinrich Bullinger, often repr. between 1541 and 1575); Daniel Rogers, *Matrimoniall Honovr: Or, The mutuall Crowne and comfort of godly, loyall, and chaste Marriage* (1642), 100.

70. Sharpe, 'Plebeian Marriage in Stuart England', 75; Alan Macfarlane, *Marriage and Love in England: Modes of Reproduction 1300–1840* (Oxford, 1986), 142–4; Martin Ingram, *Church Courts, Sex and Marriage in England, 1570–1640* (Cambridge, 1987), 200–5; Eric Josef Carlson, *Marriage and the English Reformation* (Oxford, 1994), 117–23.

71. Matthew Storey (ed.), *Two East Anglian Diaries, 1641–1729: Isaac Archer and William Coe* (Woodbridge, Suffolk, 1994), 93, 115.

72. Richard Trappes-Lomax (ed.), *The Diary and Letter Book of the Rev. Thomas Brockbank 1671–1709* (Manchester, 1930), 171, 180. Eventually, when Brockbank felt 'some inclinations to marry', he spent several months discussing the matter with his father, and several years bringing it to a conclusion, ibid. 188–9, 196–255.

73. Henry Fishwick (ed.), *The Note Book of the Rev. Thomas Jolly AD 1671–1693* (Manchester, 1894), 75, 79; Hunter and Gregory (eds.), *An Astrological Diary of the Seventeenth Century*, 150.

74. Bamford (ed.), *Royalist's Notebook* 130; Carbery (ed.), *Mrs. Elizabeth Freke Her Diary*, 21–2.

75. Amy Edith Robinson (ed.), *The Life of Richard Kidder, D.D. Bishop of Bath and Wells: Written by Himself* (Somerset Record Society; 1924), 134–44.

76. *Depositions and other Ecclesiastical Proceedings from the Courts of Durham* (Surtees Society; Durham, 1845), 234–5.

77. Ibid. 236–40.

78. Greater London Record Office, DL/C 319, fos. 172–3.

79. Ibid.

80. A. Percival Moore (ed.), 'Marriage Contracts or Espousals in the Reign of Queen Elizabeth', *Associated Architectural Societies Reports and Papers*, 30 (1909), 281.

81. Durham University Library, Archives and Special Collections, DDR V/11. fos. 162^v–163.

82. Stone, *Family, Sex and Marriage*, argued that 16th- and 17th-cent. marriages were devoid of emotional intimacy. Fundamental critiques of Stone include E. P. Thompson, 'Happy Families', *New Society* (8 Sept. 1977), 499–501, and Alan MacFarlane, review article, *History and Theory*, 18 (1979), 103–26. Jim Sharpe's analysis of ballad literature observes that 'marriage for love and freedom of choice or partner were taken for granted and held to be normal and desirable . . . even ballads portraying courtship among the masses make it clear that romantic love was felt to be an appropriate sentiment'. Sharpe, 'Plebeian Marriage in Stuart England', 73–4. Martin Ingram finds 'something very close to our idea of "romantic love", with all its heartaches and inconstancies' in early modern Wiltshire and East Anglia, Martin Ingram, 'Spousals Litigation in the English Ecclesiastical Courts *c*.1350–*c*.1640', in R. B. Outhwaite (ed.), *Marriage and Society* (1982), 50; Eric Carlson's study of marriage in Elizabethan Cambridgeshire finds that 'the most important consideration was love': *Marriage and the English Reformation*, 114. For a useful historiographical review including continental European studies of this subject, see Jeffrey R. Watt, *The Making of Modern Marriage: Matrimonial Control and the Rise of Sentiment in Neuchâtel, 1550–1800* (Ithaca, New York, 1992), 1–21.

83. Tilley, *Dictionary of the Proverbs in England*, 396–9.

84. William Gouge, *Of Domesticall Dvties* (1622; STC 12119), 196–7.

85. Dod and Cleaver, *Godly Forme of Houshold Gouernment*, sig. V5^v; Thomas Gataker, *A Good Wife God's Gift: And, A Wife Indeed* (1623; STC 11659), 11.

86. Osborn (ed.), *Autobiography of Thomas Whythorne*, 156, 159.

87. Perrin (ed.), *Autobiography of Phineas Pett*, 9–10, 137.

88. *William Whiteway of Dorchester His Diary 1618 to 1635* (Dorset Record Society; Dorchester, 1991), 25, 28, 29.

89. Parfitt and Houlbrooke (eds.), *Courtship Narrative of Leonard Wheatcroft*, 36,

78; Ferrell (ed.), 'An Imperfect Diary of a Life', 143; Carbery (ed.), *Mrs. Elizabeth Freke Her Diary*, 41–2; Trappes-Lomax (ed.), *Diary and Letter Book of the Rev. Thomas Brockbank*, 184–6.

90. See examples in *Loues Garland. Or, Posies for Rings, Hand-kerchers, and Gloues; And such pretty Tokens that Louers send their Loues* (1624; STC 16856); Margaret Spufford, *The Great Reclothing of Rural England: Petty Chapmen and their Wares in the Seventeenth Century* (1984), 88–102, 186–90.

91. F. P. Wilson (ed.), *The Batchelars Banquet* (Oxford, 1929), 86–91.

92. Brushfield (ed.), 'Financial Diary of a Citizen of Exeter', 201–4; Woodward (ed.), *Farming and Memorandum Books of Henry Best*, 122–3.

93. Henry Swinburne, *A Treatise of Spousals, or Matrimonial Contracts* (1686), 1, 207–10; Ralph Houlbrooke, 'The Making of Marriage in Mid-Tudor England: Evidence from the Records of Matrimonial Contract Litigation', *Journal of Family History*, 10 (1985), 344; Ingram, *Church Courts, Sex and Marriage*, 198; Carlson, *Marriage and the English Reformation*, 111, 136; Peter Rushton, 'The Testament of Gifts: Marriage Tokens and Disputed Contracts in North-East England, 1560–1630', *Folk-Life*, 24 (1985–6), 25–31; Diana O'Hara, 'The Language of Tokens and the Making of Marriage', *Rural History*, 3 (1992), 1–40.

94. Moore (ed.), 'Marriage Contracts or Espousals in the Reign of Queen Elizabeth', 287–9; Robert Hubbard and Elizabeth Cawnt similarly sealed their contract in 1598 by giving and receiving a piece of gold, ibid. 291.

95. Ibid. 296; *Depositions and other Ecclesiastical Proceedings from the Courts of Durham*, 234.

96. Durham University Library, Archives DDR V/8, fos. 99–99ᵛ; see also Joseph B. Gavin, '*Handley v. Newbie* alias Shields: A Marriage at Farlam in 1605', *Transactions of the Cumberland and Westmorland Antiquarian and Archaeological Society*, 70 (1970), 253–9.

97. *Depositions and other Ecclesiastical Proceedings from the Courts of Durham*, 285.

98. Oxfordshire Archives, Archdeaconry Papers, c. 5, fo. 12; E. R. Brinkworth (ed.), 'The Archdeacon's Court *Liber Actorum* 1584', *Oxfordshire Record Society*, 23–4 (1942–6), 222.

99. Moore (ed.), 'Marriage Contracts or Espousals in the Reign of Queen Elizabeth', 281–2.

100. Guido Ruggiero, *Binding Passions: Tales of Magic, Marriage, and Power at the End of the Renaissance* (New York, 1993); Keith Thomas, *Religion and the Decline of Magic* (New York, 1971), 233–4.

CHAPTER 11

1. Henry Swinburne, *A Treatise of Spousals, or Matrimonial Contracts* (1686). Scholarly examinations of marriage contracts include R. H. Helmholz, *Marriage Litigation in Medieval England* (Cambridge, 1974), 25–30; Ralph Houlbrooke, 'The Making of Marriage in Mid-Tudor England: Evidence from the Records of Matrimonial Contract Litigation', *Journal of Family History* 10 (1985), 339–52;

Martin Ingram, 'Spousals Litigation in the English Ecclesiastical Courts c.1350–c.1640', in R. B. Outhwaite (ed.), *Marriage and Society* (1982), 35–57; Martin Ingram, *Church Courts, Sex and Marriage in England, 1570–1640* (Cambridge, 1987), 189–211; and Diana O'Hara, '"Ruled by my Friends": Aspects of Marriage in the Diocese of Canterbury, c.1540–1570', *Continuity and Change*, 6 (1991), 9–41.

2. Henry Smith, *A Preparative to Marriage: The Summe whereof was spoken at a contract and inlarged after* (1591; STC 22686), title-page, 1; Smith refers readers to marriage contracts in Exodus 22: 16 and Deuteronomy 22: 28.

3. John Rylands Library, Manchester, Ms. 524, 'The Acts and Speeches of Richard Greenham', fo. 43; Richard Greenham, 'A Treatise of a Contract before Mariage', in *The Works . . . of Richard Greenham* (1599; STC 12312), 288. I am grateful to Eric Carlson for directing me to these sources.

4. Daniel Rogers, *Matrimoniall Honovr: Or, The mutuall Crowne and comfort of godly, loyall, and chaste Marriage* (1642), 104–6; John Dod and Robert Cleaver, *A Godly Forme of Houshold Gouernment* (1598, 1630 edn.; STC 5388), sig. H2; Matthew Griffith, *Bethel: Or, a Forme for Families* (1633; STC 12370), 269; William Whately, *A Care-cloth: Or a Treatise of the Cvmbers and Trovbles of Marriage* (1624; STC 25299), 31.

5. Greenham, *Works*, 289, 299.

6. William Gouge, *Of Domesticall Dvties* (1622; STC 12119), 196, 200.

7. Ibid. 198.

8. Ibid. 198, 200.

9. Griffith, *Bethel: Or, a Forme for Families*, 269–71.

10. Rogers, *Matrimoniall Honovr*, 96.

11. Henry Swinburne warned of the 'perjuries, adulteries, and bastardies' that arose from secret contracts, *Treatise of Spousals*, 194. Elizabethan bishops sometimes enquired in their visitations, 'whether you know any to have made privy contracts of matrimony, not calling two or more thereunto' as witnesses, W. H. Frere and W. M. Kennedy (eds.), *Visitation Articles and Injunctions of the Period of the Reformation*, 3 vols. (1910), iii. 85. Most parishes had nothing to report, but a few revealed characteristic problems. The churchwardens of Sidlesham, Sussex, reported in 1579 that Richard Merrit 'hath made a privy contract with Joan Lucas, widow, and now meaneth not to go forward with the same', and that 'William George of the age of 16 years hath contracted himself with one Joan Yerrish without the consent of his nighest kinsmen or others his friends in the house of his master Edward Markwork', West Sussex Record Office, Chichester Diocesan Records, Ep 1/23/5. A large proportion of the spousals cases heard before the ecclesiastical courts involved disputed contracts of this sort.

12. Rogers, *Matrimoniall Honovr*, 104–5.

13. Greenham, *Works*, 288; Gouge, *Of Domesticall Dvties*, 198–202.

14. Gouge, *Of Domesticall Dvties*, 202; Miles Coverdale, *The Christen State of Matry-monye, wherein housebandes and wyves maye lerne to kepe house together wyth loue* (1552; STC 4049), fos. 54–54^v.

15. *William Whiteway of Dorchester His Diary 1618 to 1635* (Dorset Record Society; Dorchester, 1991), 28–9.

16. It was a noteworthy event among William Carnsew's circle of Cornish gentry when 'Jane Penkevall was betrothed' to John Smith in July 1576. Gentlemen like Carnsew delighted in assisting their neighbours with marriage negotiations. In Jan. 1577 he spent several days helping 'to make a marriage for George Grainfield with Jill Vyell'. N. J. G. Pounds (ed.), 'William Carnsew of Bokelly and his Diary, 1576–7', *Royal Institution of Cornwall Journal* (1978), 45, 59. At a humbler social level the Devonshire yeoman William Honeywell used his literacy to set in writing matrimonial agreements made among his neighbours and kin. In May 1602 e.g. Honeywell helped William Casley 'to draw up his sister's assurance of marriage with Bennett Ball', and the following month he stayed overnight at Bampton on 'business . . . about marriage for Mr. Staplehills'. F. J. Snell (ed.), 'A Devonshire Yeoman's Diary', *The Antiquary*, 26 (1892), 257–8. See also Hugh Owen (ed.), 'The Diary of Bulkeley of Dronwy, Anglesea, 1630–1636', in *Anglesea Antiquarian Society and Field Club Transactions* (1937), 32. A character in Middleton's, *No Wit Like a Womans* marked the beginning of marriage, 'ev'n when my lip touched the contracting cup', quoted in John Cordy Jeaffreson, *Brides and Bridals*, 2 vols. (1872), i. 66.

17. Borthwick Institute, York, High Commission Cause Papers, 1589/7; *Depositions and other Ecclesiastical Proceedings from the Courts of Durham*, 227; Durham University Library, Archives and Special Collections, DDR V/8, fos. 185–6; V/11, fo. 162; V/12, fo. 260.

18. *Depositions and other Ecclesiastical Proceedings from the Courts of Durham*, 240–2.

19. Durham University Library, Archives, DDR V/8, fos. 75^v–76^v.

20. Durham University Library, Archives, DDR V/11, fos. 59–59^v.

21. A. Percival Moore (ed.), 'Marriage Contracts or Espousals in the Reign of Queen Elizabeth', *Associated Architectural Societies Reports and Papers*, 30 (1909), 280–2.

22. William H. Hale, *A Series of Precedents and Proceedings in Criminal Causes* (1847), 169–70.

23. Oxfordshire Archives, Archdeaconry Papers, c. 4, fo. 126^v–127.

24. Lincolnshire Archives, Court Papers, Box 59/1. no. 26.

25. Swinburne, *Treatise of Spousals*, sig. A2^v.

26. N.H., *The Ladies Dictionary* (1694), 350, 343, 349.

27. Lincolnshire Archives, Court Papers, Box 59/3, no. 5.

28. Ernest Axon (ed.), *Oliver Heywood's Life of John Angier of Denton* (Manchester, 1937), 63.

29. Michael Hunter and Annabel Gregory (eds.), *An Astrological Diary of the Seventeenth Century: Samuel Jeake of Rye 1652–1699* (Oxford, 1988), 153.

30. Coverdale, *Christen State of Matrymonye*, fo. 54^v; Greenham, *Works*, 299; Gouge, *Of Domesticall Dvties*, 202; Rogers, *Matrimoniall Honovr*, 107.

31. *The Pleasures of Matrimony* (1688), 33; Morris Palmer Tilley, *A Dictionary of the Proverbs in England in the Sixteenth and Seventeenth Centuries* (Ann Arbor, Mich., 1950), 124.

32. P. E. H. Hair, 'Bridal Pregnancy in Rural England in Earlier Centuries', *Population Studies*, 20 (1966), 233–43; id., 'Bridal Pregnancy in Earlier Rural England further Examined', *Population Studies*, 24 (1970), 59–70; E. A. Wrigley and R. S. Schofield, *The Population History of England 1541–1871* (Cambridge, Mass., 1981), 254 n. 96; David Levine and Keith Wrightson, 'The Social Context of Illegitimacy in Early Modern England', in Peter Laslett, Karla Oosterveen, and Richard M. Smith (eds.), *Bastardy and its Comparative History* (1980), 158–75; Keith Wrightson, 'The Nadir of English Illegitimacy in the Seventeenth Century', in ibid. 177–9; Ingram, *Church Courts, Sex and Marriage*, 219–37. For discussion of fecundability, the risk of pregnancy from unprotected intercourse, see Chris Wilson, 'The Proximate Determinants of Marital Fertility in England 1600–1799', in Lloyd Bonfield, Richard M. Smith, and Keith Wrightson (eds.), *The World We Have Gained: Histories of Population and Social Structure* (Oxford, 1986), 203–30.

33. James M. Osborn (ed.), *The Autobiography of Thomas Whythorne* (Oxford, 1962), 156. Proverbial wisdom advised, 'he that woos a maid must fain, lie and flatter; but he that woos a widow must down with his breeches and at her', John Ray, *A Collection of English Proverbs* (1670), 49. For the demographic context, see Vivien Brodsky, 'Widows in Late Elizabethan London: Remarriage, Economic Opportunity and Family Orientations', in Bonfield, Smith, and Wrightson (eds.), *The World We Have Gained*, 122–54.

34. Samuel Rowlands, *The Bride* [1617], in Frederick O. Waage, jun. (ed.), *Uncollected Poems . . . By Samuel Rowlands* (Gainesville, Fla., 1970), 181.

35. Examples from the 1590s abound in Oxfordshire Archives, Diocesan Papers, d. 5, fos. 35, 133, 183, 219ᵛ, etc. See also Houlbrooke, 'Making of Marriage', 345; Alan Macfarlane, *Marriage and Love in England: Modes of Reproduction 1300–1840* (Oxford, 1986), 298; O'Hara, 'Ruled by my Friends', 29.

36. Guildhall Library, Ms. 9064/13, fo. 64.

37. Guildhall Library, Ms. 9064/14, fo. 42.

38. Guildhall Library, Ms. 9064/15, fo. 196; Oxfordshire Archives, Diocesan Papers, d. 11, fo. 177.

39. Guildhall Library Ms. 9064/14, fo. 56; Oxfordshire Archives, Diocesan Papers, d. 11, fo. 228ᵛ; John Addy, *Sin and Society in the Seventeenth Century* (1989), 170, 171.

40. Lincolnshire Archives, Court Papers, Box 68/2, no. 15 [1608]; Guildhall Library Ms. 9064/18, fo. 73ᵛ.

41. Greater London Record Office, DL/C 318, p. 632; Guildhall Library, Ms. 9064/18, fo. 168ᵛ.

42. G. R. Quaife, *Wanton Wenches and Wayward Wives* (1979) revels in peasant sexuality. For a more nuanced appreciation of honour among the common people see J. A. Sharpe, *Defamation and Sexual Slander in Early Modern England: The Church Courts at York* (York, 1980); Laura Gowing, 'Gender and the Language of Insult in Early Modern London', *History Workshop Journal*, 35 (1993), 1–21.

CHAPTER 12

1. Peter Laslett, *The World We Have Lost, Further Explored* (1983), 81–90, 111–13; E. A. Wrigley and R. S. Schofield, *The Population History of England, 1541–1871* (Cambridge, Mass., 1981), 255–65, 422–4.

2. Robert C. Johnson, Mary Frear Keeler, Maija Jansson Cole, and William B. Bidwell (eds.), *Commons Debates 1628*, 4 vols. (New Haven, 1977), iii. 26; Samuel Rowlands, 'The Bride' [1617] in Frederick O. Waage, jun. (ed.), *Uncollected Poems . . . by Samuel Rowlands* (Gainesville, Fla., 1970), 157; F. P. Wilson (ed.), *The Batchelars Banquet* (Oxford, 1929), 16, 37, 67; Morris Palmer Tilley, *A Dictionary of the Proverbs in England in the Sixteenth and Seventeenth Centuries* (Ann Arbor, Mich., 1950), 389, 716.

3. Matthew Griffith, *Bethel: Or, a Forme for Families* (1633; STC 12370), 245.

4. Influential anthropological studies include David I. Kertzer, *Ritual, Politics, and Power* (New Haven, 1988); Victor W. Turner, *The Ritual Process: Structure and Anti-Structure* (Chicago, 1969); Arnold van Gennep, *The Rites of Passage* (Chicago, 1960).

5. William Gouge, *Of Domesticall Dvties* (1622; STC 12119), 210, 200.

6. Studies include Chilton Latham Powell, *English Domestic Relations 1487–1653* (New York, 1917); Susan Amussen, *An Ordered Society: Gender and Class in Early Modern England* (Oxford, 1988); Anthony Fletcher, 'The Protestant Idea of Marriage in Early Modern England', in Anthony Fletcher and Peter Roberts (eds.), *Religion, Culture and Society in Early Modern Britain* (Cambridge, 1994). For a shrewd reading of domestic conduct literature against the creative drama of the period, see Lena Cowen Orlin, *Private Matters and Public Culture in Post-Reformation England* (Ithaca, NY, 1994).

7. Patrick Hannay, *A Happy Husband or, Directions for a Maide to Choose her Mate: As also a Wives Behaviour towards her Husband after Marriage* (1619; STC 12747), sig. A2.

8. *Oxford English Dictionary*, s.v. 'husband', 'husbandman', and 'yeoman'; Thomas Smith, *De Repvblica Anglorum. The maner of Gouernement or police of the Realme of England* (1583; STC 22857), 32.

9. For gossipings and churchings see above, Chs. 4, 7, 9. For married women's honour see J. A. Sharpe, *Defamation and Sexual Slander in Early Modern England: The Church Courts at York* (York, 1980); Laura Gowing, 'Gender and the Language of Insult in Early Modern London', *History Workshop Journal*, 35 (1993), 1–21.

10. Daniel Rogers, *Matrimoniall Honovr: Or, The mutuall Crowne and comfort of godly, loyall, and chaste Marriage* (1642), 46. See the husband's complaint and his gentle wife's answer in the ballad *The Lamentation of a New Married Man* (1625?, STC 15186). The husband, who formerly 'lived in delight', now has to study 'how to please my wife'. But she replies, 'A wife hath won you credit, | A wife makes you esteemed | An honest man through marriage | You are now surely deemed.' The fruits of this transformation, aside from a domestic and financial responsibilities,

included candidacy for parish office as constable, sidesman, and churchwarden, and more favourable seating in church.

11. Lincolnshire Archives, CH P/6, concerned Agnes Bethraye of Souldrop, Bedfordshire, who was ordered in 1602 to forsake her intruded seat 'among married wives in the church' and 'to sit where other men's daughters do sit'. See also Martin Ingram, *Church Courts, Sex and Marriage in England, 1570–1640* (Cambridge, 1987), 111–12, 356; Margaret Aston, 'Segregation in Church', in W. J. Sheils and Diana Wood (eds.), *Women in the Church* (Studies in Church History, 27; Oxford, 1990), 237–94.

12. William Keatinge Clay (ed.), *Liturgical Services. Liturgies and Occasional Forms of Prayer Set Forth in the Reign of Queen Elizabeth* (Cambridge, 1847), 219.

13. William Lilly, *Mr. William Lilly's History of His Life and Times, from the Year 1602, to 1681* (1715), 20.

14. Herrick, 'A Nuptiall Song, or Epithalamie, on Sir Clipseby Crew and his Lady', in F. W. Moorman (ed.), *The Poetical Works of Robert Herrick* (Oxford, 1921), 113–14; 'Connubii Flores, or the well-wishes at Weddings', in ibid. 217–18.

15. Clay (ed.), *Liturgical Services,* 217, 219. Cf. Matthew 19: 6; Miles Coverdale, *The Christen State of Matrymonye, wherein housebandes and wyves maye lerne to kepe house together wyth loue* (1552; STC 4049), fo. 7ᵛ.

16. John Stephens, *Essayes and Characters. Ironicall and Instructive* (1615; STC 23250), 353; Sir John Suckling, 'Upon my Lord Brohalls Wedding', in Thomas Clayton (ed.), *The Works of Sir John Suckling* (Oxford, 1971), 86.

17. Rowlands, 'The Bride', 161; Thomas Gataker, *A Good Wife God's Gift: And, A Wife Indeed* (1623; STC 11659), 13–15; *Certain Sermons or Homilies Appointed to be Read in Churches* (1623; STC 13659), 240; Rogers, *Matrimoniall Honovr,* 25, 47.

18. Wilson (ed.), *The Batchelars Banquet,* 37, 67; Bodleian Library Ms. Top. Camb. e. 5, 'Diary of William Johnson, 1652–63', fos. 26–37; John Ray, *A Collection of English Proverbs* (Cambridge, 1670), 46–53; Tilley, *Dictionary of the Proverbs in England,* 4, 716. Cf. the heavy-handed saw, 'he that fetches a wife from Shrewsbury must carry her into Staffordshire or else shall live in Cumberland', and the 'old saying, that the wife brings but two merry days to her husband, the one when she is married, the other when she is buried', ibid. 723, 725.

19. See e.g. Thomas Heywood, *The Wise Woman of Hogsdon* [1638], ed. Michael H. Leonard (1980), 89, for Chartley's remarks on marriage: 'It makes a man forfeit his freedom, and makes him walk ever after with a chain at his heels, or a Jack-an-apes hanging at his elbow. Marriage is like Daedalus's labyrinth, and being once in, there's no finding the way out.'

20. Thomas Hilder, *Conjugall Counsell: or, Seasonable Advise, both to unmarried, and Married Persons* (1653), 116.

21. Oxfordshire Archives, Diocesan Papers, d. 5, fo. 50ᵛ; Herrick, 'An Epithalamie to Sir Thomas Southwell and his Ladie', Moorman (ed.), *Poetical Works of Robert Herrick,* 56.

22. Rowlands, 'The Bride', 157; Gouge, *Of Domesticall Dvties,* 200, 216–24.

23. Rowlands, 'The Bride', 155–89.

24. Huntington Library, Stowe Ms. STB Box 2 (1). I am grateful to Jo Ann Moran for drawing this letter to my attention.

25. Ibid.

26. James Shirley, *The Wedding* (1629: STC 22460), Act 1, scene 1; Joseph Hunter (ed.), *The Diary of Ralph Thoresby . . . 1677–1724*, 2 vols. (1830), i. 176; Alice Thornton, *The Autobiography of Mrs. Alice Thornton* (Surtees Society; Durham, 1875), 77, 81; British Library, Additional Ms. 27,440, 'Memoirs of Charles Allestree, 1677–1702', fo. 53ᵛ; John Gillis, *For Better for Worse: British Marriages, 1600 to the Present* (New York, 1985), 11.

27. For an early Stuart consideration of the celibate ideal, see George Herbert, 'A Priest to the Temple or, The Country Parson', in F. E. Hutchinson (ed.), *The Works of George Herbert* (Oxford, 1941), 236–7.

28. John Canne, *A Necessity of Separation from the Church of England* (Amsterdam, 1634; STC 4574), 101–2.

29. John Day, *Day's Festivals or, Twelve of His Sermons* (Oxford, 1615; STC 6426), 282; Gouge, *Of Domesticall Dvties*, 203–5.

30. John White, *The First Century of Scandalous, Malignant Priests* (1643), 50–1; A. G. Matthews, *Walker Revised. Being a Revision of John Walker's Sufferings of the Clergy during the Grand Rebellion 1642–66* (Oxford, 1948), 168.

31. Clay (ed.), *Liturgical Services*, 217.

32. Coverdale, *The Christen State of Matrymonye*, title-page, fos. 5ᵛ, 22; James Calfhill, *An Answer to John Martiall's Treatise of the Cross* [1565], ed. Richard Gibbings (Cambridge, 1846), 235; Gataker, *A Good Wife God's Gift*, 17.

33. Richard Greenham, *The Works . . . of Richard Greenham* (1599; STC 12312), 289; Rogers, *Matrimoniall Honovr*, 106; Gouge, *Of Domesticall Dvties*, 183, 208; Griffith, *Bethel: Or, a Forme for Families*, 20, 273. For idealized views of domestic and political harmony in early Stuart England, see Kevin Sharpe, *The Personal Rule of Charles I* (New Haven and London, 1992).

34. *The Petition and Articles Exhibited in Parliament against Doctor Heywood* (1641), 5; *An Answer to a Lawless Pamphlet . . . against Doctor Haywood* (1641); Matthews, *Walker Revised*, 162; Thomas Bedford, *A Treatise of the Sacraments According to the Doctrine of the Church of England* (1638; STC 1789), 54–5.

35. George R. Potter and Evelyn M. Simpson (eds.), *The Sermons of John Donne*, 10 vols. (Berkeley and Los Angeles, 1962), iii. 243.

36. C. H. Firth and R. S. Rait (eds.), *Acts and Ordinances of the Interregnum, 1642–1660*, 2 vols. (1911), i. 599; John Gauden, *Christ at the Wedding: The Pristine Sanctity and Solemnity of Christian Marriages* (1654), 2; C.C., *Sad and serious thoughts, or the sense and meaning of the late Act concerning Marriages* (1653), 4; William Secker, *A Wedding Ring Fit for the Finger: Or, the salve of Divinity On the sore of Humanity* (1658), 16.

37. The scholarly debate can be followed in Christopher Hill, *The World Turned Upside Down: Radical Ideas During the English Revolution* (New York, 1972),

247–60; John Morrill, 'The Church in England, 1642–1649', in John Morrill (ed.), *Reactions to the English Civil War* (1982), 89–114; Chris Durston, '"Unhallowed Wedlocks": The Regulation of Marriage during the English Revolution', *Historical Journal*, 31 (1988), 45–59; Christopher Durston, *The Family in the English Revolution* (Oxford, 1989), 57–86.

38. Clay (ed.), *Liturgical Services*, 217; Potter and Simpson (eds.), *Sermons of John Donne*, iii. 241–4.

39. Gouge, *Of Domesticall Dvties*, 182–4, 209; Griffith, *Bethel: Or, a Forme for Families*, 223, 237, 240. See also William Whately, *A Bride-Bvsh: Or, A Direction for Married Persons* (1619; STC 25297), 3, 18–20, for endorsement of the sexual 'covenant that passeth between yokefellows', so long as it was performed with moderation. Whately recommended married couples to read Proverbs 5: 18 and 19, 'Let thy fountain be blessed: and rejoice with the wife of thy youth. Let her be as the loving hind and pleasant roe; let her breasts satisfy thee at all times; and be thou ravished always with her love.'

40. Matthew Storey (ed.), *Two East Anglian Diaries, 1641–1729: Isaac Archer and William Coe* (Woodbridge, Suffolk, 1994), 117.

41. Gouge, *Of Domesticall Dvties*, 185; Griffith, *Bethel: Or, a Forme for Families*, 245.

42. Coverdale, *The Christen State of Matrymonye*, fos. 6–7; Gouge, *Of Domesticall Dvties*, 179, 187, 197, 210; Rogers, *Matrimoniall Honovr*, 277; Richard Meggott, *The Rib Restored: Or. The Honour of Marriage* (1656), 17, 24. See also Robert Abbot, *A Wedding Sermon Preached at Bentley* (1608; STC 55), 51; John Dod and Robert Cleaver, *A Godly Forme of Houshold Gouernment* (1598, 1630 edn.; STC 5388), sigs. F8–G; 2 Corinthians 6: 14.

43. J. Horsfall Turner (ed.), *The Rev. Oliver Heywood, B.A. 1630–1702: His Autobiography, Diaries, Anecdote and Event Books*, 4 vols. (Brighouse, 1882–5), i. 242; Hannah Woolley, *The Gentlewomans Companion; or, A Guide to the Female Sex* (1675), 103.

CHAPTER 13

1. Henry Burton, *A Tryall of Private Devotions. Or, A Diall for the Houres of Prayer* (1628; STC 4157), sig. F.

2. Frederick E. Warren (tr.), *The Sarum Missal in English*, 2 vols. (1913), ii. 143–4; H. J. Schroeder, *Canons and Decrees of the Council of Trent* (1941), 189.

3. *An Episcopal Almanack for . . . 1678* (1678); Bernard Capp, *English Almanacs 1500–1800: Astrology and the Popular Press* (Ithaca, NY, 1979), 145. Septuagesima is the third Sunday before Lent; Rogation begins on the fifth Sunday after Easter, the Sunday before Ascension; Easter Sunday itself moves on a lunar calendar between 22 Mar. and 25 Apr.; Trinity Sunday follows Whit Sunday or Pentecost, the seventh Sunday after Easter; Advent begins four Sundays before Christmas.

4. J. Charles Cox, *The Parish Registers of England* (1910), 80.

5. Edmund Gibson, *Codex Juris Ecclesiastici Anglicani* (1713), 518. See also D. Wilkins, *Concilia Magnae Britanniae*, 2 vols. (1737), ii. 176; Richard Burn, *Ecclesiastical*

Law, 4 vols. (1809), ii. 467–8; James T. Hammick, *The Marriage Law of England* (1887), 99–100.

6. James Calfhill, *An Answer to John Martiall's Treatise of the Cross* [1565], ed. Richard Gibbings (Cambridge, 1846), 241.

7. John Canne, *A Necessity of Separation from the Church of England* (Amsterdam, 1634; STC 4574), 102; Anthony Gilby, *A Pleasaunt Dialogue, Between a Souldior of Barwicke, and an English Chaplaine* (1581; STC 11888), sig. L8; David Calderwood, *The Altar of Damascus or The Patern of the English Hierarchie* (Amsterdam, 1621; STC 4352), 196.

8. Calfhill, *An Answer to John Martiall's Treatise of the Cross*, 241; Edward Cardwell, *Synodalia: A Collection of Articles of Religion, Canons, and Proceedings of Convocations* (Oxford, 1842), 133, 499; John Strype, *Life and Acts of John Whitgift*, 3 vols. (Oxford, 1822), i. 391–2; Sir Simonds D'Ewes, *The Journals of all the Parliaments During the Reign of Queen Elizabeth* (1682), 367.

9. *The Injunctions and Other Ecclesiastical Proceedings of Richard Barnes, Bishop of Durham from 1575 to 1587* (Surtees Society; Durham, 1850), 22; Walter C. Renshaw, 'Notes from the Act Books of the Archdeaconry Court of Lewes', *Sussex Archaeological Collections*, 49 (1906), 50, 62; E. R. Brinkworth (ed.), *The Archdeacon's Court Liber Actorum 1584* (Oxfordshire Record Society, 23–4; 1942–6), 36; William H. Hale (ed.), *A Series of Precedents and Proceedings in Criminal Causes* (1847), 191; Hereford Record Office, Court Books (Office), Box 17, bk. 67, fo. 54ᵛ.

10. E. A. Wrigley and R. S. Schofield, *The Population History of England, 1541–1871* (Cambridge, Mass., 1981), 298–305, 519–25.

11. Ann Kussmaul, *A General View of the Rural Economy of England, 1538–1840* (Cambridge, 1990), 3–4, 36–8, and *passim*; David Cressy, 'The Seasonality of Marriage in Old and New England', *Journal of Interdisciplinary History*, 16 (1985), 1–21.

12. The controversy can be followed in John Morrill, 'The Religious Context of the English Civil War', *Transactions of the Royal Historical Society*, 5th ser. 34 (1984), 155–78; Nicholas Tyacke, *Anti-Calvinists: The Rise of English Arminianism c.1590–1640* (Oxford, 1987); Julian Davies, *The Caroline Captivity of the Church: Charles I and the Remoulding of Anglicanism* (Oxford, 1992); Kevin Sharpe, *The Personal Rule of Charles I* (New Haven and London, 1992), 275–402; and Kenneth Fincham (ed.), *The Early Stuart Church, 1603–1642* (1993), esp. Peter Lake, 'The Laudian Style: Order, Uniformity and the Pursuit of the Beauty of Holiness in the 1630s' in ibid. 161–85.

13. William Gouge, *Of Domesticall Dvties* (1622; STC 12119), 207; Guildhall Library, Ms. 4509/1, Register of St Ann, Blackfriars, 1562–1726. The index for Feb. was 150 in the period 1600–20, 174 in the period 1621–40; the respective Mar. indices were 54 and 54.

14. John Cosin, 'Articles to be Diligently Inquired Of, and Severally Answered Unto . . . Within the Jurisdiction of the Archdeacon of the East-Riding in York [1627]' , in George Ornsby (ed.), *The Correspondence of John Cosin*, 2 vols. (Surtees Society; Durham, 1869), i. 118; John Cosin, *A Collection of Private Devotions* (1627;

STC 5816); Durham County Record Office, Register of Brancepeth, 1629–38. I am grateful to Dorothy Hamilton for directing me to this manuscript.

15. Burton, *Tryall of Private Devotions*, sigs. E4, F2.

16. Robert C. Johnson, Mary Frear Keeler, Maija Jansson Cole, and William B. Bidwell (eds.), *Commons Debates 1628*, 4 vols. (New Haven, 1977), ii. 514; iii. 26–30.

17. Ibid. iii. 26–36, 250. This was the same parliamentary session wherein reading of 'an act for the further punishment of adultery and fornication' was interrupted by raucous cries of 'commit it', ibid. 30.

18. Norfolk Record Office, VIS 6/1, fo. 46; Oxfordshire Archives, Diocesan Papers, c. 1, fo. 89.

19. C. H. Firth and R. S. Rait (eds.), *Acts and Ordinances of the Interregnum, 1642–1660*, 2 vols. (1911), i. 600; Wrigley and Schofield, *Population History of England*, 521.

20. Guildhall Library, Ms. 9583/2, bk. 4, fo. 72; Hereford Record Office, Registrar's Files, 1660–2.

21. E. S. de Beer (ed.), *The Diary of John Evelyn*, 6 vols. (Oxford, 1955), iv. 194. For a further attempt to modify the matrimonial calendar in 1714, see Cardwell, *Synodalia*, 795–6.

22. William Keatinge Clay (ed.), *Liturgical Services. Liturgies and Occasional Forms of Prayer Set Forth in the Reign of Queen Elizabeth* (Cambridge, 1847), 217; canon 62 in J. V. Bullard (ed.), *Constitutions and Canons Ecclesiastical* (1934), 282.

23. William Vaughan, *The Golden-grove, moralized in three Bookes* (2nd edn., 1609; STC 24611), bk. 2, ch. 6.

24. *Articles to be Enquyred in the Visitation in the First Yere of the Raigne of our Most Dread Soueraine Lady Elizabeth* (1559; STC 10118), no. 43; *Articles to be Enquired of Within the Diocesse of Lincolne* (1574; STC 10229), no. 18; W. H. Frere, *Visitation Articles and Injunctions of the Period of the Reformation*, 3 vols. (1910), iii. 85; William Nicholson (ed.), *The Remains of Edmund Grindal* (Cambridge, 1843), 126; 'Articles to be Enquired of Within the Dioces of London . . . 1628' in *The Works of . . . William Laud, D.D.*, 7 vols. (Oxford 1853), v. 401; *Articles of Enquiry and Direction for the Diocese of Norwich . . . 1638* (1638; STC 10299), sig. C2.

25. Charles Severn (ed.), *Diary of Rev. John Ward . . . 1648 to 1679* (1839), 172; *The Mariage of Prince Fredericke, and the Kings Daughter, the Lady Elizabeth, vpon Shouesunday last* (1613; STC 11359).

26. T. F. Thisleton-Dyer, *Church-Lore Gleanings* (1892), 124; John Gillis, *For Better for Worse: British Marriages, 1600 to the Present* (New York, 1985), 53–4.

27. Gouge, *Of Domesticall Dvties*, 202–3.

28. *The Psalmes of David in Meeter . . . Whereunto is added Prayers commonly used in the Kirke, and in private houses* (Edinburgh, 1611; STC 16591), 123–8; Firth and Rait (eds.), *Acts and Ordinances of the Interregnum*, i. 599; Thiselton-Dyer, *Church-Lore Gleanings*, 124.

29. Hale (ed.), *Series of Precedents and Proceedings*, 170; Oxfordshire Archives, Archdeaconry Papers, c. 5, fo. 52.

30. Brinkworth (ed.), *Archdeacon's Court Liber Actorum 1584*, 218–19; Oxfordshire Archives, Diocesan Papers, c. 18, fo. 64; Hale (ed.), *Series of Precedents and Proceedings*, 178, 255.

31. Oxfordshire Archives, Diocesan Papers, d. 4, fo. 192. For similar cases see Claude Jenkins (ed.), 'An Unpublished Record of Archbishop Parker's Visitation in 1573', *Archaeologia Cantiana*, 29 (1911), 279; Joseph B. Gavin, 'Handly v. Newbie alias Shields: A Marriage at Farlam in 1605', *Transactions of the Cumberland and Westmorland Antiquarian and Archaeological Society*, 2nd ser. 70 (1970), 247–68.

32. Colin W. Field, *The State of the Church in Gloucestershire, 1563* (Robertsbridge, Sussex, 1971), 2. Similar cases appear in Arthur J. Willis (ed.), *Church Life in Kent: Being Church Court Records of the Canterbury Diocese 1559–1565* (1975), 40; W. J. Sheils (ed.), *Archbishop Grindal's Visitation, 1575: Comperta et Detecta Book* (York, 1977), 40.

33. Brinkworth (ed.), *Archdeacon's Court Liber Actorum 1584*, 107; J. F. Williams (ed.), *Diocese of Norwich: Bishop Redman's Visitation 1597* (Norfolk Record Society; Norwich, 1946), 54; Greater London Record Office, DL/C 617, 478.

34. Hale (ed.), *Series of Precedents and Proceedings*, 181–2.

35. Sheils (ed.), *Archbishop Grindal's Visitation*, 23; Cambridge University Library, Ms. Mm. 4. 20, 'Act Book of the Peculiar of Tredington (Diocese of Worcester) 1576–1686', fo. 90^{v}'; A. Percival Moore (ed.), 'The Metropolitical Visitation of Archdeacon [sic] Laud', in *Associated Architectural Societies' Reports and Papers*, 29 (1907), 511; Northamptonshire Record Office, Archdeaconry Correction Book 65, fo. 38.

36. Lichfield Joint Record Office, Court Papers B/C/5, 'Lomasse v. Backe'.

37. Norfolk Record Office, MLB/2, 51; canons 101–3 of 1604, in Bullard (ed.), *Constitutions and Canons Ecclesiastical*, 305–6.

38. David Cressy, *Literacy and the Social Order: Reading and Writing in Tudor and Stuart England* (Cambridge, 1980), 109.

39. Daniel Rogers, *Matrimoniall Honovr: Or, The mutuall Crowne and comfort of godly, loyall, and chaste Marriage* (1642), 110; Guildhall Library, Ms. 4509/1, Register of St Ann, Blackfriars.

40. Canon 102 of 1604, in Bullard (ed.), *Constitutions and Canons Ecclesiastical*, 305; C. W. Foster (ed.), *Lincoln Episcopal Records in the Time of Thomas Cooper . . . A.D. 1571 to A.D. 1584* (Lincoln Record Society; Lincoln, 1912), 111–14.

41. Borthwick Institute, York, High Commission Cause Papers, 1590/16; Leicestershire Record Office, I D 41/13/16, fo. 65; Moore (ed.), 'The Metropolitical Visitation of Archdeacon [sic] Laud', 502; Borthwick Institute, York, V. 1640, fo. 64; Hereford Record Office, Court Books (Office), Box 43, bk. 166, fos. 23–24^{v}'; bk. 169, fo. 8^{v}.

42. H. R. Wilton Hall (ed.), *Records of the Old Archdeaconry of St. Albans. A Calendar of Papers A.D. 1575 to A.D. 1637* (St Albans, 1908), 137; 'Constitutions and Canons Ecclesiastical . . . 1640', in *Works of . . . William Laud*, v. 631.

43. Humphrey Prideaux, *The Case of Clandestine Mariages Stated* (1691), 4.

44. Henri Misson, *M. Misson's Memoirs and Observations in His Travels over England* (1719), 183, 351.

45. For social and economic restraints on marriage see Martin Ingram, *Church Courts, Sex and Marriage in England, 1570–1640* (Cambridge, 1987), 83, 131, 214–15, 234, 268; Gillis, *For Better for Worse*, 86–9.

46. Bullard (ed.), *Constitutions and Canons Ecclesiastical*, 304–5; *Articles to be Enquired of within the Diocese of London* (1607; STC 10257), sig. A4ᵛ; *Articles of Enquiry and Direction for the Diocese of Norwich . . . 1638*, sig. C2.

47. West Sussex Record Office, Chichester Diocesan Records, Ep 1/23/5.

48. Borthwick Institute, York, High Commission Cause Papers, 1624/13.

49. John Bossy, *The Development of the Family and Marriage in Europe* (Cambridge, 1983), 173–80.

50. Later Stuart controversialists became occupied with the legality and propriety of close-kin marriage. See e.g. John Turner, *A Letter of Resolution to a Friend, Concerning Marriage of Cousin Germans* (1682), and id., *An Argument in Defence of the Marriage of an Uncle with the Daughter of his Half-Brother by the Father's Side* (1686).

51. Canon 99, in Bullard (ed.), *Constitutions and Canons Ecclesiastical*, 304; Firth and Rait (eds.), *Acts and Ordinances of the Interregnum*, i. 599. For a brief endorsement of the prohibited degree see William Whately, *A Care-Cloth: Or a Treatise of the Cvmbers and Trovbles of Marriage* (1624; STC 25299), 30.

52. Nicholson (ed.), *Remains of Edmund Grindal*, 126; *Works of . . . William Laud*, v. 413.

53. West Sussex Record Office, Chichester Diocesan Records, Ep 1/23/5, Ep. 1/26/2; Eric Josef Carlson, *Marriage and the English Reformation* (Oxford, 1994), 234; Norfolk Record Office, VIS 5/3/1; Moore (ed.), 'The Metropolitical Visitation of Archdeacon [sic] Laud', 496; R. F. B. Hodgkinson (ed.), 'Extracts from the Act Books of the Archdeacons of Nottingham', *Transactions of the Thoroton Society*, 31 (1928), 131.

54. Dozens of parishes throughout the diocese of London lacked the table in 1665. At Isleworth, Twickenham, and Shepperton in Middlesex, they had still not been replaced in 1673; and in that year the bishop ordered 'a table of degrees of marriage to be hung up in the church' at Finchley and at Highgate, insisting on the importance of displaying it prominently; Guildhall Library, Ms. 9583/2, part 3; Ms. 9537/20, fos. 35, 36, 40, 90, 92. In 1683 the archdeacon of Essex found tables of degrees wanting in more than a dozen parishes, W. J. Pressey, 'Notes on Visitations in the Archdeaconry of Essex', *Transactions of the Essex Archaeological Society*, 19 (1939), 260–76.

55. George Benson (ed.), 'Holy Trinity Church, Goodramgate, York: Extracts from the Churchwardens' Accounts, 1557–1819', *Associated Architectural Societies Reports and Papers*, 30 (1909), 653; Lake, 'The Laudian Style', in Fincham (ed.), *Early Stuart Church*, 161–85.

56. Ingram, *Church Courts, Sex and Marriage*, 245–9; Norfolk Record Office, VIS 5/1,

ANW/3/25; Bodleian Library, Tanner. Ms. 138, fo. 64; *Calendar of State Papers Domestic 1631–2*, 41–2. Alington was the sheriff to whom Michael Dalton dedicated his *Officium Vicecomitum: The Office and Authoritie of Sherifs* (1623; STC 6212); the huge fine may have been imposed *in terrorem*, to assert the crown's interest in domestic and national good order. In 1662 the Buckinghamshire archdeaconry court cited two men for marrying their brothers' wives and ordered them to stop cohabiting, Buckinghamshire Record Office, D/A/V 6, fo. 26.

57. Nicholson (ed.), *Remains of Edmund Grindal*, 126.

58. Richard Greenham, *The Works . . . of Richard Greenham* (1599; STC 12312), 299, 291; Cosin, 'Articles to be Diligently Inquired Of', in Ornsby (ed.), *Correspondence of John Cosin*, i. 119; ii. 73.

59. John Godolphin, *Repertorium Canonicum; or an Abridgement of the Ecclesiastical laws of this Realm, Consistent with the Temporal* (1680), 626. For an Elizabethan presentment for marrying excommunicated parties, see Willis (ed.), *Church Life in Kent*, 12.

CHAPTER 14

1. Eric Josef Carlson, *Marriage and the English Reformation* (Oxford, 1984), esp. 105–41; Ralph Houlbrooke, 'The Making of Marriage in Mid-Tudor England: Evidence from the Records of Matrimonial Contract Litigation', *Journal of Family History*, 10 (1985), 339–52; Martin Ingram, *Church Courts, Sex and Marriage in England, 1570–1640* (Cambridge, 1987), esp. 125–218. See also John Gillis, 'Married but not Churched: Plebian Sexual Relations and Marital Nonconformity in Eighteenth-Century Britain', *Eighteenth-Century Life*, 9 (special issue on 'Unauthorized Sexual Behavior during the Enlightenment', ed. Robert P. Maccubbin, 1985), 31–42; John R. Gillis, *For Better, for Worse: British Marriages 1600 to the Present* (New York, 1985), 84, 98–9, 110–11; Lawrence Stone, *The Road to Divorce: England 1530–1987* (Oxford, 1990), 64–71; Lawrence Stone, *Uncertain Unions: Marriage in England 1660–1753* (Oxford, 1992), 3, 17–19; R. B. Outhwaite, *Clandestine Marriage in England, 1500–1850* (1995), 1–49.

2. J. Charles Cox, *The Parish Registers of England* (1910). The 1538 Injunctions required every parish to provide a register book in which should be written the names and dates of every person 'wedded, christened or buried', S. R. Cattley and George Townsend (eds.), *The Acts and Monuments of John Foxe*, 8 vols. (1837–41), v. 170. Canon 70 of 1604 reiterated this provision and required an annual transcript to be lodged with the diocesan authorities, J. V. Bullard (ed.), *Constitutions and Canons Ecclesiastical* (1934), 286–7.

3. Henry Swinburne, *A Treatise of Spousals, or Matrimonial Contracts* (1686); Edmund Gibson, *Codex Juris Ecclesiastici Anglicani* (1713); Richard Burn, *Ecclesiastical Law*, 4 vols. (1809); James T. Hammick, *The Marriage Law of England* (1887). For the application of the law see Christopher N. L. Brooke, *The Medieval Idea of Marriage* (Oxford, 1989); R. H. Helmholz, *Marriage Litigation in Medieval England* (Cambridge, 1974); Martin Ingram, 'Spousals Litigation in the English Ecclesiastical

courts c.1350–c.1640', in R. B. Outhwaite (ed.), *Marriage and Society: Studies in the Social History of Marriage* (New York, 1982), 35–57, esp. 37–40; Martin Ingram, 'The Reform of Popular Culture? Sex and Marriage in Early Modern England', in Barry Reay (ed.), *Popular Culture in Seventeenth Century England* (London, 1985), 129–65; R. M. Smith, 'Marriage Processes in the English Past: Some Continuities', in Lloyd Bonfield, Richard M. Smith, and Keith Wrightson (eds.), *The World We Have Gained: Histories of Population and Social Structure* (Oxford, 1986), 43–99.

4. *Statutes of the Realm*, 26 Geo. II, c. 33; Outhwaite, *Clandestine Marriage in England*, 75–97.

5. Ingram, 'Spousals Litigation', 53–5.

6. Canon 62 in Bullard (ed.), *Constitutions and Canons Ecclesiastical*, 282.

7. R. C. Latham and W. Matthews (eds.), *The Diary of Samuel Pepys*, 9 vols. (Berkeley and Los Angeles, 1970–6), vi. 176.

8. W. H. Frere, *Visitation Articles and Injunctions of the Period of the Reformation*, 3 vols. (1910), iii. 85; W. P. M. Kennedy, *Elizabethan Episcopal Administration*, 3 vols. (1924), ii. 50; iii. 202, 224; *Articles to be Enquired of within the Diocesse of Lincolne* (1574; STC 10229), no. 18.

9. John Cosin, *The Works of the Right Reverend Father in God, John Cosin*, 5 vols. (Oxford, 1843–55), v. 492; John Cosin, 'Articles to be Diligently Inquired Of, and Severally Answered Unto . . . Within the Jurisdiction of the Archdeacon of the East-Riding in York [1627]', in George Ornsby (ed.), *The Correspondence of John Cosin*, 2 vols. (Surtees Society; Durham, 1869), i. 118; 'Articles to be Enquired of Within the Dioces of London . . . 1628', in *The Works of . . . William Laud, D.D.*, 7 vols. (Oxford 1853), v. 401; *Articles of Enquiry and Direction for the Diocese of Norwich . . . 1638* (1638; STC 10299), sig. C2; *Articles to be Inquired of Within the Dioces of Ely* (1638; STC 10197), ch. 4, no. 24.

10. R. F. B. Hodgkinson (ed.), 'Extracts from the Act Books of the Archdeacons of Nottingham', *Transactions of the Thoroton Society*, 29 (1926), 31–3; Canterbury Cathedral Archives, High Commission Acts, PRC 44/3, 59–60; Borthwick Institute, York, Cause Papers, 87/1602; Hereford Record Office, Court Books (Office), Box 18, no. 71.

11. Where, asked the Elizabethan separatist Henry Barrow, did the Bible declare marriage to be an ecclesiastical action? Why should marriage be accompanied 'with such a set liturgy of collects, exhortations, psalms, anthems and blessings', when it was, more properly, a civil matter? Leland H. Carlson (ed.), *The Writings of Henry Barrow 1587–1590* (1962), 454; Chris Durston, ' "Unhallowed Wedlocks": The Regulation of Marriage during the English Revolution', *Historical Journal*, 31 (1988), 45–59.

12. William Gouge, *Of Domesticall Dvties* (1622; STC 12119), 203, 204–5.

13. Ernest Axon (ed.), *Oliver Heywood's Life of John Angier of Denton* (Manchester, 1937), 62.

14. John Gauden, who disapproved of clandestine marriages, thought the disorder

'but rare'. John Gauden, *Christ at the Wedding: the Pristine Sanctity and Solemnity of Christian Marriages* (1654), 7. Cf. Jeremy Boulton, 'Itching after Private Marryings? Marriage Customs in Seventeenth-Century London', *London Journal*, 16 (1991), 15–34; Jeremy Boulton, 'Clandestine Marriages in London: An Examination of the Neglected Urban Variable', *Urban History*, 20 (1993), 191–210.

15. Hodgkinson (ed.), 'Extracts from the Act Books of the Archdeacons of Nottingham', 29–30, 33.

16. John Bale, *A Declaration of Edmonde Bonners articles concerning the cleargye of London dyocese* (1561; STC 1289), fo. 84ᵛ; John Rylands Library, Manchester, Ms. 524, 'The Acts and Speeches of Richard Greenham', fo. 30ᵛ; Daniel Rogers, *Matrimoniall Honovr: Or, The mutuall Crowne and comfort of godly, loyall, and chaste Marriage* (1642), 110; E. Venables, 'The Primary Visitation of the Diocese of Lincolne by Bishop Neile, A.D. 1614', *Associated Architectural Societies' Reports and Papers*, 16 (1881), 48.

17. Robert Baylie, *A Dissuasive from the Errours of the Time* (1645), 26, characterized Independents' views on this topic, and the practice they had established in New England: 'Marriage to them is not only a contract merely civil, but such a one as concerns the church nothing at all; so they remit it wholly to the magistrate, or else to the parents to be solemnized in private families, and as their marriage is private, so likewise must [be] their divorces.' Cf. Gauden, *Christ at the Wedding*, 5–7.

18. *The Acts of the High Commission Court Within the Diocese of Durham* (Surtees Society; Durham, 1858), 48–9.

19. Hodgkinson (ed.), 'Extracts from the Act Books of the Archdeacons of Nottingham', 31, 33, 109, 110; *Acts of the High Commission Court Within the Diocese of Durham*, 123; Oxfordshire Archives, Diocesan Papers, c. 2, fo. 211; Walter C. Renshaw, 'Notes from the Act Books of the Archdeaconry Court of Lewes', *Sussex Archaeological Collections*, 49 (1906), 63. Thomas May of Abingdon, Berks., in 1634, in response to the charge that he and Sara May 'live together as man and wife, being not known whether they are married or not', told the court that he and his wife 'were married upon a Thursday between the hours of ten and twelve in the forenoon . . . according to the form prescribed in the Book of Common Prayer by one Mr. James Finch, then a reader of Grays Inn and curate of St. Pancras in the fields near St. Giles, London, in an upper chamber of the dwelling house of Edward Winiard, tailor, situate and being in the parish of St. Pulcher's [Sepulchre], London, without any licence from any ordinary first obtained, there being present Robert Roth of the Middle Temple, esquire, who is since dead, Edward Winiard and his wife, and another woman'. Berkshire Record Office, D/A2/c74, fo. 185. Though performed by a minister who followed the prayer book, the only record of this clandestine marriage was in the memory of the surviving participants.

20. F. R. Raines (ed.), *The State, Civil and Ecclesiastical, of the County of Lancaster, about the year 1590* (Chetham Society; Manchester, 1875), 1.

21. William H. Hale (ed.), *A Series of Precedents and Proceedings in Criminal Causes* (1847), 216.

22. On alehouse culture see Peter Clark, 'The Alehouse and the Alternative Society', in Donald Pennington and Keith Thomas (eds.), *Puritans and Revolutionaries: Essays in Seventeenth-Century History Presented to Christopher Hill* (Oxford, 1978), 47–72; Peter Clark, *The English Alehouse: A Social History, 1200–1830* (1983); Keith Wrightson, *English Society 1580–1680* (1982), 167–70; Eamon Duffy, 'The Godly and the Multitude in Stuart England', *The Seventeenth Century*, 1 (1986), 31–55; John Addy, *Sin and Society in the Seventeenth Century* (1989), 32, 169.

23. Clark, 'The Alehouse and the Alternative Society', 60; Guildhall Library, Ms. 9064/19, fos. 59^v, 62. In a similar case, Henry Franklin married Mary Shelton 'in a chamber at an inn in Northampton' after a summer feast day in 1606. None could recall the name of the minister who married them, but a witness avowed that the vicar of St Giles had promised to procure a licence, but had none. Buckinghamshire Record Office, D/A/C3, fo. 110.

24. Oxfordshire Archives, Archdeaconry Papers, c. 13, fo. 215.

25. Oxfordshire Archives, Archdeaconry Papers, c. 12, fo. 168.

26. Hodgkinson (ed.), 'Extracts from the Act Books of the Archdeacons of Nottingham', 30–3; Borthwick Institute, York, High Commission Cause Papers, 1635/3.

27. Borthwick Institute, York, Cause Papers, no. 1682; cf. no. 1388 for a similar case in 1619. See also Alison Wall, 'For Love, Money, or Politics? A Clandestine Marriage and the Elizabethan Court of Arches', *Historical Journal*, 38 (1995), 511–33.

28. Folger Shakespeare Library, Ms. L.a. 628.

29. Folger Shakespeare Library, Ms. L.a. 167. Cf. the case of Sir Edward Coke who married Lord Burghleigh's granddaughter, Elizabeth Hatton, clandestinely in 1598, 'and had the effrontery to plead ignorance of the law', A. Percival Moore (ed.), 'Marriage Contracts or Espousals in the Reign of Queen Elizabeth', *Associated Architectural Societies Reports and Papers*, 30 (1909), 268 n.

30. Hodgkinson (ed.), 'Extracts from the Act Books of the Archdeacons of Nottingham', 32; Leicestershire Record Office, 1 D/61, fo. 65.

31. Northamptonshire Record Office, Archdeaconry Correction Books, Box 61, no. 23, fos. 16, 21; Lincolnshire Archives, Court Papers, Box 58/2, nos. 3, 7, 26, 34, 41, 42, 48 etc.; Oxfordshire Archives, Diocesan Papers, d. 9, fos. 53, 53^v, 87.

32. Hodgkinson (ed.), 'Extracts from the Act Books of the Archdeacons of Nottingham', 109; A. Percival Moore (ed.), 'The Metropolitical Visitation of Archdeacon [sic] Laud', in *Associated Architectural Societies' Reports and Papers*, 29 (1907), 515, also 485, 492; Borthwick Institute, York, High Commission Act Book, 18, fo. 3; Borthwick Institute, York, V.1640, fo. 24^v.

33. Oxfordshire Archives, Cropredy Acts, c. 17, fo. 96^v.

34. Oxfordshire Archives, Archdeaconry Papers, c. 12, fo. 48^v; Joseph Foster, *Alumni Oxonienses: The Members of the University of Oxford, 1500–1714*, 4 vols. (Oxford, 1891), i. 125.

35. Greater London Record Office, DL/C 318, pp. 578, 595; DL/C 318, p. 597.

36. Roger Lee Brown, 'The Rise and Fall of the Fleet Marriages', in Outhwaite (ed.), *Marriage and Society*, 117–36.
37. Greater London Record Office, DL/C 319, fo. 172$^\text{v}$.
38. Oxfordshire Archives, Diocesan Papers, d. 4, fo. 131$^\text{v}$; Borthwick Insitute, York, High Commission Cause Papers, 1624/13.
39. Greater London Record Office, DL/C 316, fo. 113; DL/C, fo. 231.
40. Oxfordshire Archives, Archdeaconry Papers, c. 12, fo. 293$^\text{v}$.
41. T. M. Fallow (ed.), 'Some Elizabethan Visitations of the Churches belonging to the Peculiar of the Dean of York', *The Yorkshire Archaeological Journal*, 18 (1905), 213.
42. W. J. Sheils (ed.), *Archbishop Grindal's Visitation, 1575: Comperta et Detecta Book* (York, 1977), 15; Bothwick Institute, York, Y/V/CB/1, fo. 40$^\text{v}$. Similar cases appear in C. J. Kitching (ed.), *The Royal Visitation of 1559: Act Book of the Northern Province* (Surtees Society; Durham, 1975), 65, 77, 85; Hodgkinson (ed.), 'Extracts from the Act Books of the Archdeacons of Nottingham', 29–34; J. F. Williams (ed.), *Diocese of Norwich: Bishop Redman's Visitation 1597* (Norfolk Record Society; Norwich, 1946), 65.
43. e.g. the archdeacon of Cleveland in 1632, Borthwick Institute, York, C/V/CB 1, fo. 110.
44. E. R. Brinkworth (ed.), *The Archdeacon's Court: Liber Actorum 1584* (Oxfordshire Record Society; Oxford, 1942–6), 73; Lincolnshire Archives, CH.P/1, no. 12; Borthwick Institute, York, CP/1087.
45. Greater London Record Office, DL/C 315, p. 25.
46. Guildhall Library, Ms. 9064/19, fo. 53; Ms. 9064/20, fo. 189$^\text{v}$.
47. Greater London Record Office, DL/C 315, p. 47; DL/C, fos. 77a, 164; DL/C 624, p. 52. Cf. the case of Martha Harper of Ensham, Oxon., who tried hard to convince the authorities in 1671 that she was married, and that the child she had borne was not illegitimate. At her first hearing before the bishop's court she objected 'that in regard of the distance of the place where she was married from the place of her now habitation she could not make as yet any proof of her marriage', and asked for more time. Six weeks later she returned to say that 'in regard the persons who were present at her marriage are some dead and the rest unknown to her, that she cannot make that legal proof of her marriage as is alleged'. The court clearly did not believe her, and ordered her to perform penance for bastardy and fornication, Oxfordshire Archives, Diocesan Papers, c. 11, fos. 142, 156. See also the attempted back-dating of a fraudulent certificate reported in *The She Wedding; or a Mad Marriage between Mary a Seamans Mistress, and Margaret a Carpenters Wife* (1684).
48. Cambridge University Library, Ms. Mm. 4. 20, 'Act Book of the Peculiar of Tredington (Diocese of Worcester) 1576–1686', fo. 120.
49. Guildhall Library, Ms. 9537/19, fo. 72; *A Representation of the State of Christianity in England, and of its Decay and Danger from Sectaries aswel as Papists* (1674), 12.
50. Cambridge University Library, Ms. 'Act Book of the Peculiar of Tredington',

fo. 256ᵛ. Quaker practice is described in Thomas Lawrence, *Concerning Marriage. A Letter Sent to G.F.* (1663), 14.

51. Michael Hunter and Annabel Gregory (eds.), *An Astrological Diary of the Seventeenth Century: Samuel Jeake of Rye 1652–1699* (Oxford, 1988), 154; Folger Shakespeare Library, Ms. V.a. 441, 'William Westmacott: Memorabilia: or private Things to be remembered concerning my life.'

52. Henri Misson, *M. Misson's Memoirs and Observations in His Travels over England* (1719), 349–50, 183.

53. Oxfordshire Archives, Diocesan Papers c. 3, fo. 8. Similar cases are reported in E. R. C. Brinkworth (ed.), *Episcopal Visitation Book for the Archdeaconry of Buckingham, 1662* (Buckinghamshire Record Society; Aylesbury, 1947).

54. Oxfordshire Archives, Diocesan Papers, c. 3, fo. 41.

55. Oxfordshire Archives, Diocesan Papers, c. 4, fo. 107; c. 5, fo. 53.

56. Oxfordshire Archives, Diocesan Papers, c. 5, fo. 47ᵛ.

57. Oxfordshire Archives, Diocesan Papers, c. 9, fo. 204ᵛ.

58. Greater London Record Office, DL/C 328, pp. 32, 51, 54, 55, 85, etc.; W. J. Pressey, 'Notes on Visitations in the Archdeaconry of Essex', *Transactions of the Essex Archaeological Society*, 19 (1939), 260–76; Guildhall Library, Ms. 9538, fo. 70ᵛ; Borthwick Institute, York, Y/V/CB/3, fo. 509ᵛ; Y V/CH. P. See also the clandestine marriages performed by the rector of Moreton Bagot, Worcs., in David Robertson (ed.), *Diary of Francis Evans, Secretary to Bishop Lloyd, 1699–1706* (Oxford, 1903), 31, 55, 60, 62.

59. E. A. Wrigley and R. S. Schofield, *The Population History of England, 1541–1871* (Cambridge, Mass., 1981), 26–9.

60. Borthwick Institute, Cause Papers 1673, transmitted on appeal from Durham; the complexities of this case filled some 250 pp. of testimony.

CHAPTER 15

1. Christopher N. L. Brooke, *The Medieval Idea of Marriage* (Oxford, 1989), 248–9, 254–7. Many late medieval church porches had been elaborated and enlarged to accommodate wedding parties.

2. F. N. Robinson (ed.), *The Complete Works of Geoffrey Chaucer* (2nd edn., 1957), 21; Bodleian Library, Ms. Eng. hist. b. 208, 'Orders and Regulations for an Earl's House', fos. 23–30. This volume was still in use in 1589.

3. André Burguière, 'Le Rituel du mariage en France: Pratiques ecclésiastiques et pratiques populaires (XVIe–XVIIIe siècle)', *Annales E.S.C.* 33 (1978), 639; John Cordy Jeaffreson, *Brides and Bridals*, 2 vols. (1872), i. 58–9; T. F. Thiselton-Dyer, *Church-Lore Gleanings* (1982), 48–50.

4. *Missale ad vsum insignis ecclesie Sarum* (Antwerp, 1527; STC 16207); Frederick E. Warren (tr.), *The Sarum Missal in English*, 2 vols. (1913), ii. 144.

5. Ibid. ii. 145–6.

6. Ibid. 146–9. Cf. W. S. Scott, *Worship and Drama: An Inquiry into the Nature and*

Interpretation of the Dramatic Element Inherent in All Forms of Liturgical Worship, with Especial Reference to its Place in the Anglican Liturgy (1938), 77–8.

7. Warren (tr.), *Sarum Missal in English*, ii. 154; N.H., *The Ladies Dictionary* (1694), 107. Cf. the title of William Whately, *A Care-cloth: Or a Treatise of the Cvmbers and Trovbles of Marriage* (1624; STC 25299).

8. W. K. Lowther Clarke and Charles Harris (eds.), *Liturgy and Worship* (1932), 458. For a 17th-cent. account of Roman Catholic marriage ritual, including holding a sheet over the bridal couple at the altar, see Louis de Gaya, *Marriage Ceremonies: Or, The Ceremonies used in Marriages in all Parts of the World* (2nd edn., 1698), 21–8.

9. Warren (tr.), *Sarum Missal in English*, ii. 158.

10. William Vaughan, *The Golden-grove, moralized in three Bookes* (2nd edn., 1609; STC 24611), bk. 2, ch. 6.

11. William Keatinge Clay (ed.), *Liturgical Services. Liturgies and Occasional Forms of Prayer Set Forth in the Reign of Queen Elizabeth* (Cambridge, 1847), 217.

12. Ibid. 217–24.

13. Ibid. 218–19.

14. Richard Hooker, 'Of the Laws of Ecclesiastical Politie', in *The Works of that Learned and Judicious Divine, Mr. Richard Hooker* (1723), 266; John Rylands Library, Manchester, Ms. 524, 'The Acts and Speeches of Richard Greenham', fos. 48–49ᵛ; Roger Hacket, *Two Frvitfvl Sermons, Needfvll for these times* (1607; STC 12592), 5; Anthony Sparrow, *A Rationale upon the Book of Common Prayer of the Church of England* (1655; 1668 edn.), 318. For John Cosin the 'giving' of the woman showed that 'she had the consent of her parents or governors to wed herself', John Cosin, *The Works of the Right Reverend Father in God, John Cosin*, 5 vols. (Oxford, 1843–55), v. 160.

15. Clay (ed.), *Liturgical Services*, 219.

16. Ibid.

17. 'An Admonition to the Parliament [1572]' in W. H. Frere and C. E. Douglas (eds.), *Puritan Manifestoes* (1954), 27.

18. Clay (ed.), *Liturgical Services*, 219.

19. Ibid. 220–4. Folklorists report that at some North-Country weddings it was customary for the priest as well as the groom and guests to kiss the bride, William Andrews, *Old Church Lore* (Hull, 1891), 195–8; John Brand, *Observations on Popular Antiquities*, 2 vols. (1813), ii. 66–8.

20. William Gouge, *Of Domesticall Dvties* (1622; STC 12119), 205.

21. Warren (tr.), *Sarum Missal in English*, ii. 148; Henry Swinburne, *A Treatise of Spousals, or Matrimonial Contracts* (1686), 208; David Calderwood, *The Altar of Damascus or The Patern of the English Hierarchie* (Amsterdam, 1621; STC 4352), 195; Sparrow, *Rationale upon the Book of Common Prayer*, 319; N.H., *Ladies Dictionary*, 101; Thomas Browne, *Pseudodoxia Epidemica: or, Enquiries into Very Many Received Tenents and Commonly Presumed Truths* (2nd edn., 1650), 157–8.

22. Francis J. Sheernan (ed.), *Dives and Pauper* (New York, 1973), 289–90; Hooker, 'Of

the Laws of Ecclesiastical Politie', in *Works*, 267, reiterated in Sparrow, *Rationale upon the Book of Common Prayer*, 319; Swinburne, *A Treatise of Spousals, or Matrimonial Contracts*, 210.

23. Daniel Rogers, *Matrimoniall Honovr: Or, The mutuall Crowne and comfort of godly, loyall, and chaste Marriage* (1642), 24–5; C.C., *Sad and serious thoughts, or the sense and meaning of the late Act concerning Marriages* (1653), 2; Richard Meggott, *The Rib Restored: Or. The Honour of Marriage* (1656), 24. Cf. William Secker, *A Wedding Ring Fit for the Finger: Or, the salve of Divinity On the sore of Humanity* (1658).

24. Matthew Griffith, *Bethel: Or, a Forme for Families* (1633; STC 12370), 292; Henry Smith, *A Preparative to Marriage* (1591; STC 22686), 24; Thomas Clayton (ed.), *The Works of Sir John Suckling* (Oxford, 1971), 79–84.

25. Samuel Rowlands, 'The Bride' [1617], in Frederick O. Waage, jun. (ed.), *Uncollected Poems . . . by Samuel Rowlands* (Gainesville, Fla., 1970), 189; John Aubrey, 'Remains of Gentilisme and Judaisme', in John Buchanan-Brown (ed.), *John Aubrey: Three Prose Works* (Carbondale, Ill., 1972), 170; Calderwood, *Altar of Damascus*, 195; Clarke and Harris (eds.), *Liturgy and Worship*, 466; Keith Thomas, *Religion and the Decline of Magic* (New York, 1971), 39; Jeaffreson, *Brides and Bridals*, i. 90.

26. John Evans, 'An Account of the Presents Received and Expenses Incurred at the Wedding of Richard Polsted, of Albury, Esquire, and Elizabeth, Eldest Daughter of William More, of Loseley, Esquire', *Archaeologia*, 36 (1855), 44.

27. Rachel Weigall, 'An Elizabethan Gentlewoman: The Journal of Lady Mildmay, circa 1570–1617', *The Quarterly Review*, 215 (1911), 122–3; James M. Osborn (ed.), *The Autobiography of Thomas Whythorne* (Oxford, 1962), 159; *William Whiteway of Dorchester His Diary 1618 to 1635* (Dorset Record Society; Dorchester, 1991), 28, 29. See also *Loues Garland. Or, Posies for Rings, Hand-kerchers, and Gloues; And such pretty Tokens that Louers send their Loues* (1624; STC 16856).

28. F. R. Raines (ed.), *The State, Civil and Ecclesiastical, of the County of Lancaster, about the year 1590* (Chetham Society; Manchester, 1875), 7.

29. C.C., *Sad and serious thoughts*, 2; Anthony Gilby, *A Pleasant Dialogue, Between a Souldior of Barwicke, and an English Chaplaine* (1581; STC 11888), sig. M5; Hastings Robinson (ed.), *The Zurich Letters . . . During the Early Part of the Reign of Queen Elizabeth* (Parker Society; Cambridge, 1842), 163–4.

30. Frere and Douglas (eds.), *Puritan Manifestoes*, 27; Albert Peel (ed.), *The Second Parte of A Register: Being a Calendar of Manuscripts under that title intended for publication by the Puritans about 1593*, 2 vols. (Cambridge, 1915), i. 259; Leland H. Carlson (ed.), *The Writings of Henry Barrow 1587–1590* (1962), 453–4.

31. 'The Humble Petition of Ministers of the Church of England, Desiring Reformation of Certain Ceremonies and Abuses of the Church', in J. P. Kenyon (ed.), *The Stuart Constitution 1603–1688* (Cambridge, 1966), 133; William Barlow, 'The summe and substance of the conference . . . at Hampton Court', in Edward Cardwell, *A History of Conferences and other Proceedings Connected with the Revision of the Book of Common Prayer* (Oxford, 1840), 200–1.

32. *An Abridgement of that Booke which the Ministers of Lincolne Diocesse delivered to his Majestie, upon the first of December 1605* (1638; STC 15648), 96; Robert Parker, *A Scholasticall Discovrse Against Symbolizing with Antichrist in Ceremonies* (Amsterdam, 1607; STC 19294), 70, 96; Calderwood, *Altar of Damascus,* 195–6; John Canne, *A Necessity of Separation from the Church of England* (Amsterdam, 1634; STC 4574), 101.

33. William H. Hale (ed.), *A Series of Precedents and Proceedings in Criminal Causes* (1847), 185; Sidney A. Peyton (ed.), *The Churchwardens' Presentments in the Oxfordshire Peculiars of Dorchester, Thame and Banbury* (Oxfordshire Record Society; Oxford, 1928), 209; Northamptonshire Record Office, X 639/5; W. J. Sheils, *The Puritans in the Diocese of Peterborough, 1558–1610* (Northamptonshire Record Society; Northampton, 1979), 37–61; A. Percival Moore (ed.), 'The Metropolitical Visitation of Archdeacon [sic] Laud', in *Associated Architectural Societies' Reports and Papers,* 29 (1907), 521.

34. R. F. B. Hodgkinson (ed.), 'Extracts from the Act Books of the Archdeacons of Nottingham', *Transactions of the Thoroton Society,* 29 (1926), 33.

35. John Rylands Library, Manchester, Ms. 524, 'The Acts and Speeches of Richard Greenham', fo. 48, my emphasis.

36. Gouge, *Of Domesticall Dvties,* 204–6.

37. *Articles to bee enquired of by the Church-wardens and sworne-men: In the Ordinary Visitation of the Lord Bishop of Excester* (1599; STC 10204), no. 4; John Cosin, 'Articles to be Diligently Inquired Of, and Severally Answered Unto . . . Within the Jurisdiction of the Archdeacon of the East-Riding in York [1627]', in George Ornsby (ed.), *The Correspondence of John Cosin,* 2 vols. (Surtees Society; Durham, 1869), i. 119; *Articles to be Inquired of Within the Dioces of Ely* (1638; STC 10197), ch. 4, no. 24; *Articles of Enquiry and Direction for the Diocese of Norwich . . . 1638* (1638; STC 10299), sig. C2.

38. W. M. Palmer (ed.), *Episcopal Visitation Returns for Cambridgeshire: Matthew Wren, Bishop of Ely, 1638–1665* (Cambridge, 1930), 11. The churchwardens of West Grinstead, Sussex, made an almost identical return in 1636, West Sussex Record Office, Chichester Diocesan Records, Ep 1/22/1.

39. C. H. Firth and R. S. Rait (eds.), *Acts and Ordinances of the Interregnum, 1642–1660,* 2 vols. (1911), i. 601; A. G. Matthews, *Walker Revised. Being a Revision of John Walker's Sufferings of the Clergy during the Grand Rebellion 1642–66* (Oxford, 1948), 126; Christopher Durston, *The Family in the English Revolution* (Oxford, 1989), 68–86.

40. Cardwell, *History of Conferences,* 330; A. G. Matthews, *Calamy Revised, Being a Revision of Edmund Calamy's Account of the Ministers and Others Ejected and Silenced, 1660–2* (Oxford, 1934).

41. See e.g. *Articles to be Enquired of within the Archdeaconry of Middlesex* (1662), 12; 'Articles of Visitation and Enquiry Within the Diocese of Lincoln', in E. R. C. Brinkworth (ed.), *Episcopal Visitation Book for the Archdeaconry of Buckingham, 1662* (Buckinghamshire Record Society; 1947), 89.

42. Jeremy Boulton, 'Economy of Time? Wedding Days and the Working Week in the Past', *Local Population Studies*, 43 (1989), 30; T. N. Brushfield (ed.), 'The Financial Diary of a Citizen of Exeter, 1631–43', *Reports and Transactions of the Devonshire Association*, 33 (1901), 205; Oxfordshire Archives, Diocesan Papers, c. 17, fos. 78, 82; Guildhall Library, Ms. 9583/1; West Suffolk Record Office, E/14/1/13; Alan Bott (ed.), *Baptisms and Marriages at Merton College. Transcribed from the Register of St. John the Baptist's Church, Oxford* (Oxford, 1981), 116.

43. Francis Sadler, *The Exactions and Impositions of Parish Fees Discovered* (1738), 24.

44. Lincolnshire Archives, Court Papers, Box 69/1, no. 23; Greater London Record Office, DL/C 617, p. 461.

45. Greater London Record Office, DL/C 318, pp. 561, 597; Hale (ed.), *A Series of Precedents and Proceedings in Criminal Causes*, 263; Oxfordshire Archives, Diocesan Papers, c. 17, fo. 82.

46. British Library, Additional Ms. 27,440, 'Memoirs of Charles Allestree, 1677–1702', fo. 71^v; Richard Trappes-Lomax (ed.), *The Diary and Letter Book of the Rev. Thomas Brockbank 1671–1709* (Manchester, 1930), 152, 173.

CHAPTER 16

1. William Keatinge Clay (ed.), *Liturgical Services. Liturgies and Occasional Forms of Prayer Set Forth in the Reign of Queen Elizabeth* (Cambridge, 1847), 217.

2. Cf. Louis de Gaya, *Matrimonial Customs: or the Various Ceremonies, and Divers Ways of Celebrating Weddings, Practised amongst all the Nations, in the whole World* (1687), sig. A3: 'There is never a nation under the cope of heaven, how barbarous soever it be, but celebrateth the solemnity of wedlock with more than ordinary ceremonies and festival jollities.'

3. Miles Coverdale, *The Christen State of Matrymonye, wherein housebandes and wyves maye lerne to kepe house together wyth loue* (1552; STC 4049), fos. 56, 57^v.

4. Ibid. 56.

5. Ibid. 57–57^v.

6. 'An Admonition to the Parliament [1572]', in W. H. Frere and C. E. Douglas (eds.), *Puritan Manifestoes* (1954), 27.

7. Henry Smith, *The Wedding Garment* (1590; STC 22713), 7; William Bradshaw, *A Marriage Feast* (1620), printed with Thomas Gataker, *Two Marriage Sermons* (1620; STC 11680), dedication, sigs. E2^v–E4, 3–4. See also John Gauden, *Christ at the Wedding: The Pristine Sanctity and Solemnity of Christian Marriages* (1654), 3, 25; Daniel Rogers, *Matrimoniall Honovr: Or, The mutuall Crowne and comfort of godly, loyall, and chaste Marriage* (1642), 118–19.

8. William Gouge, *Of Domesticall Dvties* (1622; STC 12119), 206–7.

9. Matthew Griffith, *Bethel: Or, a Forme for Families* (1633; STC 12370), 278–9.

10. F. P. Wilson (ed.), *The Batchelars Banquet* (Oxford, 1929), 10, 16–19; Richard Brathwaite, *The Good Wife: or, A rare one amongst Women* (1618; 12747), sig. B8.

11. F. R. Raines (ed.), 'The State, Civil and Ecclesiastical, of the County of Lancaster, about the year 1590', *Chetham Society Miscellany*, 5 (1875), 4, 7; 'An Admonition to the Parliament', 27.

12. John Addy, *Sin and Society in the Seventeenth Century* (1989), 61; Richard S. Ferguson (ed.), *A Boke off Recorde or Register . . . of Kirkbie Kendall* (Kendal, 1892), 87–8, 91, 165.

13. William H. Hale (ed.), *A Series of Precedents and Proceedings in Criminal Causes* (1847), 153, 226–7; Arthur Hussey, 'Visitations of the Archdeacons of Canterbury', *Archaeologia Cantiana*, 27 (1904), 226.

14. Guildhall Library, Ms. 9064/17, fos. 87ᵛ–88.

15. *The Acts of the High Commission Court Within the Diocese of Durham* (Surtees Society; Durham, 1858), 124–5.

16. Hale (ed.), *Series of Precedents and Proceedings in Criminal Causes*, 258.

17. A. G. Matthews, *Walker Revised: Being a Revision of John Walker's Sufferings of the Clergy during the Grand Rebellion 1642–66* (Oxford, 1948), 85.

18. Thomas Deloney, 'The Pleasant History of Iohn Winchcomb, in his Younger yeares called Iacke of Newberie [1597]', in Merritt E. Lawlis (ed.), *The Novels of Thomas Deloney* (Bloomington, Ind., 1961), 28–9.

19. Ibid. 29–30.

20. John Gillis, *For Better for Worse: British Marriages, 1600 to the Present* (New York, 1985), 285–99.

21. 'The Ballad of Arthur of Bradley', in *An Antidote Against Melancholy* (1661), 16–18. 'Hey, brave Arthur Bradley' was a popular expression in Elizabethan and Jacobean England, Morris Palmer Tilley, *A Dictionary of the Proverbs in England in the Sixteenth and Seventeenth Centuries* (Ann Arbor, Mich., 1950), 19.

22. *The Winchester Wedding: or, Ralph of Reading, and Black Bess of the Green* (1670), repr. in *Ancient Songs* (1790), 295–8.

23. The recitation and presentation of epithalamia and nuptial songs was an expected treat at courtly, aristocratic, and gentle weddings. See e.g. Thomas Heywood, *A Marriage Triumphe Solemnized in an Epithalamium, In Memorie of the happie Nuptials betwixt the High and Mightie Prince Count Palatine, And the most Excellent Princesse the Lady Elizabeth* (1613; STC 13355). The wedding of Sir Francis Willoughby to Lady Cassandra Ridgeway in 1610 featured specially written verses by 'Mr. George Withers the poet', Huntington Library, Stowe Ms. STB Box 2 (1). See also Heather Dubrow, *A Happier Eden: The Politics of Marriage in the Stuart Epithalamium* (Ithaca, NY, 1990).

24. Thomas Clayton (ed.), *The Works of Sir John Suckling* (Oxford, 1971), 79–84, 279. See also Suckling 'Upon my Lord Brohall's Wedding', ibid. 86–7, 'When love and Hymen's revels are begun, | And the church ceremony's past and done.'

25. 'A Nuptial Verse to Mistress Elizabeth Lee, now Lady Tracy', in F. W. Moorman (ed.), *The Poetical Works of Robert Herrick* (Oxford, 1921), 213.

26. 'An Epithalamie to Sir Thomas Southwell and his Ladie', in ibid. 53–8; for more poetic delight in the bridal 'bed of pleasure' see Herrick's 'Connubii Flores', ibid. 217.

27. 'A Nuptial Song, or Epithalamie, on Sir Clipseby Crew and his Lady', ibid. 112–16.

28. John Gerarde, *The Herball or Generall Historie of Plantes* (1633; STC 11751), 259–60, 512–15, 854–5.

29. 'A Nuptial Song, or Epithalamie, on Sir Clipseby Crew and his Lady', 116. The poem refers to the jest of folding back the bridal bed sheets, as well as the groom's achievement of penetration and ejaculation.

30. See e.g. *The Mariage of Prince Fredericke, and the Kings Daughter, the Lady Elizabeth, vpon Shrouesunday last* (1613; STC 11359). Isaac in James Shirley's *The Wedding* (1629) remarks, 'Tailors, shoemakers, perfumers, feather-makers, and the devil and all, what a many occupations does a woman run through before she is married', Act 2, scene 1. In a later 17th-cent. account of wedding preparations, 'The seamstress, gorget-maker, and starcher, must be sent for, and the linen must be bought and ordered for the bridegroom's shirts, the bride's smock, cuffs, bands and handkerchiefs', A. Marsh, *The Ten Pleasures of Marriage* (1682), 28.

31. Henry Smith, *A Preparative to Marriage* (1591; STC 22686), 40–1; Smith, *The Wedding Garment*, 35; Gauden, *Christ at the Wedding*, 27.

32. Donald Woodward (ed.), *The Farming and Memorandum Books of Henry Best of Elmswell, 1642* (1984), 123; George Parfitt and Ralph Houlbrooke (eds.), *The Courtship Narrative of Leonard Wheatcroft, Derbyshire Yeoman* (Reading, 1986), 80, 84; E. M. Symonds (ed.), 'The Diary of John Greene (1635–57)', *English Historical Review*, 43 (1928), 392.

33. R. G. Griffiths, 'Joyce Jeffreys of Ham Castle: A Seventeenth-Century Business Gentlewoman', *Transactions of the Worcestershire Archaeological Society*, 10 (1934), 22; Alan Macfarlane (ed.), *The Diary of Ralph Josselin 1616–1683* (1976), 410; J. J. Bagley (ed.), *The Great Diurnal of Nicholas Blundell of Little Crosby, Lancashire*, i (Record Society of Lancashire and Cheshire; 1968), 37, 315.

34. F. P. Wilson (ed.), *The Batchelars Banquet* (Oxford, 1929), 10, 16–19; John Stephens, *Essays and Characters: Ironicall and Instructive* (1615; STC 23250), 353; N.H., *The Ladies Dictionary* (1694), 504; R. C. Latham and W. Matthews (eds.), *The Diary of Samuel Pepys*, 9 vols. (Berkeley and Los Angeles, 1970–6), viii. 73, 77; ix. 335.

35. Woodward (ed.), *Farming and Memorandum Books of Henry Best*, 123; John Cordy Jeaffreson, *Brides and Bridals*, 2 vols. (1872), i. 89.

36. Dorothy Gardiner (ed.), *The Oxinden Letters 1607–1642* (1933), 86; Margaret M. Verney (ed.), *Memoirs of the Verney Family from the Restoration to the Revolution 1660 to 1696* (1899), 250.

37. Henri Misson, *M. Misson's Memoirs and Observations in his Travels over England* (1719), 350.

38. Jeaffreson, *Brides and Bridals*, i. 179; T. N. Brushfield (ed.), 'The Financial Diary of a Citizen of Exeter, 1631–43', *Reports and Transactions of the Devonshire Association*, 33 (1901), 205; Macfarlane (ed.), *Diary of Ralph Josselin*, 29; Parfitt and Houlbrooke (eds.), *Courtship Narrative of Leonard Wheatcroft*, 84–5; C. Willett Cunnington, Phillis Cunnington, and Charles Beard (eds.), *A Dictionary of English Costume* (1960), 233; Norman Marlow (ed.), *The Diary of Thomas Isham of Lamport (1658–81)* (Farnborough, 1971), 61.

39. Jeaffreson, *Brides and Bridals*, i. 169, citing *Dives and Pauper*.

40. Heywood, *Marriage Triumphe*, sig B4ᵛ.

41. Margaret M. Verney (ed.), *Memoirs of the Verney Family During the Common-wealth, 1650 to 1660* (1894), 407; Richard Meggott, *The Rib Restored: Or. The Honour of Marriage* (1656), 7; Stephens, *Essays and Characters*, 355, 357; Suckling, 'Upon my Lord Brohall's Wedding', in Clayton (ed.), *The Works of Sir John Suckling*, 86.

42. Laevinus Lemnius, *An Herbal for the Bible* (1587; STC 15454), 194, 225. See also Keith Thomas, *Man and the Natural World: A History of the Modern Sensibility* (New York, 1993), 230.

43. Roger Hacket, *Two Frvitfvl Sermons, Needfvll for these times* (1607; STC 12592), 1–2.

44. William Vaughan, *The Golden-grove, moralized in three Bookes* (2nd edn., 1609; STC 24611), bk. 2, ch. 6.

45. Parfitt and Houlbrooke (eds.), *Courtship Narrative of Leonard Wheatcroft*, 80, 82, 87.

46. John Evans, 'An Account of the Presents Received and Expenses Incurred at the Wedding of Richard Polstead, of Albury, Esquire, and Elizabeth, Eldest Daughter of William More, of Losely, Esquire', *Archaeologia*, 36 (1855), 36–44; Verney (ed.), *Memoirs of the Verney Family During the Commonwealth*, 407; Symonds (ed.), 'The Diary of John Greene', 389; Latham and Matthews (eds.), *Diary of Samuel Pepys*, i. 39.

47. Ruth Bird (ed.), *The Journal of Giles Moore* (Lewes, 1971), 300, 301, 316, 327, 333, 335, 317, 318, 75, 79, 80.

48. Vaughan, *The Golden-grove*, bk. 2, ch. 6.

49. For high-church fastidiousness in this regard, see Peter Lake, 'The Laudian Style: Order, Uniformity and the Pursuit of the Beauty of Holiness in the 1630s', in Kenneth Fincham (ed.), *The Early Stuart Church, 1603–1642* (1993), 161–85.

50. T. F. Thisleton-Dyer, *Church-Lore Gleanings* (1892), 120–3; Alan Macfarlane, *Marriage and Love in England: Modes of Reproduction 1300–1840* (Oxford, 1986), 314.

51. Parfitt and Houlbrooke (eds.), *Courtship Narrative of Leonard Wheatcroft*, 87–8.

52. Thisleton-Dyer, *Church-Lore Gleanings*, 123; N.H., *Ladies Dictionary*, 505, 740.

53. N.H., *Ladies Dictionary*, 342; *The Pleasures of Matrimony* (1688), 63.

54. Woodward (ed.), *Farming and Memorandum Books of Henry Best*, 123.

55. Verney (ed.), *Memoirs of the Verney Family During the Commonwealth*, 407; Marlow (ed.), *The Diary of Thomas Isham of Lamport*, 109; Joseph Hunter (ed.), *The Diary of Ralph Thoresby . . . 1677–1724*, 2 vols. (1830), i. 179.

56. N.H., *Ladies Dictionary*, 423; Parfitt and Houlbrooke (eds.), *Courtship Narrative of Leonard Wheatcroft*, 85–6.

57. Oxfordshire Archives, Diocesan Papers, d. 6, fo. 193'; Hale (ed.), *Series of Precedents and Proceedings in Criminal Causes*, 225–6.

58. Ibid. 229; Walter C. Renshaw, 'Notes from the Act Books of the Archdeaconry Court of Lewes', *Sussex Archaeological Collections*, 49 (1906), 64.

59. Arnold van Gennep, *The Rites of Passage* (Chicago, 1960), 130–9.

60. John Aubrey, 'Remains of Gentilisme and Judaisme', in John Buchanan-Brown

(ed.), *John Aubrey: Three Prose Works* (Carbondale, Ill. 1972), 169; N.H., *Ladies Dictionary*, 108, 506–8.

61. *The Cony-catching Bride* (1643), 3.

62. John Gough Nichols (ed.), *The Diary of Henry Machyn, Citizen and Merchant-Taylor of London . . . 1550 to . . . 1563* (Camden Society; 1848), 199; Maurice Lee (ed.), *Dudley Carleton to John Chamberlain 1604–1624: Jacobean Letters* (New Brunswick, NJ, 1972), 66. A corrupt version of this report is quoted in Macfarlane, *Marriage and Love*, 313.

63. N. J. G. Pounds (ed.), 'William Carnsew of Bokelly and his Diary, 1576–7', *Royal Institution of Cornwall Journal* (1978), 16, 31, 39, 46, 50, 51, 54, 55; W. G. Perrin (ed.), *The Autobiography of Phineas Pett* (Navy Records Society; 1918), 10, 149, 164. See also Bulstrode Whitelock's account of his wedding in 1630, 'the marriage feast was great, so was the accustomed cheerfulness on such occasions, the music, dancing, revellers, all pleasing', in Ruth Spalding (ed.), *The Diary of Bulstrode Whitelock, 1605–1675* (Oxford, 1990), 61.

64. Symonds (ed.), 'The Diary of John Greene', 392.

65. Ernest Axon (ed.), *Oliver Heywood's Life of John Angier of Denton* (Manchester, 1937), 63; Macfarlane (ed.), *Diary of Ralph Josselin*, 413.

66. Parfitt and Houlbrooke (eds.), *Courtship Narrative of Leonard Wheatcroft*, 83.

67. Ibid. 87–8, 84–5.

68. See also *A Ballad of a Country Wedding*, attributed to James V of Scotland. The London collector George Thomason obtained his copy on 9 May 1660.

69. J. Horsfall Turner (ed.), *The Rev. Oliver Heywood, B.A. 1630–1702: His Autobiography, Diaries, Anecdote and Event Books*, 4 vols. (Brighouse, 1882–5), ii. 253; Verney (ed.), *Memoirs of the Verney Family from the Restoration to the Revolution*, 224; Latham and Matthews (eds.), *Diary of Samuel Pepys*, vii. 262–3.

70. Verney (ed.), *Memoirs of the Verney Family from the Restoration to the Revolution*, 190; Hunter (ed.), *Diary of Ralph Thoresby*, 114, 118, 316; British Library, Additional Ms. 27,440, 'Memoirs of Charles Allestree, 1677–1702', fo. 53ᵛ.

71. Misson, *M. Misson's Memoirs and Observations in his Travels over England*, 349–51.

72. Turner (ed.), *Rev. Oliver Heywood, B.A.*, i. 256, ii. 55, 252–3.

73. Misson, *M. Misson's Memoirs and Observations in his Travels over England*, 349–50; Parfitt and Houlbrooke (eds.), *Courtship Narrative of Leonard Wheatcroft*, 45; Verney (ed.), *Memoirs of the Verney Family from the Restoration to the Revolution*, 249.

74. Deloney, 'The Pleasant History of Iohn Winchcomb', in Lawlis (ed.), *Novels of Thomas Deloney*, 22; Stephens, *Essays and Characters*, 359.

75. Cambridge University Library, Ely Diocesan Records, B/9/15, 4: 25.

76. Subsequent proof of marriage might require evidence of consummation. The classic case in English history concerns Prince Arthur Tudor and Katherine of Aragon. A witness to a clandestine wedding in Yorkshire in 1619 attested that the couple 'did consumate the said marriage', for 'the same night after they were mar-

ried she . . . did see them lie in one and the same bed, and have carnal knowledge together as she thinketh'. Borthwick Institute, York, Cause Papers 1388.

77. Spalding (ed.), *The Diary of Bulstrode Whitelocke*, 61; Michael Hunter and Annabel Gregory (eds.), *An Astrological Diary of the Seventeenth Century: Samuel Jeake of Rye 1652–1699* (Oxford, 1988), 154.

78. N.H., *Ladies Dictionary*, 504; Frederick E. Warren (tr.), *The Sarum Missal in English*, 2 vols. (1913), ii. 160–1.

79. Latham and Matthews (eds.), *Diary of Samuel Pepys*, i. 472. An identical remark appears in *The Pleasures of Matrimony* (1688), 60. Cromwell's jest is mentioned in Keith Thomas, 'The Place of Laughter in Tudor and Stuart England', *TLS* (21 Jan. 1977), 77.

80. An established proverb held that 'more belongs to marriage than four bare legs in a bed', John Ray, *A Collection of English Proverbs* (1670), 48.

81. Latham and Matthews (eds.), *Diary of Samuel Pepys*, i. 27, ii. 23, iv. 37–8, vi. 176; N.H., *Ladies Dictionary*, 509.

82. Misson, *M. Misson's Memoirs and Observations in his Travels over England*, 352–3.

83. Parfitt and Houlbrooke (eds.), *Courtship Narrative of Leonard Wheatcroft*, 86–7; Latham and Matthews (eds.), *Diary of Samuel Pepys*, viii. 66.

CHAPTER 17

1. I have incorporated into this section a reworked version of parts of my essay, 'Death and the Social Order: The Funerary Preferences of Elizabethan Gentlemen', *Continuity and Change*, 5 (1989), 99–119.

2. Clare Gittings, *Death, Burial and the Individual in Early Modern England* (1984), 13 and *passim*.

3. Robert Pricke, *A Verie Godlie and Learned Sermon, treating of Mans mortalitie* (1608; STC 20338), sig. Cᵛ; George R. Potter and Evelyn M. Simpson (eds.), *The Sermons of John Donne*, 10 vols. (Berkeley and Los Angeles, 1962), i. 266.

4. Morris Palmer Tilley, *A Dictionary of the Proverbs in England in the Sixteenth and Seventeenth Centuries* (Ann Arbor, Mich., 1950), 145; James Cole, *Of Death. A True Description: And against it A good Preparation: Together with a sweet consolation, for the surviving mourners* (1629; STC 5533), 87.

5. Sampson Price, *The Two Twins of Birth and Death* (1624; STC 20334), 26, 28; John Dunton, *A Mourning-Ring, In Memory of Your Departed Friend* (2nd edn., 1692), 142–3.

6. Company of Parish Clerks of London, *A General Bill for this Present Year* (1665); Thomas R. Forbes, 'By What Disease or Casualty: The Changing Face of Death in London', in Charles Webster (ed.), *Health, Medicine and Mortality in the Sixteenth Century* (Cambridge, 1979), 117–39; E. A. Wrigley and R. S. Schofield, *The Population History of England, 1541–1871* (Cambridge, Mass., 1981), 181–2, 311–20, 528–33. See also Paul Slack, 'Mortality Crises and Epidemic Disease in England 1485–1610', in Webster (ed.), *Health, Medicine and Mortality*, 9–59; Roger

Schofield and E. A. Wrigley, 'Infant and Child Mortality in England in the Late Tudor and Early Stuart Period', ibid. 61–95.

7. Cole, *Of Death*, 6. Cf. Price, *Two Twins of Birth and Death*, 23.

8. William Perkins, *The Whole Treatise of the Cases of Conscience* (Cambridge, 1608; STC 19670), bk. 1, p. 139. Examples can be found in William Bullein, *A Dialogue against the fever Pestilence* [1578], ed. Mark W. Bullen and A. H. Bullen (1888), 4; *The Daunce and Song of Death* (1569; STC 6222); *Dance of Death* (1585?, STC 6223); *The Doleful Dance, and Song of Death* (1625; STC 6224); *Death's Loud Allarum* (Roxburghe Ballads, i. 78); *Death Dance* (ibid. i. 92).

9. Pricke, *A Verie Godlie and Learned Sermon, treating of Mans mortalitie*, sig. B4^v.

10. Cole, *Of Death*, 2, 25. See also Dunton, *Mourning-Ring*, 142–3; William Sherlock, *A Practical Discourse Concerning Death* (9th edn., 1696).

11. John Ray, *A Collection of English Proverbs* (1670), 6; Tilley, *Dictionary of the Proverbs in England*, 33, 407; *The Doleful Dance, and Song of Death*. For the late medieval 'dance of death' see Eamon Duffy, *The Stripping of the Altars: Traditional Religion in England c.1400–c.1580* (New Haven and London, 1992), 303–5.

12. Price, *Two Twins of Birth and Death*, 5; Potter and Simpson (eds.), *Sermons of John Donne*, iv. 53.

13. Dorothy Gardiner (ed.), *The Oxinden Letters 1607–1642* (1933), 46. See also Elizabeth Grymeston, *Miscelanea. Meditations. Memoratiues* (1604; STC 12407), sigs. C2^v, H2^v, for such aphorisms as 'death unlooseth the chains and sets us free' and 'death is the tribute all flesh must pay'.

14. Pricke, *Verie Godlie and Learned Sermon*, sig. B4^v; Price, *Two Twins of Birth and Death*, 31. See, however, Robert N. Watson, *The Rest is Silence: Death as Annihilation in the English Renaissance* (Berkeley and Los Angeles, 1994), 2–3, for the claim that a psychological 'mortality crisis' affected some authors in Jacobean England who perceived 'the Christian denial of death' as 'a manipulative illusion rather than an absolute truth'.

15. Cole, *Of Death*, 59; Sherlock, *Practical Discourse Concerning Death*, 328.

16. e.g. James Pilkington, 'A Godlie Exposition upon certain Chapters of Nehemiah', in James Scholefield (ed.), *The Works of James Pilkington* (Parker Society; Cambridge, 1842), 320; Samuel Clarke, *An Antidote Against Immoderate Mourning* (1659), 16–17, 26–7.

17. *The Map of Mortality* (1604; STC 17294).

18. Its source, of course, is Luke 16: 22, where 'the beggar died and was carried by the angels into the bosom of Abraham'. Cf. Tilley, *Dictionary of the Proverbs in England*, 1; Shakespeare, *Richard II*, Act 4, scene 1, 102; *Henry V*, Act 2, scene 3, l. 10.

19. Cole, *Of Death*, 85; Price, *Two Twins of Birth and Death*, 34–5; Samuel Hieron, *A Helpe vnto Deuotion: Containing Certain Moulds or Forms of Prayer* (1612; STC 13407), 260.

20. Thomas Playfere, *The Meane in Mourning* (1597; STC 20017), 26, 59–60. This sermon was repr. in 1607 and 1616.

21. Potter and Simpson (eds.), *Sermons of John Donne*, x. 233; Price, *Two Twins of Birth and Death*, 5–6; Dunton, *Mourning-Ring*, 98, 100, 126–7, 197.

22. Sherlock, *Practical Discourse Concerning Death*, 44–5, 58–9.

23. William Shakespeare, *Measure for Measure*, Act 3, scene 1, ll. 117–22.

24. Thomas Adams, 'The Fatal Banket' [1613] in *The Workes of Tho: Adams* (1629; STC 104), 229–30.

25. Patrick Scot, *A Table-Booke for Princes* (1621; STC 21860), 204.

26. Pricke, *Verie Godlie and Learned Sermon*, sigs. Dᵛ–D3. For discussion of the miraculous mechanics of resurrection, see Cole, *Of Death*, 37–42; Potter and Simpson (eds.), *Sermons of John Donne*, iv. 63, 69, 82, 213.

27. The characterization of the cemetery as the 'dormitory' of the dead appears in sources from Honorius of Autun in the 12th cent. to John Evelyn in the 17th. See Phillippe Aries, *The Hour of Our Death* (New York, 1981), 42; Clarke, *An Antidote Against Immoderate Mourning*, 5; E. S. de Beer (ed.), *The Diary of John Evelyn*, 6 vols. (Oxford, 1955), iii. 378.

28. Public Record Office, London, C115/N9/8876, consecration at Door, Herefordshire, 1635.

29. Duffy, *Stripping of the Altars*, 338–76; Robert Charles Hope (ed.), *The Popish Kingdome or Reign of Antichrist, written in Latine Verse by Thomas Naogeorgus, and Englyshed by Barnabe Googe* (1880), bk. 4, fo. 57.

30. John Ayre (ed.), *The Sermons of Edwin Sandys, D.D.* (Parker Society; Cambridge, 1842), 162–3.

31. Pricke, *Verie Godlie and Learned Sermon*, sigs. D4ᵛ–E.

32. Cole, *Of Death*, 140.

33. For analysis of theological debate, see Nicholas Tyacke, *Anti-Calvinists: The Rise of English Arminianism, c.1590–1640* (Oxford, 1987); Peter White, *Predestination, Policy and Polemic: Conflict and Consensus in the English Church from the Reformation to the Civil War* (Cambridge, 1992); Nicholas Tyacke, 'Anglican Attitudes: Some Recent Writings on English Religious History, from the Reformation to the Civil War', *Journal of British Studies*, 35 (1996), 139–67. Though briefly ascendant in the reign of Charles I, Arminianism triumphed in the reign of Charles II.

34. John Veron, *The Huntyng of Purgatorye to Death* (1561; STC 24683), fo. 33; John Donne, *Devotions Upon Emergent Occasions*, ed. Anthony Raspa (Montreal, 1975), 85; 1 Corinthians 6: 19.

35. William Perkins, *A Golden Chain: or, The Description of Theology* (Cambridge, 1600; STC 19646), 79; Perkins, *Whole Treatise of the Cases of Conscience*, bk. 1, pp. 148–9; Robert Hill, *The Pathway to Prayer and Pietie* (1610; STC 13473), 268.

36. Potter and Simpson (eds.), *Sermons of John Donne*, viii. 92; Clarke, *Antidote Against Immoderate Mourning*, 6.

37. Playfere, *Meane in Mourning*, 80. See also Potter and Simpson (eds.), *Sermons of John Donne*, iv. 63–5.

38. Cole, *Of Death*, 194–5. Potter and Simpson (eds.), *Sermons of John Donne*, vii. 384.

39. R. G. Griffiths, 'Joyce Jeffreys of Ham Castle: A Seventeenth-Century Business Gentlewoman', *Transactions of the Worcestershire Archaeological Society*, 10 (1934), 29.

40. *The Autobiography of Mrs. Alice Thornton* (Surtees Society; Durham, 1875), 52.

41. F. W. Bennitt (ed.), 'The Diary of Isabella, Wife of Sir Roger Twysden, Baronet, of Royden Hall, East Peckham, 1645–1651', *Archaeologia Cantiana*, 51 (1939–40), 128.

42. Richard Trappes-Lomax (ed.), *The Diary and Letter Book of the Rev. Thomas Brockbank 1671–1709* (Chetham Society; Manchester, 1930), 6, 12.

43. Alan Macfarlane (ed.), *The Diary of Ralph Josselin, 1616–1683* (1976), 113–14, 203.

44. Matthew Storey (ed.), *Two East Anglian Diaries, 1641–1729: Isaac Archer and William Coe* (Woodbridge, Suffolk, 1994), 151, 164.

45. Anthony Sparrow, *A Rationale upon the Book of Common Prayer of the Church of England* (1668), 353.

46. Veron, *Huntyng of Purgatorye*, fo. 37.

47. Michael MacDonald and Terence R. Murphy, *Sleepless Souls: Suicide in Early Modern England* (Oxford, 1990), 18–20.

48. Richard Burn, *Ecclesiastical Law*, 4 vols. (7th edn., 1809), i. 271.

49. Hill, *Pathway to Prayer and Pietie*, 197, 229. For the late medieval *ars moriendi* see Duffy, *Stripping of the Altars*, 313–27.

50. Cole, *Of Death*, 3–4, 88–9; Price, *Two Twins of Birth and Death*, 35.

51. L. C. Martin (ed.), *The Poems of Robert Herrick* (Oxford, 1956), 321; Thomas Becon, *The Sycke mans salue* (1561; STC 1757); Christopher Sutton, *Disce Mori: Learne to Dye* (1600, 1626; STC 23488); Jeremy Taylor, *The Rule and Exercises of Holy Dying* (1651). See also John More, *A Lively Anatomie of Death* (1595; STC 18073), and John Moore, *A Mappe of Mans Mortalitie* (1617; STC 18057a).

52. Donne, *Devotions Upon Emergent Occasions*, 7.

53. e.g. William Hinde, *A Faithful Remonstrance of the Holy Life and Happy Death of Iohn Bruen of Bruen-Stapleford, in the County of Chester, Esquire* (1641); Ernest Axon (ed.), *Oliver Heywood's Life of John Angier of Denton* (Manchester, 1937). See also Lucinda McCray Beier, 'The Good Death in Seventeenth-Century England', in Ralph Houlbrooke (ed.), *Death, Ritual, and Bereavement* (1989), 43–61.

54. Elizabeth Joceline, *The Mother's Legacie, To her vnborne Childe* (1624; STC 14624), 'Approbation.'

55. The Queen's College, Oxford, Ms. 390, 'Diary of Thomas Crosfield', fo. 38ᵛ.

56. *The Dead Mans Song* (1680s), Roxburghe Ballads, i. 72.

57. J. Horsfall Turner (ed.), *The Rev. Oliver Heywood, B.A. 1630–1702: His Autobiography, Diaries, Anecdote and Event Books*, 4 vols. (Brighouse, 1882–5), i. 246.

58. Trappes-Lomax (ed.), *Diary and Letter Book of the Rev. Thomas Brockbank*, 6.

59. New College, Oxford, Ms. 9502, 'Robert Woodford's Diary', 23 and 24 Aug. 1637. See also de Beer (ed.), *Diary of John Evelyn*, ii. 13, iii. 208, iv. 150; Joseph Hunter (ed.), *The Diary of Ralph Thoresby . . . 1677–1724*, 2 vols. (1830), i. 37.

60. Macfarlane (ed.), *Diary of Ralph Josselin*, 113–14.

61. Bodleian Library, Ms. Top. Camb. e. 5, 'Diary of William Johnson, 1652–63', fo. 57.

62. William Gouge, *Of Domesticall Duties* (3rd edn., 1634; STC 12121), 578.

63. Cole, *Of Death*, 90.

64. Ralph Houlbrooke, 'Death, Church and Family in England between the Late Fifteenth and the Early Eighteenth Centuries', in his *Death, Ritual, and Bereavement*, 29–31; Dan Beaver, '"Sown in Dishonour, Raised in Glory": Death, Ritual and Social Organization in Northern Gloucestershire, 1590–1690', *Social History*, 17 (1992), 393–401. Cf. late medieval deathbed will-making, in Duffy, *Stripping of the Altars*, 322–3.

65. Ann Laurence, 'Godly Grief: Individual Responses to Death in Seventeenth-Century Britain', in Houlbrooke (ed.), *Death, Ritual, and Bereavement*, 62–76; Sutton, *Disce Mori*, 288, 294.

66. Michael MacDonald, *Mystical Bedlam: Madness, Anxiety, and Healing in Seventeenth-Century England* (Cambridge, 1981), 103–4, 159–60; Jean Wilson, 'Icons of Unity', *History Today*, 43 (1993), 14–20; Company of Parish Clerks, *General Bill for . . . 1665*; Laurence, 'Godly Grief', 75. The medical condition of 'grief' was a sudden sense of loss or sadness, not necessarily caused by a loved one's death.

67. Playfere, *Meane in Mourning*, 2–9.

68. Richard Brathwaite, *Remains After Death* (1618; STC 3582), sig. K2.

69. John Weever, *Ancient Funeral Monuments* (1631; STC 25223), 16; Cole, *Of Death*, 173; Clarke, *Antidote Against Immoderate Mourning*, 5.

70. 'Robert Woodford's Diary', 24–7 Aug. 1640.

71. Ruth Spalding (ed.), *The Diary of Bulstrode Whitelock 1605–1675* (Oxford, 1990), 238–9, also 63, 399; de Beer (ed.), *Diary of John Evelyn*, iv. 302, 430, v. 207; Richard Parkinson (ed.), *The Autobiography of Henry Newcome, M.A.* (Chetham Society; Manchester, 1852), 254; Margaret M. Verney, *Memoirs of the Verney Family from the Restoration to the Revolution 1660 to 1696* (1899), 374; Mary Carbery (ed.), *Mrs. Elizabeth Freke Her Diary 1671 to 1714* (Cork, 1913), 59.

72. Turner (ed.), *The Rev. Oliver Heywood*, iii. 137; Hunter (ed.), *The Diary of Ralph Thoresby*, 83; Henry Fishwick (ed.), *The Note Book of the Rev. Thomas Jolly AD 1671–1693* (Chetham Society; Manchester, 1894), 23.

73. 'Robert Woodford's Diary', 2 June 1639; Hunter (ed.), *The Diary of Ralph Thoresby*, 71–2, 184.

74. Weever, *Ancient Funeral Monuments*, 17.

75. T. Ellison Gibson (ed.), *Crosby Records. A Cavalier's Note Book . . . of William Blundell* (1880), 211.

CHAPTER 18

1. John Ayre (ed.), *The Works of John Whitgift, D.D.*, 3 vols. (Parker Society; Cambridge, 1841–3), iii. 366, 371, 373.

2. Frederick E. Warren (ed.), *The Sarum Missal in English*, 2 vols. (1913), ii. 182; R. C. Finucane, 'Sacred Corpse, Profane Carrion: Social Ideals and Death Rituals

in the Later Middle Ages', in Joachim Whaley (ed.), *Mirrors of Mortality: Studies in the Social History of Death* (New York, 1982), 43; Clare Gittings, *Death, Burial and the Individual in Early Modern England* (1984), 31; Eamon Duffy, *The Stripping of the Altars: Traditional Religion in England c.1400–c.1580* (New Haven and London, 1992), 368–9.

3. Joseph Ketley (ed.), *The Two Liturgies, A.D. 1549, and A.D. 1552* (Parker Society; Cambridge, 1844), 144–7, 318–20; William Keating Clay (ed.), *Liturgical Services: Liturgies and Occasional Forms of Prayer Set Forth in the Reign of Queen Elizabeth* (Parker Society; Cambridge, 1847), 233–6; Geoffrey Rowell, *The Liturgy of Christian Burial* (1977), 84–8.

4. Edward Cardwell, *Documentary Annals of the Reformed Church of England*, 2 vols. (Oxford, 1844), i. 156.

5. For examples see F. G. Emmison (ed.), *Elizabethan Life: Wills of Essex Gentry and Merchants* (Chelmsford, 1978), 145, 199; id. (ed.), *Elizabethan Life: Wills of Essex Gentry and Yeomen* (Chelmsford, 1980), 159; David Cressy, 'Death and the Social Order: The Funerary Preferences of Elizabethan Gentlemen', *Continuity and Change*, 5 (1989), 104.

6. *Injunctions Geven by the Quenes Maiestie* (1559; STC 10095).

7. On the difficulties in establishing protestantism in England, compare Patrick Collinson, *The Birthpangs of Protestant England: Religious and Cultural Change in the Sixteenth and Seventeenth Centuries* (1988), and Christopher Haigh, *English Reformations: Religion, Politics and Society under the Tudors* (Oxford, 1993).

8. Canterbury Cathedral Archives, DCb J/X 1.2, fo. 57ᵛ; Cardwell, *Annals*, i. 359; W. H. Frere, *Visitation Articles and Injunctions of the Period of the Reformation*, 3 vols. (1910), iii. 215.

9. James Scholefield (ed.), *The Works of James Pilkington* (Parker Society; Cambridge, 1842), 318, 543.

10. *The Injunctions and other Ecclesiastical Proceedings of Richard Barnes, Bishop of Durham, from 1575 to 1587* (Surtees Society; Durham, 1850), 16.

11. Public Record Office, SP 12/69, fo. 52.

12. Cardwell, *Annals*, i. 371–2, 400; William Nicholson (ed.), *The Remains of Edmund Grindal* (Parker Society; Cambridge, 1843), 136.

13. W. P. M. Kennedy, *Elizabethan Episcopal Administration*, 3 vols. (1924), iii. 143; Gittings, *Death, Burial and the Individual*, 43–4.

14. F. R. Raines (ed.), *A Description of the State, Civil and Ecclesiastical, of the County of Lancaster, about the year 1590* (Chetham Society; Manchester, 1875), 5–7.

15. For examples, see John Bossy, *The English Catholic Community, 1570–1850* (1979). Roger Martin, the recusant champion of Long Melford, Suffolk, was honoured with burial inside the church. See also *The Late Commotion of Certaine Papists in Herefordshire* (1605; STC 25232.5), sig. D–Dᵛ for the early morning burial of an excommunicated recusant, with hand-bells, cross, and tapers.

16. Cited in John Addy, *Death, Money and the Vultures: Inheritance and Avarice, 1660–1750* (1992), 36–7.

17. John Aubrey, 'Remains of Gentilism and Judaisme', in John Buchanan-Brown (ed.), *John Aubrey: Three Prose Works* (Carbondale, Ill., 1972), 172–3, 178; Gittings, *Death, Burial and the Individual*, 45.

18. Joshua Stopford, *Pagano-Papismus: Or, an Exact Parallel Betweene Rome-Pagan, and Rome-Christian, in their Doctrines and Ceremonies* (1675), 278–85.

19. Theo Brown, *The Fate of the Dead: A Study in Folk-Eschatology in the West Country After the Reformation* (Totowa, NJ, 1979); Keith Thomas, *Religion and the Decline of Magic* (New York, 1971), 587–606.

20. W. H. Frere and C. E. Douglas (eds.), *Puritan Manifestoes* (1954), 28. See also Anthony Gilby, *A Pleasaunt Dialogue Between a Souldior of Barwicke and an English Chaplain* (1581; STC 11888), sigs. L8, M3ᵛ, M4, for some of the 'hundred points of Popery, yet remaining, which deform the English reformation'. For a later criticism of popish funeral practices see Stopford, *Pagan-Papismus*, 279–87.

21. Leland H. Carlson (ed.), *The Writings of Henry Barrow 1587–1590* (1962), 458–9.

22. Ibid. 459, 460.

23. Leland H. Carlson (ed.), *The Writings of Henry Barrow 1590–91* (1966), 82.

24. David Calderwood, *The Altar of Damascus or The Pattern of the English Hierarchy* (Amsterdam, 1621; STC 4532), 199–203; John Canne, *A Necessity of Separation from the Church of England* (Amsterdam, 1634; STC 4574), 102–3.

25. Such were the alleged words of John Udall of Kingston, Surrey, in 1586, cited in Albert Peel (ed.), *The Second Part of Register*, 2 vols. (Cambridge, 1915), ii. 45.

26. Cf. Richard L. Greaves, *Society and Religion in Elizabethan England* (Minneapolis, 1981), 695–703, and David E. Stannard, *The Puritan Way of Death: A Study in Religion, Culture, and Social Change* (New York, 1977), 27, 96–134, where 'puritans' are inadequately distinguished from their mainstream protestant contemporaries in England and New England.

27. See e.g. Chaderton's 1607 articles for Lincoln, in Kenneth Fincham (ed.), *Visitation Articles and Injunctions of the Early Stuart Church*, i (Church of England Record Society; Woodbridge, Suffolk, 1994), 76, and Laud's 1628 articles for London, in *The Works of ... William Laud*, 7 vols. (Oxford, 1853), v. 409.

28. William H. Hale (ed.), *A Series of Precedents and Proceedings in Criminal Causes* (1847), 197; F. G. Emmison, *Elizabethan Life: Morals and the Church Courts* (Chelmsford, 1973), 316; Marjorie K. McIntosh, *A Community Transformed: The Manor and Liberty of Havering, 1500–1620* (Cambridge, 1991), 208.

29. Rowell, *Liturgy of Christian Burial*, 91.

30. Guildhall Library, Ms. 9059/1, fo. 90.

31. Northamptonshire Record Office, Northampton, Ms. X 639/3, fo. 18ᵛ; Greater London Record Office, DL/C 617, 216; Hilda Johnstone (ed.), *Churchwardens' Presentments (17th Century), Part 1: Archdeaconry of Chichester* (Sussex Record Society; Lewes, 1947–8), 115.

32. Hale, *Series of Precedents and Proceedings*, 210; Greater London Record Office, DL/C 617, 850.

33. Lincolnshire Record Office, Lincoln, Court Papers Box 69/1 [1602], nos. 18, 23, 24.

34. e.g. at Horkstow, Lincolnshire, C. W. Foster, *The State of the Church in the Reigns of Elizabeth and James I as Illustrated by Documents Relating to the Diocese of Lincoln* (Lincolnshire Record Society; Lincoln, 1926), xxx; at Preston Capes and Ridlington, Northants, Northamptonshire Record Office, Archdeaconry Correction Books, Box 610, no. 23, fos. 95, 155ᵛ.

35. *An Abridgement of that Booke which the Ministers of Lincoln Diocess delivered to his Maiestie* (1605, STC 15646), 29.

36. Ayre (ed.), *Works of John Whitgift*, iii. 371–9; Frederic B. Tromly, ' "According to sounde religion": The Elizabethan Controversy over the Funeral Sermon', *Journal of Medieval and Reniassance Studies*, 13 (1983), 293–312.

37. Scholefield (ed.), *Works of James Pilkington*, 321.

38. e.g. John Veron, the hammer of purgatory, preached at London funerals in 1560 and 1561, John Gough Nichols (ed.), *The Diary of Henry Machyn, Citizen and Merchant-Taylor of London from A.D. 1550 to A.D. 1563* (Camden Society; 1848), 225, 257; Edwin Sandys preached a celebrated anti-purgatory sermon at a funeral in 1574, John Ayre (ed.), *The Sermons of Edwin Sandys* (Parker Society; Cambridge, 1842), 161–3.

39. Analysis of the on-line English Short-Title Catalogue (ESTC) finds just 3 funeral sermons or similar publications from the 1560s, 3 from the 1570s, 7 from the 1580s, 11 from the 1590s, 29 from the 1600s, 56 from the 1610s, 49 from the 1620s, 46 from the 1630s, 61 from the 1640s, 117 from the 1650s, 71 from the 1660s, 96 from the 1670s, 114 from the 1680s, and 150 from the 1690s. Though these are numbers of catalogued survivals, including some reprints, they clearly indicate the 17th-cent. boom in the publication of funeral sermons.

40. Robert Hill, *The Pathway to Prayer and Pietie* (1610; STC 13473), 276.

41. Dunton, *Mourning-Ring*, 23.

42. J. E. Foster (ed.), *The Diary of Samuel Newton, Alderman of Cambridge (1662–1717)* (Cambridge, 1890), 5, 6, mentions 'obit' sermons at Restoration Cambridge that memorialized Aldermanic philanthropists.

43. Edward Finch, *An Answer to the Articles Preferred Against Edward Finch* (1641), 2.

44. R. F. B. Hodgkinson (ed.), 'Extracts from the Act Books of the Archdeacons of Nottingham', *Transactions of the Thoroton Society*, 30 (Nottingham, 1927), 52; Cambridge University Library, Ms. Mm. 4.29, fo. 108.

45. Herefordshire Record Office, Hereford, Box 17, book 67, fo. 42; Sidney A Peyton (ed.), *The Churchwardens' Presentments in the Oxfordshire Peculiars of Dorchester, Thame and Banbury* (Oxfordshire Record Society; Oxford, 1928), 292, 298.

46. *The Correspondence of John Cosin*, 2 vols. (Surtees Society; Durham. 1869), i. 119–20; John Cosin, *The Works of the Right Reverend Father in God, John Cosin*, 5 vols. (Oxford, 1843–55), v. 165–71.

47. *Works of . . . William Laud*, v. 403; *Articles of Enquiry and Direction for the Diocese of Norwich* (1638; STC 10299), sig. C3.

48. Greater London Record Office, DL/C 318, fo. 228ᵛ. See also Peter Lake, 'The

Laudian Style: Order, Uniformity and the Pursuit of the Beauty of Holiness in the 1630s', in Kenneth Fincham (ed.), *The Early Stuart Church, 1603–1642* (1993), 161–85.

49. Richard Field, *Of the Church, Five Books* (2nd edn., Oxford, 1628; STC 10858), 750, 756, 761, 792–3.

50. *Articles of Enquiry and Direction for the Diocese of Norwich*, sig. C. See also *Hierurgia Anglicana: or Documents and Extracts Illustrative of the Ritual of the Church of England after the Reformation* (1848), 316–17.

51. *William Whiteway of Dorchester His Diary 1618 to 1635* (Dorset Record Society; Dorchester, 1991), 140; Cosin, *Works*, v. 169–70.

52. *Dives and Pauper* (1534 edn.; STC 19214), fos. 82–3.

53. Thomas Becon, *The Sick Mans Salve* [1561], quoted in Gordon E. Geddes, *Welcome Joy: Death in Puritan New England* (Ann Arbor, Mich., 1981), 105.

54. John Veron, *The Huntynge of Purgatorye to Death* (1561; STC 24683), fos. 34–6.

55. Ayre (ed.), *Sermons of Edwin Sandys*, 161–2; Scholefield (ed.), *Works of James Pilkington*, 320.

56. Clay (ed.), *Liturgical Services*, 202, 211.

57. Scholefield (ed.), *Works of James Pilkington*, xi. 317–19; *Dictionary of National Biography*, v. 45, 205.

58. Nicholson (ed.), *Remains of Edmund Grindal*, 458. For Grindal's funeral, which was much more elaborate than he would have wished, see Patrick Collinson, *Archbishop Grindal 1519–1583: The Struggle for a Reformed Church* (1979), 279.

59. Ayre (ed.), *The Sermons of Edwin Sandys*, 447.

60. Emmison (ed.), *Elizabethan Life: Wills of Essex Gentry and Merchants*, 174, 58, 128, 155.

61. Ibid. 106, 107; Emmison (ed.), *Elizabethan Life: Wills of Essex Gentry and Yeomen*, 36–8.

62. Francis Tate, 'Of the Antiquity, Variety and Ceremonies of Funerals in England', in Thomas Hearne (ed.), *A Collection of Curious Discourses Written by Eminent Antiquaries*, 2 vols. (1771), i. 215; Dan Beaver, ' "Sown in Dishonour, Raised in Glory": Death, Ritual and Social Organization in Northern Gloucestershire, 1590–1690', *Social History*, 17 (1992), 416–17.

63. William Perkins, *A Golden Chaine: or, The Description of Theologie, Containing the Order of the Causes of Saluation and Damnation* (Cambridge, 1600; STC 19646), 79–80.

64. Hill, *Pathway to Prayer and Pietie*, 268; Thomas Sparke, *A Brotherly Perswasion To Vnitie* (1607; STC 23020), 37.

65. William Gouge, *Of Domesticall Duties* (3rd edn., 1634; STC 12121), 482–4.

66. Patrick Scot, *A Table-Booke for Princes* (1621; STC 21860), 214–15.

67. *A Directory For the Publique Worship of God* (1646), 35, my emphasis.

68. Julian Litten, *The English Way of Death: The Common Funeral Since 1450* (1991), 158–60.

69. E. S. de Beer (ed.), *The Diary of John Evelyn*, 6 vols. (Oxford, 1955), iii. 76.

70. Richard Culmer, *A Parish Looking-Glasse for Persecutors of Ministers* (1657), 17.

71. Richard Parkinson (ed.), *The Autobiography of Henry Newcome, M.A.* (Chetham Society; Manchester, 1852), 105.

72. Edward Cardwell, *A History of Conferences . . . Connected with the Revision of the Book of Common Prayer* (Oxford, 1840), 332–3; *Correspondence of John Cosin*, ii. 75–6; *The Book of Common Prayer* (1662).

73. *Articles to be Enquired of Within the Archdeaconry of Middlesex* (1662), 13; E. R. C. Brinkworth (ed.), *Episcopal Visitation Book of the Archdeaconry of Buckingham, 1662* (Buckinghamshire Record Society; Aylesbury, 1947), 88, 91.

74. Ibid. 4, 56, 77.

75. Oxfordshire Archives, Oxford, Diocesan Papers, c. 3, fo. 9. Confessing 'that he doth serve God another way . . . and . . . that he doth not approve of the common prayer', Canon was ordered to receive instruction and to conform to ecclesiastical discipline.

76. Guildhall Library, Ms. 9583/2, part 3, fo. 48; Ms. 9583/2, part 4, nos. 125, 127, 129.

77. Guildhall Library, Ms. 9583/2, part 6, fos. 72, 78, 82; Greater London Record Office, GL/C 625, fo. 16; W. J. Pressey, 'Notes on Visitations in the Archdeaconry of Essex', *Transactions of the Essex Archaeological Society*, 20 (1930–1), 222.

78. Hilda Johnstone (ed.), *Churchwardens' Presentments (17th Century), Part 2: Archdeaconry of Lewes* (Sussex Record Society; Lewes, 1948–9), 54; J. Horsfall Turner (ed.), *The Rev. Oliver Heywood, B.A. 1630–1702: His Autobiography, Diaries, Anecdote and Event Books*, 4 vols. (Brighouse, 1882–5), ii. 250. Essex Quakers had their own burying ground at Earls Colne by the late 1670s, Alan Macfarlane, *The Family Life of Ralph Josselin* (Cambridge, 1970), 27.

79. Thomas Heywood (ed.), *The Diary of the Rev. Henry Newcome, from September 30, 1661, to September 29, 1663* (Chetham Society; Manchester, 1849), 175–6.

80. Wiltshire Record Office, Trowbridge, BSD 62, cited in Donald A. Spaeth, 'Parsons and Parishioners: Lay-Clerical Conflict and Popular Piety in Wiltshire Villages, 1660–1740', Ph.D., Brown University, 1985, p. 126.

81. Wiltshire Record Office, BSD, Bundle 3, cited in Spaeth, 'Parsons and Parishioners', 128.

82. Hilda Johnstone (ed.), *Churchwardens' Presentments (17th Century), Part 1: Archdeaconry of Chichester* (Sussex Record Society; Lewes, 1947–8), 130–1; Wiltshire Record Office, Bp. Cit. 17, cited in Spaeth, 'Parsons and Parishioners', 125; J. S. Leatherbarrow (ed.), *Churchwardens' Presentments in the Diocese of Worcester, c.1660–1760* (Worcester, 1977), 10.

83. Durham University Library, Archives and Special Collections, DDR. II/3, fo. 36.

84. Andrew Browning (ed.), *Memoirs of Sir John Reresby* (2nd edn., 1991) 409; *Depositions from the Castle at York* (Surtees Society; Durham, 1861), 279–82. I am grateful to Molly McClain and Lois Schwoerer for advice about this matter, and for pointing out that the editor of Reresby's memoirs mistakenly identifies the body as that of Henrietta Maria Wentworth, who was the Earl of Monmouth's mistress.

CHAPTER 19

1. R. C. Finucane, 'Sacred Corpse, Profane Carrion: Social Ideals and Death Rituals in the Later Middle Ages', in Joachim Whaley (ed.), *Mirrors of Mortality: Studies in the Social History of Death* (New York, 1982), 41; Richard Huntington and Peter Metcalf, *Celebrations of Death: The Anthropology of Mortuary Ritual* (Cambridge, 1979); Maurice Bloch and Jonathan Parry (eds.), *Death and the Regeneration of Life* (Cambridge, 1982). For discussion of 16th- and 17th-cent. English funerals see, in order of publication, Lawrence Stone, *The Crisis of the Aristocracy, 1558–1641* (Oxford, 1965), 572–81; Keith Thomas, *Religion and the Decline of Magic* (New York, 1971), 39, 66, 556, 601–5; David E. Stannard, *The Puritan Way of Death: A Study in Religion, Culture and Social Change* (New York, 1977), 96–134; Clare Gittings, *Death, Burial and the Individual in Early Modern England* (London, 1984); Ralph Houlbrooke (ed.), *Death, Ritual, and Bereavement* (1989); and Julian Litten, *The English Way of Death: The Common Funeral since 1450* (1991).

2. Thomas Playfere, *The Meane in Mourning* (1597; STC 20017), 81.

3. See William Henry Overall (ed.), *The Accounts of the Churchwardens of the Parish of St. Michael, Cornhill, in the City of London, from 1456 to 1608* (1868), 223–4, for the 'ordinances of the bells' and fees for knells and peals at funerals in the reign of Henry VIII.

4. Historical Manuscripts Commission, *Calendar of the Manuscripts of the Dean and Chapter of Wells*, 2 vols. (1914), ii. 265.

5. William Andrews, *Old Church Lore* (Hull, 1891), 210–11; William Nicholson (ed.), *The Remains of Edmund Grindal* (Parker Society; Cambridge, 1843), 136.

6. Kenneth Fincham (ed.), *Visitation Articles and Injunctions of the Early Stuart Church*, i (Church of England Record Society; Woodbridge, Suffolk, 1994), 76, 182.

7. F. R. Raines (ed.), *A Description of the State, Civil and Ecclesiastical, of the County of Lancaster, about the year 1590* (Chetham Society; Manchester, 1875), 5–7.

8. John Donne, *Devotions Upon Emergent Occasions*, ed. Anthony Raspa (Montreal, 1975), 83.

9. Thomas Adams, 'The Sinner's Passing Bell' [1614], in *The Workes of Tho: Adams* (1629; STC 104), 248–9.

10. Ibid. 248–9.

11. Anthony Copley, *Wits, Fits and Fancies* [1614 edn.], qu. in Andrews, *Old Church Lore*, 213; Donne, *Devotions*, 87.

12. Canterbury Cathedral Archives, Z3 8, fo. 54. W. J. Sheils (ed.), *Archbishop Grindal's Visitation, 1575: Comperta et Detecta Book* (York, 1977), 19; Raines (ed.), *Description of the State . . . of Lancaster*, 5–6.

13. Sidney A. Peyton, *The Churchwardens' Presentments in the Oxfordshire Peculiars of Dorchester, Thame and Banbury* (Oxfordshire Record Society; Oxford, 1928), 251; Oxfordshire Archives, Oxford, Diocesan Papers, c. 2, fos. 178, 179.

14. Oxfordshire Archives, Diocesan Papers, c. 17, fo. 75; Borthwick Institute, York, V. 1633, Court Book 1, fo. 115ᵛ.

15. R. G. Griffiths, 'Joyce Jeffreys of Ham Castle: A 17th Century Business Gentle-woman', *Transactions of the Worcestershire Archaeological Society*, NS 10 (1934), 21; J. J. Bagley (ed.), *The Great Diurnal of Nicholas Blundell of Little Crosby, Lancashire . . . 1702–1711* (Record Society of Lancashire and Cheshire; 1968), 15.

16. Historical Manuscripts Commission, *Wells*, ii. 363; *Records of the Borough of Nottingham, vol. V . . . 1625–1702* (London and Nottingham, 1900), 320; J. E. Foster (ed.), *Churchwardens' Accounts of St. Mary the Great, Cambridge, from 1504 to 1635* (Cambridge, 1905), 63; Mary Carbery (ed.), *Mrs. Elizabeth Freke Her Diary 1671 to 1714* (Cork, 1913), 59, 62–70.

17. E. R. C. Brinkworth (ed.), *Episcopal Visitation Book of the Archdeaconry of Buckingham, 1662* (Buckinghamshire Record Society; Aylesbury, 1947), 92; *Second Report of the Ritual Commission* (Parliamentary Papers 38; 1867–8), appendix E, p. 633.

18. John Dunton, *A Mourning-Ring, In Memory of Your Departed Friend* (2nd edn., 1692), 23. This work was written by John Dunton senior, a minister in Huntingdonshire in the reign of Charles II.

19. William Carnsew, a Cornish gentlemen, wrote in 1576 that the vicar died 'of a putrefaction of his lungs. I saw him opened.' N. J. G. Pounds (ed.), 'William Carnsew of Bokelly and his Diary, 1576–7', *Journal of the Royal Institution of Cornwall*, NS 8 (1978), 29; the Oxford fellow Thomas Crosfield recorded the death of a colleague in 1631, 'being opened by the surgeon, his lungs were found to be perished', Frederick S. Boas (ed.), *The Diary of Thomas Crosfield* (Oxford, 1935), 59; when John Evelyn's son Dick died in 1658 the diarist 'suffered the physicians to have him opened' to examine his liver and spleen, E. S. de Beer (ed.), *The Diary of John Evelyn*, 6 vols. (Oxford, 1955), ii. 209. See also David Harley, 'Political Post-Mortems and Morbid Anatomy in Seventeenth-Century England', *Social History of Medicine*, 7 (1994), 1–28. On embalming, see below, n. 25.

20. Stephen Porter, 'Death and Burial in a London Parish: St. Mary Woolnoth 1653–99', *London Journal*, 8 (1982), 76–80.

21. William H. Hale, *A Series of Precedents and Proceedings in Criminal Causes* (1847), 231; Levi Fox (ed.), 'Diary of Robert Beake Mayor of Coventry, 1655–56', *Miscellany*, 1 (Dugdale Society; Oxford, 1977), 117–18.

22. Huntington Library, San Marino, Ms. HM30665, fo. 10. 'Memorable accidents'; Lincolnshire Archives, Lincoln, Vj/28, fo. 4.

23. Ernest Axon (ed.), *Oliver Heywood's Life of John Angier of Denton* (Chetham Society; Manchester, 1937), 126; de Beer (ed.), *Diary of John Evelyn*, iv. 151.

24. Hale, *A Series of Precedents and Proceedings*, 248; Oxfordshire Archives, Diocesan Papers, c. 2, fo. 178ᵛ. R. C. Latham and W. Matthews (eds.), *The Diary of Samuel Pepys*, 11 vols. (Berkeley and Los Angeles, 1970–83), ii. 133.

25. On embalming, see Stone, *Crisis of the Aristocracy*, 572; Gittings, *Death, Burial and the Individual*, 104–5, 167; Litten, *English Way of Death*, 32–53. Other examples include Essex Record Office, Chelmsford, D/DP F240/3, 'A brief declaracon of

the chardge aswell for the openinge and embalming of the body of Thomas late Earle of Sussex'; Francis Peck, *Desiderata Curiosa* (1779), 252–3; A. Hassell Smith and Gillian M. Baker (eds.), *The Papers of Nathaniel Bacon of Stiffkey*, 3 vols. (Norwich, 1979–90), ii. 35–6; Francis Bamford (ed.), *A Royalist's Notebook: The Commonplace Book of Sir John Oglander* (1936), 26, 40.

26. Francis Tate, 'Of the Antiquity, Variety and Ceremonies of Funerals in England', in Thomas Hearne (ed.), *A Collection of Curious Discourses Written by Eminent Antiquaries*, 2 vols. (1771), i. 216.

27. John Aubrey, 'Remains of Gentilisme and Judaisme', in John Buchanan-Brown (ed.), *John Aubrey: Three Prose Works* (Carbondale, Ill., 1972), 173.

28. Henry Bourne, *Antiquitates Vulgares or the Antiquities of the Common People* (Newcastle, 1725), 16.

29. D. J. H. Clifford (ed.), *The Diaries of Lady Anne Clifford* (Stroud, 1990), 21, 72.

30. Durham University Library, Archives and Special Collections, DDR V/II, fo. 369.

31. Tate, 'Of the Antiquity, Variety and Ceremonies of Funerals', 217.

32. Smith and Baker (eds.), *Papers of Nathaniel Bacon*, ii. 34, 57; Huntington Library, Hastings Ms. Miscellany, Box 12, folder 2, fo. 77. More examples are in Hertfordshire Record Office, Hertford, D/P 93 17/1, Overseers Accounts of St Peter's, St Albans, 1663–81. I am grateful to Karen Smith Adams for this and similar references.

33. *Selections from the Household Books of the Lord William Howard of Naworth Castle* (Surtees Society; Durham, 1878), 343. R. G. Griffiths, 'Joyce Jeffreys of Ham Castle: A 17th Century Business Gentlewoman', *Transactions of the Worcestershire Archaeological Society*, NS 10 (1934), 21.

34. Edmund Hobhouse (ed.), *The Diary of a West Country Physician. AD. 1684–1726* (1935), 145–6, 149; Robert Willis Blencowe (ed.), 'Extracts from the Journal and Account-Book of Timothy Burrell . . . 1683 to 1714', *Sussex Archaeological Collections*, 3 (1850), 157.

35. Dunton, *Mourning-Ring*, 288. For more on shrouds and grave-clothes, see Gittings, *Death, Burial and the Individual*, 110–13; Litten, *English Way of Death*, 57–80.

36. Huntington Library, Hastings Ms. Miscellany, Box 8, folder 2a; Hastings Ms. Miscellany, Box 12, folder 2, fos. 21, 84, 101.

37. J. Barmby (ed.), *Churchwardens' Accounts of Pittington and other Parishes in the Diocese of Durham from A.D. 1580 to 1700* (Surtees Society; Durham, 1888), 240; T. F. Thisleton-Dyer, *Church-Lore Gleanings* (1892), 151; Gittings, *Death, Burial and the Individual*, 61.

38. *The Map of Mortalitie* (1604; STC 17294).

39. Logan Pearsall Smith, *John Donne's Sermons* (Oxford, 1919), frontispiece; Litten, *English Way of Death*, 67, pl. 31; Daniel Featley, *The Dippers Dipt* (7th edn., 1660), facing table of contents.

40. Elizabeth Joceline, *The Mothers Legacie, to her Vnborne Childe* (1624; STC 14624),

sig. A5; Ruth Spalding (ed.), *The Diary of Bulstrode Whitelock 1605–1675* (Oxford, 1990), 65.

41. John Southerden Burn, *The History of Parish Registers* (1862), 198.

42. Richard Burn, *Ecclesiastical Law*, 4 vols. (7th. edn., 1809), i. 271–2.

43. Raymond Richards, *Old Cheshire Churches: A Survey of their History, Fabric and Furniture* (London, 1947, repr. Manchester, 1973), 224. The Yorkshire diarist Abraham de la Pryme reports that straw or chaff was put into waterlogged graves 'to hinder the water being seen by the people', Charles Jackson (ed.), *The Diary of Abraham de la Pryme* (Surtees Society; Durham, 1870), 62.

44. Frances Parthenope Verney, *Memoirs of the Verney Family During the Civil War*, 2 vols. (1892), ii. 18.

45. *Statutes of the Realm*, 18–19 Car. II, c. 4; 30 Car. II, c. 3; 32 Car. II, c. 1; Burn, *History of Parish Registers*, 117; Litten, *English Way of Death*, 73–4.

46. New College, Oxford, Ms. 9502, 'Robert Woodford's Diary', entry for 6 Aug. 1638; Axon (ed.), *Oliver Heywood's Life of John Angier*, 126.

47. Ian W. Archer, *The Pursuit of Stability: Social Relations in Elizabethan London* (Cambridge, 1991), 112; Gittings, *Death, Burial and the Individual*, 116.

48. Barmby (ed.), *Churchwardens' Accounts of Pittington and other Parishes*, 33; J. F. Williams (ed.), *Diocese of Norwich: Bishop Redman's Visitation 1597* (Norfolk Record Society; Norwich, 1946), 77; J. R. Beresford (ed.), 'The Churchwarden's Accounts of Holy Trinity, Chester, 1532 to 1633', *Journal of the Chester and North Wales Architectural, Archaeological, and Historical Society*, 38 (1951), 134, 148.

49. West Sussex Record Office, Chichester, Diocesan Records, EP 1/26/2; R. F. B. Hodgkinson (ed.), 'Extracts from the Act Books of the Archdeacons of Nottingham', *Transactions of the Thoroton Society*, 31 (1928), 134; Lichfield Record Office, B/V/1/65.

50. Brinkworth (ed.), *Episcopal Visitation Book of the Archdeaconry of Buckingham*, 1; Guildhall Libary, Ms. 9583/2, part 2, fos. 2, 41; part 4, no. 63, and *passim*. See also Herefordshire Record Office, Box 43, bk. 166, fo. 2^v for deficiencies in Shropshire in 1673; W. J. Pressey, 'Notes on Visitations in the Archdeaconry of Essex', *Transactions of the Essex Archaeological Society*, 20 (1930–1), 228.

51. Litten, *English Way of Death*, fig. 68.

52. Adams, *Workes*, 230.

53. Litten, *English Way of Death*, 125; Barmby (ed.), *Churchwardens' Accounts of Pittington and other Parishes*, 169–70; Thisleton-Dyer, *Church-Lore Gleanings*, 150; Andrews, *Old Church Lore*, 219–24.

54. Litten, *English Way of Death*, 12, 86, 98.

55. Smith and Baker (eds.), *Papers of Nathaniel Bacon*, ii. 35; Verney, *Memoirs of the Verney Family During the Civil War*, ii. 18; Margaret M. Verney, *Memoirs of the Verney Family From the Restoration to the Revolution 1660 to 1696* (1899), 374. John Spencer of St Sepulchre's, London, who was cited in 1636 'for having company drinking in his house on Candlemas day and St. Mathias's day last', gave his occupation as 'coffin maker', Guildhall Library, Ms. 9059/1. fo. 11^v.

56. Essex Record Office, Chelmsford, D/DMs F9; Boas (ed.) *Diary of Thomas Crosfield*, 100, checked against The Queen's College, Oxford, Ms. K. k. 14; Latham and Matthews (eds.), *Diary of Samuel Pepys*, v. 90; Litten, *English Way of Death*, 86.

57. D. R. Hainsworth and Cherry Walker (eds.), *The Correspondence of Lord Fitzwilliam of Milton and Francis Guybon, his Steward, 1697–1709* (Northamptonshire Record Society; Northampton, 1990), 63; Bagley (ed.), *Great Diurnal of Nicholas Blundell*, 15, 314; Blencowe (ed.), 'Extracts from the Journal and Account-Book of Timothy Burrell', 157.

58. Charles Kerry, 'The Autobiography of Leonard Wheatcroft', *Journal of the Derbyshire Archaeology and Natural History Society*, 21 (1899), 53–4; Christopher Marsh, 'The Gravestone of Thomas Lawrence Revisited: Or the Family of Love and the Local Community in Balsham, 1560–1630', in Margaret Spufford (ed.), *The World of Rural Dissenters, 1520–1725* (Cambridge, 1995), 208–34.

59. Dunton, *Mourning-Ring*, 285.

60. *The Bride's Buriall* (1621?, STC 3728a); Tate, 'Of the Antiquity, Variety and Ceremonies of Funerals', 219.

61. F. G. Emmison (ed.), *Elizabethan Life: Wills of Essex Gentry and Merchants* (Chelmsford, 1978), 82, 276; id. (ed.), *Elizabethan Life: Wills of Essex Gentry and Yeomen* (Chelmsford, 1980), 128.

62. Archer, *Pursuit of Stability*, 54.

63. 'Robert Woodford's Diary', 5 Apr. 1639.

64. De Beer (ed.), *Diary of John Evelyn*, iv. 203; Hainsworth and Walker (eds.), *Correspondence of Lord Fitzwilliam of Milton*, 62.

65. J. E. Foster (ed.), *The Diary of Samuel Newton: Alderman of Cambridge (1662–1717)* (Cambridge, 1890), 18–20.

66. De Beer (ed.), *Diary of John Evelyn*, iv. 151; Carbery (ed.), *Mrs. Elizabeth Freke Her Diary*, 24.

67. Bourne, *Antiquitates Vulgares*, 19.

68. James Scholefield (ed.), *The Works of James Pilkington* (Parker Society; Cambridge, 1842), 319; John Ayre (ed.), *The Works of John Whitgift, D.D.*, 3 vols. (Parker Society; Cambridge, 1841–3), iii. 361–2.

69. De Beer (ed.), *Diary of John Evelyn*, iv. 302. See also Thomas Shipman, 'The Old Mourner', in his *Carolina: Or, Loyal Poems* (1683), 119; Gittings, *Death, Burial and the Individual*, 119–22; Randolph Trumbach, *The Rise of the Egalitarian Family* (New York, 1978), 33–41.

70. Latham and Matthews (eds.), *Diary of Samuel Pepys*, viii. 210, 242, v. 91.

71. Dunton, *Mourning-Ring*, 296, plagiarizing John Weever.

72. Ayre (ed.), *Works of John Whitgift*, iii. 368–9.

73. Playfere, *Meane in Mourning*, 81.

74. Robert Hill, *The Pathway to Prayer and Pietie* (1610; STC 13473), 276.

75. Smith and Baker (eds.), *Papers of Nathaniel Bacon*, ii. 47–56, 64; Essex Record Office, D/DP F240/4. See also the frequent reference to black gowns and black

hangings at mid-Tudor funerals in John Gough Nichols (ed.), *The Diary of Henry Machyn, Citizen and Merchant-Taylor of London from A.D. 1550 to A.D. 1563* (Camden Society; 1848), *passim*.

76. Emmison (ed.), *Elizabethan Life: Wills of Essex Gentry and Merchants*, 106, 68, 58.

77. Ibid. 127, 96, 134.

78. Folger Shakespeare Library, Washington, Folger Ms. L.a. 778, Saunders to Bagot, 12 July 1585.

79. Essex Record Office, D/DMs F9; T. N. Brushfield, 'The Financial Diary of a Citizen of Exeter, 1631–43', *Reports and Transactions of the Devonshire Association*, 33 (1901), 208.

80. Verney, *Memoirs of the Verney Family During the Civil War*, ii. 15–16; Boas (ed.) *Diary of Thomas Crosfield*, 100.

81. Latham and Matthews (eds.), *Diary of Samuel Pepys*, v. 90, ix. 452.

82. G. E. Aylmer (ed.), *The Diary of William Lawrence Covering Periods between 1662 and 1681* (Beaminster, 1961), 28. Lawrence described this event for the benefit of his brother Isaac who was trading in the Levant.

83. Joseph Hunter (ed.), *The Diary of Ralph Thoresby . . . 1677–1724*, 2 vols. (1830), i. 81.

84. Verney, *Memoirs of the Verney Family From the Restoration to the Revolution*, 327–8.

85. Hainsworth and Walker (eds.), *Correspondence of Lord Fitzwilliam of Milton*, 62–4.

86. Hobhouse (ed.), *The Diary of a West Country Physician*, 145, 148.

87. Borthwick Institute, Cause Papers Transmitted on Appeal, 1673/4, fos. 78–228.

88. Smith and Baker (eds.), *Papers of Nathaniel Bacon*, ii. 42. The funeral of Sir Fulke Greville (father of the poet) in Warwickshire in 1559 featured 'a great dole, and after, a great dinner for the rich and poor', Nichols (ed.), *Diary of Henry Machyn*, 219.

89. Anthony Sparrow, *A Rationale upon the Book of Common Prayer of the Church of England* (1668), 355; *Dives and Pauper* (1534 edn.; STC 19214), fos. 82–3. See also Stone, *Crisis of the Aristocracy*, 575; Gittings, *Death, Burial and the Individual*, 27–8, 87; Archer, *Pursuit of Stability*, 95–6, 169; Dan Beaver, '"Sown in Dishonour, Raised in Glory": Death, Ritual and Social Organization in Northern Gloucestershire, 1590–1690', *Social History*, 17 (1992), 401–2, 411.

90. Emmison (ed.), *Elizabethan Life: Wills of Essex Gentry and Merchants*, 150.

91. Ibid. 155.

92. Ibid. 21, 73, 150.

93. Ibid. 60, 82, 85, 102, 217.

94. Shipman, 'Old Mourner', 119.

95. James Cole, *Of Death. A True Description: And against it A good Preparation: Together with a sweet consolation, for the surviving mourners* (1629; STC 5533), 164.

96. Dunton, *Mourning-Ring*, 5, 23; Gittings, *Death, Burial and the Individual*, 151–64.

97. Folger Shakespeare Library, Folger Ms. L.a. 778.

98. Peck, *Desiderata Curiosa*, 255.

99. Emmison (ed.), *Elizabethan Life: Wills of Essex Gentry and Merchants*, 199; id. (ed.), *Elizabethan Life: Wills of Essex Gentry and Yeomen*, 69; id. (ed.), *Essex Wills (England)*, ii. *1565–1571* (Boston, Mass., 1983), 125.

100. id. (ed.), *Elizabethan Life: Wills of Essex Gentry and Merchants*, 245–7.

101. Brushfield, 'Financial Diary of a Citizen of Exeter', 208; Alan Macfarlane (ed.), *The Diary of Ralph Josselin 1616–1683* (1976), 396.

102. F. R. Raines (ed.), *The Journal of Nicholas Assheton* (Chetham Society; Manchester, 1848), 51–2; Essex Record Office, D/DMs F9.

103. The Queen's College, Oxford, Ms. K. k. 14, fos. 25, 86; Boas (ed.) *Diary of Thomas Crosfield*, 100.

104. Latham and Matthews (eds.), *Diary of Samuel Pepys*, v. 90–1.

105. Foster (ed.), *Diary of Samuel Newton*, 20; Verney, *Memoirs of the Verney Family From the Restoration to the Revolution*, 327.

106. J. Horsfall Turner (ed.), *The Rev. Oliver Heywood, B.A. 1630–1702; His Autobiography, Diaries, Anecdote and Event Books*, 4 vols. (Brighouse, 1882–5), i. 339.

107. William L. Sachse (ed.), *The Diary of Roger Lowe of Ashton-in-Makerfield, Lancashire 1663–74* (New Haven, 1938), 66, 82, 109.

108. Latham and Matthews (eds.), *Diary of Samuel Pepys*, ii. 179, 204.

109. William Hamper (ed.), *The Life, Diary and Correspondence of Sir William Dugdale* (1827), 106.

110. Foster (ed.), *Diary of Samuel Newton*, 8–9. For more substantial funeral provision see ibid. 25, 26.

111. Burn, *History of Parish Registers*, 109, 351.

112. Macfarlane (ed.), *Diary of Ralph Josselin*, 635.

113. Hunter (ed.), *Diary of Ralph Thoresby*, i. 38.

114. Hamper (ed.), *The Life, Diary and Correspondence of Sir William Dugdale*, 145.

115. Verney, *Memoirs of the Verney Family From the Restoration to the Revolution*, 479.

116. Verney (ed.), *Memoirs of the Verney Family During the Civil War*, i. 268. With full heraldic accomplishments, the funeral cost almost £400.

117. Boas (ed.) *Diary of Thomas Crosfield*, 9.

118. Stone, *Crisis of the Aristocracy*, 577.

119. The fashion of night-time burials was set by the aristocracy and spread to the gentle and urban élite. Among many examples, the Countess of Cumberland was buried at Appleby at night in July 1616; Sir Robert Meller was buried 'at midnight' at Bath in Sept. 1624; Thomas Crosfield attended 'the solemnity of the funeral of Sir John Walters by night' at Wolvercote, Oxon, in Dec. 1630; Sir Nicholas Saunder was buried 'by torch light' in Feb. 1649; John Evelyn's father was buried 'at night' in Jan. 1641, and so was his son in Jan. 1658; Sir William Penn's funeral took place about nine o'clock at night in Aug. 1664.

120. John Ayre (ed.), *The Sermons of Edwin Sandys* (Parker Society; Cambridge, 1841), 12; Scholefield (ed.), *Works of James Pilkington*, 319; John Veron, *The Huntyng Of Purgatorye to Death* (1561; STC 24683), fo. 35.

121. John Weever, *Ancient Funeral Monuments* (1631; STC 25223), 17–18.

122. Ibid. 11.

123. Hamper (ed.), *The Life, Diary and Correspondence of Sir William Dugdale*, 137.

124. Norman Marlow (ed.), *The Diary of Thomas Isham of Lamport (1658–81)* (Farnborough, 1971), 15. On heraldic funerals see Gittings, *Death, Burial and the Individual*, 36–7, 92–3, 166–86; Clare Gittings, 'Urban Funerals in Late Medieval and Reformation England', in Steven Bassett (ed.), *Death in Towns: Urban Responses to the Dying and the Dead, 100–1600* (Leicester, 1992), 170–83; Litten, *English Way of Death*, 161; Mervyn James, *Society, Politics and Culture: Studies in Early Modern England* (Cambridge, 1986), 176–87; J. F. R. Day, 'Death be Very Proud: Sidney, Subversion, and Elizabethan Heraldic Funerals', in Dale Hoak (ed.), *Tudor Political Culture* (Cambridge, 1995), 179–203.

125. Latham and Matthews (eds.), *Diary of Samuel Pepys*, iii. 269, iv. 21, 432, v. 90, vi. 114, 127, viii. 134, ix. 36, x. 62–3. Cf. Stannard, *Puritan Way of Death*, 110–17, for elaborate funerals of late 17th-cent. New England puritans.

126. Turner (ed.), *Rev. Oliver Heywood*, i. 284, 290, 339, 351.

127. De Beer (ed.), *Diary of John Evelyn*, iii. 490, iv. 302.

128. Ibid. v. 55–6, 357.

129. Carbery (ed.), *Mrs. Elizabeth Freke Her Diary*, 59.

130. Ibid. 62–70.

131. John Ashton, *Social Life in the Reign of Queen Anne Taken from Original Sources* (1904), 35–41, 441; Litten, *English Way of Death*, 77, 131.

132. Barmby (ed.), *Churchwardens' Accounts of Pittington and Other Parishes*, 255, 259–60.

133. Henri Misson, *M. Misson's Memoirs and Observations in his Travels over England* (1719), 90–3. See also id., *Memoires et Observations Faites par un Voyageur en Angleterre* (The Hague, 1698).

CHAPTER 20

1. Richard Burn, *Ecclesiastical Law*, 4 vols. (7th edn., 1809), i. 258, 268. See also canon 68 of the Canons of 1604, in J. V. Bullard (ed.), *Constitutions and Canons Ecclesiastical* (1934), 285.

2. John Bale, *A Declaration of Edmond Bonners Articles* (1561; STC 1289), fo. 83; Henry Barrow, 'A Brief Discoverie of the False Church' [1590] in Leland H. Carlson (ed.), *The Writings of Henry Barrow 1587–1590* (1962), 462.

3. Susan Brigden, *London and the Reformation* (Oxford, 1991), 98–9; Christopher Haigh, *English Reformations: Religion, Politics, and Society under the Tudors* (Oxford, 1993), 47–8, 77–9, 96.

4. *Statutes of the Realm*, 21 Hen. VIII, c. 6; Burn, *Ecclesiastical Law*, ii. 562; John Godolphin, *Repertorium Canonicum; or an Abridgement of the Ecclesiastical Laws* (2nd edn., 1680), 188, 423–4. See also Francis Sadler, *The Exactions and Impositions of Parish Fees Discovered* (1738).

5. Borthwick Institute, York, Dean and Chapter Cause Papers, 1627/1, 1664/1.

6. Robert Charles Hope (ed.), *The Popish Kingdome or reign of Antichrist, written in Latine Verse by Thomas Naogeorgus, and Englyshed by Barnabe Googe* (1880), bk. 4, fo. 57; James Scholefield (ed.), *The Works of James Pilkington* (Parker Society; Cambridge, 1842), 317.

7. Katherine Chidley, *The Iustification of the Independent Churches of Christ* (1641), 56–8. For more on Chidley see Patricia Crawford, *Women and Religion in England 1500–1720* (1993), 129, 132–3, 135.

8. T. C. Dale (ed.), *The Inhabitants of London in 1638* (1931), 75, 224; J. E. Foster (ed.), *Churchwardens' Accounts of St Mary the Great Cambridge from 1504 to 1635* (Cambridge, 1905), 454–5.

9. Guildhall Library, Ms. 9064/16, fo. 10; Hilda Johnstone (ed.), *Churchwardens' Presentments (17th Century), Part 1: Archdeaconry of Chichester* (Sussex Record Society; Lewes, 1947–8), 94.

10. W. M. Palmer and H. W. Saunders (eds.), *Documents Relating to Cambridgeshire Villages* (Cambridge, 1926), 75; *The Petition and Articles of Severall Charge Exhibited in Parliament against Edward Finch* (1641), 3, 4, 6, 12; Edward Finch, *An Answer to the Articles Preferred Against Edward Finch* (1641), 5.

11. *Calendar of State Papers, Domestic, 1636*, 508–9.

12. Guildhall Library, Ms. 9583/1.

13. Claude Jenkins (ed.), 'An Unpublished Record of Archbishop Parker's Visitation in 1573', *Archaeologia Cantiana*, 29 (1911), 274; Borthwick Institute, York, V. 1596–7, Court book 2, fos. 75^v, 15^v; ibid. Y/V/CB/1, fos. 33^v, 57, 59^v; ibid. Y/V/CB/2, fos. 14^v, 27.

14. Greater London Record Office, DL/C 617, 482; Borthwick Institute, York, C/V/CB 1, fo. 16^v; Guildhall Library, Ms. 9064/20, fo. 200.

15. Guildhall Library, Ms. 9583/2, part 6, fo. 72; Ms. 9583/2, part 2, fo. 47.

16. West Suffolk Record Office, E. 14/1/13, a reference I owe to Jeremy Boulton; Alan Bott (ed.), *Baptisms and Marriages at Merton College. Transcribed from the Registers of St. John the Baptist's Church, Oxford* (Oxford, 1981), 116.

17. Robert Dinn, '"Monuments Answerable to Mens Worth": Burial Patterns, Social Status and Gender in Late Medieval Bury St. Edmunds', *Journal of Ecclesiastical History*, 46 (1995), 237–55; Vanessa Harding, 'Burial Choice and Burial Location in Later Medieval London', in Steven Bassett (ed.), *Death in Towns: Urban Responses to the Dying and the Dead, 100–1600* (Leicester, 1992), 119–35.

18. John Veron, *The Huntyng of Purgatorye to Death* (1561; STC 24683), fos. 34–34^v; Scholefield (ed.), *Works of James Pilkington*, 317, 319.

19. Mary Carbery (ed.), *Mrs. Elizabeth Freke Her Diary 1671 to 1714* (Cork, 1913), 47, 32.

20. Greater London Record Office, DL/C 316, fo. 71^v.

21. F. G. Emmison (ed.), *Elizabethan Life: Wills of Essex Gentry and Merchants* (Chelmsford, 1978), 99, 60.

22. Ibid. 126, 19.

23. Ibid. 109; id. (ed.), *Elizabethan Life: Wills of Essex Gentry and Yeomen* (Chelmsford, 1980), 46. For similar bequests in Elizabethan and Stuart Gloucestershire,

see Dan Beaver, '"Sown in Dishonour, Raised in Glory": Death, Ritual and Social Organization in Northern Gloucestershire, 1590–1690', *Social History*, 17 (1992), 406–8.

24. Emmison (ed.), *Elizabethan Life: Wills of Essex Gentry and Merchants*, 6, 8.

25. Ibid. 1.

26. Burn, *Ecclesiastical Law*, i. 256–8.

27. Robert Hill, *The Pathway to Prayer and Pietie* (1610; STC 13473), 270.

28. W. P. M. Kennedy, *Elizabethan Episcopal Administration*, 3 vols. (1924), iii. 152.

29. Foster (ed.), *Churchwardens' Accounts of St Mary the Great Cambridge*, 191.

30. *Articles of Enquiry and Direction for the Diocese of Norwich* (1638; STC 10299), sig. A2.

31. Sidney A. Peyton (ed.), *The Churchwardens' Presentments in the Oxfordshire Peculiars of Dorchester, Thame and Banbury* (Oxfordshire Record Society; Oxford, 1928), 289–90; Norfolk Record Office, Norwich, VIS 5/1, n.f.; ibid. VIS 6/1, fo. 38ᵛ. For similar complaints in Oxfordshire in 1628 see Oxfordshire Archives, Diocesan Papers, C.17, fo. 22; and at Castle Donington, Leicestershire, 1633, Alice Dryden, *Memorials of Old Leicestershire* (1911), 158.

32. Cambridge University Library Ms. Mm. 4. 29, fo. 100ᵛ; Lincolnshire Archives, Vj/29, fo. 81.

33. J. Barmby (ed.), *Churchwardens' Accounts of Pittington and other Parishes in the Diocese of Durham from A.D. 1580 to 1700* (Surtees Society; Durham, 1888), 310–11.

34. John Dunton, *A Mourning-Ring, In Memory of Your Departed Friend* (2nd edn., 1692), 103–4, 290.

35. E. S. de Beer (ed.), *The Diary of John Evelyn*, 6 vols. (Oxford, 1955), iv. 304.

36. George R. Potter and Evelyn M. Simpson (eds.), *The Sermons of John Donne*, 10 vols. (Berkeley and Los Angeles, 1962), i. 266.

37. For examples of accommodation, see Borthwick Institute, York, Y/V/CB/1, fo. 34ᵛ; Durham University Library, Archives and Special Collections, DCD/ SJB 7, fo. 6ᵛ; Guildhall Library, Ms. 9064/18, fo. 97ᵛ; Berkshire Record Office, Reading, D/A2. C74, fos. 406–407ᵛ; Oxfordshire Archives, Archdeaconry Papers C.23, fo. 163.

38. *The Late Commotion of Certaine Papists in Herefordshire* (1605; STC 25232.5); Oxfordshire Archives, Diocesan Papers, C.2, fos. 144ᵛ–147, 167, 172, 178–179ᵛ, 192–194ᵛ; Borthwick Institute, York, C/V/CB 2, fo. 77ᵛ; Ronald A. Marchant, *The Church Under the Law; Justice, Administration and Discipline in the Diocese of York 1560–1640* (Cambridge, 1969), 139 n, 220 n.

39. Margaret Blundell (ed.), *Cavalier Letters of William Blundell to his Friends 1620–1698* (1933), 244–5.

40. For Quaker burying grounds in Essex, Sussex, and Yorkshire, see Guildhall Library, Ms. 9583/2, parts 3 and 4; Hilda Johnstone (ed.), *Churchwardens' Presentments (17th Century), Part 2: Archdeaconry of Lewes* (Sussex Record Society; Lewes, 1948–9), 54; J. Horsfall Turner (ed.), *The Rev. Oliver Heywood, B.A. 1630–1702: His Autobiography, Diaries, Anecdote and Event Books*, 4 vols. (Brighouse, 1882–5), ii. 250.

41. R. C. Finucane, 'Sacred Corpse, Profane Carrion: Social Ideals and Death Rituals in the Later Middle Ages', in Joachim Whaley (ed.), *Mirrors of Mortality: Studies in the Social History of Death* (New York, 1982), 43; George S. Tyack, *Lore and Legend of the English Church* (1899), 65–6, 80; 'Mary Tattlewell', *The Womens Sharpe Revenge* (1640; STC 23706), 104; Francis Tate, 'Of the Antiquity, Variety and Ceremonies of Funerals in England', in Thomas Hearne (ed.), *A Collection of Curious Discourses Written by Eminent Antiquaries*, 2 vols. (1771), i. 218.

42. Dinn, 'Monuments Answerable to Mens Worth', 249–50, 246; Clare Gittings, *Death, Burial and the Individual in Early Modern England* (1984), 139.

43. Palmer and Saunders (eds.), *Documents Relating to Cambridgeshire Villages*, 60; W. M. Palmer (ed.), *Episcopal Visitation Returns for Cambridgeshire: Matthew Wren, Bishop of Ely, 1638–1665* (Cambridge, 1930), 51.

44. *Articles of Enquiry and Direction for the Diocese of Norwich*, sigs. A3, C3.

45. Jenkins (ed.), 'An Unpublished Record of Archbishop Parker's Visitation', 282; E. R. Brinkworth (ed.), *The Archdeacon's Court: Liber Actorum, 1584* (Oxfordshire Record Society; Oxford, 1942), 51.

46. Buckinghamshire Record Office, Aylesbury, D/A/C 4, fo. 136; D/A/C/5, fo. 153; Alice Dryden, *Memorials of Old Leicestershire* (1911), 164; R. F. B. Hodgkinson (ed.), 'Extracts from the Act Books of the Archdeacons of Nottingham', *Transactions of the Thoroton Society*, 31 (Nottingham, 1928), 134.

47. *Articles to be Enquired of, within the Diocesse of Lincolne* (Cambridge, 1598; STC 10235), 1.

48. *Articles of Enquiry and Direction for the Diocese of Norwich*, sigs. A3–A3^v.

49. Hodgkinson (ed.), 'Extracts from the Act Books of the Archdeacons of Nottingham', 139–42.

50. Norfolk Record Office, VIS 5/3/2 (1627), p. 66; Greater London Record Office, DL/C 318, p. 587; DL/C 625, fo. 27.

51. P. Braby, 'Churchwardens' Presentments from the Vale of Evesham, 1660–1717: Part I', *Vale of Evesham Historical Society Research Papers*, 5 (1975), 76; W. J. Pressey, 'Notes on Visitations in the Archdeaconry of Essex', *Transactions of the Essex Archaeological Society*, 19 (1930), 264; Buckinghamshire Record Society, D/A/V 6, fos. 41, 50^v, 55; D/A/V 7, fo. 39.

52. Guilldhall Library, Ms. 9064/16, fo. 95; Dinn, 'Monuments Answerable to Mens Worth', 245–6, mentions the existence of grave-markers in the 15th cent.

53. *Articles to be Inquired of Within the Diocese of Ely* (1638; STC 10197), no. 17.

54. Lawrence Stone, *Crisis of the Aristocracy* (Oxford, 1965), 579–81; Gittings, *Death, Burial and the Individual*, 144–7; Nigel Llewellyn, *The Art of Death: Visual Culture in the English Death Ritual c.1500–c.1800* (1991), 101–21; Jean Wilson, 'Icons of Unity', *History Today*, 43 (1993), 14–20; Felicity Heal and Clive Holmes, *The Gentry of England and Wales, 1500–1700* (Stanford, Calif., 1994), 1–3, 20–2, 338–40.

55. Emmison (ed.), *Elizabethan Life: Wills of Essex Gentry and Merchants*, 111, 81–2, 212.

56. Scholefield (ed.), *Works of James Pilkington*, 317; Potter and Simpson (eds.), *Sermons of John Donne*, ii. 296.

57. Coke, *Institutes*, cited in Burn, *Ecclesiastical Law*, i. 272; Hill, *Pathway to Prayer and Pietie*, 272.

58. John Weever, *Ancient Funeral Monuments* (1631; STC 25223), 10–11.

59. Edmund Gurnay, *Gurnay Redivivus, or an Appendix unto the Homily Against Images in Churches* (1660), 89. See also id., *Toward the Vindication of the Second Commandment* (Cambridge, 1639; STC 12531).

60. *Articles to be Inquired of Within the Diocese of Ely*, no. 17.

61. John Aubrey, 'Remains of Gentilism and Judaisme', in John Buchanan-Brown (ed.), *John Aubrey: Three Prose Works* (Carbondale, Ill., 1972), 174; T. F. Thisleton-Dyer, *Church-Lore Gleanings* (1892), 161, 162^r.

62. Dorothy Gardiner (ed.), *The Oxinden Letters 1607–1642 Being the Correspondence of Henry Oxinden of Barham and his Circle* (1933), 21; Folger Shakespeare Library, Folger Ms. X.d. 428 (187).

63. Edmund Hobhouse (ed.), *The Diary of a West Country Physician. AD. 1684–1726* (1935), 149; Carbery (ed.), *Mrs. Elizabeth Freke Her Diary*, 47.

64. W. J. Pressey, 'Notes on Visitations in the Archdeaconry of Essex', *Transactions of the Essex Archaeological Society* 21 (1933–4), 326.

65. *Articles of Enquiry and Direction for the Diocese of Norwich*, sig. A3^v.

66. Patrick Scot, *A Table-Booke for Princes* (1621; STC 21860), 212.

CONCLUSION

1. *Certaine Questions by Way of Conference betwixt a Chauncelor and a Kinswoman of His Concerning Churching of Women* (Middleburg?, 1601; STC 20557), 15–16.

2. William Keatinge Clay (ed.), *Liturgical Services. Liturgies and Occasional Forms of Prayer Set Forth in the Reign of Queen Elizabeth* (Cambridge, 1847), 217.

3. Robert Pricke, *A Verie Godlie and Learned Sermon, treating of Mans mortalitie* (1608; STC 20338), sig. B4^v; John Veron, *The Huntyng of Purgatorye to Death* (1561; STC 24683), fo. 37.

Bibliography

DIARIES AND FAMILY PAPERS

Allestree, Charles, 'Memoirs of Charles Allestree 1677–1702', British Library, Additional Ms. 27,440.

Archer, Isaac, 'Isaac Archer's Diary', Cambridge University Library, Additional Ms. 8499; in Matthew Storey (ed.), *Two East Anglian Diaries, 1641–1729; Isaac Archer and William Coe* (Woodbridge, Suffolk, 1994).

Ashcombe, William, 'Memorable Accidents of Sir William Ashcombe, 1591–1625', Huntington Library, San Marino, Ms. HM 30665.

Ashmole, Elias, *Elias Ashmole (1617–1692): His Autobiographical and Historical Notes*, ed. C. H. Josten (Oxford, 1966).

Assheton, Nicholas, *The Journal of Nicholas Assheton*, ed. F. R. Raines (Chetham Society; Manchester, 1848).

Bacon, Nathaniel, *The Papers of Nathaniel Bacon of Stiffkey*, 3 vols., ed. A. Hassell Smith and Gillian M. Baker (Norwich, 1979–90).

Bagot family letters, Folger Shakespeare Library, Folger Mss. L.a.

Bathurst, Anne, 'Diary of Anne Bathurst', Bodleian Library, Oxford, Rawlinson Mss. 1262–3.

Beake, Robert, 'Diary of Robert Beake Mayor of Coventry, 1655–1656', ed. Levi Fox, *Miscellany I* (Dugdale Society; Oxford, 1977), 111–37.

Best, Henry, *The Farming and Memorandum Books of Henry Best of Elmswell, 1642*, ed. Donald Woodward (1984).

Blundell, Nicholas, *The Great Diurnal of Nicholas Blundell of Little Crosby, Lancashire*, i. *1702– 1711*, ed. J. J. Bagley (Record Society of Lancashire and Cheshire; 1968).

Blundell, William, *Cavalier Letters of William Blundell to his Friends 1620–1698*, ed. Margaret Blundell (1933); *Crosby Records. A Cavalier's Note Book . . . of William Blundell*, ed. T. Ellison Gibson (1880).

Brockbank, Thomas, *The Diary and Letter Book of the Rev. Thomas Brockbank, 1671–1709*, ed. Richard Trappes-Lomax (Chetham Society; Manchester, 1930).

Bulkeley, Robert, 'The Diary of Bulkeley of Dronwy, Anglesea, 1630–1636', ed. Hugh Owen, *Anglesea Antiquarian Society and Field Club Transactions* (1937), 26–187.

Burrell, Timothy, 'Extracts from the Journal and Account-Book of Timothy Burrell . . . 1683 to 1714', ed. Robert Willis Blencowe, *Sussex Archaeological Collections*, 3 (1850), 117–72.

Cannon, John, 'John Cannon's Memoirs', Somerset Record Office, Taunton, DD/SAS/C/1193.

Carleton, Dudley, *Dudley Carleton to John Chamberlain 1604–1624: Jacobean Letters*, ed. Maurice Lee (New Brunswick, NJ, 1972).

Carnsew, William, 'William Carnsew of Bokelly and his Diary, 1576–7', ed. N. J. G. Pounds, *Royal Institution of Cornwall Journal* (1978), 14–60.

Cartwright, Thomas, *The Diary of Thomas Cartwright, Bishop of Chester . . . 1686–87*, ed. Joseph Hunter (Camden Society; 1843).

Clifford, Anne, *The Diaries of Lady Anne Clifford*, ed. D. J. H. Clifford (Stroud, 1990).

Cole, William, *The Blecheley Diary of the Rev. William Cole 1765–6*, ed. Francis Griffin Stokes (1931).

Cosin, John, *The Correspondence of John Cosin*, ed. George Ornsby, 2 vols. (Surtees Society; Durham, 1869).

Crosfield, Thomas, 'The Diary of Thomas Crosfield', The Queen's College, Oxford, Ms. 390; *The Diary of Thomas Crosfield*, ed. Frederick S. Boas (Oxford, 1935).

De la Pryme, Abraham, *The Diary of Abraham de la Pryme*, ed. Charles Jackson (Surtees Society; Durham, 1870).

Dowsing, William, *The Journal of William Dowsing*, ed. E. H. White (Ipswich, 1885).

Drake, William, 'William Drake's Journal, 1631–42', The Huntington Library, Ms. HM 55603.

Drury, Walter, 'Walter Drury's Almanacks', Norfolk Record Office, Hare Ms. 3527b.

Dugdale, William, *The Life, Diary and Correspondence of Sir William Dugdale*, ed. William Hamper (1827).

Egerton, Elizabeth, 'Devotional Pieces by Elizabeth Countess of Bridgewater', British Library, Egerton Ms. 607.

Evans, Francis, *Diary of Francis Evans, Secretary to Bishop Lloyd, 1699–1706*, ed. David Robertson (Oxford, 1903).

Evelyn, John, *The Diary of John Evelyn*, ed. E. S. de Beer, 6 vols. (Oxford, 1955).

Eyre, Adam, 'A Dyurnall, or Catalogue of all my accions and expences from the 1st of January 1646/7', in *Yorkshire Diaries and Autobiographies in the Seventeenth and Eighteenth Centuries*, ed. H. J. Morehouse (Surtees Society; Durham, 1877).

Fitzwilliam, William, *The Correspondence of Lord Fitzwilliam of Milton and Francis Guybon, his Steward, 1697–1709*, ed. D. R. Hainsworth and Cherry Walker (Northamptonshire Record Society; Northampton, 1990).

Forman, Simon, *The Autobiography and Personal Diary of Dr. Simon Forman . . . 1552 to 1602*, ed. James Orchard Halliwell (1849).

Freke, Elizabeth, *Mrs. Elizabeth Freke Her Diary 1671 to 1714*, ed. Mary Carbery (Cork, 1913).

Fytton family, *Gossip from a Muniment Room: Being Passages in the Lives of Anne and Mary Fytton 1574 to 1618*, ed. Lady Newdigate-Newdegate (1897).

Gerard, John, *John Gerard. The Autobiography of an Elizabethan*, tr. Philip Caraman (1951).

Greene, John, 'The Diary of John Greene (1635–57)', ed. E. M. Symonds, *English Historical Review*, 43 (1928), 385–94, 598–604; 44 (1929), 106–17.

Hayne, John, 'The Financial Diary of a Citizen of Exeter, 1631–43', ed. T. N. Brushfield, *Reports and Transactions of the Devonshire Association*, 33 (1901), 187–269.

Heywood, Oliver, *The Rev. Oliver Heywood, B.A. 1630–1702; His Autobiography, Diaries, Anecdote and Event Books*, ed. J. Horsfall Turner, 4 vols. (Brighouse, 1882–5).

Hickman, Rose, 'Certain old storyes recorded by an aged Gentlewoman', British

Library, Add. Ms. 45,027; in Maria Dowling and Joy Shakespeare, 'Religion and Politics in Mid Tudor England through the Eyes of an English Protestant Woman: The Recollections of Rose Hickman', *Bulletin of the Institute of Historical Research*, 55 (1982), 94–102.

Hoby, Margaret, *Diary of Lady Margaret Hoby 1599–1605*, ed. Dorothy M. Meads (1930).

Honeywell, William, 'A Devonshire Yeoman's Diary', ed. William F. J. Snell, *The Antiquary*, 26 (1892), 254–9.

Hooke, Robert, *The Diary of Robert Hooke . . . 1672–1680*, ed. Henry W. Robinson and Walter Adams (1935).

Howard, William, *Selections from the Household Books of the Lord William Howard of Naworth Castle* (Surtees Society; Durham, 1878).

Isham, Thomas, *The Diary of Thomas Isham of Lamport (1658–81)*, ed. Norman Marlow (Farnborough, 1971).

Jeake, Samuel, *An Astrological Diary of the Seventeenth Century: Samuel Jeake of Rye 1652–1699*, ed. Michael Hunter and Annabel Gregory (Oxford, 1988).

Jeffries, Joyce, 'Accounts of Joyce Jeffries, 1638–46', British Library, Egerton Ms. 3054; in R. G. Griffiths, 'Joyce Jeffreys of Ham Castle: A Seventeenth-Century Business Gentlewoman', *Transactions of the Worcestershire Archaeological Society*, 10 (1934), 1–32; 11 (1035), 1–13; 12 (1935), 1–17.

Johnson, William, 'Diary of William Johnson, 1652–63', Bodleian Library, Oxford, Ms. Top. Camb. e. 5.

Jolly, Thomas, *The Notebook of the Rev. Thomas Jolly AD 1671–1693*, ed. Henry Fishwick (Chetham Society; Manchester, 1894).

Josselin, Ralph, *The Diary of Ralph Josselin 1616–1683*, ed. Alan Macfarlane (1976).

Kidder, Richard, *The Life of Richard Kidder, D.D. Bishop of Bath and Wells: Written by Himself*, ed. Amy Edith Robinson (Somerset Record Society; 1924).

Lawrence, William, *The Diary of William Lawrence Covering Periods between 1662 and 1681*, ed. G. E. Aylmer (Beaminster, Dorset, 1961).

Lilly, William, *Mr. William Lilly's History of His Life and Times, from the Year 1602 to 1681* (1715).

'A London Midwife's Account Book, 1694–1716', Bodleian Library, Oxford, Rawlinson Ms. D.1141.

Lowe, Roger, *The Diary of Roger Lowe of Ashton-in-Makerfield, Lancashire 1663–74*, ed. William L. Sachse (New Haven, 1938).

Machyn, Henry, *The Diary of Henry Machyn, Citizen and Merchant-Taylor of London, from A.D. 1550 to A.D. 1563*, ed. John Gough Nichols (Camden Society; 1848).

Mainwaring, Thomas, 'Diary of Thomas Mainwaring', Cheshire Record Office, Chester, DDX 384/1.

Manningham, John, *The Diary of John Manningham of the Middle Temple, 1602–1603*, ed. Robert Parker Sorlien (Hanover, NH, 1976).

Mildmay, Grace, 'An Elizabethan Gentlewoman: The Journal of Lady Mildmay, circa 1570–1617', ed. Rachel Weigall, *The Quarterly Review*, 215 (1911), 119–38.

Misson, Henri, *Memoires et Observations Faites par un Voyageur en Angleterre* (The Hague, 1698); *M. Misson's Memoirs and Observations in his Travels over England* (1719).

Moore, Giles, *The Journal of Giles Moore*, ed. Ruth Bird (Lewes, 1971).

Morris, Claver, *The Diary of a West Country Physician. AD 1684–1726*, ed. Edmund Hobhouse (1935).

Newcome, Henry, *The Autobiography of Henry Newcome, M.A.*, ed. Richard Parkinson (Chetham Society; Manchester, 1852).

—— *The Diary of the Rev. Henry Newcome, from September 30, 1661, to September 29, 1663*, ed. Thomas Heywood (Chetham Society; Manchester, 1849).

Newton, Samuel, *The Diary of Samuel Newton, Alderman of Cambridge (1662–1717)*, ed. J. E. Foster (Cambridge, 1890).

Oglander, John, *A Royalist's Notebook: The Commonplace Book of Sir John Oglander*, ed. Francis Bamford (1936).

Oxinden family, *The Oxinden Letters 1607–1642*, ed. Dorothy Gardiner (1933).

Parker, Matthew, *Correspondence of Matthew Parker*, ed. John Bruce and Thomas Thomason Perowne (Parker Society; Cambridge, 1853).

Pepys, Samuel, *The Diary of Samuel Pepys*, ed. R. C. Latham and W. Matthews, 9 vols. (Berkeley and Los Angeles, Calif., 1970–6).

Pett, Phineas, *The Autobiography of Phineas Pett*, ed. W. G. Perrin (Navy Records Society; 1918).

Rawdon family letters, Hastings Irish Papers, The Huntington Library, Ms. HA 15615–20.

Reresby, John, *Memoirs of Sir John Reresby*, ed. Andrew Browning (Glasgow, 1936; 2nd edn., 1991).

Rogers, Richard, 'The Diary of Richard Rogers', in M. M. Knappen (ed.), *Two Elizabethan Puritan Diaries* (1933, repr. Gloucester, Mass., 1966).

Sewell, Samuel, *The Diary of Samuel Sewall 1674–1729*, ed. M. Halsey Thomas, 2 vols. (New York, 1973).

Shanne, Richard, 'Of certain extraordinarie things chauncing in my tyme and remembrance', British Library, Additional Ms. 38,599.

Strange family, *The Derby Household Books*, ed. F. R. Raines (Chetham Society; Manchester, 1853).

Thoresby, Ralph, *The Diary of Ralph Thoresby . . . 1677–1724*, ed. Joseph Hunter, 2 vols. (1830).

Thornton, Alice, *The Autobiography of Mrs. Alice Thornton* (Surtees Society; Durham, 1875).

—— 'Alice Thornton's Book of Remembrances', in Elspeth Graham, Hilary Hinds, Elaine Hobby, and Helen Wilcox (eds.), *Her Own Life: Autobiographical Writings by Seventeenth-Century Englishwomen* (1989).

Thynne, *Two Elizabethan Women: Correspondence of Joan and Maria Thynne 1575–1611*, ed. Alison D. Wall (Wiltshire Record Society; Devizes, 1983).

Twysden, Isabella, 'The Diary of Isabella, Wife of Sir Roger Twysden, Baronet, of

Royden Hall, East Peckham, 1645–1651', ed. F. W. Bennitt, *Archaeologia Cantiana*, 51 (1939–40), 113–36.

Verney family, *Memoirs of the Verney Family During the Civil War*, ed. Frances Parthenope Verney, 2 vols. (1892).

—— *Memoirs of the Verney Family During the Commonwealth 1560 to 1660*, ed. Margaret M. Verney (1894).

—— *Memoirs of the Verney Family from the Restoration to the Revolution 1660 to 1696*, ed. Margaret M. Verney (1899).

Wallington, Nehemiah, 'Nehemiah Wallington, Writing Book 1654', Folger Shakespeare Library, Ms. V.a. 436, 1.

Ward, John, *Diary of the Rev. John Ward . . . 1648 to 1679*, ed. Charles Severn (1839).

Westmacott, William, 'William Westmacott. Memorabilia: or private Things to be remembered concerning my life', Folger Shakespeare Library, Ms. V.a. 441.

Wheatcroft, Leonard, *The Courtship Narrative of Leonard Wheatcroft, Derbyshire Yeoman*, ed. George Parfitt and Ralph Houlbrooke (Reading, 1986).

—— Charles Kerry, 'Leonard Wheatcroft of Ashover', *Journal of the Derbyshire Archaeology and Natural History Society*, 18 (1896), 29–80; 21 (1899), 26–60.

Whitelock, Bulstrode, *The Diary of Bulstrode Whitelock, 1605–1675*, ed. Ruth Spalding (Oxford, 1990).

Whiteway, William, 'Diary of William Whiteway', British Library, Egerton Ms. 784; *William Whiteway of Dorchester His Diary 1618 to 1635* (Dorset Record Society; Dorchester, 1991).

Whithead, Henry, *Sir Henry Whithead's Letter Book*, i. *1601–1614* (Winchester, 1976).

Willoughby family, 'Willoughby-Ridgeway Letters', The Huntington Library, Stowe Mss., STB Box 2.

Woodford, Robert, 'Robert Woodforde's Diary', New College, Oxford, Ms. 9502.

Woodford, Samuel, 'An Imperfect Diary of a Life: The 1662 Diary of Samuel Woodforde', ed. Lori Anne Ferrell, *Yale University Library Gazette*, 63 (1989), 137–44.

Woodforde, James, *The Diary of a Country Parson: The Reverend James Woodforde, 1758–1802*, ed. John Beresford, 5 vols. (Oxford, 1926–31).

Wyatt, Thomas, 'Diary of Thomas Wyatt, 'Bodleian Library, Oxford, Ms. Top. Oxon. c. 378.

Wythorne, Thomas, *The Autobiography of Thomas Whythorne*, ed. James M. Osborn (Oxford, 1962).

CONTEMPORARY AUTHORS

Abbot, Robert, *A Wedding Sermon Preached at Bentley* (1608; STC 55).

An Abridgement of that Book which the Ministers of Lincoln Diocess delivered to his Maiestie upon the first of December last, 1605 (1605; STC 15646).

Adams, Thomas, *The Workes of Thomas Adams: Being the Svmme of His Sermons* (1629; STC 104).

An Admonition to the Parliament (Hemel Hempstead?, 1572; STC 10847).

A.M., *A Rich Closet of Physical Secrets* (1652).

Ames, William, *A Fresh Svit Against Human Ceremonies in Gods Worship* (Amsterdam?, 1633; STC 555).

Annesley, Samuel (ed.), *A Continuation of Morning-Exercise Questions and Cases of Conscience* (1683).

An Answer to a Lawless Pamphlet . . . against Doctor Haywood (1641).

Aristotle, *The Problemes of Aristotle* (1597; STC 764).

The Art of Courtship (1686).

Arwaker, Edmund, *The Ministration of Publick Baptism of Infants to be used in the Church, or A Disswasive from Baptising Children in Private* (1689).

Aubrey, John, 'Remaines of Gentilisme and Judaisme', in John Buchanan-Brown (ed.), *John Aubrey: Three Prose Works* (Carbondale, Ill., 1972).

Bale, John, A *Declaration of Edmonde Bonners articles concerning the cleargye of London dyocese* (1561; STC 1289).

'The Ballad of Arthur of Bradley', in *An Antidote Against Melancholy* (1661).

A Ballad of a Country Wedding (1660?).

Banister, John, *The Historie of Man, sucked from the sappe of the most approued Anathomistes* (1578; STC 1359).

Barclay, Robert, *Baptism and the Lord's Supper Substantially Asserted* (1696).

Barret, Robert, *A Companion for Midwives, Child-Bearing Women, and Nurses* (1699).

Barrough, Philip, *The Method of Physick* (1652).

Barrow, Henry, *The Writings of Henry Barrow 1587–1590*, ed. Leland H. Carlson (1962).

—— *The Writings of Henry Barrow 1590–91*, ed. Leland H. Carlson (1966).

The Batchelars Banquet, ed. F. P. Wilson (Oxford, 1929).

Baylie, Robert, *A Dissuasive from the Errours of the Time* (1645).

Baxter, Richard, *A Christian Directory: Or, A Summ of Practical Theologie, and Cases of Conscience* (1678).

—— *The Practical Works of Richard Baxter*, 4 vols. (Ligonier, Pa., 1990).

—— *Reliquiae Baxterianae* (1696).

Beadle, John, *The Journall or Diary of a Thankfull Christian* (1656).

Becon, Thomas, *The Sycke mans salue* (1561; STC 1757).

Bedford, Thomas, *A Treatise of the Sacraments According to the Doctrin of the Church of England* (1638; STC 1789).

Bentley, Thomas, *The Monvment of Matrones: Conteining seuen seuerall Lamps of Virginitie* (1582; STC 1892–3).

Birket, John, *The God-father's Advice to his Son: Shewing the Necessity of performing the Baptismal Vow* (1700).

Blancard, Stephen, *A Physical Dictionary* (1684).

Boorde, Andrew, *The Breuiary of Healthe, for all maner of sickenesses and diseases the which may be in man or woman* (1552, 1598; STC 3374, STC 3378).

Bourne, Henry, *Antiquitates Vulgares or the Antiquities of the Common People* (Newcastle, 1725).

Bourne, Reuben, *The Contented Cuckold, or, the Woman's Advocate: A Comedy* (1692).

Bradshaw, William, *A Marriage Feast* (1620), printed with Thomas Gataker, *Two Marriage Sermons* (1620; STC 11680).

—— *A Shorte Treatise, Of the Crosse in Baptism* (Amsterdam, 1604; STC 3526).

Brathwaite, Richard, *The Good Wife: or, A rare one amongst Women* (1618; 12747).

—— *Remains After Death* (1618; STC 3582).

The Bride's Buriall (1621?, STC 3728a).

Brome, Richard, *A Joviall Crew: Or, The Merry Beggars* (1652).

Browne, Thomas, *Pseudodoxia Epidemica: Or, Enquiries into Very Many Received Tenents and Commonly Presumed Truths* (2nd edn., 1650).

Browne, Tobias, *The Hasty-Wedding; or, William's Patience Rewarded* (1685?).

Bullein, William, *A Dialogue against the fever Pestilence*, ed. Mark W. Bullen and A. H. Bullen (1888).

Bunworth, Richard, *The Doctoresse: A plain and easie method of curing those diseases which are peculiar to Women* (1656).

Burges, John, *An Answer Reioyned to that much applauded Pamphlet of a Namelesse Author* (1631; STC 4113).

Burton, Henry, *A Tryall of Private Devotions: Or, A Diall for the Houres of Prayer* (1628; STC 4157).

Calderwood, David, *Altare Damascenum ceu Politia Ecclesiae Anglicanae* (Amsterdam?, 1623; STC 4353).

—— *The Altare of Damascus or The Patern of the English Hierarchie* (1621; STC 4352).

Calfhill, James, *An Answer to John Martiall's Treatise of the Cross* ed. Richard Gibbings (Parker Society; Cambridge, 1846).

Canne, John, *A Necessity of Separation from the Church of England* (Amsterdam, 1634; STC 4574).

The Card of Courtship: or, The Language of Love (1653).

Cartwright, Thomas, *A Replye to an answere made of M. Doctor Whitgifte* (Hemel Hempstead?, 1573; STC 4711).

—— *The second replie agaynst Maister Doctor Whitgiftes second answer* (Heidelberg, 1575; STC 4714).

Cavendish, Margaret (Duchess of Newcastle), *CCXI Sociable Letters* (1664).

—— *Playes* (1662).

C.C., *Sad and serious thoughts, or the sense and meaning of the late Act concerning Marriages* (1653).

Cellier, Elizabeth, *To Dr. —, An Answer to his Queries concerning the Colledg of Midwives* (1688).

Certaine Questions by Way of Conference betwixt a Chauncelor and a Kinswoman of His Concerning Churching of Women (Middleburg?, 1601; STC 20557).

'Certayne considerations aboute the churchinge of weomen otherwise Cawled puryfication and covered with the name of thankesgivinge', Dr Williams's Library, London, 'Old Loose Papers', 47–8.

C.H., *A Fairing for Young-men, or The careless Lover* (1655?).

Chamberlen, Peter, *A Voice in Rhama: Or, The Crie of Women and Children* (1647).

Charnock, Stephen, *A Supplement to the Several Discourses upon Various Divine Subjects* (1683).

Chaucer, Geoffrey, *The Complete Works of Geoffrey Chaucer*, ed. Geoffrey F. N. Robinson (2nd edn., 1957).

Chidley, Katherine, *The Iustification of the Independent Churches of Christ* (1641).

Clarke, Samuel, *An Antidote Against Immoderate Mourning* (1659).

Clinton, Elizabeth, *The Covntesse of Lincolnes Nvrserie* (1622; STC 5432).

Cole, James, *Of Death. A True Description: And against it A good Preparation: Together with a sweet Consolation, for the surviving Mourners* (1629; STC 5533).

Collier, Thomas, *The Font-Guard Routed* (1652).

Collinges, John, *The Improvableness of Water-Baptism* (1681).

Comber, Thomas, *A Brief Discourse Upon the Offices of Baptism and Confirmation* (1674).

—— *A Companion to the Altar* (1675).

Compton, Henry, *Episcopalia: or, Letters . . . to the Clergy of this Diocese* (1686).

The Cony-catching Bride (1643).

Cook, William, *The Font Uncover'd for Infant-Baptisme* (1651).

Copley, Anthony, *Wits, Fits and Fancies* (1614; STC 5741).

Cosin, John, *A Collection of Private Devotions* (1627; STC 5816).

—— *John Cosin. A Collection of Private Devotions*, ed. P. G. Stanwood (Oxford, 1967).

—— *The Works of the Right Reverend Father in God, John Cosin*, 5 vols. (Oxford, 1843–55).

Couch, John, *Anabaptistarum Scrupuli: or, An Answer to a Kentish Anabaptist* (1650).

Coverdale, Miles, *The Christen State of Matrymonye, wherein housebandes and wyves maye lerne to kepe house together wyth loue* (1552; STC 4049).

The crie of the poore for the death of the Right Honourable Earle of Huntington (1596; STC 12929).

Crooke, Helkiah, *Microcosmographia. A Description of the Body of Man* (2nd edn., 1631; STC 6063).

Culmer, Richard, *Cathedral Newes from Canterbury* (1644).

—— *A Parish Looking-Glasse for Persecutors of Ministers* (1657).

Culpeper, Nicholas, *A Directory for Midwives: Or, A Guide for Women, In their Conception, Bearing, and Suckling their Children* (1651).

Dalton, Michael, *Officium Vicecomitum: The Office and Authoritie of Sherifs* (1623; STC 6212).

Dance of Death (1585?; STC 6223).

Darcie, Abraham, *The Originall of Idolatries: or, The Birth of Heresies* (1624; STC 4747).

The Daunce and Song of Death (1569; STC 6222).

Day, John, *Day's Festivals or, Twelve of His Sermons* (Oxford, 1615; STC 6426).

The Dead Mans Song (1680s?).

Death Dance (1680s?).

Death's Loud Allarum (1680s?).

A Declaration of a Strange and Wonderfull Monster (1646).

De Gaya, Louis, *Marriage Ceremonies: Or, The Ceremonies used in Marriages in all Parts of the World* (2nd edn., 1698).

—— *Matrimoniall Customs: or the Various Ceremonies, and Divers Ways of Celebrating Weddings, Practised amongst all the Nations, in the whole World* (1687).

Deloney, Thomas, *The Novels of Thomas Deloney*, ed. Merritt E. Lawlis (Bloomington, Ind., 1961).

Dent, Arthur, *A Pastime for Parents* (1612; STC 6624.4).

—— *The Plaine Mans Path-way to Heauen* (1612; STC 6630.5).

Dives and Pauper (1534; STC 19214); *Dives and Pauper*, ed. Francis J. Sheernan (New York, 1973).

Dod, John, and Robert Cleaver, *A Godly Forme of Houshold Gouernment* (1630; STC 5388).

The Doleful Dance, and Song of Death (1625; STC 6224).

Donne, John, *Devotions Upon Emergent Occasions*, ed. Anthony Raspa (Montreal, 1975).

—— *The Sermons of John Donne*, ed. George R. Potter and Evelyn M. Simpson, 10 vols. (Berkeley and Los Angeles, 1962).

Dow, Christopher, *Innovations Unjustly Charged upon the Present Church and State* (1637; STC 7090).

Drayton, Michael, *The Works of Michael Drayton*, ed. J. William Hebel, 5 vols. (Oxford, 1961).

Dunton, John, *A Mourning-Ring, In Memory of Your Departed Friend* (2nd edn., 1692).

Edwards,Thomas, *Gangraena: Or a Catalogue and Discovery of many of the Errours, Heresies, Blasphemies and Pernicious Practices of the Sectaries of this time* (1646).

—— *The Third Part of Gangraena* (1646).

The English Midwife Enlarged (1682).

An Episcopal Almanack for . . . 1678 (1678).

Featley, Daniel, *Ancilla Pietatis: or, The Hand-Maid to Private Devotion* (1626; STC 10725).

—— *Clavis Mystica: A Key Opening Divers Difficult and Mysterious Texts of Holy Scripture* (1636; STC 10730).

—— *The Dippers Dipt* (7th edn., 1660).

F.F., *An Excellent Ballad Upon a Wedding* (1698).

Field, Richard, *Of the Church, Five Books* (2nd edn., Oxford, 1628; STC 10858).

Finch, Edward, *An Answer to the Articles Preferd Against Edward Finch* (1641).

Fonteyn (Fontanus), Nicholas, *The Womans Doctour* (1652).

Foxe, John, *The Acts and Monuments of John Foxe*, ed. Stephen Reed Cattley and George Townsend, 8 vols. (1837–41).

Frank, Mark, *LI Sermons* (1672).

Gataker, Thomas, *A Good Wife God's Gift: And, A Wife Indeed* (1623; STC 11659).

—— *Two Marriage Sermons* (1620; STC 11680).

Gauden, John, *Christ at the Wedding: The Pristine Sanctity and Solemnity of Christian Marriages* (1654).

Geninges, John, *The Life and Death of Mr. E. Geninges* (St Omer, 1614; STC 11728).

Gerarde, John, *The Herball or General Historie of Plantes* (1633; STC 11751, 1636; STC 11752).

Gilby, Anthony, *A Pleasaunt Dialogue, Between a Souldior of Barwicke, and an English Chaplaine* (1581; STC 11888).

Googe, Barnaby, *The Popish Kingdome or reign of Antichrist, written in Latine Verse by Thomas Naogeorgus, and Englyshed by Barnabe Googe*, ed. Robert Charles Hope (1880).

The Gossips Feast or Morral Tales (1647).

The Gossips Meeting. Or, The Merry Market Women of Taunton (c.1674).

Gother, John, *A Discourse of the Use of Images: In Relation to the Church of England and the Church of Rome* (1687).

Gouge, William, *Of Domesticall Dvties* (1622; STC 12119).

—— *Of Domesticall Duties* (3rd edn., 1634; STC 12121).

Greenham, Richard, 'The Acts and Speeches of Richard Greenham', John Rylands Library, Manchester, Ms. 524.

—— *The Works . . . of Richard Greenham* (1599; STC 12312).

Greenwood, John, *M. Some laid open in his coulers* (1590; STC 12342).

Griffith, Matthew, *Bethel: Or, a Forme for Families* (1633; STC 12370).

Grindal, Edmund, *The Remains of Edmund Grindal*, ed. William Nicholson (Parker Society; Cambridge, 1843).

Grymeston, Elizabeth, *Miscelanea. Meditations. Memoratiues* (1604; STC 12407).

Guillemeau, Jacques, *Child-Birth, or The Happy Deliverie of Women* (London, 1612; STC 12496).

Gurnay, Edmund, *Gurnay Redivivus, or an Appendix unto the Homily Against Images in Churches* (1660).

—— *Toward the Vindication of the Second Commandment* (Cambridge, 1639; STC 12531).

Hacket, Roger, *Two Frvitfvl Sermons, Needfvll for these times* (1607; STC 12592).

Hannay, Patrick, *A Happy Husband or, Directions for a Maide to Choose her Mate: As also a Wives Behaviour towards her Husband after Marriage* (1619; STC 12747).

Harvey, William, *Anatomical Exercitations, Concerning the Generation of Living Creatures* (1653).

Herbert, George, *The Works of George Herbert*, ed. F. E. Hutchinson (Oxford, 1941).

—— *George Herbert and Henry Vaughan*, ed. Louis L. Martz (Oxford, 1986).

Herrick, Robert, *Hesperides: or, The Works both Humane and Divine* (1648).

—— *The Poetical Works of Robert Herrick*, ed. F. W. Moorman (Oxford, 1921).

—— *The Poetical Works of Robert Herrick*, ed. L. C. Martin (Oxford, 1956).

Hewardine, Thomas, *The Countrey-Curate to the Countrey-People* (1701).

—— *Some Plain Letters in the Defence of Infant Baptism* (1699).

Heywood, Oliver, *Oliver Heywood's Life of John Angier of Denton*, ed. Ernest Axon (Chetham Society; Manchester, 1937).

Heywood, Thomas, *A Marriage Triumphe Solemnized in an Epithalamium, In Memorie of the happie Nuptials betwixt the High and Mightie Prince Count Palatine, And the most Excellent Princessse the Lady Elizabeth* (1613; STC 13355).

—— *The Wise Woman of Hogsdon* (1638; STC 13370).

—— *The Wise Woman of Hogsdon*, ed. Michael H. Leonard (1980).

Hickeringhill, Edmund, *The Ceremony-Monger, His Character* (1689).

Hieron, Samuel, *A Helpe vnto Deuotion: Containing Certain Moulds or Forms of Prayer* (1612; STC 13407).

Hilder, Thomas, *Conjugall Counsell: Or, Seasonable Advise, both to unmarried, and Married Persons* (1653).

Hill, Robert, *The Pathway to Prayer and Pietie* (1610; STC 13473).

Hinde, William, *A Faithful Remonstrance of the Holy Life and Happy Death of Iohn Bruen of Bruen-Stapleford* (1641).

Hooke, Christopher, *The Child-birth or Womans Lecture* (1590; STC 13702).

Hooker, Richard, *The Works of that Learned and Judicious Divine, Mr. Richard Hooker* (1723).

Huarte, John, *Examen de Ingenios: The Examination of mens wits* (1594; STC 13890).

Joceline, Elizabeth, *The Mothers Legacie, to her Vnborne Childe* (1624; STC 14624).

Jones, John, *The Arte and Science of Preseruing Bodie and Soule in Healthe, Wisedom, and Catholike Religion* (1579; STC 14724).

Jonson, Ben, *Epicoene, or The Silent Woman* (1620; STC 14764).

Lambard, William, *Eirenarcha, Or the Office of the Iustices of Peace . . . enlarged* (1610; STC 15172).

The Lamentation of a New Married Man (1625?, STC 15186).

The Late Commotion of Certaine Papists in Herefordshire (1605; STC 25232.5).

Latimer, Hugh, *Sermons by Hugh Latimer*, ed. George Elwes Corrie (Parker Society; Cambridge, 1844).

Laud, William, *The Works of . . . William Laud, D.D.*, ed. W. Scott and J. Bliss, 7 vols. (Oxford, 1847–60).

Lawrence, Thomas, *Concerning Marriage: A Letter Sent to G.F.* (1663).

Lechford, Thomas, *New Englands Advice to Old England* (1644).

Lemnius, Laevinus, *An Herbal for the Bible* (1587; STC 15454).

Loues Garland. Or, Posies for Rings, Hand-kerchers, and Gloues; And such pretty Tokens that Louers send their Loues (1624; STC 16856).

Lupton, Thomas, *A Thousand Notable Things of Sundrie Sorts* (1631; STC 16961).

The Map of Mortalitie (1604; STC 17294).

The Mariage of Prince Fredericke, and the Kings Daughter, the Lady Elizabeth, vpon Shouesunday last (1613; STC 11359).

The Married Mens Feast. Or, The Banquet at Barnet (1671).

Marsh, A., *The Ten Pleasures of Marriage* (1682).

Match me this Wedding: Or, A health that was drunke in Sider and Perrie (1640?, STC 21503).

Mauriceau, Francis, *The Accomplisht Midwife* (1673).

—— *The Diseases of Women with Child and in Child-bed* (1672, 1683).

Meggott, Richard, *The Rib Restored: Or. The Honour of Marriage* (1656).

The Mid-wives Just Complaint (1646).

The Mid-wives Just Petition (1643).

Milton, John, *The Poetical Works of John Milton*, ed. H. C. Beeching (Oxford, 1900).

—— *The Works of John Milton; Anti-Prelatical Tracts*, ed. Harry Morgan Ayres (New York, 1931).

Moffett, Thomas, *Health's Improvement* (1655).

Moore, John, *A Mappe of Mans Mortalitie* (1617; STC 18057a).

More, John, *A Lively Anatomie of Death* (1595; STC 18073).

Morton, Thomas, *A Defence of the Innocencie of the Three Ceremonies of the Church of England* (1618; STC 18179).

The Murderous Midwife, with her Roasted Punishement (1673).

A Newe Boke Conteyninge An exortacion to the sicke. The sycke mans prayer. A prayer with thanks, at ye purification of women. A Consolation at buriall (1548, 1561; STC 3362, STC 3363.3).

Newcome, Henry, *The Compleat Mother: Or An Earnest Perswasive to all Mothers (especially those of Rank and Quality) to Nurse their own Children* (1695).

N.H., *The Ladies Dictionary, Being a General Entertainment for the Fair-Sex* (1694).

Niccholes, Alexander, *A Discourse of Marriage and Wiving* (1615; STC 18514).

Nowell, Alexander, *A Catechisme or First Instruction and Learning of Christian Religion* (1570; STC 18708).

Oliver, John, *A Present for Teeming Women: Or, Scripture-Directions for Women with Child, how to prepare for the hour of Travel* (1663).

—— *A Present to be Given to Teeming Women: By their Husbands or Friends* (1669).

Palmer, Geoffrey, *Les Reports de Sir Gefrey Palmer* (1678).

Parker, Robert, *A Scholasticall Discovrse Against Symbolizing with Antichrist in Ceremonies, Especially in the Signe of the Crosse* (Amsterdam?, 1607; STC 19294).

Parkinson, John, *Paradisi In Sole, Paradisus Terrestris: A Garden of all sorts of pleasant flowers* (1629; STC 19300).

Parrot, Henry, *The Gossips Greeting* (1620; STC 19331).

Patrick, Simon, *Aqua Genitalis: A Discourse Concerning Baptism* (1667).

Pechey, John, *The Compleat Midwife's Practice Enlarged* (5th edn., 1698).

—— *A General Treatise of the Diseases of Maids, Big-Bellied Women, Child-bed Women, and Widows* (1696).

—— *Some Observations Made upon the Maldiva Nut: Shewing Its Admirable Virtue in giving an Easie, Safe and Speedy Delivery to Women in Child-bed* (1694).

Perkins, William, *A Golden Chaine; or, The Description of Theologie, Containing the Order of the Causes of Saluation and Damnation* (Cambridge, 1600; STC 19646).

—— *The Whole Treatise of the Cases of Conscience* (Cambridge, 1608; STC 19670).

The Petition and Articles Exhibited in Parliament against Doctor Heywood (1641).

The Petition and Articles or Severall Charge Exhibited in Parliament against Edward Finch (1641).

Phillips, Edward, *The Mysteries of Love and Eloquence* (1658).

'Philomusus', *The Academy of Complements* (1640; STC 19883).

Pierce, Thomas, *A Collection of Sermons upon Several Occasions* (Oxford, 1671).

Pilkington, James, *The Works of James Pilkington*, ed. James Scholefield (Parker Society; Cambridge, 1842).

Playfere, Thomas, *The Meane in Mourning* (1597; STC 20016).

A Pleasand New Ballad of Tobias (1680s?).

The Pleasures of Matrimony (1688).

The praise of our Country Barly-Brake: or, Cupids advisement for Young-men to take Vp this loving old sport, Called Barly-Brake (1680s?).

Price, Sampson, *The Two Twins of Birth and Death* (1624; STC 20334).

Pricke, Robert, *A Verie Godlie and Learned Sermon, treating of Mans mortalitie* (1608; STC 20338).

Prideaux, Humphrey, *The Case of Clandestine Marriages Stated* (1691).

Primrose, James, *De Vulgi in Medicina Erroribus* (1638; STC 20384).

—— *Popular Errours. Or the Errours of the People in Physick* (1651).

The Problemes of Aristotle (1597; STC 764).

Prynne, William, *Canterburies Doome: or, The First Part of a Compleat History of the Commitment, Charge, Tryall, Condemnnation, Execution of William Laud* (1646).

Pulton, Ferdinando (ed.), *A Kalender, Or Table, Comprehending the effect of all the Statutes* (1612; STC 9549).

Ray, John, *A Collection of English Proverbs* (1670).

A Representation of the State of Christianity in England, and of its Decay and Danger from Sectaries aswel as Papists (1674).

Resbury, Nathaniel, *The Case of the Cross in Baptism Considered* (1684).

Rider, John, *Riders Dictionarie, Corrected and Augmented* (1640; STC 21036b).

Ridley, Nicholas, *The Works of Nicholas Ridley*, ed. Henry Christmas (Parker Society; Cambridge, 1841).

Roesslin, Eucharius, *The Birth of Man-Kinde; Otherwise Named The Womans Book* (tr. Thomas Raynold, 1604; STC 21161. 1626; STC 21163).

Rogers, Daniel, *Matrimoniall Honovr: Or, The mutuall Crowne and comfort of godly, loyall, and chaste Marriage* (1642).

Rowlands, Samuel, *Heavens Glory, Seeke It* (1628; STC 21383).

—— *Uncollected Poems . . . By Samuel Rowlands*, ed. Frederick O. Waage, jun. (Gainesville, Fla., 1970).

—— *A Whole Crew of Kind Gossips, all met to be Merry* (1609; STC 21413).

Rueff, Jacob, *The Expert Midwife* (1637; STC 21442).

Sadler, Francis, *The Exactions and Impositions of Parish Fees Discovered* (1738).

Sadler, John, *The Sicke Womans Private Looking-Glasse* (1636; STC 21544).

Sandys, Edmund, *The Sermons of Edwin Sandys*, ed. John Ayre (Parker Society; Cambridge, 1842).

Scot, Patrick, *A Table-Booke for Princes* (1621; STC 21860).

Secker, William, *A Wedding Ring Fit for the Finger: Or, the salve of Divinity On the sore of Humanity* (1658).

Selden, John, *Table Talk of John Selden*, ed. Frederick Pollock (1927).

Sermon, William, *The Ladies Companion, Or the English Midwife* (1671).

Shakespeare, William, *Works*.

Sharp, Jane, *The Midwives Book: Or the Whole Art of Midwifery Discovered* (1671).

The She Wedding; or a Mad-Marriage, between Mary a Seamans Mistress, and Margaret a Carpenters Wife (1684).

Sherlock, William, *A Practical Discourse Concerning Death* (9th edn., 1696).

—— *A Practical Discourse of Religious Assemblies* (2nd edn., 1682).

Shipman, Thomas, *Carolina: Or, Loyal Poems* (1683).

Shirley, James, *The Wedding* (1629: STC 22460).

Sicke Womans Private Looking-Glasse (1636; STC 21544).

Smart, Peter, *A Catalogue of Superstitious Innovations in the change of Services and Ceremonies* (1642).

—— *A Short Treatise of Altars* (1643).

—— *The Vanitie and Downefall of Superstitious Popish Ceremonies* (Edinburgh, 1628; STC 22643).

Smith, Henry, *A Preparative to Marriage: The Summe whereof was spoken at a contract and inlarged after* (1591; STC 22686).

—— *The Wedding Garment* (1590; STC 22713).

Smith, Thomas, *De Repvublica Anglorum: The maner of Gouernement or police of the Realme of England* (1583; STC 22857).

Sowerby, Leonard, *The Ladies Dispensatory, Containing the Natures, Vertues, and Qualities of all Herbs* (1652).

Sparke, Edward, *Scintilla Altaris. Primitive Devotion in the Feasts and Fasts of the Church of England* (6th edn., 1678).

Sparke, Thomas, *A Brotherly Perswasion to Vnitie, and Vniformitie in Ivdgement* (1607; STC 23020).

Sparrow, Anthony, *A Rationale upon the Book of Common Prayer of the Church of England* (1668).

Stephens, John, *Essayes and Characters. Ironicall and Instructive* (1615; STC 23250).

Stopford, Joshua, *Pagano-Papismus: Or, an Exact Parallel Betweene Rome-Pagan, and Rome-Christian, in their Doctrines and Ceremonies* (1675).

The Story of David and Bersheba (1680s?).

Stradling, George, *Sermons and Discourses upon Several Occasions* (1692).

A Strange and Lamentable Accident that happened lately at Mears Ashby in Northamptonshire (1642).

A Strange and Wonderful Example of Gods Judements, Shewed upon Iames Brathwaight of Shoreditch (1645).

Strange Newes out of Kent, of a Monstrous and misshapen Child, borne in Olde Sand-wich (1609; STC 14934).

Strong, Martin, *The Indecency and Unlawfulness of Baptizing Children in Private, Without Necessity, and with the Public Form* (1692).

Stubs, Philip, *Of Publick Baptism* (1693; 2nd edn., 1699).

Suckling, John, *The Works of Sir John Suckling*, ed. Thomas Clayton (Oxford, 1971).

Susanna's Apology Against the Elders, in Elspeth Graham, Hilary Hinds, Elaine Hobby, and Helen Wilcox (eds.), *Her Own Life: Autobiographical Writings by Seventeenth-Century Englishwomen* (1989).

Sutton, Christopher, *Disce Mori: Learne to Dye* (1600, 1626; STC 23488).

Sutton, Thomas, *The Christians Iewell fit to adorne the heart* (1624; STC 23499).

Swinburne, Henry, *A Treatise of Spousals, or Matrimonial Contracts* (1686).

Tanner, John, *The Hidden Treasures of the Art of Physick* (1659).

Tate, Francis, 'Of the Antiquity, Variety and Ceremonies of Funerals in England', in Thomas Hearne (ed.), *A Collection of Curious Discourses Written by Eminent Antiquaries*, 2 vols. (1771), i. 215–20.

'Tattle-well, Mary, and Ioane Hit-him-home', *The Womens Sharpe Revenge* (1640; STC 23706).

Taylor, Jeremy, *The Rule and Exercises of Holy Dying* (1651).

Taylor, John, *A Swarme of Sectaries and Schismatiques* (1641).

The Ten Pleasures of Marriage (1682).

Tilney, Edmund, *A brief and pleasant discourse of duties in Mariage* (1571; STC 24077).

Turner, John, *An Argument in Defence of the Marriage of an Uncle with the Daughter of his Half-Brother by the Father's Side* (1686).

—— *A Letter of Resolution to a Friend, Concerning Marriage of Cousin Germans* (1682).

Vaughan, William, *The Golden-grove, moralized in three Bookes* (2nd edn., 1608; STC 24611).

Veron, John, *The Huntyng of Purgatorye to Death* (1561; STC 24683).

Ward, Ned, *The London-Spy, Compleat, in Eighteen Parts* (1703).

Webb, George, *Catalogus Protestantium: Or, The Protestants Kalendar* (1624; STC 25161).

Weever, John, *Ancient Funeral Monuments* (1631; STC 25223).

Whately, William, *A Bride-Bvsh: Or, A Direction for Married Persons* (1619; STC 25297).

—— *A Care-cloth: Or a Treatise of the Cvmbers and Trovbles of Marriage* (1624; STC 25299).

Whetstone, George, *An Heptameron of Ciuill Discourses* (1582; STC 25337).

White, John, *The First Century of Scandalous, Malignant Priests* (1643).

Whitgift, John, *The Works of John Whitgift*, ed. John Ayre, 3 vols. (Parker Society; Cambridge, 1851–3).

The Wicked Midwife, the cruell Mother, and the harmlesse Daughter (c.1640; STC 17915.7).

Widdowes, Giles, *The Schismatical Puritan: A Sermon Preached at Witney* (2nd edn., Oxford 1631; STC 25595).

Willughby, Percival, *Observations in Midwifery*, ed. Henry Blenkinsop (Warwick, 1863).

The Winchester Wedding: Or, Ralph of Reading, and Black Bess of the Green (1670); repr. in *Ancient Songs* (1790).

Wither, George, *Halelviah* (1641).

W.M., *The Queens Closet Opened* (1674).

Wolveridge, James, *Speculum Matricis Hybernicum; Or, The Irish Midwives Handmaid* (1670).

Woolley, Hannah, *The Gentlewoman's Companion; Or, A Guide to the Female Sex* (1675).

The Zurich Letters, ed. Hastings Robinson, 2 vols. (Parker Society; Cambridge, 1842–5).

ECCLESIASTICAL PROCEEDINGS

Aduertisements partly for due order in the publique administration of common praiers (1565; STC 10028).

Articles Agreed Upon by the Arch-Bishops and Bishops of both Provinces, and the whole Cleargie (1630; STC 10055).

Articles Ecclesiasticall to be Inquired of . . . within the diocese of Hereford (Oxford, 1586; STC 10215).

Articles of Enquiry and Direction for the Diocese of Norwich . . . 1638 (1638; STC 10299).

Articles of Enquiry . . . for the Diocese of Ely (1662).

Articles to bee enquired of by the Church-wardens and sworne-men: In the Ordinary Visitation of the Lord Bishop of Excester (1599; STC 10204).

Articles to bee enquired of by the Minister, Church-wardens, and Side-men . . . within the Arch-Deaconry of Lincolne (1600; STC 10245.8).

Articles to be inquired of, in the first Metropoliticall visitation (1616; STC 10147.5).

Articles to be Inquired of in the Metropolitical Visitation . . . for the Dioces of London (1636; STC 10265.5).

Articles to be Enquired of . . . in the Primary Visitation of . . . Simon Lord Bishop of Chichester (1690).

Articles to be Enquyred in the Visitation in the First Yere of the Raigne of our Most Dread Soueraine Lady Elizabeth (1559; STC 10118).

Articles to be Enquired of Within the Archdeaconry of Middlesex (1662).

Articles to be Enquired of Within the Archdeaconry of Yorke (1635; STC 10382).

Articles to be Inquired of Within the Dioces of Ely (1638; STC 10197).

Articles to be Enquired of Within the Diocesse of Lincolne (1574; STC 10229).

Articles to be Enquired of Within the Diocesse of Lincoln (1588; STC 10232).

Articles to be Enqvired of, within the Diocesse of Lincolne (Cambridge, 1598; STC 10235).

Articles to be Enqvired of within the Dioces of London (1607; STC 10257).

Articles to be Enquired of Within the Dioces of London (1628; STC 10263).

Articles to be enquired of within the Dioces of Winchester, in the Metropolitical visitation (1590; STC 10355).

Articles to be enquired of within the Prouince of Yorke (1571; STC 10375).

Articles Whereupon it was agreed by the Archbishoppes and Bishoppes of both provinces and the whole cleargie (1571; STC 10036a).

'Benedictio super mulieres post partum ante ostium ecclesie', Bodleian Library, Oxford, Tanner Ms. 5.

The Booke of Common Prayer, and Administration of the Sacraments, and other Rites and Ceremonies of the Church of England (1578; STC 16308).

The Booke of Common Prayer (1604; STC 16326).

The Book of Common Prayer (1662).

Bullard, J. V. (ed.), *Constitutions and Canons Ecclesiastical 1604* (1934).

Burn, John Southerden, *The High Commission. Notices of the Court, and its Proceedings* (1865).

Cardwell, Edward (ed.), *Documentary Annals of the Reformed Church of England*, 2 vols. (Oxford, 1844).

—— *A History of Conferences, and other Proceedings connected with the Revision of the Book of Common Prayer* (Oxford, 1840; 3rd edn., Oxford, 1849).

—— *Synodalia: A Collection of Articles of Religion, Canons, and Proceedings of Convocations* (Oxford, 1842).

Certaine Sermons or Homilies Appointed to be Read in Churches (1623; STC 13659).

Clay, William Keatinge (ed.), *Liturgical Services: Liturgies and Occasional Forms of Prayer Set Forth in the Reign of Queen Elizabeth* (Cambridge, 1847).

Constitutions and Canons Ecclesiastical (1612; STC 10072).

A Directory For the Publique Worship of God (1646).

Fincham, Kenneth (ed.), *Visitation Articles and Injunctions of the Early Stuart Church*, (Church of England Record Society; Woodbridge, Suffolk, 1994).

Fisher, J. D. C., *Christian Initiation: Baptism in the Medieval West* (1963).

—— *Christian Initiation: The Reformation Period* (1970).

A Form of Prayer with Thanksgiving for the Safe Delivery of the Queen, and happy Birth of the Young Prince (1688).

A Form, or Order of Thanksgiving, and Prayer . . . upon Occasion of the Queen's being with Child (1688).

Frere, W. H., and W. M. Kennedy (eds.), *Visitation Articles and Injunctions of the Period of the Reformation*, 3 vols. (1910).

Gibson, Edmund, *Codex Juris Ecclesiastici Anglicani* (1713).

Godolphin, John, *Repertorium Canonicum; Or an Abridgement of the Ecclesiastical Laws of this Realm, Consistent with the Temporal* (2nd edn., 1680).

Hierurgia Anglicana: Or Documents and Extracts Illustrative of the Ritual of the Church of England After the Reformation (1848).

Historical Manuscripts Commission, *Calendar of the Manuscripts of the Dean and Chapter of Wells*, 2 vols. (1914).

Iniunctions Geven by the Quenes Maiestie (1559; STC 10095).

Iniunctions Giuen by the most reuerende father in Christ, Edmonde . . . in his Metropoliticall visitation of the Prouince of Yorke (1571; STC 10375).

'Injunctions and Visitation Articles', *Second Report of the Ritual Commission* (Parliamentary Papers 38; 1867–8), appendix E.

Injunctions Given by . . . Bishop of Lincolne (1577; STC 10230).

Keeling, William (ed.), *Liturgiae Britannicae, or The Several Editions of the Book of Common Prayer . . . Arranged to Shew their Respective Variations* (2nd edn., 1851).

Kennedy, W. P. M., *Elizabethan Episcopal Adminstration*, 3 vols. (1924).

Ketley, Joseph (ed.), *The Two Liturgies, A.D. 1549, and A.D. 1552* (Parker Society; Cambridge, 1844).

Maskell, William, *Monumenta Ritualia Ecclesiae Anglicanae: The Occasional Offices of the Church of England According to the Old Use of Salisbury*, 3 vols. (Oxford, 1882).

Missale Ad Usum Insignis Ecclesie Sarum (Rouen, 1519 (STC 16201); Antwerp, 1527 (STC 16207); London, 1555 (STC 16218)).

The Psalmes of David in Meeter . . . Whereunto is added Prayers commonly used in the Kirke, and in private houses (Edinburgh, 1611; STC 16591).

Prayers Appointed to be vsed in the Church at Morning and Evening Prayer by every Minister, For the Queenes safe deliverance (1605; STC 16534).

Prayers and Thanksgiving to bee vsed by all the Kings Maiesties louing Subiects For the happy deliverance of his Maiestie, the Queene, Prince, and states of Parliament, from the most Traiterous and bloody intended Massacre by Gunpowder, the fift of November, 1605 (1605; STC 16494).

Schroeder, H. J., *Canons and Decrees of the Council of Trent* (1941).

Strype, John, *Annals of the Reformation*, 3 vols. (Oxford, 1824).

A Thanksgiuing and Prayer for the safe Child-bearing of the Queenes Maiestie (1629; STC 16548.3).

A Thanksgiuing and Prayer for the safe Child-bearing of the Queenes Maiestie (1631; STC 16549.5).

A Thanksgiving for the Queenes Maiesties Safe Deliverance (1605; STC 16535).

Warren, Frederick E. (tr.), *The Sarum Missal in English*, 2 vols. (1913).

Wilkins, D., *Concilia Magnae Britanniae*, 2 vols. (1737).

Diocese of Bath and Wells:

'Act Books, 1615–37', Somerset Record Office, Taunton, D/D/Ca. 191–313.

Jenkins, Claude (ed.), 'Act Books of the Archdeacon of Taunton, 1623–4', Somerset Record Society, *Collecteana II* (1928), 47–175.

Diocese and Province of Canterbury:

'Act Book of the High Commission Court within the Diocese of Canterbury, 1584–1603', Canterbury Cathedral Archives, PRC 44/3.

'Canterbury Diocesan Records, 1560–1700', Canterbury Cathedral Archives, DCb J/X, Y, Z.

Hussey, Arthur (ed.), 'Visitations of the Archdeacons of Canterbury', *Archaeologia Cantiana*, 27 (1904), 213–29.

Jenkins, Claude (ed.), 'An Unpublished Record of Archbishop Parker's Visitation in 1573', *Archaeologia Cantiana*, 29 (1911), 270–318.

Willis, Arthur J., *Church Life in Kent: Being Church Court Records of the Canterbury Diocese, 1559–1565* (London and Chichester, 1975).

Diocese of Carlisle:

'Visitation books, 1663–65', Cumbria Record Office, Carlisle, DRC/5/2.

Diocese of Chester:

'Consistory Court Papers, 1525–1731', Cheshire Record Office, Chester, EDC 5.

Beresford, J. R. (ed.), 'The Churchwarden's Accounts of Holy Trinity, Chester, 1532 to 1633', *Journal of the Chester and North Wales Architectural, Archaeological, and Historical Society*, 38 (1951), 94–171.

Diocese of Chichester:

'Churchwardens' Presentments, 1573–1698', West Sussex Record Office, Chichester, EP.1/23.

'Church Inspections, 1636–40', West Sussex Record Office, EP.1/26/2.

'Detection Books, 1589–1610', West Sussex Record Office, EP.1/17/7–13.

'Consistory Court Acts, 1592–3', British Library, Additional Ms. 33,410.

Johnstone, Hilda (ed.), *Churchwardens' Presentments (17th Century) Part 1: Archdeaconry of Chichester* (Sussex Record Society; Lewes, 1947–8).

—— *Churchwardens' Presentments (17th Century) Part 2: Archdeaconry of Lewes* (Sussex Record Society; Lewes, 1948–9).

Renshaw, Walter C., 'Notes from the Act Books of the Archdeaconry Court of Lewes', *Sussex Archaeological Collections*, 49 (1906), 47–65.

Diocese of Coventry and Lichfield:

'Court Papers, 1636', Lichfield Record Office, B/C/5.

'Visitation Acta, 1635–39', Lichfield Record Office, B/V/1 55–66.

Diocese of Durham:

'Consistory Court Depositions, 1605–31', University of Durham Archives, DDR V/8–12.

'Diocesan Visitations, 1601–18', University of Durham Archives, DDR 11/5–7.

'Diocesan Visitations, 1662–70', University of Durham Archives, DDR II/3.

'Durham Archdeaconry Correction Book, 1637', University of Durham Archives, DCD/SJB 7.

The Acts of the High Commission Court Within the Diocese of Durham (Surtees Society; Durham, 1857).

Depositions and other Ecclesiastical Proceedings from the Courts of Durham (Surtees Society; Durham, 1845).

The Injunctions and other Ecclesiastical Proceedings of Richard Barnes, Bishop of Durham, from 1577 to 1587 (Surtees Society; Durham, 1850).

Barmby, J. (ed.), *Churchwardens' Accounts of Pittington and other Parishes in the Diocese of Durham* (Surtees Society: Durham, 1888).

Diocese of Ely:

'Visitation Books, 1638–66', Cambridge University Library, Ely Diocesan Records B/9/5–52.

'Churchwardens' Presentments, Diocese of Ely, 1554–1679', Bodleian Library, Ms. Gough. Eccl. Top. 3.

Bradshaw, Henry (ed.), 'Notes on the Episcopal Visitation of the Archdeaconrry of Ely in 1685', *Cambridgeshire Antiquarian Communications,* 3 (1879), 323–62.

Foster, J. E. (ed.), *Churchwardens' Accounts of St. Mary the Great, Cambridge, from 1504 to 1635* (Cambridge, 1905).

Hall, Hubert (ed.), 'Some Elizabethan Penances in the Diocese of Ely', *Transactions of Royal Historical Society,* 3rd ser. 1 (1907), 263–77.

Palmer, W. M. (ed.), *Episcopal Visitation Returns for Cambridgeshire: Matthew Wren, Bishop of Ely, 1638–1665* (Cambridge, 1930).

Diocese of Gloucester:

Field, Colin W., *The State of the Church in Gloucestershire, 1563* (Robertsbridge, Sussex, 1971).

Price, F. D. (ed.), *The Commission for Ecclesiastical Causes within the Dioceses of Bristol and Gloucester, 1574* (Bristol and Gloucestershire Archaeological Society; Bristol, 1972).

Diocese of Hereford:

'Office Court Books, 1558–1700', Hereford Record Office, Boxes 11–44, Books 47–174.

'Cause Papers, 1613–1703', Hereford Record Office, Cause Papers, Boxes 1–10.

'Registrar's Files, 1660–74', Hereford Record Office.

Diocese of Lincoln:

'Court Papers, 1570–1664', Lincolnshire Archives, Lincoln, Ch./P 1–12; CP 58/2–69/2.

'Visitation records, 1631–36', Lincolnshire Archives, Vj/27–29.

'Licences to Midwives, etc. 1683–1773', Lincolnshire Archives, Lic/M/1.

'Archdeacon of Bedford visitation court, 1617', Bedfordshire Record Office, A.B.C. 5.

'Leicester Archdeaconry Act Books, 1569–71', Leicestershire Record Office, 1 D41/13/5–7.

'Cause Papers, 1570–83', Leicestershire Record Office, 1 D41/4.

'Churchwardens' Presentments, 1632–35', Leicestershire Record Office, 1 D41/21.

'Correction Court records, 1634', Leicestershire Record Office, 1 D41/13/61

Foster, C. W. (ed.), *Lincoln Episcopal Records in the Time of Thomas Cooper . . . A.D. 1571 to A.D. 1584* (Lincoln Record Society; Lincoln, 1912).

—— *The State of the Church in the Reigns of Elizabeth and James I as Illustrated by Documents Relating to the Diocese of Lincoln* (Lincoln Record Society; Lincoln, 1926).

Moore, A. Percival (ed.), 'The Metropolitical Visitation of Archdeacon [sic] Laud', in *Associated Architectural Societies' Reports and Papers,* 29 (1907), 479–534.

Venables, E., 'The Primary Visitation of the Diocese of Lincoln by Bishop Neile, A.D. 1614', *Associated Architectural Societies' Reports and Papers*, 16 (1881), 31–54.

Diocese of London:

'Archdeaconry Acts, 1635–40', Guildhall Library, London, Mss. 9059/1–2.

'Commissary Acta, 1582–1641', Guildhall Library, London, Mss. 9064/12–21.

'Churchwardens' Presentments, 1630–1680', Guildhall Library, London, Mss. 9583/1–5.

'Visitation books, 1637–93', Guildhall Library, London, Mss. 9537/15–20, 9538

'Consistory Court, Office Acts, 1605–1706', Greater London Record Office, DL/C 304–29, DL/C 618–26.

Hale, William H. (ed.), *A Series of Precedents and Proceedings in Criminal Causes, extending from the year 1475 to 1640; extracted from the Act-Books of the Ecclesiastical Courts of the Diocese of London* (1847).

Hall, H. R. Wilton, *Records of the Old Archdeaconry of St. Albans: A Calendar of Papers A.D. 1575 to A.D. 1637* (St Albans, 1908).

Overall, William Henry (ed.), *The Accounts of the Churchwardens of the Parish of St. Michael, Cornhill, in the City of London, from 1456 to 1608* (1868).

Pressey, W. J., 'Notes on Visitations in the Archdeaconry of Essex', *Transactions of the Essex Archaeological Society*, 19 (1930), 260–76; 20 (1930–1), 216–42; 21 (1933–4), 306–26; 22 (1936–40), 113–25, 316–29; 23 (1942), 145–64.

Diocese of Norwich:

'Archdeaconry of Norwich visitations and comperta, 1614–23', Norfolk Record Office, Norwich, ANW/6/7, ANW/3/25.

'Consistory Court Miscellany, 1615–19', Norfolk Record Office, CON/8.

'Visitation books, 1620–29', Norfolk Record Office, VIS 5/1–3, VIS 6/1.

'Testimonials for Midwives, etc., 1660–90', Norfolk Record Office, TES/1–3.

Houlbrooke, R. A. (ed.), *The Letter Book of John Parkhurst, Bishop of Norwich . . . 1571–5* (Norfolk Record Society; Norwich, 1974–5).

Williams, J. F. (ed.), *Diocese of Norwich: Bishop Redman's Visitation 1597* (Norfolk Record Society; Norwich, 1946).

Diocese of Oxford:

'Archdeaconry of Oxford Acts, 1581–1681', Oxfordshire Archives, Oxford, Archdeaconry Papers, c. 4–22.

'Archdeaconry Presentments, 1619–96', Oxfordshire Archives, Archdeaconry Papers, b. 1a.

'Diocesan Acts, 1593–1677', Oxfordshire Archives, Diocesan Papers, c. 1–12, d. 4–12.

'Banbury Acts, 1625–38', Oxfordshire Archives, Diocesan Papers, c. 16, c. 155.

'Cropredy Acts, 1626–36', Oxfordshire Archives, Diocesan Papers, c. 17.

'Thame Acts, 1584–1622', Oxfordshire Archives, Diocesan Papers, c. 18.

'Archdeaconry of Berkshire, Liber Actorum 1630–35', Berkshire Record Office, Reading, D/A2/c 71–75.

'Archdeaconry of Buckinghamshire Acts, 1561–1630', Buckinghamshire Record Office, Aylesbury, D/A/C 2–6.

'Archdeaconry of Buckinghamshire Visitations, 1633–72', Buckinghamshire Record Office, D/A/V 2–9.

Brinkworth, E. R. (ed.), *The Archdeacon's Court Liber Actorum 1584*, 2 vols. (Oxfordshire Record Society; Oxford, 1942–6).

Brinkworth, E. R. C. (ed.), *Episcopal Visitation Book for the Archdeaconry of Buckingham, 1662* (Buckinghamshire Record Society; Aylesbury, 1947).

Howse, Violet M. (ed.), *Stanford in the Vale Churchwardens' Accounts 1552–1725* (Oxford, 1987).

Peyton, Sidney A. (ed.), *The Churchwardens' Presentments in the Oxfordshire Peculiars of Dorchester, Thame and Banbury* (Oxfordshire Record Society, Oxford, 1928).

Diocese of Peterborough:

'Northamptonshire Archdeaconry Visitation Returns, 1561–97', Northamptonshire Record Office, Northampton, X.639/1–5.

'Archdeaconry Correction Books, 1588–1635', Northamptonshire Record Office.

Diocese of Salisbury:

'Diocesan Act Book, 1615–19', Wiltshire Record Office, Trowbridge, D1/39/2/9.

'Office Acts, 1599–1602', Wiltshire Record Office, D2/4/1/8.

'Dean of Salisbury, Act Book, 1628', Wiltshire Record Office, D/5/19/32.

Nevill, Edmund R. (ed.), 'The Chrysom Book of St. Thomas, New Sarum', *Wiltshire Notes and Queries*, 5 (1908), 462–8, 510–14, 561–6; 6 (1911), 19–25, 57–60, 107–10, 208–11, 302–5, 344–8, 391–5, 455–9, 492–8, 547–50.

Swayne, Henry James Fowle (ed.), *Churchwardens' Accounts of S. Edmund and S. Thomas, Sarum, 1443–1702* (Salisbury, 1896).

Diocese of Winchester:

Willis, Arthur J. *Winchester Consistory Court Depositions 1561–1602* (Hambleden, Kent, 1960).

Diocese of Worcester:

'Act Book of the Peculiar of Tredington (Diocese of Worcester) 1576–1686', Cambridge University Library, Ms. Mm. 4. 20.

Braby, P., 'Churchwardens' Presentments from the Vale of Evesham, 1660–1717: Part I', *Vale of Evesham Historical Society Research Papers*, 5 (1975), 61–79; 6 (1977), 101–16.

Leatherbarrow, J. S. (ed.), *Churchwardens' Presentments in the Diocese of Worcester, c.1660–1760* (Worcester Historical Society; Worcester, 1977).

Diocese and Province of York:

'Visitation Court Books, 1567–1640', Borthwick Institute, York.

'Archdeaconry of Cleveland Court Books, 1632–41', Borthwick Institute, York.

'Archdeaconry of York Court Books, 1598–1684', Borthwick Institute, York.

'Cause Papers, 1562–1697', Borthwick Institute, York.

'High Commission Cause Papers, 1561–1641', Borthwick Institute, York.

Benson, George (ed.), 'Holy Trinity Church, Goodramgate, York. Extracts from the Churchwardens' Accounts, 1557–1819', *Associated Architectural Societies Reports and Papers*, 30 (1909), 641–53.

Fallow, T. M. (ed.), 'Some Elizabethan Visitations of the Churches belonging to the Peculiar of the Dean of York', *The Yorkshire Archaeological Journal*, 18 (1905), 197–232, 313–40.

Hodgkinson, R. F. B. (ed.), 'Extracts from the Act Books of the Archdeacons of Nottingham', *Transactions of the Thoroton Society*, 29 (1926), 19–67; 30 (1927), 11–57; 31 (1928), 108–53.

Kitching, C. J. (ed.), *The Royal Visitation of 1559: Act Book of the Northern Province* (Surtees Society; Durham, 1975).

Sheils, W. J. (ed.), *Archbishop Grindal's Visitation, 1575: Comperta et Detecta Book* (York, 1977).

Wood, A. C. (ed.), 'The Nottinghamshire Presentment Bills of 1587', *Thoroton Society Record Series*, 11 (1945), 1–42.

OTHER PRIMARY SOURCES

Ballam, Harry, and Roy Lewis (eds.), *The Visitor's Book: England and the English as Others Have Seen Them AD 1500 to 1950* (1950).

Bateson, Mary (ed.), *Records of the Borough of Leicester . . . 1509–1603* (Cambridge, 1905).

The Book of Oaths (1689).

Calendar of State Papers, Domestic.

Cockburn, J. S. (ed.), *Calendar of Assize Records, Surrey Indictments, Elizabeth I* (1979).

A Collection of Ordinances and Regulations for the Government of the Royal Household, Made in Divers Reigns (1790).

Company of Parish Clerks of London, *A General Bill for this Present Year* (1665).

Dale, T. C. (ed.), *The Inhabitants of London in 1638* (1931).

Depositions from the Castle at York (Surtees Society; Durham, 1861).

D'Ewes, Sir Simonds, *The Journals of all the Parliaments During the Reign of Queen Elizabeth* (1682).

Emmison, F. G. (ed.), *Elizabethan Life: Wills of Essex Gentry and Merchants* (Chelmsford, 1978).

—— (ed.), *Elizabethan Life: Wills of Essex Gentry and Yeomen* (Chelmsford, 1980).

—— (ed.), *Essex Wills (England)*, ii. *1565–1571* (Boston, Mass., 1983).

Ferguson, Richard S. (ed.), *A Boke off Recorde or Register . . . of Kirkbiekendall . . . 1575* (Kendal, 1892).

Firth, C. H., and R. S. Rait (eds.), *Acts and Ordinances of the Interregnum, 1642–1660*, 2 vols. (1911).

Frere, W. H., and C. E. Douglas (eds.), *Puritan Manifestoes* (1954).

Hearne, Thomas (ed.), *A Collection of Curious Discourses Written by Eminent Antiquaries*, 2 vols. (1771).

Holmes, Clive (ed.), *The Suffolk Committees for Scandalous Ministers 1644–1646* (Suffolk Records Society; Ipswich, 1970).

Jeaffreson, John Cordy (ed.), *Middlesex County Records*, 4 vols. (1886–92).

Johnson, H. C. (ed.), *Wiltshire County Records. Minutes and Proceedings in Sessions 1563 and 1574 to 1592* (Devizes, 1949).

Johnson, Robert C., Mary Frear Keeler, Maija Jansson Cole, and William B. Bidwell (eds.), *Commons Debates 1628*, 4 vols. (New Haven, 1977).

Kenyon, J. P., *The Stuart Constitution* (Cambridge, 1966).

Larkin, James F., and Paul L. Hughes (eds.), *Stuart Royal Proclamations*, i. *Royal Proclamations of King James I, 1603–1625* (Oxford, 1973).

'Orders and Regulations for an Earl's House', Bodleian Library, Oxford, Ms. Eng. hist. b. 208.

Palmer, W. M., and H. W. Saunders (eds.), *Documents Relating to Cambridgeshire Villages* (Cambridge, 1926).

Peel, Albert (ed.), *The Second Part of a Register: Being a Calendar of Manuscripts under that title intended for publication by the Puritans about 1593*, 2 vols. (Cambridge, 1915).

'Proceedings against Malignants in Wiltshire, 1646', British Library, Additional Ms. 22,084.

Raines, F. R. (ed.), *A Description of the State, Civil and Ecclesiastical, of the County of Lancaster about the year 1590* (Chetham Society; Manchester, 1875).

Raymond, Joad (ed.), *Making the News: An Anthology of the Newsbooks of Revolutionary England, 1641–1660* (New York, 1993).

Raymond, Robert Lord, *Reports of Cases Argued and Adjudged in the Courts of King's Bench and Common Pleas* (1743).

Records of the Borough of Nottingham, vol. 5 . . . 1625–1702 (London and Nottingham, 1900).

Statutes of the Realm.

Tanner Mss. 5, 35, 38, 42, 62, 68, 124, 125, 138, 140, 280, Bodleian Library, Oxford.

Usher, Roland G. (ed.), *The Presbyterian Movement in the reign of Queen Elizabeth as Illustrated by the Minute Book of the Dedham Classis 1582–1589* (Camden Society, 1905).

SELECT SECONDARY SOURCES

Addleshaw, G. W. O., and Frederick Etchells, *The Architectural Setting of Anglican Worship* (1948).

Addy, John, *Death, Money and the Vultures: Inheritance and Avarice, 1660–1750* (1992).

—— *Sin and Society in the Seventeenth Century* (1989).

Amussen, S. D., 'Gender, Family and the Social Order, 1560–1725', in Anthony Fletcher and John Stevenson (eds.), *Order and Disorder in Early Modern England* (Cambridge, 1985), 196–217.

Amussen, Susan, *An Ordered Society: Gender and Class in Early Modern England* (Oxford, 1988).

Anderson, Bonnie S., and Judith P. Zinsser (eds.), *A History of Their Own: Women in Europe from Prehistory to the Present,* 2 vols. (New York, 1988).

Andrews, William, *Old Church Lore* (Hull, 1891).

Archer, Ian W., *The Pursuit of Stability: Social Relations in Elizabethan London* (Cambridge, 1991).

Aries, Philippe, *The Hour of Our Death* (New York, 1981).

Ashton, John, *Social Life in the Reign of Queen Anne Taken from Original Sources* (1904).

Aston, Margaret, 'Segregation in Church', in W. J. Sheils and Diana Wood (eds.), *Women in the Church* (Studies in Church History, 27; Oxford, 1990), 237–94.

Atkinson, Colin B., and William P. Stoneman, '"These griping greefes and pinching pangs": Attitudes to Childbirth in Thomas Bentley's *The Monument of Matrones* (1582)', *Sixteenth Century Journal,* 21 (1990), 193–203.

Aveling, Hugh, *Northern Catholics: The Catholic Recusants of the North Riding of Yorkshire 1558–1790* (1966).

Bardsley, Charles Wareing, *Curiosities of Puritan Nomenclature* (1897).

Beaver, Dan, '"Sown in Dishonour, Raised in Glory": Death, Ritual and Social Organization in Northern Gloucestershire, 1590–1690', *Social History,* 17 (1992), 389–419.

Beier, Lucinda McCray, 'The Good Death in Seventeenth-Century England', in Ralph Houlbrooke (ed.), *Death, Ritual, and Bereavement* (1989), 43–61.

Ben-Amos, Illana Krausman, *Adolescence and Youth in Early Modern England* (New Haven and London, 1994).

Benedek, Thomas G., 'The Changing Relationship between Midwives and Physicians during the Renaissance', *Bulletin of the History of Medicine,* 51 (1977), 550–64.

Berry, B. Midi, and R. S. Schofield, 'Age at Baptism in Pre-industrial England', *Population Studies,* 25 (1971), 453–63.

Bloch, Maurice, and Jonathan Parry (eds.), *Death and the Regeneration of Life* (Cambridge, 1982).

Bond, Francis, *Fonts and Font Covers* (Oxford, 1908).

Bongaarts, John, 'Why Birth Rates are so Low', *Population and Development Review,* 1 (1975), 289–96.

Bossy, John, *The Development of the Family and Marriage in Europe* (Cambridge, 1983).

—— *The English Catholic Community, 1570–1850* (1979).

—— 'Godparenthood: The Fortunes of a Social Institution in Early Modern Christianity', in Kaspar von Greyerz (ed.), *Religion and Society in Early Modern Europe* (1984), 194–201.

Boulton, Jeremy, 'Clandestine Marriages in London: An Examination of the Neglected Urban Variable', *Urban History,* 20 (1993), 191–210.

—— 'Economy of Time? Wedding Days and the Working Week in the Past', *Local Population Studies,* 43 (1989), 28–46.

Boulton, Jeremy, 'Itching after Private Marryings? Marriage Customs in Seventeenth-Century London', *London Journal*, 16 (1991), 15–34.

—— *Neighbourhood and Society: A London Suburb in the Seventeenth Century* (Cambridge, 1987).

Brand, John, *Observations on Popular Antiquities*, 2 vols. (1813).

Brigden, Susan, *London and the Reformation* (Oxford, 1991).

Brodsky, Vivien, 'Widows in Late Elizabethan London: Remarriage, Economic Opportunity and Family Orientations', in Lloyd Bonfield, Richard M. Smith, and Keith Wrightson (eds.), *The World We Have Gained: Histories of Population and Social Structure* (Oxford, 1986), 122–54.

Bromiley, G. W., *Baptism and the Anglican Reformers* (1953).

Brooke, Christopher N. L., *The Medieval Idea of Marriage* (Oxford, 1989).

Brown, Roger Lee, 'The Rise and Fall of the Fleet Marriages', in R. B. Outhwaite (ed.), *Marriage and Society* (1982), 117–36.

Brown, Theo, *The Fate of the Dead: A Study in Folk-Eschatology in the West Country After the Reformation* (Totowa, NJ, 1979).

Burguière, André, 'Le Rituel du mariage en France: Pratiques ecclésiastiques et pratiques populaires (XVIe–XVIIIe siècle)', *Annales E.S.C.* 33 (1978), 637–49.

Burn, John Southerden, *The History of Parish Registers in England* (1862).

Burn, Richard, *Ecclesiastical Law*, 4 vols. (7th edn., 1809).

Capp, Bernard, *English Almanacs 1500–1800: Astrology and the Popular Press* (Ithaca, NY, 1979).

Carlson, Eric, 'Courtship in Tudor England', *History Today*, 43 (1993), 23–9.

—— *Marriage and the English Reformation* (Oxford, 1994).

—— 'Marriage Reform and the Elizabethan High Commission', *Sixteenth Century Journal*, 21 (1990), 437–51.

Clark, Alice, *Working Life of Women in the Seventeenth Century* (1919, repr. 1982).

Clark, David, *Between Pulpit and Pew: Folk Religion in a North Yorkshire Fishing Village* (Cambridge, 1982).

Clark, Peter, 'The Alehouse and the Alternative Society', in Donald Pennington and Keith Thomas (eds.), *Puritans and Revoltionaries: Essays in Seventeenth-Century History Presented to Christopher Hill* (Oxford, 1978), 47–72.

—— *The English Alehouse: A Social History, 1200–1830* (1983)

Clarke, W. K. Lowther, and Charles Harris (eds.), *Liturgy and Worship: A Companion to the Prayer Books of the Anglican Communion* (1932).

Collinson, Patrick, *Archbishop Grindal 1519–1583: The Struggle for a Reformed Church* (1979).

—— *The Birthpangs of Protestant England: Religious and Cultural Change in the Sixteenth and Seventeenth Centuries* (1988).

—— *The Religion of Protestants: the Church in English Society, 1559–1625* (Oxford, 1982).

Cook, Ann Jennalie, *Making a Match: Courtship in Shakespeare and his Society* (Princeton, NJ, 1991).

Coster, Will, 'Kinship and Community in Yorkshire, 1500–1700', D.Phil. thesis, University of York, 1992.

—— 'Purity, Profanity and Puritanism: The Churching of Women, 1500–1700', in W. J. Sheils and Diana Wood (eds.), *Women in the Church* (Studies in Church History, 27; Oxford, 1990), 377–87.

Cox, J. Charles, *English Church Fittings, Furniture and Accessories* (1923).

—— *The Parish Registers of England* (1910).

—— and Alfred Harvey, *English Church Furniture* (1908).

Crawford, Patricia, 'Attitudes to Menstruation in Seventeenth-Century England', *Past and Present*, 91 (1981), 47–73.

—— 'The Construction and Experience of Maternity in Seventeenth-Century England', in Valerie Fildes (ed.), *Women as Mothers in Pre-Industrial England* (1990), 3–38.

—— 'Sexual Knowledge in England, 1500–1750', in Roy Porter and Mikulas Teich (eds.), *Sexual Knowledge, Sexual Science: The History of Attitudes to Sexuality* (Cambridge, 1994), 82–106.

—— *Women and Religion in England 1500–1720* (1993).

Cressy, David, *Bonfires and Bells: National Memory and the Protestant Calendar in Elizabethan and Stuart England* (1989).

—— 'Books as Totems in Seventeenth-Century England and New England', *The Journal of Library History*, 21 (1986), 92–106.

—— 'De la Fiction dans les Archives? Ou le Monstre de 1569', *Annales E.S.C.* 48 (1993), 1309–29.

—— 'Death and the Social Order: The Funerary Preferences of Elizabethan Gentlemen', *Continuity and Change*, 5 (1989), 99–119.

—— 'Gender Trouble and Cross-Dressing in Early Modern England', *Journal of British Studies*, 35 (1996), 438–65.

—— 'Kinship and Kin Interaction in Early Modern England', *Past and Present*, 113 (1986), 38–69.

—— *Literacy and the Social Order: Reading and Writing in Tudor and Stuart England* (Cambridge, 1980).

—— 'Purification, Thanksgiving and the Churching of Women in Post-Reformation England', *Past and Present*, 141 (1993), 106–46.

—— 'The Seasonality of Marriage in Old and New England', *Journal of Interdisciplinary History*, 16 (1985), 1–21.

Cunnington, C. Willett, Phillis Cunnington, and Charles Beard (eds.), *A Dictionary of English Costume* (1960).

Davies, J. G., *The Architectural Setting of Baptism* (1962).

Davies, Julian, *The Caroline Captivity of the Church: Charles I and the Remoulding of Anglicanism* (Oxford, 1992).

Davis, Natalie Zemon, *Society and Culture in Early Modern France* (Stanford, Calif., 1975).

Day, J. F. R., 'Death Be Very Proud: Sidney, Subversion, and Elizabethan Heraldic Funerals', in Dale Hoak (ed.), *Tudor Political Culture* (Cambridge, 1995), 179–203.

Dayton, Cornelia Hughes, 'Taking the Trade: Abortion and Gender Relations in an Eighteenth-Century New England Village', *William and Mary Quarterly*, 48 (1991), 19–49.

Dinn, Robert, '"Monuments Answerable to Mens Worth": Burial Patterns, Social Status and Gender in Late Medieval Bury St. Edmunds', *Journal of Ecclesiastical History*, 46 (1995), 237–55

Donnison, Jean, *Midwives and Medical Men: A History of the Struggle for the Control of Childbirth* (1977).

Dryden, Alice, *Memorials of Old Leicestershire* (1911).

Dubrow, Heather, *A Happier Eden: The Politics of Marriage in the Stuart Epithalamium* (Ithaca, NY, 1990).

—— 'Navel Battles: Interpreting Renaissance Gynecological Manuals', *ANQ* 5 (1992), 67–71.

Duden, Barbara, *Disembodying Women: Perspectives on Pregnancy and the Unborn* (Cambridge, Mass., 1993).

Duffy, Eamon, 'The Godly and the Multitude in Stuart England', *The Seventeenth Century*, 1 (1986), 31–55.

—— *The Stripping of the Altars: Traditional Religion in England c.1400–c.1580* (New Haven and London, 1992).

Durston, Christopher, *The Family in the English Revolution* (Oxford, 1989).

—— '"Unhallowed Wedlocks": The Regulation of Marriage during the English Revolution', *Historical Journal*, 31 (1988), 45–59.

Eccles, Audrey, *Obstetrics and Gynaecology in Tudor and Stuart England* (Kent, Ohio, 1982).

Ehrenreich, Barbara, and Deirdre English, *Witches, Midwives and Nurses: A History of Women Healers* (Old Westbury, NY, 1973).

Elliot, Viven Brodsky, 'Mobility and Marriage in Pre-Industrial England', Ph.D. thesis, University of Cambridge, 1979.

Emmison, F. G., *Elizabethan Life: Morals and the Church Courts* (Chelmsford, 1973).

Erickson, Amy Louise, *Women and Property in Early Modern England* (1993).

—— 'Common Law Versus Common Practice: The Use of Marriage Settlements in Early Modern England', *Economic History Review*, 2nd ser. 43 (1990), 21–39.

Erickson, Robert A., *Mother Midnight: Birth, Sex, and Fate in Eighteenth-Century Fiction* (New York, 1986).

Evans, John, 'An Account of the Presents Received and Expenses Incurred at the Wedding of Richard Polsted, of Albury, Esquire, and Elizabeth, Eldest Daughter of William More, of Loseley, Esquire', *Archaeologia*, 36 (1855), 33–52.

Evans, John T., *Seventeenth-Century Norwich: Politics, Religion, and Government, 1620–1690* (Oxford, 1979).

Evenden, Doreen, 'Mothers and their Midwives in Seventeenth-Century London', in Hilary Marland (ed.), *The Art of Midwifery: Early Modern Midwives in Europe* (1993), 9–26.

Fildes, Valerie A., *Breasts, Bottles and Babies: A History of Infant Feeding* (Edinburgh, 1986).

—— *Wet Nursing: A History from Antiquity to the Present* (Oxford, 1988).

Fincham, Kenneth (ed.), *The Early Stuart Church, 1603–1642* (1993).

—— *Prelate as Pastor: The Episcopate of James I* (Oxford, 1990).

Finucane, R. C., 'Sacred Corpse, Profane Carrion: Social Ideals and Death Rituals in the Later Middle Ages', in Joachim Whaley (ed.), *Mirrors of Mortality: Studies in the Social History of Death* (New York, 1982), 40–60.

Fletcher, Anthony, 'The Protestant Idea of Marriage in Early Modern England', in Anthony Fletcher and Peter Roberts (eds.), *Religion, Culture and Society in Early Modern Britain* (Cambridge, 1994).

—— and John Stevenson (eds.), *Order and Disorder in Early Modern England* (Cambridge, 1985).

Forbes, Thomas R., 'By What Disease or Casualty: The Changing Face of Death in London', in Charles Webster (ed.), *Health, Medicine and Mortality in the Sixteenth Century* (Cambridge, 1979), 117–39.

—— *The Midwife and the Witch* (New Haven and London, 1966).

Fraser, Antonia, *Mary Queen of Scots* (1970).

—— *The Weaker Vessel* (New York, 1984).

Gardiner, Ann Barbeau, 'Elizabeth Cellier in 1688 on Envious Doctors and Heroic Midwives Ancient and Modern', *Eighteenth-Century Life*, 14 (1990), 24–34.

Gavin, Joseph B., '*Handley* v. *Newbie* alias Shields: A Marriage at Farlam in 1605', *Transactions of the Cumberland and Westmorland Antiquarian and Archaeological Society*, 70 (1970), 253–9.

Geddes, Gordon E., *Welcome Joy: Death in Puritan New England* (Ann Arbor, Mich., 1981).

Gélis, Jacques, *History of Childbirth: Fertility, Pregnancy and Birth in Early Modern Europe* (Cambridge, 1991).

Gillis, John, *For Better for Worse: British Marriages, 1600 to the Present* (New York, 1985).

—— 'Married but not Churched: Plebeian Sexual Relations and Marital Nonconformity in Eighteenth-Century Britain', *Eighteenth-Century Life*, 9 (special issue on 'Unauthorized Sexual Behavior during the Enlightenment', ed. Robert P. Maccubbin, 1985), 31–42.

Gittings, Clare, *Death, Burial and the Individual in Early Modern England* (1984).

—— 'Urban Funerals in Late Medieval and Reformation England', in Steven Bassett (ed.), *Death in Towns: Urban Responses to the Dying and the Dead, 100–1600* (Leicester, 1992), 170–83.

Gowing, Laura, 'Gender and the Language of Insult in Early Modern London', *History Workshop Journal*, 35 (1993), 1–21.

Greaves, Richard L., *Society and Religion in Elizabethan England* (Minneapolis, 1981).

Green, I. M., *The Re-Establishment of the Church of England 1660–1663* (Oxford, 1978).

Griffiths, Paul, *Youth and Authority: Formative Experiences in England, 1560–1640* (Oxford, 1996).

Guy, John R., 'The Episcopal Licensing of Physicians, Surgeons and Midwives', *Bulletin of the History of Medicine*, 56 (1982), 528–42.

Haas, Louis, 'Boccaccio, Baptismal Kinship and Spiritual Incest', *Renaissance and Reformation*, NS 13 (1989), 343–56.

Haigh, Christopher, *English Reformations: Religion, Politics, and Society under the Tudors* (Oxford, 1993).

Hair, P. E. H., 'Bridal Pregnancy in Earlier Rural England further Examined', *Population Studies*, 24 (1970), 59–70.

—— 'Bridal Pregnancy in Rural England in Earlier Centuries', *Population Studies*, 20 (1966), 233–43.

Hajzyk, Helena, 'The Church in Lincolnshire c.1595–1640', Cambridge Ph.D. thesis, 1980.

Hammick, James T., *The Marriage Law of England* (1887).

Hammond, Gerald, *Fleeting Things: English Poets and Poems 1616–1660* (1990).

Harding, Vanessa, 'Burial Choice and Burial Location in Later Medieval London', in Steven Bassett (ed.), *Death in Towns: Urban Responses to the Dying and the Dead, 100–1600* (Leicester, 1992), 119–35.

Harley, David, 'From Providence to Nature: The Moral Theology and Godly Practice of Maternal Breastfeeding in Stuart England', *Bulletin of the History of Medicine*, 69 (1995), 198–223.

—— 'Historians as Demonologists: The Myth of the Midwife-Witch', *Social History of Medicine*, 3 (1990), 1–26.

—— 'Political Post-Mortems and Morbid Anatomy in Seventeenth-Century England', *Social History of Medicine*, 7 (1994), 1–28.

—— 'Provincial Midwives in England: Lancashire and Cheshire, 1660–1760', in Hilary Marland (ed.), *The Art of Midwifery: Early Modern Midwives in Europe* (1993), 27–48.

Heal, Felicity, *Hospitality in Early Modern England* (Oxford, 1990).

—— and Clive Holmes, *The Gentry of England and Wales, 1500–1700* (Stanford, Calif., 1994).

Helmholz, R. H., *Marriage Litigation in Medieval England* (Cambridge, 1974).

Hencke, James T., *Courtesans and Cuckolds: A Glossary of Renaissance Dramatic Bawdy (Exclusive of Shakespeare)* (New York, 1979).

Hill, Christopher, *The World Turned Upside Down: Radical Ideas During the English Revolution* (New York, 1972).

Hoffer, Peter C., and N. E. H. Hull, *Murdering Mothers: Infanticide in England and New England 1558–1803* (New York, 1981).

Holmes, Clive, 'Popular Culture? Witches, Magistrates, and Divines in Early Modern England', in Steven L. Kaplan (ed.), *Understanding Popular Culture* (Berlin, 1984), 85–111.

Houlbrooke, Ralph (ed.), *Death, Ritual, and Bereavement* (1989).

—— 'The Making of Marriage in Mid-Tudor England: Evidence from the Records of Matrimonial Contract Litigation', *Journal of Family History*, 10 (1985), 339–52.

Huntington, Richard, and Peter Metcalf, *Celebrations of Death: The Anthropology of Mortuary Ritual* (Cambridge, 1979).

Hutton, Ronald, *The Pagan Religions of the Ancient British Isles: Their Nature and Legacy* (Oxford, 1991).

—— *The Rise and Fall of Merry England: The Ritual Year 1400–1700* (Oxford, 1994).

Ingram, Martin, *Church Courts, Sex and Marriage in England, 1570–1640* (Cambridge, 1987).

—— 'The Reform of Popular Culture? Sex and Marriage in Early Modern England', in Barry Reay (ed.), *Popular Culture in Seventeenth Century England* (London, 1985), 129–65.

—— 'Spousals Litigation in the English Ecclesiastical Courts c.1350–c.1640', in R. B. Outhwaite (ed.), *Marriage and Society* (1982), 35–57.

Jagger, Peter J., *Christian Initiation 1552–1969* (1970).

—— *Clouded Witness: Initiation in the Church of England in the Mid-Victorian Period, 1850–1875* (Allison Park, Pa., 1982).

James, Mervyn, *Society, Politics and Culture: Studies in Early Modern England* (Cambridge, 1986).

James, William H., 'The Incidence of Spontaneous Abortion', *Population Studies*, 24 (1970), 241–5.

Jeaffreson, John Cordy, *Brides and Bridals*, 2 vols. (1872).

Karant-Nunn, Susan C., 'Churching, a Women's Rite: Ritual Modification in Reformation Germany', conference paper, Wolfenbuttel, June 1991, to be included in a volume ed. R. W. Scribner and R. Po-Chia Hsia and published by the Herzog August Bibliothek.

Kelly, Henry Ansgar, *The Devil at Baptism: Ritual, Theology and Drama* (Ithaca, NY, 1985).

Kertzer, David I., *Rituals, Politics, and Power* (New Haven, 1988).

King, Helen, 'The Politick Midwife: Models of Midwifery in the Work of Elizabeth Cellier', in Hilary Marland (ed.), *The Art of Midwifery: Early Modern Midwives in Europe* (1993), 115–30.

Klapisch-Zuber, Christiane, *Women, Family and Ritual in Renaissance Italy* (Chicago, 1985).

Knodel, John, 'Breast Feeding and Population Growth', *Science*, 198 (1977), 111–15.

Kussmaul, Ann, *A General View of the Rural Economy of England, 1538–1840* (Cambridge, 1990).

Laget, Mireille, *Naissances: L'Accouchement avant l'âge de la clinique* (Paris, 1982).

Lake, Peter, *Anglicans and Puritans? Presbyterianism and English Conformist Thought from Whitgift to Hooker* (1988).

—— 'The Laudian Style: Order, Uniformity and the Pursuit of the Beauty of Holiness in the 1630s', in Kenneth Fincham (ed.), *The Early Stuart Church, 1603–1642* (1993), 161–85.

Lake, Peter, *Moderate Puritans and the Elizabethan Church* (Cambridge, 1982).

Larner, Christina, *Witchcraft and Religion: The Politics of Popular Belief* (Oxford, 1984).

Laslett, Peter, *The World We Have Lost, Further Explored* (1983).

Laurence, Anne, 'The Cradle to the Grave: English Observation of Irish Social Customs in the Seventeenth Century', *The Seventeenth Century*, 3 (1988), 63–84.

—— 'Godly Grief: Individual Responses to Death in Seventeenth-Century Britain', in Ralph Houlbrooke (ed.), *Death, Ritual, and Bereavement* (1989), 62–76.

Levine, David, and Keith Wrightson, 'The Social Context of Illegitimacy in Early Modern England', in Peter Laslett, Karla Oosterveen, and Richard M. Smith (eds.), *Bastardy and its Comparative History* (Cambridge, Mass., 1980), 158–75.

Litten, Julian, *The English Way of Death: The Common Funeral Since 1450* (1991).

Llewellyn, Nigel, *The Art of Death: Visual Culture in the English Death Ritual c.1500– c.1800* (1991).

Loudon, Irvine, *Death in Childbirth: An International Study of Maternal Care and Maternal Mortality 1800–1950* (Oxford, 1992).

MacDonald, Michael, *Mystical Bedlam: Madness, Anxiety, and Healing in Seventeenth-Century England* (Cambridge, 1981).

—— and Terence R. Murphy, *Sleepless Souls: Suicide in Early Modern England* (Oxford, 1990).

Macfarlane, Alan, *The Family Life of Ralph Josselin: A Seventeenth-Century Clergyman. An Essay in Historical Anthropology* (Cambridge, 1970).

—— 'Illegitimacy and Illegitimates in English History', in Peter Laslett, Karla Oosterveen, and Richard M. Smith (eds.), *Bastardy and its Comparative History* (Cambridge, Mass., 1980), 71–85.

—— *Marriage and Love in England: Modes of Reproduction 1300–1840* (Oxford, 1986).

McGregor, J. F., 'The Baptists: Fount of All Heresy', in J. F. McGregor and Barry Reay (eds.), *Radical Religion in the English Revolution* (Oxford, 1984).

McIntosh, Marjorie K., *A Community Transformed: The Manor and Liberty of Havering, 1500–1620* (Cambridge, 1991).

McLaren, Angus, *Reproductive Rituals: The Perception of Fertility in England from the Sixteenth to the Nineteenth Centuries* (1984).

McLaren, Dorothy, 'Marital Fertility and Lactation, 1570–1720', in Mary Prior (ed.), *Women in English Society, 1500–1800* (1985),

Marchant, Ronald A., *The Church Under the Law: Justice, Administration and Discipline in the Diocese of York 1560–1640* (Cambridge, 1969).

Marcus, Leah, *The Politics of Mirth: Jonson, Herrick, Milton, Marvell, and the Defense of Old Holiday Pastimes* (Chicago, 1986).

Marland, Hilary (ed.), *The Art of Midwifery: Early Modern Midwives in Europe* (1993).

Marsh, Christopher, 'The Gravestone of Thomas Lawrence Revisited: Or the Family of Love and the Local Community in Balsham, 1560–1630', in Margaret Spufford (ed.), *The World of Rural Dissenters, 1520–1725* (Cambridge, 1995), 208–34.

Matthews, A. G., *Calamy Revised, Being a Revision of Edmund Calamy's Account of the Ministers and Others Ejected and Silenced, 1660–2* (Oxford, 1934).

—— *Walker Revised: Being a Revision of John Walker's Sufferings of the Clergy during the Grand Rebellion 1642–60* (Oxford, 1948).

Mertes, Kate, *The English Noble Household 1250–1600* (Oxford, 1988).

Mollat, Michel (ed.), *Le Rôle du sel dans l'histoire* (Paris, 1968).

Moore, A. Percival, 'Leicestershire Churches in the Time of Charles I', in Alice Dryden (ed.), *Memorials of Old Leicestershire* (1911).

—— (ed.), 'Marriage Contracts or Espousals in the Reign of Queen Elizabeth', *Associated Architectural Societies Reports and Papers*, 30 (1909), 261–98.

Morrill, John, 'The Church in England 1642–1649', in his *The Nature of the English Revolution* (1993), 148–75.

—— 'The Religious Context of the English Civil War', *Transactions of the Royal Historical Society*, 5th ser. 34 (1984), 155–78.

—— 'William Dowsing, the Bureaucratic Puritan', in John Morrill, Paul Slack, and Daniel Woolf (eds.), *Public Duty and Private Conscience in Seventeenth-Century England* (Oxford, 1993), 173–203.

Morris, Rupert H., *Chester in the Plantagenet and Tudor Reigns* (Chester, 1893).

O'Hara, Diana, 'The Language of Tokens and the Making of Marriage', *Rural History*, 3 (1992), 1–40.

—— '"Ruled by My Friends": Aspects of Marriage in the Diocese of Canterbury, c.1540–1570', *Continuity and Change*, 6 (1991), 9–41.

Obelkevich, James, 'Proverbs and Social History', in Peter Burke and Roy Porter (eds.), *The Social History of Language* (Cambridge, 1987), 43–72.

—— *Religion and Rural Society: South Lindsay 1825–75* (Oxford, 1976).

Old, Hughes Oliphant, *The Shaping of the Reformed Baptismal Rite in the Sixteenth Century* (Grand Rapids, Mich., 1992).

Orlin, Lena Cowen, *Private Matters and Public Culture in Post-Reformation England* (Ithaca, NY, 1994).

Otten, Charlotte F., 'Women's Prayers in Childbirth in Sixteenth-Century England', *Women and Language*, 16 (1993), 18–21.

Outhwaite, R. B., *Clandestine Marriage in England, 1500–1850* (1995).

—— (ed.), *Marriage and Society: Studies in the Social History of Marriage* (New York, 1982).

Oxorn, Harry, *Human Labor and Birth* (5th edn., Norwalk, Conn., 1986).

Paige, Karen Erickson, and Jeffery M. Paige, *The Politics of Reproductive Ritual* (Berkeley and Los Angeles, 1981).

Paster, Gail Kern, *The Body Embarrassed: Drama and the Disciplines of Shame in Early Modern England* (Ithaca, NY, 1993).

Peck, Francis, *Desiderata Curiosa* (1779).

Pickering, W. S. F., 'The Persistence of Rites of Passage: Towards an Explanation', *British Journal of Sociology*, 25 (1974), 63–78.

Pollock, Linda, 'Embarking on a Rough Passage: The Experience of Pregnancy in Early Modern Society', in Valerie Fildes (ed.), *Women as Mothers in Pre-Industrial England* (1990), 39–67.

Pollock, Linda, 'Living on the Stage of the World: The Concept of Privacy among the Elite of Early Modern England', in Adrian Wilson (ed.), *Rethinking Social History: English Society 1570–1920 and its Interpretations* (Manchester, 1993), 78–96.

—— *With Faith and Physic: The Life of a Tudor Gentlewoman. Lady Grace Mildmay 1552–1620* (1993).

Porter, Enid, *Cambridgeshire Customs and Folklore* (1969).

Porter, Stephen, 'Death and Burial in a London Parish: St. Mary Woolnoth 1653–99', *London Journal*, 8 (1982), 76–80.

—— 'Death and Burial in Seventeenth-Century Oxford', *Oxfordshire Local History*, 1 (1980), 2–7.

Powell, Chilton Latham, *English Domestic Relations 1487–1653* (New York, 1917).

Procter, Francis, *A History of the Book of Common Prayer* (1875).

Pruett, John H., *The Parish Clergy under the Later Stuarts: The Leicestershire Experience* (Urbana and Chicago, 1978).

Quaife, G. R., *Wanton Wenches and Wayward Wives: Peasants and Illicit Sex in Early Seventeenth Century England* (1979).

Reay, Barry (ed.), *Popular Culture in Seventeenth-Century England* (1985).

Richards, Raymond, *Old Cheshire Churches: A Survey of their History, Fabric and Furniture with Records of the Older Monuments* (1947).

Riddle, John M., 'Oral Contraceptives and Early-Term Abortifacients During Classical Antiquity and the Middle Ages', *Past and Present*, 132 (1991), 3–32.

—— *Contraception and Abortion from the Ancient World to the Renaissance* (Cambridge, Mass., 1992).

Rosen, Barbara (ed.), *Witchcraft in England, 1558–1618* (Amherst, Mass., 1991).

Rowell, Geoffrey, *The Liturgy of Christian Burial* (1977).

Rowland, Beryl, *Medieval Woman's Guide to Health: The First English Gynecological Handbook* (Kent, Ohio, 1981).

Ruggiero, Guido, *Binding Passions: Tales of Magic, Marriage, and Power at the End of the Renaissance* (New York, 1993).

Rupp, Gordon, *Religion in England 1688–1791* (Oxford, 1986).

Rushton, Peter, 'Property, Power and Family Networks: The Problem of Disputed Marriage in Early Modern England', *Journal of Family History*, 11 (1986), 205–19.

—— 'Purification or Social Control? Ideologies of Reproduction and the Churching of Women after Childbirth', in Eva Garamarnikow (ed.), *The Public and the Private* (1983), 118–31.

—— 'The Testament of Gifts: Marriage Tokens and Disputed Contracts in North-East England, 1560–1630', *Folk-Life*, 24 (1985–6), 25–31.

Russell, Conrad, *Parliaments and English Politics 1621–1629* (Oxford, 1979).

Salmon, Marylyn, 'The Cultural Significance of Breastfeeding and Infant Care in Early Modern England and America', *Journal of Social History*, 28 (1994), 247–69.

Schnorrenberg, Barbara Brandon, 'Is Childbirth Any Place for a Woman? The Decline of Midwifery in Eighteenth-Century England', *Studies in Eighteenth-Century Culture*, 10 (1981), 393–408.

Schnucker, R. V., 'The English Puritans and Pregnancy, Delivery and Breast Feeding', *History of Childhood Quarterly*, 1 (1974), 637–58.

Schofield, Roger, 'Did the Mothers Really Die? Three Centuries of Maternal Mortality in "The World We Have Lost"', in Lloyd Bonfield, Richard M. Smith, and Keith Wrightson (eds.), *The World We Have Gained: Histories of Population and Social Structure* (Oxford, 1986), 231–60.

—— and E. A. Wrigley, 'Infant and Child Mortality in England in the Late Tudor and Early Stuart Period', in Charles Webster (ed.), *Health, Medicine and Mortality in the Sixteenth Century* (Cambridge, 1979), 61–95.

Scott, W. S., *Worship and Drama: An Inquiry into the Nature and Interpretation of the Dramatic Element Inherent in All Forms of Liturgical Worship, with Especial Reference to its Place in the Anglican Liturgy* (1938).

Sharpe, J. A., *Defamation and Sexual Slander in Early Modern England: The Church Courts at York* (York, 1980).

—— *Early Modern England: A Social History 1550–1760* (1987).

—— 'Plebeian Marriage in Stuart England: Some Evidence from Popular Literature', *Transactions of the Royal Historical Society*, 5th ser. 36 (1986), 69–90.

Sharpe, Kevin, *The Personal Rule of Charles I* (New Haven and London, 1992).

Sheils, W. J., *The Puritans in the Diocese of Peterborough 1558–1610* (Northamptonshire Record Society; Northampton, 1979).

Shorter, Edward, *A History of Women's Bodies* (New York, 1982).

Slack, Paul, 'Mortality Crises and Epidemic Disease in England 1485–1610', in Charles Webster (ed.), *Health, Medicine and Mortality in the Sixteenth Century* (Cambridge, 1979), 9–59.

Smith, Daniel Scott, 'Child-Naming Practices as Cultural and Familial Indicators', *Local Population Studies*, 32 (1984), 17–27.

—— 'Child-Naming Practices, Kinship Ties, and Change in Family Attitudes in Hingham, Massachusetts, 1641 to 1880', *Journal of Social History*, 18 (1985), 541–66.

Smith, Harold, *The Ecclesiastical History of Essex Under the Long Parliament and Commonwealth* (Colchester, 1932).

Smith, Hilda, 'Gynecology and Ideology in Seventeenth-Century England', in Berenice A. Carroll (ed.), *Liberating Women's History: Theoretical and Critical Essays* (Urbana, Ill., 1976), 97–114.

Smith, James E., and Jim Oeppen, 'Estimating Numbers of Kin in Historical England Using Microsimulation', in David S. Reher and Roger Schofield (eds.), *Old and New Methods in Historical Demography* (Oxford, 1993), 280–317.

Smith, R. M., 'Marriage Processes in the English Past: Some Continuities', in Lloyd Bonfield, Richard M. Smith, and Keith Wrightson (eds.), *The World We Have Gained: Histories of Population and Social Structure* (Oxford, 1986), 43–99.

Spaeth, Donald A., 'Parsons and Parishioners: Lay-Clerical Conflict and Popular Piety in Wiltshire Villages, 1660–1740', Ph.D. thesis, Brown University, 1985.

Spufford, Margaret, *The Great Reclothing of Rural England: Petty Chapmen and their Wares in the Seventeenth Century* (1984).

Spurr, John, *The Restoration Church of England, 1646–1689* (New Haven and London, 1991).

Stannard, David E., *The Puritan Way of Death: A Study in Religion, Culture, and Social Change* (New York, 1977).

Steig, Margaret, *Laud's Laboratory: The Diocese of Bath and Wells in the Early Seventeenth Century* (East Brunswick, NJ, 1982).

Stone, Lawrence, *The Crisis of the Aristocracy, 1558–1641* (Oxford, 1965).

—— *The Family, Sex and Marriage in England, 1500–1800* (1977; New York, 1979).

—— *Road to Divorce: England 1530–1987* (Oxford, 1990).

—— *Uncertain Unions: Marriage in England 1660–1753* (Oxford, 1992).

Strype, John, *Life and Acts of John Whitgift*, 3 vols. (Oxford, 1822).

Thisleton-Dyer, T. F., *Church-Lore Gleanings* (1892).

—— *Domestic Folk-Lore* (1881).

Thomas, Keith, 'Cases of Conscience in Seventeenth-Century England', in John Morrill, Paul Slack, and Daniel Woolf (eds.), *Public Duty and Private Conscience in Seventeenth-Century England* (Oxford, 1993).

—— *Man and the Natural World: A History of the Modern Sensibility* (New York, 1993).

—— 'The Place of Laughter in Tudor and Stuart England', *TLS* (21 Jan. 1977), 77–81.

—— *Religion and the Decline of Magic* (New York, 1971).

Thompson, Roger, *Sex in Middlesex: Popular Mores in Massachusetts County, 1649–1699* (Amherst, Mass., 1986).

Tilley, Morris Palmer, *A Dictionary of the Proverbs in England in the Sixteenth and Seventeenth Centuries* (Ann Arbor, Mich. 1950).

Tromly, Frederic B., ' "According to sounde religion": The Elizabethan Controversy over the Funeral Sermon', *Journal of Medieval and Reniassance Studies*, 13 (1983), 293–312.

Trumbach, Randolph, *The Rise of the Egalitarian Family* (New York, 1978).

Turner, Victor, *Dramas, Fields, and Metaphors: Symbolic Action in Human Society* (Ithaca, NY, 1974).

—— *The Ritual Process: Structure and Anti-Structure* (Chicago, 1969).

Tyack, George S., *Lore and Legend of the English Church* (1899).

Tyacke, Nicholas, 'Anglican Attitudes: Some Recent Writings on English Religious History, from the Reformation to the Civil War', *Journal of British Studies*, 35 (1996), 139–67.

—— *Anti-Calvinists: The Rise of English Arminianism c.1590–1640* (Oxford, 1987; 2nd edn., Oxford, 1990).

—— *The Fortunes of English Puritanism, 1603–1640* (1990).

Underdown, David, *Fire From Heaven: Life in an English Town in the Seventeenth Century* (New Haven and London, 1992).

—— *Revel, Riot and Rebellion: Popular Politics and Culture in England 1603–1660* (Oxford, 1985).

Usher, Roland G., *The Rise and Fall of the High Commission* (1913; revised edn., Oxford, 1968).

Van Gennep, Arnold, *The Rites of Passage* (Chicago, 1960).

Von Arx, Walter, 'The Churching of Women after Childbirth: History and Significance', in David Power and Luis Maldonado (eds.), *Liturgy and Human Passage* (New York, 1979), 63–72.

Von Friedeburg, Robert, 'Reformation of Manners and the Social Composition of Offenders in an East Anglian Cloth Village: Earls Colne, Essex, 1531–1642', *Journal of British Studies*, 29 (1990), 347–85.

Walker, Barbara G., *The Crone; Women of Age, Wisdom and Power* (San Francisco, 1985).

Wall, Alison, 'For Love, Money, or Politics? A Clandestine Marriage and the Elizabethan Court of Arches', *Historical Journal*, 38 (1995), 511–33.

Watson, Robert N., *The Rest is Silence: Death as Annihilation in the English Renaissance* (Berkeley and Los Angeles, 1994).

Watt, Jeffrey R., *The Making of Modern Marriage: Matrimonial Control and the Rise of Sentiment in Neuchâtel, 1550–1800* (Ithaca, NY, 1992).

Webster, Charles (ed.), *Health, Medicine and Mortality in the Sixteenth Century* (Cambridge, 1979).

Whaley, Joachim (ed.), *Mirrors of Mortality: Studies in the Social History of Death* (New York, 1982).

White, Peter, *Predestination, Policy and Polemic: Conflict and Consensus in the English Church from the Reformation to the Civil War* (Cambridge, 1992).

Wilson, Adrian, 'The Ceremony of Childbirth and its Interpretation', in Valerie Fildes (ed.), *Women as Mothers in Pre-Industrial England* (1990), 68–107.

—— *The Making of Man-midwifery: Childbirth in England, 1660–1770* (1995).

—— 'Participant or Patient? Seventeenth Century Childbirth from the Mother's Point of View', in Roy Porter (ed.), *Patients and Practitioners: Lay Perceptions of Medicine in Pre-Industrial Society* (Cambridge, 1986), 129–44.

—— 'The Perils of Early Modern Procreation: Childbirth With or Without Fear?', *British Journal for Eighteenth-Century Studies*, 16 (1993), 1–19.

Wilson, Chris, 'The Proximate Determinants of Marital Fertility in England 1600–1799', in Lloyd Bonfield, Richard M. Smith, and Keith Wrightson (eds.), *The World We Have Gained: Histories of Population and Social Structure* (Oxford, 1986), 203–30.

Wilson, Jean, 'Icons of Unity', *History Today*, 43 (1993), 14–20.

Wright, Susan, 'Family Life and Society in Sixteenth and Early Seventeenth Century Salisbury', Ph.D. thesis, University of Leicester, 1982.

Wrightson, Keith, *English Society 1580–1680* (1982).

—— 'Infanticide in Earlier Seventeenth-Century England', *Local Population Studies*, 15 (1975), 10–22.

—— 'The Nadir of English Illegitimacy in the Seventeenth Century', in Peter Laslett,

Karla Oosterveen, and Richard M. Smith (eds.), *Bastardy and its Comparative History* (Cambridge, Mass., 1980), 176–91.

Wrigley, E. A., 'Births and Baptisms: The Use of Anglican Baptism Registers as a Source of Information about the Numbers of Births in England before the Beginning of Civil Registration', *Population Studies*, 31 (1977), 281–312.

—— and R. S. Schofield, *The Population History of England, 1541–1871* (Cambridge, Mass., 1981).

Yates, Nigel, *Buildings, Faith, and Worship: The Liturgical Arrangement of Anglican Churches, 1600–1900* (Oxford, 1991).

Index